CW01022964

Common Worship

Daily Eucharistic Lectionary

Common Worship

Daily Eucharistic Lectionary

CANTERBURY PRESS

Norwich

Compilation copyright © Simon Kershaw 2008

First published in 2008 by the Canterbury Press Norwich
(a publishing imprint of Hymns Ancient & Modern Limited,
a registered charity)
108-114 Golden Lane, London, EC14 0TG.
www.canterburypress.co.uk

Third Impression 2018

For further copyright and permission information see page 821

A catalogue record for this book is available from the British Library

ISBN 978 1 85311 896 8

Designed by **crucix** www.crucix.com
and typeset in Gill Sans and Joanna

Printed and bound by CPI Group (UK) Ltd, Croydon, CR0 4YY

CONTENTS

INTRODUCTION

The readings in this book are taken from the Daily Eucharistic Lectionary, authorized by the General Synod of the Church of England in 2005, which is a slight revision of the lectionary published in *The Alternative Service Book 1980*. That lectionary was, in turn, derived from the 1969 *Ordo Lectionum Missae* of the Roman Catholic Church, with the intention that the same readings be read on the same days in both Churches. The adoption in 1997 by the Church of England of a Sunday lectionary based on the Revised Common Lectionary, which itself derives from the Roman Sunday lectionary, has meant that this weekday lectionary now fits more conveniently with the Church of England's own calendar and Sunday lectionary.

This introduction gives an overview of the principles behind the selection of readings in the weekday lectionary and any decisions which the minister may have to make in using it.

About the Daily Eucharistic Lectionary

The readings of the Daily Eucharistic Lectionary complement those of the Sunday lectionary, enabling a larger amount of the Bible to be read over the course of two years. Almost all weekdays are provided with two readings: first, a reading from the Old Testament or from the New Testament other than the Gospels; and, secondly, a reading from one of the Gospels. Christmas Eve and the days of Holy Week are provided with both an Old Testament and a New Testament reading in addition to a reading from the Gospels. The first reading is, in each case, followed by a psalm or portion of a psalm which serves as a response to the reading.

In Advent and Christmas and during the first part of Epiphany (until the Baptism of Christ) and again during Lent and Eastertide the selection of readings and psalms is the same every year. In the rest of the Epiphany season (from the Baptism of Christ until the feast of the Presentation of Christ in the Temple, or Candlemas) and in the remainder of the year (between the Presentation and Lent, and between Pentecost and Advent; the periods called 'Ordinary Time') the selection of first readings and psalms is spread over a two-year cycle. The readings for *Year 1* are used in calendar years with an odd number, and the readings for *Year 2* in calendar years with an even number. The Gospel readings are the same in each year.

The Selection of Readings

Advent

At the start of Advent, up to 16 December, readings are provided for each weekday by name. In the first two weeks the first reading is from Isaiah, read in sequence, and the psalm and the Gospel are chosen to relate to that reading. From Thursday in the second week the Gospel reading focuses on John the Baptist, and the first reading is chosen from the Old Testament to relate to that.

From 17 December until Christmas Eve, readings are assigned to each specific date in the calendar, and, reflecting the approach of Christmas, focus on the events leading up to the birth of Christ, as told in Matthew and Luke, together with various Messianic prophecies from the Old Testament.

Christmas and Epiphany (until the Baptism of Christ)

The weekday lectionary resumes on 29 December, after Christmas Day and the festivals that follow it. The first reading is taken from 1 John (the opening chapter of which is read on 27 December, the Feast of St John) and this continues until the festival of the Baptism of Christ, on the Sunday after the Epiphany. The Gospel readings relate the childhood of Jesus (from Luke), the first appearance of Jesus (from John 1) and then his first manifestations in the four Gospels.

Lent

In the early part of Lent, up to the Fourth Sunday, various Lenten themes are covered, the readings for each day being chosen to complement one another. From the fourth week of Lent there is a semi-continuous reading of John's Gospel, chapters 4 to 11.

In each of the third, fourth and fifth weeks of Lent there is an alternative set of readings that may be used if desired. These sets are particularly appropriate in Years B and C of the Sunday lectionary scheme, because they provide an opportunity to hear each year the Gospel passages that are read on the Sundays of those weeks in Year A. On the Fourth Sunday in any year this Sunday Gospel passage may be displaced by the readings for Mothering Sunday, so that this alternative set is appropriate in all three years in the fourth week of Lent. The passages tell the stories of the Samaritan woman, the man born blind, and the raising of Lazarus.

Easter

In Eastertide, the first reading is a semi-continuous series from the Acts of the Apostles. The Gospel readings in the first week of Easter relate the resurrection appearances. In the rest of the Easter season, the Gospel is a semi-continuous reading of John, complementing the passages that were read at the end of Lent.

Between the Baptism of Christ and Lent, and between Pentecost and Advent

Between the feast of the Presentation of Christ and the start of Lent, and again between Pentecost and the start of Advent, is Ordinary Time. During these periods, and also for the period of Epiphany between the Baptism of Christ and the Presentation, the lectionary provides a two-year cycle of first readings and psalms, together with a repeated yearly cycle of Gospel readings. Mark 1–12 is read in weeks 1 to 9. Then the passages from Matthew not in Mark are read in weeks 10 to 21, and the passages from Luke not in Mark in weeks 22 to 34.

The first reading contains, over the course of two years, a substantial selection from both the Old Testament and the New Testament. In Year 1, twenty weeks are provided with readings from the Old Testament, and fourteen with readings from the New Testament. In Year 2, the figures are eighteen weeks and sixteen weeks, respectively. The Old Testament passages give a selection from nearly every book, omitting only 1 Chronicles, Esther (a passage of which is read in Lent), the Song of Songs, Obadiah and Zephaniah (some of which is read in Advent). These readings provide an overview of the history of salvation. The New Testament readings are from the letters of Paul and the other apostles, and a large selection of the letters is read over the course of two years. Finally, the book of Revelation is read in the last two weeks of Year 2.

The tables on pages 11–13 show the distribution of readings through the year: first during the period Advent to the Baptism of Christ, and during Lent and Easter; and then for the two years covering the Baptism of Christ until Lent, and Pentecost until Advent.

The Psalms

A psalm is provided for each day, arranged for responsorial use. Occasionally a canticle from elsewhere in the Old Testament or from the New Testament is provided, though in these cases a psalm is usually printed as an alternative. The psalm (or canticle) is intended as a meditative response to the first reading and is selected because of its relationship to that reading. The response is often a verse from the psalm, or a simpler form of a verse, or, on a few occasions, a verse from the first reading or elsewhere. This response is intended to encourage the active participation of the people in the Liturgy of the Word: it should be sung by all if possible, but may otherwise be spoken by the people.

Frequently only a portion of a psalm is set for each day, rather than the whole psalm. The choice of verses often provides a more contiguous portion of psalmody than is specified in the Roman lectionary. This is explained below in the section on differences from the Roman lectionary.

The Apocrypha

The lectionary contains some readings from the Apocrypha. In the seasons, there are occasional passages from Ecclesiasticus, Esther, the Song of the Three, and Susanna, whilst in Year 1 of Ordinary Time there are sequences from Ecclesiasticus, Tobit, Baruch, Wisdom, and 1 and 2 Maccabees. In almost all cases, alternative canonical readings are provided.

Differences in this Lectionary

This lectionary derives, as has been said, from the Roman Catholic Church's Ordo Lectionum Missae (the Order of Readings for Mass). It was first adapted for the Church of England in The Alternative Service Book 1980, and was further revised in 2000 and 2005. The intention of the adaptations is that the same readings should be read on the same days as in the Roman Catholic Church, despite any differences in the calendars of the two Churches. However, there are some alterations compared with the Roman lectionary and these are listed on the next page.

- The choice of psalm verses provides a more 'consolidated' portion of psalmody: in the original lectionary the verses selected for each day are often non-continuous, making it difficult to recite the portion from a psalter. Slightly different verse selections make this easier.
- The lectionary contains passages from the Apocrypha. Recent practice in the Church of England has been to provide canonical readings as an alternative to readings from the Apocrypha, and this policy is followed in almost all cases in this lectionary.
- The lectionary sometimes provides a canticle as a response to the first reading, rather than a psalm. Where this canticle is not one that has traditionally been used in the Church of England a psalm or portion of a psalm is provided as an alternative in almost all cases, or in two places (Monday and Tuesday of Week 20 in Year 2) as a replacement.
- In a few places a slightly longer or slightly different selection of verses is prescribed for a reading.
- Some very minor changes are made as a consequence of differences between the Sunday lectionaries of the two Churches. For example, there is no need to provide an alternative Gospel reading on Monday of the fifth week of Lent in Year C (which in the Roman lectionary would be the same as that on the preceding Sunday).

Holy Days

When a Principal Feast or Holy Day, or a Festival, falls on a weekday then the readings and other material appropriate to that day replace those from the Daily Eucharistic Lectionary. The minister may be selective in the Lesser Festivals that are observed, and may keep some or all as commemorations. Where a Lesser Festival is observed as such, the appropriate readings and psalm may supersede those in the Daily Eucharistic Lectionary, but this is not required. The displaced readings may be added to those of the preceding or the following day at the minister's discretion to maintain continuity.

Companion Volumes

Readings for saints' days and other commemorations, according to the calendars of the Church of England, the Church of Ireland, the Scottish Episcopal Church and the Church in Wales, may be found in the companion volume, Exciting Holiness, which also includes brief biographical or historical notes on each commemoration. Readings for Sundays, and for Principal Feasts, other Principal Holy Days and Festivals may be found in the series entitled The Word of the Lord which comprises a volume for each of the years A, B and C, together with a fourth volume for special occasions. A further volume contains all the Gospel readings for use at the Principal Service and is called The Gospel of the Lord.

Reading Scheme: Year 1 and Year 2

The tables on this and the following two pages provide an overview of the distribution of biblical books through the two years of the lectionary. The tables should be read in conjunction with the description of the reading scheme on the preceding pages.

The table on this page covers the period when the readings for both years are the same. The tables on pages 12 and 13 cover the period when the first reading and psalm differ between the two years.

Week	First Reading	Gospel Reading
Advent 1	Isaiah 2 − 30	mostly Matthew
Advent 2	Isaiah 35 − 48; Ecclesiasticus	mostly Matthew
Advent 3		
17–24 December		Matthew 1; Luke 1
Christmas	1 John 2 − 3	Luke 2; John 1
Epiphany	1 John 3 − 5	
(until the Baptism of Christ)		
Lent 1		
Lent 2		
Lent 3		
Lent 4		John 4 − 7
Lent 5		John 8 − 11
Easter 1	Acts 2 − 4	
Easter 2	Acts 4 − 6	John 3 − 6
Easter 3	Acts 6 − 9	John 6
Easter 4	Acts 11 − 13	John 10 − 14
Easter 5	Acts 14 − 16	John 14 − 15
Easter 6	Acts 16 − 18	John 15 − 16
Easter 7	Acts 19 − 28	John 16 − 21

Blank entries in this table indicate that readings are selected from a variety of books, rather than being read in sequence.

Reading Scheme: Year 1

Week	First Reading	Gospel Reading
1	Hebrews	Mark 1.14 – 2.17
2		2.18 – 3.21
3		3.22 – end of 4
4		5.1 – 6.34
5	Genesis 1 – 11	6.53 – 8.10
6		8.11 – 9.13
7	Ecclesiasticus	9.14 – 10.16
8		10.17 – end of 11
9	Tobit	12
10	2 Corinthians	Matthew 5.1–37
11		5.38 – end of 6
12	Genesis 12 – 50	7.1 – 8.17
13		8.18 – 9.17
14		9.18 – 10.33
15	Exodus	10.34 – 12.21
16		12.38 – 13.30
17	Exodus; Leviticus	13.31 – 14.12
18	Numbers; Deuteronomy	14.13 – 17.20
19	Deuteronomy; Joshua	17.22 – 19.15
20	Judges; Ruth	19.16 – 23.12
21	1 Thessalonians	23.13 – 25.30
22	1 Thessalonians; Colossians	Luke 4.16 – 6.5
23	Colossians; 1 Timothy	6.6–end
24	1 Timothy	7.1 – 8.15
25	Ezra; Haggai; Zechariah	8.16 – 9.45
26	Zechariah; Nehemiah; Baruch	9.46 – 10.24
27	Jonah; Malachi; Joel	10.25 – 11.28
28	Romans	11.29 – 12.12
29		12.13 – 13.9
30		13.10 – 14.11
31		14.12 – 16.15
32	Wisdom	17.1 – 18.8
33	1 and 2 Maccabees	18.35 – 20.40
34	Daniel	21.1–36

Blank entries in this table indicate that readings continue in sequence from the line above.

Reading Scheme: Year 2

Week	First Reading	Gospel Reading
1	1 Samuel	Mark 1.14 – 2.17
2	1 Samuel; 2 Samuel	2.18 – 3.21
3	2 Samuel	3.22 – end of 4
4	2 Samuel; 1 Kings 1 – 16	5.1 – 6.34
5	1 Kings 1 – 16	6.53 – 8.10
6	James	8.11 – 9.13
7		9.14 – 10.16
8	1 Peter; Jude	10.17 – end of 11
9	2 Peter; 2 Timothy	12
10	1 Kings 17 – 21	Matthew 5.1–37
11	1 Kings 17 – 21; 2 Kings	5.38 – end of 6
12	2 Kings; Lamentations	7.1 – 8.17
13	Amos	8.18 – 9.17
14	Hosea; Isaiah	9.18 – 10.33
15	Isaiah; Micah	10.34 – 12.21
16	Micah; Jeremiah	12.38 – 13.30
17	Jeremiah	13.31 – 14.12
18	Jeremiah; Nahum; Habakkuk	14.13 – 17.20
19	Ezekiel	17.22 – 19.15
20		19.16 – 23.12
21	2 Thessalonians; 1 Corinthians	23.13 – 25.30
22	1 Corinthians	Luke 4.16 – 6.5
23		6.6–end
24		7.1 – 8.15
25	Proverbs; Ecclesiastes	8.16 – 9.45
26	Job	9.46 – 10.24
27	Galatians	10.25 – 11.28
28	Galatians; Ephesians	11.29 – 12.12
29	Ephesians	12.13 – 13.9
30	Ephesians; Philippians	13.10 – 14.11
31	Philippians	14.12 – 16.15
32	Titus; Philemon; 2 and 3 John	17.1 – 18.8
33	Revelation	18.35 – 20.40
34		21.1–36

Blank entries in this table indicate that readings continue in sequence from the line above.

Movable Feasts: 2008–25

Year	Sunday year	DEL year	Ash Wednesday	Easter Day	Ascension Day	Pentecost	Week OT resumes	Advent Sunday	
2008	A	2	6 February	23 March	1 May	11 May	6	30 November	(Year B begins)
2009	B	1	25 February	12 April	21 May	31 May	9	29 November	(Year C begins)
2010	C	2	17 February	4 April	13 May	23 May	8	28 November	(Year A begins)
2011	A	1	9 March	24 April	2 June	12 June	11	27 November	(Year B begins)
2012	B	2	22 February	8 April	17 May	27 May	8	2 December	(Year C begins)
2013	C	1	13 February	31 March	9 May	19 May	7	1 December	(Year A begins)
2014	A	2	5 March	20 April	29 May	8 June	10	30 November	(Year B begins)
2015	B	1	18 February	5 April	14 May	24 May	8	29 November	(Year C begins)
2016	C	2	10 February	27 March	5 May	15 May	7	27 November	(Year A begins)
2017	A	1	1 March	16 April	25 May	4 June	9	3 December	(Year B begins)
2018	B	2	14 February	1 April	10 May	20 May	7	2 December	(Year C begins)
2019	C	1	6 March	21 April	30 May	9 June	10	1 December	(Year A begins)
2020	A	2	26 February	12 April	21 May	31 May	9	29 November	(Year B begins)
2021	B	1	17 February	4 April	13 May	23 May	8	28 November	(Year C begins)
2022	C	2	2 March	17 April	26 May	5 June	10	27 November	(Year A begins)
2023	A	1	22 February	9 April	18 May	28 May	8	3 December	(Year B begins)
2024	B	2	14 February	31 March	9 May	19 May	7	1 December	(Year C begins)
2025	C	1	5 March	20 April	29 May	8 June	10	30 November	(Year A begins)

Movable Feasts: 2026–43

Year	Sunday year	DEL year	Ash Wednesday	Easter Day	Ascension Day	Pentecost	Week OT resumes	Advent Sunday	
2026	A	2	18 February	5 April	14 May	24 May	8	29 November	(Year B begins)
2027	B	1	10 February	28 March	6 May	16 May	7	28 November	(Year C begins)
2028	C	2	1 March	16 April	25 May	4 June	9	3 December	(Year A begins)
2029	A	1	14 February	1 April	10 May	20 May	7	2 December	(Year B begins)
2030	B	2	6 March	21 April	30 May	9 June	10	1 December	(Year C begins)
2031	C	1	26 February	13 April	22 May	1 June	9	30 November	(Year A begins)
2032	A	2	11 February	28 March	6 May	16 May	7	28 November	(Year B begins)
2033	B	1	2 March	17 April	26 May	5 June	10	27 November	(Year C begins)
2034	C	2	22 February	9 April	18 May	28 May	8	3 December	(Year A begins)
2035	A	1	7 February	25 March	3 May	13 May	6	2 December	(Year B begins)
2036	B	2	27 February	13 April	22 May	1 June	9	30 November	(Year C begins)
2037	C	1	18 February	5 April	14 May	24 May	8	29 November	(Year A begins)
2038	A	2	10 March	25 April	3 June	13 June	11	28 November	(Year B begins)
2039	B	1	23 February	10 April	19 May	29 May	9	27 November	(Year C begins)
2040	C	2	15 February	1 April	10 May	20 May	7	2 December	(Year A begins)
2041	A	1	6 March	21 April	30 May	9 June	10	1 December	(Year B begins)
2042	B	2	19 February	6 April	15 May	25 May	8	30 November	(Year C begins)
2043	C	1	11 February	29 March	7 May	17 May	7	29 November	(Year A begins)

USING THIS BOOK

Lectionary Years

In this volume the two years of the lectionary are printed together. The readings labelled *Year 1* are used in years with an odd number, and readings labelled *Year 2* in years with an even number. When the same readings are used in both years, they are labelled *Year 1 and Year 2*. This almost always applies to the Gospel readings as these do not follow a two-year cycle. In a very small number of cases, different readings are provided depending on the three-year Sunday lectionary: these are labelled *Year A*, *Year B* and *Year C*. Year A begins on the First Sunday of Advent in years whose number is exactly divisible by three; the table on pages 14–15 indicates the lectionary year in the three-year scheme which applies from January until Advent, and the year which starts each Advent.

Lectionary Weeks

The readings for the seasons of Advent, Christmas, Epiphany (up to the Baptism of Christ), Lent and Easter are printed first; these readings are the same in each year of the cycle, except for a few occasions where there are differences depending on the Sunday lectionary year.

In the first part of Advent the readings depend on the liturgical calendar. For the date of the First Sunday of Advent, which begins this season, see the table on pages 14–15. From 17 December until the Baptism of Christ the readings are fixed to specific dates. In Lent and Eastertide the readings again depend on the liturgical calendar. The table on pages 14–15 indicates the dates of Ash Wednesday and Pentecost, between which these seasons fall.

After these readings, those for the rest of the year are printed. In this period (from the Baptism of Christ until the Presentation of Christ; and in Ordinary Time) the readings are fixed to ranges of secular calendar dates, and these dates are indicated in the heading of each day. The weeks are numbered consecutively from 1 to 34. Weeks 1 to 3, and Monday and Tuesday in week 4, always fall before Lent, and from week 11 all dates are after Pentecost. In between, some weeks may in any given year fall either before Lent or after Pentecost, and in some years one week may be omitted altogether.

The table on pages 14–15 indicates the week with which the lectionary resumes after Pentecost in each year. The minister and reader will need to pay careful attention to the headings against each day to determine the correct reading.

The Sunday at the start of each week falls in the range of dates indicated in the table opposite. This table also shows the page on which the readings for the subsequent weekdays commence.

Weeks of the Year

About the readings

The following typographic conventions should be noted.

Round brackets ( ) which are included in the Biblical texts are part of the Bible translation. The text enclosed in the brackets should always be read.

Square brackets [ ] indicate that the text within them may be omitted, as permitted by the lectionary and noted in the passage citation after the reading. Square brackets are also used in the psalm responses (see below).

An **arrow** → at the foot of a page indicates that the reading or psalm continues over the page.

Where the lectionary provides alternative readings or psalms and canticles this is indicated by the rubrics *Either* and *or* before the alternatives.

Psalm Responses

The response for each psalm is normally a verse or part-verse from that psalm. Sometimes that verse is then omitted from the psalm as printed, and the response is then marked **R***, with an asterisk * in the text of the psalm marking the place of the omitted verse. When the omitted verse is from the start of the specified portion no asterisk marker is printed in the text of the psalm. If the psalm is used without a congregational response the reader may recite the omitted verse at the appropriate point.

Before the psalm the reader may introduce the response with words such as 'The response to the psalm is:' followed by the response, and the congregation may then repeat it back. This immediate repetition helps to memorize the words.

Many of the responses are provided in short and long versions: the portion in square brackets may be omitted if the shorter version is preferred, for example when the response is not printed but must be remembered.

Responses marked *cf* indicate adapted or compressed text; otherwise the response follows the text of the Common Worship psalter or *The New Revised Standard Version* without alteration. The responses are not themselves part of the authorized lectionary, and other responses may be used if desired.

Gospel Acclamations

Acclamations for the Gospel reading can be found on pages 813–818. These are drawn from the provision in the main *Common Worship* volume, and the *Times and Seasons* volume. Other acclamations may be used, and if more variety is desired, then it may often be appropriate to adapt the psalm response.

Dates

For much of the year, the lectionary is tied to dates in the secular calendar, either to a specific date or to a range of dates. These dates are indicated in the heading for each day. Where a range of dates is printed, these are to be interpreted inclusively.

AUTHORIZATION

The Common Worship Weekday Lectionary, of which the Daily Eucharistic Lectionary forms part, is authorized pursuant to Canon B2 of the Canons of the Church of England for use until further resolution of the General Synod.

Authorization extends to the references to the readings and psalms or canticles, which may be read from any version whose use is not prohibited. In this edition the text of *The New Revised Standard Version* of the Bible is used for the readings, and the text of the Common Worship psalter for the psalms. Canticles follow the text printed in *Common Worship: Daily Prayer* where possible. Other canticles are adapted from a number of Bible translations, chiefly *The New Revised Standard Version*.

THE DAILY EUCHARISTIC LECTIONARY

ADVENT

First Week of Advent: Monday
between 28 November and 4 December

Year B and Year C

A reading from the prophecy of Isaiah.

The word that Isaiah son of Amoz saw concerning Judah and Jerusalem.
In days to come
the mountain of the LORD's house
shall be established as the highest of the mountains,
and shall be raised above the hills;
all the nations shall stream to it.
Many peoples shall come and say,
'Come, let us go up to the mountain of the LORD,
to the house of the God of Jacob;
that he may teach us his ways
and that we may walk in his paths.'
For out of Zion shall go forth instruction,
and the word of the LORD from Jerusalem.
He shall judge between the nations,
and shall arbitrate for many peoples;
they shall beat their swords into ploughshares,
and their spears into pruning-hooks;
nation shall not lift up sword against nation,
neither shall they learn war any more.
O house of Jacob,
come, let us walk in the light of the LORD!

This is the word of the Lord.   Isaiah 2.1–5

Year A

A reading from the prophecy of Isaiah.

On that day the branch of the LORD shall be beautiful and glorious, and the fruit of the land shall be the pride and glory of the survivors of Israel. Whoever is left in Zion and remains in Jerusalem will be called holy, everyone who has been recorded for life in Jerusalem, once the Lord has washed away the filth of the daughters of Zion and cleansed the bloodstains of Jerusalem from its midst by a spirit of judgement and by a spirit of burning. Then the LORD will create over the whole site of Mount Zion and over its places of assembly a cloud by day and smoke and the shining of a flaming fire by night. Indeed, over all the glory there will be a canopy. It will serve as a pavilion, a shade by day from the heat, and a refuge and a shelter from the storm and rain.

This is the word of the Lord.   Isaiah 4.2–end

Responsorial Psalm

R [I was glad when they said to me:]
Let us go to the house of the Lord.

Psalm 122.1

I was glad when they said to me,
'Let us go to the house of the Lord.'
And now our feet are standing
within your gates, O Jerusalem.   R

Jerusalem, built as a city
that is at unity in itself.
Thither the tribes go up,
the tribes of the Lord.   R

As is decreed for Israel,
to give thanks to the name of the Lord.
For there are set the thrones of judgement,
the thrones of the house of David.   R

O pray for the peace of Jerusalem:
'May they prosper who love you.
Peace be within your walls
and tranquillity within your palaces.'   R

For my kindred and companions' sake,
I will pray that peace be with you.
For the sake of the house of the Lord our God,
I will seek to do you good.   R

Psalm 122

Hear the Gospel of our Lord Jesus Christ according to Matthew.

When Jesus entered Capernaum, a centurion came to him, appealing to him and saying, 'Lord, my servant is lying at home paralysed, in terrible distress.' And he said to him, 'I will come and cure him.' The centurion answered, 'Lord, I am not worthy to have you come under my roof; but only speak the word, and my servant will be healed. For I also am a man under authority, with soldiers under me; and I say to one, "Go", and he goes, and to another, "Come", and he comes, and to my slave, "Do this", and the slave does it.' When Jesus heard him, he was amazed and said to those who followed him, 'Truly I tell you, in no one in Israel have I found such faith. I tell you, many will come from east and west and will eat with Abraham and Isaac and Jacob in the kingdom of heaven.'

This is the Gospel of the Lord.

Matthew 8.5–11

First Week of Advent: Tuesday
between 29 November and 5 December

Year 1 and Year 2

A reading from the prophecy of Isaiah.

A shoot shall come out from the stock of Jesse,
    and a branch shall grow out of his roots.
The spirit of the LORD shall rest on him,
    the spirit of wisdom and understanding,
    the spirit of counsel and might,
    the spirit of knowledge and the fear of the LORD.
His delight shall be in the fear of the LORD.

He shall not judge by what his eyes see,
    or decide by what his ears hear;
but with righteousness he shall judge the poor,
    and decide with equity for the meek of the earth;
he shall strike the earth with the rod of his mouth,
    and with the breath of his lips he shall kill the wicked.
Righteousness shall be the belt around his waist,
    and faithfulness the belt around his loins.

The wolf shall live with the lamb,
    the leopard shall lie down with the kid,
the calf and the lion and the fatling together,
    and a little child shall lead them.
The cow and the bear shall graze,
    their young shall lie down together;
    and the lion shall eat straw like the ox.
The nursing child shall play over the hole of the asp,
    and the weaned child shall put its hand on the adder's den.
They will not hurt or destroy
    on all my holy mountain;
for the earth will be full of the knowledge of the LORD
    as the waters cover the sea.

On that day the root of Jesse shall stand as a signal to the peoples; the nations shall inquire of him, and his dwelling shall be glorious.

This is the word of the Lord.   *Isaiah 11.1–10*

Responsorial Psalm

R **Righteousness and peace shall flourish:**
[till the moon shall be no more].   *cf Psalm 72.7*

Give the king your judgements, O God,
and your righteousness to the son of a king.
Then shall he judge your people righteously
and your poor with justice. **R**

May the mountains bring forth peace,
and the little hills righteousness for the people.
May he defend the poor among the people,
deliver the children of the needy and crush the oppressor. **R**

Blessed be the Lord, the God of Israel,
who alone does wonderful things.
And blessed be his glorious name for ever.
May all the earth be filled with his glory. **R**   *Psalm 72.1–4, 18–19*

Hear the Gospel of our Lord Jesus Christ according to Luke.

Jesus rejoiced in the Holy Spirit and said, 'I thank you, Father, Lord of heaven
and earth, because you have hidden these things from the wise and the
intelligent and have revealed them to infants; yes, Father, for such was your
gracious will. All things have been handed over to me by my Father; and no
one knows who the Son is except the Father, or who the Father is except the
Son and anyone to whom the Son chooses to reveal him.'

Then turning to the disciples, Jesus said to them privately, 'Blessed are
the eyes that see what you see! For I tell you that many prophets and kings
desired to see what you see, but did not see it, and to hear what you hear,
but did not hear it.'

This is the Gospel of the Lord.   *Luke 10.21–24*

First Week of Advent: Wednesday
between 30 November and 6 December

Year 1 and Year 2

A reading from the prophecy of Isaiah.

On this mountain the LORD of hosts will make for all peoples
    a feast of rich food, a feast of well-matured wines,
    of rich food filled with marrow, of well-matured wines strained clear.
And he will destroy on this mountain
    the shroud that is cast over all peoples,
    the sheet that is spread over all nations;
he will swallow up death for ever.
Then the Lord GOD will wipe away the tears from all faces,
    and the disgrace of his people he will take away from all the earth,
    for the LORD has spoken.
It will be said on that day,
    Lo, this is our God; we have waited for him,
        so that he might save us.
    This is the LORD for whom we have waited;
    let us be glad and rejoice in his salvation.
For the hand of the LORD will rest on this mountain.

This is the word of the Lord.   *Isaiah 25.6–10a*

Responsorial Psalm

R   **I will dwell in the house of the Lord for ever.**   *Psalm 23.6b*

The Lord is my shepherd;
therefore can I lack nothing.
He makes me lie down in green pastures
and leads me beside still waters.   **R**

He shall refresh my soul
and guide me in the paths of righteousness
for his name's sake.   **R**

Though I walk through the valley of the shadow of death,
I will fear no evil;
for you are with me;
your rod and your staff, they comfort me.   **R**

You spread a table before me
in the presence of those who trouble me;
you have anointed my head with oil
and my cup shall be full.   **R**

Surely goodness and loving mercy shall follow me
all the days of my life,
and I will dwell in the house of the Lord for ever.   **R**   *Psalm 23*

Hear the Gospel of our Lord Jesus Christ according to Matthew.

Jesus passed along the Sea of Galilee, and he went up the mountain, where he sat down. Great crowds came to him, bringing with them the lame, the maimed, the blind, the mute, and many others. They put them at his feet, and he cured them, so that the crowd was amazed when they saw the mute speaking, the maimed whole, the lame walking, and the blind seeing. And they praised the God of Israel.

Then Jesus called his disciples to him and said, 'I have compassion for the crowd, because they have been with me now for three days and have nothing to eat; and I do not want to send them away hungry, for they might faint on the way.' The disciples said to him, 'Where are we to get enough bread in the desert to feed so great a crowd?' Jesus asked them, 'How many loaves have you?' They said, 'Seven, and a few small fish.' Then ordering the crowd to sit down on the ground, he took the seven loaves and the fish; and after giving thanks he broke them and gave them to the disciples, and the disciples gave them to the crowds. And all of them ate and were filled; and they took up the broken pieces left over, seven baskets full.

This is the Gospel of the Lord. Matthew 15.29–37

First Week of Advent: Thursday between 1 and 7 December

Year 1 and Year 2

A reading from the prophecy of Isaiah.

On that day this song will be sung in the land of Judah:
> We have a strong city;
>> he sets up victory
>> like walls and bulwarks.
> Open the gates,
>> so that the righteous nation that keeps faith
>> may enter in.
> Those of steadfast mind you keep in peace –
>> in peace because they trust in you.
> Trust in the LORD for ever,
>> for in the LORD GOD
>> you have an everlasting rock.
> For he has brought low
>> the inhabitants of the height;
>> the lofty city he lays low.
> He lays it low to the ground,
>> casts it to the dust.
> The foot tramples it,
>> the feet of the poor,
>> the steps of the needy.

This is the word of the Lord. Isaiah 26.1–6

Responsorial Psalm

R **Blessed is he who comes in the name of the Lord.** Psalm 118.26a

The Lord has punished me sorely,
but he has not given me over to death.
Open to me the gates of righteousness,
that I may enter and give thanks to the Lord.   R

This is the gate of the Lord;
the righteous shall enter through it.
I will give thanks to you, for you have answered me
and have become my salvation.   R

The stone which the builders rejected
has become the chief cornerstone.
This is the Lord's doing,
and it is marvellous in our eyes.   R

This is the day that the Lord has made;
we will rejoice and be glad in it.
Come, O Lord, and save us we pray.
Come, Lord, send us now prosperity.   R

Blessed is he
who comes in the name of the Lord;
we bless you from the house of the Lord.
The Lord is God; he has given us light.   R   Psalm 118.18–27a

Hear the Gospel of our Lord Jesus Christ according to Matthew.

Jesus said to his disciples, 'Not everyone who says to me, "Lord, Lord", will
enter the kingdom of heaven, but only one who does the will of my Father
in heaven.

'Everyone then who hears these words of mine and acts on them will be
like a wise man who built his house on rock. The rain fell, the floods came,
and the winds blew and beat on that house, but it did not fall, because it had
been founded on rock. And everyone who hears these words of mine and
does not act on them will be like a foolish man who built his house on sand.
The rain fell, and the floods came, and the winds blew and beat against that
house, and it fell – and great was its fall!'

This is the Gospel of the Lord.   Matthew 7.21, 24–27

First Week of Advent: Friday between 2 and 8 December

Year 1 and Year 2

A reading from the prophecy of Isaiah.

The Lord said:
    Shall not Lebanon in a very little while
        become a fruitful field,
        and the fruitful field be regarded as a forest?
On that day the deaf shall hear
        the words of a scroll,
and out of their gloom and darkness
        the eyes of the blind shall see.
The meek shall obtain fresh joy in the LORD,
        and the neediest people shall exult in the Holy One of Israel.
For the tyrant shall be no more,
        and the scoffer shall cease to be;
        all those alert to do evil shall be cut off –
those who cause a person to lose a lawsuit,
        who set a trap for the arbiter in the gate,
        and without grounds deny justice to the one in the right.

Therefore thus says the LORD, who redeemed Abraham, concerning the house of Jacob:
    No longer shall Jacob be ashamed,
        no longer shall his face grow pale.
For when he sees his children,
        the work of my hands, in his midst,
        they will sanctify my name;
they will sanctify the Holy One of Jacob,
        and will stand in awe of the God of Israel.
And those who err in spirit will come to understanding,
        and those who grumble will accept instruction.

This is the word of the Lord.
        Isaiah 29.17–end

Responsorial Psalm

R **The Lord is my light and my salvation:**
    [he is the strength of my life].
        cf Psalm 27.1

The Lord is my light and my salvation;
whom then shall I fear?
The Lord is the strength of my life;
of whom then shall I be afraid? R →

When the wicked,
even my enemies and my foes,
came upon me to eat up my flesh,
they stumbled and fell.   R

R   **The Lord is my light and my salvation:**
[he is the strength of my life].

Though a host encamp against me,
my heart shall not be afraid,
and though there rise up war against me,
yet will I put my trust in him.   R

One thing have I asked of the Lord
and that alone I seek:
that I may dwell in the house of the Lord
all the days of my life.   R

I believe that I shall see the goodness of the Lord
in the land of the living.
Wait for the Lord; be strong and he shall comfort your heart;
wait patiently for the Lord.   R   Psalm 27.1–4, 16–17

Hear the Gospel of our Lord Jesus Christ according to Matthew.

As Jesus went on, two blind men followed him, crying loudly, 'Have mercy on us, Son of David!' When he entered the house, the blind men came to him; and Jesus said to them, 'Do you believe that I am able to do this?' They said to him, 'Yes, Lord.' Then he touched their eyes and said, 'According to your faith let it be done to you.' And their eyes were opened. Then Jesus sternly ordered them, 'See that no one knows of this.' But they went away and spread the news about him throughout that district.

This is the Gospel of the Lord.   Matthew 9.27–31

First Week of Advent: Saturday between 3 and 9 December

Year 1 and Year 2

A reading from the prophecy of Isaiah.

Truly, O people in Zion, inhabitants of Jerusalem, you shall weep no more. He will surely be gracious to you at the sound of your cry; when he hears it, he will answer you. Though the Lord may give you the bread of adversity and the water of affliction, yet your Teacher will not hide himself any more, but your eyes shall see your Teacher. And when you turn to the right or when you turn to the left, your ears shall hear a word behind you, saying, 'This is the way; walk in it.'

He will give rain for the seed with which you sow the ground, and grain, the produce of the ground, which will be rich and plenteous. On that day your cattle will graze in broad pastures; and the oxen and donkeys that till the ground will eat silage, which has been winnowed with shovel and fork. On every lofty mountain and every high hill there will be brooks running with water – on a day of the great slaughter, when the towers fall. Moreover, the light of the moon will be like the light of the sun, and the light of the sun will be sevenfold, like the light of seven days, on the day when the LORD binds up the injuries of his people, and heals the wounds inflicted by his blow.

This is the word of the Lord.   *Isaiah 30.19–21, 23–26*

Responsorial Psalm

R **The Lord is a God of justice:**
  [blessed are those who hope in him].   *Isaiah 30.18b*

Happy are those who have the God of Jacob for their help,
whose hope is in the Lord their God;
who made heaven and earth, the sea and all that is in them;
who keeps his promise for ever.   **R**

Who gives justice to those that suffer wrong
and bread to those who hunger.
The Lord looses those that are bound;
the Lord opens the eyes of the blind;
the Lord lifts up those who are bowed down.   **R**

The Lord loves the righteous;
the Lord watches over the stranger in the land;
he upholds the orphan and widow;
but the way of the wicked he turns upside down.   **R**   *Psalm 146.4–9*

Hear the Gospel of our Lord Jesus Christ according to Matthew.

Jesus went about all the cities and villages, teaching in their synagogues, and proclaiming the good news of the kingdom, and curing every disease and every sickness. When he saw the crowds, he had compassion for them, because they were harassed and helpless, like sheep without a shepherd. Then he said to his disciples, 'The harvest is plentiful, but the labourers are few; therefore ask the Lord of the harvest to send out labourers into his harvest.'

Then Jesus summoned his twelve disciples and gave them authority over unclean spirits, to cast them out, and to cure every disease and every sickness. These twelve he sent out with the following instructions: 'Go to the lost sheep of the house of Israel. As you go, proclaim the good news, "The kingdom of heaven has come near." Cure the sick, raise the dead, cleanse the lepers, cast out demons. You received without payment; give without payment.'

This is the Gospel of the Lord.   *Matthew 9.35 – 10.1, 6–8*

Year 1 and Year 2

A reading from the prophecy of Isaiah.

The wilderness and the dry land shall be glad,
  the desert shall rejoice and blossom;
like the crocus it shall blossom abundantly,
  and rejoice with joy and singing.
The glory of Lebanon shall be given to it,
  the majesty of Carmel and Sharon.
They shall see the glory of the LORD,
  the majesty of our God.

Strengthen the weak hands,
  and make firm the feeble knees.
Say to those who are of a fearful heart,
  'Be strong, do not fear!
Here is your God.
  He will come with vengeance,
with terrible recompense.
  He will come and save you.'

Then the eyes of the blind shall be opened,
  and the ears of the deaf unstopped;
then the lame shall leap like a deer,
  and the tongue of the speechless sing for joy.
For waters shall break forth in the wilderness,
  and streams in the desert;
the burning sand shall become a pool,
  and the thirsty ground springs of water;
the haunt of jackals shall become a swamp,
  the grass shall become reeds and rushes.

A highway shall be there,
  and it shall be called the Holy Way;
the unclean shall not travel on it,
  but it shall be for God's people;
  no traveller, not even fools, shall go astray.
No lion shall be there,
  nor shall any ravenous beast come up on it;
they shall not be found there,
  but the redeemed shall walk there.
And the ransomed of the LORD shall return,
  and come to Zion with singing;
everlasting joy shall be upon their heads;
  they shall obtain joy and gladness,
  and sorrow and sighing shall flee away.

This is the word of the Lord.

Isaiah 35

R **The Lord was gracious to his land:**
   [and restored the fortunes of Jacob].   *cf Psalm 85.1*

Show us your mercy, O Lord,
and grant us your salvation.
I will listen
to what the Lord God will say.   **R**

For he shall speak peace to his people and to the faithful,
that they turn not again to folly.
Truly, his salvation is near to those who fear him,
that his glory may dwell in our land.   **R**

Mercy and truth are met together,
righteousness and peace have kissed each other.
Truth shall spring up from the earth
and righteousness look down from heaven.   **R**

The Lord will indeed give all that is good,
and our land will yield its increase.
Righteousness shall go before him
and direct his steps in the way.   **R**   *Psalm 85.7—end*

Hear the Gospel of our Lord Jesus Christ according to Luke.

One day, while Jesus was teaching, Pharisees and teachers of the law were sitting nearby (they had come from every village of Galilee and Judea and from Jerusalem); and the power of the Lord was with him to heal. Just then some men came, carrying a paralysed man on a bed. They were trying to bring him in and lay him before Jesus; but finding no way to bring him in because of the crowd, they went up on the roof and let him down with his bed through the tiles into the middle of the crowd in front of Jesus. When he saw their faith, he said, 'Friend, your sins are forgiven you.' Then the scribes and the Pharisees began to question, 'Who is this who is speaking blasphemies? Who can forgive sins but God alone?'

When Jesus perceived their questionings, he answered them, 'Why do you raise such questions in your hearts? Which is easier, to say, "Your sins are forgiven you", or to say, "Stand up and walk"? But so that you may know that the Son of Man has authority on earth to forgive sins' — he said to the one who was paralysed — 'I say to you, stand up and take your bed and go to your home.' Immediately he stood up before them, took what he had been lying on, and went to his home, glorifying God. Amazement seized all of them, and they glorified God and were filled with awe, saying, 'We have seen strange things today.'

This is the Gospel of the Lord.   *Luke 5.17—26*

Second Week of Advent: Tuesday between 6 and 12 December

Year 1 and Year 2

A reading from the prophecy of Isaiah.

Comfort, O comfort my people,
    says your God.
Speak tenderly to Jerusalem,
    and cry to her
that she has served her term,
    that her penalty is paid,
that she has received from the Lord's hand
    double for all her sins.
A voice cries out:
'In the wilderness prepare the way of the Lord,
    make straight in the desert a highway for our God.
Every valley shall be lifted up,
    and every mountain and hill be made low;
the uneven ground shall become level,
    and the rough places a plain.
Then the glory of the Lord shall be revealed,
    and all people shall see it together,
    for the mouth of the Lord has spoken.'
A voice says, 'Cry out!'
    And I said, 'What shall I cry?'
All people are grass,
    their constancy is like the flower of the field.
The grass withers, the flower fades,
    when the breath of the LORD blows upon it;
    surely the people are grass.
The grass withers, the flower fades;
    but the word of our God will stand for ever.
Get you up to a high mountain,
    O Zion, herald of good tidings;
lift up your voice with strength,
    O Jerusalem, herald of good tidings,
    lift it up, do not fear;
say to the cities of Judah,
    'Here is your God!'
See, the Lord GOD comes with might,
    and his arm rules for him;
his reward is with him,
    and his recompense before him.
He will feed his flock like a shepherd;
    he will gather the lambs in his arms,
and carry them in his bosom,
    and gently lead the mother sheep.

This is the word of the Lord.　　　　　　　　　　　Isaiah 40.1–11

Responsorial Psalm

R* **Sing to the Lord a new song;**
[sing to the Lord, all the earth].   *Psalm 96.1*

Tell it out among the nations that the Lord is king.
He has made the world so firm that it cannot be moved;
he will judge the peoples with equity.   R

Let the heavens rejoice and let the earth be glad;
let the sea thunder and all that is in it;
let the fields be joyful and all that is in them;
let all the trees of the wood shout for joy before the Lord.   R

For he comes, he comes to judge the earth;
with righteousness he will judge the world
and the peoples with his truth.   R   *Psalm 96.1, 10—end*

Hear the Gospel of our Lord Jesus Christ according to Matthew.

Jesus said to his disciples, 'What do you think? If a shepherd has a hundred sheep, and one of them has gone astray, does he not leave the ninety-nine on the mountains and go in search of the one that went astray? And if he finds it, truly I tell you, he rejoices over it more than over the ninety-nine that never went astray. So it is not the will of your Father in heaven that one of these little ones should be lost.'

This is the Gospel of the Lord.   *Matthew 18.12—14*

Second Week of Advent: Wednesday between 7 and 13 December

Year 1 and Year 2

A reading from the prophecy of Isaiah.

To whom then will you compare me,
    or who is my equal? says the Holy One.
Lift up your eyes on high and see:
    Who created these?
He who brings out their host and numbers them,
    calling them all by name;
because he is great in strength,
    mighty in power,
    not one is missing.

Why do you say, O Jacob,
    and speak, O Israel,
'My way is hidden from the LORD,
    and my right is disregarded by my God'?
Have you not known? Have you not heard?   →

The LORD is the everlasting God,
　　the Creator of the ends of the earth.
He does not faint or grow weary;
　　his understanding is unsearchable.
He gives power to the faint,
　　and strengthens the powerless.
Even youths will faint and be weary,
　　and the young will fall exhausted;
but those who wait for the LORD shall renew their strength,
　　they shall mount up with wings like eagles,
they shall run and not be weary,
　　they shall walk and not faint.

This is the word of the Lord.   Isaiah 40.25–end

Responsorial Psalm

R　**Bless the Lord, O my soul**
　　[and give thanks for all his blessings].   cf Psalm 103.2

The Lord is full of compassion and mercy,
slow to anger and of great kindness.
He will not always accuse us,
neither will he keep his anger for ever.　**R**

He has not dealt with us according to our sins,
nor rewarded us according to our wickedness.
For as the heavens are high above the earth,
so great is his mercy upon those who fear him.　**R**

As far as the east is from the west,
so far has he set our sins from us.
As a father has compassion on his children,
so is the Lord merciful towards those who fear him.　**R**　　Psalm 103.8–13

Hear the Gospel of our Lord Jesus Christ according to Matthew.

Jesus said, 'Come to me, all you that are weary and are carrying heavy burdens, and I will give you rest. Take my yoke upon you, and learn from me; for I am gentle and humble in heart, and you will find rest for your souls. For my yoke is easy, and my burden is light.'

This is the Gospel of the Lord.   Matthew 11.28–end

Second Week of Advent: Thursday between 8 and 14 December

Year 1 and Year 2

A reading from the prophecy of Isaiah.

For I, the LORD your God,
    hold your right hand;
it is I who say to you, 'Do not fear,
    I will help you.'

Do not fear, you worm Jacob,
    you insect Israel!
I will help you, says the LORD;
    your Redeemer is the Holy One of Israel.
Now, I will make of you a threshing-sledge,
    sharp, new, and having teeth;
you shall thresh the mountains and crush them,
    and you shall make the hills like chaff.
You shall winnow them and the wind shall carry them away,
    and the tempest shall scatter them.
Then you shall rejoice in the LORD;
    in the Holy One of Israel you shall glory.

When the poor and needy seek water,
    and there is none,
    and their tongue is parched with thirst,
I the LORD will answer them,
    I the God of Israel will not forsake them.
I will open rivers on the bare heights,
    and fountains in the midst of the valleys;
I will make the wilderness a pool of water,
    and the dry land springs of water.
I will put in the wilderness the cedar,
    the acacia, the myrtle, and the olive;
I will set in the desert the cypress,
    the plane and the pine together,
so that all may see and know,
    all may consider and understand,
that the hand of the LORD has done this,
    the Holy One of Israel has created it.

This is the word of the Lord.

Isaiah 41.13–20

R* **I will exalt you, O God my King,
[and bless your name for ever].**   cf Psalm 145.1

The Lord is gracious and merciful,
long-suffering and of great goodness.
The Lord is loving to everyone
and his mercy is over all his creatures.   **R**

All your works praise you, O Lord,
and your faithful servants bless you.
They tell of the glory of your kingdom
and speak of your mighty power.   **R**

To make known to all peoples your mighty acts
and the glorious splendour of your kingdom.
Your kingdom is an everlasting kingdom;
your dominion endures throughout all ages.   **R**   Psalm 145.1, 8–13

Hear the Gospel of our Lord Jesus Christ according to Matthew.

Jesus said to the crowds, 'Truly I tell you, among those born of women no
one has arisen greater than John the Baptist; yet the least in the kingdom of
heaven is greater than he. From the days of John the Baptist until now the
kingdom of heaven has suffered violence, and the violent take it by force. For
all the prophets and the law prophesied until John came; and if you are willing
to accept it, he is Elijah who is to come. Let anyone with ears listen!'

This is the Gospel of the Lord.   Matthew 11.11–15

Second Week of Advent: Friday between 9 and 15 December

Year 1 and Year 2

A reading from the prophecy of Isaiah.

Thus says the LORD,
  your Redeemer, the Holy One of Israel:
I am the LORD your God,
  who teaches you for your own good,
  who leads you in the way you should go.
O that you had paid attention to my commandments!
  Then your prosperity would have been like a river,
  and your success like the waves of the sea;
your offspring would have been like the sand,
  and your descendants like its grains;
their name would never be cut off
  or destroyed from before me.

This is the word of the Lord.   Isaiah 48.17–19

Responsorial Psalm

R **The Lord teaches us what is good:**
   [our delight is in the law of the Lord].   cf Isaiah 48.17, Psalm 1.3a

Blessed are they who have not walked
in the counsel of the wicked,
nor lingered in the way of sinners,
nor sat in the assembly of the scornful.
Their delight is in the law of the Lord
and they meditate on his law day and night.   R

Like a tree planted by streams of water
bearing fruit in due season,
with leaves that do not wither,
whatever they do, it shall prosper.   R

As for the wicked, it is not so with them;
they are like chaff which the wind blows away.
Therefore the wicked shall not be able to stand in the judgement,
nor the sinner in the congregation of the righteous.
For the Lord knows the way of the righteous,
but the way of the wicked shall perish.   R   Psalm 1

Hear the Gospel of our Lord Jesus Christ according to Matthew.

Jesus said to the crowds, 'To what will I compare this generation? It is like
children sitting in the market-places and calling to one another,
    "We played the flute for you, and you did not dance;
        we wailed, and you did not mourn."
'For John came neither eating nor drinking, and they say, "He has a demon";
the Son of Man came eating and drinking, and they say, "Look, a glutton and
a drunkard, a friend of tax-collectors and sinners!" Yet wisdom is vindicated
by her deeds.'

This is the Gospel of the Lord.   Matthew 11.16–19

Second Week of Advent: Saturday between 10 and 16 December

Year 1 and Year 2

Either

A reading from the book Ecclesiasticus.

Then Elijah arose, a prophet like fire,
    and his word burned like a torch.
He brought a famine upon them,
    and by his zeal he made them few in number.
By the word of the Lord he shut up the heavens,
    and also three times brought down fire.
How glorious you were, Elijah, in your wondrous deeds!
    Whose glory is equal to yours?
You were taken up by a whirlwind of fire,
    in a chariot with horses of fire.
At the appointed time, it is written, you are destined
    to calm the wrath of God before it breaks out in fury,
to turn the hearts of parents to their children,
    and to restore the tribes of Jacob.
Happy are those who saw you
    and were adorned with your love!
    For we also shall surely live.

This is the word of the Lord.   Ecclesiasticus 48.1–4, 9–11

or

A reading from the Second Book of the Kings.

Elijah said to Elisha, 'Tell me what I may do for you, before I am taken from you.' Elisha said, 'Please let me inherit a double share of your spirit.' He responded, 'You have asked a hard thing; yet, if you see me as I am being taken from you, it will be granted you; if not, it will not.' As they continued walking and talking, a chariot of fire and horses of fire separated the two of them, and Elijah ascended in a whirlwind into heaven. Elisha kept watching and crying out, 'Father, father! The chariots of Israel and its horsemen!' But when he could no longer see him, he grasped his own clothes and tore them in two pieces.

This is the word of the Lord.   2 Kings 2.9–12

Responsorial Psalm

R **Make your face shine upon us, O Lord:**
   [restore us, and we shall be saved].   cf *Psalm* 80.4, 8, 20

Hear, O Shepherd of Israel,
you that led Joseph like a flock;
shine forth, you that are enthroned upon the cherubim,
before Ephraim, Benjamin and Manasseh. R

Stir up your mighty strength
and come to our salvation.
Turn us again, O God;
show the light of your countenance, and we shall be saved. R

Let your hand be upon the man at your right hand,
the son of man you made so strong for yourself.
And so will we not go back from you;
give us life, and we shall call upon your name. R   *Psalm* 80.1–4, 18–19

Hear the Gospel of our Lord Jesus Christ according to Matthew.

The disciples asked Jesus, 'Why, then, do the scribes say that Elijah must come first?' He replied, 'Elijah is indeed coming and will restore all things; but I tell you that Elijah has already come, and they did not recognize him, but they did to him whatever they pleased. So also the Son of Man is about to suffer at their hands.' Then the disciples understood that he was speaking to them about John the Baptist.

This is the Gospel of the Lord.   *Matthew* 17.10–13

Third Week of Advent: Monday between 12 and 16 December

From 17 December to Christmas readings are provided for each specific date. See page 52 ff.

Year 1 and Year 2

A reading from the book Numbers.

Balaam looked up and saw Israel camping tribe by tribe. Then the spirit of God came upon him, and he uttered his oracle, saying:
'The oracle of Balaam son of Beor,
    the oracle of the man whose eye is clear,
the oracle of one who hears the words of God,
    who sees the vision of the Almighty,
    who falls down, but with eyes uncovered:
how fair are your tents, O Jacob,
    your encampments, O Israel!
Like palm groves that stretch far away,
    like gardens beside a river,
like aloes that the LORD has planted,
    like cedar trees beside the waters.
Water shall flow from his buckets,
    and his seed shall have abundant water,
his king shall be higher than Agag,
    and his kingdom shall be exalted.'

So he uttered his oracle, saying:
'The oracle of Balaam son of Beor,
    the oracle of the man whose eye is clear,
the oracle of one who hears the words of God,
    and knows the knowledge of the Most High,
who sees the vision of the Almighty,
    who falls down, but with his eyes uncovered:
I see him, but not now;
    I behold him, but not near –
a star shall come out of Jacob,
    and a sceptre shall rise out of Israel;
it shall crush the borderlands of Moab,
    and the territory of all the Shethites.'

This is the word of the Lord.   Numbers 24.2–7, 15–17

Responsorial Psalm

R **To you, O Lord, I lift up my soul;
[My God, in you I trust].**

Make me to know your ways, O Lord,
and teach me your paths.
Lead me in your truth and teach me,
for you are the God of my salvation;
for you have I hoped all the day long. R

Remember, Lord, your compassion and love,
for they are from everlasting.
Remember not the sins of my youth or my transgressions,
but think on me in your goodness, O Lord,
according to your steadfast love. R

Gracious and upright is the Lord;
therefore shall he teach sinners in the way.
He will guide the humble in doing right
and teach his way to the lowly. R

Psalm 25.3–8

Hear the Gospel of our Lord Jesus Christ according to Matthew.

When Jesus entered the temple, the chief priests and the elders of the people came to him as he was teaching, and said, 'By what authority are you doing these things, and who gave you this authority?' Jesus said to them, 'I will also ask you one question; if you tell me the answer, then I will also tell you by what authority I do these things. Did the baptism of John come from heaven, or was it of human origin?' And they argued with one another, 'If we say, "From heaven", he will say to us, "Why then did you not believe him?" But if we say, "Of human origin", we are afraid of the crowd; for all regard John as a prophet.' So they answered Jesus, 'We do not know.' And he said to them, 'Neither will I tell you by what authority I am doing these things.'

This is the Gospel of the Lord.

Matthew 21.23–27

Third Week of Advent: Tuesday between 13 and 16 December

From 17 December to Christmas readings are provided for each specific date. See page 52 ff.

Year 1 and Year 2

A reading from the prophecy of Zephaniah.

Ah, soiled, defiled,
    oppressing city!
It has listened to no voice;
    it has accepted no correction.
It has not trusted in the LORD;
    it has not drawn near to its God.

At that time I will change the speech of the peoples
    to a pure speech,
that all of them may call on the name of the LORD
    and serve him with one accord.
From beyond the rivers of Ethiopia
    my suppliants, my scattered ones,
    shall bring my offering.

On that day you shall not be put to shame
    because of all the deeds by which you have rebelled against me;
for then I will remove from your midst
    your proudly exultant ones,
and you shall no longer be haughty
    in my holy mountain.
For I will leave in the midst of you
    a people humble and lowly.
They shall seek refuge in the name of the LORD –
    the remnant of Israel;
they shall do no wrong
    and utter no lies,
nor shall a deceitful tongue
    be found in their mouths.
Then they will pasture and lie down,
    and no one shall make them afraid.

This is the word of the Lord. *Zephaniah 3.1–2, 9–13*

Responsorial Psalm

R **Taste and see that the Lord is good:**
   [happy are all who trust in him].   cf Psalm 34.8

I will bless the Lord at all times;
his praise shall ever be in my mouth.
My soul shall glory in the Lord;
let the humble hear and be glad.   R

O magnify the Lord with me;
let us exalt his name together.
I sought the Lord and he answered me
and delivered me from all my fears.   R

Look upon him and be radiant
and your faces shall not be ashamed.
This poor soul cried, and the Lord heard me
and saved me from all my troubles.   R

But evil shall slay the wicked
and those who hate the righteous will be condemned.
The Lord ransoms the life of his servants
and will condemn none who seek refuge in him.   R   Psalm 34.1–6, 21–22

Hear the Gospel of our Lord Jesus Christ according to Matthew.

Jesus said to the chief priests and the elders of the people, 'What do you think?
A man had two sons; he went to the first and said, "Son, go and work in the
vineyard today." He answered, "I will not"; but later he changed his mind and
went. The father went to the second and said the same; and he answered, "I
go, sir"; but he did not go. Which of the two did the will of his father?' They
said, 'The first.' Jesus said to them, 'Truly I tell you, the tax-collectors and
the prostitutes are going into the kingdom of God ahead of you. For John
came to you in the way of righteousness and you did not believe him, but
the tax-collectors and the prostitutes believed him; and even after you saw it,
you did not change your minds and believe him.'

This is the Gospel of the Lord.   Matthew 21.28–32

Third Week of Advent: Wednesday between 14 and 16 December

From 17 December to Christmas readings are provided for each specific date. See page 52 ff.

Year 1 and Year 2

A reading from the prophecy of Isaiah.

There is no one besides me;
    I am the LORD, and there is no other.
I form light and create darkness,
    I make weal and create woe;
    I the LORD do all these things.

Shower, O heavens, from above,
    and let the skies rain down righteousness;
let the earth open, that salvation may spring up,
    and let it cause righteousness to sprout up also;
    I the LORD have created it.

For thus says the LORD,
who created the heavens
    (he is God!),
who formed the earth and made it
    (he established it;
he did not create it a chaos,
    he formed it to be inhabited!):
I am the LORD, and there is no other.
    There is no other god besides me,
a righteous God and a Saviour;
    there is no one besides me.

Turn to me and be saved,
    all the ends of the earth!
    For I am God, and there is no other.
By myself I have sworn,
    from my mouth has gone forth in righteousness
    a word that shall not return:
'To me every knee shall bow,
    every tongue shall swear.'

Only in the LORD, it shall be said of me,
    are righteousness and strength;
all who were incensed against him
    shall come to him and be ashamed.
In the LORD all the offspring of Israel
    shall triumph and glory.

This is the word of the Lord.

Isaiah 45.6b–8, 18, 21b–end

Responsorial Psalm

R **The Lord was gracious to his land:**
   [and restored the fortunes of Jacob].   cf Psalm 85.1

Show us your mercy, O Lord,
and grant us your salvation.
I will listen
to what the Lord God will say.   R

For he shall speak peace to his people and to the faithful,
that they turn not again to folly.
Truly, his salvation is near to those who fear him,
that his glory may dwell in our land.   R

Mercy and truth are met together,
righteousness and peace have kissed each other.
Truth shall spring up from the earth
and righteousness look down from heaven.   R

The Lord will indeed give all that is good,
and our land will yield its increase.
Righteousness shall go before him
and direct his steps in the way.   R   Psalm 85.7—end

Hear the Gospel of our Lord Jesus Christ according to Luke.

John summoned two of his disciples and sent them to the Lord to ask, 'Are
you the one who is to come, or are we to wait for another?' When the men
had come to him, they said, 'John the Baptist has sent us to you to ask, "Are
you the one who is to come, or are we to wait for another?"' Jesus had just
then cured many people of diseases, plagues, and evil spirits, and had given
sight to many who were blind. And he answered them, 'Go and tell John what
you have seen and heard: the blind receive their sight, the lame walk, the lepers are cleansed, the deaf hear, the dead are raised, the poor have good news
brought to them. And blessed is anyone who takes no offence at me.'

This is the Gospel of the Lord.   Luke 7.18b—23

Third Week of Advent: Thursday between 15 and 16 December

From 17 December to Christmas readings are provided for each specific date. See page 52 ff.

Year 1 and Year 2

A reading from the prophecy of Isaiah.

Sing, O barren one who did not bear;
　　burst into song and shout,
　　you who have not been in labour!
For the children of the desolate woman will be more
　　than the children of her that is married, says the LORD.
Enlarge the site of your tent,
　　and let the curtains of your habitations be stretched out;
do not hold back; lengthen your cords
　　and strengthen your stakes.
For you will spread out to the right and to the left,
　　and your descendants will possess the nations
　　and will settle the desolate towns.

Do not fear, for you will not be ashamed;
　　do not be discouraged, for you will not suffer disgrace;
for you will forget the shame of your youth,
　　and the disgrace of your widowhood you will remember no more.
For your Maker is your husband,
　　the LORD of hosts is his name;
the Holy One of Israel is your Redeemer,
　　the God of the whole earth he is called.
For the LORD has called you
　　like a wife forsaken and grieved in spirit,
like the wife of a man's youth when she is cast off,
　　says your God.
For a brief moment I abandoned you,
　　but with great compassion I will gather you.
In overflowing wrath for a moment
　　I hid my face from you,
but with everlasting love I will have compassion on you,
　　says the LORD, your Redeemer.

This is like the days of Noah to me:
　　Just as I swore that the waters of Noah
　　would never again go over the earth,
so I have sworn that I will not be angry with you
　　and will not rebuke you.
For the mountains may depart
　　and the hills be removed,
but my steadfast love shall not depart from you,
　　and my covenant of peace shall not be removed,
　　says the LORD, who has compassion on you.

This is the word of the Lord.   *Isaiah 54.1–10*

Responsorial Psalm

R **I will exalt you, O Lord:**
   [because you have raised me up].   Psalm 30.1a

I will exalt you, O Lord, because you have raised me up
and have not let my foes triumph over me.
O Lord my God, I cried out to you
and you have healed me. **R**

You brought me up, O Lord, from the dead;
you restored me to life from among those that go down to the Pit.
Sing to the Lord, you servants of his;
give thanks to his holy name. **R**

For his wrath endures but the twinkling of an eye,
his favour for a lifetime.
Heaviness may endure for a night,
but joy comes in the morning. **R**

You have turned my mourning into dancing;
you have put off my sackcloth and girded me with gladness;
therefore my heart sings to you without ceasing;
O Lord my God, I will give you thanks for ever. **R**   Psalm 30.1–5, 11–end

Hear the Gospel of our Lord Jesus Christ according to Luke.

When John's messengers had gone, Jesus began to speak to the crowds about John: 'What did you go out into the wilderness to look at? A reed shaken by the wind? What then did you go out to see? Someone dressed in soft robes? Look, those who put on fine clothing and live in luxury are in royal palaces. What then did you go out to see? A prophet? Yes, I tell you, and more than a prophet. This is the one about whom it is written,
   "See, I am sending my messenger ahead of you,
      who will prepare your way before you."
'I tell you, among those born of women no one is greater than John; yet the least in the kingdom of God is greater than he.' (And all the people who heard this, including the tax-collectors, acknowledged the justice of God, because they had been baptized with John's baptism. But by refusing to be baptized by him, the Pharisees and the lawyers rejected God's purpose for themselves.)

This is the Gospel of the Lord.   Luke 7.24–30

Third Week of Advent: Friday 16 December

From 17 December to Christmas readings are provided for each specific date. See page 52 ff.

Year 1 and Year 2

A reading from the prophecy of Isaiah.

Thus says the LORD:
Maintain justice, and do what is right,
　　for soon my salvation will come,
　　and my deliverance be revealed.
Happy is the mortal who does this,
　　the one who holds it fast,
who keeps the sabbath, not profaning it,
　　and refrains from doing any evil.
Do not let the foreigner joined to the LORD say,
　　'The LORD will surely separate me from his people';

And the foreigners who join themselves to the LORD,
　　to minister to him, to love the name of the LORD,
　　and to be his servants,
all who keep the sabbath, and do not profane it,
　　and hold fast my covenant –
these I will bring to my holy mountain,
　　and make them joyful in my house of prayer;
their burnt-offerings and their sacrifices
　　will be accepted on my altar;
for my house shall be called a house of prayer
　　for all peoples.
Thus says the Lord GOD,
　　who gathers the outcasts of Israel,
I will gather others to them
　　besides those already gathered.

This is the word of the Lord.　　　　　　　　　　*Isaiah 56.1–3a, 6–8*

Responsorial Psalm

R* **Let the peoples praise you, O God,
[let all the peoples praise you].** *Psalm 67.3, 5*

God be gracious to us and bless us
and make his face to shine upon us,
that your way may be known upon earth,
your saving power among all nations.   R*

O let the nations rejoice and be glad,
for you will judge the peoples righteously
and govern the nations upon earth.   R*

Then shall the earth bring forth her increase,
and God, our own God, will bless us.
God will bless us,
and all the ends of the earth shall fear him.   R   *Psalm 67*

Hear the Gospel of our Lord Jesus Christ according to John.

Jesus said to the Jews, 'You sent messengers to John, and he testified to the truth. Not that I accept such human testimony, but I say these things so that you may be saved. He was a burning and shining lamp, and you were willing to rejoice for a while in his light. But I have a testimony greater than John's. The works that the Father has given me to complete, the very works that I am doing, testify on my behalf that the Father has sent me.'

This is the Gospel of the Lord. *John 5.33–36*

17 December

From 17 December to Christmas readings are provided for each specific date. These readings do not supersede those for the Fourth Sunday of Advent.

Year 1 and Year 2

A reading from the book Genesis.

Assemble and hear, O sons of Jacob;
    listen to Israel your father.
'Judah, your brothers shall praise you;
    your hand shall be on the neck of your enemies;
    your father's sons shall bow down before you.
Judah is a lion's whelp;
    from the prey, my son, you have gone up.
He crouches down, he stretches out like a lion,
    like a lioness – who dares rouse him up?
The sceptre shall not depart from Judah,
    nor the ruler's staff from between his feet,
until tribute comes to him;
    and the obedience of the peoples is his.'

This is the word of the Lord. Genesis 49.2, 8–10

Responsorial Psalm

R **Righteousness and peace shall flourish:**
    [till the moon shall be no more]. cf Psalm 72.7

Give the king your judgements, O God,
and your righteousness to the son of a king.
Then shall he judge your people righteously
and your poor with justice. **R**

May the mountains bring forth peace,
and the little hills righteousness for the people.
May he defend the poor among the people,
deliver the children of the needy and crush the oppressor. **R**

May he live as long as the sun and moon endure,
from one generation to another. **R**

Blessed be the Lord, the God of Israel,
who alone does wonderful things.
And blessed be his glorious name for ever.
May all the earth be filled with his glory. **R** Psalm 72.1–5, 18–19

Hear the Gospel of our Lord Jesus Christ according to Matthew.

An account of the genealogy of Jesus the Messiah, the son of David, the son of Abraham.

Abraham was the father of Isaac, and Isaac the father of Jacob, and Jacob the father of Judah and his brothers, and Judah the father of Perez and Zerah by Tamar, and Perez the father of Hezron, and Hezron the father of Aram, and Aram the father of Aminadab, and Aminadab the father of Nahshon, and Nahshon the father of Salmon, and Salmon the father of Boaz by Rahab, and Boaz the father of Obed by Ruth, and Obed the father of Jesse, and Jesse the father of King David.

And David was the father of Solomon by the wife of Uriah, and Solomon the father of Rehoboam, and Rehoboam the father of Abijah, and Abijah the father of Asaph, and Asaph the father of Jehoshaphat, and Jehoshaphat the father of Joram, and Joram the father of Uzziah, and Uzziah the father of Jotham, and Jotham the father of Ahaz, and Ahaz the father of Hezekiah, and Hezekiah the father of Manasseh, and Manasseh the father of Amos, and Amos the father of Josiah, and Josiah the father of Jechoniah and his brothers, at the time of the deportation to Babylon.

And after the deportation to Babylon: Jechoniah was the father of Salathiel, and Salathiel the father of Zerubbabel, and Zerubbabel the father of Abiud, and Abiud the father of Eliakim, and Eliakim the father of Azor, and Azor the father of Zadok, and Zadok the father of Achim, and Achim the father of Eliud, and Eliud the father of Eleazar, and Eleazar the father of Matthan, and Matthan the father of Jacob, and Jacob the father of Joseph the husband of Mary, of whom Jesus was born, who is called the Messiah.

So all the generations from Abraham to David are fourteen generations; and from David to the deportation to Babylon, fourteen generations; and from the deportation to Babylon to the Messiah, fourteen generations.

This is the Gospel of the Lord.   Matthew 1.1–17

18 December

From 17 December to Christmas readings are provided for each specific date. These readings do not supersede those for the Fourth Sunday of Advent.

Year 1 and Year 2

A reading from the prophecy of Jeremiah.

The days are surely coming, says the LORD, when I will raise up for David a righteous Branch, and he shall reign as king and deal wisely, and shall execute justice and righteousness in the land. In his days Judah will be saved and Israel will live in safety. And this is the name by which he will be called: 'The LORD is our righteousness.'

Therefore, the days are surely coming, says the LORD, when it shall no longer be said, 'As the LORD lives who brought the people of Israel up out of the land of Egypt', but 'As the LORD lives who brought out and led the offspring of the house of Israel out of the land of the north and out of all the lands where he had driven them.' Then they shall live in their own land.

This is the word of the Lord.   Jeremiah 23.5–8

Responsorial Psalm

R **Righteousness and peace shall flourish:**
  [till the moon shall be no more].   cf Psalm 72.7

Give the king your judgements, O God,
and your righteousness to the son of a king.
Then shall he judge your people righteously
and your poor with justice.   R

For he shall deliver the poor that cry out,
the needy and those who have no helper.
He shall have pity on the weak and poor;
he shall preserve the lives of the needy.   R

Blessed be the Lord, the God of Israel,
who alone does wonderful things.
And blessed be his glorious name for ever.
May all the earth be filled with his glory.   R   Psalm 72.1–2, 12–13, 18–end

Hear the Gospel of our Lord Jesus Christ according to Matthew.

Now the birth of Jesus the Messiah took place in this way. When his mother Mary had been engaged to Joseph, but before they lived together, she was found to be with child from the Holy Spirit. Her husband Joseph, being a righteous man and unwilling to expose her to public disgrace, planned to dismiss her quietly. But just when he had resolved to do this, an angel of the Lord appeared to him in a dream and said, 'Joseph, son of David, do not be afraid to take Mary as your wife, for the child conceived in her is from the Holy Spirit. She will bear a son, and you are to name him Jesus, for he will save his people from their sins.' All this took place to fulfil what had been spoken by the Lord through the prophet:

'Look, the virgin shall conceive and bear a son,
    and they shall name him Emmanuel',

which means, 'God is with us.' When Joseph awoke from sleep, he did as the angel of the Lord commanded him; he took her as his wife.

This is the Gospel of the Lord.   Matthew 1.18–24

19 December

From 17 December to Christmas readings are provided for each specific date. These readings do not supersede those for the Fourth Sunday of Advent.

Year 1 and Year 2

A reading from the book Judges.

There was a certain man of Zorah, of the tribe of the Danites, whose name was Manoah. His wife was barren, having borne no children. And the angel of the LORD appeared to the woman and said to her, 'Although you are barren, having borne no children, you shall conceive and bear a son. Now be careful not to drink wine or strong drink, or to eat anything unclean, for you shall conceive and bear a son. No razor is to come on his head, for the boy shall be a nazirite to God from birth. It is he who shall begin to deliver Israel from the hand of the Philistines.' Then the woman came and told her husband, 'A man of God came to me, and his appearance was like that of an angel of God, most awe-inspiring; I did not ask him where he came from, and he did not tell me his name; but he said to me, "You shall conceive and bear a son. So then drink no wine or strong drink, and eat nothing unclean, for the boy shall be a nazirite to God from birth to the day of his death."'

The woman bore a son, and named him Samson. The boy grew, and the LORD blessed him. The spirit of the LORD began to stir him in Mahaneh-dan, between Zorah and Eshtaol.

This is the word of the Lord.   Judges 13.2–7, 24–end

R **Deliver me, O Lord, and set me free:**
 [come quickly to my help]. *cf Psalm 71.2a, 12b*

Be for me a stronghold to which I may ever resort;
send out to save me, for you are my rock and my fortress.
Deliver me, my God, from the hand of the wicked,
from the grasp of the evildoer and the oppressor. R

For you are my hope, O Lord God,
my confidence, even from my youth.
Upon you have I leaned from my birth,
when you drew me from my mother's womb. R

My praise shall be always of you.
I have become a portent to many,
but you are my refuge and my strength.
Let my mouth be full of your praise
and your glory all the day long. R *Psalm 71.3–8*

Hear the Gospel of our Lord Jesus Christ according to Luke.

In the days of King Herod of Judea, there was a priest named Zechariah, who belonged to the priestly order of Abijah. His wife was a descendant of Aaron, and her name was Elizabeth. Both of them were righteous before God, living blamelessly according to all the commandments and regulations of the Lord. But they had no children, because Elizabeth was barren, and both were getting on in years.

Once when he was serving as priest before God and his section was on duty, he was chosen by lot, according to the custom of the priesthood, to enter the sanctuary of the Lord and offer incense. Now at the time of the incense-offering, the whole assembly of the people was praying outside. Then there appeared to him an angel of the Lord, standing at the right side of the altar of incense. When Zechariah saw him, he was terrified; and fear overwhelmed him. But the angel said to him, 'Do not be afraid, Zechariah, for your prayer has been heard. Your wife Elizabeth will bear you a son, and you will name him John. You will have joy and gladness, and many will rejoice at his birth, for he will be great in the sight of the Lord. He must never drink wine or strong drink; even before his birth he will be filled with the Holy Spirit. He will turn many of the people of Israel to the Lord their God. With the spirit and power of Elijah he will go before him, to turn the hearts of parents to their children, and the disobedient to the wisdom of the righteous, to make ready a people prepared for the Lord.' Zechariah said to the angel, 'How will I know that this is so? For I am an old man, and my wife is getting on in years.' The angel replied, 'I am Gabriel. I stand in the presence of God, and I have been sent to speak to you and to bring you this good news. But now, because you did not believe my words, which will be fulfilled in their time, you will become mute, unable to speak, until the day these things occur.'

Meanwhile, the people were waiting for Zechariah, and wondered at his delay in the sanctuary. When he did come out, he could not speak to them, and they realized that he had seen a vision in the sanctuary. He kept motioning to them and remained unable to speak. When his time of service was ended, he went to his home.

After those days his wife Elizabeth conceived, and for five months she remained in seclusion. She said, 'This is what the Lord has done for me when he looked favourably on me and took away the disgrace I have endured among my people.'

This is the Gospel of the Lord.   *Luke 1.5–25*

20 December

From 17 December to Christmas readings are provided for each specific date. These readings do not supersede those for the Fourth Sunday of Advent.

Year 1 and Year 2

A reading from the prophecy of Isaiah.

The LORD spoke to Ahaz, saying, Ask a sign of the LORD your God; let it be deep as Sheol or high as heaven. But Ahaz said, I will not ask, and I will not put the LORD to the test. Then Isaiah said: 'Hear then, O house of David! Is it too little for you to weary mortals, that you weary my God also? Therefore the Lord himself will give you a sign. Look, the young woman is with child and shall bear a son, and shall name him Immanuel.'

This is the word of the Lord.   *Isaiah 7.10–14*

Responsorial Psalm

R **The Lord of hosts is the king of glory:**
   [the king of glory shall come in].   *cf Psalm 24.10b, 7b*

The earth is the Lord's and all that fills it,
the compass of the world and all who dwell therein.
For he has founded it upon the seas
and set it firm upon the rivers of the deep.   **R**

'Who shall ascend the hill of the Lord,
or who can rise up in his holy place?
Those who have clean hands and a pure heart,
who have not lifted up their soul to an idol,
nor sworn an oath to a lie.   **R**

'They shall receive a blessing from the Lord,
a just reward from the God of their salvation.'
Such is the company of those who seek him,
of those who seek your face, O God of Jacob.   **R**   *Psalm 24.1–6*

Hear the Gospel of our Lord Jesus Christ according to Luke.

In the sixth month the angel Gabriel was sent by God to a town in Galilee called Nazareth, to a virgin engaged to a man whose name was Joseph, of the house of David. The virgin's name was Mary. And he came to her and said, 'Greetings, favoured one! The Lord is with you.' But she was much perplexed by his words and pondered what sort of greeting this might be. The angel said to her, 'Do not be afraid, Mary, for you have found favour with God. And now, you will conceive in your womb and bear a son, and you will name him Jesus. He will be great, and will be called the Son of the Most High, and the Lord God will give to him the throne of his ancestor David. He will reign over the house of Jacob for ever, and of his kingdom there will be no end.' Mary said to the angel, 'How can this be, since I am a virgin?' The angel said to her, 'The Holy Spirit will come upon you, and the power of the Most High will overshadow you; therefore the child to be born will be holy; he will be called Son of God. And now, your relative Elizabeth in her old age has also conceived a son; and this is the sixth month for her who was said to be barren. For nothing will be impossible with God.' Then Mary said, 'Here am I, the servant of the Lord; let it be with me according to your word.' Then the angel departed from her.

This is the Gospel of the Lord.   Luke 1.26–38

21 December

From 17 December to Christmas readings are provided for each specific date. These readings do not supersede those for the Fourth Sunday of Advent.

Year 1 and Year 2

A reading from the prophecy of Zephaniah.

Sing aloud, O daughter Zion;
    shout, O Israel!
Rejoice and exult with all your heart,
    O daughter Jerusalem!
The LORD has taken away the judgements against you,
    he has turned away your enemies.
The king of Israel, the LORD, is in your midst;
    you shall fear disaster no more.
On that day it shall be said to Jerusalem:
Do not fear, O Zion;
    do not let your hands grow weak.
The LORD, your God, is in your midst,
    a warrior who gives victory;
he will rejoice over you with gladness,
    he will renew you in his love;

he will exult over you with loud singing
    as on a day of festival.
I will remove disaster from you,
    so that you will not bear reproach for it.

This is the word of the Lord. *Zephaniah 3.14–18*

Responsorial Psalm

R* **Rejoice in the Lord, O you righteous:**
[it is good to sing his praises]. *cf Psalm 33.1*

Praise the Lord with the lyre;
on the ten-stringed harp sing his praise.
Sing for him a new song;
play skilfully, with shouts of praise.   **R**

For the word of the Lord is true
and all his works are sure.
But the counsel of the Lord shall endure for ever
and the designs of his heart from generation to generation.   **R**

Happy the nation whose God is the Lord
and the people he has chosen for his own.
Our soul waits longingly for the Lord;
he is our help and our shield.   **R**

Indeed, our heart rejoices in him;
in his holy name have we put our trust.
Let your loving-kindness, O Lord, be upon us,
as we have set our hope on you.   **R** *Psalm 33.1–4, 11–12, 20–end*

Hear the Gospel of our Lord Jesus Christ according to Luke.

Mary set out and went with haste to a Judean town in the hill country, where she entered the house of Zechariah and greeted Elizabeth. When Elizabeth heard Mary's greeting, the child leapt in her womb. And Elizabeth was filled with the Holy Spirit and exclaimed with a loud cry, 'Blessed are you among women, and blessed is the fruit of your womb. And why has this happened to me, that the mother of my Lord comes to me? For as soon as I heard the sound of your greeting, the child in my womb leapt for joy. And blessed is she who believed that there would be a fulfilment of what was spoken to her by the Lord.'

This is the Gospel of the Lord. *Luke 1.39–45*

22 December

From 17 December to Christmas readings are provided for each specific date. These readings do not supersede those for the Fourth Sunday of Advent.

Year 1 and Year 2

A reading from the First Book of Samuel.

When Hannah had weaned Samuel, she took him up with her, along with a three-year-old bull, an ephah of flour, and a skin of wine. She brought him to the house of the LORD at Shiloh; and the child was young. Then they slaughtered the bull, and they brought the child to Eli. And she said, 'Oh, my lord! As you live, my lord, I am the woman who was standing here in your presence, praying to the LORD. For this child I prayed; and the LORD has granted me the petition that I made to him. Therefore I have lent him to the LORD; as long as he lives, he is given to the LORD.' She left him there for the LORD.

This is the word of the Lord. 1 Samuel 1.24–end

Responsorial Psalm

R **Blessed be the name of the Lord:**
  [from this time forth and for evermore]. Psalm 113.2

Give praise, you servants of the Lord,
O praise the name of the Lord.
Blessed be the name of the Lord,
from this time forth and for evermore. **R**

From the rising of the sun to its setting
let the name of the Lord be praised.
The Lord is high above all nations
and his glory above the heavens. **R**

Who is like the Lord our God,
that has his throne so high,
yet humbles himself to behold
the things of heaven and earth? **R**

He raises the poor from the dust
and lifts the needy from the ashes,
to set them with princes,
with the princes of his people.
He gives the barren woman a place in the house
and makes her a joyful mother of children. **R** Psalm 113

Hear the Gospel of our Lord Jesus Christ according to Luke.

Mary said,
'My soul magnifies the Lord,
and my spirit rejoices in God my Saviour,
for he has looked with favour on the lowliness of his servant.
    Surely, from now on all generations will call me blessed;
for the Mighty One has done great things for me,
    and holy is his name.
His mercy is for those who fear him
    from generation to generation.
He has shown strength with his arm;
    he has scattered the proud in the thoughts of their hearts.
He has brought down the powerful from their thrones,
    and lifted up the lowly;
he has filled the hungry with good things,
    and sent the rich away empty.
He has helped his servant Israel,
    in remembrance of his mercy,
according to the promise he made to our ancestors,
    to Abraham and to his descendants for ever.'

And Mary remained with Elizabeth for about three months and then returned to her home.

This is the Gospel of the Lord.   Luke 1.46–56

23 December

From 17 December to Christmas readings are provided for each specific date. These readings do not supersede those for the Fourth Sunday of Advent.

Year 1 and Year 2

A reading from the prophecy of Malachi.

See, I am sending my messenger to prepare the way before me, and the Lord whom you seek will suddenly come to his temple. The messenger of the covenant in whom you delight – indeed, he is coming, says the LORD of hosts. But who can endure the day of his coming, and who can stand when he appears?

For he is like a refiner's fire and like fullers' soap; he will sit as a refiner and purifier of silver, and he will purify the descendants of Levi and refine them like gold and silver, until they present offerings to the LORD in righteousness. Then the offering of Judah and Jerusalem will be pleasing to the LORD as in the days of old and as in former years.

Lo, I will send you the prophet Elijah before the great and terrible day of the LORD comes. He will turn the hearts of parents to their children and the hearts of children to their parents, so that I will not come and strike the land with a curse.

This is the word of the Lord.   Malachi 3.1–4, 4.5–end

R **To you, O Lord, I lift up my soul;
   [My God, in you I trust].**

cf Psalm 25.1a

Make me to know your ways, O Lord,
and teach me your paths.
Lead me in your truth and teach me,
for you are the God of my salvation;
for you have I hoped all the day long. **R**

Remember, Lord, your compassion and love,
for they are from everlasting.
Remember not the sins of my youth
or my transgressions. **R**

But think on me in your goodness, O Lord,
according to your steadfast love.
Gracious and upright is the Lord;
therefore shall he teach sinners in the way. **R**

He will guide the humble in doing right
and teach his way to the lowly.
All the paths of the Lord are mercy and truth
to those who keep his covenant and his testimonies. **R**   *Psalm 25.3–9*

Hear the Gospel of our Lord Jesus Christ according to Luke.

The time came for Elizabeth to give birth, and she bore a son. Her neighbours and relatives heard that the Lord had shown his great mercy to her, and they rejoiced with her.

On the eighth day they came to circumcise the child, and they were going to name him Zechariah after his father. But his mother said, 'No; he is to be called John.' They said to her, 'None of your relatives has this name.' Then they began motioning to his father to find out what name he wanted to give him. He asked for a writing-tablet and wrote, 'His name is John.' And all of them were amazed. Immediately his mouth was opened and his tongue freed, and he began to speak, praising God. Fear came over all their neighbours, and all these things were talked about throughout the entire hill country of Judea. All who heard them pondered them and said, 'What then will this child become?' For, indeed, the hand of the Lord was with him.

This is the Gospel of the Lord.   *Luke 1.57–66*

24 December: Christmas Eve

From 17 December to Christmas readings are provided for each specific date. These readings do not supersede those for the Fourth Sunday of Advent.

Year 1 and Year 2

A reading from the Second Book of Samuel.

When King David was settled in his house, and the LORD had given him rest from all his enemies around him, the king said to the prophet Nathan, 'See now, I am living in a house of cedar, but the ark of God stays in a tent.' Nathan said to the king, 'Go, do all that you have in mind; for the LORD is with you.'

But that same night the word of the LORD came to Nathan: Go and tell my servant David: Thus says the LORD: Are you the one to build me a house to live in? Now therefore thus you shall say to my servant David: Thus says the LORD of hosts: I took you from the pasture, from following the sheep to be prince over my people Israel; and I have been with you wherever you went, and have cut off all your enemies from before you; and I will make for you a great name, like the name of the great ones of the earth. And I will appoint a place for my people Israel and will plant them, so that they may live in their own place, and be disturbed no more; and evildoers shall afflict them no more, as formerly, from the time that I appointed judges over my people Israel; and I will give you rest from all your enemies. Moreover, the LORD declares to you that the LORD will make you a house. Your house and your kingdom shall be made sure for ever before me; your throne shall be established for ever.

This is the word of the Lord.   2 Samuel 7.1–5, 8–11, 16

Responsorial Psalm

R* **Your love, O God, is established for ever:**
   [your faithfulness as firm as the heavens].   cf Psalm 89.2

You spoke once in a vision
and said to your faithful people:
I have set a youth above the mighty;
I have raised a young man over the people.   **R**

I have found David my servant;
with my holy oil have I anointed him.
My hand shall hold him fast
and my arm shall strengthen him.   **R**

No enemy shall deceive him,
nor any wicked person afflict him.
I will strike down his foes before his face
and beat down those that hate him.   **R**   →

My truth also and my steadfast love shall be with him,
and in my name shall his head be exalted.
I will set his dominion upon the sea
and his right hand upon the rivers.   R

R* **Your love, O God, is established for ever:**
[your faithfulness as firm as the heavens].

He shall call to me, 'You are my Father,
my God, and the rock of my salvation;'
And I will make him my firstborn,
the most high above the kings of the earth.   R   Psalm 89.2, 19–27

A reading from the Acts of the Apostles

Paul stood up and with a gesture began to speak: 'You Israelites, and others
who fear God, listen. The God of this people Israel chose our ancestors and
made the people great during their stay in the land of Egypt, and with uplifted
arm he led them out of it. For about forty years he put up with them in the
wilderness. After he had destroyed seven nations in the land of Canaan, he
gave them their land as an inheritance for about four hundred and fifty years.
After that he gave them judges until the time of the prophet Samuel. Then they
asked for a king; and God gave them Saul son of Kish, a man of the tribe of
Benjamin, who reigned for forty years. When he had removed him, he made
David their king. In his testimony about him he said, "I have found David, son
of Jesse, to be a man after my heart, who will carry out all my wishes." Of
this man's posterity God has brought to Israel a Saviour, Jesus, as he promised;
before his coming John had already proclaimed a baptism of repentance to
all the people of Israel. And as John was finishing his work, he said, "What
do you suppose that I am? I am not he. No, but one is coming after me; I am
not worthy to untie the thong of the sandals on his feet."

'My brothers, you descendants of Abraham's family, and others who fear
God, to us the message of this salvation has been sent.'

This is the word of the Lord.   Acts 13.16–26

Hear the Gospel of our Lord Jesus Christ according to Luke.

John's father Zechariah was filled with the Holy Spirit and spoke this prophecy:
'Blessed be the Lord God of Israel,
for he has looked favourably on his people and redeemed them.
He has raised up a mighty saviour for us
in the house of his servant David,
as he spoke through the mouth of his holy prophets from of old,
that we would be saved from our enemies
and from the hand of all who hate us.
Thus he has shown the mercy promised to our ancestors,
and has remembered his holy covenant,
the oath that he swore to our ancestor Abraham,
to grant us that we, being rescued from the hands of our enemies,
might serve him without fear, in holiness and righteousness
before him all our days.
And you, child, will be called the prophet of the Most High;
for you will go before the Lord to prepare his ways,
to give knowledge of salvation to his people
by the forgiveness of their sins.
By the tender mercy of our God,
the dawn from on high will break upon us,
to give light to those who sit in darkness and in the shadow of death,
to guide our feet into the way of peace.'

This is the Gospel of the Lord.

Luke 1.67–79

CHRISTMAS

25 December: Christmas Day
26 December: Stephen, Deacon, First Martyr
27 December: John, Apostle and Evangelist
28 December: the Holy Innocents

Provision is made for the period 25–28 December in the lectionary for Principal Feasts and Festivals.

29 December: Fifth Day of Christmas

From 29 December until 5 January readings are provided for each specific date. These readings do not supersede those for the First or Second Sundays of Christmas.

Year 1 and Year 2

A reading from the First Letter of John.

We may be sure that we know God, if we obey his commandments. Whoever says, 'I have come to know him', but does not obey his commandments, is a liar, and in such a person the truth does not exist; but whoever obeys his word, truly in this person the love of God has reached perfection. By this we may be sure that we are in him: whoever says, 'I abide in him', ought to walk just as he walked.

Beloved, I am writing you no new commandment, but an old commandment that you have had from the beginning; the old commandment is the word that you have heard. Yet I am writing you a new commandment that is true in him and in you, because the darkness is passing away and the true light is already shining. Whoever says, 'I am in the light', while hating a brother or sister, is still in the darkness. Whoever loves a brother or sister lives in the light, and in such a person there is no cause for stumbling. But whoever hates another believer is in the darkness, walks in the darkness, and does not know the way to go, because the darkness has brought on blindness.

This is the word of the Lord.   1 John 2.3–11

Responsorial Psalm

R **Let the heavens rejoice and the earth be glad.** *cf Psalm 96.11a*

Sing to the Lord a new song;
sing to the Lord, all the earth.
Sing to the Lord and bless his name;
tell out his salvation from day to day. **R**

Declare his glory among the nations
and his wonders among all peoples.
For great is the Lord and greatly to be praised;
he is more to be feared than all gods. **R** *Psalm 96.1–4*

Hear the Gospel of our Lord Jesus Christ according to Luke.

When the time came for their purification according to the law of Moses, Mary and Joseph brought Jesus up to Jerusalem to present him to the Lord (as it is written in the law of the Lord, 'Every firstborn male shall be designated as holy to the Lord'), and they offered a sacrifice according to what is stated in the law of the Lord, 'a pair of turtle-doves or two young pigeons.'

Now there was a man in Jerusalem whose name was Simeon; this man was righteous and devout, looking forward to the consolation of Israel, and the Holy Spirit rested on him. It had been revealed to him by the Holy Spirit that he would not see death before he had seen the Lord's Messiah. Guided by the Spirit, Simeon came into the temple; and when the parents brought in the child Jesus, to do for him what was customary under the law, Simeon took him in his arms and praised God, saying,

'Master, now you are dismissing your servant in peace,
according to your word;
for my eyes have seen your salvation,
which you have prepared in the presence of all peoples,
a light for revelation to the Gentiles
and for glory to your people Israel.'

And the child's father and mother were amazed at what was being said about him. Then Simeon blessed them and said to his mother Mary, 'This child is destined for the falling and the rising of many in Israel, and to be a sign that will be opposed so that the inner thoughts of many will be revealed – and a sword will pierce your own soul too.'

This is the Gospel of the Lord. *Luke 2.22–35*

30 December: Sixth Day of Christmas

From 29 December until 5 January readings are provided for each specific date. These readings do not supersede those for the First or Second Sundays of Christmas.

Year 1 and Year 2

A reading from the First Letter of John.

I am writing to you, little children,
> because your sins are forgiven on account of his name.
I am writing to you, fathers,
> because you know him who is from the beginning.
I am writing to you, young people,
> because you have conquered the evil one.
I write to you, children,
> because you know the Father.
I write to you, fathers,
> because you know him who is from the beginning.
I write to you, young people,
> because you are strong
> and the word of God abides in you,
> > and you have overcome the evil one.

Do not love the world or the things in the world. The love of the Father is not in those who love the world; for all that is in the world – the desire of the flesh, the desire of the eyes, the pride in riches – comes not from the Father but from the world. And the world and its desire are passing away, but those who do the will of God live for ever.

This is the word of the Lord.   1 John 2.12–17

Responsorial Psalm

**R* O worship the Lord in the beauty of holiness:
[let the whole earth tremble before him].**   Psalm 96.9

Ascribe to the Lord, you families of the peoples,
ascribe to the Lord honour and strength.
Ascribe to the Lord the honour due to his name;
bring offerings and come into his courts.   **R***

Tell it out among the nations that the Lord is king.
He has made the world so firm that it cannot be moved;
he will judge the peoples with equity.   **R**   Psalm 96.7–10

Hear the Gospel of our Lord Jesus Christ according to Luke.

There was a prophet, Anna the daughter of Phanuel, of the tribe of Asher. She was of a great age, having lived with her husband for seven years after her marriage, then as a widow to the age of eighty-four. She never left the temple but worshipped there with fasting and prayer night and day. At that moment she came, and began to praise God and to speak about the child to all who were looking for the redemption of Jerusalem.

When they had finished everything required by the law of the Lord, they returned to Galilee, to their own town of Nazareth. The child grew and became strong, filled with wisdom; and the favour of God was upon him.

This is the Gospel of the Lord.   Luke 2.36–40

31 December: Seventh Day of Christmas

From 29 December until 5 January readings are provided for each specific date. These readings do not supersede those for the First or Second Sundays of Christmas.

Year 1 and Year 2

A reading from the First Letter of John.

Children, it is the last hour! As you have heard that antichrist is coming, so now many antichrists have come. From this we know that it is the last hour. They went out from us, but they did not belong to us; for if they had belonged to us, they would have remained with us. But by going out they made it plain that none of them belongs to us. But you have been anointed by the Holy One, and all of you have knowledge. I write to you, not because you do not know the truth, but because you know it, and you know that no lie comes from the truth.

This is the word of the Lord.   1 John 2.18–21

Responsorial Psalm

R **Let the heavens rejoice and the earth be glad.**   cf Psalm 96.11a

Sing to the Lord a new song;
sing to the Lord, all the earth.
Let the heavens rejoice and let the earth be glad.   **R**

Let the sea thunder and all that is in it;
let the fields be joyful and all that is in them;
let all the trees of the wood shout for joy before the Lord.   **R**

For he comes, he comes to judge the earth;
with righteousness he will judge the world
and the peoples with his truth.   **R**   Psalm 96.1, 11–end

Hear the Gospel of our Lord Jesus Christ according to John.

In the beginning was the Word, and the Word was with God, and the Word was God. He was in the beginning with God. All things came into being through him, and without him not one thing came into being. What has come into being in him was life, and the life was the light of all people. The light shines in the darkness, and the darkness did not overcome it.

There was a man sent from God, whose name was John. He came as a witness to testify to the light, so that all might believe through him. He himself was not the light, but he came to testify to the light. The true light, which enlightens everyone, was coming into the world.

He was in the world, and the world came into being through him; yet the world did not know him. He came to what was his own, and his own people did not accept him. But to all who received him, who believed in his name, he gave power to become children of God, who were born, not of blood or of the will of the flesh or of the will of man, but of God.

And the Word became flesh and lived among us, and we have seen his glory, the glory as of a father's only son, full of grace and truth. (John testified to him and cried out, 'This was he of whom I said, "He who comes after me ranks ahead of me because he was before me."') From his fullness we have all received, grace upon grace. The law indeed was given through Moses; grace and truth came through Jesus Christ. No one has ever seen God. It is God the only Son, who is close to the Father's heart, who has made him known.

This is the Gospel of the Lord. John 1.1–18

1 January: The Naming and Circumcision of Jesus

Provision is made for 1 January in the lectionary for Festivals.

If, for pastoral reasons, the Epiphany is celebrated on the Sunday between 2 and 5 January, the following readings are not used after that Sunday.

2 January: Ninth Day of Christmas

From 29 December until 5 January readings are provided for each specific date. These readings do not supersede those for the First or Second Sundays of Christmas.

Year 1 and Year 2

A reading from the First Letter of John.

Who is the liar but the one who denies that Jesus is the Christ? This is the antichrist, the one who denies the Father and the Son. No one who denies the Son has the Father; everyone who confesses the Son has the Father also. Let what you heard from the beginning abide in you. If what you heard from the beginning abides in you, then you will abide in the Son and in the Father. And this is what he has promised us, eternal life.

I write these things to you concerning those who would deceive you. As for you, the anointing that you received from him abides in you, and so you do not need anyone to teach you. But as his anointing teaches you about all things, and is true and is not a lie, and just as it has taught you, abide in him.

And now, little children, abide in him, so that when he is revealed we may have confidence and not be put to shame before him at his coming.

This is the word of the Lord. 1 John 2.22–28

Responsorial Psalm

R **Sound praises to the Lord, all the earth;
[break into song and make music].** cf Psalm 98.5

Sing to the Lord a new song,
for he has done marvellous things.
His own right hand and his holy arm
have won for him the victory. R

The Lord has made known his salvation;
his deliverance has he openly shown
in the sight of the nations. R

He has remembered his mercy and faithfulness
towards the house of Israel,
and all the ends of the earth have seen
the salvation of our God. R Psalm 98.1–4

Hear the Gospel of our Lord Jesus Christ according to John.

This is the testimony given by John when the Jews sent priests and Levites from Jerusalem to ask him, 'Who are you?' He confessed and did not deny it, but confessed, 'I am not the Messiah.' And they asked him, 'What then? Are you Elijah?' He said, 'I am not.' 'Are you the prophet?' He answered, 'No.' Then they said to him, 'Who are you? Let us have an answer for those who sent us. What do you say about yourself?' He said,

'I am the voice of one crying out in the wilderness,
"Make straight the way of the Lord" ',
as the prophet Isaiah said.

Now they had been sent from the Pharisees. They asked him, 'Why then are you baptizing if you are neither the Messiah, nor Elijah, nor the prophet?' John answered them, 'I baptize with water. Among you stands one whom you do not know, the one who is coming after me; I am not worthy to untie the thong of his sandal.' This took place in Bethany across the Jordan where John was baptizing.

This is the Gospel of the Lord. John 1.19–28

3 January: Tenth Day of Christmas

From 29 December until 5 January readings are provided for each specific date. These readings do not supersede those for the First or Second Sundays of Christmas.

Year 1 and Year 2

A reading from the First Letter of John.

If you know that God is righteous, you may be sure that everyone who does right has been born of him. See what love the Father has given us, that we should be called children of God; and that is what we are. The reason the world does not know us is that it did not know him. Beloved, we are God's children now; what we will be has not yet been revealed. What we do know is this: when he is revealed, we will be like him, for we will see him as he is. And all who have this hope in him purify themselves, just as he is pure.

Everyone who commits sin is guilty of lawlessness; sin is lawlessness. You know that he was revealed to take away sins, and in him there is no sin. No one who abides in him sins; no one who sins has either seen him or known him.

This is the word of the Lord.
1 John 2.29 – 3.6

Responsorial Psalm

R* **Sound praises to the Lord, all the earth;**
  [break into song and make music].
cf Psalm 98.5

His own right hand and his holy arm
have won for him the victory.
The Lord has made known his salvation;
his deliverance has he openly shown in the sight of the nations.   **R**

He has remembered his mercy and faithfulness
towards the house of Israel;
and all the ends of the earth have seen
the salvation of our God.   **R***

Make music to the Lord with the lyre,
with the lyre and the voice of melody.
With trumpets and the sound of the horn
sound praises before the Lord, the King.   **R**
Psalm 98.2–7

Hear the Gospel of our Lord Jesus Christ according to John.

John saw Jesus coming towards him and declared, 'Here is the Lamb of God who takes away the sin of the world! This is he of whom I said, "After me comes a man who ranks ahead of me because he was before me." I myself did not know him; but I came baptizing with water for this reason, that he might be revealed to Israel.' And John testified, 'I saw the Spirit descending from heaven like a dove, and it remained on him. I myself did not know him, but the one who sent me to baptize with water said to me, "He on whom you see the Spirit descend and remain is the one who baptizes with the Holy Spirit." And I myself have seen and have testified that this is the Son of God.'

This is the Gospel of the Lord.

John 1.29–34

4 January: Eleventh Day of Christmas

From 29 December until 5 January readings are provided for each specific date. These readings do not supersede those for the First or Second Sundays of Christmas.

Year 1 and Year 2

A reading from the First Letter of John.

Little children, let no one deceive you. Everyone who does what is right is righteous, just as God is righteous. Everyone who commits sin is a child of the devil; for the devil has been sinning from the beginning. The Son of God was revealed for this purpose, to destroy the works of the devil. Those who have been born of God do not sin, because God's seed abides in them; they cannot sin, because they have been born of God. The children of God and the children of the devil are revealed in this way: all who do not do what is right are not from God, nor are those who do not love their brothers and sisters.

This is the word of the Lord.

1 John 3.7–10

Responsorial Psalm

R **Sound praises to the Lord, all the earth;**
  [break into song and make music].

cf *Psalm* 98.5

Sing to the Lord a new song,
for he has done marvellous things.
Let the sea thunder and all that fills it,
the world and all that dwell upon it.   **R**

Let the rivers clap their hands
and let the hills ring out together before the Lord,
for he comes to judge the earth.
In righteousness shall he judge the world
and the peoples with equity.   **R**

Psalm 98.1, 8–end

Hear the Gospel of our Lord Jesus Christ according to John.

John was standing with two of his disciples, and as he watched Jesus walk by, he exclaimed, 'Look, here is the Lamb of God!' The two disciples heard him say this, and they followed Jesus. When Jesus turned and saw them following, he said to them, 'What are you looking for?' They said to him, 'Rabbi' (which translated means Teacher), 'where are you staying?' He said to them, 'Come and see.' They came and saw where he was staying, and they remained with him that day. It was about four o'clock in the afternoon. One of the two who heard John speak and followed him was Andrew, Simon Peter's brother. He first found his brother Simon and said to him, 'We have found the Messiah' (which is translated Anointed). He brought Simon to Jesus, who looked at him and said, 'You are Simon son of John. You are to be called Cephas' (which is translated Peter).

This is the Gospel of the Lord.   John 1.35–42

5 January: Twelfth Day of Christmas

From 29 December until 5 January readings are provided for each specific date. These readings do not supersede those for the First or Second Sundays of Christmas.

Year 1 and Year 2

A reading from the First Letter of John.

This is the message you have heard from the beginning, that we should love one another. We must not be like Cain who was from the evil one and murdered his brother. And why did he murder him? Because his own deeds were evil and his brother's righteous. Do not be astonished, brothers and sisters, that the world hates you. We know that we have passed from death to life because we love one another. Whoever does not love abides in death. All who hate a brother or sister are murderers, and you know that murderers do not have eternal life abiding in them. We know love by this, that he laid down his life for us – and we ought to lay down our lives for one another. How does God's love abide in anyone who has the world's goods and sees a brother or sister in need and yet refuses help?

Little children, let us love, not in word or speech, but in truth and action. And by this we will know that we are from the truth and will reassure our hearts before him whenever our hearts condemn us; for God is greater than our hearts, and he knows everything. Beloved, if our hearts do not condemn us, we have boldness before God.

This is the word of the Lord.   1 John 3.11–21

Responsorial Psalm

R **Be joyful in the Lord, all the earth:**
   [give thanks and bless his name].   *cf Psalm* 100.1a, 3b

O be joyful in the Lord, all the earth;
serve the Lord with gladness
and come before his presence with a song. **R**

Know that the Lord is God;
it is he that has made us and we are his;
we are his people and the sheep of his pasture. **R**

Enter his gates with thanksgiving
and his courts with praise;
give thanks to him and bless his name. **R**

For the Lord is gracious;
his steadfast love is everlasting,
and his faithfulness endures from generation to generation. **R**

Psalm 100

Hear the Gospel of our Lord Jesus Christ according to John.

Jesus decided to go to Galilee. He found Philip and said to him, 'Follow me.'
Now Philip was from Bethsaida, the city of Andrew and Peter. Philip found
Nathanael and said to him, 'We have found him about whom Moses in the law
and also the prophets wrote, Jesus son of Joseph from Nazareth.' Nathanael
said to him, 'Can anything good come out of Nazareth?' Philip said to him,
'Come and see.' When Jesus saw Nathanael coming towards him, he said of
him, 'Here is truly an Israelite in whom there is no deceit!' Nathanael asked
him, 'Where did you come to know me?' Jesus answered, 'I saw you under
the fig tree before Philip called you.' Nathanael replied, 'Rabbi, you are the Son
of God! You are the King of Israel!' Jesus answered, 'Do you believe because
I told you that I saw you under the fig tree? You will see greater things than
these.' And he said to him, 'Very truly, I tell you, you will see heaven opened
and the angels of God ascending and descending upon the Son of Man.'

This is the Gospel of the Lord.   *John* 1.43–*end*

The Feast of the Epiphany is normally celebrated on 6 January, and readings are appointed for the weekdays 7–12 January (page 80 ff).

For pastoral reasons, the Epiphany may be celebrated on the Sunday between 2 and 8 January. If the Epiphany is celebrated on the Sunday between 2 and 5 January, readings are appointed for the weekdays after the celebration (page 80 ff).

If, for pastoral reasons, the Epiphany is celebrated on Sunday 7 January, or on Sunday 8 January, then the following readings are used on the weekdays after 5 January and before the celebration of the Epiphany. On these occasions, the readings for the weekdays after the Epiphany (page 80 ff) are not used; the Baptism of Christ is celebrated on the following day, Monday 8 or 9 January, and the lectionary then continues from Tuesday of Week 1 (page 249 ff).

6 January *(when the Epiphany is celebrated on Sunday 7 or 8 January)*

If, for pastoral reasons, the Epiphany is celebrated on Sunday 7 January, or on Sunday 8 January, the following readings are used on 6 January.

Year 1 and Year 2

A reading from the First Letter of John.

Who is it that conquers the world but the one who believes that Jesus is the Son of God?

This is the one who came by water and blood, Jesus Christ, not with the water only but with the water and the blood. And the Spirit is the one that testifies, for the Spirit is the truth. There are three that testify: the Spirit and the water and the blood, and these three agree. If we receive human testimony, the testimony of God is greater; for this is the testimony of God that he has testified to his Son. Those who believe in the Son of God have the testimony in their hearts. Those who do not believe in God have made him a liar by not believing in the testimony that God has given concerning his Son. And this is the testimony: God gave us eternal life, and this life is in his Son. Whoever has the Son has life; whoever does not have the Son of God does not have life.

I write these things to you who believe in the name of the Son of God, so that you may know that you have eternal life.

This is the word of the Lord.   1 John 5.5–13

Responsorial Psalm

R* **Sing praise to the Lord, O Jerusalem:**
[praise your God, O Zion]. *Psalm 147.13*

The Lord has strengthened the bars of your gates
and has blest your children within you.
He has established peace in your borders
and satisfies you with the finest wheat. **R**

He sends forth his command to the earth
and his word runs very swiftly.
He gives snow like wool
and scatters the hoarfrost like ashes. **R**

He casts down his hailstones like morsels of bread;
who can endure his frost?
He sends forth his word and melts them;
he blows with his wind and the waters flow. **R**

He declares his word to Jacob,
his statutes and judgements to Israel.
He has not dealt so with any other nation;
they do not know his laws. **R** *Psalm 147.13–end*

Hear the Gospel of our Lord Jesus Christ according to Mark.

John proclaimed, 'The one who is more powerful than I is coming after me;
I am not worthy to stoop down and untie the thong of his sandals. I have
baptized you with water; but he will baptize you with the Holy Spirit.'

In those days Jesus came from Nazareth of Galilee and was baptized by
John in the Jordan. And just as he was coming up out of the water, he saw
the heavens torn apart and the Spirit descending like a dove on him. And
a voice came from heaven, 'You are my Son, the Beloved; with you I am
well pleased.'

This is the Gospel of the Lord. *Mark 1.7–11*

7 January *(when the Epiphany is celebrated on Sunday 8 January)*

If, for pastoral reasons, the Epiphany is celebrated on Sunday 8 January, the following readings are used on Saturday 7 January.

Year 1 and Year 2

A reading from the First Letter of John.

This is the boldness we have in the Son of God, that if we ask anything according to his will, he hears us. And if we know that he hears us in whatever we ask, we know that we have obtained the requests made of him. If you see your brother or sister committing what is not a mortal sin, you will ask, and God will give life to such a one – to those whose sin is not mortal. There is sin that is mortal; I do not say that you should pray about that. All wrongdoing is sin, but there is sin that is not mortal.

We know that those who are born of God do not sin, but the one who was born of God protects them, and the evil one does not touch them. We know that we are God's children, and that the whole world lies under the power of the evil one. And we know that the Son of God has come and has given us understanding so that we may know him who is true; and we are in him who is true, in his Son Jesus Christ. He is the true God and eternal life.

Little children, keep yourselves from idols.

This is the word of the Lord.   1 John 5.14–end

Responsorial Psalm

R* **O sing to the Lord a new song:**
     [sing his praise in the congregation of the faithful].   Psalm 149.1

Let Israel rejoice in their maker;
let the children of Zion be joyful in their king.
Let them praise his name in the dance;
let them sing praise to him with timbrel and lyre.   **R**

For the Lord has pleasure in his people
and adorns the poor with salvation.
Let the faithful be joyful in glory;
let them rejoice in their ranks.   **R**   Psalm 149.1–5

Hear the Gospel of our Lord Jesus Christ according to John.

There was a wedding in Cana of Galilee, and the mother of Jesus was there. Jesus and his disciples had also been invited to the wedding. When the wine gave out, the mother of Jesus said to him, 'They have no wine.' And Jesus said to her, 'Woman, what concern is that to you and to me? My hour has not yet come.' His mother said to the servants, 'Do whatever he tells you.' Now standing there were six stone water-jars for the Jewish rites of purification, each holding twenty or thirty gallons. Jesus said to them, 'Fill the jars with water.' And they filled them up to the brim. He said to them, 'Now draw some out, and take it to the chief steward.' So they took it. When the steward tasted the water that had become wine, and did not know where it came from (though the servants who had drawn the water knew), the steward called the bridegroom and said to him, 'Everyone serves the good wine first, and then the inferior wine after the guests have become drunk. But you have kept the good wine until now.' Jesus did this, the first of his signs, in Cana of Galilee, and revealed his glory; and his disciples believed in him.

This is the Gospel of the Lord.   John 2.1–11

When, for pastoral reasons, the Epiphany is celebrated on Sunday 7 or 8 January, then the Baptism of Christ is celebrated on the following day, Monday 8 or 9 January, and the lectionary continues from Tuesday of Week 1 (page 249 ff). In this case, the readings for the days after the Epiphany (page 80 ff) are not used.

EPIPHANY

6 January: The Epiphany
(*or* Epiphany Sunday)

Provision is made for the Epiphany in the lectionary for Principal Feasts.

If the Epiphany is celebrated on 6 January, the following readings are used on the dates indicated between the Epiphany and the Baptism of Christ.

If, for pastoral reasons, the Epiphany is celebrated on the Sunday between 2 and 5 January, after that Sunday the following readings are used on the weekdays indicated.

If, for pastoral reasons, the Epiphany is celebrated on Sunday 7 or 8 January, then the Baptism of Christ is celebrated on the following day, Monday 8 or 9 January, and the lectionary continues from Tuesday of Week 1 (page 249 ff). In this case, the following readings for the days after the Epiphany are not used.

7 January *(if before the Baptism of Christ)*
(*or* Monday after Epiphany Sunday)

Year 1 and Year 2

A reading from the First Letter of John.

We receive from God whatever we ask, because we obey his commandments and do what pleases him.

And this is his commandment, that we should believe in the name of his Son Jesus Christ and love one another, just as he has commanded us. All who obey his commandments abide in him, and he abides in them. And by this we know that he abides in us, by the Spirit that he has given us.

Beloved, do not believe every spirit, but test the spirits to see whether they are from God; for many false prophets have gone out into the world. By this you know the Spirit of God: every spirit that confesses that Jesus Christ has come in the flesh is from God, and every spirit that does not confess Jesus is not from God. And this is the spirit of the antichrist, of which you have heard that it is coming; and now it is already in the world. Little children, you are from God, and have conquered them; for the one who is in you is greater than the one who is in the world. They are from the world; therefore what they say is from the world, and the world listens to them. We are from God. Whoever knows God listens to us, and whoever is not from God does not listen to us. From this we know the spirit of truth and the spirit of error.

This is the word of the Lord.   1 John 3.22 – 4.6

Responsorial Psalm

R **I will give you the nations for your inheritance:**
[the ends of the earth for your possession]. *cf Psalm* 2.8

I will proclaim the decree of the Lord;
he said to me: 'You are my Son; this day have I begotten you.
Ask of me and I will give you the nations for your inheritance
and the ends of the earth for your possession. **R**

'You shall break them with a rod of iron
and dash them in pieces like a potter's vessel.'
Now therefore be wise, O kings;
be prudent, you judges of the earth. **R**

Serve the Lord with fear, and with trembling kiss his feet,
lest he be angry and you perish from the way,
for his wrath is quickly kindled.
Happy are all they who take refuge in him. **R** *Psalm* 2.7–*end*

Hear the Gospel of our Lord Jesus Christ according to Matthew.

When Jesus heard that John had been arrested, he withdrew to Galilee. He
left Nazareth and made his home in Capernaum by the lake, in the territory
of Zebulun and Naphtali, so that what had been spoken through the prophet
Isaiah might be fulfilled:
'Land of Zebulun, land of Naphtali,
  on the road by the sea, across the Jordan, Galilee of the Gentiles –
the people who sat in darkness
  have seen a great light,
and for those who sat in the region and shadow of death
  light has dawned.'
From that time Jesus began to proclaim, 'Repent, for the kingdom of heaven
has come near.'

Jesus went throughout Galilee, teaching in their synagogues and proclaiming
the good news of the kingdom and curing every disease and every sickness
among the people. So his fame spread throughout all Syria, and they brought
to him all the sick, those who were afflicted with various diseases and pains,
demoniacs, epileptics, and paralytics, and he cured them. And great crowds
followed him from Galilee, the Decapolis, Jerusalem, Judea, and from beyond
the Jordan.

This is the Gospel of the Lord. *Matthew* 4.12–17, 23–*end*

8 January *(if before the Baptism of Christ)*

(*or* Tuesday after Epiphany Sunday)

Year 1 and Year 2

A reading from the First Letter of John.

Beloved, let us love one another, because love is from God; everyone who loves is born of God and knows God. Whoever does not love does not know God, for God is love. God's love was revealed among us in this way: God sent his only Son into the world so that we might live through him. In this is love, not that we loved God but that he loved us and sent his Son to be the atoning sacrifice for our sins.

This is the word of the Lord.   1 John 4.7–10

Responsorial Psalm

R   **Righteousness and peace shall flourish:**
    [till the moon shall be no more].   cf Psalm 72.7

Give the king your judgements, O God,
and your righteousness to the son of a king.
Then shall he judge your people righteously
and your poor with justice.

May the mountains bring forth peace,
and the little hills righteousness for the people.
May he defend the poor among the people,
deliver the children of the needy and crush the oppressor.

May he live as long as the sun and moon endure,
from one generation to another.
May he come down like rain upon the mown grass,
like the showers that water the earth.

In his time shall righteousness flourish, and abundance of peace
till the moon shall be no more.
May his dominion extend from sea to sea
and from the River to the ends of the earth.   **R**   Psalm 72.1–8

Hear the Gospel of our Lord Jesus Christ according to Mark.

As Jesus went ashore, he saw a great crowd; and he had compassion for them, because they were like sheep without a shepherd; and he began to teach them many things. When it grew late, his disciples came to him and said, 'This is a deserted place, and the hour is now very late; send them away so that they may go into the surrounding country and villages and buy something for themselves to eat.' But he answered them, 'You give them something to eat.' They said to him, 'Are we to go and buy two hundred denarii worth of bread, and give it to them to eat?' And he said to them, 'How many loaves have you? Go and see.' When they had found out, they said, 'Five, and two fish.' Then he ordered them to get all the people to sit down in groups on the green grass. So they sat down in groups of hundreds and of fifties. Taking the five loaves and the two fish, he looked up to heaven, and blessed and broke the loaves, and gave them to his disciples to set before the people; and he divided the two fish among them all. And all ate and were filled; and they took up twelve baskets full of broken pieces and of the fish. Those who had eaten the loaves numbered five thousand men.

This is the Gospel of the Lord.

Mark 6.34–44

9 January *(if before the Baptism of Christ)*
(*or* Wednesday after Epiphany Sunday)
Year 1 and Year 2

A reading from the First Letter of John.

Beloved, since God loved us so much, we also ought to love one another. No one has ever seen God; if we love one another, God lives in us, and his love is perfected in us.

By this we know that we abide in him and he in us, because he has given us of his Spirit. And we have seen and do testify that the Father has sent his Son as the Saviour of the world. God abides in those who confess that Jesus is the Son of God, and they abide in God. So we have known and believe the love that God has for us.

God is love, and those who abide in love abide in God, and God abides in them. Love has been perfected among us in this: that we may have boldness on the day of judgement, because as he is, so are we in this world. There is no fear in love, but perfect love casts out fear; for fear has to do with punishment, and whoever fears has not reached perfection in love.

This is the word of the Lord.

1 John 4.11–18

R **Righteousness and peace shall flourish:**
   [till the moon shall be no more].   *cf Psalm 72.7*

Give the king your judgements, O God,
and your righteousness to the son of a king.   R

The kings of Tarshish and of the isles shall pay tribute;
the kings of Sheba and Seba shall bring gifts.
All kings shall fall down before him;
all nations shall do him service.   R

For he shall deliver the poor that cry out,
the needy and those who have no helper.
He shall have pity on the weak and poor;
he shall preserve the lives of the needy.   R   *Psalm 72.1, 10–13*

Hear the Gospel of our Lord Jesus Christ according to Mark.

Jesus made his disciples get into the boat and go on ahead to the other side,
to Bethsaida, while he dismissed the crowd. After saying farewell to them, he
went up on the mountain to pray.

When evening came, the boat was out on the lake, and he was alone on
the land. When he saw that they were straining at the oars against an adverse
wind, he came towards them early in the morning, walking on the lake. He
intended to pass them by. But when they saw him walking on the lake, they
thought it was a ghost and cried out; for they all saw him and were terrified.
But immediately he spoke to them and said, 'Take heart, it is I; do not be
afraid.' Then he got into the boat with them and the wind ceased. And they
were utterly astounded, for they did not understand about the loaves, but
their hearts were hardened.

This is the Gospel of the Lord.   *Mark 6.45–52*

10 January *(if before the Baptism of Christ)*

(*or* Thursday after Epiphany Sunday)

Year 1 and Year 2

A reading from the First Letter of John.

We love because God first loved us. Those who say, 'I love God', and hate
their brothers or sisters, are liars; for those who do not love a brother or
sister whom they have seen, cannot love God whom they have not seen. The
commandment we have from him is this: those who love God must love their
brothers and sisters also.

Everyone who believes that Jesus is the Christ has been born of God, and
everyone who loves the parent loves the child. By this we know that we love

the children of God, when we love God and obey his commandments. For the love of God is this, that we obey his commandments. And his commandments are not burdensome, for whatever is born of God conquers the world. And this is the victory that conquers the world, our faith.

This is the word of the Lord.

1 John 4.19 − 5.4

Responsorial Psalm

R **Righteousness and peace shall flourish:**
   [till the moon shall be no more].

cf Psalm 72.7

Give the king your judgements, O God,
and your righteousness to the son of a king.   **R**

May his name remain for ever
and be established as long as the sun endures;
may all nations be blest in him
and call him blessed.   **R**

Blessed be the Lord, the God of Israel,
who alone does wonderful things.
And blessed be his glorious name for ever.
May all the earth be filled with his glory.   **R**

Psalm 72.1, 17−end

Hear the Gospel of our Lord Jesus Christ according to Luke.

Jesus, filled with the power of the Spirit, returned to Galilee, and a report about him spread through all the surrounding country. He began to teach in their synagogues and was praised by everyone.

When he came to Nazareth, where he had been brought up, he went to the synagogue on the sabbath day, as was his custom. He stood up to read, and the scroll of the prophet Isaiah was given to him. He unrolled the scroll and found the place where it was written:

'The Spirit of the Lord is upon me,
   because he has anointed me
   to bring good news to the poor.
He has sent me to proclaim release to the captives
   and recovery of sight to the blind,
   to let the oppressed go free,
to proclaim the year of the Lord's favour.'

And he rolled up the scroll, gave it back to the attendant, and sat down. The eyes of all in the synagogue were fixed on him. Then he began to say to them, 'Today this scripture has been fulfilled in your hearing.' All spoke well of him and were amazed at the gracious words that came from his mouth. They said, 'Is not this Joseph's son?'

This is the Gospel of the Lord.

Luke 4.14−22

11 January *(if before the Baptism of Christ)*
(*or* Friday after Epiphany Sunday)

Year 1 and Year 2

A reading from the First Letter of John.

Who is it that conquers the world but the one who believes that Jesus is the Son of God? This is the one who came by water and blood, Jesus Christ, not with the water only but with the water and the blood. And the Spirit is the one that testifies, for the Spirit is the truth. There are three that testify: the Spirit and the water and the blood, and these three agree. If we receive human testimony, the testimony of God is greater; for this is the testimony of God that he has testified to his Son. Those who believe in the Son of God have the testimony in their hearts. Those who do not believe in God have made him a liar by not believing in the testimony that God has given concerning his Son. And this is the testimony: God gave us eternal life, and this life is in his Son. Whoever has the Son has life; whoever does not have the Son of God does not have life.

I write these things to you who believe in the name of the Son of God, so that you may know that you have eternal life.

This is the word of the Lord.   1 John 5.5–13

Responsorial Psalm

R* **Sing praise to the Lord, O Jerusalem:
[praise your God, O Zion].**   Psalm 147.13

The Lord has strengthened the bars of your gates
and has blest your children within you.
He has established peace in your borders
and satisfies you with the finest wheat.   **R**

He sends forth his command to the earth
and his word runs very swiftly.
He gives snow like wool
and scatters the hoarfrost like ashes.   **R**

He casts down his hailstones like morsels of bread;
who can endure his frost?
He sends forth his word and melts them;
he blows with his wind and the waters flow.   **R**

He declares his word to Jacob,
his statutes and judgements to Israel.
He has not dealt so with any other nation;
they do not know his laws.   **R**   Psalm 147.13–end

Hear the Gospel of our Lord Jesus Christ according to Luke.

Once, when Jesus was in one of the cities, there was a man covered with leprosy. When he saw Jesus, he bowed with his face to the ground and begged him, 'Lord, if you choose, you can make me clean.' Then Jesus stretched out his hand, touched him, and said, 'I do choose. Be made clean.' Immediately the leprosy left him. And he ordered him to tell no one. 'Go', he said, 'and show yourself to the priest, and, as Moses commanded, make an offering for your cleansing, for a testimony to them.' But now more than ever the word about Jesus spread abroad; many crowds would gather to hear him and to be cured of their diseases. But he would withdraw to deserted places and pray.

This is the Gospel of the Lord.   Luke 5.12–16

12 January *(if before the Baptism of Christ)*
(*or* Saturday after Epiphany Sunday)

Year 1 and Year 2

A reading from the First Letter of John.

This is the boldness we have in God, that if we ask anything according to his will, he hears us. And if we know that he hears us in whatever we ask, we know that we have obtained the requests made of him. If you see your brother or sister committing what is not a mortal sin, you will ask, and God will give life to such a one – to those whose sin is not mortal. There is sin that is mortal; I do not say that you should pray about that. All wrongdoing is sin, but there is sin that is not mortal.

We know that those who are born of God do not sin, but the one who was born of God protects them, and the evil one does not touch them. We know that we are God's children, and that the whole world lies under the power of the evil one. And we know that the Son of God has come and has given us understanding so that we may know him who is true; and we are in him who is true, in his Son Jesus Christ. He is the true God and eternal life.

Little children, keep yourselves from idols.

This is the word of the Lord.   1 John 5.14–end

Responsorial Psalm

R* **O sing to the Lord a new song:**
[sing his praise in the congregation of the faithful].   Psalm 149.1

Let Israel rejoice in their maker;
let the children of Zion be joyful in their king.
Let them praise his name in the dance;
let them sing praise to him with timbrel and lyre.   **R**

For the Lord has pleasure in his people
and adorns the poor with salvation.
Let the faithful be joyful in glory;
let them rejoice in their ranks.   **R**   Psalm 149.1–5

Hear the Gospel of our Lord Jesus Christ according to John.

Jesus and his disciples went into the Judean countryside, and he spent some time there with them and baptized. John also was baptizing at Aenon near Salim because water was abundant there; and people kept coming and were being baptized – John, of course, had not yet been thrown into prison. Now a discussion about purification arose between John's disciples and a Jew. They came to John and said to him, 'Rabbi, the one who was with you across the Jordan, to whom you testified, here he is baptizing, and all are going to him.' John answered, 'No one can receive anything except what has been given from heaven. You yourselves are my witnesses that I said, "I am not the Messiah, but I have been sent ahead of him." He who has the bride is the bridegroom. The friend of the bridegroom, who stands and hears him, rejoices greatly at the bridegroom's voice. For this reason my joy has been fulfilled. He must increase, but I must decrease.'

This is the Gospel of the Lord.   John 3.22–30

After the Baptism of Christ (which is observed on the Sunday after 6 January, or – if the Epiphany has been celebrated on Sunday 7 or 8 January – on Monday 8 or 9 January) the lectionary continues with readings from Week 1 (page 247 ff).

In years in which 6 January is a Sunday, that day is both the Feast of the Epiphany and the First Sunday of Epiphany, and the Baptism of Christ is celebrated on Sunday 13 January, which is the Second Sunday of Epiphany. In those years, the readings appointed for 7–12 January (page 80 ff) are used in the week following the Epiphany, the readings for Week 1 (page 247 ff) in the week following the Baptism of Christ, and the readings for Week 2 (page 263 ff) and Week 3 (page 279 ff) in the remaining weeks of Epiphany.

LENT

Ash Wednesday

Provision is made for Ash Wednesday in the lectionary for Principal Holy Days.

Thursday after Ash Wednesday

Year 1 and Year 2

A reading from the book Deuteronomy.

Moses said to the people: See, I have set before you today life and prosperity, death and adversity. If you obey the commandments of the LORD your God that I am commanding you today, by loving the LORD your God, walking in his ways, and observing his commandments, decrees, and ordinances, then you shall live and become numerous, and the LORD your God will bless you in the land that you are entering to possess. But if your heart turns away and you do not hear, but are led astray to bow down to other gods and serve them, I declare to you today that you shall perish; you shall not live long in the land that you are crossing the Jordan to enter and possess. I call heaven and earth to witness against you today that I have set before you life and death, blessings and curses. Choose life so that you and your descendants may live, loving the LORD your God, obeying him, and holding fast to him; for that means life to you and length of days, so that you may live in the land that the LORD swore to give to your ancestors, to Abraham, to Isaac, and to Jacob.

This is the word of the Lord.   Deuteronomy 30.15–end

Responsorial Psalm

R **The Lord teaches us what is good:**
   [our delight is in the law of the Lord].   *cf Isaiah 48.17, Psalm 1.3a*

Blessed are they who have not walked
in the counsel of the wicked,
nor lingered in the way of sinners,
nor sat in the assembly of the scornful.
Their delight is in the law of the Lord
and they meditate on his law day and night.   R

Like a tree planted by streams of water
bearing fruit in due season,
with leaves that do not wither,
whatever they do, it shall prosper.   R   →

As for the wicked, it is not so with them;
they are like chaff which the wind blows away.
Therefore the wicked shall not be able to stand in the judgement,
nor the sinner in the congregation of the righteous.
For the Lord knows the way of the righteous,
but the way of the wicked shall perish.   R   *Psalm* 1

R   **The Lord teaches us what is good:**
    [our delight is in the law of the Lord].

Hear the Gospel of our Lord Jesus Christ according to Luke.

Jesus said to his disciples, 'The Son of Man must undergo great suffering, and
be rejected by the elders, chief priests, and scribes, and be killed, and on the
third day be raised.'

Then he said to them all, 'If any want to become my followers, let them
deny themselves and take up their cross daily and follow me. For those who
want to save their life will lose it, and those who lose their life for my sake
will save it. What does it profit them if they gain the whole world, but lose
or forfeit themselves?'

This is the Gospel of the Lord.   Luke 9.22–25

Friday after Ash Wednesday

Year 1 and Year 2

A reading from the prophecy of Isaiah.

Shout out, do not hold back!
    Lift up your voice like a trumpet!
Announce to my people their rebellion,
    to the house of Jacob their sins.
Yet day after day they seek me
    and delight to know my ways,
as if they were a nation that practised righteousness
    and did not forsake the ordinance of their God;
they ask of me righteous judgements,
    they delight to draw near to God.
'Why do we fast, but you do not see?
    Why humble ourselves, but you do not notice?'
Look, you serve your own interest on your fast-day,
    and oppress all your workers.
Look, you fast only to quarrel and to fight
    and to strike with a wicked fist.
Such fasting as you do today
    will not make your voice heard on high.

Is such the fast that I choose,
　　a day to humble oneself?
Is it to bow down the head like a bulrush,
　　and to lie in sackcloth and ashes?
Will you call this a fast,
　　a day acceptable to the LORD?

Is not this the fast that I choose:
　　to loose the bonds of injustice,
　　to undo the thongs of the yoke,
to let the oppressed go free,
　　and to break every yoke?
Is it not to share your bread with the hungry,
　　and bring the homeless poor into your house;
when you see the naked, to cover them,
　　and not to hide yourself from your own kin?
Then your light shall break forth like the dawn,
　　and your healing shall spring up quickly;
your vindicator shall go before you,
　　the glory of the LORD shall be your rearguard.
Then you shall call, and the LORD will answer;
　　you shall cry for help, and he will say, Here I am.

This is the word of the Lord.
Isaiah 58.1–9a

Responsorial Psalm

R　**A broken and contrite heart, O God,
　　you will not despise.**
Psalm 51.18b

Have mercy on me, O God,
in your great goodness;
according to the abundance of your compassion
blot out my offences.　**R**

Wash me thoroughly from my wickedness
and cleanse me from my sin.
For I acknowledge my faults
and my sin is ever before me.　**R**

Against you only have I sinned
and done what is evil in your sight,
so that you are justified in your sentence
and righteous in your judgement.　**R**

For you desire no sacrifice, else I would give it;
you take no delight in burnt offerings.
The sacrifice of God is a broken spirit;
a broken and contrite heart, O God, you will not despise.　**R**
Psalm 51.1–5, 17–18

Hear the Gospel of our Lord Jesus Christ according to Matthew.

The disciples of John came to Jesus, saying, 'Why do we and the Pharisees fast often, but your disciples do not fast?' And Jesus said to them, 'The wedding-guests cannot mourn as long as the bridegroom is with them, can they? The days will come when the bridegroom is taken away from them, and then they will fast.'

This is the Gospel of the Lord. *Matthew 9.14–15*

Saturday after Ash Wednesday

Year 1 and Year 2

A reading from the prophecy of Isaiah.

If you remove the yoke from among you,
    the pointing of the finger, the speaking of evil,
if you offer your food to the hungry
    and satisfy the needs of the afflicted,
then your light shall rise in the darkness
    and your gloom be like the noonday.
The LORD will guide you continually,
    and satisfy your needs in parched places,
    and make your bones strong;
and you shall be like a watered garden,
    like a spring of water,
    whose waters never fail.
Your ancient ruins shall be rebuilt;
    you shall raise up the foundations of many generations;
you shall be called the repairer of the breach,
    the restorer of streets to live in.

If you refrain from trampling the sabbath,
    from pursuing your own interests on my holy day;
if you call the sabbath a delight
    and the holy day of the LORD honourable;
if you honour it, not going your own ways,
    serving your own interests, or pursuing your own affairs;
then you shall take delight in the LORD,
    and I will make you ride upon the heights of the earth;
I will feed you with the heritage of your ancestor Jacob,
    for the mouth of the LORD has spoken.

This is the word of the Lord. *Isaiah 58.9b–end*

Responsorial Psalm

R **Teach me your way, O Lord,**
and I will walk in your truth. Psalm 86.11a

Incline your ear, O Lord, and answer me,
for I am poor and in misery.
Preserve my soul, for I am faithful;
save your servant, for I put my trust in you. **R**

Be merciful to me, O Lord, for you are my God;
I call upon you all the day long.
Gladden the soul of your servant,
for to you, O Lord, I lift up my soul. **R**

For you, Lord, are good and forgiving,
abounding in steadfast love to all who call upon you.
Give ear, O Lord, to my prayer
and listen to the voice of my supplication. **R**

In the day of my distress I will call upon you,
for you will answer me. **R** Psalm 86.1–7

Hear the Gospel of our Lord Jesus Christ according to Luke.

Jesus went out and saw a tax-collector named Levi, sitting at the tax booth;
and he said to him, 'Follow me.' And he got up, left everything, and followed him.

Then Levi gave a great banquet for him in his house; and there was a large
crowd of tax-collectors and others sitting at the table with them. The Pharisees
and their scribes were complaining to his disciples, saying, 'Why do you eat
and drink with tax-collectors and sinners?' Jesus answered, 'Those who are
well have no need of a physician, but those who are sick; I have come to call
not the righteous but sinners to repentance.'

This is the Gospel of the Lord. Luke 5.27–32

First Week of Lent: Monday

Year 1 and Year 2

A reading from the book Leviticus.

The LORD spoke to Moses, saying:
Speak to all the congregation of the people of Israel and say to them: You shall be holy, for I the LORD your God am holy.

You shall not steal; you shall not deal falsely; and you shall not lie to one another. And you shall not swear falsely by my name, profaning the name of your God: I am the LORD.

You shall not defraud your neighbour; you shall not steal; and you shall not keep for yourself the wages of a labourer until morning. You shall not revile the deaf or put a stumbling-block before the blind; you shall fear your God: I am the LORD.

You shall not render an unjust judgement; you shall not be partial to the poor or defer to the great: with justice you shall judge your neighbour. You shall not go around as a slanderer among your people, and you shall not profit by the blood of your neighbour: I am the LORD.

You shall not hate in your heart anyone of your kin; you shall reprove your neighbour, or you will incur guilt yourself. You shall not take vengeance or bear a grudge against any of your people, but you shall love your neighbour as yourself: I am the LORD.

This is the word of the Lord. *Leviticus 19.1–2, 11–18*

Responsorial Psalm

R **The judgements of the Lord are true:**
   more to be desired than gold. *cf Psalm 19.9b, 10a*

The law of the Lord is perfect,
reviving the soul;
the testimony of the Lord is sure
and gives wisdom to the simple. R

The statutes of the Lord are right
and rejoice the heart;
the commandment of the Lord is pure
and gives light to the eyes. R

The fear of the Lord is clean
and endures for ever;
the judgements of the Lord are true
and righteous altogether. R

More to be desired are they than gold,
more than much fine gold,
sweeter also than honey,
dripping from the honeycomb. R

By them also is your servant taught
and in keeping them there is great reward.
Who can tell how often they offend?
O cleanse me from my secret faults!   R

Keep your servant also from presumptuous sins
lest they get dominion over me;
so shall I be undefiled,
and innocent of great offence.   R

Let the words of my mouth
and the meditation of my heart
be acceptable in your sight,
O Lord, my strength and my redeemer.   R   *Psalm* 19.7–*end*

Hear the Gospel of our Lord Jesus Christ according to Matthew.

Jesus said to his disciples, 'When the Son of Man comes in his glory, and all the angels with him, then he will sit on the throne of his glory. All the nations will be gathered before him, and he will separate people one from another as a shepherd separates the sheep from the goats, and he will put the sheep at his right hand and the goats at the left.

'Then the king will say to those at his right hand, "Come, you that are blessed by my Father, inherit the kingdom prepared for you from the foundation of the world; for I was hungry and you gave me food, I was thirsty and you gave me something to drink, I was a stranger and you welcomed me, I was naked and you gave me clothing, I was sick and you took care of me, I was in prison and you visited me." Then the righteous will answer him, "Lord, when was it that we saw you hungry and gave you food, or thirsty and gave you something to drink? And when was it that we saw you a stranger and welcomed you, or naked and gave you clothing? And when was it that we saw you sick or in prison and visited you?" And the king will answer them, "Truly I tell you, just as you did it to one of the least of these who are members of my family, you did it to me."

'Then he will say to those at his left hand, "You that are accursed, depart from me into the eternal fire prepared for the devil and his angels; for I was hungry and you gave me no food, I was thirsty and you gave me nothing to drink, I was a stranger and you did not welcome me, naked and you did not give me clothing, sick and in prison and you did not visit me." Then they also will answer, "Lord, when was it that we saw you hungry or thirsty or a stranger or naked or sick or in prison, and did not take care of you?" Then he will answer them, "Truly I tell you, just as you did not do it to one of the least of these, you did not do it to me." And these will go away into eternal punishment, but the righteous into eternal life.'

This is the Gospel of the Lord.   *Matthew* 25.31–*end*

First Week of Lent: Tuesday

Year I and Year 2

A reading from the prophecy of Isaiah.

For as the rain and the snow come down from heaven,
    and do not return there until they have watered the earth,
making it bring forth and sprout,
    giving seed to the sower and bread to the eater,
so shall my word be that goes out from my mouth;
    it shall not return to me empty,
but it shall accomplish that which I purpose,
    and succeed in the thing for which I sent it.

This is the word of the Lord.   *Isaiah 55.10–11*

Responsorial Psalm

R **The eyes of the Lord are upon the righteous:**
    [and his ears are open to their cry]   *Psalm 34.15*

I sought the Lord and he answered me
and delivered me from all my fears.
Look upon him and be radiant
and your faces shall not be ashamed. **R**

This poor soul cried, and the Lord heard me
and saved me from all my troubles. **R**

But evil shall slay the wicked
and those who hate the righteous will be condemned.
The Lord ransoms the life of his servants
and will condemn none who seek refuge in him. **R**   *Psalm 34.4–6, 21–22*

Hear the Gospel of our Lord Jesus Christ according to Matthew.

Jesus said to his disciples, 'When you are praying, do not heap up empty phrases as the Gentiles do; for they think that they will be heard because of their many words. Do not be like them, for your Father knows what you need before you ask him. Pray then in this way:
    'Our Father in heaven,
        hallowed be your name.
        Your kingdom come.
        Your will be done,
            on earth as it is in heaven.
        Give us this day our daily bread.
        And forgive us our debts,
            as we also have forgiven our debtors.

And do not bring us to the time of trial,
but rescue us from the evil one.
'For if you forgive others their trespasses, your heavenly Father will also forgive you; but if you do not forgive others, neither will your Father forgive your trespasses.'

This is the Gospel of the Lord.   Matthew 6.7–15

First Week of Lent: Wednesday

Year I and Year 2

A reading from the Book of Jonah.

The word of the LORD came to Jonah a second time, saying, 'Get up, go to Nineveh, that great city, and proclaim to it the message that I tell you.' So Jonah set out and went to Nineveh, according to the word of the LORD. Now Nineveh was an exceedingly large city, a three days' walk across. Jonah began to go into the city, going a day's walk. And he cried out, 'Forty days more, and Nineveh shall be overthrown!' And the people of Nineveh believed God; they proclaimed a fast, and everyone, great and small, put on sackcloth.

When the news reached the king of Nineveh, he rose from his throne, removed his robe, covered himself with sackcloth, and sat in ashes. Then he had a proclamation made in Nineveh: 'By the decree of the king and his nobles: No human being or animal, no herd or flock, shall taste anything. They shall not feed, nor shall they drink water. Human beings and animals shall be covered with sackcloth, and they shall cry mightily to God. All shall turn from their evil ways and from the violence that is in their hands. Who knows? God may relent and change his mind; he may turn from his fierce anger, so that we do not perish.'

When God saw what they did, how they turned from their evil ways, God changed his mind about the calamity that he had said he would bring upon them; and he did not do it.

This is the word of the Lord.   Jonah 3

Responsorial Psalm

R   **A broken and contrite heart, O God,
you will not despise.**   *Psalm 51.18b*

Have mercy on me, O God,
in your great goodness;
according to the abundance of your compassion
blot out my offences.   R

Wash me thoroughly from my wickedness
and cleanse me from my sin.
For I acknowledge my faults
and my sin is ever before me.   R

Against you only have I sinned
and done what is evil in your sight,
so that you are justified in your sentence
and righteous in your judgement.   R

For you desire no sacrifice, else I would give it;
you take no delight in burnt offerings.
The sacrifice of God is a broken spirit;
a broken and contrite heart, O God, you will not despise.   R

Psalm 51.1–5, 17–18

Hear the Gospel of our Lord Jesus Christ according to Luke.

Jesus said to the crowds, 'This generation is an evil generation; it asks for a
sign, but no sign will be given to it except the sign of Jonah. For just as Jonah
became a sign to the people of Nineveh, so the Son of Man will be to this
generation. The queen of the South will rise at the judgement with the people
of this generation and condemn them, because she came from the ends of the
earth to listen to the wisdom of Solomon, and see, something greater than
Solomon is here! The people of Nineveh will rise up at the judgement with
this generation and condemn it, because they repented at the proclamation
of Jonah, and see, something greater than Jonah is here!'

This is the Gospel of the Lord.   *Luke 11.29–32*

First Week of Lent: Thursday

Year I and Year 2

Either

A reading from the Book of Esther.

Queen Esther, seized with deadly anxiety, fled to the Lord. She took off her splendid apparel and put on the garments of distress and mourning, and instead of costly perfumes she covered her head with ashes and dung, and she utterly humbled her body; every part that she loved to adorn she covered with her tangled hair.

She prayed to the Lord God of Israel, and said: 'O my Lord, you only are our king; help me, who am alone and have no helper but you, for my danger is in my hand. Ever since I was born I have heard in the tribe of my family that you, O Lord, took Israel out of all the nations, and our ancestors from among all their forebears, for an everlasting inheritance, and that you did for them all that you promised. Remember, O Lord; make yourself known in this time of our affliction, and give me courage, O King of the gods and Master of all dominion! Put eloquent speech in my mouth before the lion, and turn his heart to hate the man who is fighting against us, so that there may be an end of him and those who agree with him. But save us by your hand, and help me, who am alone and have no helper but you, O Lord.'

This is the word of the Lord. *Esther 14.1–5, 12–14*

or

A reading from the prophecy of Isaiah.

Seek the LORD while he may be found,
    call upon him while he is near;
let the wicked forsake their way,
    and the unrighteous their thoughts;
let them return to the LORD, that he may have mercy on them,
    and to our God, for he will abundantly pardon.
For my thoughts are not your thoughts,
    nor are your ways my ways, says the LORD.
For as the heavens are higher than the earth,
    so are my ways higher than your ways
    and my thoughts than your thoughts.

This is the word of the Lord. *Isaiah 55.6–9*

R **Your loving-kindness, O Lord, endures for ever;**
 [forsake not the work of your hands]. *Psalm 138.8b*

I will give thanks to you, O Lord, with my whole heart;
before the gods will I sing praise to you.
I will bow down towards your holy temple and praise your name,
because of your love and faithfulness. **R**

For you have glorified your name
and your word above all things.
In the day that I called to you, you answered me;
you put new strength in my soul. **R**

All the kings of the earth shall praise you, O Lord,
for they have heard the words of your mouth.
They shall sing of the ways of the Lord,
that great is the glory of the Lord. **R**

Though the Lord be high,
he watches over the lowly;
as for the proud,
he regards them from afar. **R**

Though I walk in the midst of trouble,
you will preserve me;
you will stretch forth your hand against the fury of my enemies;
your right hand will save me. **R**

The Lord shall make good his purpose for me;
your loving-kindness, O Lord, endures for ever;
forsake not the work of your hands. **R** *Psalm 138*

Hear the Gospel of our Lord Jesus Christ according to Matthew.

Jesus said to his disciples, 'Ask, and it will be given to you; search, and you
will find; knock, and the door will be opened for you. For everyone who asks
receives, and everyone who searches finds, and for everyone who knocks, the
door will be opened. Is there anyone among you who, if your child asks for
bread, will give a stone? Or if the child asks for a fish, will give a snake? If
you then, who are evil, know how to give good gifts to your children, how
much more will your Father in heaven give good things to those who ask
him! In everything do to others as you would have them do to you; for this
is the law and the prophets.'

This is the Gospel of the Lord. *Matthew 7.7–12*

First Week of Lent: Friday

Year 1 and Year 2

A reading from the prophecy of Ezekiel.

The word of the LORD came to me: If the wicked turn away from all their sins that they have committed and keep all my statutes and do what is lawful and right, they shall surely live; they shall not die. None of the transgressions that they have committed shall be remembered against them; for the righteousness that they have done they shall live. Have I any pleasure in the death of the wicked, says the Lord GOD, and not rather that they should turn from their ways and live? But when the righteous turn away from their righteousness and commit iniquity and do the same abominable things that the wicked do, shall they live? None of the righteous deeds that they have done shall be remembered; for the treachery of which they are guilty and the sin they have committed, they shall die.

Yet you say, 'The way of the Lord is unfair.' Hear now, O house of Israel: Is my way unfair? Is it not your ways that are unfair? When the righteous turn away from their righteousness and commit iniquity, they shall die for it; for the iniquity that they have committed they shall die. Again, when the wicked turn away from the wickedness they have committed and do what is lawful and right, they shall save their life. Because they considered and turned away from all the transgressions that they had committed, they shall surely live; they shall not die.

This is the word of the Lord. *Ezekiel 18.21–28*

Responsorial Psalm

R **My soul waits for the Lord,**
   [more than the night watch for the morning]. *Psalm 130.5*

Out of the depths have I cried to you, O Lord;
Lord, hear my voice;
let your ears consider well the voice of my supplication. **R**

If you, Lord, were to mark what is done amiss,
O Lord, who could stand?
But there is forgiveness with you,
so that you shall be feared. **R**

I wait for the Lord; my soul waits for him;
in his word is my hope.
My soul waits for the Lord,
more than the night watch for the morning,
more than the night watch for the morning. **R**

O Israel, wait for the Lord,
for with the Lord there is mercy;
with him is plenteous redemption
and he shall redeem Israel from all their sins. **R** *Psalm 130*

Hear the Gospel of our Lord Jesus Christ according to Matthew.

Jesus said to his disciples, 'I tell you, unless your righteousness exceeds that of the scribes and Pharisees, you will never enter the kingdom of heaven.

'You have heard that it was said to those of ancient times, "You shall not murder"; and "whoever murders shall be liable to judgement." But I say to you that if you are angry with a brother or sister, you will be liable to judgement; and if you insult a brother or sister, you will be liable to the council; and if you say, "You fool", you will be liable to the hell of fire.

'So when you are offering your gift at the altar, if you remember that your brother or sister has something against you, leave your gift there before the altar and go; first be reconciled to your brother or sister, and then come and offer your gift. Come to terms quickly with your accuser while you are on the way to court with him, or your accuser may hand you over to the judge, and the judge to the guard, and you will be thrown into prison. Truly I tell you, you will never get out until you have paid the last penny.'

This is the Gospel of the Lord.   Matthew 5.20–26

First Week of Lent: Saturday

Year 1 and Year 2

A reading from the book Deuteronomy.

Moses said to the people: This very day the LORD your God is commanding you to observe these statutes and ordinances; so observe them diligently with all your heart and with all your soul. Today you have obtained the LORD's agreement: to be your God; and for you to walk in his ways, to keep his statutes, his commandments, and his ordinances, and to obey him. Today the LORD has obtained your agreement: to be his treasured people, as he promised you, and to keep his commandments; for him to set you high above all nations that he has made, in praise and in fame and in honour; and for you to be a people holy to the LORD your God, as he promised.

This is the word of the Lord.   Deuteronomy 26.16–end

Responsorial Psalm

R **Blessed are those who walk in the law of the Lord.** cf Psalm 119.1

Blessed are those whose way is pure,
who walk in the law of the Lord.
Blessed are those who keep his testimonies
and seek him with their whole heart. R

Those who do no wickedness,
but walk in his ways.
You, O Lord, have charged
that we should diligently keep your commandments. R

O that my ways were made so direct
that I might keep your statutes.
Then should I not be put to shame,
because I have regard for all your commandments. R

I will thank you with an unfeigned heart,
when I have learned your righteous judgements.
I will keep your statutes;
O forsake me not utterly. R Psalm 119.1–8

Hear the Gospel of our Lord Jesus Christ according to Matthew.

Jesus said to his disciples, 'You have heard that it was said, "You shall love your neighbour and hate your enemy." But I say to you, Love your enemies and pray for those who persecute you, so that you may be children of your Father in heaven; for he makes his sun rise on the evil and on the good, and sends rain on the righteous and on the unrighteous. For if you love those who love you, what reward do you have? Do not even the tax-collectors do the same? And if you greet only your brothers and sisters, what more are you doing than others? Do not even the Gentiles do the same? Be perfect, therefore, as your heavenly Father is perfect.'

This is the Gospel of the Lord. Matthew 5.43–end

Second Week of Lent: Monday

Year 1 and Year 2

A reading from the Book of Daniel.

I, Daniel, prayed to the LORD my God and made confession, saying,
'Ah, Lord, great and awesome God, keeping covenant and steadfast love with those who love you and keep your commandments, we have sinned and done wrong, acted wickedly and rebelled, turning aside from your commandments and ordinances. We have not listened to your servants the prophets, who spoke in your name to our kings, our princes, and our ancestors, and to all the people of the land.
'Righteousness is on your side, O Lord, but open shame, as at this day, falls on us, the people of Judah, the inhabitants of Jerusalem, and all Israel, those who are near and those who are far away, in all the lands to which you have driven them, because of the treachery that they have committed against you. Open shame, O LORD, falls on us, our kings, our officials, and our ancestors, because we have sinned against you. To the Lord our God belong mercy and forgiveness, for we have rebelled against him, and have not obeyed the voice of the LORD our God by following his laws, which he set before us by his servants the prophets.'

This is the word of the Lord. Daniel 9.4–10

Responsorial Psalm

R **Righteousness is on your side, O Lord:**
 [mercy and forgiveness belong to you]. cf Daniel 9.7, 9

Remember not against us our former sins;
let your compassion make haste to meet us,
for we are brought very low. **R**

Help us, O God of our salvation,
for the glory of your name;
deliver us, and wipe away our sins
for your name's sake. **R**

Let the sorrowful sighing of the prisoners
come before you,
and by your mighty arm
preserve those who are condemned to die. **R**

But we that are your people
and the sheep of your pasture
will give you thanks for ever,
and tell of your praise from generation to generation. **R**

Psalm 79.8–9, 12, 14

Hear the Gospel of our Lord Jesus Christ according to Luke.

Jesus said to his disciples, 'Be merciful, just as your Father is merciful. Do not judge, and you will not be judged; do not condemn, and you will not be condemned. Forgive, and you will be forgiven; give, and it will be given to you. A good measure, pressed down, shaken together, running over, will be put into your lap; for the measure you give will be the measure you get back.'

This is the Gospel of the Lord.   Luke 6.36–38

Second Week of Lent: Tuesday

Year 1 and Year 2

A reading from the prophecy of Isaiah.

Hear the word of the LORD,
    you rulers of Sodom!
Listen to the teaching of our God,
    you people of Gomorrah!
Wash yourselves; make yourselves clean;
      remove the evil of your doings
      from before my eyes;
cease to do evil,
    learn to do good;
seek justice,
    rescue the oppressed,
defend the orphan,
    plead for the widow.

Come now, let us argue it out,
    says the LORD:
though your sins are like scarlet,
    they shall be like snow;
though they are red like crimson,
    they shall become like wool.
If you are willing and obedient,
    you shall eat the good of the land;
but if you refuse and rebel,
    you shall be devoured by the sword;
    for the mouth of the LORD has spoken.

This is the word of the Lord.   Isaiah 1.10, 16–20

Responsorial Psalm

R **I will show my salvation
to those who keep my way.**   *cf Psalm 50.24b*

'I will not reprove you for your sacrifices,
for your burnt offerings are always before me.'
But to the wicked, says God:
'Why do you recite my statutes
and take my covenant upon your lips,
since you refuse to be disciplined
and have cast my words behind you? R

'When you saw a thief, you made friends with him
and you threw in your lot with adulterers.
You have loosed your lips for evil
and harnessed your tongue to deceit.
You sit and speak evil of your brother;
you slander your own mother's son. R

'These things have you done, and should I keep silence?
Did you think that I am even such a one as yourself?
But no, I must reprove you,
and set before your eyes the things that you have done. R

'You that forget God, consider this well,
lest I tear you apart and there is none to deliver you.
Whoever offers me the sacrifice of thanksgiving honours me
and to those who keep my way
will I show the salvation of God.' R   *Psalm 50.8, 16–end*

Hear the Gospel of our Lord Jesus Christ according to Matthew.

Jesus said to the crowds and to his disciples, 'The scribes and the Pharisees sit on Moses' seat; therefore, do whatever they teach you and follow it; but do not do as they do, for they do not practise what they teach. They tie up heavy burdens, hard to bear, and lay them on the shoulders of others; but they themselves are unwilling to lift a finger to move them. They do all their deeds to be seen by others; for they make their phylacteries broad and their fringes long. They love to have the place of honour at banquets and the best seats in the synagogues, and to be greeted with respect in the market-places, and to have people call them rabbi. But you are not to be called rabbi, for you have one teacher, and you are all students. And call no one your father on earth, for you have one Father – the one in heaven. Nor are you to be called instructors, for you have one instructor, the Messiah. The greatest among you will be your servant. All who exalt themselves will be humbled, and all who humble themselves will be exalted.'

This is the Gospel of the Lord.   *Matthew 23.1–12*

Second Week of Lent: Wednesday

Year 1 and Year 2

A reading from the prophecy of Jeremiah.

The people said, 'Come, let us make plots against Jeremiah – for instruction shall not perish from the priest, nor counsel from the wise, nor the word from the prophet. Come, let us bring charges against him, and let us not heed any of his words.'
> Give heed to me, O LORD,
>> and listen to what my adversaries say!
> Is evil a recompense for good?
>> Yet they have dug a pit for my life.
> Remember how I stood before you
>> to speak good for them,
>> to turn away your wrath from them.

This is the word of the Lord.   Jeremiah 18.18–20

Responsorial Psalm

R **My trust is in you, O Lord;**
   [I have said, 'You are my God.']   cf Psalm 31.14

Take me out of the net that they have laid secretly for me,
for you are my strength.
Into your hands I commend my spirit,
for you have redeemed me, O Lord God of truth.   **R**

But my trust is in you, O Lord.
I have said, 'You are my God,
my times are in your hand.   **R**

'Deliver me from the hand of my enemies,
and from those who persecute me.
Make your face to shine upon your servant,
and save me for your mercy's sake.'   **R**

Lord, let me not be confounded
for I have called upon you;
but let the wicked be put to shame;
let them be silent in the grave.   **R**

Let the lying lips be put to silence
that speak against the righteous
with arrogance, disdain and contempt.   **R**   Psalm 31.4–5, 14–18

Hear the Gospel of our Lord Jesus Christ according to Matthew.

While Jesus was going up to Jerusalem, he took the twelve disciples aside by themselves, and said to them on the way, 'See, we are going up to Jerusalem, and the Son of Man will be handed over to the chief priests and scribes, and they will condemn him to death; then they will hand him over to the Gentiles to be mocked and flogged and crucified; and on the third day he will be raised.'

Then the mother of the sons of Zebedee came to him with her sons, and kneeling before him, she asked a favour of him. And he said to her, 'What do you want?' She said to him, 'Declare that these two sons of mine will sit, one at your right hand and one at your left, in your kingdom.' But Jesus answered, 'You do not know what you are asking. Are you able to drink the cup that I am about to drink?' They said to him, 'We are able.' He said to them, 'You will indeed drink my cup, but to sit at my right hand and at my left, this is not mine to grant, but it is for those for whom it has been prepared by my Father.'

When the ten heard it, they were angry with the two brothers. But Jesus called them to him and said, 'You know that the rulers of the Gentiles lord it over them, and their great ones are tyrants over them. It will not be so among you; but whoever wishes to be great among you must be your servant, and whoever wishes to be first among you must be your slave; just as the Son of Man came not to be served but to serve, and to give his life a ransom for many.'

This is the Gospel of the Lord. Matthew 20.17–28

Second Week of Lent: Thursday

Year 1 and Year 2

A reading from the prophecy of Jeremiah.

Thus says the LORD:
Cursed are those who trust in mere mortals
 and make mere flesh their strength,
  whose hearts turn away from the LORD.
They shall be like a shrub in the desert,
 and shall not see when relief comes.
They shall live in the parched places of the wilderness,
 in an uninhabited salt land.

Blessed are those who trust in the LORD,
 whose trust is the LORD.
They shall be like a tree planted by water,
 sending out its roots by the stream.

It shall not fear when heat comes,
and its leaves shall stay green;
in the year of drought it is not anxious,
and it does not cease to bear fruit.

The heart is devious above all else;
it is perverse –
who can understand it?
I the LORD test the mind
and search the heart,
to give to all according to their ways,
according to the fruit of their doings.

This is the word of the Lord.   *Jeremiah 17.5–10*

Responsorial Psalm

R **Blessed are those who trust in the Lord:**
   [their delight is in the law of the Lord].   *Jeremiah 17.7a, Psalm 1.3a*

Blessed are they who have not walked
in the counsel of the wicked,
nor lingered in the way of sinners,
nor sat in the assembly of the scornful.
Their delight is in the law of the Lord
and they meditate on his law day and night. **R**

Like a tree planted by streams of water
bearing fruit in due season,
with leaves that do not wither,
whatever they do, it shall prosper. **R**

As for the wicked, it is not so with them;
they are like chaff which the wind blows away.
Therefore the wicked shall not be able to stand in the judgement,
nor the sinner in the congregation of the righteous.
For the Lord knows the way of the righteous,
but the way of the wicked shall perish. **R**   *Psalm 1*

Hear the Gospel of our Lord Jesus Christ according to Luke.

Jesus said to the Pharisees, 'There was a rich man who was dressed in purple and fine linen and who feasted sumptuously every day. And at his gate lay a poor man named Lazarus, covered with sores, who longed to satisfy his hunger with what fell from the rich man's table; even the dogs would come and lick his sores. The poor man died and was carried away by the angels to be with Abraham. The rich man also died and was buried.

'In Hades, where he was being tormented, he looked up and saw Abraham far away with Lazarus by his side. He called out, "Father Abraham, have mercy on me, and send Lazarus to dip the tip of his finger in water and cool my tongue; for I am in agony in these flames." But Abraham said, "Child, remember that during your lifetime you received your good things, and Lazarus in like manner evil things; but now he is comforted here, and you are in agony. Besides all this, between you and us a great chasm has been fixed, so that those who might want to pass from here to you cannot do so, and no one can cross from there to us."

'He said, "Then, father, I beg you to send him to my father's house – for I have five brothers – that he may warn them, so that they will not also come into this place of torment." Abraham replied, "They have Moses and the prophets; they should listen to them." He said, "No, father Abraham; but if someone goes to them from the dead, they will repent." He said to him, "If they do not listen to Moses and the prophets, neither will they be convinced even if someone rises from the dead." '

This is the Gospel of the Lord.   Luke 16.19–end

Second Week of Lent: Friday

Year 1 and Year 2

A reading from the book Genesis.

Israel loved Joseph more than any other of his children, because he was the son of his old age; and he had made him a long robe with sleeves. But when his brothers saw that their father loved him more than all his brothers, they hated him, and could not speak peaceably to him.

Now his brothers went to pasture their father's flock near Shechem. And Israel said to Joseph, 'Are not your brothers pasturing the flock at Shechem? Come, I will send you to them.' He answered, 'Here I am.' The man said, 'They have gone away, for I heard them say, "Let us go to Dothan." ' So Joseph went after his brothers, and found them at Dothan. They saw him from a distance, and before he came near to them, they conspired to kill him. They said to one another, 'Here comes this dreamer. Come now, let us kill him and throw him into one of the pits; then we shall say that a wild animal has devoured him, and we shall see what will become of his dreams.'

But when Reuben heard it, he delivered him out of their hands, saying, 'Let us not take his life.' Reuben said to them, 'Shed no blood; throw him into this pit here in the wilderness, but lay no hand on him' – that he might rescue him out of their hand and restore him to his father. So when Joseph came to his brothers, they stripped him of his robe, the long robe with sleeves that he wore; and they took him and threw him into a pit. The pit was empty; there was no water in it.

Then they sat down to eat; and looking up they saw a caravan of Ishmaelites coming from Gilead, with their camels carrying gum, balm, and resin, on their way to carry it down to Egypt. Then Judah said to his brothers, 'What profit is there if we kill our brother and conceal his blood? Come, let us sell him to the Ishmaelites, and not lay our hands on him, for he is our brother, our own flesh.' And his brothers agreed. When some Midianite traders passed by, they drew Joseph up, lifting him out of the pit, and sold him to the Ishmaelites for twenty pieces of silver. And they took Joseph to Egypt.

This is the word of the Lord. *Genesis 37.3–4, 12–13, 17–28*

Responsorial Psalm

R **Remember the marvels the Lord has done:**
   [his wonders and the judgements he has given]. *cf Psalm 105.5*

Then God called down famine over the land
and broke every staff of bread.
But he had sent a man before them,
Joseph, who was sold as a slave. **R**

They shackled his feet with fetters;
his neck was ringed with iron.
Until all he foretold came to pass,
the word of the Lord tested him. **R**

The king sent and released him;
the ruler of peoples set him free.
He appointed him lord of his household
and ruler of all he possessed,
to instruct his princes as he willed
and to teach his counsellors wisdom. **R** *Psalm 105.16–22*

Hear the Gospel of our Lord Jesus Christ according to Matthew.

Jesus said to the chief priests and the elders of the people, 'Listen to another parable. There was a landowner who planted a vineyard, put a fence around it, dug a wine press in it, and built a watch-tower. Then he leased it to tenants and went to another country. When the harvest time had come, he sent his slaves to the tenants to collect his produce. But the tenants seized his slaves and beat one, killed another, and stoned another. Again he sent other slaves, more than the first; and they treated them in the same way. Finally he sent his son to them, saying, "They will respect my son." But when the tenants saw the son, they said to themselves, "This is the heir; come, let us kill him and get his inheritance." So they seized him, threw him out of the vineyard, and killed him. Now when the owner of the vineyard comes, what will he do to those tenants?' They said to him, 'He will put those wretches to a miserable death, and lease the vineyard to other tenants who will give him the produce at the harvest time.'

Jesus said to them, 'Have you never read in the scriptures:
"The stone that the builders rejected
    has become the cornerstone;
  this was the Lord's doing,
    and it is amazing in our eyes"?
Therefore I tell you, the kingdom of God will be taken away from you and given to a people that produces the fruits of the kingdom.'

When the chief priests and the Pharisees heard his parables, they realized that he was speaking about them. They wanted to arrest him, but they feared the crowds, because they regarded him as a prophet.

This is the Gospel of the Lord.
                                       Matthew 21.33–43, 45–46

Second Week of Lent: Saturday

Year 1 and Year 2

A reading from the prophecy of Micah.

Shepherd your people with your staff,
    the flock that belongs to you,
which lives alone in a forest
    in the midst of a garden land;
let them feed in Bashan and Gilead
    as in the days of old.
As in the days when you came out of the land of Egypt,
    show us marvellous things.

Who is a God like you, pardoning iniquity
    and passing over the transgression
    of the remnant of your possession?

He does not retain his anger for ever,
　　because he delights in showing clemency.
He will again have compassion upon us;
　　he will tread our iniquities under foot.
You will cast all our sins
　　into the depths of the sea.
You will show faithfulness to Jacob
　　and unswerving loyalty to Abraham,
as you have sworn to our ancestors
　　from the days of old.

This is the word of the Lord.　　　　　　　　　　Micah 7.14–15, 18–20

Responsorial Psalm

R　**Bless the Lord, O my soul,**
　　[and bless his holy name].　　　　　　　　cf Psalm 103.1

Bless the Lord, O my soul,
and all that is within me bless his holy name.
Bless the Lord, O my soul,
and forget not all his benefits.　**R**

Who forgives all your sins
and heals all your infirmities;
who redeems your life from the Pit
and crowns you with faithful love and compassion.　**R**

He will not always accuse us,
neither will he keep his anger for ever.
He has not dealt with us according to our sins,
nor rewarded us according to our wickedness.　**R**

For as the heavens are high above the earth,
so great is his mercy upon those who fear him.
As far as the east is from the west,
so far has he set our sins from us.　**R**　　　　Psalm 103.1–4, 9–12

Hear the Gospel of our Lord Jesus Christ according to Luke.

All the tax-collectors and sinners were coming near to listen to Jesus. And the Pharisees and the scribes were grumbling and saying, 'This fellow welcomes sinners and eats with them.'

So he told them this parable: 'There was a man who had two sons. The younger of them said to his father, "Father, give me the share of the property that will belong to me." So he divided his property between them. A few days later the younger son gathered all he had and travelled to a distant country, and there he squandered his property in dissolute living.

'When he had spent everything, a severe famine took place throughout that country, and he began to be in need. So he went and hired himself out to one of the citizens of that country, who sent him to his fields to feed the pigs. He would gladly have filled himself with the pods that the pigs were eating; and no one gave him anything. But when he came to himself he said, "How many of my father's hired hands have bread enough and to spare, but here I am dying of hunger! I will get up and go to my father, and I will say to him, 'Father, I have sinned against heaven and before you; I am no longer worthy to be called your son; treat me like one of your hired hands.'" So he set off and went to his father.

'But while he was still far off, his father saw him and was filled with compassion; he ran and put his arms around him and kissed him. Then the son said to him, "Father, I have sinned against heaven and before you; I am no longer worthy to be called your son." But the father said to his slaves, "Quickly, bring out a robe – the best one – and put it on him; put a ring on his finger and sandals on his feet. And get the fatted calf and kill it, and let us eat and celebrate; for this son of mine was dead and is alive again; he was lost and is found!" And they began to celebrate.

'Now his elder son was in the field; and when he came and approached the house, he heard music and dancing. He called one of the slaves and asked what was going on. He replied, "Your brother has come, and your father has killed the fatted calf, because he has got him back safe and sound." Then he became angry and refused to go in. His father came out and began to plead with him. But he answered his father, "Listen! For all these years I have been working like a slave for you, and I have never disobeyed your command; yet you have never given me even a young goat so that I might celebrate with my friends. But when this son of yours came back, who has devoured your property with prostitutes, you killed the fatted calf for him!"

'Then the father said to him, "Son, you are always with me, and all that is mine is yours. But we had to celebrate and rejoice, because this brother of yours was dead and has come to life; he was lost and has been found."'

This is the Gospel of the Lord.   Luke 15.1–3, 11–end

Third Week of Lent: any day

The following readings may replace those provided on any day (except St Joseph's Day and the Annunciation) during the Third Week of Lent, especially in Years B and C when the Gospel passage about the Samaritan woman is not read on the Third Sunday of Lent.

A reading from the book of the Exodus.

From the wilderness of Sin the whole congregation of the Israelites journeyed by stages, as the LORD commanded. They camped at Rephidim, but there was no water for the people to drink. The people quarrelled with Moses, and said, 'Give us water to drink.' Moses said to them, 'Why do you quarrel with me? Why do you test the LORD?' But the people thirsted there for water; and the people complained against Moses and said, 'Why did you bring us out of Egypt, to kill us and our children and livestock with thirst?' So Moses cried out to the LORD, 'What shall I do with this people? They are almost ready to stone me.' The LORD said to Moses, 'Go on ahead of the people, and take some of the elders of Israel with you; take in your hand the staff with which you struck the Nile, and go. I will be standing there in front of you on the rock at Horeb. Strike the rock, and water will come out of it, so that the people may drink.' Moses did so, in the sight of the elders of Israel. He called the place Massah and Meribah, because the Israelites quarrelled and tested the LORD, saying, 'Is the LORD among us or not?'

This is the word of the Lord. *Exodus 17.1–7*

Responsorial Psalm

R **Come, let us sing to the Lord;**
 and rejoice in the rock of our salvation. *cf Psalm 95.1*

O come, let us sing to the Lord;
let us heartily rejoice in the rock of our salvation.
Let us come into his presence with thanksgiving
and be glad in him with psalms. **R**

Come, let us worship and bow down
and kneel before the Lord our Maker.
For he is our God;
we are the people of his pasture and the sheep of his hand. **R**

O that today you would listen to his voice:
'Harden not your hearts as at Meribah,
on that day at Massah in the wilderness,
when your forebears tested me, and put me to the proof,
though they had seen my works. **R**

'Forty years long I detested that generation and said,
"This people are wayward in their hearts;
they do not know my ways."
So I swore in my wrath,
"They shall not enter into my rest." ' **R** *Psalm 95.1–2, 6–end*

Hear the Gospel of our Lord Jesus Christ according to John.

Jesus came to a Samaritan city called Sychar, near the plot of ground that Jacob had given to his son Joseph. Jacob's well was there, and Jesus, tired out by his journey, was sitting by the well. It was about noon.

A Samaritan woman came to draw water, and Jesus said to her, 'Give me a drink'. (His disciples had gone to the city to buy food.) The Samaritan woman said to him, 'How is it that you, a Jew, ask a drink of me, a woman of Samaria?' (Jews do not share things in common with Samaritans.) Jesus answered her, 'If you knew the gift of God, and who it is that is saying to you, "Give me a drink", you would have asked him, and he would have given you living water.'

The woman said to him, 'Sir, you have no bucket, and the well is deep. Where do you get that living water? Are you greater than our ancestor Jacob, who gave us the well, and with his sons and his flocks drank from it?' Jesus said to her, 'Everyone who drinks of this water will be thirsty again, but those who drink of the water that I will give them will never be thirsty. The water that I will give will become in them a spring of water gushing up to eternal life.' The woman said to him, 'Sir, give me this water, so that I may never be thirsty or have to keep coming here to draw water.'

Jesus said to her, 'Go, call your husband, and come back.' The woman answered him, 'I have no husband.' Jesus said to her, 'You are right in saying, "I have no husband"; for you have had five husbands, and the one you have now is not your husband. What you have said is true!' The woman said to him, 'Sir, I see that you are a prophet. Our ancestors worshipped on this mountain, but you say that the place where people must worship is in Jerusalem.'

Jesus said to her, 'Woman, believe me, the hour is coming when you will worship the Father neither on this mountain nor in Jerusalem. You worship what you do not know; we worship what we know, for salvation is from the Jews. But the hour is coming, and is now here, when the true worshippers will worship the Father in spirit and truth, for the Father seeks such as these to worship him. God is spirit, and those who worship him must worship in spirit and truth.' The woman said to him, 'I know that Messiah is coming' (who is called Christ). 'When he comes, he will proclaim all things to us.' Jesus said to her, 'I am he, the one who is speaking to you.'

Just then his disciples came. They were astonished that he was speaking with a woman, but no one said, 'What do you want?' or, 'Why are you speaking with her?' Then the woman left her water-jar and went back to the city. She said to the people, 'Come and see a man who told me everything I have ever done! He cannot be the Messiah, can he?' They left the city and were on their way to him.

Meanwhile the disciples were urging him, 'Rabbi, eat something.' But he said to them, 'I have food to eat that you do not know about.' So the disciples said to one another, 'Surely no one has brought him something to eat?' Jesus said to them, 'My food is to do the will of him who sent me and to complete his work. Do you not say, "Four months more, then comes the harvest"? But I tell you, look around you, and see how the fields are ripe for harvesting. The reaper is already receiving wages and is gathering fruit for eternal life, so that sower and reaper may rejoice together. For here the saying holds true, "One sows and another reaps." I sent you to reap that for which you did not labour. Others have laboured, and you have entered into their labour.'

Many Samaritans from that city believed in him because of the woman's testimony, 'He told me everything I have ever done.' So when the Samaritans came to him, they asked him to stay with them; and he stayed there for two days. And many more believed because of his word. They said to the woman, 'It is no longer because of what you said that we believe, for we have heard for ourselves, and we know that this is truly the Saviour of the world.'

This is the Gospel of the Lord.   John 4.5–42

Third Week of Lent: Monday

Year 1 and Year 2

A reading from the Second Book of the Kings.

Naaman, commander of the army of the king of Aram, was a great man and in high favour with his master, because by him the LORD had given victory to Aram. The man, though a mighty warrior, suffered from leprosy. Now the Arameans on one of their raids had taken a young girl captive from the land of Israel, and she served Naaman's wife. She said to her mistress, 'If only my lord were with the prophet who is in Samaria! He would cure him of his leprosy.' So Naaman went in and told his lord just what the girl from the land of Israel had said. And the king of Aram said, 'Go then, and I will send along a letter to the king of Israel.'

He went, taking with him ten talents of silver, six thousand shekels of gold, and ten sets of garments. He brought the letter to the king of Israel, which read, 'When this letter reaches you, know that I have sent to you my servant Naaman, that you may cure him of his leprosy.' When the king of Israel read the letter, he tore his clothes and said, 'Am I God, to give death or life, that this man sends word to me to cure a man of his leprosy? Just look and see how he is trying to pick a quarrel with me.'

But when Elisha the man of God heard that the king of Israel had torn his clothes, he sent a message to the king, 'Why have you torn your clothes? Let him come to me, that he may learn that there is a prophet in Israel.' So Naaman came with his horses and chariots, and halted at the entrance of Elisha's house. Elisha sent a messenger to him, saying, 'Go, wash in the Jordan seven times, and your flesh shall be restored and you shall be clean.' But Naaman became angry and went away, saying, 'I thought that for me he would surely come out, and stand and call on the name of the LORD his God, and would wave his hand over the spot, and cure the leprosy! Are not Abana and Pharpar, the rivers of Damascus, better than all the waters of Israel? Could I not wash in them, and be clean?' He turned and went away in a rage.

But his servants approached and said to him, 'Father, if the prophet had commanded you to do something difficult, would you not have done it? How much more, when all he said to you was, "Wash, and be clean"?' So he went down and immersed himself seven times in the Jordan, according to the word of the man of God; his flesh was restored like the flesh of a young boy, and he was clean.

Then he returned to the man of God, he and all his company; he came and stood before him and said, 'Now I know that there is no God in all the earth except in Israel; please accept a present from your servant.'

This is the word of the Lord.   2 Kings 5.1–15

Responsorial Psalm

R **My soul is athirst for God, the living God:**
  [the God of my joy and gladness]. cf Psalm 42.2a, 43.4a

As the deer longs for the water brooks,
so longs my soul for you, O God.
My soul is athirst for God, even for the living God;
when shall I come before the presence of God? R

Give judgement for me, O God,
and defend my cause against an ungodly people;
deliver me from the deceitful
and the wicked. R

For you are the God of my refuge;
why have you cast me from you,
and why go I so heavily,
while the enemy oppresses me? R

O send out your light and your truth,
that they may lead me,
and bring me to your holy hill
and to your dwelling. R

That I may go to the altar of God,
to the God of my joy and gladness;
and on the lyre I will give thanks to you,
O God my God. R Psalm 42.1–2, 43.1–4

Hear the Gospel of our Lord Jesus Christ according to Luke.

Jesus came to Nazareth and spoke in the synagogue, 'Truly I tell you, no prophet is accepted in the prophet's home town. But the truth is, there were many widows in Israel in the time of Elijah, when the heaven was shut up for three years and six months, and there was a severe famine over all the land; yet Elijah was sent to none of them except to a widow at Zarephath in Sidon. There were also many lepers in Israel in the time of the prophet Elisha, and none of them was cleansed except Naaman the Syrian.'

When they heard this, all in the synagogue were filled with rage. They got up, drove him out of the town, and led him to the brow of the hill on which their town was built, so that they might hurl him off the cliff. But he passed through the midst of them and went on his way.

This is the Gospel of the Lord. Luke 4.24–30

Third Week of Lent: Tuesday

Year 1 and Year 2

Either

A reading from the Song of the Three.

Azariah stood still in the fire and prayed aloud:
> For your name's sake do not give us up for ever,
>> and do not annul your covenant.
> Do not withdraw your mercy from us,
> for the sake of Abraham your beloved
>> and for the sake of your servant Isaac
>> and Israel your holy one,
> to whom you promised
>> to multiply their descendants like the stars of heaven
>> and like the sand on the shore of the sea.
> For we, O Lord, have become fewer than any other nation,
>> and are brought low this day in all the world because of our sins.
> In our day we have no ruler, or prophet, or leader,
>> no burnt-offering, or sacrifice, or oblation, or incense,
>> no place to make an offering before you and to find mercy.
> Yet with a contrite heart and a humble spirit may we be accepted,
>> as though it were with burnt-offerings of rams and bulls,
>> or with tens of thousands of fat lambs;
>> such may our sacrifice be in your sight today,
>> and may we unreservedly follow you,
>> for no shame will come to those who trust in you.
> And now with all our heart we follow you;
>> we fear you and seek your presence.
> Do not put us to shame,
>> but deal with us in your patience
>> and in your abundant mercy.
> Deliver us in accordance with your marvellous works,
>> and bring glory to your name, O Lord.

This is the word of the Lord.   *Song of the Three 2, 11–20*

or

A reading from the Book of Daniel.

Daniel said:
'Blessed be the name of God from age to age,
for wisdom and power are his.
He changes times and seasons,
deposes kings and sets up kings;
he gives wisdom to the wise
and knowledge to those who have understanding.
He reveals deep and hidden things;
he knows what is in the darkness,
and light dwells with him.
To you, O God of my ancestors,
I give thanks and praise,
for you have given me wisdom and power,
and have now revealed to me what we asked of you,
for you have revealed to us what the king ordered.'

This is the word of the Lord.

Daniel 2.20–23

Responsorial Psalm

R **With contrite heart and humble spirit
we come to you, O Lord.**

cf *Song of the Three* 16

Make me to know your ways, O Lord,
and teach me your paths.
Lead me in your truth and teach me,
for you are the God of my salvation;
for you have I hoped all the day long. **R**

Remember, Lord, your compassion and love,
for they are from everlasting.
Remember not the sins of my youth or my transgressions,
but think on me in your goodness, O Lord,
according to your steadfast love. **R**

Gracious and upright is the Lord;
therefore shall he teach sinners in the way.
He will guide the humble in doing right
and teach his way to the lowly. **R**

All the paths of the Lord are mercy and truth
to those who keep his covenant and his testimonies.
For your name's sake, O Lord,
be merciful to my sin, for it is great. **R**

Psalm 25.3–10

Hear the Gospel of our Lord Jesus Christ according to Matthew.

Peter came and said to Jesus, 'Lord, if another member of the church sins against me, how often should I forgive? As many as seven times?'

Jesus said to him, 'Not seven times, but, I tell you, seventy-seven times. For this reason the kingdom of heaven may be compared to a king who wished to settle accounts with his slaves. When he began the reckoning, one who owed him ten thousand talents was brought to him; and, as he could not pay, his lord ordered him to be sold, together with his wife and children and all his possessions, and payment to be made.

'So the slave fell on his knees before him, saying, "Have patience with me, and I will pay you everything." And out of pity for him, the lord of that slave released him and forgave him the debt. But that same slave, as he went out, came upon one of his fellow-slaves who owed him a hundred denarii; and seizing him by the throat, he said, "Pay what you owe." Then his fellow-slave fell down and pleaded with him, "Have patience with me, and I will pay you." But he refused; then he went and threw him into prison until he should pay the debt. When his fellow-slaves saw what had happened, they were greatly distressed, and they went and reported to their lord all that had taken place. Then his lord summoned him and said to him, "You wicked slave! I forgave you all that debt because you pleaded with me. Should you not have had mercy on your fellow-slave, as I had mercy on you?" And in anger his lord handed him over to be tortured until he should pay his entire debt. So my heavenly Father will also do to every one of you, if you do not forgive your brother or sister from your heart.'

This is the Gospel of the Lord.   Matthew 18.21–end

Third Week of Lent: Wednesday

Year 1 and Year 2

A reading from the book Deuteronomy.

Moses said to the people: So now, Israel, give heed to the statutes and ordinances that I am teaching you to observe, so that you may live to enter and occupy the land that the LORD, the God of your ancestors, is giving you.

See, just as the LORD my God has charged me, I now teach you statutes and ordinances for you to observe in the land that you are about to enter and occupy. You must observe them diligently, for this will show your wisdom and discernment to the peoples, who, when they hear all these statutes, will say, 'Surely this great nation is a wise and discerning people!' For what other great nation has a god so near to it as the LORD our God is whenever we call to him? And what other great nation has statutes and ordinances as just as this entire law that I am setting before you today?

But take care and watch yourselves closely, so as neither to forget the things that your eyes have seen nor to let them slip from your mind all the days of your life; make them known to your children and your children's children.

This is the word of the Lord. Deuteronomy 4.1, 5–9

Responsorial Psalm

R* **Sing praise to the Lord, O Jerusalem:**
[praise your God, O Zion]. Psalm 147.13

The Lord has strengthened the bars of your gates
and has blest your children within you.
He has established peace in your borders
and satisfies you with the finest wheat.   **R**

He sends forth his command to the earth
and his word runs very swiftly.
He gives snow like wool
and scatters the hoarfrost like ashes.   **R**

He casts down his hailstones like morsels of bread;
who can endure his frost?
He sends forth his word and melts them;
he blows with his wind and the waters flow.   **R**

He declares his word to Jacob,
his statutes and judgements to Israel.
He has not dealt so with any other nation;
they do not know his laws.   **R** Psalm 147.13–end

Hear the Gospel of our Lord Jesus Christ according to Matthew.

Jesus said to his disciples, 'Do not think that I have come to abolish the law or the prophets; I have come not to abolish but to fulfil. For truly I tell you, until heaven and earth pass away, not one letter, not one stroke of a letter, will pass from the law until all is accomplished. Therefore, whoever breaks one of the least of these commandments, and teaches others to do the same, will be called least in the kingdom of heaven; but whoever does them and teaches them will be called great in the kingdom of heaven.'

This is the Gospel of the Lord. Matthew 5.17–19

Third Week of Lent: Thursday

Year 1 and Year 2

A reading from the prophecy of Jeremiah.

Thus says the LORD of hosts, the God of Israel: This command I gave them,
'Obey my voice, and I will be your God, and you shall be my people; and walk
only in the way that I command you, so that it may be well with you.' Yet they
did not obey or incline their ear, but, in the stubbornness of their evil will,
they walked in their own counsels, and looked backwards rather than forwards.
From the day that your ancestors came out of the land of Egypt until this day,
I have persistently sent all my servants the prophets to them, day after day;
yet they did not listen to me, or pay attention, but they stiffened their necks.
They did worse than their ancestors did.

So you shall speak all these words to them, but they will not listen to you.
You shall call to them, but they will not answer you. You shall say to them:
This is the nation that did not obey the voice of the LORD their God, and did
not accept discipline; truth has perished; it is cut off from their lips.

This is the word of the Lord. *Jeremiah 7.23–28*

Responsorial Psalm

R **Come, let us sing to the Lord;**
and rejoice in the rock of our salvation. cf Psalm 95.1

O come, let us sing to the Lord;
let us heartily rejoice in the rock of our salvation.
Let us come into his presence with thanksgiving
and be glad in him with psalms. **R**

Come, let us worship and bow down
and kneel before the Lord our Maker.
For he is our God;
we are the people of his pasture and the sheep of his hand. **R**

O that today you would listen to his voice:
'Harden not your hearts as at Meribah,
on that day at Massah in the wilderness,
when your forebears tested me, and put me to the proof,
though they had seen my works. **R**

'Forty years long I detested that generation and said,
"This people are wayward in their hearts;
they do not know my ways."
So I swore in my wrath,
"They shall not enter into my rest." ' **R** Psalm 95.1–2, 6–end

Hear the Gospel of our Lord Jesus Christ according to Luke.

Jesus was casting out a demon that was mute; when the demon had gone out, the one who had been mute spoke, and the crowds were amazed. But some of them said, 'He casts out demons by Beelzebul, the ruler of the demons.' Others, to test him, kept demanding from him a sign from heaven. But he knew what they were thinking and said to them, 'Every kingdom divided against itself becomes a desert, and house falls on house. If Satan also is divided against himself, how will his kingdom stand? – for you say that I cast out the demons by Beelzebul. Now if I cast out the demons by Beelzebul, by whom do your exorcists cast them out? Therefore they will be your judges. But if it is by the finger of God that I cast out the demons, then the kingdom of God has come to you. When a strong man, fully armed, guards his castle, his property is safe. But when one stronger than he attacks him and overpowers him, he takes away his armour in which he trusted and divides his plunder. Whoever is not with me is against me, and whoever does not gather with me scatters.'

This is the Gospel of the Lord.   Luke 11.14–23

Third Week of Lent: Friday

Year 1 and Year 2

A reading from the prophecy of Hosea.

Return, O Israel, to the Lord your God,
 for you have stumbled because of your iniquity.
Take words with you
 and return to the LORD;
say to him,
 'Take away all guilt;
accept that which is good,
 and we will offer
 the fruit of our lips.
Assyria shall not save us;
 we will not ride upon horses;
we will say no more, "Our God",
 to the work of our hands.
In you the orphan finds mercy.'

I will heal their disloyalty;
 I will love them freely,
 for my anger has turned from them.
I will be like the dew to Israel;
 he shall blossom like the lily,
 he shall strike root like the forests of Lebanon. →

His shoots shall spread out;
   his beauty shall be like the olive tree,
   and his fragrance like that of Lebanon.
They shall again live beneath my shadow,
   they shall flourish as a garden;
they shall blossom like the vine,
   their fragrance shall be like the wine of Lebanon.

O Ephraim, what have I to do with idols?
   It is I who answer and look after you.
I am like an evergreen cypress;
   your faithfulness comes from me.
Those who are wise understand these things;
   those who are discerning know them.
For the ways of the LORD are right,
   and the upright walk in them,
   but transgressors stumble in them.

This is the word of the Lord.   Hosea 14

Responsorial Psalm

R **The ways of the Lord are right,
    [and the upright walk in them].**   Hosea 14.9b

I heard a voice I did not know, that said:
'I eased their shoulder from the burden;
   their hands were set free from bearing the load.
You called upon me in trouble and I delivered you.   **R**

'I answered you from the secret place of thunder
and proved you at the waters of Meribah.
Hear, O my people, and I will admonish you:
O Israel, if you would but listen to me!   **R**

'There shall be no strange god among you;
you shall not worship a foreign god.
I am the Lord your God,
   who brought you up from the land of Egypt;
open your mouth wide and I shall fill it.   **R**

'O that my people would listen to me,
that Israel would walk in my ways!
But Israel would I feed with the finest wheat
and with honey from the rock would I satisfy them.'   **R**

                                    Psalm 81.6–10, 13, 16

Hear the Gospel of our Lord Jesus Christ according to Mark.

One of the scribes came near Jesus and asked him, 'Which commandment is the first of all?' Jesus answered, 'The first is, "Hear, O Israel: the Lord our God, the Lord is one; you shall love the Lord your God with all your heart, and with all your soul, and with all your mind, and with all your strength." The second is this, "You shall love your neighbour as yourself." There is no other commandment greater than these.' Then the scribe said to him, 'You are right, Teacher; you have truly said that "he is one, and besides him there is no other"; and "to love him with all the heart, and with all the understanding, and with all the strength", and "to love one's neighbour as oneself", – this is much more important than all whole burnt-offerings and sacrifices.' When Jesus saw that he answered wisely, he said to him, 'You are not far from the kingdom of God.' After that no one dared to ask him any question.

This is the Gospel of the Lord.   Mark 12.28–34

Third Week of Lent: Saturday

Year 1 and Year 2

A reading from the prophecy of Hosea.

I will return again to my place
    until they acknowledge their guilt and seek my face.
    In their distress they will beg my favour:

'Come, let us return to the LORD;
    for it is he who has torn, and he will heal us;
    he has struck down, and he will bind us up.
After two days he will revive us;
    on the third day he will raise us up,
    that we may live before him.
Let us know, let us press on to know the LORD;
    his appearing is as sure as the dawn;
he will come to us like the showers,
    like the spring rains that water the earth.'

What shall I do with you, O Ephraim?
    What shall I do with you, O Judah?
Your love is like a morning cloud,
    like the dew that goes away early.
Therefore I have hewn them by the prophets,
    I have killed them by the words of my mouth,
    and my judgement goes forth as the light.
For I desire steadfast love and not sacrifice,
    the knowledge of God rather than burnt-offerings.

This is the word of the Lord.   Hosea 5.15 – 6.6

Responsorial Psalm

R **Come, let us return to the Lord:**
   [he will heal us and bind up our wounds].   cf Hosea 6.1

Have mercy on me, O God, in your great goodness;
according to the abundance of your compassion
    blot out my offences.
Wash me thoroughly from my wickedness
and cleanse me from my sin. R

For you desire no sacrifice, else I would give it;
you take no delight in burnt offerings.
The sacrifice of God is a broken spirit;
a broken and contrite heart, O God, you will not despise. R

O be favourable and gracious to Zion;
build up the walls of Jerusalem.
Then you will accept sacrifices offered in righteousness,
the burnt offerings and oblations;
then shall they offer up bulls on your altar. R   *Psalm 51.1–2, 17–end*

Hear the Gospel of our Lord Jesus Christ according to Luke.

Jesus told this parable to some who trusted in themselves that they were
righteous and regarded others with contempt: 'Two men went up to the temple
to pray, one a Pharisee and the other a tax-collector. The Pharisee, standing by
himself, was praying thus, "God, I thank you that I am not like other people:
thieves, rogues, adulterers, or even like this tax-collector. I fast twice a week;
I give a tenth of all my income." But the tax-collector, standing far off, would
not even look up to heaven, but was beating his breast and saying, "God, be
merciful to me, a sinner!" I tell you, this man went down to his home justified
rather than the other; for all who exalt themselves will be humbled, but all
who humble themselves will be exalted.'

This is the Gospel of the Lord.   Luke 18.9–14

Fourth Week of Lent: any day

The following readings may replace those provided on any day (except St Joseph's Day and the Annunciation) during the Fourth Week of Lent, especially in Years B and C when the Gospel passage about the man born blind is not read on the Fourth Sunday of Lent.

A reading from the prophecy of Micah.

As for me, I will look to the LORD,
    I will wait for the God of my salvation;
    my God will hear me.

Do not rejoice over me, O my enemy;
    when I fall, I shall rise;
when I sit in darkness,
    the LORD will be a light to me.
I must bear the indignation of the LORD,
    because I have sinned against him,
until he takes my side
    and executes judgement for me.
He will bring me out to the light;
    I shall see his vindication.

This is the word of the Lord.

Micah 7.7–9

Responsorial Psalm

R **The Lord is my light and my salvation:**
  [he is the strength of my life].

cf Psalm 27.1

The Lord is my light and my salvation;
whom then shall I fear?
The Lord is the strength of my life;
of whom then shall I be afraid?   **R**

Hear my voice, O Lord, when I call;
have mercy upon me and answer me.
My heart tells of your word, 'Seek my face.'
Your face, Lord, will I seek.   **R**

I believe that I shall see the goodness of the Lord
    in the land of the living.
Wait for the Lord;
be strong and he shall comfort your heart;
wait patiently for the Lord.   **R**

Psalm 27.1, 9–10, 16–17

Hear the Gospel of our Lord Jesus Christ according to John.

As Jesus walked along, he saw a man blind from birth. His disciples asked him, 'Rabbi, who sinned, this man or his parents, that he was born blind?' Jesus answered, 'Neither this man nor his parents sinned; he was born blind so that God's works might be revealed in him. We must work the works of him who sent me while it is day; night is coming when no one can work. As long as I am in the world, I am the light of the world.' When he had said this, he spat on the ground and made mud with the saliva and spread the mud on the man's eyes, saying to him, 'Go, wash in the pool of Siloam' (which means Sent). Then he went and washed and came back able to see. The neighbours and those who had seen him before as a beggar began to ask, 'Is this not the man who used to sit and beg?' Some were saying, 'It is he.' Others were saying, 'No, but it is someone like him.' He kept saying, 'I am the man.' But they kept asking him, 'Then how were your eyes opened?' He answered, 'The man called Jesus made mud, spread it on my eyes, and said to me, "Go to Siloam and wash." Then I went and washed and received my sight.' They said to him, 'Where is he?' He said, 'I do not know.'

They brought to the Pharisees the man who had formerly been blind. Now it was a sabbath day when Jesus made the mud and opened his eyes. Then the Pharisees also began to ask him how he had received his sight. He said to them, 'He put mud on my eyes. Then I washed, and now I see.' Some of the Pharisees said, 'This man is not from God, for he does not observe the sabbath.' But others said, 'How can a man who is a sinner perform such signs?' And they were divided. So they said again to the blind man, 'What do you say about him? It was your eyes he opened.' He said, 'He is a prophet.'

The Jews did not believe that he had been blind and had received his sight until they called the parents of the man who had received his sight and asked them, 'Is this your son, who you say was born blind? How then does he now see?' His parents answered, 'We know that this is our son, and that he was born blind; but we do not know how it is that now he sees, nor do we know who opened his eyes. Ask him; he is of age. He will speak for himself.' His parents said this because they were afraid of the Jews; for the Jews had already agreed that anyone who confessed Jesus to be the Messiah would be put out of the synagogue. Therefore his parents said, 'He is of age; ask him.'

So for the second time they called the man who had been blind, and they said to him, 'Give glory to God! We know that this man is a sinner.' He answered, 'I do not know whether he is a sinner. One thing I do know, that though I was blind, now I see.' They said to him, 'What did he do to you? How did he open your eyes?' He answered them, 'I have told you already, and you would not listen. Why do you want to hear it again? Do you also want to become his disciples?' Then they reviled him, saying, 'You are his disciple, but we are disciples of Moses. We know that God has spoken to Moses, but as for this man, we do not know where he comes from.' The man answered, 'Here is an astonishing thing! You do not know where he comes from, and yet he opened my eyes. We know that God does not listen to sinners, but he does listen to one who worships him and obeys his will. Never since the world began has it been heard that anyone opened the eyes of a person born blind. If this man were not from God, he could do nothing.' They answered him, 'You were born entirely in sins, and are you trying to teach us?' And they drove him out.

Jesus heard that they had driven him out, and when he found him, he said, 'Do you believe in the Son of Man?' He answered, 'And who is he, sir? Tell me, so that I may believe in him.' Jesus said to him, 'You have seen him, and the one speaking with you is he.' He said, 'Lord, I believe.' And he worshipped him. Jesus said, 'I came into this world for judgement so that those who do not see may see, and those who do see may become blind.' Some of the Pharisees near him heard this and said to him, 'Surely we are not blind, are we?' Jesus said to them, 'If you were blind, you would not have sin. But now that you say, "We see", your sin remains.'

This is the Gospel of the Lord.

John 9

Fourth Week of Lent: Monday

Year 1 and Year 2

A reading from the prophecy of Isaiah.

For I am about to create new heavens
    and a new earth;
the former things shall not be remembered
    or come to mind.
But be glad and rejoice for ever
    in what I am creating;
for I am about to create Jerusalem as a joy,
    and its people as a delight.
I will rejoice in Jerusalem,
    and delight in my people;
no more shall the sound of weeping be heard in it,
    or the cry of distress.
No more shall there be in it
    an infant that lives but a few days,
    or an old person who does not live out a lifetime;
for one who dies at a hundred years will be considered a youth,
    and one who falls short of a hundred will be considered accursed.
They shall build houses and inhabit them;
    they shall plant vineyards and eat their fruit.

This is the word of the Lord.

Isaiah 65.17–21

Responsorial Psalm

R* **[My heart sings to you without ceasing:]**
O God, I will praise you for ever. *cf Psalm 30.12*

I will exalt you, O Lord, because you have raised me up
and have not let my foes triumph over me.
O Lord my God, I cried out to you
and you have healed me. **R**

You brought me up, O Lord, from the dead;
you restored me to life from among those that go down to the Pit.
Sing to the Lord, you servants of his;
give thanks to his holy name. **R**

For his wrath endures but the twinkling of an eye,
his favour for a lifetime.
Heaviness may endure for a night,
but joy comes in the morning. **R**

To you, O Lord, I cried;
to the Lord I made my supplication.
You have turned my mourning into dancing;
you have put off my sackcloth and girded me with gladness. **R***

Psalm 30.1–5, 8, 11–end

Hear the Gospel of our Lord Jesus Christ according to John.

Jesus went from Sychar in Samaria to Galilee (for Jesus himself had testified that a prophet has no honour in the prophet's own country). When he came to Galilee, the Galileans welcomed him, since they had seen all that he had done in Jerusalem at the festival; for they too had gone to the festival.

Then he came again to Cana in Galilee where he had changed the water into wine. Now there was a royal official whose son lay ill in Capernaum. When he heard that Jesus had come from Judea to Galilee, he went and begged him to come down and heal his son, for he was at the point of death. Then Jesus said to him, 'Unless you see signs and wonders you will not believe.' The official said to him, 'Sir, come down before my little boy dies.' Jesus said to him, 'Go; your son will live.' The man believed the word that Jesus spoke to him and started on his way. As he was going down, his slaves met him and told him that his child was alive. So he asked them the hour when he began to recover, and they said to him, 'Yesterday at one in the afternoon the fever left him.' The father realized that this was the hour when Jesus had said to him, 'Your son will live.' So he himself believed, along with his whole household. Now this was the second sign that Jesus did after coming from Judea to Galilee.

This is the Gospel of the Lord. *John 4.43–end*

Fourth Week of Lent: Tuesday

Year 1 and Year 2

A reading from the prophecy of Ezekiel.

In my vision the man brought me back to the entrance of the temple; there, water was flowing from below the threshold of the temple towards the east (for the temple faced east); and the water was flowing down from below the south end of the threshold of the temple, south of the altar. Then he brought me out by way of the north gate, and led me round on the outside to the outer gate that faces towards the east; and the water was coming out on the south side.

Going on eastwards with a cord in his hand, the man measured one thousand cubits, and then led me through the water; and it was ankle-deep. Again he measured one thousand, and led me through the water; and it was knee-deep. Again he measured one thousand, and led me through the water; and it was up to the waist. Again he measured one thousand, and it was a river that I could not cross, for the water had risen; it was deep enough to swim in, a river that could not be crossed. He said to me, 'Mortal, have you seen this?'

Then he led me back along the bank of the river. As I came back, I saw on the bank of the river a great many trees on one side and on the other. He said to me, 'This water flows towards the eastern region and goes down into the Arabah; and when it enters the sea, the sea of stagnant waters, the water will become fresh. Wherever the river goes, every living creature that swarms will live, and there will be very many fish, once these waters reach there. It will become fresh; and everything will live where the river goes. On the banks, on both sides of the river, there will grow all kinds of trees for food. Their leaves will not wither nor their fruit fail, but they will bear fresh fruit every month, because the water for them flows from the sanctuary. Their fruit will be for food, and their leaves for healing.'

This is the word of the Lord. *Ezekiel 47.1–9, 12*

Responsorial Psalm

R **The Lord of hosts is with us;**
   the God of Jacob is our stronghold. *Psalm 46.7*

God is our refuge and strength,
a very present help in trouble;
therefore we will not fear, though the earth be moved,
and though the mountains tremble in the heart of the sea. **R**

Though the waters rage and swell,
and though the mountains quake at the towering seas.
There is a river whose streams make glad the city of God,
the holy place of the dwelling of the Most High. **R** →

God is in the midst of her;
therefore shall she not be removed;
God shall help her at the break of day.
The nations are in uproar and the kingdoms are shaken,
but God utters his voice and the earth shall melt away. R

R **The Lord of hosts is with us;**
   the God of Jacob is our stronghold.

The Lord of hosts is with us;
the God of Jacob is our stronghold.
Come and behold the works of the Lord,
what destruction he has wrought upon the earth. R   *Psalm 46.1–8*

Hear the Gospel of our Lord Jesus Christ according to John.

There was a festival of the Jews, and Jesus went up to Jerusalem. Now in
Jerusalem by the Sheep Gate there is a pool, called in Hebrew Beth-zatha,
which has five porticoes. In these lay many invalids – blind, lame, and paralysed.
One man was there who had been ill for thirty-eight years. When Jesus saw
him lying there and knew that he had been there a long time, he said to him,
'Do you want to be made well?' The sick man answered him, 'Sir, I have no
one to put me into the pool when the water is stirred up; and while I am
making my way, someone else steps down ahead of me.' Jesus said to him,
'Stand up, take your mat and walk.' At once the man was made well, and he
took up his mat and began to walk.

Now that day was a sabbath. So the Jews said to the man who had been
cured, 'It is the sabbath; it is not lawful for you to carry your mat.' But he
answered them, 'The man who made me well said to me, "Take up your mat
and walk."' They asked him, 'Who is the man who said to you, "Take it up
and walk"?' Now the man who had been healed did not know who it was,
for Jesus had disappeared in the crowd that was there. Later Jesus found him
in the temple and said to him, 'See, you have been made well! Do not sin any
more, so that nothing worse happens to you.' The man went away and told
the Jews that it was Jesus who had made him well. Therefore the Jews started
persecuting Jesus, because he was doing such things on the sabbath.

This is the Gospel of the Lord.   *John 5.1–3, 5–16*

Fourth Week of Lent: Wednesday

Year 1 and Year 2

A reading from the prophecy of Isaiah.

Thus says the LORD:
In a time of favour I have answered you,
    on a day of salvation I have helped you;
I have kept you and given you
    as a covenant to the people,
to establish the land,
    to apportion the desolate heritages;
saying to the prisoners, 'Come out',
    to those who are in darkness, 'Show yourselves.'
They shall feed along the ways,
    on all the bare heights shall be their pasture;
they shall not hunger or thirst,
    neither scorching wind nor sun shall strike them down,
for he who has pity on them will lead them,
    and by springs of water will guide them.
And I will turn all my mountains into a road,
    and my highways shall be raised up.
Lo, these shall come from far away,
    and lo, these from the north and from the west,
    and these from the land of Syene.

Sing for joy, O heavens, and exult, O earth;
    break forth, O mountains, into singing!
For the LORD has comforted his people,
    and will have compassion on his suffering ones.

But Zion said, 'The LORD has forsaken me,
    my Lord has forgotten me.'
Can a woman forget her nursing-child,
    or show no compassion for the child of her womb?
Even these may forget,
    yet I will not forget you.

This is the word of the Lord.

Isaiah 49.8–15

Responsorial Psalm

R* **The Lord is righteous in all his ways**
and loving in all his works. *Psalm* 145.18

The Lord is gracious and merciful,
long-suffering and of great goodness.
The Lord is loving to everyone
and his mercy is over all his creatures.   R

All your works praise you, O Lord,
and your faithful servants bless you.
They tell of the glory of your kingdom
and speak of your mighty power.   R

To make known to all peoples your mighty acts
and the glorious splendour of your kingdom.
Your kingdom is an everlasting kingdom;
your dominion endures throughout all ages.   R

The Lord is sure in all his words
and faithful in all his deeds.
The Lord upholds all those who fall
and lifts up all those who are bowed down.   R

The eyes of all wait upon you, O Lord,
and you give them their food in due season.
You open wide your hand
and fill all things living with plenty.   R* *Psalm* 145.8–18

Hear the Gospel of our Lord Jesus Christ according to John.

Jesus said to the Jews, 'My Father is still working, and I also am working.' For this reason the Jews were seeking all the more to kill him, because he was not only breaking the sabbath, but was also calling God his own Father, thereby making himself equal to God.

Jesus said to them, 'Very truly, I tell you, the Son can do nothing on his own, but only what he sees the Father doing; for whatever the Father does, the Son does likewise. The Father loves the Son and shows him all that he himself is doing; and he will show him greater works than these, so that you will be astonished. Indeed, just as the Father raises the dead and gives them life, so also the Son gives life to whomsoever he wishes. The Father judges no one but has given all judgement to the Son, so that all may honour the Son just as they honour the Father. Anyone who does not honour the Son does not honour the Father who sent him. Very truly, I tell you, anyone who hears my word and believes him who sent me has eternal life, and does not come under judgement, but has passed from death to life.

'Very truly, I tell you, the hour is coming, and is now here, when the dead will hear the voice of the Son of God, and those who hear will live. For just as the Father has life in himself, so he has granted the Son also to have life in himself; and he has given him authority to execute judgement, because he is the Son of Man. Do not be astonished at this; for the hour is coming when all who are in their graves will hear his voice and will come out – those who have done good, to the resurrection of life, and those who have done evil, to the resurrection of condemnation.

'I can do nothing on my own. As I hear, I judge; and my judgement is just, because I seek to do not my own will but the will of him who sent me.'

This is the Gospel of the Lord.   John 5.17–30

Fourth Week of Lent: Thursday

Year I and Year 2

A reading from the Book of the Exodus.

The LORD said to Moses, 'Go down at once! Your people, whom you brought up out of the land of Egypt, have acted perversely; they have been quick to turn aside from the way that I commanded them; they have cast for themselves an image of a calf, and have worshipped it and sacrificed to it, and said, "These are your gods, O Israel, who brought you up out of the land of Egypt!" ' The LORD said to Moses, 'I have seen this people, how stiff-necked they are. Now let me alone, so that my wrath may burn hot against them and I may consume them; and of you I will make a great nation.'

But Moses implored the LORD his God, and said, 'O LORD, why does your wrath burn hot against your people, whom you brought out of the land of Egypt with great power and with a mighty hand? Why should the Egyptians say, "It was with evil intent that he brought them out to kill them in the mountains, and to consume them from the face of the earth"? Turn from your fierce wrath; change your mind and do not bring disaster on your people. Remember Abraham, Isaac, and Israel, your servants, how you swore to them by your own self, saying to them, "I will multiply your descendants like the stars of heaven, and all this land that I have promised I will give to your descendants, and they shall inherit it for ever." ' And the LORD changed his mind about the disaster that he planned to bring on his people.

This is the word of the Lord.   Exodus 32.7–14

Responsorial Psalm

R **Remember me, Lord,**
  when you show favour to your people. cf Psalm 106.4a

They made a calf at Horeb
and worshipped the molten image;
thus they exchanged their glory
for the image of an ox that feeds on hay.   R

They forgot God their saviour,
who had done such great things in Egypt,
wonderful deeds in the land of Ham
and fearful things at the Red Sea.   R

So he would have destroyed them,
had not Moses his chosen
stood before him in the breach,
to turn away his wrath from consuming them.   R Psalm 106.19–23

Hear the Gospel of our Lord Jesus Christ according to John.

Jesus said to the Jews, 'If I testify about myself, my testimony is not true. There is another who testifies on my behalf, and I know that his testimony to me is true. You sent messengers to John, and he testified to the truth. Not that I accept such human testimony, but I say these things so that you may be saved. He was a burning and shining lamp, and you were willing to rejoice for a while in his light. But I have a testimony greater than John's. The works that the Father has given me to complete, the very works that I am doing, testify on my behalf that the Father has sent me. And the Father who sent me has himself testified on my behalf. You have never heard his voice or seen his form, and you do not have his word abiding in you, because you do not believe him whom he has sent.

'You search the scriptures because you think that in them you have eternal life; and it is they that testify on my behalf. Yet you refuse to come to me to have life. I do not accept glory from human beings. But I know that you do not have the love of God in you. I have come in my Father's name, and you do not accept me; if another comes in his own name, you will accept him. How can you believe when you accept glory from one another and do not seek the glory that comes from the one who alone is God? Do not think that I will accuse you before the Father; your accuser is Moses, on whom you have set your hope. If you believed Moses, you would believe me, for he wrote about me. But if you do not believe what he wrote, how will you believe what I say?'

This is the Gospel of the Lord. John 5.31–end

Fourth Week of Lent: Friday

Year 1 and Year 2

Either

A reading from the Wisdom of Solomon.

The ungodly reasoned unsoundly, saying to themselves,
'Short and sorrowful is our life,
and there is no remedy when a life comes to its end,
and no one has been known to return from Hades.
Let us lie in wait for the righteous man,
because he is inconvenient to us and opposes our actions;
he reproaches us for sins against the law,
and accuses us of sins against our training.
He professes to have knowledge of God,
and calls himself a child of the Lord.
He became to us a reproof of our thoughts;
the very sight of him is a burden to us,
because his manner of life is unlike that of others,
and his ways are strange.
We are considered by him as something base,
and he avoids our ways as unclean;
he calls the last end of the righteous happy,
and boasts that God is his father.
Let us see if his words are true,
and let us test what will happen at the end of his life;
for if the righteous man is God's child, he will help him,
and will deliver him from the hand of his adversaries.
Let us test him with insult and torture,
so that we may find out how gentle he is,
and make trial of his forbearance.
Let us condemn him to a shameful death,
for, according to what he says, he will be protected.'

Thus they reasoned, but they were led astray,
for their wickedness blinded them,
and they did not know the secret purposes of God,
nor hoped for the wages of holiness,
nor discerned the prize for blameless souls.

This is the word of the Lord.   *Wisdom 2.1, 12–22*

or

A reading from the prophecy of Jeremiah.

When Jeremiah had finished speaking all that the LORD had commanded him to speak to all the people, then the priests and the prophets and all the people laid hold of him, saying, 'You shall die! Why have you prophesied in the name of the LORD, saying, "This house shall be like Shiloh, and this city shall be desolate, without inhabitant"?' And all the people gathered around Jeremiah in the house of the LORD.

When the officials of Judah heard these things, they came up from the king's house to the house of the LORD and took their seat in the entry of the New Gate of the house of the LORD. Then the priests and the prophets said to the officials and to all the people, 'This man deserves the sentence of death because he has prophesied against this city, as you have heard with your own ears.'

This is the word of the Lord.   Jeremiah 26.8–11

Responsorial Psalm

R **The Lord is near to the brokenhearted.**   *Psalm 34.18a*

The eyes of the Lord are upon the righteous
and his ears are open to their cry.
The face of the Lord is against those who do evil,
to root out the remembrance of them from the earth.   **R**

The righteous cry and the Lord hears them
and delivers them out of all their troubles.
The Lord is near to the brokenhearted
and will save those who are crushed in spirit.   **R**

Many are the troubles of the righteous;
from them all will the Lord deliver them.
He keeps all their bones,
so that not one of them is broken.   **R**

But evil shall slay the wicked
and those who hate the righteous will be condemned.
The Lord ransoms the life of his servants
and will condemn none who seek refuge in him.   **R**   *Psalm 34.15–end*

Hear the Gospel of our Lord Jesus Christ according to John.

Jesus went about in Galilee. He did not wish to go about in Judea because the Jews were looking for an opportunity to kill him. Now the Jewish festival of Booths was near. But after his brothers had gone to the festival, then he also went, not publicly but as it were in secret.

Now some of the people of Jerusalem were saying, 'Is not this the man whom they are trying to kill? And here he is, speaking openly, but they say nothing to him! Can it be that the authorities really know that this is the Messiah? Yet we know where this man is from; but when the Messiah comes, no one will know where he is from.' Then Jesus cried out as he was teaching in the temple, 'You know me, and you know where I am from. I have not come on my own. But the one who sent me is true, and you do not know him. I know him, because I am from him, and he sent me.' Then they tried to arrest him, but no one laid hands on him, because his hour had not yet come.

This is the Gospel of the Lord.   John 7.1–2, 10, 25–30

Fourth Week of Lent: Saturday

Year 1 and Year 2

A reading from the prophecy of Jeremiah.

It was the LORD who made it known to me, and I knew;
> then you showed me their evil deeds.
But I was like a gentle lamb
> led to the slaughter.
And I did not know it was against me
> that they devised schemes, saying,
'Let us destroy the tree with its fruit,
> let us cut him off from the land of the living,
> so that his name will no longer be remembered!'
But you, O LORD of hosts, who judge righteously,
> who try the heart and the mind,
let me see your retribution upon them,
> for to you I have committed my cause.

This is the word of the Lord.   Jeremiah 11.18–20

**R* God is my shield that is over me;
he saves the true of heart.**

Psalm 7.10

O Lord my God, in you I take refuge;
save me from all who pursue me, and deliver me,
lest they rend me like a lion and tear me in pieces
while there is no one to help me.   **R**

Give judgement for me
according to my righteousness, O Lord,
and according to the innocence that is in me.   **R**

Let the malice of the wicked come to an end,
but establish the righteous;
for you test the mind and heart, O righteous God.   **R***   *Psalm 7.1–2, 8–10*

Hear the Gospel of our Lord Jesus Christ according to John.

When they heard Jesus speak, some in the crowd said, 'This is really the prophet.'
Others said, 'This is the Messiah.' But some asked, 'Surely the Messiah does
not come from Galilee, does he? Has not the scripture said that the Messiah
is descended from David and comes from Bethlehem, the village where David
lived?' So there was a division in the crowd because of him. Some of them
wanted to arrest him, but no one laid hands on him.

Then the temple police went back to the chief priests and Pharisees, who
asked them, 'Why did you not arrest him?' The police answered, 'Never has
anyone spoken like this!' Then the Pharisees replied, 'Surely you have not been
deceived too, have you? Has any one of the authorities or of the Pharisees
believed in him? But this crowd, which does not know the law – they are
accursed.' Nicodemus, who had gone to Jesus before, and who was one of
them, asked, 'Our law does not judge people without first giving them a
hearing to find out what they are doing, does it?' They replied, 'Surely you
are not also from Galilee, are you? Search and you will see that no prophet
is to arise from Galilee.'

This is the Gospel of the Lord.

John 7.40–end

Fifth Week of Lent: any day

Passiontide begins on the Fifth Sunday of Lent.

The following readings may replace those provided on any day (except St Joseph's Day and the Annunciation) during the Fifth Week of Lent, especially in Years B and C when the Gospel passage about Lazarus is not read on the Fifth Sunday of Lent.

A reading from the Second book of the Kings.

The son of the Shunammite woman went out one day to his father among the reapers. He complained to his father, 'Oh, my head, my head!' The father said to his servant, 'Carry him to his mother.' He carried him and brought him to his mother; the child sat on her lap until noon, and he died. She went up and laid him on the bed of the man of God, closed the door on him, and left.

When Elisha came into the house, he saw the child lying dead on his bed. So he went in and closed the door on the two of them, and prayed to the LORD. Then he got up on the bed and lay upon the child, putting his mouth upon his mouth, his eyes upon his eyes, and his hands upon his hands; and while he lay bent over him, the flesh of the child became warm. He got down, walked once to and fro in the room, then got up again and bent over him; the child sneezed seven times, and the child opened his eyes. Elisha summoned Gehazi and said, 'Call the Shunammite woman.' So he called her. When she came to him, he said, 'Take your son.' She came and fell at his feet, bowing to the ground; then she took her son and left.

This is the word of the Lord.   2 Kings 4.18–21, 32–37

Responsorial Psalm

R   **Keep me as the apple of your eye;**
  [hide me under the shadow of your wings].   Psalm 17.8

Hear my just cause, O Lord; consider my complaint;
listen to my prayer, which comes not from lying lips.
Let my vindication come forth from your presence;
let your eyes behold what is right.   **R**

Weigh my heart, examine me by night,
refine me, and you will find no impurity in me.
My mouth does not trespass for earthly rewards;
I have heeded the words of your lips.   **R**

My footsteps hold fast in the ways of your commandments;
my feet have not stumbled in your paths.
I call upon you, O God, for you will answer me;
incline your ear to me, and listen to my words.   **R**   →

Show me your marvellous loving-kindness,
O Saviour of those who take refuge at your right hand
from those who rise up against them.   R

R   **Keep me as the apple of your eye;**
   [hide me under the shadow of your wings].

Keep me as the apple of your eye;
hide me under the shadow of your wings.
As for me, I shall see your face in righteousness;
when I awake and behold your likeness, I shall be satisfied.   R

Psalm 17.1–8, 16

Hear the Gospel of our Lord Jesus Christ according to John.

Now a certain man was ill, Lazarus of Bethany, the village of Mary and her
sister Martha. Mary was the one who anointed the Lord with perfume and
wiped his feet with her hair; her brother Lazarus was ill. So the sisters sent a
message to Jesus, 'Lord, he whom you love is ill.' But when Jesus heard it, he
said, 'This illness does not lead to death; rather it is for God's glory, so that
the Son of God may be glorified through it.' Accordingly, though Jesus loved
Martha and her sister and Lazarus, after having heard that Lazarus was ill, he
stayed two days longer in the place where he was.

Then after this he said to the disciples, 'Let us go to Judea again.' The
disciples said to him, 'Rabbi, the Jews were just now trying to stone you,
and are you going there again?' Jesus answered, 'Are there not twelve hours
of daylight? Those who walk during the day do not stumble, because they
see the light of this world. But those who walk at night stumble, because the
light is not in them.' After saying this, he told them, 'Our friend Lazarus has
fallen asleep, but I am going there to awaken him.' The disciples said to him,
'Lord, if he has fallen asleep, he will be all right.' Jesus, however, had been
speaking about his death, but they thought that he was referring merely to
sleep. Then Jesus told them plainly, 'Lazarus is dead. For your sake I am glad
I was not there, so that you may believe. But let us go to him.' Thomas, who
was called the Twin, said to his fellow-disciples, 'Let us also go, that we may
die with him.'

When Jesus arrived, he found that Lazarus had already been in the tomb
for four days. Now Bethany was near Jerusalem, some two miles away, and
many of the Jews had come to Martha and Mary to console them about their
brother. When Martha heard that Jesus was coming, she went and met him,
while Mary stayed at home. Martha said to Jesus, 'Lord, if you had been here,
my brother would not have died. But even now I know that God will give
you whatever you ask of him.' Jesus said to her, 'Your brother will rise again.'
Martha said to him, 'I know that he will rise again in the resurrection on the
last day.' Jesus said to her, 'I am the resurrection and the life. Those who believe
in me, even though they die, will live, and everyone who lives and believes in

me will never die. Do you believe this?' She said to him, 'Yes, Lord, I believe that you are the Messiah, the Son of God, the one coming into the world.'

When she had said this, she went back and called her sister Mary, and told her privately, 'The Teacher is here and is calling for you.' And when she heard it, she got up quickly and went to him. Now Jesus had not yet come to the village, but was still at the place where Martha had met him. The Jews who were with her in the house, consoling her, saw Mary get up quickly and go out. They followed her because they thought that she was going to the tomb to weep there. When Mary came where Jesus was and saw him, she knelt at his feet and said to him, 'Lord, if you had been here, my brother would not have died.' When Jesus saw her weeping, and the Jews who came with her also weeping, he was greatly disturbed in spirit and deeply moved. He said, 'Where have you laid him?' They said to him, 'Lord, come and see.' Jesus began to weep. So the Jews said, 'See how he loved him!' But some of them said, 'Could not he who opened the eyes of the blind man have kept this man from dying?'

Then Jesus, again greatly disturbed, came to the tomb. It was a cave, and a stone was lying against it. Jesus said, 'Take away the stone.' Martha, the sister of the dead man, said to him, 'Lord, already there is a stench because he has been dead for four days.' Jesus said to her, 'Did I not tell you that if you believed, you would see the glory of God?' So they took away the stone. And Jesus looked upwards and said, 'Father, I thank you for having heard me. I knew that you always hear me, but I have said this for the sake of the crowd standing here, so that they may believe that you sent me.' When he had said this, he cried with a loud voice, 'Lazarus, come out!' The dead man came out, his hands and feet bound with strips of cloth, and his face wrapped in a cloth. Jesus said to them, 'Unbind him, and let him go.'

Many of the Jews therefore, who had come with Mary and had seen what Jesus did, believed in him.

This is the Gospel of the Lord.

John 11.1–45

Fifth Week of Lent: Monday

Year 1 and Year 2

Either

A reading from the Book of Susanna.

[There was a man living in Babylon whose name was Joakim. He married the daughter of Hilkiah, named Susanna, a very beautiful woman and one who feared the Lord. Her parents were righteous, and had trained their daughter according to the law of Moses. Joakim was very rich, and had a fine garden adjoining his house; the Jews used to come to him because he was the most honoured of them all.

That year two elders from the people were appointed as judges. Concerning them the Lord had said: 'Wickedness came forth from Babylon, from elders who were judges, who were supposed to govern the people.' These men were frequently at Joakim's house, and all who had a case to be tried came to them there.

When the people left at noon, Susanna would go into her husband's garden to walk. Every day the two elders used to see her, going in and walking about, and they began to lust for her. They suppressed their consciences and turned away their eyes from looking to Heaven or remembering their duty to administer justice.

Once, while they were watching for an opportune day, she went in as before with only two maids, and wished to bathe in the garden, for it was a hot day. No one was there except the two elders, who had hidden themselves and were watching her. She said to her maids, 'Bring me olive oil and ointments, and shut the garden doors so that I can bathe.'

When the maids had gone out, the two elders got up and ran to her. They said, 'Look, the garden doors are shut, and no one can see us. We are burning with desire for you; so give your consent, and lie with us. If you refuse, we will testify against you that a young man was with you, and this was why you sent your maids away.'

Susanna groaned and said, 'I am completely trapped. For if I do this, it will mean death for me; if I do not, I cannot escape your hands. I choose not to do it; I will fall into your hands, rather than sin in the sight of the Lord.'

Then Susanna cried out with a loud voice, and the two elders shouted against her. And one of them ran and opened the garden doors. When the people in the house heard the shouting in the garden, they rushed in at the side door to see what had happened to her. And when the elders told their story, the servants felt very much ashamed, for nothing like this had ever been said about Susanna.

The next day, when the people gathered at the house of her husband Joakim, the two elders came, full of their wicked plot to have Susanna put to death. In the presence of the people they said, 'Send for Susanna daughter of Hilkiah, the wife of Joakim.' So they sent for her. And she came with her parents, her children, and all her relatives. Those who were with her and all who saw her were weeping.

Then the two elders stood up before the people and laid their hands on her head. Through her tears she looked up towards Heaven, for her heart trusted in the Lord. The elders said, 'While we were walking in the garden alone, this woman came in with two maids, shut the garden doors, and dismissed the maids. Then a young man, who was hiding there, came to her and lay with her. We were in a corner of the garden, and when we saw this wickedness we ran to them. Although we saw them embracing, we could not hold the man, because he was stronger than we are, and he opened the doors and got away. We did, however, seize this woman and asked who the young man was, but she would not tell us. These things we testify.' Because they were elders of the people and judges, the assembly believed them.]

Susanna was condemned to death. Then she cried out with a loud voice, and said, 'O eternal God, you know what is secret and are aware of all things before they come to be; you know that these men have given false evidence against me. And now I am to die, though I have done none of the wicked things that they have charged against me!'

The Lord heard her cry. Just as she was being led off to execution, God stirred up the holy spirit of a young lad named Daniel, and he shouted with a loud voice, 'I want no part in shedding this woman's blood!'

All the people turned to him and asked, 'What is this you are saying?' Taking his stand among them he said, 'Are you such fools, O Israelites, as to condemn a daughter of Israel without examination and without learning the facts? Return to court, for these men have given false evidence against her.'

So all the people hurried back. And the rest of the elders said to him, 'Come, sit among us and inform us, for God has given you the standing of an elder.' Daniel said to them, 'Separate them far from each other, and I will examine them.'

When they were separated from each other, he summoned one of them and said to him, 'You old relic of wicked days, your sins have now come home, which you have committed in the past, pronouncing unjust judgements, condemning the innocent and acquitting the guilty, though the Lord said, "You shall not put an innocent and righteous person to death." Now then, if you really saw this woman, tell me this: Under what tree did you see them being intimate with each other?' He answered, 'Under a mastic tree.' And Daniel said, 'Very well! This lie has cost you your head, for the angel of God has received the sentence from God and will immediately cut you in two.'

Then, putting him to one side, he ordered them to bring the other. And he said to him, 'You offspring of Canaan and not of Judah, beauty has beguiled you and lust has perverted your heart. This is how you have been treating the daughters of Israel, and they were intimate with you through fear; but a daughter of Judah would not tolerate your wickedness. Now then, tell me: Under what tree did you catch them being intimate with each other?' He answered, 'Under an evergreen oak.' Daniel said to him, 'Very well! This lie →

has cost you also your head, for the angel of God is waiting with his sword to split you in two, so as to destroy you both.'

Then the whole assembly raised a great shout and blessed God, who saves those who hope in him. And they took action against the two elders, because out of their own mouths Daniel had convicted them of bearing false witness; they did to them as they had wickedly planned to do to their neighbour. Acting in accordance with the law of Moses, they put them to death. Thus innocent blood was spared that day.

This is the word of the Lord.   Susanna 1–9, 15–17, 19–30, 33–62 [or 41b–62]

or

A reading from the Book of Joshua.

Joshua son of Nun sent two men secretly from Shittim as spies, saying, 'Go, view the land, especially Jericho.' So they went, and entered the house of a prostitute whose name was Rahab, and spent the night there. The king of Jericho was told, 'Some Israelites have come here tonight to search out the land.' Then the king of Jericho sent orders to Rahab, 'Bring out the men who have come to you, who entered your house, for they have come only to search out the whole land.' But the woman took the two men and hid them. Then she said, 'True, the men came to me, but I did not know where they came from. And when it was time to close the gate at dark, the men went out. Where the men went I do not know. Pursue them quickly, for you can overtake them.' She had, however, brought them up to the roof and hidden them with the stalks of flax that she had laid out on the roof. So the men pursued them on the way to the Jordan as far as the fords. As soon as the pursuers had gone out, the gate was shut.

Before they went to sleep, she came up to them on the roof and said to the men: 'I know that the LORD has given you the land, and that dread of you has fallen on us, and that all the inhabitants of the land melt in fear before you. For we have heard how the LORD dried up the water of the Red Sea before you when you came out of Egypt, and what you did to the two kings of the Amorites that were beyond the Jordan, to Sihon and Og, whom you utterly destroyed. As soon as we heard it, our hearts failed, and there was no courage left in any of us because of you. The LORD your God is indeed God in heaven above and on earth below. Now then, since I have dealt kindly with you, swear to me by the LORD that you in turn will deal kindly with my family. Give me a sign of good faith that you will spare my father and mother, my brothers and sisters, and all who belong to them, and deliver our lives from death.' The men said to her, 'Our life for yours! If you do not tell this business of ours, then we will deal kindly and faithfully with you when the LORD gives us the land.'

This is the word of the Lord.   Joshua 2.1–14

Responsorial Psalm

R **I will dwell in the house of the Lord for ever.** *Psalm 23.6b*

The Lord is my shepherd;
therefore can I lack nothing.
He makes me lie down in green pastures
and leads me beside still waters. R

He shall refresh my soul
and guide me in the paths of righteousness
for his name's sake. R

Though I walk through the valley of the shadow of death,
I will fear no evil;
for you are with me;
your rod and your staff, they comfort me. R

You spread a table before me
in the presence of those who trouble me;
you have anointed my head with oil
and my cup shall be full. R

Surely goodness and loving mercy shall follow me
all the days of my life,
and I will dwell in the house of the Lord for ever. R *Psalm 23*

Hear the Gospel of our Lord Jesus Christ according to John.

Jesus went to the Mount of Olives. Early in the morning he came again to the temple. All the people came to him and he sat down and began to teach them. The scribes and the Pharisees brought a woman who had been caught in adultery; and making her stand before all of them, they said to him, 'Teacher, this woman was caught in the very act of committing adultery. Now in the law Moses commanded us to stone such women. Now what do you say?' They said this to test him, so that they might have some charge to bring against him. Jesus bent down and wrote with his finger on the ground. When they kept on questioning him, he straightened up and said to them, 'Let anyone among you who is without sin be the first to throw a stone at her.' And once again he bent down and wrote on the ground. When they heard it, they went away, one by one, beginning with the elders; and Jesus was left alone with the woman standing before him. Jesus straightened up and said to her, 'Woman, where are they? Has no one condemned you?' She said, 'No one, sir.' And Jesus said, 'Neither do I condemn you. Go your way, and from now on do not sin again.'

This is the Gospel of the Lord. *John 8.1–11*

Fifth Week of Lent: Tuesday

Year 1 and Year 2

A reading from the book Numbers.

From Mount Hor the Israelites set out by the way to the Red Sea, to go around the land of Edom; but the people became impatient on the way. The people spoke against God and against Moses, 'Why have you brought us up out of Egypt to die in the wilderness? For there is no food and no water, and we detest this miserable food.' Then the LORD sent poisonous serpents among the people, and they bit the people, so that many Israelites died. The people came to Moses and said, 'We have sinned by speaking against the LORD and against you; pray to the LORD to take away the serpents from us.' So Moses prayed for the people. And the LORD said to Moses, 'Make a poisonous serpent, and set it on a pole; and everyone who is bitten shall look at it and live.' So Moses made a serpent of bronze, and put it upon a pole; and whenever a serpent bit someone, that person would look at the serpent of bronze and live.

This is the word of the Lord.   Numbers 21.4–9

Responsorial Psalm

R* **O Lord, hear my prayer**
   and let my crying come before you.   *Psalm* 102.1

Hide not your face from me
in the day of my distress.
Incline your ear to me;
when I call, make haste to answer me.   **R**

Then shall the nations fear your name, O Lord,
and all the kings of the earth your glory,
when the Lord has built up Zion
and shown himself in glory.   **R**

When he has turned to the prayer of the destitute
and has not despised their plea.
This shall be written for those that come after,
and a people yet unborn shall praise the Lord.   **R**

For he has looked down from his holy height;
from the heavens he beheld the earth,
that he might hear the sighings of the prisoner
and set free those condemned to die.   **R**

That the name of the Lord may be proclaimed in Zion
and his praises in Jerusalem,
when peoples are gathered together
and kingdoms also, to serve the Lord.   **R**   *Psalm* 102.1–3, 16–23

Hear the Gospel of our Lord Jesus Christ according to John.

Jesus said to the Pharisees, 'I am going away, and you will search for me, but you will die in your sin. Where I am going, you cannot come.' Then the Jews said, 'Is he going to kill himself? Is that what he means by saying, "Where I am going, you cannot come"?' He said to them, 'You are from below, I am from above; you are of this world, I am not of this world. I told you that you would die in your sins, for you will die in your sins unless you believe that I am he.' They said to him, 'Who are you?'

Jesus said to them, 'Why do I speak to you at all? I have much to say about you and much to condemn; but the one who sent me is true, and I declare to the world what I have heard from him.' They did not understand that he was speaking to them about the Father. So Jesus said, 'When you have lifted up the Son of Man, then you will realize that I am he, and that I do nothing on my own, but I speak these things as the Father instructed me. And the one who sent me is with me; he has not left me alone, for I always do what is pleasing to him.' As he was saying these things, many believed in him.

This is the Gospel of the Lord.   John 8.21–30

Fifth Week of Lent: Wednesday

Year 1 and Year 2

A reading from the Book of Daniel.

Nebuchadnezzar said, 'Is it true, O Shadrach, Meshach, and Abednego, that you do not serve my gods and you do not worship the golden statue that I have set up? Now if you are ready when you hear the sound of the horn, pipe, lyre, trigon, harp, drum, and entire musical ensemble to fall down and worship the statue that I have made, well and good. But if you do not worship, you shall immediately be thrown into a furnace of blazing fire, and who is the god that will deliver you out of my hands?'

Shadrach, Meshach, and Abednego answered the king, 'O Nebuchadnezzar, we have no need to present a defence to you in this matter. If our God whom we serve is able to deliver us from the furnace of blazing fire and out of your hand, O king, let him deliver us. But if not, be it known to you, O king, that we will not serve your gods and we will not worship the golden statue that you have set up.'

Then Nebuchadnezzar was so filled with rage against Shadrach, Meshach, and Abednego that his face was distorted. He ordered the furnace to be heated up seven times more than was customary, and ordered some of the strongest guards in his army to bind Shadrach, Meshach, and Abednego and to throw them into the furnace of blazing fire.

Then King Nebuchadnezzar was astonished and rose up quickly. He said to his counsellors, 'Was it not three men that we threw bound into the fire?' They answered the king, 'True, O king.' He replied, 'But I see four men unbound,   →

walking in the middle of the fire, and they are not hurt; and the fourth has the appearance of a god.' Nebuchadnezzar said, 'Blessed be the God of Shadrach, Meshach, and Abednego, who has sent his angel and delivered his servants who trusted in him. They disobeyed the king's command and yielded up their bodies rather than serve and worship any god except their own God.'

This is the word of the Lord.   Daniel 3.14–20, 24–25, 28

Canticle

R **You are worthy to be praised and exalted for ever.**

Blessed are you, the God of our ancestors.   [R]
Blessed is your holy and glorious name.   [R]
Blessed are you, in your holy and glorious temple.   R

Blessed are you who look into the depths.   [R]
Blessed are you, enthroned on the cherubim.   [R]
Blessed are you on the throne of your kingdom.   [R]
Blessed are you in the heights of heaven.   R   *Song of the Three 29–34*

Hear the Gospel of our Lord Jesus Christ according to John.

Jesus said to the Jews who had believed in him, 'If you continue in my word, you are truly my disciples; and you will know the truth, and the truth will make you free.' They answered him, 'We are descendants of Abraham and have never been slaves to anyone. What do you mean by saying, "You will be made free"?'

Jesus answered them, 'Very truly, I tell you, everyone who commits sin is a slave to sin. The slave does not have a permanent place in the household; the son has a place there for ever. So if the Son makes you free, you will be free indeed. I know that you are descendants of Abraham; yet you look for an opportunity to kill me, because there is no place in you for my word. I declare what I have seen in the Father's presence; as for you, you should do what you have heard from the Father.'

They answered him, 'Abraham is our father.' Jesus said to them, 'If you were Abraham's children, you would be doing what Abraham did, but now you are trying to kill me, a man who has told you the truth that I heard from God. This is not what Abraham did. You are indeed doing what your father does.' They said to him, 'We are not illegitimate children; we have one father, God himself.' Jesus said to them, 'If God were your Father, you would love me, for I came from God and now I am here. I did not come on my own, but he sent me.'

This is the Gospel of the Lord.   John 8.31–42

Fifth Week of Lent: Thursday

Year 1 and Year 2

A reading from the book Genesis.

Abram fell on his face; and God said to him, 'As for me, this is my covenant with you: You shall be the ancestor of a multitude of nations. No longer shall your name be Abram, but your name shall be Abraham; for I have made you the ancestor of a multitude of nations. I will make you exceedingly fruitful; and I will make nations of you, and kings shall come from you. I will establish my covenant between me and you, and your offspring after you throughout their generations, for an everlasting covenant, to be God to you and to your offspring after you. And I will give to you, and to your offspring after you, the land where you are now an alien, all the land of Canaan, for a perpetual holding; and I will be their God.'

God said to Abraham, 'As for you, you shall keep my covenant, you and your offspring after you throughout their generations.'

This is the word of the Lord.   Genesis 17.3–9

Responsorial Psalm

R **The Lord remembers his covenant:**
   the covenant he made with Abraham.   cf Psalm 105.8a, 9a

Seek the Lord and his strength;
seek his face continually.
Remember the marvels he has done,
his wonders and the judgements of his mouth.   **R**

O seed of Abraham his servant,
O children of Jacob his chosen.
He is the Lord our God;
his judgements are in all the earth.   **R**

He has always been mindful of his covenant,
the promise that he made for a thousand generations:
the covenant he made with Abraham,
the oath that he swore to Isaac.   **R**   Psalm 105.4–9

Hear the Gospel of our Lord Jesus Christ according to John.

Jesus said to the Jews, 'Very truly, I tell you, whoever keeps my word will never see death.' The Jews said to him, 'Now we know that you have a demon. Abraham died, and so did the prophets; yet you say, "Whoever keeps my word will never taste death." Are you greater than our father Abraham, who died? The prophets also died. Who do you claim to be?' Jesus answered, 'If I glorify myself, my glory is nothing. It is my Father who glorifies me, he of whom you say, "He is our God", though you do not know him. But I know him; if I were to say that I do not know him, I would be a liar like you. But I do know him and I keep his word. Your ancestor Abraham rejoiced that he would see my day; he saw it and was glad.' Then the Jews said to him, 'You are not yet fifty years old, and have you seen Abraham?' Jesus said to them, 'Very truly, I tell you, before Abraham was, I am.' So they picked up stones to throw at him, but Jesus hid himself and went out of the temple.

This is the Gospel of the Lord.   John 8.51–end

Fifth Week of Lent: Friday

Year 1 and Year 2

A reading from the prophecy of Jeremiah.

For I hear many whispering:
    'Terror is all around!
Denounce him! Let us denounce him!'
    All my close friends
    are watching for me to stumble.
'Perhaps he can be enticed,
    and we can prevail against him,
    and take our revenge on him.'
But the LORD is with me like a dread warrior;
    therefore my persecutors will stumble,
    and they will not prevail.
They will be greatly shamed,
    for they will not succeed.
Their eternal dishonour
    will never be forgotten.
O LORD of hosts, you test the righteous,
    you see the heart and the mind;
let me see your retribution upon them,
    for to you I have committed my cause.

Sing to the LORD;
    praise the LORD!
For he has delivered the life of the needy
    from the hands of evildoers.

This is the word of the Lord.   Jeremiah 20.10–13

Responsorial Psalm

R **O God, you are my rock and my refuge,**
[you are my shield and strong defence].   *cf Psalm* 18.2

I love you, O Lord my strength.
The Lord is my crag, my fortress and my deliverer,
my God, my rock in whom I take refuge,
my shield, the horn of my salvation and my stronghold.   **R**

I cried to the Lord in my anguish
and I was saved from my enemies.
The cords of death entwined me
and the torrents of destruction overwhelmed me.   **R**

The cords of the Pit fastened about me
and the snares of death entangled me.
In my distress I called upon the Lord
and cried out to my God for help.   **R**   *Psalm* 18.1–6

Hear the Gospel of our Lord Jesus Christ according to John.

The Jews took up stones again to stone Jesus. He replied, 'I have shown you
many good works from the Father. For which of these are you going to stone
me?' The Jews answered, 'It is not for a good work that we are going to stone
you, but for blasphemy, because you, though only a human being, are making
yourself God.' Jesus answered, 'Is it not written in your law, "I said, you are
gods"? If those to whom the word of God came were called "gods" – and the
scripture cannot be annulled – can you say that the one whom the Father has
sanctified and sent into the world is blaspheming because I said, "I am God's
Son"? If I am not doing the works of my Father, then do not believe me. But
if I do them, even though you do not believe me, believe the works, so that
you may know and understand that the Father is in me and I am in the Father.'
Then they tried to arrest him again, but he escaped from their hands.

He went away again across the Jordan to the place where John had been
baptizing earlier, and he remained there. Many came to him, and they were
saying, 'John performed no sign, but everything that John said about this man
was true.' And many believed in him there.

This is the Gospel of the Lord.   *John* 10.31–end

Fifth Week of Lent: Saturday

Year 1 and Year 2

A reading from the prophecy of Ezekiel.

Thus says the LORD God: I will take the people of Israel from the nations among which they have gone, and will gather them from every quarter, and bring them to their own land. I will make them one nation in the land, on the mountains of Israel; and one king shall be king over them all. Never again shall they be two nations, and never again shall they be divided into two kingdoms. They shall never again defile themselves with their idols and their detestable things, or with any of their transgressions. I will save them from all the apostasies into which they have fallen, and will cleanse them. Then they shall be my people, and I will be their God.

My servant David shall be king over them; and they shall all have one shepherd. They shall follow my ordinances and be careful to observe my statutes. They shall live in the land that I gave to my servant Jacob, in which your ancestors lived; they and their children and their children's children shall live there for ever; and my servant David shall be their prince for ever. I will make a covenant of peace with them; it shall be an everlasting covenant with them; and I will bless them and multiply them, and will set my sanctuary among them for evermore. My dwelling-place shall be with them; and I will be their God, and they shall be my people. Then the nations shall know that I the LORD sanctify Israel, when my sanctuary is among them for evermore.

This is the word of the Lord.   Ezekiel 37.21—end

Either

Canticle

R   **The Lord will watch over us**
  as a shepherd watches the flock.   cf Jeremiah 31.10b

Hear the word of the Lord, O nations,
and declare it in the coastlands far away;
say, 'He who scattered Israel will gather him,
and will watch over him as a shepherd watches the flock.'   **R**

For the Lord has ransomed Jacob,
and redeemed him from hands too strong for him.
They shall come and sing aloud on the height of Zion,
and they shall be radiant at the goodness of the Lord.   **R**

They shall be radiant over the grain, the wine, and the oil,
and over the young of the flock and the herd;
their life shall be like a watered garden,
and they shall never languish again.   **R**

Then shall the young women rejoice in the dance,
and young men and old shall be glad together.
I will turn their mourning into joy,
I will comfort them, and give them gladness for sorrow. R

Jeremiah 31.10–13

or

Responsorial Psalm

R **My help comes from the Lord,**
[the maker of heaven and earth].

Psalm 121.2

I lift up my eyes to the hills;
from where is my help to come?
My help comes from the Lord,
the maker of heaven and earth. R

He will not suffer your foot to stumble;
he who watches over you will not sleep.
Behold, he who keeps watch over Israel
shall neither slumber nor sleep. R

The Lord himself watches over you;
the Lord is your shade at your right hand,
so that the sun shall not strike you by day,
neither the moon by night. R

The Lord shall keep you from all evil;
it is he who shall keep your soul.
The Lord shall keep watch over your going out
    and your coming in,
from this time forth for evermore. R

Psalm 121

Hear the Gospel of our Lord Jesus Christ according to John.

Many of the Jews who had come with Mary and had seen what Jesus did,
believed in him. But some of them went to the Pharisees and told them what
he had done. So the chief priests and the Pharisees called a meeting of the
council, and said, 'What are we to do? This man is performing many signs.
If we let him go on like this, everyone will believe in him, and the Romans
will come and destroy both our holy place and our nation.' But one of them,
Caiaphas, who was high priest that year, said to them, 'You know nothing at
all! You do not understand that it is better for you to have one man die for
the people than to have the whole nation destroyed.' He did not say this on
his own, but being high priest that year he prophesied that Jesus was about
to die for the nation, and not for the nation only, but to gather into one the
dispersed children of God. So from that day on they planned to put him
to death. →

Jesus therefore no longer walked about openly among the Jews, but went from there to a town called Ephraim in the region near the wilderness; and he remained there with the disciples.

Now the Passover of the Jews was near, and many went up from the country to Jerusalem before the Passover to purify themselves. They were looking for Jesus and were asking one another as they stood in the temple, 'What do you think? Surely he will not come to the festival, will he?' Now the chief priests and the Pharisees had given orders that anyone who knew where Jesus was should let them know, so that they might arrest him.

This is the Gospel of the Lord. John 11.45–end

HOLY WEEK

Monday of Holy Week

All Years

A reading from the prophecy of Isaiah.

Here is my servant, whom I uphold,
　　my chosen, in whom my soul delights;
I have put my spirit upon him;
　　he will bring forth justice to the nations.
He will not cry or lift up his voice,
　　or make it heard in the street;
a bruised reed he will not break,
　　and a dimly burning wick he will not quench;
　　he will faithfully bring forth justice.
He will not grow faint or be crushed
　　until he has established justice in the earth;
　　and the coastlands wait for his teaching.

Thus says God, the LORD,
　　who created the heavens and stretched them out,
　　who spread out the earth and what comes from it,
who gives breath to the people upon it
　　and spirit to those who walk in it:
I am the LORD, I have called you in righteousness,
　　I have taken you by the hand and kept you;
I have given you as a covenant to the people,
　　a light to the nations,
　　to open the eyes that are blind,
to bring out the prisoners from the dungeon,
　　from the prison those who sit in darkness.
I am the LORD, that is my name;
　　my glory I give to no other,
　　nor my praise to idols.
See, the former things have come to pass,
　　and new things I now declare;
before they spring forth,
　　I tell you of them.

This is the word of the Lord.

Isaiah 42.1–9

R* **Lord, with you is the well of life:**
　　[in your light shall we see light].　　　　　　　*cf Psalm 36.9*

Your love, O Lord, reaches to the heavens
and your faithfulness to the clouds.
Your righteousness stands like the strong mountains,
your justice like the great deep;
you, Lord, shall save both man and beast.　**R**

How precious is your loving mercy, O God!
All mortal flesh shall take refuge
under the shadow of your wings.
They shall be satisfied with the abundance of your house;
they shall drink from the river of your delights.　**R***

O continue your loving-kindness to those who know you
and your righteousness to those who are true of heart.
Let not the foot of pride come against me,
nor the hand of the ungodly thrust me away.　**R**　　　*Psalm 36.5–11*

A reading from the Letter to the Hebrews.

When Christ came as a high priest of the good things that have come, then
through the greater and perfect tent (not made with hands, that is, not of this
creation), he entered once for all into the Holy Place, not with the blood of
goats and calves, but with his own blood, thus obtaining eternal redemption.
For if the blood of goats and bulls, with the sprinkling of the ashes of a heifer,
sanctifies those who have been defiled so that their flesh is purified, how
much more will the blood of Christ, who through the eternal Spirit offered
himself without blemish to God, purify our conscience from dead works to
worship the living God!

　　For this reason he is the mediator of a new covenant, so that those who
are called may receive the promised eternal inheritance, because a death has
occurred that redeems them from the transgressions under the first covenant.

This is the word of the Lord.　　　　　　　　　　*Hebrews 9.11–15*

Hear the Gospel of our Lord Jesus Christ according to John.

Six days before the Passover Jesus came to Bethany, the home of Lazarus, whom
he had raised from the dead. There they gave a dinner for him. Martha served,
and Lazarus was one of those at the table with him. Mary took a pound of
costly perfume made of pure nard, anointed Jesus' feet, and wiped them with
her hair. The house was filled with the fragrance of the perfume. But Judas
Iscariot, one of his disciples (the one who was about to betray him), said,
'Why was this perfume not sold for three hundred denarii and the money

given to the poor?' (He said this not because he cared about the poor, but because he was a thief; he kept the common purse and used to steal what was put into it.) Jesus said, 'Leave her alone. She bought it so that she might keep it for the day of my burial. You always have the poor with you, but you do not always have me.'

When the great crowd of the Jews learned that he was there, they came not only because of Jesus but also to see Lazarus, whom he had raised from the dead. So the chief priests planned to put Lazarus to death as well, since it was on account of him that many of the Jews were deserting and were believing in Jesus.

This is the Gospel of the Lord.   John 12.1–11

Tuesday of Holy Week

All Years

A reading from the prophecy of Isaiah.

Listen to me, O coastlands,
    pay attention, you peoples from far away!
The LORD called me before I was born,
    while I was in my mother's womb he named me.
He made my mouth like a sharp sword,
    in the shadow of his hand he hid me;
he made me a polished arrow,
    in his quiver he hid me away.
And he said to me, 'You are my servant,
    Israel, in whom I will be glorified.'
But I said, 'I have laboured in vain,
    I have spent my strength for nothing and vanity;
yet surely my cause is with the LORD,
    and my reward with my God.'

And now the LORD says,
    who formed me in the womb to be his servant,
to bring Jacob back to him,
    and that Israel might be gathered to him,
for I am honoured in the sight of the LORD,
    and my God has become my strength –
he says,
'It is too light a thing that you should be my servant
    to raise up the tribes of Jacob
    and to restore the survivors of Israel;
I will give you as a light to the nations,
    that my salvation may reach to the end of the earth.'   →

Thus says the LORD,
    the Redeemer of Israel and his Holy One,
to one deeply despised, abhorred by the nations,
    the slave of rulers,
'Kings shall see and stand up,
    princes, and they shall prostrate themselves,
because of the LORD, who is faithful,
    the Holy One of Israel, who has chosen you.'

This is the word of the Lord.   *Isaiah 49.1–7*

Responsorial Psalm

**R   O Lord, you are my refuge and my strength,
     [let my mouth be full of your praise].**   *cf Psalm 71.7b, 8a*

In you, O Lord, do I seek refuge;
let me never be put to shame.
In your righteousness, deliver me and set me free;
incline your ear to me and save me.   **R**

Be for me a stronghold to which I may ever resort;
send out to save me, for you are my rock and my fortress.
Deliver me, my God, from the hand of the wicked,
from the grasp of the evildoer and the oppressor.   **R**

For you are my hope, O Lord God,
my confidence, even from my youth.
Upon you have I leaned from my birth,
when you drew me from my mother's womb;
my praise shall be always of you.   **R**

I have become a portent to many,
but you are my refuge and my strength.
Let my mouth be full of your praise
and your glory all the day long.   **R**

[Do not cast me away in the time of old age;
forsake me not when my strength fails.
For my enemies are talking against me,
and those who lie in wait for my life take counsel together.   **R**

They say, 'God has forsaken him;
pursue him and take him,
because there is none to deliver him.'
O God, be not far from me;
come quickly to help me, O my God.   **R**

Let those who are against me
be put to shame and disgrace;
let those who seek to do me evil
be covered with scorn and reproach.
But as for me I will hope continually
and will praise you more and more. **R]** *Psalm 71.1–8, [9–14]*

A reading from the First Letter of Paul to the Corinthians.

The message about the cross is foolishness to those who are perishing, but to
us who are being saved it is the power of God. For it is written,
   'I will destroy the wisdom of the wise,
      and the discernment of the discerning I will thwart.'
Where is the one who is wise? Where is the scribe? Where is the debater
of this age? Has not God made foolish the wisdom of the world? For since,
in the wisdom of God, the world did not know God through wisdom, God
decided, through the foolishness of our proclamation, to save those who
believe. For Jews demand signs and Greeks desire wisdom, but we proclaim
Christ crucified, a stumbling-block to Jews and foolishness to Gentiles, but
to those who are the called, both Jews and Greeks, Christ the power of God
and the wisdom of God. For God's foolishness is wiser than human wisdom,
and God's weakness is stronger than human strength.

   Consider your own call, brothers and sisters: not many of you were wise
by human standards, not many were powerful, not many were of noble birth.
But God chose what is foolish in the world to shame the wise; God chose
what is weak in the world to shame the strong; God chose what is low and
despised in the world, things that are not, to reduce to nothing things that are,
so that no one might boast in the presence of God. He is the source of your
life in Christ Jesus, who became for us wisdom from God, and righteousness
and sanctification and redemption, in order that, as it is written, 'Let the one
who boasts, boast in the Lord.'

This is the word of the Lord.   *1 Corinthians 1.18–31*

Hear the Gospel of our Lord Jesus Christ according to John.

Among those who went up to worship at the festival were some Greeks. They
came to Philip, who was from Bethsaida in Galilee, and said to him, 'Sir, we
wish to see Jesus.' Philip went and told Andrew; then Andrew and Philip
went and told Jesus. Jesus answered them, 'The hour has come for the Son
of Man to be glorified. Very truly, I tell you, unless a grain of wheat falls into
the earth and dies, it remains just a single grain; but if it dies, it bears much
fruit. Those who love their life lose it, and those who hate their life in this
world will keep it for eternal life. Whoever serves me must follow me, and
where I am, there will my servant be also. Whoever serves me, the Father
will honour.   →

'Now my soul is troubled. And what should I say – "Father, save me from this hour"? No, it is for this reason that I have come to this hour. Father, glorify your name.' Then a voice came from heaven, 'I have glorified it, and I will glorify it again.' The crowd standing there heard it and said that it was thunder. Others said, 'An angel has spoken to him.' Jesus answered, 'This voice has come for your sake, not for mine. Now is the judgement of this world; now the ruler of this world will be driven out. And I, when I am lifted up from the earth, will draw all people to myself.' He said this to indicate the kind of death he was to die. The crowd answered him, 'We have heard from the law that the Messiah remains for ever. How can you say that the Son of Man must be lifted up? Who is this Son of Man?' Jesus said to them, 'The light is with you for a little longer. Walk while you have the light, so that the darkness may not overtake you. If you walk in the darkness, you do not know where you are going. While you have the light, believe in the light, so that you may become children of light.'

After Jesus had said this, he departed and hid from them.

This is the Gospel of the Lord.   John 12.20–36

Wednesday of Holy Week

All Years

A reading from the prophecy of Isaiah.

The Lord GOD has given me
  the tongue of a teacher,
that I may know how to sustain
  the weary with a word.
Morning by morning he wakens –
  wakens my ear
  to listen as those who are taught.
The Lord GOD has opened my ear,
  and I was not rebellious,
  I did not turn backwards.
I gave my back to those who struck me,
  and my cheeks to those who pulled out the beard;
I did not hide my face
  from insult and spitting.

The Lord GOD helps me;
  therefore I have not been disgraced;
therefore I have set my face like flint,
  and I know that I shall not be put to shame;
  he who vindicates me is near.
Who will contend with me?
  Let us stand up together.

Who are my adversaries?
    Let them confront me.
It is the Lord GOD who helps me;
    who will declare me guilty?

This is the word of the Lord.
Isaiah 50.4–9a

Responsorial Psalm

R* **O God, make speed to save me;**
   O Lord, make haste to help me.
Psalm 70.1

Let those who seek my life
be put to shame and confusion;
let them be turned back and disgraced
who wish me evil. **R**

Let those who mock and deride me
turn back because of their shame.
But let all who seek you rejoice and be glad in you;
let those who love your salvation say always,
'Great is the Lord!' **R**

As for me, I am poor and needy;
come to me quickly, O God.
You are my help and my deliverer;
O Lord, do not delay. **R**
Psalm 70

A reading from the Letter to the Hebrews.

Since we are surrounded by so great a cloud of witnesses, let us also lay aside
every weight and the sin that clings so closely, and let us run with perseverance
the race that is set before us, looking to Jesus the pioneer and perfecter of
our faith, who for the sake of the joy that was set before him endured the
cross, disregarding its shame, and has taken his seat at the right hand of the
throne of God.

Consider him who endured such hostility against himself from sinners,
so that you may not grow weary or lose heart.

This is the word of the Lord.
Hebrews 12.1–3

Hear the Gospel of our Lord Jesus Christ according to John.

Jesus was troubled in spirit, and declared, 'Very truly, I tell you, one of you
will betray me.' The disciples looked at one another, uncertain of whom he
was speaking. One of his disciples – the one whom Jesus loved – was reclining
next to him; Simon Peter therefore motioned to him to ask Jesus of whom
he was speaking. So while reclining next to Jesus, he asked him, 'Lord, who
is it?' Jesus answered, 'It is the one to whom I give this piece of bread when →

I have dipped it in the dish.' So when he had dipped the piece of bread, he gave it to Judas son of Simon Iscariot. After he received the piece of bread, Satan entered into him. Jesus said to him, 'Do quickly what you are going to do.' Now no one at the table knew why he said this to him. Some thought that, because Judas had the common purse, Jesus was telling him, 'Buy what we need for the festival'; or, that he should give something to the poor. So, after receiving the piece of bread, he immediately went out. And it was night.

When he had gone out, Jesus said, 'Now the Son of Man has been glorified, and God has been glorified in him. If God has been glorified in him, God will also glorify him in himself and will glorify him at once.'

This is the Gospel of the Lord.   John 13.21–32

Maundy Thursday

All Years

A reading from the book of the Exodus.

The LORD said to Moses and Aaron in the land of Egypt:

This month shall mark for you the beginning of months; it shall be the first month of the year for you. Tell the whole congregation of Israel that on the tenth of this month they are to take a lamb for each family, a lamb for each household. If a household is too small for a whole lamb, it shall join its closest neighbour in obtaining one; the lamb shall be divided in proportion to the number of people who eat of it.

[Your lamb shall be without blemish, a year-old male; you may take it from the sheep or from the goats. You shall keep it until the fourteenth day of this month; then the whole assembled congregation of Israel shall slaughter it at twilight. They shall take some of the blood and put it on the two doorposts and the lintel of the houses in which they eat it. They shall eat the lamb that same night; they shall eat it roasted over the fire with unleavened bread and bitter herbs. Do not eat any of it raw or boiled in water, but roasted over the fire, with its head, legs, and inner organs. You shall let none of it remain until the morning; anything that remains until the morning you shall burn.]

This is how you shall eat it: your loins girded, your sandals on your feet, and your staff in your hand; and you shall eat it hurriedly. It is the passover of the LORD. For I will pass through the land of Egypt that night, and I will strike down every firstborn in the land of Egypt, both human beings and animals; on all the gods of Egypt I will execute judgements: I am the LORD. The blood shall be a sign for you on the houses where you live: when I see the blood, I will pass over you, and no plague shall destroy you when I strike the land of Egypt.

This day shall be a day of remembrance for you. You shall celebrate it as a festival to the LORD; throughout your generations you shall observe it as a perpetual ordinance.

This is the word of the Lord.   Exodus 12.1–4 [5–10] 11–14

Responsorial Psalm

R **I will lift up the cup of salvation:**
[and call upon the name of the Lord].   Psalm 116.11

I love the Lord,
for he has heard the voice of my supplication;
because he inclined his ear to me
on the day I called to him.   **R**

How shall I repay the Lord
for all the benefits he has given to me?
I will lift up the cup of salvation
and call upon the name of the Lord.   **R**

I will fulfil my vows to the Lord
in the presence of all his people.
Precious in the sight of the Lord
is the death of his faithful servants.   **R**

O Lord, I am your servant,
your servant, the child of your handmaid;
you have freed me from my bonds.
I will offer to you a sacrifice of thanksgiving
and call upon the name of the Lord.   **R**

I will fulfil my vows to the Lord
in the presence of all his people,
in the courts of the house of the Lord,
in the midst of you, O Jerusalem.   **R**   Psalm 116.1, 10–17

A reading from the First Letter of Paul to the Corinthians.

I received from the Lord what I also handed on to you, that the Lord Jesus on the night when he was betrayed took a loaf of bread, and when he had given thanks, he broke it and said, 'This is my body that is for you. Do this in remembrance of me.' In the same way he took the cup also, after supper, saying, 'This cup is the new covenant in my blood. Do this, as often as you drink it, in remembrance of me.' For as often as you eat this bread and drink the cup, you proclaim the Lord's death until he comes.

This is the word of the Lord.   1 Corinthians 11.23–26

Hear the Gospel of our Lord Jesus Christ according to John.

Before the festival of the Passover, Jesus knew that his hour had come to depart from this world and go to the Father. Having loved his own who were in the world, he loved them to the end. The devil had already put it into the heart of Judas son of Simon Iscariot to betray him. And during supper Jesus, knowing that the Father had given all things into his hands, and that he had come from God and was going to God, got up from the table, took off his outer robe, and tied a towel around himself. Then he poured water into a basin and began to wash the disciples' feet and to wipe them with the towel that was tied around him. He came to Simon Peter, who said to him, 'Lord, are you going to wash my feet?' Jesus answered, 'You do not know now what I am doing, but later you will understand.' Peter said to him, 'You will never wash my feet.' Jesus answered, 'Unless I wash you, you have no share with me.' Simon Peter said to him, 'Lord, not my feet only but also my hands and my head!' Jesus said to him, 'One who has bathed does not need to wash, except for the feet, but is entirely clean. And you are clean, though not all of you.' For he knew who was to betray him; for this reason he said, 'Not all of you are clean.'

After he had washed their feet, had put on his robe, and had returned to the table, he said to them, 'Do you know what I have done to you? You call me Teacher and Lord – and you are right, for that is what I am. So if I, your Lord and Teacher, have washed your feet, you also ought to wash one another's feet. For I have set you an example, that you also should do as I have done to you. Very truly, I tell you, servants are not greater than their master, nor are messengers greater than the one who sent them. If you know these things, you are blessed if you do them.

'Now the Son of Man has been glorified, and God has been glorified in him. If God has been glorified in him, God will also glorify him in himself and will glorify him at once. Little children, I am with you only a little longer. You will look for me; and as I said to the Jews so now I say to you, "Where I am going, you cannot come." I give you a new commandment, that you love one another. Just as I have loved you, you also should love one another. By this everyone will know that you are my disciples, if you have love for one another.'

This is the Gospel of the Lord. John 13.1–17, 31b–35

Good Friday

It is a widespread custom for there not to be a celebration of the Eucharist on Good Friday, but for the consecrated bread and wine remaining from the Maundy Thursday Eucharist to be given in communion.

A reading from the prophecy of Isaiah.

See, my servant shall prosper;
    he shall be exalted and lifted up,
    and shall be very high.
Just as there were many who were astonished at him
    — so marred was his appearance, beyond human semblance,
    and his form beyond that of mortals —
so he shall startle many nations;
    kings shall shut their mouths because of him;
for that which had not been told them they shall see,
    and that which they had not heard they shall contemplate.
Who has believed what we have heard?
    And to whom has the arm of the Lord been revealed?
For he grew up before him like a young plant,
    and like a root out of dry ground;
he had no form or majesty that we should look at him,
    nothing in his appearance that we should desire him.
He was despised and rejected by others;
    a man of suffering and acquainted with infirmity;
and as one from whom others hide their faces
    he was despised, and we held him of no account.

Surely he has borne our infirmities
    and carried our diseases;
yet we accounted him stricken,
    struck down by God, and afflicted.
But he was wounded for our transgressions,
    crushed for our iniquities;
upon him was the punishment that made us whole,
    and by his bruises we are healed.
All we like sheep have gone astray;
    we have all turned to our own way,
and the Lord has laid on him
    the iniquity of us all.

He was oppressed, and he was afflicted,
    yet he did not open his mouth;
like a lamb that is led to the slaughter,
    and like a sheep that before its shearers is silent,
    so he did not open his mouth.
By a perversion of justice he was taken away. →

Who could have imagined his future?
For he was cut off from the land of the living,
    stricken for the transgression of my people.
They made his grave with the wicked
    and his tomb with the rich,
although he had done no violence,
    and there was no deceit in his mouth.

Yet it was the will of the LORD to crush him with pain.
When you make his life an offering for sin,
    he shall see his offspring, and shall prolong his days;
through him the will of the LORD shall prosper.
    Out of his anguish he shall see light;
he shall find satisfaction through his knowledge.
    The righteous one, my servant, shall make many righteous,
    and he shall bear their iniquities.
Therefore I will allot him a portion with the great,
    and he shall divide the spoil with the strong;
because he poured out himself to death,
    and was numbered with the transgressors;
yet he bore the sin of many,
    and made intercession for the transgressors.

This is the word of the Lord.   *Isaiah 52.13 − 53.12*

Responsorial Psalm

R **My God, my God, why have you forsaken me?**   *Psalm 22.1a*

My God, my God, why have you forsaken me,
and are so far from my salvation,
from the words of my distress?
O my God, I cry in the daytime,
but you do not answer;
and by night also, but I find no rest. **R**

Yet you are the Holy One,
enthroned upon the praises of Israel.
Our forebears trusted in you;
they trusted, and you delivered them.
They cried out to you and were delivered;
they put their trust in you and were not confounded. **R**

But as for me, I am a worm and no man,
scorned by all and despised by the people.
All who see me laugh me to scorn;
they curl their lips and wag their heads, saying,
'He trusted in the Lord; let him deliver him;
let him deliver him, if he delights in him.' **R**

But it is you that took me out of the womb
and laid me safe upon my mother's breast.
On you was I cast ever since I was born;
you are my God even from my mother's womb.
Be not far from me, for trouble is near at hand
and there is none to help.   R

[Mighty oxen come around me;
fat bulls of Bashan close me in on every side.
They gape upon me with their mouths,
as it were a ramping and a roaring lion.   R

I am poured out like water;
all my bones are out of joint;
my heart has become like wax
melting in the depths of my body.   R

My mouth is dried up like a potsherd;
my tongue cleaves to my gums;
you have laid me in the dust of death.
For the hounds are all about me,
the pack of evildoers close in on me;
they pierce my hands and my feet.   R

I can count all my bones;
they stand staring and looking upon me.
They divide my garments among them;
they cast lots for my clothing.
Be not far from me, O Lord;
you are my strength; hasten to help me.   R

Deliver my soul from the sword,
my poor life from the power of the dog.
Save me from the lion's mouth,
from the horns of wild oxen.
You have answered me!   R]

[I will tell of your name to my people;
in the midst of the congregation will I praise you.
Praise the Lord, you that fear him;
O seed of Jacob, glorify him;
stand in awe of him, O seed of Israel.   R

For he has not despised nor abhorred the suffering of the poor;
neither has he hidden his face from them;
but when they cried to him he heard them.
From you comes my praise in the great congregation;
I will perform my vows
in the presence of those that fear you.   R   →

The poor shall eat and be satisfied;
those who seek the Lord shall praise him;
their hearts shall live for ever.
All the ends of the earth
shall remember and turn to the Lord,
and all the families of the nations shall bow before him. R

R **My God, my God, why have you forsaken me?**

For the kingdom is the Lord's
and he rules over the nations.
How can those who sleep in the earth
bow down in worship,
or those who go down to the dust kneel before him? R

He has saved my life for himself;
my descendants shall serve him;
this shall be told of the Lord for generations to come.
They shall come and make known his salvation,
to a people yet unborn,
declaring that he, the Lord, has done it. R]

Psalm 22 [or 22.1–11 or 22.1–21]

Either

A reading from the Letter to the Hebrews.

The Holy Spirit testifies to us, for after saying,
  'This is the covenant that I will make with them
    after those days, says the Lord:
  I will put my laws in their hearts,
    and I will write them on their minds',
he also adds,
  'I will remember their sins and their lawless deeds no more.'
Where there is forgiveness of these, there is no longer any offering for sin.

Therefore, my friends, since we have confidence to enter the sanctuary by the blood of Jesus, by the new and living way that he opened for us through the curtain (that is, through his flesh), and since we have a great priest over the house of God, let us approach with a true heart in full assurance of faith, with our hearts sprinkled clean from an evil conscience and our bodies washed with pure water. Let us hold fast to the confession of our hope without wavering, for he who has promised is faithful. And let us consider how to provoke one another to love and good deeds, not neglecting to meet together, as is the habit of some, but encouraging one another, and all the more as you see the Day approaching.

This is the word of the Lord.

Hebrews 10.15–25

or

A reading from the Letter to the Hebrews.

Since we have a great high priest who has passed through the heavens, Jesus, the Son of God, let us hold fast to our confession. For we do not have a high priest who is unable to sympathize with our weaknesses, but we have one who in every respect has been tested as we are, yet without sin. Let us therefore approach the throne of grace with boldness, so that we may receive mercy and find grace to help in time of need.

In the days of his flesh, Jesus offered up prayers and supplications, with loud cries and tears, to the one who was able to save him from death, and he was heard because of his reverent submission. Although he was a Son, he learned obedience through what he suffered; and having been made perfect, he became the source of eternal salvation for all who obey him.

This is the word of the Lord.   Hebrews 4.14–end, 5.7–9

There is no response to the introduction of the Passion reading.

The Passion of our Lord Jesus Christ according to John.

Jesus went out with his disciples across the Kidron valley to a place where there was a garden, which he and his disciples entered. Now Judas, who betrayed him, also knew the place, because Jesus often met there with his disciples. So Judas brought a detachment of soldiers together with police from the chief priests and the Pharisees, and they came there with lanterns and torches and weapons. Then Jesus, knowing all that was to happen to him, came forward and asked them, 'For whom are you looking?' They answered, 'Jesus of Nazareth.' Jesus replied, 'I am he.' Judas, who betrayed him, was standing with them. When Jesus said to them, 'I am he', they stepped back and fell to the ground. Again he asked them, 'For whom are you looking?' And they said, 'Jesus of Nazareth.' Jesus answered, 'I told you that I am he. So if you are looking for me, let these men go.' This was to fulfil the word that he had spoken, 'I did not lose a single one of those whom you gave me.' Then Simon Peter, who had a sword, drew it, struck the high priest's slave, and cut off his right ear. The slave's name was Malchus. Jesus said to Peter, 'Put your sword back into its sheath. Am I not to drink the cup that the Father has given me?'

So the soldiers, their officer, and the Jewish police arrested Jesus and bound him. First they took him to Annas, who was the father-in-law of Caiaphas, the high priest that year. Caiaphas was the one who had advised the Jews that it was better to have one person die for the people.

Simon Peter and another disciple followed Jesus. Since that disciple was known to the high priest, he went with Jesus into the courtyard of the high priest, but Peter was standing outside at the gate. So the other disciple, who was known to the high priest, went out, spoke to the woman who guarded the gate, and brought Peter in. The woman said to Peter, 'You are not also one of this man's disciples, are you?' He said, 'I am not.' Now the slaves and the →

police had made a charcoal fire because it was cold, and they were standing round it and warming themselves. Peter also was standing with them and warming himself.

Then the high priest questioned Jesus about his disciples and about his teaching. Jesus answered, 'I have spoken openly to the world; I have always taught in synagogues and in the temple, where all the Jews come together. I have said nothing in secret. Why do you ask me? Ask those who heard what I said to them; they know what I said.' When he had said this, one of the police standing nearby struck Jesus on the face, saying, 'Is that how you answer the high priest?' Jesus answered, 'If I have spoken wrongly, testify to the wrong. But if I have spoken rightly, why do you strike me?' Then Annas sent him bound to Caiaphas the high priest.

Now Simon Peter was standing and warming himself. They asked him, 'You are not also one of his disciples, are you?' He denied it and said, 'I am not.' One of the slaves of the high priest, a relative of the man whose ear Peter had cut off, asked, 'Did I not see you in the garden with him?' Again Peter denied it, and at that moment the cock crowed.

Then they took Jesus from Caiaphas to Pilate's headquarters. It was early in the morning. They themselves did not enter the headquarters, so as to avoid ritual defilement and to be able to eat the Passover. So Pilate went out to them and said, 'What accusation do you bring against this man?' They answered, 'If this man were not a criminal, we would not have handed him over to you.' Pilate said to them, 'Take him yourselves and judge him according to your law.' The Jews replied, 'We are not permitted to put anyone to death.' (This was to fulfil what Jesus had said when he indicated the kind of death he was to die.)

Then Pilate entered the headquarters again, summoned Jesus, and asked him, 'Are you the King of the Jews?' Jesus answered, 'Do you ask this on your own, or did others tell you about me?' Pilate replied, 'I am not a Jew, am I? Your own nation and the chief priests have handed you over to me. What have you done?' Jesus answered, 'My kingdom is not from this world. If my kingdom were from this world, my followers would be fighting to keep me from being handed over to the Jews. But as it is, my kingdom is not from here.' Pilate asked him, 'So you are a king?' Jesus answered, 'You say that I am a king. For this I was born, and for this I came into the world, to testify to the truth. Everyone who belongs to the truth listens to my voice.' Pilate asked him, 'What is truth?'

After he had said this, he went out to the Jews again and told them, 'I find no case against him. But you have a custom that I release someone for you at the Passover. Do you want me to release for you the King of the Jews?' They shouted in reply, 'Not this man, but Barabbas!' Now Barabbas was a bandit.

Then Pilate took Jesus and had him flogged. And the soldiers wove a crown of thorns and put it on his head, and they dressed him in a purple robe. They kept coming up to him, saying, 'Hail, King of the Jews!' and striking him on the face. Pilate went out again and said to them, 'Look, I am bringing him out to you to let you know that I find no case against him.' So Jesus came out, wearing the crown of thorns and the purple robe. Pilate said to them, 'Here is the man!' When the chief priests and the police saw him, they shouted, 'Crucify him! Crucify him!' Pilate said to them, 'Take him yourselves and crucify him; I find no case against him.' The Jews answered him, 'We have a law, and according to that law he ought to die because he has claimed to be the Son of God.'

Now when Pilate heard this, he was more afraid than ever. He entered his headquarters again and asked Jesus, 'Where are you from?' But Jesus gave him no answer. Pilate therefore said to him, 'Do you refuse to speak to me? Do you not know that I have power to release you, and power to crucify you?' Jesus answered him, 'You would have no power over me unless it had been given you from above; therefore the one who handed me over to you is guilty of a greater sin.' From then on Pilate tried to release him, but the Jews cried out, 'If you release this man, you are no friend of the emperor. Everyone who claims to be a king sets himself against the emperor.'

When Pilate heard these words, he brought Jesus outside and sat on the judge's bench at a place called The Stone Pavement, or in Hebrew Gabbatha. Now it was the day of Preparation for the Passover; and it was about noon. He said to the Jews, 'Here is your King!' They cried out, 'Away with him! Away with him! Crucify him!' Pilate asked them, 'Shall I crucify your King?' The chief priests answered, 'We have no king but the emperor.' Then he handed him over to them to be crucified.

So they took Jesus; and carrying the cross by himself, he went out to what is called The Place of the Skull, which in Hebrew is called Golgotha. There they crucified him, and with him two others, one on either side, with Jesus between them. Pilate also had an inscription written and put on the cross. It read, 'Jesus of Nazareth, the King of the Jews.' Many of the Jews read this inscription, because the place where Jesus was crucified was near the city; and it was written in Hebrew, in Latin, and in Greek. Then the chief priests of the Jews said to Pilate, 'Do not write, "The King of the Jews", but, "This man said, I am King of the Jews." ' Pilate answered, 'What I have written I have written.' When the soldiers had crucified Jesus, they took his clothes and divided them into four parts, one for each soldier. They also took his tunic; now the tunic was seamless, woven in one piece from the top. So they said to one another, 'Let us not tear it, but cast lots for it to see who will get it.' This was to fulfil what the scripture says,

'They divided my clothes among themselves,
    and for my clothing they cast lots.'

And that is what the soldiers did.

Meanwhile, standing near the cross of Jesus were his mother, and his mother's sister, Mary the wife of Clopas, and Mary Magdalene. When Jesus saw his mother and the disciple whom he loved standing beside her, he said to his mother, 'Woman, here is your son.' Then he said to the disciple, 'Here is your mother.' And from that hour the disciple took her into his own home. →

After this, when Jesus knew that all was now finished, he said (in order to fulfil the scripture), 'I am thirsty.' A jar full of sour wine was standing there. So they put a sponge full of the wine on a branch of hyssop and held it to his mouth. When Jesus had received the wine, he said, 'It is finished.' Then he bowed his head and gave up his spirit.

Since it was the day of Preparation, the Jews did not want the bodies left on the cross during the sabbath, especially because that sabbath was a day of great solemnity. So they asked Pilate to have the legs of the crucified men broken and the bodies removed. Then the soldiers came and broke the legs of the first and of the other who had been crucified with him. But when they came to Jesus and saw that he was already dead, they did not break his legs. Instead, one of the soldiers pierced his side with a spear, and at once blood and water came out. (He who saw this has testified so that you also may believe. His testimony is true, and he knows that he tells the truth.) These things occurred so that the scripture might be fulfilled, 'None of his bones shall be broken.' And again another passage of scripture says, 'They will look on the one whom they have pierced.'

After these things, Joseph of Arimathea, who was a disciple of Jesus, though a secret one because of his fear of the Jews, asked Pilate to let him take away the body of Jesus. Pilate gave him permission; so he came and removed his body. Nicodemus, who had at first come to Jesus by night, also came, bringing a mixture of myrrh and aloes, weighing about a hundred pounds. They took the body of Jesus and wrapped it with the spices in linen cloths, according to the burial custom of the Jews. Now there was a garden in the place where he was crucified, and in the garden there was a new tomb in which no one had ever been laid. And so, because it was the Jewish day of Preparation, and the tomb was nearby, they laid Jesus there.

This is the Passion of the Lord.   John 18 – 19

There is no response at the end of the Passion reading.

Easter Eve

According to ancient custom there is no celebration of the Eucharist on Easter Eve.

Either

A reading from the Book of Job.

A mortal, born of woman, few of days and full of trouble,
  comes up like a flower and withers,
  flees like a shadow and does not last.
Do you fix your eyes on such a one?
  Do you bring me into judgement with you?
Who can bring a clean thing out of an unclean?
  No one can.
Since their days are determined,
  and the number of their months is known to you,
  and you have appointed the bounds that they cannot pass,
look away from them, and desist,
  that they may enjoy, like labourers, their days.

For there is hope for a tree,
  if it is cut down, that it will sprout again,
  and that its shoots will not cease.
Though its root grows old in the earth,
  and its stump dies in the ground,
yet at the scent of water it will bud
  and put forth branches like a young plant.
But mortals die, and are laid low;
  humans expire, and where are they?
As waters fail from a lake,
  and a river wastes away and dries up,
so mortals lie down and do not rise again;
  until the heavens are no more, they will not awake
  or be roused out of their sleep.
O that you would hide me in Sheol,
  that you would conceal me until your wrath is past,
  that you would appoint me a set time, and remember me!
If mortals die, will they live again?
  All the days of my service I would wait
  until my release should come.

This is the word of the Lord.   Job 14.1–14

or

A reading from the book of Lamentations.

I am one who has seen affliction
    under the rod of God's wrath;
he has driven and brought me
    into darkness without any light;
against me alone he turns his hand,
    again and again, all day long.

He has made my flesh and my skin waste away,
    and broken my bones;
he has besieged and enveloped me
    with bitterness and tribulation;
he has made me sit in darkness
    like the dead of long ago.

He has walled me about so that I cannot escape;
    he has put heavy chains on me;
though I call and cry for help,
    he shuts out my prayer;
he has blocked my ways with hewn stones,
    he has made my paths crooked.

The thought of my affliction and my homelessness
    is wormwood and gall!
My soul continually thinks of it
    and is bowed down within me.
But this I call to mind,
    and therefore I have hope:

The steadfast love of the LORD never ceases,
    his mercies never come to an end;
they are new every morning;
    great is your faithfulness.
'The LORD is my portion,' says my soul,
    'therefore I will hope in him.'

This is the word of the Lord.   Lamentations 3.1–9, 19–24

R **Let your face shine upon us, O Lord;
[save us in your unfailing love].** *cf Psalm 31.16*

In you, O Lord, have I taken refuge;
let me never be put to shame;
deliver me in your righteousness.
Incline your ear to me;
make haste to deliver me. **R**

Be my strong rock, a fortress to save me,
for you are my rock and my stronghold;
guide me, and lead me for your name's sake.
Take me out of the net
that they have laid secretly for me,
for you are my strength. **R**

My times are in your hand;
deliver me from the hand of my enemies,
and from those who persecute me.
Make your face to shine upon your servant,
and save me for your mercy's sake. **R** *Psalm 31.1–4, 15–16*

A reading from the First Letter of Peter.

Since Christ suffered in the flesh, arm yourselves also with the same intention (for whoever has suffered in the flesh has finished with sin), so as to live for the rest of your earthly life no longer by human desires but by the will of God. You have already spent enough time in doing what the Gentiles like to do, living in licentiousness, passions, drunkenness, revels, carousing, and lawless idolatry. They are surprised that you no longer join them in the same excesses of dissipation, and so they blaspheme. But they will have to give an account to him who stands ready to judge the living and the dead. For this is the reason the gospel was proclaimed even to the dead, so that, though they had been judged in the flesh as everyone is judged, they might live in the spirit as God does.

The end of all things is near; therefore be serious and discipline yourselves for the sake of your prayers. Above all, maintain constant love for one another, for love covers a multitude of sins.

This is the word of the Lord. *1 Peter 4.1–8*

Either

Hear the Gospel of our Lord Jesus Christ according to Matthew.

When it was evening, there came a rich man from Arimathea, named Joseph, who was also a disciple of Jesus. He went to Pilate and asked for the body of Jesus; then Pilate ordered it to be given to him. So Joseph took the body and wrapped it in a clean linen cloth and laid it in his own new tomb, which he had hewn in the rock. He then rolled a great stone to the door of the tomb and went away. Mary Magdalene and the other Mary were there, sitting opposite the tomb.

The next day, that is, after the day of Preparation, the chief priests and the Pharisees gathered before Pilate and said, 'Sir, we remember what that impostor said while he was still alive, "After three days I will rise again." Therefore command that the tomb be made secure until the third day; otherwise his disciples may go and steal him away, and tell the people, "He has been raised from the dead", and the last deception would be worse than the first.' Pilate said to them, 'You have a guard of soldiers; go, make it as secure as you can.' So they went with the guard and made the tomb secure by sealing the stone.

This is the Gospel of the Lord.   Matthew 27.57–66

or

Hear the Gospel of our Lord Jesus Christ according to John.

Joseph of Arimathea, who was a disciple of Jesus, though a secret one because of his fear of the Jews, asked Pilate to let him take away the body of Jesus. Pilate gave him permission; so he came and removed his body. Nicodemus, who had at first come to Jesus by night, also came, bringing a mixture of myrrh and aloes, weighing about a hundred pounds. They took the body of Jesus and wrapped it with the spices in linen cloths, according to the burial custom of the Jews. Now there was a garden in the place where he was crucified, and in the garden there was a new tomb in which no one had ever been laid. And so, because it was the Jewish day of Preparation, and the tomb was nearby, they laid Jesus there.

This is the Gospel of the Lord.   John 19.38–end

EASTER

First Week of Easter: Monday

Year 1 and Year 2

A reading from the Acts of the Apostles.

On the day of Pentecost, Peter, standing with the eleven, raised his voice and addressed the crowd: 'Men of Judea and all who live in Jerusalem, let this be known to you, and listen to what I say.

'You that are Israelites, listen to what I have to say: Jesus of Nazareth, a man attested to you by God with deeds of power, wonders, and signs that God did through him among you, as you yourselves know – this man, handed over to you according to the definite plan and foreknowledge of God, you crucified and killed by the hands of those outside the law. But God raised him up, having freed him from death, because it was impossible for him to be held in its power. For David says concerning him,

"I saw the Lord always before me,
for he is at my right hand so that I will not be shaken;
therefore my heart was glad, and my tongue rejoiced;
moreover, my flesh will live in hope.
For you will not abandon my soul to Hades,
or let your Holy One experience corruption.
You have made known to me the ways of life;
you will make me full of gladness with your presence."

'Fellow Israelites, I may say to you confidently of our ancestor David that he both died and was buried, and his tomb is with us to this day. Since he was a prophet, he knew that God had sworn with an oath to him that he would put one of his descendants on his throne. Foreseeing this, David spoke of the resurrection of the Messiah, saying,

"He was not abandoned to Hades,
nor did his flesh experience corruption."
This Jesus God raised up, and of that all of us are witnesses.'

This is the word of the Lord.   *Acts 2.14, 22–32*

Responsorial Psalm

R **He was not abandoned to Hades,
nor did his flesh experience corruption.** *Acts 2.31, cf Psalm 16.9*

or

R **Alleluia, alleluia, alleluia!**

Preserve me, O God,
for in you have I taken refuge;
I have said to the Lord, 'You are my lord,
all my good depends on you.' **R**

All my delight is upon the godly that are in the land,
upon those who are noble in heart.
I will bless the Lord who has given me counsel,
and in the night watches he instructs my heart. **R**

I have set the Lord always before me;
he is at my right hand; I shall not fall.
Wherefore my heart is glad and my spirit rejoices;
my flesh also shall rest secure. **R**

For you will not abandon my soul to Death,
nor suffer your faithful one to see the Pit;
you will show me the path of life.
In your presence is the fullness of joy
and in your right hand are pleasures for evermore. **R**

Psalm 16.1–2, 6–end

Hear the Gospel of our Lord Jesus Christ according to Matthew.

Mary Magdalene and the other Mary left the tomb quickly with fear and great joy, and ran to tell the disciples. Suddenly Jesus met them and said, 'Greetings!' And they came to him, took hold of his feet, and worshipped him. Then Jesus said to them, 'Do not be afraid; go and tell my brothers to go to Galilee; there they will see me.'

While they were going, some of the guard went into the city and told the chief priests everything that had happened. After the priests had assembled with the elders, they devised a plan to give a large sum of money to the soldiers, telling them, 'You must say, "His disciples came by night and stole him away while we were asleep." If this comes to the governor's ears, we will satisfy him and keep you out of trouble.' So they took the money and did as they were directed. And this story is still told among the Jews to this day.

This is the Gospel of the Lord. *Matthew 28.8–15*

First Week of Easter: Tuesday

Year 1 and Year 2

A reading from the Acts of the Apostles.

Peter said to the crowd, 'Let the entire house of Israel know with certainty that God has made him both Lord and Messiah, this Jesus whom you crucified.'

Now when they heard this, they were cut to the heart and said to Peter and to the other apostles, 'Brothers, what should we do?' Peter said to them, 'Repent, and be baptized every one of you in the name of Jesus Christ so that your sins may be forgiven; and you will receive the gift of the Holy Spirit. For the promise is for you, for your children, and for all who are far away, everyone whom the Lord our God calls to him.' And he testified with many other arguments and exhorted them, saying, 'Save yourselves from this corrupt generation.' So those who welcomed his message were baptized, and that day about three thousand persons were added.

This is the word of the Lord.   *Acts 2.36–41*

Responsorial Psalm

R **Let your loving-kindness, O Lord, be upon us,**
   [as we have set our hope on you].   *Psalm 33.22*

   or

R **Alleluia, alleluia, alleluia!**

The word of the Lord is true
and all his works are sure.
He loves righteousness and justice;
the earth is full of the loving-kindness of the Lord.   **R**

Behold, the eye of the Lord
   is upon those who fear him,
on those who wait in hope for his steadfast love,
to deliver their soul from death
and to feed them in time of famine.   **R**

Our soul waits longingly for the Lord;
he is our help and our shield.
Indeed, our heart rejoices in him;
in his holy name have we put our trust.
Let your loving-kindness, O Lord, be upon us,
as we have set our hope on you.   **R**   *Psalm 33.4–5, 18–end*

Hear the Gospel of our Lord Jesus Christ according to John.

Mary Magdalene stood weeping outside the tomb. As she wept, she bent over to look into the tomb; and she saw two angels in white, sitting where the body of Jesus had been lying, one at the head and the other at the feet. They said to her, 'Woman, why are you weeping?' She said to them, 'They have taken away my Lord, and I do not know where they have laid him.' When she had said this, she turned round and saw Jesus standing there, but she did not know that it was Jesus. Jesus said to her, 'Woman, why are you weeping? For whom are you looking?' Supposing him to be the gardener, she said to him, 'Sir, if you have carried him away, tell me where you have laid him, and I will take him away.' Jesus said to her, 'Mary!' She turned and said to him in Hebrew, 'Rabbouni!' (which means Teacher). Jesus said to her, 'Do not hold on to me, because I have not yet ascended to the Father. But go to my brothers and say to them, "I am ascending to my Father and your Father, to my God and your God."' Mary Magdalene went and announced to the disciples, 'I have seen the Lord'; and she told them that he had said these things to her.

This is the Gospel of the Lord.   John 20.11–18

First Week of Easter: Wednesday

Year 1 and Year 2

A reading from the Acts of the Apostles.

One day Peter and John were going up to the temple at the hour of prayer, at three o'clock in the afternoon. And a man lame from birth was being carried in. People would lay him daily at the gate of the temple called the Beautiful Gate so that he could ask for alms from those entering the temple. When he saw Peter and John about to go into the temple, he asked them for alms. Peter looked intently at him, as did John, and said, 'Look at us.' And he fixed his attention on them, expecting to receive something from them. But Peter said, 'I have no silver or gold, but what I have I give you; in the name of Jesus Christ of Nazareth, stand up and walk.' And he took him by the right hand and raised him up; and immediately his feet and ankles were made strong. Jumping up, he stood and began to walk, and he entered the temple with them, walking and leaping and praising God. All the people saw him walking and praising God, and they recognized him as the one who used to sit and ask for alms at the Beautiful Gate of the temple; and they were filled with wonder and amazement at what had happened to him.

This is the word of the Lord.   Acts 3.1–10

R* **Sing to the Lord, sing praises,**
  [and tell of his marvellous works].   cf Psalm 105.2

  or

R **Alleluia, alleluia, alleluia!**

O give thanks to the Lord and call upon his name;
make known his deeds among the peoples.*
Rejoice in the praise of his holy name;
let the hearts of them rejoice who seek the Lord. **R**

Seek the Lord and his strength;
seek his face continually.
Remember the marvels he has done,
his wonders and the judgements of his mouth. **R**

O seed of Abraham his servant,
O children of Jacob his chosen:
he is the Lord our God;
his judgements are in all the earth. **R**

He has always been mindful of his covenant,
the promise that he made for a thousand generations:
the covenant he made with Abraham,
the oath that he swore to Isaac. **R**   Psalm 105.1–9

Hear the Gospel of our Lord Jesus Christ according to Luke.

On the first day of the week two of the disciples were going to a village
called Emmaus, about seven miles from Jerusalem, and talking with each
other about all the things that had happened. While they were talking and
discussing, Jesus himself came near and went with them, but their eyes were
kept from recognizing him. And he said to them, 'What are you discussing
with each other while you walk along?' They stood still, looking sad. Then one
of them, whose name was Cleopas, answered him, 'Are you the only stranger
in Jerusalem who does not know the things that have taken place there in
these days?' He asked them, 'What things?'

They replied, 'The things about Jesus of Nazareth, who was a prophet
mighty in deed and word before God and all the people, and how our chief
priests and leaders handed him over to be condemned to death and crucified
him. But we had hoped that he was the one to redeem Israel. Yes, and besides
all this, it is now the third day since these things took place. Moreover, some
women of our group astounded us. They were at the tomb early this morning,
and when they did not find his body there, they came back and told us that
they had indeed seen a vision of angels who said that he was alive. Some of
those who were with us went to the tomb and found it just as the women
had said; but they did not see him.' Then he said to them, 'Oh, how foolish   →

you are, and how slow of heart to believe all that the prophets have declared! Was it not necessary that the Messiah should suffer these things and then enter into his glory?' Then beginning with Moses and all the prophets, he interpreted to them the things about himself in all the scriptures.

As they came near the village to which they were going, he walked ahead as if he were going on. But they urged him strongly, saying, 'Stay with us, because it is almost evening and the day is now nearly over.' So he went in to stay with them. When he was at the table with them, he took bread, blessed and broke it, and gave it to them. Then their eyes were opened, and they recognized him; and he vanished from their sight. They said to each other, 'Were not our hearts burning within us while he was talking to us on the road, while he was opening the scriptures to us?'

That same hour they got up and returned to Jerusalem; and they found the eleven and their companions gathered together. They were saying, 'The Lord has risen indeed, and he has appeared to Simon!' Then they told what had happened on the road, and how he had been made known to them in the breaking of the bread.

This is the Gospel of the Lord.   Luke 24.13–35

First Week of Easter: Thursday

Year 1 and Year 2

A reading from the Acts of the Apostles.

All the people ran together to Peter and John in the portico called Solomon's Portico, utterly astonished. When Peter saw it, he addressed the people, 'You Israelites, why do you wonder at this, or why do you stare at us, as though by our own power or piety we had made him walk? The God of Abraham, the God of Isaac, and the God of Jacob, the God of our ancestors has glorified his servant Jesus, whom you handed over and rejected in the presence of Pilate, though he had decided to release him. But you rejected the Holy and Righteous One and asked to have a murderer given to you, and you killed the Author of life, whom God raised from the dead. To this we are witnesses. And by faith in his name, his name itself has made this man strong, whom you see and know; and the faith that is through Jesus has given him this perfect health in the presence of all of you.

'And now, friends, I know that you acted in ignorance, as did also your rulers. In this way God fulfilled what he had foretold through all the prophets, that his Messiah would suffer. Repent therefore, and turn to God so that your sins may be wiped out, so that times of refreshing may come from the presence of the Lord, and that he may send the Messiah appointed for you, that is, Jesus, who must remain in heaven until the time of universal restoration that God announced long ago through his holy prophets. Moses said, "The Lord your God will raise up for you from your own people a prophet like me. You must listen to whatever he tells you. And it will be that everyone who does not listen to that prophet will be utterly rooted out from the people." And all the prophets, as many as have spoken, from Samuel and those after him, also predicted these days.

'You are the descendants of the prophets and of the covenant that God gave to your ancestors, saying to Abraham, "And in your descendants all the families of the earth shall be blessed." When God raised up his servant, he sent him first to you, to bless you by turning each of you from your wicked ways.'

This is the word of the Lord.   *Acts 3.11–end*

Responsorial Psalm

R* **O Lord our governor,**
    how glorious is your name in all the world!   *Psalm 8.1*
    or

R   **Alleluia, alleluia, alleluia!**

Your majesty above the heavens is praised
out of the mouths of babes at the breast.
You have founded a stronghold against your foes,
that you might still the enemy and the avenger. **R**

When I consider your heavens, the work of your fingers,
the moon and the stars that you have ordained,
what is man, that you should be mindful of him;
the son of man, that you should seek him out? **R**

You have made him little lower than the angels
and crown him with glory and honour.
You have given him dominion over the works of your hands
and put all things under his feet. **R**

All sheep and oxen,
even the wild beasts of the field,
the birds of the air, the fish of the sea
and whatsoever moves in the paths of the sea. **R**   *Psalm 8*

Hear the Gospel of our Lord Jesus Christ according to Luke.

The two disciples told the eleven and their companions what had happened on the road, and how Jesus had been made known to them in the breaking of the bread.

While they were talking about this, Jesus himself stood among them and said to them, 'Peace be with you.' They were startled and terrified, and thought that they were seeing a ghost. He said to them, 'Why are you frightened, and why do doubts arise in your hearts? Look at my hands and my feet; see that it is I myself. Touch me and see; for a ghost does not have flesh and bones as you see that I have.' And when he had said this, he showed them his hands and his feet. While in their joy they were disbelieving and still wondering, he said to them, 'Have you anything here to eat?' They gave him a piece of broiled fish, and he took it and ate in their presence.

Then he said to them, 'These are my words that I spoke to you while I was still with you – that everything written about me in the law of Moses, the prophets, and the psalms must be fulfilled.' Then he opened their minds to understand the scriptures, and he said to them, 'Thus it is written, that the Messiah is to suffer and to rise from the dead on the third day, and that repentance and forgiveness of sins is to be proclaimed in his name to all nations, beginning from Jerusalem. You are witnesses of these things.'

This is the Gospel of the Lord.   Luke 24.35–48

First Week of Easter: Friday

Year 1 and Year 2

A reading from the Acts of the Apostles.

While Peter and John were speaking to the people, the priests, the captain of the temple, and the Sadducees came to them, much annoyed because they were teaching the people and proclaiming that in Jesus there is the resurrection of the dead. So they arrested them and put them in custody until the next day, for it was already evening. But many of those who heard the word believed; and they numbered about five thousand.

The next day their rulers, elders, and scribes assembled in Jerusalem, with Annas the high priest, Caiaphas, John, and Alexander, and all who were of the high-priestly family. When they had made the prisoners stand in their midst, they inquired, 'By what power or by what name did you do this?' Then Peter, filled with the Holy Spirit, said to them, 'Rulers of the people and elders, if we are questioned today because of a good deed done to someone who was sick and are asked how this man has been healed, let it be known to all of you, and to all the people of Israel, that this man is standing before you in good health by the name of Jesus Christ of Nazareth, whom you crucified, whom God raised from the dead. This Jesus is

"the stone that was rejected by you, the builders;
  it has become the cornerstone."
There is salvation in no one else, for there is no other name under heaven
given among mortals by which we must be saved.'

This is the word of the Lord.   Acts 4.1–12

Responsorial Psalm

R* **The stone which the builders rejected
  has become the chief cornerstone.**   Psalm 118.22

  or

R **Alleluia, alleluia, alleluia!**

O give thanks to the Lord, for he is good;
his mercy endures for ever.
Let Israel now proclaim,
'His mercy endures for ever.'   **R**

Let the house of Aaron now proclaim,
'His mercy endures for ever.'
Let those who fear the Lord proclaim,
'His mercy endures for ever.'   **R***

This is the Lord's doing,
and it is marvellous in our eyes.
This is the day that the Lord has made;
we will rejoice and be glad in it.   **R**

Come, O Lord, and save us we pray.
Come, Lord, send us now prosperity.
Blessed is he who comes in the name of the Lord;
we bless you from the house of the Lord.   **R**   Psalm 118.1–4, 22–26

Hear the Gospel of our Lord Jesus Christ according to John.

Jesus showed himself again to the disciples by the Sea of Tiberias; and he showed himself in this way. Gathered there together were Simon Peter, Thomas called the Twin, Nathanael of Cana in Galilee, the sons of Zebedee, and two others of his disciples. Simon Peter said to them, 'I am going fishing.' They said to him, 'We will go with you.' They went out and got into the boat, but that night they caught nothing.

Just after daybreak, Jesus stood on the beach; but the disciples did not know that it was Jesus. Jesus said to them, 'Children, you have no fish, have you?' They answered him, 'No.' He said to them, 'Cast the net to the right side of the boat, and you will find some.' So they cast it, and now they were not able to haul it in because there were so many fish. That disciple whom Jesus loved said to Peter, 'It is the Lord!' When Simon Peter heard that it was the Lord, he put on some clothes, for he was naked, and jumped into the lake. But the other disciples came in the boat, dragging the net full of fish, for they were not far from the land, only about a hundred yards off.

When they had gone ashore, they saw a charcoal fire there, with fish on it, and bread. Jesus said to them, 'Bring some of the fish that you have just caught.' So Simon Peter went aboard and hauled the net ashore, full of large fish, a hundred and fifty-three of them; and though there were so many, the net was not torn. Jesus said to them, 'Come and have breakfast.' Now none of the disciples dared to ask him, 'Who are you?' because they knew it was the Lord. Jesus came and took the bread and gave it to them, and did the same with the fish. This was now the third time that Jesus appeared to the disciples after he was raised from the dead.

This is the Gospel of the Lord.   John 21.1–14

First Week of Easter: Saturday

Year 1 and Year 2

A reading from the Acts of the Apostles.

When the rulers, elders, and scribes saw the boldness of Peter and John and realized that they were uneducated and ordinary men, they were amazed and recognized them as companions of Jesus. When they saw the man who had been cured standing beside them, they had nothing to say in opposition. So they ordered them to leave the council while they discussed the matter with one another. They said, 'What will we do with them? For it is obvious to all who live in Jerusalem that a notable sign has been done through them; we cannot deny it. But to keep it from spreading further among the people, let us warn them to speak no more to anyone in this name.'

So they called them and ordered them not to speak or teach at all in the name of Jesus. But Peter and John answered them, 'Whether it is right in God's sight to listen to you rather than to God, you must judge; for we cannot keep from speaking about what we have seen and heard.' After threatening them again, they let them go, finding no way to punish them because of the people, for all of them praised God for what had happened.

This is the word of the Lord. *Acts 4.13–21*

Responsorial Psalm

R   **Give thanks to the Lord, for he is good;**
   [his mercy endures for ever]. *Psalm 118.1*

   or

R   **Alleluia, alleluia, alleluia!**

O give thanks to the Lord, for he is good;
his mercy endures for ever.
Let Israel now proclaim,
'His mercy endures for ever.'   R

Let the house of Aaron now proclaim,
'His mercy endures for ever.'
Let those who fear the Lord proclaim,
'His mercy endures for ever.'   R

The Lord is my strength and my song,
and he has become my salvation.
Joyful shouts of salvation
sound from the tents of the righteous.   R

'The right hand of the Lord does mighty deeds;
the right hand of the Lord raises up;
the right hand of the Lord does mighty deeds.'
I shall not die, but live
and declare the works of the Lord.   R

The Lord has punished me sorely,
but he has not given me over to death.
Open to me the gates of righteousness,
that I may enter and give thanks to the Lord.   R

This is the gate of the Lord;
the righteous shall enter through it.
I will give thanks to you, for you have answered me
and have become my salvation.   R   *Psalm 118.1–4, 14–21*

Hear the Gospel of our Lord Jesus Christ according to Mark.

After Jesus rose early on the first day of the week, he appeared first to Mary Magdalene, from whom he had cast out seven demons. She went out and told those who had been with him, while they were mourning and weeping. But when they heard that he was alive and had been seen by her, they would not believe it.

After this he appeared in another form to two of them, as they were walking into the country. And they went back and told the rest, but they did not believe them.

Later he appeared to the eleven themselves as they were sitting at the table; and he upbraided them for their lack of faith and stubbornness, because they had not believed those who saw him after he had risen. And he said to them, 'Go into all the world and proclaim the good news to the whole creation.'

This is the Gospel of the Lord.

Mark 16.9–15

Second Week of Easter: Monday

Year 1 and Year 2

A reading from the Acts of the Apostles.

After Peter and John were released, they went to their friends and reported what the chief priests and the elders had said to them. When they heard it, they raised their voices together to God and said, 'Sovereign Lord, who made the heaven and the earth, the sea, and everything in them, it is you who said by the Holy Spirit through our ancestor David, your servant:
"Why did the Gentiles rage,
and the peoples imagine vain things?
The kings of the earth took their stand,
and the rulers have gathered together
against the Lord and against his Messiah."
For in this city, in fact, both Herod and Pontius Pilate, with the Gentiles and the peoples of Israel, gathered together against your holy servant Jesus, whom you anointed, to do whatever your hand and your plan had predestined to take place. And now, Lord, look at their threats, and grant to your servants to speak your word with all boldness, while you stretch out your hand to heal, and signs and wonders are performed through the name of your holy servant Jesus.' When they had prayed, the place in which they were gathered together was shaken; and they were all filled with the Holy Spirit and spoke the word of God with boldness.

This is the word of the Lord.   Acts 4.23–31

Responsorial Psalm

R   **The kings of the earth rise up**
    against the Lord and his anointed.   cf Psalm 2.2

    or

R   **Alleluia!**

Why are the nations in tumult,
and why do the peoples devise a vain plot?   **R**

The kings of the earth rise up,
and the rulers take counsel together,
against the Lord and against his anointed:
'Let us break their bonds asunder
and cast away their cords from us.'   **R**

He who dwells in heaven shall laugh them to scorn;
the Lord shall have them in derision.
Then shall he speak to them in his wrath
and terrify them in his fury:
'Yet have I set my king
upon my holy hill of Zion.'   **R**   →

I will proclaim the decree of the Lord;
he said to me: 'You are my Son;
this day have I begotten you.'   R

R   **The kings of the earth rise up
against the Lord and his anointed.**

or

R   **Alleluia!**

'Ask of me and I will give you the nations for your inheritance
and the ends of the earth for your possession.
You shall break them with a rod of iron
and dash them in pieces like a potter's vessel.'   R   *Psalm 2.1–9*

Hear the Gospel of our Lord Jesus Christ according to John.

There was a Pharisee named Nicodemus, a leader of the Jews. He came to
Jesus by night and said to him, 'Rabbi, we know that you are a teacher who
has come from God; for no one can do these signs that you do apart from
the presence of God.' Jesus answered him, 'Very truly, I tell you, no one can
see the kingdom of God without being born from above.' Nicodemus said
to him, 'How can anyone be born after having grown old? Can one enter a
second time into the mother's womb and be born?' Jesus answered, 'Very
truly, I tell you, no one can enter the kingdom of God without being born of
water and Spirit. What is born of the flesh is flesh, and what is born of the
Spirit is spirit. Do not be astonished that I said to you, "You must be born
from above." The wind blows where it chooses, and you hear the sound of
it, but you do not know where it comes from or where it goes. So it is with
everyone who is born of the Spirit.'

This is the Gospel of the Lord.   *John 3.1–8*

Second Week of Easter: Tuesday

Year I and Year 2

A reading from the Acts of the Apostles.

The whole group of those who believed were of one heart and soul, and no
one claimed private ownership of any possessions, but everything they owned
was held in common. With great power the apostles gave their testimony to
the resurrection of the Lord Jesus, and great grace was upon them all. There
was not a needy person among them, for as many as owned lands or houses
sold them and brought the proceeds of what was sold. They laid it at the apostles' feet, and it was distributed to each as any had need. There was a Levite,
a native of Cyprus, Joseph, to whom the apostles gave the name Barnabas
(which means 'son of encouragement'). He sold a field that belonged to him,
then brought the money, and laid it at the apostles' feet.

This is the word of the Lord.   *Acts 4.32–end*

Responsorial Psalm

R **The Lord has put on his glory**
   and girded himself with strength. *Psalm 93.1b*

  or

R **Alleluia!**

The Lord is king and has put on glorious apparel;
the Lord has put on his glory
and girded himself with strength. R

He has made the whole world so sure
that it cannot be moved.
Your throne has been established from of old;
you are from everlasting. R

The floods have lifted up, O Lord,
the floods have lifted up their voice;
the floods lift up their pounding waves. R

Mightier than the thunder of many waters,
mightier than the breakers of the sea,
the Lord on high is mightier.
Your testimonies are very sure;
holiness adorns your house, O Lord, for ever. R *Psalm 93*

Hear the Gospel of our Lord Jesus Christ according to John.

Jesus said to Nicodemus, 'Do not be astonished that I said to you, "You must be born from above." The wind blows where it chooses, and you hear the sound of it, but you do not know where it comes from or where it goes. So it is with everyone who is born of the Spirit.' Nicodemus said to him, 'How can these things be?' Jesus answered him, 'Are you a teacher of Israel, and yet you do not understand these things?

'Very truly, I tell you, we speak of what we know and testify to what we have seen; yet you do not receive our testimony. If I have told you about earthly things and you do not believe, how can you believe if I tell you about heavenly things? No one has ascended into heaven except the one who descended from heaven, the Son of Man. And just as Moses lifted up the serpent in the wilderness, so must the Son of Man be lifted up, that whoever believes in him may have eternal life.'

This is the Gospel of the Lord. *John 3.7–15*

Second Week of Easter: Wednesday

Year 1 and Year 2

A reading from the Acts of the Apostles.

The high priest and all who were with him (that is, the sect of the Sadducees), being filled with jealousy, arrested the apostles and put them in the public prison. But during the night an angel of the Lord opened the prison doors, brought them out, and said, 'Go, stand in the temple and tell the people the whole message about this life.' When they heard this, they entered the temple at daybreak and went on with their teaching.

When the high priest and those with him arrived, they called together the council and the whole body of the elders of Israel, and sent to the prison to have them brought. But when the temple police went there, they did not find them in the prison; so they returned and reported, 'We found the prison securely locked and the guards standing at the doors, but when we opened them, we found no one inside.' Now when the captain of the temple and the chief priests heard these words, they were perplexed about them, wondering what might be going on. Then someone arrived and announced, 'Look, the men whom you put in prison are standing in the temple and teaching the people!' Then the captain went with the temple police and brought them, but without violence, for they were afraid of being stoned by the people.

This is the word of the Lord.   *Acts 5.17–26*

Responsorial Psalm

R **Taste and see that the Lord is good:**
   [happy are all who trust in him].   *cf Psalm 34.8*

   or

R **Alleluia!**

I will bless the Lord at all times;
his praise shall ever be in my mouth.
My soul shall glory in the Lord;
let the humble hear and be glad.   **R**

O magnify the Lord with me;
let us exalt his name together.
I sought the Lord and he answered me
and delivered me from all my fears.   **R**

Look upon him and be radiant
and your faces shall not be ashamed.
This poor soul cried, and the Lord heard me
and saved me from all my troubles.   **R**

The angel of the Lord encamps around those who fear him
and delivers them.
O taste and see that the Lord is gracious;
blessed is the one who trusts in him. **R**   *Psalm 34.1–8*

Hear the Gospel of our Lord Jesus Christ according to John.

Jesus said to Nicodemus, 'God so loved the world that he gave his only Son, so
that everyone who believes in him may not perish but may have eternal life.

'Indeed, God did not send the Son into the world to condemn the world,
but in order that the world might be saved through him. Those who believe
in him are not condemned; but those who do not believe are condemned
already, because they have not believed in the name of the only Son of God.
And this is the judgement, that the light has come into the world, and people
loved darkness rather than light because their deeds were evil. For all who do
evil hate the light and do not come to the light, so that their deeds may not
be exposed. But those who do what is true come to the light, so that it may
be clearly seen that their deeds have been done in God.'

This is the Gospel of the Lord.   *John 3.16–21*

Second Week of Easter: Thursday

Year 1 and Year 2

A reading from the Acts of the Apostles.

When the temple police had brought the apostles, they had them stand before
the council. The high priest questioned them, saying, 'We gave you strict
orders not to teach in this name, yet here you have filled Jerusalem with your
teaching and you are determined to bring this man's blood on us.'

But Peter and the apostles answered, 'We must obey God rather than any
human authority. The God of our ancestors raised up Jesus, whom you had
killed by hanging him on a tree. God exalted him at his right hand as Leader
and Saviour, so that he might give repentance to Israel and forgiveness of sins.
And we are witnesses to these things, and so is the Holy Spirit whom God
has given to those who obey him.'

When they heard this, they were enraged and wanted to kill them.

This is the word of the Lord.   *Acts 5.27–33*

R   **Taste and see that the Lord is good:**
    [happy are all who trust in him].   cf Psalm 34.8
    or
R   **Alleluia!**

I will bless the Lord at all times;
his praise shall ever be in my mouth.
The eyes of the Lord are upon the righteous
and his ears are open to their cry.   **R**

The face of the Lord is against those who do evil,
to root out the remembrance of them from the earth.
The righteous cry and the Lord hears them
and delivers them out of all their troubles.   **R**

The Lord is near to the brokenhearted
and will save those who are crushed in spirit.
Many are the troubles of the righteous;
from them all will the Lord deliver them.   **R**

He keeps all their bones,
so that not one of them is broken.
But evil shall slay the wicked
and those who hate the righteous will be condemned.
The Lord ransoms the life of his servants
and will condemn none who seek refuge in him.   **R**   Psalm 34.1, 15–end

Hear the Gospel of our Lord Jesus Christ according to John.

John the Baptist said, 'The one who comes from above is above all; the one
who is of the earth belongs to the earth and speaks about earthly things. The
one who comes from heaven is above all. He testifies to what he has seen and
heard, yet no one accepts his testimony. Whoever has accepted his testimony
has certified this, that God is true. He whom God has sent speaks the words
of God, for he gives the Spirit without measure. The Father loves the Son and
has placed all things in his hands. Whoever believes in the Son has eternal life;
whoever disobeys the Son will not see life, but must endure God's wrath.'

This is the Gospel of the Lord.   John 3.31–end

Second Week of Easter: Friday

Year 1 and Year 2

A reading from the Acts of the Apostles.

A Pharisee in the council named Gamaliel, a teacher of the law, respected by all the people, stood up and ordered the men to be put outside for a short time. Then he said to them, 'Fellow-Israelites, consider carefully what you propose to do to these men. For some time ago Theudas rose up, claiming to be somebody, and a number of men, about four hundred, joined him; but he was killed, and all who followed him were dispersed and disappeared. After him Judas the Galilean rose up at the time of the census and got people to follow him; he also perished, and all who followed him were scattered. So in the present case, I tell you, keep away from these men and let them alone; because if this plan or this undertaking is of human origin, it will fail; but if it is of God, you will not be able to overthrow them – in that case you may even be found fighting against God!'

They were convinced by him, and when they had called in the apostles, they had them flogged. Then they ordered them not to speak in the name of Jesus, and let them go. As they left the council, they rejoiced that they were considered worthy to suffer dishonour for the sake of the name. And every day in the temple and at home they did not cease to teach and proclaim Jesus as the Messiah.

This is the word of the Lord. *Acts 5.34–end*

Responsorial Psalm

R **The Lord is my light and my salvation:**
 [he is the strength of my life]. *cf Psalm 27.1*

 or

R **Alleluia!**

The Lord is my light and my salvation;
whom then shall I fear?
The Lord is the strength of my life;
of whom then shall I be afraid?   R

When the wicked,
even my enemies and my foes,
came upon me to eat up my flesh,
they stumbled and fell.   R

Though a host encamp against me,
my heart shall not be afraid,
and though there rise up war against me,
yet will I put my trust in him.   R   →

One thing have I asked of the Lord and that alone I seek:
that I may dwell in the house of the Lord all the days of my life,
to behold the fair beauty of the Lord
and to seek his will in his temple.   R

R   **The Lord is my light and my salvation:
[he is the strength of my life].**

or

R   **Alleluia!**

I believe that I shall see the goodness of the Lord
    in the land of the living.
Wait for the Lord;
be strong and he shall comfort your heart;
wait patiently for the Lord.   R   *Psalm 27.1–5, 16–17*

Hear the Gospel of our Lord Jesus Christ according to John.

Jesus went to the other side of the Sea of Galilee, also called the Sea of Tiberias.
A large crowd kept following him, because they saw the signs that he was
doing for the sick. Jesus went up the mountain and sat down there with his
disciples. Now the Passover, the festival of the Jews, was near. When he looked
up and saw a large crowd coming towards him, Jesus said to Philip, 'Where
are we to buy bread for these people to eat?' He said this to test him, for he
himself knew what he was going to do. Philip answered him, 'Six months'
wages would not buy enough bread for each of them to get a little.' One of
his disciples, Andrew, Simon Peter's brother, said to him, 'There is a boy
here who has five barley loaves and two fish. But what are they among so
many people?' Jesus said, 'Make the people sit down.' Now there was a great
deal of grass in the place; so they sat down, about five thousand in all. Then
Jesus took the loaves, and when he had given thanks, he distributed them to
those who were seated; so also the fish, as much as they wanted. When they
were satisfied, he told his disciples, 'Gather up the fragments left over, so that
nothing may be lost.' So they gathered them up, and from the fragments of
the five barley loaves, left by those who had eaten, they filled twelve baskets.
When the people saw the sign that he had done, they began to say, 'This is
indeed the prophet who is to come into the world.'

When Jesus realized that they were about to come and take him by force
to make him king, he withdrew again to the mountain by himself.

This is the Gospel of the Lord.   *John 6.1–15*

Second Week of Easter: Saturday

Year 1 and Year 2

A reading from the Acts of the Apostles.

During those days, when the disciples were increasing in number, the Hellenists complained against the Hebrews because their widows were being neglected in the daily distribution of food. And the twelve called together the whole community of the disciples and said, 'It is not right that we should neglect the word of God in order to wait at tables. Therefore, friends, select from among yourselves seven men of good standing, full of the Spirit and of wisdom, whom we may appoint to this task, while we, for our part, will devote ourselves to prayer and to serving the word.' What they said pleased the whole community, and they chose Stephen, a man full of faith and the Holy Spirit, together with Philip, Prochorus, Nicanor, Timon, Parmenas, and Nicolaus, a proselyte of Antioch. They had these men stand before the apostles, who prayed and laid their hands on them.

The word of God continued to spread; the number of the disciples increased greatly in Jerusalem, and a great many of the priests became obedient to the faith.

This is the word of the Lord. Acts 6.1–7

Responsorial Psalm

R **Rejoice in the Lord, O you righteous:
   [it is good to sing his praises].** cf Psalm 33.1

   or

R **Alleluia!**

Rejoice in the Lord, O you righteous,
for it is good for the just to sing praises.
Praise the Lord with the lyre;
on the ten-stringed harp sing his praise.
Sing for him a new song;
play skilfully, with shouts of praise. **R**

For the word of the Lord is true
and all his works are sure.
He loves righteousness and justice;
the earth is full of the loving-kindness of the Lord. **R**

Behold, the eye of the Lord
is upon those who fear him,
on those who wait in hope for his steadfast love,
to deliver their soul from death
and to feed them in time of famine. **R** Psalm 33.1–5, 18–19

Hear the Gospel of our Lord Jesus Christ according to John.

When evening came, the disciples went down to the lake, got into a boat, and started across the lake to Capernaum. It was now dark, and Jesus had not yet come to them. The lake became rough because a strong wind was blowing. When they had rowed about three or four miles, they saw Jesus walking on the lake and coming near the boat, and they were terrified. But he said to them, 'It is I; do not be afraid.' Then they wanted to take him into the boat, and immediately the boat reached the land towards which they were going.

This is the Gospel of the Lord.   John 6.16–21

Third Week of Easter: Monday

Year 1 and Year 2

A reading from the Acts of the Apostles.

Stephen, full of grace and power, did great wonders and signs among the people. Then some of those who belonged to the synagogue of the Freedmen (as it was called), Cyrenians, Alexandrians, and others of those from Cilicia and Asia, stood up and argued with Stephen. But they could not withstand the wisdom and the Spirit with which he spoke. Then they secretly instigated some men to say, 'We have heard him speak blasphemous words against Moses and God.' They stirred up the people as well as the elders and the scribes; then they suddenly confronted him, seized him, and brought him before the council. They set up false witnesses who said, 'This man never stops saying things against this holy place and the law; for we have heard him say that this Jesus of Nazareth will destroy this place and will change the customs that Moses handed on to us.' And all who sat in the council looked intently at him, and they saw that his face was like the face of an angel.

This is the word of the Lord.   Acts 6.8–end

Responsorial Psalm

R **Blessed are those who walk in the law of the Lord.**   cf Psalm 119.1

   or

R **Alleluia!**

O do good to your servant that I may live,
and so shall I keep your word.
Open my eyes, that I may see
the wonders of your law.   **R**

I am a stranger upon earth;
hide not your commandments from me.
My soul is consumed at all times
with fervent longing for your judgements.   **R**

You have rebuked the arrogant;
cursed are those who stray from your commandments.
Turn from me shame and rebuke,
for I have kept your testimonies.   **R**

Rulers also sit and speak against me,
but your servant meditates on your statutes.
For your testimonies are my delight;
they are my faithful counsellors.   **R**   Psalm 119.17–24

Hear the Gospel of our Lord Jesus Christ according to John.

The crowd that had stayed on the other side of the lake saw that there had been only one boat there. They also saw that Jesus had not got into the boat with his disciples, but that his disciples had gone away alone. Then some boats from Tiberias came near the place where they had eaten the bread after the Lord had given thanks. So when the crowd saw that neither Jesus nor his disciples were there, they themselves got into the boats and went to Capernaum looking for Jesus.

When they found him on the other side of the lake, they said to him, 'Rabbi, when did you come here?' Jesus answered them, 'Very truly, I tell you, you are looking for me, not because you saw signs, but because you ate your fill of the loaves. Do not work for the food that perishes, but for the food that endures for eternal life, which the Son of Man will give you. For it is on him that God the Father has set his seal.' Then they said to him, 'What must we do to perform the works of God?' Jesus answered them, 'This is the work of God, that you believe in him whom he has sent.'

This is the Gospel of the Lord.   John 6.22–29

Third Week of Easter: Tuesday

Year 1 and Year 2

A reading from the Acts of the Apostles.

Stephen said to the council, 'You stiff-necked people, uncircumcised in heart and ears, you are for ever opposing the Holy Spirit, just as your ancestors used to do. Which of the prophets did your ancestors not persecute? They killed those who foretold the coming of the Righteous One, and now you have become his betrayers and murderers. You are the ones that received the law as ordained by angels, and yet you have not kept it.'

When they heard these things, they became enraged and ground their teeth at Stephen. But filled with the Holy Spirit, he gazed into heaven and saw the glory of God and Jesus standing at the right hand of God. 'Look,' he said, 'I see the heavens opened and the Son of Man standing at the right hand of God!' But they covered their ears, and with a loud shout all rushed together against him. Then they dragged him out of the city and began to stone him; and the witnesses laid their coats at the feet of a young man named Saul. While they were stoning Stephen, he prayed, 'Lord Jesus, receive my spirit.' Then he knelt down and cried out in a loud voice, 'Lord, do not hold this sin against them.' When he had said this, he died. And Saul approved of their killing him.

This is the word of the Lord.   Acts 7.51 – 8.1a

Responsorial Psalm

R **Let your face shine upon us, O Lord;
[save us in your unfailing love].**   *cf Psalm 31.16*

or

R **Alleluia!**

In you, O Lord, have I taken refuge;
let me never be put to shame;
deliver me in your righteousness.
Incline your ear to me;
make haste to deliver me. R

Be my strong rock, a fortress to save me,
for you are my rock and my stronghold;
guide me, and lead me for your name's sake.
Take me out of the net
that they have laid secretly for me. R

For you are my strength:
into your hands I commend my spirit,
for you have redeemed me, O Lord God of truth.
Make your face to shine upon your servant,
and save me for your mercy's sake. R   *Psalm 31.1–5, 16*

Hear the Gospel of our Lord Jesus Christ according to John.

The crowd said to Jesus, 'What sign are you going to give us then, so that we may see it and believe you? What work are you performing? Our ancestors ate the manna in the wilderness; as it is written, "He gave them bread from heaven to eat." ' Then Jesus said to them, 'Very truly, I tell you, it was not Moses who gave you the bread from heaven, but it is my Father who gives you the true bread from heaven. For the bread of God is that which comes down from heaven and gives life to the world.' They said to him, 'Sir, give us this bread always.'

    Jesus said to them, 'I am the bread of life. Whoever comes to me will never be hungry, and whoever believes in me will never be thirsty.'

This is the Gospel of the Lord.   *John 6.30–35*

Third Week of Easter: Wednesday

Year 1 and Year 2

A reading from the Acts of the Apostles.

That day a severe persecution began against the church in Jerusalem, and all except the apostles were scattered throughout the countryside of Judea and Samaria. Devout men buried Stephen and made loud lamentation over him. But Saul was ravaging the church by entering house after house; dragging off both men and women, he committed them to prison.

Now those who were scattered went from place to place, proclaiming the word. Philip went down to the city of Samaria and proclaimed the Messiah to them. The crowds with one accord listened eagerly to what was said by Philip, hearing and seeing the signs that he did, for unclean spirits, crying with loud shrieks, came out of many who were possessed; and many others who were paralysed or lame were cured. So there was great joy in that city.

This is the word of the Lord. Acts 8.1b–8

Responsorial Psalm

R **Be joyful in God, all the earth;**
   [sing the glory of his praise]. cf Psalm 66.1

   or

R **Alleluia!**

Be joyful in God, all the earth;
sing the glory of his name;
sing the glory of his praise.
Say to God, 'How awesome are your deeds!   **R**

'Because of your great strength
your enemies shall bow before you.
All the earth shall worship you,
sing to you, sing praise to your name.'   **R**

Come now and behold the works of God,
how wonderful he is in his dealings with humankind.
He turned the sea into dry land;
the river they passed through on foot.   **R**

There we rejoiced in him;
in his might he rules for ever.
His eyes keep watch over the nations;
let no rebel rise up against him.   **R** Psalm 66.1–6

Hear the Gospel of our Lord Jesus Christ according to John.

Jesus said to the crowd, 'I am the bread of life. Whoever comes to me will never be hungry, and whoever believes in me will never be thirsty. But I said to you that you have seen me and yet do not believe. Everything that the Father gives me will come to me, and anyone who comes to me I will never drive away; for I have come down from heaven, not to do my own will, but the will of him who sent me. And this is the will of him who sent me, that I should lose nothing of all that he has given me, but raise it up on the last day. This is indeed the will of my Father, that all who see the Son and believe in him may have eternal life; and I will raise them up on the last day.'

This is the Gospel of the Lord.   John 6.35–40

Third Week of Easter: Thursday

Year 1 and Year 2

A reading from the Acts of the Apostles.

An angel of the Lord said to Philip, 'Get up and go towards the south to the road that goes down from Jerusalem to Gaza.' (This is a wilderness road.) So he got up and went. Now there was an Ethiopian eunuch, a court official of the Candace, queen of the Ethiopians, in charge of her entire treasury. He had come to Jerusalem to worship and was returning home; seated in his chariot, he was reading the prophet Isaiah. Then the Spirit said to Philip, 'Go over to this chariot and join it.' So Philip ran up to it and heard him reading the prophet Isaiah. He asked, 'Do you understand what you are reading?' He replied, 'How can I, unless someone guides me?' And he invited Philip to get in and sit beside him. Now the passage of the scripture that he was reading was this:

'Like a sheep he was led to the slaughter,
    and like a lamb silent before its shearer,
    so he does not open his mouth.
In his humiliation justice was denied him.
    Who can describe his generation?
      For his life is taken away from the earth.'

The eunuch asked Philip, 'About whom, may I ask you, does the prophet say this, about himself or about someone else?' Then Philip began to speak, and starting with this scripture, he proclaimed to him the good news about Jesus. As they were going along the road, they came to some water; and the eunuch said, 'Look, here is water! What is to prevent me from being baptized?' He commanded the chariot to stop, and both of them, Philip and the eunuch, went down into the water, and Philip baptized him. When they came up out of the water, the Spirit of the Lord snatched Philip away; the eunuch saw him no more, and went on his way rejoicing. But Philip found himself at Azotus, and as he was passing through the region, he proclaimed the good news to all the towns until he came to Caesarea.

This is the word of the Lord.   Acts 8.26–end

R **Be joyful in God, all the earth;**
[sing the glory of his praise].   cf Psalm 66.1

or

R **Alleluia!**

Bless our God, O you peoples;
make the voice of his praise to be heard,
who holds our souls in life
and suffers not our feet to slip.   R

Come and listen, all you who fear God,
and I will tell you what he has done for my soul.
I called out to him with my mouth
and his praise was on my tongue.   R

If I had nursed evil in my heart,
the Lord would not have heard me,
but in truth God has heard me;
he has heeded the voice of my prayer.   R

Blessed be God, who has not rejected my prayer,
nor withheld his loving mercy from me.   R   *Psalm 66.7–8, 14–end*

Hear the Gospel of our Lord Jesus Christ according to John.

Jesus said to the crowd, 'No one can come to me unless drawn by the Father
who sent me; and I will raise that person up on the last day. It is written in
the prophets, "And they shall all be taught by God." Everyone who has heard
and learned from the Father comes to me. Not that anyone has seen the Father
except the one who is from God; he has seen the Father. Very truly, I tell you,
whoever believes has eternal life. I am the bread of life. Your ancestors ate the
manna in the wilderness, and they died. This is the bread that comes down
from heaven, so that one may eat of it and not die. I am the living bread that
came down from heaven. Whoever eats of this bread will live for ever; and
the bread that I will give for the life of the world is my flesh.'

This is the Gospel of the Lord.   *John 6.44–51*

Third Week of Easter: Friday

Year I and Year 2

A reading from the Acts of the Apostles.

Saul, still breathing threats and murder against the disciples of the Lord, went to the high priest and asked him for letters to the synagogues at Damascus, so that if he found any who belonged to the Way, men or women, he might bring them bound to Jerusalem.

Now as he was going along and approaching Damascus, suddenly a light from heaven flashed around him. He fell to the ground and heard a voice saying to him, 'Saul, Saul, why do you persecute me?' He asked, 'Who are you, Lord?' The reply came, 'I am Jesus, whom you are persecuting. But get up and enter the city, and you will be told what you are to do.' The men who were travelling with him stood speechless because they heard the voice but saw no one. Saul got up from the ground, and though his eyes were open, he could see nothing; so they led him by the hand and brought him into Damascus. For three days he was without sight, and neither ate nor drank.

Now there was a disciple in Damascus named Ananias. The Lord said to him in a vision, 'Ananias.' He answered, 'Here I am, Lord.' The Lord said to him, 'Get up and go to the street called Straight, and at the house of Judas look for a man of Tarsus named Saul. At this moment he is praying, and he has seen in a vision a man named Ananias come in and lay his hands on him so that he might regain his sight.' But Ananias answered, 'Lord, I have heard from many about this man, how much evil he has done to your saints in Jerusalem; and here he has authority from the chief priests to bind all who invoke your name.' But the Lord said to him, 'Go, for he is an instrument whom I have chosen to bring my name before Gentiles and kings and before the people of Israel; I myself will show him how much he must suffer for the sake of my name.'

So Ananias went and entered the house. He laid his hands on Saul and said, 'Brother Saul, the Lord Jesus, who appeared to you on your way here, has sent me so that you may regain your sight and be filled with the Holy Spirit.' And immediately something like scales fell from his eyes, and his sight was restored. Then he got up and was baptized, and after taking some food, he regained his strength.

For several days he was with the disciples in Damascus, and immediately he began to proclaim Jesus in the synagogues, saying, 'He is the Son of God.'

This is the word of the Lord.   *Acts 9.1–20*

R **He will bring God's name to all the nations;
[to kings and to the people of Israel].**   *cf Acts 9.15*

or

R **Alleluia!**

O praise the Lord, all you nations;
praise him, all you peoples.   R

For great is his steadfast love towards us,
and the faithfulness of the Lord endures for ever.   R   *Psalm 117*

Hear the Gospel of our Lord Jesus Christ according to John.

The Jews disputed among themselves, saying, 'How can this man give us his flesh to eat?' So Jesus said to them, 'Very truly, I tell you, unless you eat the flesh of the Son of Man and drink his blood, you have no life in you. Those who eat my flesh and drink my blood have eternal life, and I will raise them up on the last day; for my flesh is true food and my blood is true drink. Those who eat my flesh and drink my blood abide in me, and I in them. Just as the living Father sent me, and I live because of the Father, so whoever eats me will live because of me. This is the bread that came down from heaven, not like that which your ancestors ate, and they died. But the one who eats this bread will live for ever.' He said these things while he was teaching in the synagogue at Capernaum.

This is the Gospel of the Lord.   *John 6.52–59*

Third Week of Easter: Saturday

Year 1 and Year 2

A reading from the Acts of the Apostles.

The church throughout Judea, Galilee, and Samaria had peace and was built up. Living in the fear of the Lord and in the comfort of the Holy Spirit, it increased in numbers.

Now as Peter went here and there among all the believers, he came down also to the saints living in Lydda. There he found a man named Aeneas, who had been bedridden for eight years, for he was paralysed. Peter said to him, 'Aeneas, Jesus Christ heals you; get up and make your bed!' And immediately he got up. And all the residents of Lydda and Sharon saw him and turned to the Lord.

Now in Joppa there was a disciple whose name was Tabitha, which in Greek is Dorcas. She was devoted to good works and acts of charity. At that time she became ill and died. When they had washed her, they laid her in a room upstairs. Since Lydda was near Joppa, the disciples, who heard that Peter was there, sent two men to him with the request, 'Please come to us without delay.' So Peter got up and went with them; and when he arrived, they took him to the room upstairs. All the widows stood beside him, weeping and showing tunics and other clothing that Dorcas had made while she was with them. Peter put all of them outside, and then he knelt down and prayed. He turned to the body and said, 'Tabitha, get up.' Then she opened her eyes, and seeing Peter, she sat up. He gave her his hand and helped her up. Then calling the saints and widows, he showed her to be alive. This became known throughout Joppa, and many believed in the Lord.

This is the word of the Lord. Acts 9.31–42

Responsorial Psalm

R **I will offer to you a sacrifice of thanksgiving:**
  [and call upon the name of the Lord]. Psalm 116.15
  or

R **Alleluia!**

How shall I repay the Lord
for all the benefits he has given to me?
I will lift up the cup of salvation
and call upon the name of the Lord. **R**

I will fulfil my vows to the Lord
in the presence of all his people.
Precious in the sight of the Lord
is the death of his faithful servants. **R**

O Lord, I am your servant,
your servant, the child of your handmaid;
you have freed me from my bonds.
I will offer to you a sacrifice of thanksgiving
and call upon the name of the Lord. **R** Psalm 116.10–15

Hear the Gospel of our Lord Jesus Christ according to John.

When many of the disciples heard Jesus, they said, 'This teaching is difficult; who can accept it?' But Jesus, being aware that his disciples were complaining about it, said to them, 'Does this offend you? Then what if you were to see the Son of Man ascending to where he was before? It is the spirit that gives life; the flesh is useless. The words that I have spoken to you are spirit and life. But among you there are some who do not believe.' For Jesus knew from the first who were the ones that did not believe, and who was the one that would betray him. And he said, 'For this reason I have told you that no one can come to me unless it is granted by the Father.'

Because of this many of his disciples turned back and no longer went about with him. So Jesus asked the twelve, 'Do you also wish to go away?' Simon Peter answered him, 'Lord, to whom can we go? You have the words of eternal life. We have come to believe and know that you are the Holy One of God.'

This is the Gospel of the Lord. John 6.60–69

Fourth Week of Easter: Monday

Year 1 and Year 2

A reading from the Acts of the Apostles.

The apostles and the believers who were in Judea heard that the Gentiles had also accepted the word of God. So when Peter went up to Jerusalem, the circumcised believers criticized him, saying, 'Why did you go to uncircumcised men and eat with them?' Then Peter began to explain it to them, step by step, saying, 'I was in the city of Joppa praying, and in a trance I saw a vision. There was something like a large sheet coming down from heaven, being lowered by its four corners; and it came close to me. As I looked at it closely I saw four-footed animals, beasts of prey, reptiles, and birds of the air. I also heard a voice saying to me, "Get up, Peter; kill and eat." But I replied, "By no means, Lord; for nothing profane or unclean has ever entered my mouth." But a second time the voice answered from heaven, "What God has made clean, you must not call profane." This happened three times; then everything was pulled up again to heaven.

'At that very moment three men, sent to me from Caesarea, arrived at the house where we were. The Spirit told me to go with them and not to make a distinction between them and us. These six brothers also accompanied me, and we entered the man's house. He told us how he had seen the angel standing in his house and saying, "Send to Joppa and bring Simon, who is called Peter; he will give you a message by which you and your entire household will be saved."

'And as I began to speak, the Holy Spirit fell upon them just as it had upon us at the beginning. And I remembered the word of the Lord, how he had said, "John baptized with water, but you will be baptized with the Holy Spirit." If then God gave them the same gift that he gave us when we believed in the Lord Jesus Christ, who was I that I could hinder God?' When they heard this, they were silenced. And they praised God, saying, 'Then God has given even to the Gentiles the repentance that leads to life.'

This is the word of the Lord.   *Acts 11.1–18*

Responsional Psalm

R **My soul is athirst for God, the living God:**
   [the God of my joy and gladness].   *cf Psalm 42.2a, 43.4a*

   or

R **Alleluia!**

As the deer longs for the water brooks,
so longs my soul for you, O God.
My soul is athirst for God, even for the living God;
when shall I come before the presence of God? R

Give judgement for me, O God,
and defend my cause against an ungodly people;
deliver me from the deceitful
and the wicked. **R**

For you are the God of my refuge;
why have you cast me from you,
and why go I so heavily,
while the enemy oppresses me? **R**

O send out your light and your truth,
that they may lead me,
and bring me to your holy hill
and to your dwelling. **R**

That I may go to the altar of God,
to the God of my joy and gladness;
and on the lyre I will give thanks to you,
O God my God. **R**   *Psalm 42.1–2, 43.1–4*

Year B and Year C

Hear the Gospel of our Lord Jesus Christ according to John.

Jesus said to the Pharisees, 'Very truly, I tell you, anyone who does not enter
the sheepfold by the gate but climbs in by another way is a thief and a bandit.
The one who enters by the gate is the shepherd of the sheep. The gatekeeper
opens the gate for him, and the sheep hear his voice. He calls his own sheep
by name and leads them out. When he has brought out all his own, he goes
ahead of them, and the sheep follow him because they know his voice. They
will not follow a stranger, but they will run from him because they do not
know the voice of strangers.' Jesus used this figure of speech with them, but
they did not understand what he was saying to them.

So again Jesus said to them, 'Very truly, I tell you, I am the gate for the
sheep. All who came before me are thieves and bandits; but the sheep did not
listen to them. I am the gate. Whoever enters by me will be saved, and will
come in and go out and find pasture. The thief comes only to steal and kill
and destroy. I came that they may have life, and have it abundantly.'

This is the Gospel of the Lord.   *John 10.1–10*

Hear the Gospel of our Lord Jesus Christ according to John.

Jesus said to the Pharisees, 'I am the good shepherd. The good shepherd lays down his life for the sheep. The hired hand, who is not the shepherd and does not own the sheep, sees the wolf coming and leaves the sheep and runs away – and the wolf snatches them and scatters them. The hired hand runs away because a hired hand does not care for the sheep. I am the good shepherd. I know my own and my own know me, just as the Father knows me and I know the Father. And I lay down my life for the sheep. I have other sheep that do not belong to this fold. I must bring them also, and they will listen to my voice. So there will be one flock, one shepherd. For this reason the Father loves me, because I lay down my life in order to take it up again. No one takes it from me, but I lay it down of my own accord. I have power to lay it down, and I have power to take it up again. I have received this command from my Father.'

This is the Gospel of the Lord. John 10.11–18

Fourth Week of Easter: Tuesday

Year 1 and Year 2

A reading from the Acts of the Apostles.

Those who were scattered because of the persecution that took place over Stephen travelled as far as Phoenicia, Cyprus, and Antioch, and they spoke the word to no one except Jews. But among them were some men of Cyprus and Cyrene who, on coming to Antioch, spoke to the Hellenists also, proclaiming the Lord Jesus. The hand of the Lord was with them, and a great number became believers and turned to the Lord.

News of this came to the ears of the church in Jerusalem, and they sent Barnabas to Antioch. When he came and saw the grace of God, he rejoiced, and he exhorted them all to remain faithful to the Lord with steadfast devotion; for he was a good man, full of the Holy Spirit and of faith. And a great many people were brought to the Lord. Then Barnabas went to Tarsus to look for Saul, and when he had found him, he brought him to Antioch. So it was that for an entire year they associated with the church and taught a great many people, and it was in Antioch that the disciples were first called 'Christians'.

This is the word of the Lord. Acts 11.19–26

Responsorial Psalm

R **Glorious things are spoken of you,**
   Zion, city of our God.   Psalm 87.2

   or

R **Alleluia!**

His foundation is on the holy mountains.
The Lord loves the gates of Zion
more than all the dwellings of Jacob.
Glorious things are spoken of you,
Zion, city of our God.   R

I record Egypt and Babylon as those who know me;
behold Philistia, Tyre and Ethiopia:
in Zion were they born.
And of Zion it shall be said, 'Each one was born in her,
and the Most High himself has established her.'   R

The Lord will record as he writes up the peoples,
'This one also was born there.'
And as they dance they shall sing,
'All my fresh springs are in you.'   R   Psalm 87

Hear the Gospel of our Lord Jesus Christ according to John.

At that time the festival of the Dedication took place in Jerusalem. It was
winter, and Jesus was walking in the temple, in the portico of Solomon. So
the Jews gathered around him and said to him, 'How long will you keep us in
suspense? If you are the Messiah, tell us plainly.' Jesus answered, 'I have told
you, and you do not believe. The works that I do in my Father's name testify
to me; but you do not believe, because you do not belong to my sheep. My
sheep hear my voice. I know them, and they follow me. I give them eternal
life, and they will never perish. No one will snatch them out of my hand.
What my Father has given me is greater than all else, and no one can snatch
it out of the Father's hand. The Father and I are one.'

This is the Gospel of the Lord.   John 10.22–30

Fourth Week of Easter: Wednesday

Year 1 and Year 2

A reading from the Acts of the Apostles.

The word of God continued to advance and gain adherents. Then after
completing their mission Barnabas and Saul returned to Jerusalem and brought
with them John, whose other name was Mark.   →

Now in the church at Antioch there were prophets and teachers: Barnabas, Simeon who was called Niger, Lucius of Cyrene, Manaen a member of the court of Herod the ruler, and Saul. While they were worshipping the Lord and fasting, the Holy Spirit said, 'Set apart for me Barnabas and Saul for the work to which I have called them.' Then after fasting and praying they laid their hands on them and sent them off.

So, being sent out by the Holy Spirit, they went down to Seleucia; and from there they sailed to Cyprus. When they arrived at Salamis, they proclaimed the word of God in the synagogues of the Jews. And they had John also to assist them.

This is the word of the Lord.   *Acts 12.24 – 13.5*

Responsorial Psalm

R* **Let the peoples praise you, O God,**
   [let all the peoples praise you].   *Psalm 67.3, 5*

   or

R **Alleluia!**

God be gracious to us and bless us
and make his face to shine upon us,
that your way may be known upon earth,
your saving power among all nations.   **R***

O let the nations rejoice and be glad,
for you will judge the peoples righteously
and govern the nations upon earth.   **R***

Then shall the earth bring forth her increase,
and God, our own God, will bless us.
God will bless us,
and all the ends of the earth shall fear him.   **R**   *Psalm 67*

Hear the Gospel of our Lord Jesus Christ according to John.

Jesus cried aloud: 'Whoever believes in me believes not in me but in him who sent me. And whoever sees me sees him who sent me. I have come as light into the world, so that everyone who believes in me should not remain in the darkness. I do not judge anyone who hears my words and does not keep them, for I came not to judge the world, but to save the world. The one who rejects me and does not receive my word has a judge; on the last day the word that I have spoken will serve as judge, for I have not spoken on my own, but the Father who sent me has himself given me a commandment about what to say and what to speak. And I know that his commandment is eternal life. What I speak, therefore, I speak just as the Father has told me.'

This is the Gospel of the Lord.   *John 12.44—end*

Fourth Week of Easter: Thursday

Year 1 and Year 2

A reading from the Acts of the Apostles.

Paul and his companions set sail from Paphos and came to Perga in Pamphylia. John, however, left them and returned to Jerusalem; but they went on from Perga and came to Antioch in Pisidia. And on the sabbath day they went into the synagogue and sat down. After the reading of the law and the prophets, the officials of the synagogue sent them a message, saying, 'Brothers, if you have any word of exhortation for the people, give it.' So Paul stood up and with a gesture began to speak:

'You Israelites, and others who fear God, listen. The God of this people Israel chose our ancestors and made the people great during their stay in the land of Egypt, and with uplifted arm he led them out of it. For about forty years he put up with them in the wilderness. After he had destroyed seven nations in the land of Canaan, he gave them their land as an inheritance for about four hundred and fifty years. After that he gave them judges until the time of the prophet Samuel. Then they asked for a king; and God gave them Saul son of Kish, a man of the tribe of Benjamin, who reigned for forty years. When he had removed him, he made David their king. In his testimony about him he said, "I have found David, son of Jesse, to be a man after my heart, who will carry out all my wishes." Of this man's posterity God has brought to Israel a Saviour, Jesus, as he promised; before his coming John had already proclaimed a baptism of repentance to all the people of Israel. And as John was finishing his work, he said, "What do you suppose that I am? I am not he. No, but one is coming after me; I am not worthy to untie the thong of the sandals on his feet." '

This is the word of the Lord.   *Acts 13.13–25*

Responsorial Psalm

R   **I shall sing for ever of your love, O Lord.**   *cf Psalm 89.1*

   or

R   **Alleluia!**

My song shall be always of the loving-kindness of the Lord:
with my mouth will I proclaim your faithfulness
throughout all generations.
I will declare that your love is established for ever;
you have set your faithfulness as firm as the heavens.   **R**

'I have found David my servant;
with my holy oil have I anointed him.
My hand shall hold him fast
and my arm shall strengthen him.   **R**   →

'No enemy shall deceive him,
nor any wicked person afflict him.
I will strike down his foes before his face
and beat down those that hate him.   R

R   **I shall sing for ever of your love, O Lord.**

or

R   **Alleluia!**

'My truth also and my steadfast love shall be with him,
and in my name shall his head be exalted.
I will set his dominion upon the sea
and his right hand upon the rivers.
He shall call to me, "You are my Father,
my God, and the rock of my salvation." '   R   Psalm 89.1–2, 20–26

Hear the Gospel of our Lord Jesus Christ according to John.

After he had washed the disciples' feet, Jesus said, 'Very truly, I tell you, servants are not greater than their master, nor are messengers greater than the one
who sent them. If you know these things, you are blessed if you do them. I
am not speaking of all of you; I know whom I have chosen. But it is to fulfil
the scripture, "The one who ate my bread has lifted his heel against me." I tell
you this now, before it occurs, so that when it does occur, you may believe
that I am he. Very truly, I tell you, whoever receives one whom I send receives
me; and whoever receives me receives him who sent me.'

This is the Gospel of the Lord.   John 13.16–20

Fourth Week of Easter: Friday

Year 1 and Year 2

A reading from the Acts of the Apostles.

Paul said in the synagogue, 'My brothers, you descendants of Abraham's
family, and others who fear God, to us the message of this salvation has
been sent. Because the residents of Jerusalem and their leaders did not
recognize him or understand the words of the prophets that are read every
sabbath, they fulfilled those words by condemning him. Even though they
found no cause for a sentence of death, they asked Pilate to have him killed.
When they had carried out everything that was written about him, they
took him down from the tree and laid him in a tomb. But God raised him
from the dead; and for many days he appeared to those who came up
with him from Galilee to Jerusalem, and they are now his witnesses to the
people. And we bring you the good news that what God promised to our

ancestors he has fulfilled for us, their children, by raising Jesus; as also it is written in the second psalm,
"You are my Son;
today I have begotten you." '

This is the word of the Lord.   Acts 13.26–33

Responsorial Psalm

R **You are my Son;
this day have I begotten you.**   Psalm 2.7b

    or

R **Alleluia!**

Why are the nations in tumult,
and why do the peoples devise a vain plot?
The kings of the earth rise up,
and the rulers take counsel together,
against the Lord and against his anointed.   R

'Let us break their bonds asunder
and cast away their cords from us.'
He who dwells in heaven shall laugh them to scorn;
the Lord shall have them in derision.   R

Then shall he speak to them in his wrath
and terrify them in his fury:
'Yet have I set my king
upon my holy hill of Zion.'   R

I will proclaim the decree of the Lord;
he said to me: 'You are my Son; this day have I begotten you.
Ask of me and I will give you the nations for your inheritance
and the ends of the earth for your possession.   R

'You shall break them with a rod of iron
and dash them in pieces like a potter's vessel.'
Now therefore be wise, O kings;
be prudent, you judges of the earth.   R

Serve the Lord with fear, and with trembling kiss his feet,
lest he be angry and you perish from the way,
for his wrath is quickly kindled.
Happy are all they who take refuge in him.   R   Psalm 2

Hear the Gospel of our Lord Jesus Christ according to John.

Jesus said to his disciples, 'Do not let your hearts be troubled. Believe in God, believe also in me. In my Father's house there are many dwelling-places. If it were not so, would I have told you that I go to prepare a place for you? And if I go and prepare a place for you, I will come again and will take you to myself, so that where I am, there you may be also. And you know the way to the place where I am going.' Thomas said to him, 'Lord, we do not know where you are going. How can we know the way?' Jesus said to him, 'I am the way, and the truth, and the life. No one comes to the Father except through me.'

This is the Gospel of the Lord.   John 14.1–6

Fourth Week of Easter: Saturday

Year 1 and Year 2

A reading from the Acts of the Apostles.

The next sabbath almost the whole city of Antioch gathered to hear the word of the Lord. But when the Jews saw the crowds, they were filled with jealousy; and blaspheming, they contradicted what was spoken by Paul. Then both Paul and Barnabas spoke out boldly, saying, 'It was necessary that the word of God should be spoken first to you. Since you reject it and judge yourselves to be unworthy of eternal life, we are now turning to the Gentiles. For so the Lord has commanded us, saying,

"I have set you to be a light for the Gentiles,
so that you may bring salvation to the ends of the earth." '

When the Gentiles heard this, they were glad and praised the word of the Lord; and as many as had been destined for eternal life became believers. Thus the word of the Lord spread throughout the region. But the Jews incited the devout women of high standing and the leading men of the city, and stirred up persecution against Paul and Barnabas, and drove them out of their region. So they shook the dust off their feet in protest against them, and went to Iconium. And the disciples were filled with joy and with the Holy Spirit.

This is the word of the Lord.   Acts 13.44–end

R* **Sound praises to the Lord, all the earth;**
   [break into song and make music].   cf Psalm 98.5

   or

R **Alleluia!**

Sing to the Lord a new song,
for he has done marvellous things.
His own right hand and his holy arm
have won for him the victory.   **R**

The Lord has made known his salvation;
his deliverance has he openly shown
in the sight of the nations.   **R**

He has remembered his mercy and faithfulness
towards the house of Israel,
and all the ends of the earth have seen
the salvation of our God.   **R***   Psalm 98.1–5

Hear the Gospel of our Lord Jesus Christ according to John.

Jesus said to his disciples, 'If you know me, you will know my Father also.
From now on you do know him and have seen him.'
     Philip said to him, 'Lord, show us the Father, and we will be satisfied.'
Jesus said to him, 'Have I been with you all this time, Philip, and you still
do not know me? Whoever has seen me has seen the Father. How can you
say, "Show us the Father"? Do you not believe that I am in the Father and
the Father is in me? The words that I say to you I do not speak on my own;
but the Father who dwells in me does his works. Believe me that I am in the
Father and the Father is in me; but if you do not, then believe me because
of the works themselves.
     'Very truly, I tell you, the one who believes in me will also do the works
that I do and, in fact, will do greater works than these, because I am going to
the Father. I will do whatever you ask in my name, so that the Father may be
glorified in the Son. If in my name you ask me for anything, I will do it.'

This is the Gospel of the Lord.   John 14.7–14

Fifth Week of Easter: Monday

Year 1 and Year 2

A reading from the Acts of the Apostles.

When an attempt was made by both Gentiles and Jews, with their rulers, to maltreat the apostles and to stone them, they learned of it and fled to Lystra and Derbe, cities of Lycaonia, and to the surrounding country; and there they continued proclaiming the good news.

In Lystra there was a man sitting who could not use his feet and had never walked, for he had been crippled from birth. He listened to Paul as he was speaking. And Paul, looking at him intently and seeing that he had faith to be healed, said in a loud voice, 'Stand upright on your feet.' And the man sprang up and began to walk. When the crowds saw what Paul had done, they shouted in the Lycaonian language, 'The gods have come down to us in human form!' Barnabas they called Zeus, and Paul they called Hermes, because he was the chief speaker. The priest of Zeus, whose temple was just outside the city, brought oxen and garlands to the gates; he and the crowds wanted to offer sacrifice. When the apostles Barnabas and Paul heard of it, they tore their clothes and rushed out into the crowd, shouting, 'Friends, why are you doing this? We are mortals just like you, and we bring you good news, that you should turn from these worthless things to the living God, who made the heaven and the earth and the sea and all that is in them. In past generations he allowed all the nations to follow their own ways; yet he has not left himself without a witness in doing good – giving you rains from heaven and fruitful seasons, and filling you with food and your hearts with joy.' Even with these words, they scarcely restrained the crowds from offering sacrifice to them.

This is the word of the Lord.   *Acts 14.5–18*

Responsorial Psalm

R* **Give thanks to the Lord, for he is good;
[his mercy endures for ever].**   *Psalm 118.1*

or

R **Alleluia!**

Let Israel now proclaim,
'His mercy endures for ever.'
Let the house of Aaron now proclaim,
'His mercy endures for ever.'   **R**

The Lord is my strength and my song,
and he has become my salvation.
Joyful shouts of salvation
sound from the tents of the righteous.   **R**   *Psalm 118.1–3, 14–15*

Hear the Gospel of our Lord Jesus Christ according to John.

Jesus said to his disciples, 'They who have my commandments and keep them are those who love me; and those who love me will be loved by my Father, and I will love them and reveal myself to them.'

Judas (not Iscariot) said to him, 'Lord, how is it that you will reveal yourself to us, and not to the world?' Jesus answered him, 'Those who love me will keep my word, and my Father will love them, and we will come to them and make our home with them. Whoever does not love me does not keep my words; and the word that you hear is not mine, but is from the Father who sent me.

'I have said these things to you while I am still with you. But the Advocate, the Holy Spirit, whom the Father will send in my name, will teach you everything, and remind you of all that I have said to you.'

This is the Gospel of the Lord.   John 14.21–26

Fifth Week of Easter: Tuesday

Year 1 and Year 2

A reading from the Acts of the Apostles.

Jews came from Antioch and Iconium and won over the crowds. Then they stoned Paul and dragged him out of the city, supposing that he was dead. But when the disciples surrounded him, he got up and went into the city. The next day he went on with Barnabas to Derbe.

After they had proclaimed the good news to that city and had made many disciples, they returned to Lystra, then on to Iconium and Antioch. There they strengthened the souls of the disciples and encouraged them to continue in the faith, saying, 'It is through many persecutions that we must enter the kingdom of God.' And after they had appointed elders for them in each church, with prayer and fasting they entrusted them to the Lord in whom they had come to believe.

Then they passed through Pisidia and came to Pamphylia. When they had spoken the word in Perga, they went down to Attalia. From there they sailed back to Antioch, where they had been commended to the grace of God for the work that they had completed. When they arrived, they called the church together and related all that God had done with them, and how he had opened a door of faith for the Gentiles. And they stayed there with the disciples for some time.

This is the word of the Lord.   Acts 14.19–end

Responsorial Psalm

R* **The Lord is righteous in all his ways
and loving in all his works.**

Psalm 145.18

or

R **Alleluia!**

All your works praise you, O Lord,
and your faithful servants bless you.
They tell of the glory of your kingdom
and speak of your mighty power. **R**

To make known to all peoples your mighty acts
and the glorious splendour of your kingdom.
Your kingdom is an everlasting kingdom;
your dominion endures throughout all ages. **R**

The Lord is sure in all his words
and faithful in all his deeds.
The Lord upholds all those who fall
and lifts up all those who are bowed down. **R**

The eyes of all wait upon you, O Lord,
and you give them their food in due season.
You open wide your hand
and fill all things living with plenty. **R***

The Lord is near to those who call upon him,
to all who call upon him faithfully.
He fulfils the desire of those who fear him;
he hears their cry and saves them. **R**

The Lord watches over those who love him,
but all the wicked shall he destroy.
My mouth shall speak the praise of the Lord,
and let all flesh bless his holy name for ever and ever. **R**

Psalm 145.10—end

Hear the Gospel of our Lord Jesus Christ according to John.

Jesus said to his disciples, 'Peace I leave with you; my peace I give to you. I do not give to you as the world gives. Do not let your hearts be troubled, and do not let them be afraid. You heard me say to you, "I am going away, and I am coming to you." If you loved me, you would rejoice that I am going to the Father, because the Father is greater than I. And now I have told you this before it occurs, so that when it does occur, you may believe. I will no longer talk much with you, for the ruler of this world is coming. He has no power over me; but I do as the Father has commanded me, so that the world may know that I love the Father.'

This is the Gospel of the Lord.

John 14.27—end

Fifth Week of Easter: Wednesday

Year 1 and Year 2

A reading from the Acts of the Apostles.

Certain individuals came down from Judea and were teaching the brothers, 'Unless you are circumcised according to the custom of Moses, you cannot be saved.' And after Paul and Barnabas had no small dissension and debate with them, Paul and Barnabas and some of the others were appointed to go up to Jerusalem to discuss this question with the apostles and the elders. So they were sent on their way by the church, and as they passed through both Phoenicia and Samaria, they reported the conversion of the Gentiles, and brought great joy to all the believers. When they came to Jerusalem, they were welcomed by the church and the apostles and the elders, and they reported all that God had done with them. But some believers who belonged to the sect of the Pharisees stood up and said, 'It is necessary for them to be circumcised and ordered to keep the law of Moses.' The apostles and the elders met together to consider this matter.

This is the word of the Lord.   *Acts 15.1–6*

Responsorial Psalm

R **[I was glad when they said to me:]**
   Let us go to the house of the Lord.   *Psalm 122.1*

   or

R **Alleluia!**

I was glad when they said to me,
'Let us go to the house of the Lord.'
And now our feet are standing
within your gates, O Jerusalem.   **R**

Jerusalem, built as a city
that is at unity in itself.
Thither the tribes go up,
the tribes of the Lord.   **R**

As is decreed for Israel,
to give thanks to the name of the Lord.
For there are set the thrones of judgement,
the thrones of the house of David.   **R**   *Psalm 122.1–5*

Hear the Gospel of our Lord Jesus Christ according to John.

Jesus said to his disciples, 'I am the true vine, and my Father is the vine-grower. He removes every branch in me that bears no fruit. Every branch that bears fruit he prunes to make it bear more fruit. You have already been cleansed by the word that I have spoken to you. Abide in me as I abide in you. Just as the branch cannot bear fruit by itself unless it abides in the vine, neither can   →

you unless you abide in me. I am the vine, you are the branches. Those who abide in me and I in them bear much fruit, because apart from me you can do nothing. Whoever does not abide in me is thrown away like a branch and withers; such branches are gathered, thrown into the fire, and burned. If you abide in me, and my words abide in you, ask for whatever you wish, and it will be done for you. My Father is glorified by this, that you bear much fruit and become my disciples.'

This is the Gospel of the Lord.   John 15.1–8

Fifth Week of Easter: Thursday

Year I and Year 2

A reading from the Acts of the Apostles.

After there had been much debate, Peter stood up and said to the apostles and elders, 'My brothers, you know that in the early days God made a choice among you, that I should be the one through whom the Gentiles would hear the message of the good news and become believers. And God, who knows the human heart, testified to them by giving them the Holy Spirit, just as he did to us; and in cleansing their hearts by faith he has made no distinction between them and us. Now therefore why are you putting God to the test by placing on the neck of the disciples a yoke that neither our ancestors nor we have been able to bear? On the contrary, we believe that we will be saved through the grace of the Lord Jesus, just as they will.'

The whole assembly kept silence, and listened to Barnabas and Paul as they told of all the signs and wonders that God had done through them among the Gentiles. After they finished speaking, James replied, 'My brothers, listen to me. Simeon has related how God first looked favourably on the Gentiles, to take from among them a people for his name. This agrees with the words of the prophets, as it is written,
"After this I will return,
and I will rebuild the dwelling of David, which has fallen;
from its ruins I will rebuild it,
and I will set it up,
so that all other peoples may seek the Lord –
even all the Gentiles over whom my name has been called.
Thus says the Lord,
who has been making these things known from long ago."
'Therefore I have reached the decision that we should not trouble those Gentiles who are turning to God, but we should write to them to abstain only from things polluted by idols and from fornication and from whatever has been strangled and from blood. For in every city, for generations past, Moses has had those who proclaim him, for he has been read aloud every sabbath in the synagogues.'

This is the word of the Lord.   Acts 15.7–21

R **Sing to the Lord a new song;**
   [sing to the Lord, all the earth].   *Psalm* 96.1
   or

R **Alleluia!**

Sing to the Lord a new song;
sing to the Lord, all the earth.
Sing to the Lord and bless his name;
tell out his salvation from day to day. R

Declare his glory among the nations
and his wonders among all peoples.
Ascribe to the Lord, you families of the peoples;
ascribe to the Lord honour and strength. R

Ascribe to the Lord the honour due to his name;
bring offerings and come into his courts.
O worship the Lord in the beauty of holiness;
let the whole earth tremble before him. R

Tell it out among the nations that the Lord is king.
He has made the world so firm that it cannot be moved;
he will judge the peoples with equity. R   *Psalm* 96.1–3, 7–10

Hear the Gospel of our Lord Jesus Christ according to John.

Jesus said to his disciples, 'As the Father has loved me, so I have loved you;
abide in my love. If you keep my commandments, you will abide in my love,
just as I have kept my Father's commandments and abide in his love. I have
said these things to you so that my joy may be in you, and that your joy may
be complete.'

This is the Gospel of the Lord.   *John* 15.9–11

Fifth Week of Easter: Friday

Year 1 and Year 2

A reading from the Acts of the Apostles.

The apostles and the elders, with the consent of the whole church, decided to
choose men from among their members and to send them to Antioch with
Paul and Barnabas. They sent Judas called Barsabbas, and Silas, leaders among
the brothers, with the following letter:
   'The brothers, both the apostles and the elders, to the believers of Gentile
origin in Antioch and Syria and Cilicia, greetings. Since we have heard that
certain persons who have gone out from us, though with no instructions →

from us, have said things to disturb you and have unsettled your minds, we have decided unanimously to choose representatives and send them to you, along with our beloved Barnabas and Paul, who have risked their lives for the sake of our Lord Jesus Christ. We have therefore sent Judas and Silas, who themselves will tell you the same things by word of mouth. For it has seemed good to the Holy Spirit and to us to impose on you no further burden than these essentials: that you abstain from what has been sacrificed to idols and from blood and from what is strangled and from fornication. If you keep yourselves from these, you will do well. Farewell.'

So they were sent off and went down to Antioch. When they gathered the congregation together, they delivered the letter. When its members read it, they rejoiced at the exhortation.

This is the word of the Lord. Acts 15.22–31

Responsorial Psalm

R* **O God, be exalted above the heavens,**
[let your glory be over all the earth]. cf Psalm 57.12
   or

R **Alleluia!**

My heart is ready, O God, my heart is ready;
I will sing and give you praise.
Awake, my soul; awake, harp and lyre,
that I may awaken the dawn.   **R**

I will give you thanks, O Lord, among the peoples;
I will sing praise to you among the nations.
For your loving-kindness is as high as the heavens,
and your faithfulness reaches to the clouds.   **R*** Psalm 57.8–end

Hear the Gospel of our Lord Jesus Christ according to John.

Jesus said to his disciples, 'This is my commandment, that you love one another as I have loved you. No one has greater love than this, to lay down one's life for one's friends. You are my friends if you do what I command you. I do not call you servants any longer, because the servant does not know what the master is doing; but I have called you friends, because I have made known to you everything that I have heard from my Father. You did not choose me but I chose you. And I appointed you to go and bear fruit, fruit that will last, so that the Father will give you whatever you ask him in my name. I am giving you these commands so that you may love one another.'

This is the Gospel of the Lord. John 15.12–17

Fifth Week of Easter: Saturday

Year I and Year 2

A reading from the Acts of the Apostles.

Paul went on to Derbe and to Lystra, where there was a disciple named Timothy, the son of a Jewish woman who was a believer; but his father was a Greek. He was well spoken of by the believers in Lystra and Iconium. Paul wanted Timothy to accompany him; and he took him and had him circumcised because of the Jews who were in those places, for they all knew that his father was a Greek. As they went from town to town, they delivered to them for observance the decisions that had been reached by the apostles and elders who were in Jerusalem. So the churches were strengthened in the faith and increased in numbers daily.

They went through the region of Phrygia and Galatia, having been forbidden by the Holy Spirit to speak the word in Asia. When they had come opposite Mysia, they attempted to go into Bithynia, but the Spirit of Jesus did not allow them; so, passing by Mysia, they went down to Troas. During the night Paul had a vision: there stood a man of Macedonia pleading with him and saying, 'Come over to Macedonia and help us.' When he had seen the vision, we immediately tried to cross over to Macedonia, being convinced that God had called us to proclaim the good news to them.

This is the word of the Lord.   Acts 16.1–10

Responsorial Psalm

R   **Be joyful in the Lord, all the earth:**
    [give thanks and bless his name].   cf Psalm 100.1a, 3b

    or

R   **Alleluia!**

O be joyful in the Lord, all the earth;
serve the Lord with gladness
and come before his presence with a song.   **R**

Know that the Lord is God;
it is he that has made us and we are his;
we are his people and the sheep of his pasture.   **R**

Enter his gates with thanksgiving
and his courts with praise;
give thanks to him and bless his name.   **R**

For the Lord is gracious;
his steadfast love is everlasting,
and his faithfulness endures from generation to generation.   **R**

                                                                Psalm 100

Hear the Gospel of our Lord Jesus Christ according to John.

Jesus said to his disciples, 'If the world hates you, be aware that it hated me before it hated you. If you belonged to the world, the world would love you as its own. Because you do not belong to the world, but I have chosen you out of the world – therefore the world hates you. Remember the word that I said to you, "Servants are not greater than their master." If they persecuted me, they will persecute you; if they kept my word, they will keep yours also. But they will do all these things to you on account of my name, because they do not know him who sent me.'

This is the Gospel of the Lord.   John 15.18–21

Sixth Week of Easter: Monday

Year 1 and Year 2

A reading from the Acts of the Apostles.

We set sail from Troas and took a straight course to Samothrace, the following day to Neapolis, and from there to Philippi, which is a leading city of the district of Macedonia and a Roman colony. We remained in this city for some days. On the sabbath day we went outside the gate by the river, where we supposed there was a place of prayer; and we sat down and spoke to the women who had gathered there. A certain woman named Lydia, a worshipper of God, was listening to us; she was from the city of Thyatira and a dealer in purple cloth. The Lord opened her heart to listen eagerly to what was said by Paul. When she and her household were baptized, she urged us, saying, 'If you have judged me to be faithful to the Lord, come and stay at my home.' And she prevailed upon us.

This is the word of the Lord.   Acts 16.11–15

Responsorial Psalm

R* **Sing to the Lord a new song:**
     [sing his praise in the congregation of the faithful].   Psalm 149.1
     or

R   **Alleluia!**

Let Israel rejoice in their maker;
let the children of Zion be joyful in their king.
Let them praise his name in the dance;
let them sing praise to him with timbrel and lyre.   **R**

For the Lord has pleasure in his people
and adorns the poor with salvation.
Let the faithful be joyful in glory;
let them rejoice in their ranks.   **R**   Psalm 149.1–5

Hear the Gospel of our Lord Jesus Christ according to John.

Jesus said to his disciples, 'When the Advocate comes, whom I will send to you from the Father, the Spirit of truth who comes from the Father, he will testify on my behalf. You also are to testify because you have been with me from the beginning.

'I have said these things to you to keep you from stumbling. They will put you out of the synagogues. Indeed, an hour is coming when those who kill you will think that by doing so they are offering worship to God. And they will do this because they have not known the Father or me. But I have said these things to you so that when their hour comes you may remember that I told you about them. I did not say these things to you from the beginning, because I was with you.'

This is the Gospel of the Lord.   John 15.26 – 16.4

Sixth Week of Easter: Tuesday

Year 1 and Year 2

A reading from the Acts of the Apostles.

The crowd joined in attacking Paul and Silas, and the magistrates had them stripped of their clothing and ordered them to be beaten with rods. After they had given them a severe flogging, they threw them into prison and ordered the jailer to keep them securely. Following these instructions, he put them in the innermost cell and fastened their feet in the stocks.

About midnight Paul and Silas were praying and singing hymns to God, and the prisoners were listening to them. Suddenly there was an earthquake, so violent that the foundations of the prison were shaken; and immediately all the doors were opened and everyone's chains were unfastened. When the jailer woke up and saw the prison doors wide open, he drew his sword and was about to kill himself, since he supposed that the prisoners had escaped. But Paul shouted in a loud voice, 'Do not harm yourself, for we are all here.' The jailer called for lights, and rushing in, he fell down trembling before Paul and Silas. Then he brought them outside and said, 'Sirs, what must I do to be saved?' They answered, 'Believe on the Lord Jesus, and you will be saved, you and your household.' They spoke the word of the Lord to him and to all who were in his house. At the same hour of the night he took them and washed their wounds; then he and his entire family were baptized without delay. He brought them up into the house and set food before them; and he and his entire household rejoiced that he had become a believer in God.

This is the word of the Lord. Acts 16.22–34

Responsorial Psalm

R **Your loving-kindness, O Lord, endures for ever;**
  [forsake not the work of your hands]. Psalm 138.8b

  or

R **Alleluia!**

I will give thanks to you, O Lord, with my whole heart;
before the gods will I sing praise to you.
I will bow down towards your holy temple and praise your name,
because of your love and faithfulness.   R

For you have glorified your name
and your word above all things.
In the day that I called to you, you answered me;
you put new strength in my soul.   R

All the kings of the earth shall praise you, O Lord,
for they have heard the words of your mouth.
They shall sing of the ways of the Lord,
that great is the glory of the Lord. **R**

Though the Lord be high,
he watches over the lowly;
as for the proud,
he regards them from afar. **R**

Though I walk in the midst of trouble,
you will preserve me;
you will stretch forth your hand against the fury of my enemies;
your right hand will save me. **R**

The Lord shall make good his purpose for me;
your loving-kindness, O Lord, endures for ever;
forsake not the work of your hands. **R**   Psalm 138

Hear the Gospel of our Lord Jesus Christ according to John.

Jesus said to his disciples, 'Now I am going to him who sent me; yet none of
you asks me, "Where are you going?" But because I have said these things to
you, sorrow has filled your hearts. Nevertheless, I tell you the truth: it is to
your advantage that I go away, for if I do not go away, the Advocate will not
come to you; but if I go, I will send him to you. And when he comes, he will
prove the world wrong about sin and righteousness and judgement: about sin,
because they do not believe in me; about righteousness, because I am going
to the Father and you will see me no longer; about judgement, because the
ruler of this world has been condemned.'

This is the Gospel of the Lord.   John 16.5–11

Sixth Week of Easter: Wednesday

Year 1 and Year 2

A reading from the Acts of the Apostles.

Those who conducted Paul brought him as far as Athens; and after receiving
instructions to have Silas and Timothy join him as soon as possible, they
left him.

Then Paul stood in front of the Areopagus and said, 'Athenians, I see how
extremely religious you are in every way. For as I went through the city and
looked carefully at the objects of your worship, I found among them an altar
with the inscription, "To an unknown god." What therefore you worship as
unknown, this I proclaim to you. The God who made the world and everything
in it, he who is Lord of heaven and earth, does not live in shrines made by   →

human hands, nor is he served by human hands, as though he needed anything, since he himself gives to all mortals life and breath and all things. From one ancestor he made all nations to inhabit the whole earth, and he allotted the times of their existence and the boundaries of the places where they would live, so that they would search for God and perhaps grope for him and find him — though indeed he is not far from each one of us. For "In him we live and move and have our being"; as even some of your own poets have said,
    "For we too are his offspring."
Since we are God's offspring, we ought not to think that the deity is like gold, or silver, or stone, an image formed by the art and imagination of mortals. While God has overlooked the times of human ignorance, now he commands all people everywhere to repent, because he has fixed a day on which he will have the world judged in righteousness by a man whom he has appointed, and of this he has given assurance to all by raising him from the dead.'

When they heard of the resurrection of the dead, some scoffed; but others said, 'We will hear you again about this.' At that point Paul left them. But some of them joined him and became believers, including Dionysius the Areopagite and a woman named Damaris, and others with them. After this Paul left Athens and went to Corinth.

This is the word of the Lord.   *Acts 17.15, 22 — 18.1*

Responsorial Psalm

R **The name of the Lord is exalted,
    [his splendour above earth and heaven].**   cf *Psalm 148.13*
        or

R **Alleluia!**

Praise the Lord from the heavens;
praise him in the heights.
Praise him, all you his angels;
praise him, all his host.   **R**

Kings of the earth and all peoples,
princes and all rulers of the world;
young men and women,
old and young together;
let them praise the name of the Lord.   **R**

For his name only is exalted,
his splendour above earth and heaven.
He has raised up the horn of his people
and praise for all his faithful servants,
the children of Israel, a people who are near him.   **R**

Psalm 148.1–2, 11–end

Hear the Gospel of our Lord Jesus Christ according to John.

Jesus said to his disciples, 'I still have many things to say to you, but you cannot bear them now. When the Spirit of truth comes, he will guide you into all the truth; for he will not speak on his own, but will speak whatever he hears, and he will declare to you the things that are to come. He will glorify me, because he will take what is mine and declare it to you. All that the Father has is mine. For this reason I said that he will take what is mine and declare it to you.'

This is the Gospel of the Lord.   John 16.12–15

Sixth Week of Easter: Thursday – Ascension Day

Provision is made for Ascension Day in the lectionary for Principal Feasts.

Sixth Week of Easter: Friday

Year 1 and Year 2

A reading from the Acts of the Apostles.

One night the Lord said to Paul in a vision, 'Do not be afraid, but speak and do not be silent; for I am with you, and no one will lay a hand on you to harm you, for there are many in this city who are my people.' He stayed there for a year and six months, teaching the word of God among them.

But when Gallio was proconsul of Achaia, the Jews made a united attack on Paul and brought him before the tribunal. They said, 'This man is persuading people to worship God in ways that are contrary to the law.' Just as Paul was about to speak, Gallio said to the Jews, 'If it were a matter of crime or serious villainy, I would be justified in accepting the complaint of you Jews; but since it is a matter of questions about words and names and your own law, see to it yourselves; I do not wish to be a judge of these matters.' And he dismissed them from the tribunal. Then all of them seized Sosthenes, the official of the synagogue, and beat him in front of the tribunal. But Gallio paid no attention to any of these things.

After staying there for a considerable time, Paul said farewell to the believers and sailed for Syria, accompanied by Priscilla and Aquila. At Cenchreae he had his hair cut, for he was under a vow.

This is the word of the Lord.   Acts 18.9–18

Responsorial Psalm

R **God has gone up with a merry noise,**
 [the Lord with the sound of the trumpet].   *Psalm 47.5*

 or

R **Alleluia!**

Clap your hands together, all you peoples;
O sing to God with shouts of joy.
For the Lord Most High is to be feared;
he is the great King over all the earth. R

He subdued the peoples under us
and the nations under our feet.
He has chosen our heritage for us,
the pride of Jacob, whom he loves. R

God has gone up with a merry noise,
the Lord with the sound of the trumpet.
O sing praises to God, sing praises;
sing praises to our King, sing praises. R   *Psalm 47.1–6*

Hear the Gospel of our Lord Jesus Christ according to John.

Jesus said to his disciples, 'Very truly, I tell you, you will weep and mourn,
but the world will rejoice; you will have pain, but your pain will turn into joy.
When a woman is in labour, she has pain, because her hour has come. But
when her child is born, she no longer remembers the anguish because of the
joy of having brought a human being into the world. So you have pain now;
but I will see you again, and your hearts will rejoice, and no one will take your
joy from you. On that day you will ask nothing of me. Very truly, I tell you, if
you ask anything of the Father in my name, he will give it to you.'

This is the Gospel of the Lord.   *John 16.20–23*

Sixth Week of Easter: Saturday

Year 1 and Year 2

A reading from the Acts of the Apostles.

When Paul had landed at Caesarea, he went up to Jerusalem and greeted the
church, and then went down to Antioch. After spending some time there
he departed and went from place to place through the region of Galatia and
Phrygia, strengthening all the disciples.

   Now there came to Ephesus a Jew named Apollos, a native of Alexandria.
He was an eloquent man, well-versed in the scriptures. He had been instructed
in the Way of the Lord; and he spoke with burning enthusiasm and taught
accurately the things concerning Jesus, though he knew only the baptism

of John. He began to speak boldly in the synagogue; but when Priscilla and Aquila heard him, they took him aside and explained the Way of God to him more accurately. And when he wished to cross over to Achaia, the believers encouraged him and wrote to the disciples to welcome him. On his arrival he greatly helped those who through grace had become believers, for he powerfully refuted the Jews in public, showing by the scriptures that the Messiah is Jesus.

This is the word of the Lord.   *Acts* 18.22–end

Responsorial Psalm

R **God has gone up with a merry noise,**
   [the Lord with the sound of the trumpet].   *Psalm* 47.5
   or

R **Alleluia!**

Clap your hands together, all you peoples;
O sing to God with shouts of joy.
For the Lord Most High is to be feared;
he is the great King over all the earth.   **R**

For God is the King of all the earth;
sing praises with all your skill.
God reigns over the nations;
God has taken his seat upon his holy throne.   **R**

The nobles of the peoples are gathered together
with the people of the God of Abraham.
For the powers of the earth belong to God
and he is very highly exalted.   **R**   *Psalm* 47.1–2, 7–end

Hear the Gospel of our Lord Jesus Christ according to John.

Jesus said to his disciples, 'On that day you will ask nothing of me. Very truly, I tell you, if you ask anything of the Father in my name, he will give it to you. Until now you have not asked for anything in my name. Ask and you will receive, so that your joy may be complete.

'I have said these things to you in figures of speech. The hour is coming when I will no longer speak to you in figures, but will tell you plainly of the Father. On that day you will ask in my name. I do not say to you that I will ask the Father on your behalf; for the Father himself loves you, because you have loved me and have believed that I came from God. I came from the Father and have come into the world; again, I am leaving the world and am going to the Father.'

This is the Gospel of the Lord.   *John* 16.23–28

Seventh Week of Easter: Monday

Year 1 and Year 2

A reading from the Acts of the Apostles.

While Apollos was in Corinth, Paul passed through the inland regions and came to Ephesus, where he found some disciples. He said to them, 'Did you receive the Holy Spirit when you became believers?' They replied, 'No, we have not even heard that there is a Holy Spirit.' Then he said, 'Into what then were you baptized?' They answered, 'Into John's baptism.' Paul said, 'John baptized with the baptism of repentance, telling the people to believe in the one who was to come after him, that is, in Jesus.' On hearing this, they were baptized in the name of the Lord Jesus. When Paul had laid his hands on them, the Holy Spirit came upon them, and they spoke in tongues and prophesied – altogether there were about twelve of them.

He entered the synagogue and for three months spoke out boldly, and argued persuasively about the kingdom of God.

This is the word of the Lord.   *Acts 19.1–8*

Responsorial Psalm

R **Sing to God, sing praises to his name;**
   [the Lord is his name; rejoice before him].   *cf Psalm 68.4*

   or

R **Alleluia!**

Let God arise and let his enemies be scattered;
let those that hate him flee before him.
As the smoke vanishes, so may they vanish away;
as wax melts at the fire,
so let the wicked perish at the presence of God.   **R**

But let the righteous be glad and rejoice before God;
let them make merry with gladness.
Sing to God, sing praises to his name;
exalt him who rides on the clouds.
The Lord is his name; rejoice before him.   **R**

Father of the fatherless, defender of widows,
God in his holy habitation!
God gives the solitary a home
and brings forth prisoners to songs of welcome,
but the rebellious inhabit a burning desert.   **R**   *Psalm 68.1–6*

Hear the Gospel of our Lord Jesus Christ according to John.

The disciples said to Jesus, 'Now you are speaking plainly, not in any figure of speech! Now we know that you know all things, and do not need to have anyone question you; by this we believe that you came from God.'

Jesus answered them, 'Do you now believe? The hour is coming, indeed it has come, when you will be scattered, each one to his home, and you will leave me alone. Yet I am not alone because the Father is with me. I have said this to you, so that in me you may have peace. In the world you face persecution. But take courage; I have conquered the world!'

This is the Gospel of the Lord.   John 16.29–end

Seventh Week of Easter: Tuesday

Year 1 and Year 2

A reading from the Acts of the Apostles.

From Miletus Paul sent a message to Ephesus, asking the elders of the church to meet him. When they came to him, he said to them:

'You yourselves know how I lived among you the entire time from the first day that I set foot in Asia, serving the Lord with all humility and with tears, enduring the trials that came to me through the plots of the Jews. I did not shrink from doing anything helpful, proclaiming the message to you and teaching you publicly and from house to house, as I testified to both Jews and Greeks about repentance towards God and faith towards our Lord Jesus. And now, as a captive to the Spirit, I am on my way to Jerusalem, not knowing what will happen to me there, except that the Holy Spirit testifies to me in every city that imprisonment and persecutions are waiting for me. But I do not count my life of any value to myself, if only I may finish my course and the ministry that I received from the Lord Jesus, to testify to the good news of God's grace.

'And now I know that none of you, among whom I have gone about proclaiming the kingdom, will ever see my face again. Therefore I declare to you this day that I am not responsible for the blood of any of you, for I did not shrink from declaring to you the whole purpose of God.'

This is the word of the Lord.   Acts 20.17–27

Responsorial Psalm

R **Sing to God, sing praises to his name;
[the Lord is his name; rejoice before him].**   cf *Psalm* 68.4

or

R **Alleluia!**

You sent down a gracious rain, O God;
you refreshed your inheritance when it was weary.
Your people came to dwell there;
in your goodness, O God, you provide for the poor.   R

Blessed be the Lord who bears our burdens day by day,
for God is our salvation.
God is for us the God of our salvation;
God is the Lord who can deliver from death.   R   *Psalm* 68.9–10, 18–19

Hear the Gospel of our Lord Jesus Christ according to John.

Jesus looked up to heaven and said, 'Father, the hour has come; glorify your Son so that the Son may glorify you, since you have given him authority over all people, to give eternal life to all whom you have given him. And this is eternal life, that they may know you, the only true God, and Jesus Christ whom you have sent. I glorified you on earth by finishing the work that you gave me to do. So now, Father, glorify me in your own presence with the glory that I had in your presence before the world existed.

'I have made your name known to those whom you gave me from the world. They were yours, and you gave them to me, and they have kept your word. Now they know that everything you have given me is from you; for the words that you gave to me I have given to them, and they have received them and know in truth that I came from you; and they have believed that you sent me. I am asking on their behalf; I am not asking on behalf of the world, but on behalf of those whom you gave me, because they are yours. All mine are yours, and yours are mine; and I have been glorified in them. And now I am no longer in the world, but they are in the world, and I am coming to you. Holy Father, protect them in your name that you have given me, so that they may be one, as we are one.'

This is the Gospel of the Lord.   John 17.1–11

Seventh Week of Easter: Wednesday

Year 1 and Year 2

A reading from the Acts of the Apostles.

Paul said to the elders of the church of Ephesus, 'Keep watch over yourselves and over all the flock, of which the Holy Spirit has made you overseers, to shepherd the church of God that he obtained with the blood of his own Son. I know that after I have gone, savage wolves will come in among you, not sparing the flock. Some even from your own group will come distorting the truth in order to entice the disciples to follow them. Therefore be alert, remembering that for three years I did not cease night or day to warn everyone with tears.

'And now I commend you to God and to the message of his grace, a message that is able to build you up and to give you the inheritance among all who are sanctified. I coveted no one's silver or gold or clothing. You know for yourselves that I worked with my own hands to support myself and my companions. In all this I have given you an example that by such work we must support the weak, remembering the words of the Lord Jesus, for he himself said, "It is more blessed to give than to receive." '

When he had finished speaking, he knelt down with them all and prayed. There was much weeping among them all; they embraced Paul and kissed him, grieving especially because of what he had said, that they would not see him again. Then they brought him to the ship.

This is the word of the Lord.   Acts 20.28–end

Responsorial Psalm

R **Sing to God, sing praises to his name;**
  [the Lord is his name; rejoice before him].   cf Psalm 68.4
  or

R **Alleluia!**

Send forth your strength, O God;
establish, O God, what you have wrought in us.
For your temple's sake in Jerusalem
kings shall bring their gifts to you.   R

Sing to God, you kingdoms of the earth;
make music in praise of the Lord;
he rides on the ancient heaven of heavens
and sends forth his voice, a mighty voice.   R

Ascribe power to God, whose splendour is over Israel,
whose power is above the clouds.
How terrible is God in his holy sanctuary,
the God of Israel, who gives power and strength to his people!
Blessed be God.   R   Psalm 68.27–28, 32–end

Hear the Gospel of our Lord Jesus Christ according to John.

Jesus said, 'Holy Father, protect them in your name that you have given me, so that they may be one, as we are one. While I was with them, I protected them in your name that you have given me. I guarded them, and not one of them was lost except the one destined to be lost, so that the scripture might be fulfilled. But now I am coming to you, and I speak these things in the world so that they may have my joy made complete in themselves. I have given them your word, and the world has hated them because they do not belong to the world, just as I do not belong to the world. I am not asking you to take them out of the world, but I ask you to protect them from the evil one. They do not belong to the world, just as I do not belong to the world. Sanctify them in the truth; your word is truth. As you have sent me into the world, so I have sent them into the world. And for their sakes I sanctify myself, so that they also may be sanctified in truth.'

This is the Gospel of the Lord.   John 17.11–19

Seventh Week of Easter: Thursday

Year 1 and Year 2

A reading from the Acts of the Apostles.

Since the tribune wanted to find out what Paul was being accused of by the Jews, the next day he released him and ordered the chief priests and the entire council to meet. He brought Paul down and had him stand before them.

When Paul noticed that some were Sadducees and others were Pharisees, he called out in the council, 'Brothers, I am a Pharisee, a son of Pharisees. I am on trial concerning the hope of the resurrection of the dead.' When he said this, a dissension began between the Pharisees and the Sadducees, and the assembly was divided. (The Sadducees say that there is no resurrection, or angel, or spirit; but the Pharisees acknowledge all three.) Then a great clamour arose, and certain scribes of the Pharisees' group stood up and contended, 'We find nothing wrong with this man. What if a spirit or an angel has spoken to him?' When the dissension became violent, the tribune, fearing that they would tear Paul to pieces, ordered the soldiers to go down, take him by force, and bring him into the barracks.

That night the Lord stood near him and said, 'Keep up your courage! For just as you have testified for me in Jerusalem, so you must bear witness also in Rome.'

This is the word of the Lord.   Acts 22.30, 23.6–11

Responsorial Psalm

R **Preserve me, O God,
for in you have I taken refuge.**   Psalm 16.1

or

R **Alleluia!**

Preserve me, O God,
for in you have I taken refuge;
I have said to the Lord, 'You are my lord,
all my good depends on you.'   R

My share has fallen in a fair land;
indeed, I have a goodly heritage.
I will bless the Lord who has given me counsel,
and in the night watches he instructs my heart.   R

I have set the Lord always before me;
he is at my right hand; I shall not fall.
Wherefore my heart is glad and my spirit rejoices;
my flesh also shall rest secure.   R

For you will not abandon my soul to Death,
nor suffer your faithful one to see the Pit;
you will show me the path of life.
In your presence is the fullness of joy
and in your right hand are pleasures for evermore.   R   Psalm 16.1, 5–end

Hear the Gospel of our Lord Jesus Christ according to John.

Jesus said, 'I ask not only on behalf of these, but also on behalf of those
who will believe in me through their word, that they may all be one. As you,
Father, are in me and I am in you, may they also be in us, so that the world
may believe that you have sent me. The glory that you have given me I have
given them, so that they may be one, as we are one, I in them and you in
me, that they may become completely one, so that the world may know that
you have sent me and have loved them even as you have loved me. Father, I
desire that those also, whom you have given me, may be with me where I
am, to see my glory, which you have given me because you loved me before
the foundation of the world.

'Righteous Father, the world does not know you, but I know you; and
these know that you have sent me. I made your name known to them, and I
will make it known, so that the love with which you have loved me may be
in them, and I in them.'

This is the Gospel of the Lord.   John 17.20–end

Seventh Week of Easter: Friday

Year 1 and Year 2

A reading from the Acts of the Apostles.

King Agrippa and Bernice arrived at Caesarea to welcome Festus. Since they were staying there for several days, Festus laid Paul's case before the king, saying, 'There is a man here who was left in prison by Felix. When I was in Jerusalem, the chief priests and the elders of the Jews informed me about him and asked for a sentence against him. I told them that it was not the custom of the Romans to hand over anyone before the accused had met the accusers face to face and had been given an opportunity to make a defence against the charge. So when they met here, I lost no time, but on the next day took my seat on the tribunal and ordered the man to be brought. When the accusers stood up, they did not charge him with any of the crimes that I was expecting. Instead they had certain points of disagreement with him about their own religion and about a certain Jesus, who had died, but whom Paul asserted to be alive. Since I was at a loss how to investigate these questions, I asked whether he wished to go to Jerusalem and be tried there on these charges. But when Paul had appealed to be kept in custody for the decision of his Imperial Majesty, I ordered him to be held until I could send him to the emperor.'

This is the word of the Lord.   *Acts 25.13–21*

Responsorial Psalm

R **Bless the Lord, O my soul,**
   [and bless his holy name].   *cf Psalm 103.1*

   or

R **Alleluia!**

Bless the Lord, O my soul,
and all that is within me bless his holy name.
Bless the Lord, O my soul,
and forget not all his benefits.   **R**

For as the heavens are high above the earth,
so great is his mercy upon those who fear him.
As far as the east is from the west,
so far has he set our sins from us.   **R**

The Lord has established his throne in heaven,
and his kingdom has dominion over all.
Bless the Lord, you angels of his,
you mighty ones who do his bidding
and hearken to the voice of his word.   **R**   *Psalm 103.1–2, 11–12, 19–20*

Hear the Gospel of our Lord Jesus Christ according to John.

Jesus said to Simon Peter, 'Simon son of John, do you love me more than these?' He said to him, 'Yes, Lord; you know that I love you.' Jesus said to him, 'Feed my lambs.' A second time he said to him, 'Simon son of John, do you love me?' He said to him, 'Yes, Lord; you know that I love you.' Jesus said to him, 'Tend my sheep.' He said to him the third time, 'Simon son of John, do you love me?'

Peter felt hurt because he said to him the third time, 'Do you love me?' And he said to him, 'Lord, you know everything; you know that I love you.' Jesus said to him, 'Feed my sheep. Very truly, I tell you, when you were younger, you used to fasten your own belt and to go wherever you wished. But when you grow old, you will stretch out your hands, and someone else will fasten a belt around you and take you where you do not wish to go.' (He said this to indicate the kind of death by which he would glorify God.) After this he said to him, 'Follow me.'

This is the Gospel of the Lord.   John 21.15–19

Seventh Week of Easter: Saturday

Year 1 and Year 2

A reading from the Acts of the Apostles.

When we came into Rome, Paul was allowed to live by himself, with the soldier who was guarding him.

Three days later he called together the local leaders of the Jews. When they had assembled, he said to them, 'Brothers, though I had done nothing against our people or the customs of our ancestors, yet I was arrested in Jerusalem and handed over to the Romans. When they had examined me, the Romans wanted to release me, because there was no reason for the death penalty in my case. But when the Jews objected, I was compelled to appeal to the emperor – even though I had no charge to bring against my nation. For this reason therefore I have asked to see you and speak with you, since it is for the sake of the hope of Israel that I am bound with this chain.'

He lived there for two whole years at his own expense and welcomed all who came to him, proclaiming the kingdom of God and teaching about the Lord Jesus Christ with all boldness and without hindrance.

This is the word of the Lord.   Acts 28.16–20, 30–end

R **The upright shall behold the face of the Lord.** cf Psalm 11.8

or

R **Alleluia!**

The Lord is in his holy temple;
the Lord's throne is in heaven.
His eyes behold,
his eyelids try every mortal being. **R**

The Lord tries the righteous as well as the wicked,
but those who delight in violence his soul abhors.
Upon the wicked he shall rain coals of fire and burning sulphur;
scorching wind shall be their portion to drink. **R**

For the Lord is righteous;
he loves righteous deeds,
and those who are upright
shall behold his face. **R** Psalm 11.4–end

Hear the Gospel of our Lord Jesus Christ according to John.

Peter turned and saw the disciple whom Jesus loved following them; he was the one who had reclined next to Jesus at the supper and had said, 'Lord, who is it that is going to betray you?' When Peter saw him, he said to Jesus, 'Lord, what about him?' Jesus said to him, 'If it is my will that he remain until I come, what is that to you? Follow me!' So the rumour spread in the community that this disciple would not die. Yet Jesus did not say to him that he would not die, but, 'If it is my will that he remain until I come, what is that to you?'

This is the disciple who is testifying to these things and has written them, and we know that his testimony is true. But there are also many other things that Jesus did; if every one of them were written down, I suppose that the world itself could not contain the books that would be written.

This is the Gospel of the Lord. John 21.20–end

BETWEEN THE BAPTISM OF CHRIST AND LENT AND BETWEEN PENTECOST AND ADVENT

The following readings are used from the day after the Baptism of Christ.

Week 1: Monday between 8 and 14 January

Year 1

A reading from the Letter to the Hebrews.

Long ago God spoke to our ancestors in many and various ways by the prophets, but in these last days he has spoken to us by a Son, whom he appointed heir of all things, through whom he also created the worlds. He is the reflection of God's glory and the exact imprint of God's very being, and he sustains all things by his powerful word. When he had made purification for sins, he sat down at the right hand of the Majesty on high, having become as much superior to angels as the name he has inherited is more excellent than theirs. For to which of the angels did God ever say,
  'You are my Son;
    today I have begotten you'?
Or again,
  'I will be his Father,
    and he will be my Son'?
And again, when he brings the firstborn into the world, he says,
  'Let all God's angels worship him.'

This is the word of the Lord.   Hebrews 1.1–6

Responsorial Psalm

R* **The Lord is king: let the earth rejoice;**
  [let the multitude of the isles be glad].   Psalm 97.1

Clouds and darkness are round about him;
righteousness and justice are the foundation of his throne.
The heavens declared his righteousness,
and all the peoples have seen his glory.   **R**

Confounded be all who worship carved images
and delight in mere idols.
Bow down before him, all you gods.   **R**

Zion heard and was glad, and the daughters of Judah rejoiced,
because of your judgements, O Lord.
For you, Lord, are most high over all the earth;
you are exalted far above all gods.   **R**

The Lord loves those who hate evil;
he preserves the lives of his faithful
and delivers them from the hand of the wicked.   **R**   Psalm 97.1–2, 6–10

A reading from the First Book of Samuel.

There was a certain man of Ramathaim, a Zuphite from the hill country of Ephraim, whose name was Elkanah son of Jeroham son of Elihu son of Tohu son of Zuph, an Ephraimite. He had two wives; the name of one was Hannah, and the name of the other Peninnah. Peninnah had children, but Hannah had no children.

Now this man used to go up year by year from his town to worship and to sacrifice to the LORD of hosts at Shiloh, where the two sons of Eli, Hophni and Phinehas, were priests of the LORD. On the day when Elkanah sacrificed, he would give portions to his wife Peninnah and to all her sons and daughters; but to Hannah he gave a double portion, because he loved her, though the LORD had closed her womb. Her rival used to provoke her severely, to irritate her, because the LORD had closed her womb. So it went on year after year; as often as she went up to the house of the LORD, she used to provoke her. Therefore Hannah wept and would not eat. Her husband Elkanah said to her, 'Hannah, why do you weep? Why do you not eat? Why is your heart sad? Am I not more to you than ten sons?'

This is the word of the Lord. 1 Samuel 1.1–8

Responsorial Psalm

R **I will offer to you a sacrifice of thanksgiving:
[and call upon the name of the Lord].** Psalm 116.15

How shall I repay the Lord
for all the benefits he has given to me?
I will lift up the cup of salvation
and call upon the name of the Lord. **R**

I will fulfil my vows to the Lord
in the presence of all his people.
Precious in the sight of the Lord
is the death of his faithful servants. **R**

O Lord, I am your servant,
your servant, the child of your handmaid;
you have freed me from my bonds.
I will offer to you a sacrifice of thanksgiving
and call upon the name of the Lord. **R** Psalm 116.10–15

Hear the Gospel of our Lord Jesus Christ according to Mark.

After John was arrested, Jesus came to Galilee, proclaiming the good news of God, and saying, 'The time is fulfilled, and the kingdom of God has come near; repent, and believe in the good news.'

As Jesus passed along the Sea of Galilee, he saw Simon and his brother Andrew casting a net into the lake – for they were fishermen. And Jesus said to them, 'Follow me and I will make you fish for people.' And immediately they left their nets and followed him. As he went a little farther, he saw James son of Zebedee and his brother John, who were in their boat mending the nets. Immediately he called them; and they left their father Zebedee in the boat with the hired men, and followed him.

This is the Gospel of the Lord.   Mark 1.14–20

Week 1: Tuesday between 9 and 15 January

Year 1

A reading from the Letter to the Hebrews.

God did not subject the coming world, about which we are speaking, to angels. But someone has testified somewhere,

'What are human beings that you are mindful of them,
    or mortals, that you care for them?
You have made them for a little while lower than the angels;
    you have crowned them with glory and honour,
    subjecting all things under their feet.'
Now in subjecting all things to them, God left nothing outside their control. As it is, we do not yet see everything in subjection to them, but we do see Jesus, who for a little while was made lower than the angels, now crowned with glory and honour because of the suffering of death, so that by the grace of God he might taste death for everyone.

It was fitting that God, for whom and through whom all things exist, in bringing many children to glory, should make the pioneer of their salvation perfect through sufferings. For the one who sanctifies and those who are sanctified all have one Father. For this reason Jesus is not ashamed to call them brothers and sisters, saying,

'I will proclaim your name to my brothers and sisters,
    in the midst of the congregation I will praise you.'

This is the word of the Lord.   Hebrews 2.5–12

R* **O Lord our governor,**
how glorious is your name in all the world! *Psalm 8.1*

Your majesty above the heavens is praised
out of the mouths of babes at the breast.
You have founded a stronghold against your foes,
that you might still the enemy and the avenger. **R**

When I consider your heavens, the work of your fingers,
the moon and the stars that you have ordained,
what is man, that you should be mindful of him;
the son of man, that you should seek him out? **R**

You have made him little lower than the angels
and crown him with glory and honour.
You have given him dominion over the works of your hands
and put all things under his feet. **R**

All sheep and oxen,
even the wild beasts of the field,
the birds of the air, the fish of the sea
and whatsoever moves in the paths of the sea. **R** *Psalm 8*

Year 2

A reading from the First Book of Samuel.

After Hannah and her husband, Elkanah, had eaten and drunk at Shiloh, Hannah rose and presented herself before the LORD. Now Eli the priest was sitting on the seat beside the doorpost of the temple of the LORD. She was deeply distressed and prayed to the LORD, and wept bitterly. She made this vow: 'O LORD of hosts, if only you will look on the misery of your servant, and remember me, and not forget your servant, but will give to your servant a male child, then I will set him before you as a nazirite until the day of his death. He shall drink neither wine nor intoxicants, and no razor shall touch his head.'

As she continued praying before the LORD, Eli observed her mouth. Hannah was praying silently; only her lips moved, but her voice was not heard; therefore Eli thought she was drunk. So Eli said to her, 'How long will you make a drunken spectacle of yourself? Put away your wine.' But Hannah answered, 'No, my lord, I am a woman deeply troubled; I have drunk neither wine nor strong drink, but I have been pouring out my soul before the LORD. Do not regard your servant as a worthless woman, for I have been speaking out of my great anxiety and vexation all this time.' Then Eli answered, 'Go in peace; the God of Israel grant the petition you have made to him.' And she said, 'Let your servant find favour in your sight.' Then the woman went to her quarters, ate and drank with her husband, and her countenance was sad no longer.

They rose early in the morning and worshipped before the LORD; then they went back to their house at Ramah. Elkanah knew his wife Hannah, and the LORD remembered her. In due time Hannah conceived and bore a son. She named him Samuel, for she said, 'I have asked him of the LORD.'

This is the word of the Lord.   1 Samuel 1.9–20

Either

Canticle

R **My heart exults in the Lord;**
   [my strength is exalted in my God].   1 Samuel 2.1

My heart exults in the Lord;
my strength is exalted in my God.
My mouth derides my enemies,
because I rejoice in your salvation.   **R**

The bows of the mighty are broken,
but the weak are clothed in strength.
Those who were full now work for bread,
but those who were hungry are well fed.   **R**

The childless woman has borne sevenfold,
but she who has many children is forlorn.
You, Lord, give life and death;
you bring down to the grave and you raise up.   **R**

Both the poor and the rich are of your making;
you bring low and you also exalt.
You raise up the poor from the dust;
and lift the needy from the ash heap.   **R**

You make them sit with princes
and inherit a place of honour.
For the pillars of the earth are the yours
and on them you have set the world.   **R**   1 Samuel 2.1, 4–8

or

Canticle

R **The Almighty has done great things for me
[and holy is his name].** Luke 1.49

My soul proclaims the greatness of the Lord,
my spirit rejoices in God my Saviour;
he has looked with favour on his lowly servant.
From this day all generations will call me blessed.   R

The Almighty has done great things for me
and holy is his name.
He has mercy on those who fear him,
from generation to generation.   R

He has shown strength with his arm
and has scattered the proud in their conceit,
casting down the mighty from their thrones
and lifting up the lowly.   R

He has filled the hungry with good things
and sent the rich away empty.
He has come to the aid of his servant Israel,
to remember his promise of mercy,
the promise made to our ancestors,
to Abraham and his children for ever.   R Luke 1.46b–55

Year 1 and Year 2

Hear the Gospel of our Lord Jesus Christ according to Mark.

Jesus and his disciples went to Capernaum; and when the sabbath came, he
entered the synagogue and taught. They were astounded at his teaching, for he
taught them as one having authority, and not as the scribes. Just then there was
in their synagogue a man with an unclean spirit, and he cried out, 'What have
you to do with us, Jesus of Nazareth? Have you come to destroy us? I know
who you are, the Holy One of God.' But Jesus rebuked him, saying, 'Be silent,
and come out of him!' And the unclean spirit, throwing him into convulsions
and crying with a loud voice, came out of him. They were all amazed, and they
kept on asking one another, 'What is this? A new teaching – with authority!
He commands even the unclean spirits, and they obey him.' At once his fame
began to spread throughout the surrounding region of Galilee.

This is the Gospel of the Lord. Mark 1.21–28

Week 1: Wednesday between 10 and 16 January

Year 1

A reading from the Letter to the Hebrews.

Since the children share flesh and blood, Jesus himself likewise shared the same things, so that through death he might destroy the one who has the power of death, that is, the devil, and free those who all their lives were held in slavery by the fear of death. For it is clear that he did not come to help angels, but the descendants of Abraham. Therefore he had to become like his brothers and sisters in every respect, so that he might be a merciful and faithful high priest in the service of God, to make a sacrifice of atonement for the sins of the people. Because he himself was tested by what he suffered, he is able to help those who are being tested.

This is the word of the Lord.   Hebrews 2.14–end

Responsorial Psalm

R* **Sing to the Lord, sing praises,**
   [and tell of his marvellous works].   *cf Psalm* 105.2

O give thanks to the Lord and call upon his name;
make known his deeds among the peoples.*
Rejoice in the praise of his holy name;
let the hearts of them rejoice who seek the Lord.   **R**

Seek the Lord and his strength;
seek his face continually.
Remember the marvels he has done,
his wonders and the judgements of his mouth.   **R**

O seed of Abraham his servant,
O children of Jacob his chosen:
he is the Lord our God;
his judgements are in all the earth.   **R**

He has always been mindful of his covenant,
the promise that he made for a thousand generations:
the covenant he made with Abraham,
the oath that he swore to Isaac.   **R**   *Psalm* 105.1–9

Year 2

A reading from the First Book of Samuel.

The boy Samuel was ministering to the Lord under Eli. The word of the Lord was rare in those days; visions were not widespread.

   At that time Eli, whose eyesight had begun to grow dim so that he could not see, was lying down in his room; the lamp of God had not yet gone out,   →

and Samuel was lying down in the temple of the LORD, where the ark of God was. Then the LORD called, 'Samuel! Samuel!' and he said, 'Here I am!' and ran to Eli, and said, 'Here I am, for you called me.' But he said, 'I did not call; lie down again.' So he went and lay down. The LORD called again, 'Samuel!' Samuel got up and went to Eli, and said, 'Here I am, for you called me.' But he said, 'I did not call, my son; lie down again.' Now Samuel did not yet know the LORD, and the word of the LORD had not yet been revealed to him. The LORD called Samuel again, a third time. And he got up and went to Eli, and said, 'Here I am, for you called me.' Then Eli perceived that the LORD was calling the boy. Therefore Eli said to Samuel, 'Go, lie down; and if he calls you, you shall say, "Speak, LORD, for your servant is listening."' So Samuel went and lay down in his place.

Now the LORD came and stood there, calling as before, 'Samuel! Samuel!' And Samuel said, 'Speak, for your servant is listening.'

As Samuel grew up, the LORD was with him and let none of his words fall to the ground. And all Israel from Dan to Beer-sheba knew that Samuel was a trustworthy prophet of the LORD.

This is the word of the Lord.   I Samuel 3.I–I0, I9–20

Responsorial Psalm

R* **Blessed is the one who trusts in the Lord,**
   [and does not turn to the proud that follow false gods].   Psalm 40.4

I waited patiently for the Lord;
he inclined to me and heard my cry.
He brought me out of the roaring pit,
out of the mire and clay;
he set my feet upon a rock and made my footing sure.   R

He has put a new song in my mouth,
a song of praise to our God;
many shall see and fear
and put their trust in the Lord.   R*

Sacrifice and offering you do not desire
but my ears you have opened;
burnt offering and sacrifice for sin you have not required;
then said I: 'Lo, I come.   R

'In the scroll of the book it is written of me
that I should do your will, O my God;
I delight to do it: your law is within my heart.'   R

I have declared your righteousness in the great congregation;
behold, I did not restrain my lips,
and that, O Lord, you know.   R   Psalm 40.I–4, 7–I0

Hear the Gospel of our Lord Jesus Christ according to Mark.

As soon as Jesus and his disciples left the synagogue, they entered the house of Simon and Andrew, with James and John. Now Simon's mother-in-law was in bed with a fever, and they told him about her at once. He came and took her by the hand and lifted her up. Then the fever left her, and she began to serve them.

That evening, at sunset, they brought to him all who were sick or possessed with demons. And the whole city was gathered around the door. And he cured many who were sick with various diseases, and cast out many demons; and he would not permit the demons to speak, because they knew him.

In the morning, while it was still very dark, he got up and went out to a deserted place, and there he prayed. And Simon and his companions hunted for him. When they found him, they said to him, 'Everyone is searching for you.' He answered, 'Let us go on to the neighbouring towns, so that I may proclaim the message there also; for that is what I came out to do.' And he went throughout Galilee, proclaiming the message in their synagogues and casting out demons.

This is the Gospel of the Lord.   Mark 1.29–39

Week 1: Thursday between 11 and 17 January

Year 1

A reading from the Letter to the Hebrews.

The Holy Spirit says,
  'Today, if you hear his voice,
  do not harden your hearts as in the rebellion,
    as on the day of testing in the wilderness,
  where your ancestors put me to the test,
    though they had seen my works for forty years.
  Therefore I was angry with that generation,
  and I said, "They always go astray in their hearts,
    and they have not known my ways."
  As in my anger I swore,
    "They will not enter my rest." '
Take care, brothers and sisters, that none of you may have an evil, unbelieving heart that turns away from the living God. But exhort one another every day, as long as it is called 'today', so that none of you may be hardened by the deceitfulness of sin. For we have become partners of Christ, if only we hold our first confidence firm to the end.

This is the word of the Lord.   Hebrews 3.7–14

Responsorial Psalm

R* **Come, let us sing to the Lord;**
   and rejoice in the rock of our salvation.   *cf Psalm 95.1*

O that today you would listen to his voice:
Harden not your hearts as at Meribah,
on that day at Massah in the wilderness,
when your forebears tested me, and put me to the proof,
though they had seen my works.   R

Forty years long I detested that generation and said,
'This people are wayward in their hearts;
they do not know my ways.'
So I swore in my wrath,
'They shall not enter into my rest.'   R   *Psalm 95.1, 8–end*

Year 2

A reading from the First Book of Samuel.

In those days the Philistines mustered for war against Israel, and Israel went out to battle against them; they encamped at Ebenezer, and the Philistines encamped at Aphek. The Philistines drew up in line against Israel, and when the battle was joined, Israel was defeated by the Philistines, who killed about four thousand men on the field of battle. When the troops came to the camp, the elders of Israel said, 'Why has the LORD put us to rout today before the Philistines? Let us bring the ark of the covenant of the LORD here from Shiloh, so that he may come among us and save us from the power of our enemies.' So the people sent to Shiloh, and brought from there the ark of the covenant of the LORD of hosts, who is enthroned on the cherubim. The two sons of Eli, Hophni and Phinehas, were there with the ark of the covenant of God.

When the ark of the covenant of the LORD came into the camp, all Israel gave a mighty shout, so that the earth resounded. When the Philistines heard the noise of the shouting, they said, 'What does this great shouting in the camp of the Hebrews mean?' When they learned that the ark of the LORD had come to the camp, the Philistines were afraid; for they said, 'Gods have come into the camp.' They also said, 'Woe to us! For nothing like this has happened before. Woe to us! Who can deliver us from the power of these mighty gods? These are the gods who struck the Egyptians with every sort of plague in the wilderness. Take courage, and be men, O Philistines, in order not to become slaves to the Hebrews as they have been to you; be men and fight.'

So the Philistines fought; Israel was defeated, and they fled, everyone to his home. There was a very great slaughter, for there fell of Israel thirty thousand foot-soldiers. The ark of God was captured; and the two sons of Eli, Hophni and Phinehas, died.

This is the word of the Lord.   *1 Samuel 4.1–11*

Responsorial Psalm

R **We gloried in God all day long,**
   [and were ever praising your name].   *Psalm* 44.9

But now you have rejected us and brought us to shame,
and go not out with our armies.
You have made us turn our backs on our enemies,
and our enemies have despoiled us. R

You have made us like sheep to be slaughtered,
and have scattered us among the nations.
You have sold your people for a pittance
and made no profit on their sale. R

You have made us the taunt of our neighbours,
the scorn and derision of those that are round about us.
You have made us a byword among the nations;
among the peoples they wag their heads. R

Rise up! Why sleep, O Lord?
Awake, and do not reject us for ever.
Why do you hide your face
and forget our grief and oppression? R   *Psalm* 44.10–15, 24–25

Year 1 and Year 2

Hear the Gospel of our Lord Jesus Christ according to Mark.

A leper came to Jesus begging him, and kneeling he said to him, 'If you choose,
you can make me clean.' Moved with pity, Jesus stretched out his hand and
touched him, and said to him, 'I do choose. Be made clean!' Immediately the
leprosy left him, and he was made clean. After sternly warning him he sent him
away at once, saying to him, 'See that you say nothing to anyone; but go, show
yourself to the priest, and offer for your cleansing what Moses commanded,
as a testimony to them.' But he went out and began to proclaim it freely, and
to spread the word, so that Jesus could no longer go into a town openly, but
stayed out in the country; and people came to him from every quarter.

This is the Gospel of the Lord.   *Mark* 1.40–end

Week 1: Friday between 12 and 18 January

Year 1

A reading from the Letter to the Hebrews.

While the promise of entering God's rest is still open, let us take care that none of you should seem to have failed to reach it. For indeed the good news came to us just as to the Israelites; but the message they heard did not benefit them, because they were not united by faith with those who listened. For we who have believed enter that rest, just as God has said,

'As in my anger I swore,
"They shall not enter my rest"',

though his works were finished at the foundation of the world. For in one place it speaks about the seventh day as follows: 'And God rested on the seventh day from all his works.' And again in this place it says, 'They shall not enter my rest.' Let us therefore make every effort to enter that rest, so that no one may fall through such disobedience as theirs.

This is the word of the Lord. Hebrews 4.1–5, 11

Responsorial Psalm

R **We will recount the praises of the Lord,
   [and the wonderful works he has done].** cf Psalm 78.4

Such as we have heard and known,
which our forebears have told us,
we will not hide from their children,
but will recount to generations to come:
the praises of the Lord and his power
and the wonderful works he has done. **R**

He laid a solemn charge on Jacob
and made it a law in Israel,
which he commanded them to teach their children;
that the generations to come might know,
and the children yet unborn. **R**

That they in turn might tell it to their children;
so that they might put their trust in God
and not forget the deeds of God,
but keep his commandments. **R**

And not be like their forebears,
a stubborn and rebellious generation,
a generation whose heart was not steadfast,
and whose spirit was not faithful to God. **R** Psalm 78.3–8

Year 2

A reading from the First Book of Samuel.

All the elders of Israel gathered together and came to Samuel at Ramah, and said to him, 'You are old and your sons do not follow in your ways; appoint for us, then, a king to govern us, like other nations.' But the thing displeased Samuel when they said, 'Give us a king to govern us.' Samuel prayed to the LORD, and the LORD said to Samuel, 'Listen to the voice of the people in all that they say to you; for they have not rejected you, but they have rejected me from being king over them.

So Samuel reported all the words of the LORD to the people who were asking him for a king. He said, 'These will be the ways of the king who will reign over you: he will take your sons and appoint them to his chariots and to be his horsemen, and to run before his chariots; and he will appoint for himself commanders of thousands and commanders of fifties, and some to plough his ground and to reap his harvest, and to make his implements of war and the equipment of his chariots. He will take your daughters to be perfumers and cooks and bakers. He will take the best of your fields and vineyards and olive orchards and give them to his courtiers. He will take one-tenth of your grain and of your vineyards and give it to his officers and his courtiers. He will take your male and female slaves, and the best of your cattle and donkeys, and put them to his work. He will take one-tenth of your flocks, and you shall be his slaves. And in that day you will cry out because of your king, whom you have chosen for yourselves; but the LORD will not answer you in that day.'

But the people refused to listen to the voice of Samuel; they said, 'No! but we are determined to have a king over us, so that we also may be like other nations, and that our king may govern us and go out before us and fight our battles.' When Samuel had heard all the words of the people, he repeated them in the ears of the LORD. The LORD said to Samuel, 'Listen to their voice and set a king over them.' Samuel then said to the people of Israel, 'Each of you return home.'

This is the word of the Lord. 1 Samuel 8.4–7, 10–end

Responsorial Psalm

R **Your love, O God, is established for ever:**
   [your faithfulness as firm as the heavens]. cf Psalm 89.2

Happy are the people who know the shout of triumph:
they walk, O Lord, in the light of your countenance.
In your name they rejoice all the day long
and are exalted in your righteousness. **R**

For you are the glory of their strength,
and in your favour you lift up our heads.
Truly the Lord is our shield;
the Holy One of Israel is our king. **R** Psalm 89.15–18

Hear the Gospel of our Lord Jesus Christ according to Mark.

When Jesus returned to Capernaum, it was reported that he was at home. So many gathered around that there was no longer room for them, not even in front of the door; and he was speaking the word to them. Then some people came, bringing to him a paralysed man, carried by four of them. And when they could not bring him to Jesus because of the crowd, they removed the roof above him; and after having dug through it, they let down the mat on which the paralytic lay. When Jesus saw their faith, he said to the paralytic, 'Son, your sins are forgiven.' Now some of the scribes were sitting there, questioning in their hearts, 'Why does this fellow speak in this way? It is blasphemy! Who can forgive sins but God alone?' At once Jesus perceived in his spirit that they were discussing these questions among themselves; and he said to them, 'Why do you raise such questions in your hearts? Which is easier, to say to the paralytic, "Your sins are forgiven", or to say, "Stand up and take your mat and walk"? But so that you may know that the Son of Man has authority on earth to forgive sins' – he said to the paralytic – 'I say to you, stand up, take your mat and go to your home.' And he stood up, and immediately took the mat and went out before all of them; so that they were all amazed and glorified God, saying, 'We have never seen anything like this!'

This is the Gospel of the Lord.   Mark 2.1–12

Week 1: Saturday between 13 and 19 January

Year 1

A reading from the Letter to the Hebrews.

The word of God is living and active, sharper than any two-edged sword, piercing until it divides soul from spirit, joints from marrow; it is able to judge the thoughts and intentions of the heart. And before him no creature is hidden, but all are naked and laid bare to the eyes of the one to whom we must render an account.

Since, then, we have a great high priest who has passed through the heavens, Jesus, the Son of God, let us hold fast to our confession. For we do not have a high priest who is unable to sympathize with our weaknesses, but we have one who in every respect has been tested as we are, yet without sin. Let us therefore approach the throne of grace with boldness, so that we may receive mercy and find grace to help in time of need.

This is the word of the Lord.   Hebrews 4.12–end

R **The judgements of the Lord are true:**
   more to be desired than gold. *cf Psalm* 19.9b, 10a

The law of the Lord is perfect, reviving the soul;
the testimony of the Lord is sure
and gives wisdom to the simple. **R**

The statutes of the Lord are right and rejoice the heart;
the commandment of the Lord is pure
and gives light to the eyes. **R**

The fear of the Lord is clean and endures for ever;
the judgements of the Lord are true
and righteous altogether. **R**

More to be desired are they than gold,
more than much fine gold,
sweeter also than honey,
dripping from the honeycomb. **R**

By them also is your servant taught
and in keeping them there is great reward.
Who can tell how often they offend?
O cleanse me from my secret faults! **R**

Keep your servant also from presumptuous sins
lest they get dominion over me;
so shall I be undefiled,
and innocent of great offence. **R**

Let the words of my mouth
and the meditation of my heart
be acceptable in your sight,
O Lord, my strength and my redeemer. **R** *Psalm* 19.7—end

Year 2

A reading from the First Book of Samuel.

There was a man of Benjamin whose name was Kish son of Abiel son of Zeror son of Becorath son of Aphiah, a Benjaminite, a man of wealth. He had a son whose name was Saul, a handsome young man. There was not a man among the people of Israel more handsome than he; he stood head and shoulders above everyone else.

Now the donkeys of Kish, Saul's father, had strayed. So Kish said to his son Saul, 'Take one of the boys with you; go and look for the donkeys.' He passed through the hill country of Ephraim and passed through the land of Shalishah, but they did not find them. And they passed through the land of Shaalim, but they were not there. Then he passed through the land of Benjamin, but they →

did not find them. When Samuel saw Saul, the LORD told him, 'Here is the man of whom I spoke to you. He it is who shall rule over my people.' Then Saul approached Samuel inside the gate, and said, 'Tell me, please, where is the house of the seer?' Samuel answered Saul, 'I am the seer; go up before me to the shrine, for today you shall eat with me, and in the morning I will let you go and will tell you all that is on your mind.'

Samuel took a phial of oil and poured it on his head, and kissed him; he said, 'The LORD has anointed you ruler over his people Israel. You shall reign over the people of the LORD and you will save them from the hand of their enemies all around.'

This is the word of the Lord.   1 Samuel 9.1–4, 17–19, 10.1a

Responsorial Psalm

R **Be exalted, O Lord, in your might;**
   [we will make music and sing of your power].   Psalm 21.13

The king shall rejoice in your strength, O Lord;
how greatly shall he rejoice in your salvation!
You have given him his heart's desire
and have not denied the request of his lips.   **R**

For you come to meet him with blessings of goodness
and set a crown of pure gold upon his head.
He asked of you life and you gave it him,
length of days, for ever and ever.   **R**

His honour is great because of your salvation;
glory and majesty have you laid upon him.
You have granted him everlasting felicity
and will make him glad with joy in your presence.   **R**   Psalm 21.1–6

Year 1 and Year 2

Hear the Gospel of our Lord Jesus Christ according to Mark.

Jesus went out again beside the lake; the whole crowd gathered around him, and he taught them. As he was walking along, he saw Levi son of Alphaeus sitting at the tax booth, and he said to him, 'Follow me.' And he got up and followed him.

And as he sat at dinner in Levi's house, many tax-collectors and sinners were also sitting with Jesus and his disciples – for there were many who followed him. When the scribes of the Pharisees saw that he was eating with sinners and tax-collectors, they said to his disciples, 'Why does he eat with tax-collectors and sinners?' When Jesus heard this, he said to them, 'Those who are well have no need of a physician, but those who are sick; I have come to call not the righteous but sinners.'

This is the Gospel of the Lord.   Mark 2.13–17

Week 2: Monday between 15 and 21 January

Year I

A reading from the Letter to the Hebrews.

Every high priest chosen from among mortals is put in charge of things pertaining to God on their behalf, to offer gifts and sacrifices for sins. He is able to deal gently with the ignorant and wayward, since he himself is subject to weakness; and because of this he must offer sacrifice for his own sins as well as for those of the people. And one does not presume to take this honour, but takes it only when called by God, just as Aaron was.

So also Christ did not glorify himself in becoming a high priest, but was appointed by the one who said to him,
'You are my Son,
today I have begotten you';
as he says also in another place,
'You are a priest for ever,
according to the order of Melchizedek.'

In the days of his flesh, Jesus offered up prayers and supplications, with loud cries and tears, to the one who was able to save him from death, and he was heard because of his reverent submission. Although he was a Son, he learned obedience through what he suffered; and having been made perfect, he became the source of eternal salvation for all who obey him, having been designated by God a high priest according to the order of Melchizedek.

This is the word of the Lord.   Hebrews 5.1–10

Responsorial Psalm

R **You are a priest for ever
[a priest after the order of Melchizedek].**   *cf Psalm 110.4b*

The Lord said to my lord, 'Sit at my right hand,
until I make your enemies your footstool.'
May the Lord stretch forth the sceptre of your power;
rule from Zion in the midst of your enemies. **R**

'Noble are you on this day of your birth;
on the holy mountain, from the womb of the dawn
the dew of your new birth is upon you.'
The Lord has sworn and will not retract:
'You are a priest for ever after the order of Melchizedek.' **R**

Psalm 110.1–4

A reading from the First Book of Samuel.

Samuel said to Saul, 'Stop! I will tell you what the LORD said to me last night.' He replied, 'Speak.'

  Samuel said, 'Though you are little in your own eyes, are you not the head of the tribes of Israel? The LORD anointed you king over Israel. And the LORD sent you on a mission, and said, "Go, utterly destroy the sinners, the Amalekites, and fight against them until they are consumed." Why then did you not obey the voice of the LORD? Why did you swoop down on the spoil, and do what was evil in the sight of the LORD?' Saul said to Samuel, 'I have obeyed the voice of the LORD, I have gone on the mission on which the LORD sent me, I have brought Agag the king of Amalek, and I have utterly destroyed the Amalekites. But from the spoil the people took sheep and cattle, the best of the things devoted to destruction, to sacrifice to the LORD your God in Gilgal.' And Samuel said,

'Has the LORD as great delight in burnt-offerings and sacrifices,
    as in obedience to the voice of the LORD?
Surely, to obey is better than sacrifice,
    and to heed than the fat of rams.
For rebellion is no less a sin than divination,
    and stubbornness is like iniquity and idolatry.
Because you have rejected the word of the LORD,
    he has also rejected you from being king.'

This is the word of the Lord.   1 *Samuel* 15.16–23

Responsorial Psalm

R **I will show my salvation
   to those who keep my way.**   cf *Psalm* 50.24b

'I will not reprove you for your sacrifices,
    for your burnt offerings are always before me.
I will take no bull out of your house,
    nor he-goat out of your folds,
for all the beasts of the forest are mine,
    the cattle upon a thousand hills.' **R**

But to the wicked, says God:
'Why do you recite my statutes
and take my covenant upon your lips,
since you refuse to be disciplined
and have cast my words behind you? **R**

'Whoever offers me the sacrifice of thanksgiving honours me
and to those who keep my way
will I show the salvation of God.' **R**   *Psalm* 50.8–10, 16–17, 24

Hear the Gospel of our Lord Jesus Christ according to Mark.

John's disciples and the Pharisees were fasting; and people came and said to him, 'Why do John's disciples and the disciples of the Pharisees fast, but your disciples do not fast?' Jesus said to them, 'The wedding-guests cannot fast while the bridegroom is with them, can they? As long as they have the bridegroom with them, they cannot fast. The days will come when the bridegroom is taken away from them, and then they will fast on that day.

'No one sews a piece of unshrunk cloth on an old cloak; otherwise, the patch pulls away from it, the new from the old, and a worse tear is made. And no one puts new wine into old wineskins; otherwise, the wine will burst the skins, and the wine is lost, and so are the skins; but one puts new wine into fresh wineskins.'

This is the Gospel of the Lord.   Mark 2.18–22

Week 2: Tuesday between 16 and 22 January

Year 1

A reading from the Letter to the Hebrews.

God is not unjust; he will not overlook your work and the love that you showed for his sake in serving the saints, as you still do. And we want each one of you to show the same diligence, so as to realize the full assurance of hope to the very end, so that you may not become sluggish, but imitators of those who through faith and patience inherit the promises.

When God made a promise to Abraham, because he had no one greater by whom to swear, he swore by himself, saying, 'I will surely bless you and multiply you.' And thus Abraham, having patiently endured, obtained the promise. Human beings, of course, swear by someone greater than themselves, and an oath given as confirmation puts an end to all dispute. In the same way, when God desired to show even more clearly to the heirs of the promise the unchangeable character of his purpose, he guaranteed it by an oath, so that through two unchangeable things, in which it is impossible that God would prove false, we who have taken refuge might be strongly encouraged to seize the hope set before us. We have this hope, a sure and steadfast anchor of the soul, a hope that enters the inner shrine behind the curtain, where Jesus, a forerunner on our behalf, has entered, having become a high priest for ever according to the order of Melchizedek.

This is the word of the Lord.   Hebrews 6.10–end

R **The works of God are truth and justice:**
   [he is gracious and full of compassion].   *cf Psalm* 111.*7a, 4b*

I will give thanks to the Lord with my whole heart,
in the company of the faithful and in the congregation.
The works of the Lord are great,
sought out by all who delight in them.   R

His work is full of majesty and honour
and his righteousness endures for ever.
He appointed a memorial for his marvellous deeds;
the Lord is gracious and full of compassion.   R

He gave food to those who feared him;
he is ever mindful of his covenant.
He showed his people the power of his works
in giving them the heritage of the nations.   R

The works of his hands are truth and justice;
all his commandments are sure.
They stand fast for ever and ever;
they are done in truth and equity.   R

He sent redemption to his people;
he commanded his covenant for ever;
holy and awesome is his name.
The fear of the Lord is the beginning of wisdom;
a good understanding have those who live by it;
his praise endures for ever.   R   *Psalm* 111

Year 2

A reading from the First Book of Samuel.

The LORD said to Samuel, 'How long will you grieve over Saul? I have rejected him from being king over Israel. Fill your horn with oil and set out; I will send you to Jesse the Bethlehemite, for I have provided for myself a king among his sons.' Samuel said, 'How can I go? If Saul hears of it, he will kill me.' And the LORD said, 'Take a heifer with you, and say, "I have come to sacrifice to the LORD." Invite Jesse to the sacrifice, and I will show you what you shall do; and you shall anoint for me the one whom I name to you.' Samuel did what the LORD commanded, and came to Bethlehem. The elders of the city came to meet him trembling, and said, 'Do you come peaceably?' He said, 'Peaceably; I have come to sacrifice to the LORD; sanctify yourselves and come with me to the sacrifice.' And he sanctified Jesse and his sons and invited them to the sacrifice.

    When they came, he looked on Eliab and thought, 'Surely the LORD's anointed is now before the LORD.' But the LORD said to Samuel, 'Do not look on his appearance or on the height of his stature, because I have rejected him; for the LORD does not see as mortals see; they look on the outward appearance, but the LORD looks on the heart.' Then Jesse called Abinadab, and made him pass before Samuel. He said, 'Neither has the LORD chosen this one.' Then Jesse made Shammah pass by. And he said, 'Neither has the LORD chosen this one.' Jesse made seven of his sons pass before Samuel, and Samuel said to Jesse, 'The LORD has not chosen any of these.' Samuel said to Jesse, 'Are all your sons here?' And he said, 'There remains yet the youngest, but he is keeping the sheep.' And Samuel said to Jesse, 'Send and bring him; for we will not sit down until he comes here.' He sent and brought him in. Now he was ruddy, and had beautiful eyes, and was handsome. The LORD said, 'Rise and anoint him; for this is the one.' Then Samuel took the horn of oil, and anointed him in the presence of his brothers; and the spirit of the LORD came mightily upon David from that day forward. Samuel then set out and went to Ramah.

This is the word of the Lord.   1 Samuel 16.1–13

Responsorial Psalm

R **Your love, O God, is established for ever:**
   [your faithfulness as firm as the heavens].   cf Psalm 89.2

You spoke once in a vision
and said to your faithful people:
I have set a youth above the mighty;
I have raised a young man over the people.   R

I have found David my servant;
with my holy oil have I anointed him.
My hand shall hold him fast
and my arm shall strengthen him.   R

No enemy shall deceive him,
nor any wicked person afflict him.
I will strike down his foes before his face
and beat down those that hate him.   R

My truth also and my steadfast love shall be with him,
and in my name shall his head be exalted.
I will set his dominion upon the sea
and his right hand upon the rivers.   R

He shall call to me, 'You are my Father,
my God, and the rock of my salvation;'
And I will make him my firstborn,
the most high above the kings of the earth.   R   Psalm 89.19–27

Hear the Gospel of our Lord Jesus Christ according to Mark.

One sabbath Jesus was going through the cornfields; and as they made their way his disciples began to pluck heads of grain. The Pharisees said to him, 'Look, why are they doing what is not lawful on the sabbath?' And he said to them, 'Have you never read what David did when he and his companions were hungry and in need of food? He entered the house of God, when Abiathar was high priest, and ate the bread of the Presence, which it is not lawful for any but the priests to eat, and he gave some to his companions.' Then he said to them, 'The sabbath was made for humankind, and not humankind for the sabbath; so the Son of Man is lord even of the sabbath.'

This is the Gospel of the Lord. Mark 2.23–end

Week 2: Wednesday between 17 and 23 January

Year 1

A reading from the Letter to the Hebrews.

This 'King Melchizedek of Salem, priest of the Most High God, met Abraham as he was returning from defeating the kings and blessed him'; and to him Abraham apportioned 'one-tenth of everything'. His name, in the first place, means 'king of righteousness'; next he is also king of Salem, that is, 'king of peace'. Without father, without mother, without genealogy, having neither beginning of days nor end of life, but resembling the Son of God, he remains a priest for ever.

It is even more obvious when another priest arises, resembling Melchizedek, one who has become a priest, not through a legal requirement concerning physical descent, but through the power of an indestructible life. For it is attested of him,

'You are a priest for ever,
according to the order of Melchizedek.'

This is the word of the Lord. Hebrews 7.1–3, 15–17

Responsorial Psalm

R **You are a priest for ever
[a priest after the order of Melchizedek].** cf Psalm 110.4b

The Lord said to my lord, 'Sit at my right hand,
until I make your enemies your footstool.'
May the Lord stretch forth the sceptre of your power;
rule from Zion in the midst of your enemies. **R**

'Noble are you on this day of your birth;
on the holy mountain, from the womb of the dawn
the dew of your new birth is upon you.'
The Lord has sworn and will not retract:
'You are a priest for ever after the order of Melchizedek.' R

Psalm 110.1–4

Year 2

A reading from the First Book of Samuel.

David said to Saul, 'Let no one's heart fail because of him; your servant will
go and fight with this Philistine.' Saul said to David, 'You are not able to go
against this Philistine to fight with him; for you are just a boy, and he has
been a warrior from his youth.' David said, 'The LORD, who saved me from
the paw of the lion and from the paw of the bear, will save me from the hand
of this Philistine.' So Saul said to David, 'Go, and may the LORD be with you!'
Then he took his staff in his hand, and chose five smooth stones from the
wadi, and put them in his shepherd's bag, in the pouch; his sling was in his
hand, and he drew near to the Philistine.

The Philistine came on and drew near to David, with his shield-bearer in
front of him. When the Philistine looked and saw David, he disdained him, for
he was only a youth, ruddy and handsome in appearance. The Philistine said
to David, 'Am I a dog, that you come to me with sticks?' And the Philistine
cursed David by his gods. The Philistine said to David, 'Come to me, and I
will give your flesh to the birds of the air and to the wild animals of the field.'
But David said to the Philistine, 'You come to me with sword and spear and
javelin; but I come to you in the name of the LORD of hosts, the God of the
armies of Israel, whom you have defied. This very day the LORD will deliver
you into my hand, and I will strike you down and cut off your head; and I
will give the dead bodies of the Philistine army this very day to the birds of
the air and to the wild animals of the earth, so that all the earth may know
that there is a God in Israel, and that all this assembly may know that the
LORD does not save by sword and spear; for the battle is the LORD's and he
will give you into our hand.'

When the Philistine drew nearer to meet David, David ran quickly towards
the battle line to meet the Philistine. David put his hand in his bag, took out
a stone, slung it, and struck the Philistine on his forehead; the stone sank
into his forehead, and he fell face down on the ground.

So David prevailed over the Philistine with a sling and a stone, striking
down the Philistine and killing him; there was no sword in David's hand.
Then David ran and stood over the Philistine; he grasped his sword, drew it
out of its sheath, and killed him; then he cut off his head with it. When the
Philistines saw that their champion was dead, they fled.

This is the word of the Lord.   1 Samuel 17.32–33, 37, 40–51

Responsorial Psalm

R **Blessed be the Lord my rock,**
  [my stronghold and my deliverer]. *cf Psalm 144.1a, 2b*

Blessed be the Lord my rock,
who teaches my hands for war
and my fingers for battle. **R**

My steadfast help and my fortress,
my stronghold and my deliverer,
my shield in whom I trust,
who subdues the peoples under me. **R**

O God, I will sing to you a new song;
I will play to you on a ten-stringed harp;
you that give salvation to kings
and have delivered David your servant. **R** *Psalm 144.1–2, 9–10*

Year 1 and Year 2

Hear the Gospel of our Lord Jesus Christ according to Mark.

Jesus entered the synagogue, and a man was there who had a withered hand. They watched him to see whether he would cure him on the sabbath, so that they might accuse him. And he said to the man who had the withered hand, 'Come forward.' Then he said to them, 'Is it lawful to do good or to do harm on the sabbath, to save life or to kill?' But they were silent. He looked around at them with anger; he was grieved at their hardness of heart and said to the man, 'Stretch out your hand.' He stretched it out, and his hand was restored. The Pharisees went out and immediately conspired with the Herodians against him, how to destroy him.

This is the Gospel of the Lord. *Mark 3.1–6*

Week 2: Thursday between 18 and 24 January

Year 1

A reading from the Letter to the Hebrews.

Jesus is able for all time to save those who approach God through him, since he always lives to make intercession for them.

For it was fitting that we should have such a high priest, holy, blameless, undefiled, separated from sinners, and exalted above the heavens. Unlike the other high priests, he has no need to offer sacrifices day after day, first for his own sins, and then for those of the people; this he did once for all when he offered himself. For the law appoints as high priests those who are subject to weakness, but the word of the oath, which came later than the law, appoints a Son who has been made perfect for ever.

Now the main point in what we are saying is this: we have such a high priest, one who is seated at the right hand of the throne of the Majesty in the heavens, a minister in the sanctuary and the true tent that the Lord, and not any mortal, has set up. For every high priest is appointed to offer gifts and sacrifices; hence it is necessary for this priest also to have something to offer. Now if he were on earth, he would not be a priest at all, since there are priests who offer gifts according to the law. They offer worship in a sanctuary that is a sketch and shadow of the heavenly one; for Moses, when he was about to erect the tent, was warned, 'See that you make everything according to the pattern that was shown you on the mountain.' But Jesus has now obtained a more excellent ministry, and to that degree he is the mediator of a better covenant, which has been enacted through better promises.

This is the word of the Lord.   *Hebrews 7.25 – 8.6*

Responsorial Psalm

R   **Great are the wonders you have done, O God:**
    [none can compare with you].   *cf Psalm 40.5*

Sacrifice and offering you do not desire
but my ears you have opened;
burnt offering and sacrifice for sin you have not required;
then said I: 'Lo, I come.   R

'In the scroll of the book it is written of me
that I should do your will, O my God;
I delight to do it: your law is within my heart.'   R

I have declared your righteousness in the great congregation;
behold, I did not restrain my lips,
and that, O Lord, you know.   R

Let all who seek you rejoice in you and be glad;
let those who love your salvation say always,
'The Lord is great.'   R

Though I am poor and needy,
the Lord cares for me.
You are my helper and my deliverer;
O my God, make no delay.   R   *Psalm 40.7–10, 17–end*

Year 2

A reading from the First Book of Samuel.

As they were coming home, when David returned from killing the Philistine, the women came out of all the towns of Israel, singing and dancing, to meet King Saul, with tambourines, with songs of joy, and with musical instruments. And the women sang to one another as they made merry,   →

'Saul has killed his thousands,
    and David his tens of thousands.'
Saul was very angry, for this saying displeased him. He said, 'They have ascribed
to David tens of thousands, and to me they have ascribed thousands; what
more can he have but the kingdom?' So Saul eyed David from that day on.

Saul spoke to his son Jonathan and to all his servants about killing David.
But Saul's son Jonathan took great delight in David. Jonathan told David, 'My
father Saul is trying to kill you; therefore be on guard tomorrow morning; stay
in a secret place and hide yourself. I will go out and stand beside my father
in the field where you are, and I will speak to my father about you; if I learn
anything I will tell you.' Jonathan spoke well of David to his father Saul, saying
to him, 'The king should not sin against his servant David, because he has
not sinned against you, and because his deeds have been of good service to
you; for he took his life in his hand when he attacked the Philistine, and the
LORD brought about a great victory for all Israel. You saw it, and rejoiced; why
then will you sin against an innocent person by killing David without cause?'
Saul heeded the voice of Jonathan; Saul swore, 'As the LORD lives, he shall not
be put to death.' So Jonathan called David and related all these things to him.
Jonathan then brought David to Saul, and he was in his presence as before.

This is the word of the Lord.   1 Samuel 18.6–9, 19.1–7

Responsorial Psalm

R **In God I trust and will not fear.**   *Psalm 56.10b*

Have mercy on me, O God, for they trample over me;
all day long they assault and oppress me.
My adversaries trample over me all the day long;
many are they that make proud war against me.   R

You have counted up my groaning;
put my tears into your bottle;
are they not written in your book?   R

Then shall my enemies turn back
on the day when I call upon you;
this I know, for God is on my side.   R

In God whose word I praise,
in the Lord whose word I praise,
in God I trust and will not fear:
what can flesh do to me?   R

To you, O God, will I fulfil my vows;
to you will I present my offerings of thanks,
for you will deliver my soul from death
and my feet from falling,
that I may walk before God in the light of the living.   R

                                                    Psalm 56.1–2, 8–end

Hear the Gospel of our Lord Jesus Christ according to Mark.

Jesus departed with his disciples to the lake, and a great multitude from Galilee followed him; hearing all that he was doing, they came to him in great numbers from Judea, Jerusalem, Idumea, beyond the Jordan, and the region around Tyre and Sidon. He told his disciples to have a boat ready for him because of the crowd, so that they would not crush him; for he had cured many, so that all who had diseases pressed upon him to touch him. Whenever the unclean spirits saw him, they fell down before him and shouted, 'You are the Son of God!' But he sternly ordered them not to make him known.

This is the Gospel of the Lord.   Mark 3.7–12

Week 2: Friday between 19 and 25 January

Year 1

A reading from the Letter to the Hebrews.

Jesus has now obtained a more excellent ministry, and to that degree he is the mediator of a better covenant, which has been enacted through better promises. For if that first covenant had been faultless, there would have been no need to look for a second one. God finds fault with them when he says:
'The days are surely coming, says the Lord,
    when I will establish a new covenant with the house of Israel
    and with the house of Judah;
not like the covenant that I made with their ancestors,
    on the day when I took them by the hand
        to lead them out of the land of Egypt;
for they did not continue in my covenant,
    and so I had no concern for them, says the Lord.
This is the covenant that I will make with the house of Israel
    after those days, says the Lord:
I will put my laws in their minds,
    and write them on their hearts,
and I will be their God,
    and they shall be my people.
And they shall not teach one another
    or say to each other, "Know the Lord",
for they shall all know me,
    from the least of them to the greatest.
For I will be merciful towards their iniquities,
    and I will remember their sins no more.'
In speaking of 'a new covenant', he has made the first one obsolete. And what is obsolete and growing old will soon disappear.

This is the word of the Lord.   Hebrews 8.6–end

Responsorial Psalm

R **The Lord was gracious to his land;**
  and restored the fortunes of Jacob. cf *Psalm* 85.1

Show us your mercy, O Lord,
and grant us your salvation.
I will listen
to what the Lord God will say. **R**

For he shall speak peace to his people and to the faithful,
that they turn not again to folly.
Truly, his salvation is near to those who fear him,
that his glory may dwell in our land. **R**

Mercy and truth are met together,
righteousness and peace have kissed each other.
Truth shall spring up from the earth
and righteousness look down from heaven. **R**

The Lord will indeed give all that is good,
and our land will yield its increase.
Righteousness shall go before him
and direct his steps in the way. **R** *Psalm* 85.7–*end*

Year 2

A reading from the First Book of Samuel.

Saul came to the sheepfolds beside the road, where there was a cave; and he went in to relieve himself. Now David and his men were sitting in the innermost parts of the cave. The men of David said to him, 'Here is the day of which the LORD said to you, "I will give your enemy into your hand, and you shall do to him as it seems good to you."' Then David went and stealthily cut off a corner of Saul's cloak. Afterwards David was stricken to the heart because he had cut off a corner of Saul's cloak. He said to his men, 'The LORD forbid that I should do this thing to my lord, the LORD's anointed, to raise my hand against him; for he is the LORD's anointed.' So David scolded his men severely and did not permit them to attack Saul. Then Saul got up and left the cave, and went on his way.

Afterwards David also rose up and went out of the cave and called after Saul, 'My lord the king!' When Saul looked behind him, David bowed with his face to the ground, and did obeisance. David said to Saul, 'Why do you listen to the words of those who say, "David seeks to do you harm"? This very day your eyes have seen how the LORD gave you into my hand in the cave; and some urged me to kill you, but I spared you. I said, "I will not raise my hand against my lord; for he is the LORD's anointed." See, my father, see the corner of your cloak in my hand; for by the fact that I cut off the corner of your cloak, and did not kill you, you may know for certain that there is no wrong or treason in my hands. I have not sinned against you, though you are hunting me to take my life. May the LORD judge between me and you! May the LORD avenge me on you; but my hand shall not be against you. As the ancient proverb says, "Out of the wicked comes forth wickedness"; but my hand shall not be against you. Against whom has the king of Israel come out? Whom do you pursue? A dead dog? A single flea? May the LORD therefore be judge, and give sentence between me and you. May he see to it, and plead my cause, and vindicate me against you.'

When David had finished speaking these words to Saul, Saul said, 'Is that your voice, my son David?' Saul lifted up his voice and wept. He said to David, 'You are more righteous than I; for you have repaid me good, whereas I have repaid you evil. Today you have explained how you have dealt well with me, in that you did not kill me when the LORD put me into your hands. For who has ever found an enemy, and sent the enemy safely away? So may the LORD reward you with good for what you have done to me this day. Now I know that you shall surely be king, and that the kingdom of Israel shall be established in your hand. Swear to me therefore by the LORD that you will not cut off my descendants after me, and that you will not wipe out my name from my father's house.' So David swore this to Saul.

This is the word of the Lord.   *1 Samuel 24.3–22a*

Responsorial Psalm

R* **O God, be exalted above the heavens,**
   [let your glory be over all the earth].   *cf Psalm 57.12*

Be merciful to me, O God, be merciful to me,
for my soul takes refuge in you;
in the shadow of your wings will I take refuge
until the storm of destruction has passed by.   **R**

My heart is ready, O God, my heart is ready;
I will sing and give you praise.
Awake, my soul; awake, harp and lyre,
that I may awaken the dawn.   **R**

I will give you thanks, O Lord, among the peoples;
I will sing praise to you among the nations.
For your loving-kindness is as high as the heavens,
and your faithfulness reaches to the clouds.   **R***   *Psalm 57.1–2, 8–end*

Hear the Gospel of our Lord Jesus Christ according to Mark.

Jesus went up the mountain and called to him those whom he wanted, and they came to him. And he appointed twelve, whom he also named apostles, to be with him, and to be sent out to proclaim the message, and to have authority to cast out demons. So he appointed the twelve: Simon (to whom he gave the name Peter); James son of Zebedee and John the brother of James (to whom he gave the name Boanerges, that is, Sons of Thunder); and Andrew, and Philip, and Bartholomew, and Matthew, and Thomas, and James son of Alphaeus, and Thaddaeus, and Simon the Cananaean, and Judas Iscariot, who betrayed him.

This is the Gospel of the Lord. Mark 3.13–19

Week 2: Saturday between 20 and 26 January

Year 1

A reading from the Letter to the Hebrews.

A tent was constructed, the first one, in which were the lampstand, the table, and the bread of the Presence; this is called the Holy Place. Behind the second curtain was a tent called the Holy of Holies.

But when Christ came as a high priest of the good things that have come, then through the greater and perfect tent (not made with hands, that is, not of this creation), he entered once for all into the Holy Place, not with the blood of goats and calves, but with his own blood, thus obtaining eternal redemption. For if the blood of goats and bulls, with the sprinkling of the ashes of a heifer, sanctifies those who have been defiled so that their flesh is purified, how much more will the blood of Christ, who through the eternal Spirit offered himself without blemish to God, purify our conscience from dead works to worship the living God!

This is the word of the Lord. Hebrews 9.2–3, 11–14

Responsorial Psalm

R **God has gone up with a merry noise,**
   [the Lord with the sound of the trumpet].   *Psalm 47.5*

Clap your hands together, all you peoples;
O sing to God with shouts of joy.
For the Lord Most High is to be feared;
he is the great King over all the earth. R

He subdued the peoples under us
and the nations under our feet.
He has chosen our heritage for us,
the pride of Jacob, whom he loves. R

God has gone up with a merry noise,
the Lord with the sound of the trumpet.
O sing praises to God, sing praises;
sing praises to our King, sing praises. R

For God is the King of all the earth;
sing praises with all your skill.
God reigns over the nations;
God has taken his seat upon his holy throne. R   *Psalm 47.1–8*

Year 2

A reading from the Second Book of Samuel.

After the death of Saul, when David had returned from defeating the Amalekites, David remained two days in Ziklag. On the third day, a man came from Saul's camp, with his clothes torn and dirt on his head. When he came to David, he fell to the ground and did obeisance. David said to him, 'Where have you come from?' He said to him, 'I have escaped from the camp of Israel.' David said to him, 'How did things go? Tell me!' He answered, 'The army fled from the battle, but also many of the army fell and died; and Saul and his son Jonathan also died.'

Then David took hold of his clothes and tore them; and all the men who were with him did the same. They mourned and wept, and fasted until evening for Saul and for his son Jonathan, and for the army of the LORD and for the house of Israel, because they had fallen by the sword.

David intoned this lamentation over Saul and his son Jonathan. (He ordered that The Song of the Bow be taught to the people of Judah; it is written in the Book of Jashar.) He said:

Your glory, O Israel, lies slain upon your high places!
    How the mighty have fallen!
Saul and Jonathan, beloved and lovely!
    In life and in death they were not divided; →

they were swifter than eagles,
they were stronger than lions.
O daughters of Israel, weep over Saul,
who clothed you with crimson, in luxury,
who put ornaments of gold on your apparel.

How the mighty have fallen
in the midst of the battle!

Jonathan lies slain upon your high places.
I am distressed for you, my brother Jonathan;
greatly beloved were you to me;
your love to me was wonderful,
passing the love of women.

How the mighty have fallen,
and the weapons of war perished!

This is the word of the Lord.   2 Samuel 1.1–4, 11–12, 17–19, 23–end

Responsorial Psalm

R **Make your face shine upon us, O Lord:
[restore us, and we shall be saved].**   cf Psalm 80.4, 8, 20

Hear, O Shepherd of Israel,
you that led Joseph like a flock;
shine forth, you that are enthroned upon the cherubim,
before Ephraim, Benjamin and Manasseh.   **R**

Stir up your mighty strength
and come to our salvation.
Turn us again, O God;
show the light of your countenance, and we shall be saved.   **R**

O Lord God of hosts,
how long will you be angry at your people's prayer?
You feed them with the bread of tears;
you give them abundance of tears to drink.   **R**   Psalm 80.1–6

Year 1 and Year 2

Hear the Gospel of our Lord Jesus Christ according to Mark.

Jesus went home, and the crowd came together again, so that they could not
even eat. When his family heard it, they went out to restrain him, for people
were saying, 'He has gone out of his mind.'

This is the Gospel of the Lord.   Mark 3.20–21

Week 3: Monday between 22 and 28 January

Year 1

A reading from the Letter to the Hebrews.

Christ is the mediator of a new covenant, so that those who are called may receive the promised eternal inheritance, because a death has occurred that redeems them from the transgressions under the first covenant. For Christ did not enter a sanctuary made by human hands, a mere copy of the true one, but he entered into heaven itself, now to appear in the presence of God on our behalf. Nor was it to offer himself again and again, as the high priest enters the Holy Place year after year with blood that is not his own; for then he would have had to suffer again and again since the foundation of the world. But as it is, he has appeared once for all at the end of the age to remove sin by the sacrifice of himself. And just as it is appointed for mortals to die once, and after that the judgement, so Christ, having been offered once to bear the sins of many, will appear a second time, not to deal with sin, but to save those who are eagerly waiting for him.

This is the word of the Lord. *Hebrews 9.15, 24–end*

Responsorial Psalm

R* **Sound praises to the Lord, all the earth;**
[break into song and make music]. *cf Psalm 98.5*

Sing to the Lord a new song,
for he has done marvellous things.
His own right hand and his holy arm
have won for him the victory.   **R**

The Lord has made known his salvation;
his deliverance has he openly shown
in the sight of the nations.   **R**

He has remembered his mercy and faithfulness
towards the house of Israel,
and all the ends of the earth have seen
the salvation of our God.   **R***

Make music to the Lord with the lyre,
with the lyre and the voice of melody.
With trumpets and the sound of the horn
sound praises before the Lord, the King.   **R** *Psalm 98.1–7*

A reading from the Second Book of Samuel.

All the tribes of Israel came to David at Hebron, and said, 'Look, we are your bone and flesh. For some time, while Saul was king over us, it was you who led out Israel and brought it in. The LORD said to you: It is you who shall be shepherd of my people Israel, you who shall be ruler over Israel.' So all the elders of Israel came to the king at Hebron; and King David made a covenant with them at Hebron before the LORD, and they anointed David king over Israel. David was thirty years old when he began to reign, and he reigned for forty years. At Hebron he reigned over Judah for seven years and six months; and at Jerusalem he reigned over all Israel and Judah for thirty-three years.

The king and his men marched to Jerusalem against the Jebusites, the inhabitants of the land, who said to David, 'You will not come in here, even the blind and the lame will turn you back' – thinking, 'David cannot come in here.' Nevertheless, David took the stronghold of Zion, which is now the city of David. And David became greater and greater, for the LORD, the God of hosts, was with him.

This is the word of the Lord.   *2 Samuel 5.1–7, 10*

Responsorial Psalm

R **Your love, O God, is established for ever:**
   [your faithfulness as firm as the heavens].   cf Psalm 89.2

You spoke once in a vision and said to your faithful people:
I have set a youth above the mighty;
I have raised a young man over the people.   R

I have found David my servant;
with my holy oil have I anointed him.
My hand shall hold him fast
and my arm shall strengthen him.   R

No enemy shall deceive him,
nor any wicked person afflict him.
I will strike down his foes before his face
and beat down those that hate him.   R

My truth also and my steadfast love shall be with him,
and in my name shall his head be exalted.
I will set his dominion upon the sea
and his right hand upon the rivers.   R

He shall call to me, 'You are my Father,
my God, and the rock of my salvation;'
And I will make him my firstborn,
the most high above the kings of the earth.   R   *Psalm 89.19–27*

Year 1 and Year 2

Hear the Gospel of our Lord Jesus Christ according to Mark.

The scribes who came down from Jerusalem said, 'He has Beelzebul, and by the ruler of the demons he casts out demons.' And Jesus called them to him, and spoke to them in parables, 'How can Satan cast out Satan? If a kingdom is divided against itself, that kingdom cannot stand. And if a house is divided against itself, that house will not be able to stand. And if Satan has risen up against himself and is divided, he cannot stand, but his end has come. But no one can enter a strong man's house and plunder his property without first tying up the strong man; then indeed the house can be plundered.

'Truly I tell you, people will be forgiven for their sins and whatever blasphemies they utter; but whoever blasphemes against the Holy Spirit can never have forgiveness, but is guilty of an eternal sin' – for they had said, 'He has an unclean spirit.'

This is the Gospel of the Lord.

Mark 3.22–30

Week 3: Tuesday between 23 and 29 January

Year 1

A reading from the Letter to the Hebrews.

Since the law has only a shadow of the good things to come and not the true form of these realities, it can never, by the same sacrifices that are continually offered year after year, make perfect those who approach. Otherwise, would they not have ceased being offered, since the worshippers, cleansed once for all, would no longer have any consciousness of sin? But in these sacrifices there is a reminder of sin year after year. For it is impossible for the blood of bulls and goats to take away sins. Consequently, when Christ came into the world, he said,

'Sacrifices and offerings you have not desired,
　　but a body you have prepared for me;
in burnt-offerings and sin-offerings
　　you have taken no pleasure.
Then I said, "See, God, I have come to do your will, O God"
　　(in the scroll of the book it is written of me).'
When he said above, 'You have neither desired nor taken pleasure in sacrifices and offerings and burnt-offerings and sin-offerings' (these are offered according to the law), then he added, 'See, I have come to do your will.' He abolishes the first in order to establish the second. And it is by God's will that we have been sanctified through the offering of the body of Jesus Christ once for all.

This is the word of the Lord.

Hebrews 10.1–10

**R* Blessed is the one who trusts in the Lord,
 [and does not turn to the proud that follow false gods].**   *Psalm* 40.4

I waited patiently for the Lord;
 he inclined to me and heard my cry.
He brought me out of the roaring pit,
 out of the mire and clay;
he set my feet upon a rock and made my footing sure.   **R**

He has put a new song in my mouth,
 a song of praise to our God;
many shall see and fear
 and put their trust in the Lord.   **R***

Sacrifice and offering you do not desire
 but my ears you have opened;
burnt offering and sacrifice for sin you have not required;
 then said I: 'Lo, I come.   **R**

'In the scroll of the book it is written of me
 that I should do your will, O my God;
I delight to do it: your law is within my heart.'   **R**

I have declared your righteousness in the great congregation;
 behold, I did not restrain my lips,
and that, O Lord, you know.   **R**   *Psalm* 40.1–4, 7–10

Year 2

A reading from the Second Book of Samuel.

It was told King David, 'The LORD has blessed the household of Obed-edom
and all that belongs to him, because of the ark of God.' So David went and
brought up the ark of God from the house of Obed-edom to the city of David
with rejoicing; and when those who bore the ark of the LORD had gone six
paces, he sacrificed an ox and a fatling. David danced before the LORD with all
his might; David was girded with a linen ephod. So David and all the house
of Israel brought up the ark of the LORD with shouting, and with the sound
of the trumpet.

They brought in the ark of the LORD, and set it in its place, inside the tent
that David had pitched for it; and David offered burnt-offerings and offerings
of well-being before the LORD. When David had finished offering the burnt-
offerings and the offerings of well-being, he blessed the people in the name
of the LORD of hosts, and distributed food among all the people, the whole
multitude of Israel, both men and women, to each a cake of bread, a portion of
meat, and a cake of raisins. Then all the people went back to their homes.

This is the word of the Lord.   2 *Samuel* 6.12–15, 17–19

R **The Lord of hosts is the king of glory:**
[the king of glory shall come in]. *cf Psalm 24.10b, 7b*

Lift up your heads, O gates;
be lifted up, you everlasting doors;
and the King of glory shall come in. R

'Who is the King of glory?'
'The Lord, strong and mighty,
the Lord who is mighty in battle.' R

Lift up your heads, O gates;
be lifted up, you everlasting doors;
and the King of glory shall come in. R

'Who is this King of glory?'
'The Lord of hosts,
he is the King of glory.' R *Psalm 24.7—end*

Year I and Year 2

Hear the Gospel of our Lord Jesus Christ according to Mark.

The mother and brothers of Jesus came; and standing outside, they sent to him and called him. A crowd was sitting around him; and they said to him, 'Your mother and your brothers and sisters are outside, asking for you.' And he replied, 'Who are my mother and my brothers?' And looking at those who sat around him, he said, 'Here are my mother and my brothers! Whoever does the will of God is my brother and sister and mother.'

This is the Gospel of the Lord. *Mark 3.31—end*

Week 3: Wednesday between 24 and 30 January

Year I

A reading from the Letter to the Hebrews.

Every priest stands day after day at his service, offering again and again the same sacrifices that can never take away sins. But when Christ had offered for all time a single sacrifice for sins, 'he sat down at the right hand of God', and since then has been waiting 'until his enemies would be made a footstool for his feet.' For by a single offering he has perfected for all time those who are sanctified. And the Holy Spirit also testifies to us, for after saying,
'This is the covenant that I will make with them
after those days, says the Lord:
I will put my laws in their hearts,
and I will write them on their minds', →

he also adds,

'I will remember their sins and their lawless deeds no more.'

Where there is forgiveness of these, there is no longer any offering for sin.

This is the word of the Lord. *Hebrews 10.11–18*

Responsorial Psalm

R **You are a priest for ever**
[a priest after the order of Melchizedek]. *cf Psalm 110.4b*

The Lord said to my lord, 'Sit at my right hand,
until I make your enemies your footstool.'
May the Lord stretch forth the sceptre of your power;
rule from Zion in the midst of your enemies. **R**

'Noble are you on this day of your birth;
on the holy mountain, from the womb of the dawn
the dew of your new birth is upon you.'
The Lord has sworn and will not retract:
'You are a priest for ever after the order of Melchizedek.' **R**

Psalm 110.1–4

Year 2

A reading from the Second Book of Samuel.

The word of the LORD came to Nathan: Go and tell my servant David: Thus says the LORD: Are you the one to build me a house to live in? I have not lived in a house since the day I brought up the people of Israel from Egypt to this day, but I have been moving about in a tent and a tabernacle. Wherever I have moved about among all the people of Israel, did I ever speak a word with any of the tribal leaders of Israel, whom I commanded to shepherd my people Israel, saying, 'Why have you not built me a house of cedar?'

Now therefore thus you shall say to my servant David: Thus says the LORD of hosts: I took you from the pasture, from following the sheep to be prince over my people Israel; and I have been with you wherever you went, and have cut off all your enemies from before you; and I will make for you a great name, like the name of the great ones of the earth. And I will appoint a place for my people Israel and will plant them, so that they may live in their own place, and be disturbed no more; and evildoers shall afflict them no more, as formerly, from the time that I appointed judges over my people Israel; and I will give you rest from all your enemies.

Moreover, the LORD declares to you that the LORD will make you a house. When your days are fulfilled and you lie down with your ancestors, I will raise up your offspring after you, who shall come forth from your body, and I will establish his kingdom. He shall build a house for my name, and I will establish the throne of his kingdom for ever. I will be a father to him, and he shall be a son to me. When he commits iniquity, I will punish him with a rod such as mortals use, with blows inflicted by human beings. But I will not take my steadfast love from him, as I took it from Saul, whom I put away from before you. Your house and your kingdom shall be made sure for ever before me; your throne shall be established for ever. In accordance with all these words and with all this vision, Nathan spoke to David.

This is the word of the Lord.   2 Samuel 7.4–17

Responsorial Psalm

R   **Your love, O God, is established for ever:**
  [your faithfulness as firm as the heavens].   cf Psalm 89.2

You spoke once in a vision
and said to your faithful people:
I have set a youth above the mighty;
I have raised a young man over the people.   R

I have found David my servant;
with my holy oil have I anointed him.
My hand shall hold him fast
and my arm shall strengthen him.   R

No enemy shall deceive him,
nor any wicked person afflict him.
I will strike down his foes before his face
and beat down those that hate him.   R

My truth also and my steadfast love shall be with him,
and in my name shall his head be exalted.
I will set his dominion upon the sea
and his right hand upon the rivers.   R

He shall call to me, 'You are my Father,
my God, and the rock of my salvation;'
And I will make him my firstborn,
the most high above the kings of the earth.   R   Psalm 89.19–27

Year 1 and Year 2

Hear the Gospel of our Lord Jesus Christ according to Mark.

Jesus began to teach beside the lake. Such a very large crowd gathered around him that he got into a boat on the lake and sat there, while the whole crowd was beside the lake on the land. He began to teach them many things in parables, and in his teaching he said to them: 'Listen! A sower went out to sow. And as he sowed, some seed fell on the path, and the birds came and ate it up. Other seed fell on rocky ground, where it did not have much soil, and it sprang up quickly, since it had no depth of soil. And when the sun rose, it was scorched; and since it had no root, it withered away. Other seed   →

fell among thorns, and the thorns grew up and choked it, and it yielded no grain. Other seed fell into good soil and brought forth grain, growing up and increasing and yielding thirty and sixty and a hundredfold.' And he said, 'Let anyone with ears to hear listen!'

When he was alone, those who were around him along with the twelve asked him about the parables. And he said to them, 'To you has been given the secret of the kingdom of God, but for those outside, everything comes in parables; in order that

"they may indeed look, but not perceive,
    and may indeed listen, but not understand;
so that they may not turn again and be forgiven." '

And he said to them, 'Do you not understand this parable? Then how will you understand all the parables? The sower sows the word. These are the ones on the path where the word is sown: when they hear, Satan immediately comes and takes away the word that is sown in them. And these are the ones sown on rocky ground: when they hear the word, they immediately receive it with joy. But they have no root, and endure only for a while; then, when trouble or persecution arises on account of the word, immediately they fall away. And others are those sown among the thorns: these are the ones who hear the word, but the cares of the world, and the lure of wealth, and the desire for other things come in and choke the word, and it yields nothing. And these are the ones sown on the good soil: they hear the word and accept it and bear fruit, thirty and sixty and a hundredfold.'

This is the Gospel of the Lord.   Mark 4.1–20

Week 3: Thursday between 25 and 31 January

Year I

A reading from the Letter to the Hebrews.

Since we have confidence to enter the sanctuary by the blood of Jesus, by the new and living way that he opened for us through the curtain (that is, through his flesh), and since we have a great priest over the house of God, let us approach with a true heart in full assurance of faith, with our hearts sprinkled clean from an evil conscience and our bodies washed with pure water. Let us hold fast to the confession of our hope without wavering, for he who has promised is faithful. And let us consider how to provoke one another to love and good deeds, not neglecting to meet together, as is the habit of some, but encouraging one another, and all the more as you see the Day approaching.

This is the word of the Lord.   Hebrews 10.19–25

Responsorial Psalm

R **Those who trust in God will understand truth
[and the faithful will abide in love].**   cf *Wisdom* 3.9

The earth is the Lord's and all that fills it,
the compass of the world and all who dwell therein.
For he has founded it upon the seas
and set it firm upon the rivers of the deep. **R**

'Who shall ascend the hill of the Lord,
or who can rise up in his holy place?
Those who have clean hands and a pure heart,
who have not lifted up their soul to an idol,
nor sworn an oath to a lie. **R**

'They shall receive a blessing from the Lord,
a just reward from the God of their salvation.'
Such is the company of those who seek him,
of those who seek your face, O God of Jacob. **R**   *Psalm* 24.1–6

Year 2

A reading from the Second Book of Samuel.

King David went in and sat before the LORD, and said, 'Who am I, O Lord
GOD, and what is my house, that you have brought me thus far? And yet this
was a small thing in your eyes, O Lord GOD; you have spoken also of your
servant's house for a great while to come. May this be instruction for the
people, O Lord GOD! And you established your people Israel for yourself to
be your people for ever; and you, O LORD, became their God. And now, O
Lord GOD, as for the word that you have spoken concerning your servant and
concerning his house, confirm it for ever; do as you have promised. Thus your
name will be magnified for ever in the saying, "The LORD of hosts is God over
Israel"; and the house of your servant David will be established before you.
For you, O LORD of hosts, the God of Israel, have made this revelation to your
servant, saying, "I will build you a house"; therefore your servant has found
courage to pray this prayer to you. And now, O Lord GOD, you are God, and
your words are true, and you have promised this good thing to your servant;
now therefore may it please you to bless the house of your servant, so that
it may continue for ever before you; for you, O Lord GOD, have spoken, and
with your blessing shall the house of your servant be blessed for ever.'

This is the word of the Lord.   *2 Samuel* 7.18–19, 24–end

Responsorial Psalm

R **The Lord God will give him
the throne of his father David.** cf Luke 1.32

Lord, remember for David
all the hardships he endured;
how he swore an oath to the Lord
and vowed a vow to the Mighty One of Jacob. R

'I will not come within the shelter of my house,
nor climb up into my bed;
I will not allow my eyes to sleep,
nor let my eyelids slumber,
until I find a place for the Lord,
a dwelling for the Mighty One of Jacob.' R

The Lord has sworn an oath to David,
a promise from which he will not shrink:
'Of the fruit of your body
shall I set upon your throne. R

'If your children keep my covenant
and my testimonies that I shall teach them,
their children also shall sit
upon your throne for evermore.' R

For the Lord has chosen Zion for himself;
he has desired her for his habitation:
'This shall be my resting place for ever;
here will I dwell, for I have longed for her.' R Psalm 132.1–5, 11–15

Year 1 and Year 2

Hear the Gospel of our Lord Jesus Christ according to Mark.

Jesus said to the twelve and those around him, 'Is a lamp brought in to be put under the bushel basket, or under the bed, and not on the lampstand? For there is nothing hidden, except to be disclosed; nor is anything secret, except to come to light. Let anyone with ears to hear listen!' And he said to them, 'Pay attention to what you hear; the measure you give will be the measure you get, and still more will be given you. For to those who have, more will be given; and from those who have nothing, even what they have will be taken away.'

This is the Gospel of the Lord. Mark 4.21–25

Week 3: Friday between 26 January and 1 February

Year 1

A reading from the Letter to the Hebrews.

Recall those earlier days when, after you had been enlightened, you endured a hard struggle with sufferings, sometimes being publicly exposed to abuse and persecution, and sometimes being partners with those so treated. For you had compassion for those who were in prison, and you cheerfully accepted the plundering of your possessions, knowing that you yourselves possessed something better and more lasting. Do not, therefore, abandon that confidence of yours; it brings a great reward. For you need endurance, so that when you have done the will of God, you may receive what was promised. For yet
  'in a very little while,
      the one who is coming will come and will not delay;
  but my righteous one will live by faith.
      My soul takes no pleasure in anyone who shrinks back.'
But we are not among those who shrink back and so are lost, but among those who have faith and so are saved.

This is the word of the Lord.   Hebrews 10.32–end

Responsorial Psalm

R* **The salvation of the righteous comes from the Lord;**
   [he is their stronghold in the time of trouble].   *Psalm 37.40*

Trust in the Lord and be doing good;
dwell in the land and be nourished with truth.
Let your delight be in the Lord
and he will give you your heart's desire.   **R**

Commit your way to the Lord and put your trust in him,
and he will bring it to pass.
He will make your righteousness as clear as the light
and your just dealing as the noonday.   **R***

The Lord shall stand by them and deliver them;
he shall deliver them from the wicked and shall save them,
because they have put their trust in him.   **R**   *Psalm 37.3–6, 40–end*

A reading from the Second Book of Samuel.

In the spring of the year, the time when kings go out to battle, David sent Joab with his officers and all Israel with him; they ravaged the Ammonites, and besieged Rabbah. But David remained at Jerusalem.

It happened, late one afternoon, when David rose from his couch and was walking about on the roof of the king's house, that he saw from the roof a woman bathing; the woman was very beautiful. David sent someone to inquire about the woman. It was reported, 'This is Bathsheba daughter of Eliam, the wife of Uriah the Hittite.' So David sent messengers to fetch her, and she came to him, and he lay with her. (Now she was purifying herself after her period.) Then she returned to her house. The woman conceived; and she sent and told David, 'I am pregnant.'

So David sent word to Joab, 'Send me Uriah the Hittite.' And Joab sent Uriah to David. When Uriah came to him, David asked how Joab and the people fared, and how the war was going. Then David said to Uriah, 'Go down to your house, and wash your feet.' Uriah went out of the king's house, and there followed him a present from the king. But Uriah slept at the entrance of the king's house with all the servants of his lord, and did not go down to his house. When they told David, 'Uriah did not go down to his house', David said to Uriah, 'You have just come from a journey. Why did you not go down to your house?' David invited him to eat and drink in his presence and made him drunk; and in the evening he went out to lie on his couch with the servants of his lord, but he did not go down to his house.

In the morning David wrote a letter to Joab, and sent it by the hand of Uriah. In the letter he wrote, 'Set Uriah in the forefront of the hardest fighting, and then draw back from him, so that he may be struck down and die.' As Joab was besieging the city, he assigned Uriah to the place where he knew there were valiant warriors. The men of the city came out and fought with Joab; and some of the servants of David among the people fell. Uriah the Hittite was killed as well.

This is the word of the Lord.   2 Samuel 11.1–10, 13–17

Responsorial Psalm

R **Make me a clean heart, O God,**
   [and renew a right spirit within me].   *Psalm 51.11*

Have mercy on me, O God, in your great goodness;
according to the abundance of your compassion
blot out my offences. **R**

Wash me thoroughly from my wickedness
and cleanse me from my sin.
For I acknowledge my faults
and my sin is ever before me. **R**

Against you only have I sinned
and done what is evil in your sight,
so that you are justified in your sentence
and righteous in your judgement.   R

I have been wicked even from my birth,
a sinner when my mother conceived me.
Make me hear of joy and gladness,
that the bones you have broken may rejoice.   R   *Psalm 51.1–6, 9*

Year 1 and Year 2

Hear the Gospel of our Lord Jesus Christ according to Mark.

Jesus said to the twelve and those around him, 'The kingdom of God is as if someone would scatter seed on the ground, and would sleep and rise night and day, and the seed would sprout and grow, he does not know how. The earth produces of itself, first the stalk, then the head, then the full grain in the head. But when the grain is ripe, at once he goes in with his sickle, because the harvest has come.'

He also said, 'With what can we compare the kingdom of God, or what parable will we use for it? It is like a mustard seed, which, when sown upon the ground, is the smallest of all the seeds on earth; yet when it is sown it grows up and becomes the greatest of all shrubs, and puts forth large branches, so that the birds of the air can make nests in its shade.'

With many such parables he spoke the word to them, as they were able to hear it; he did not speak to them except in parables, but he explained everything in private to his disciples.

This is the Gospel of the Lord.   *Mark 4.26–34*

Week 3: Saturday between 27 January and 2 February

Year 1

A reading from the Letter to the Hebrews.

Faith is the assurance of things hoped for, the conviction of things not seen. Indeed, by faith our ancestors received approval.

By faith Abraham obeyed when he was called to set out for a place that he was to receive as an inheritance; and he set out, not knowing where he was going. By faith he stayed for a time in the land he had been promised, as in a foreign land, living in tents, as did Isaac and Jacob, who were heirs with him of the same promise. For he looked forward to the city that has foundations, whose architect and builder is God. By faith he received power of procreation, even though he was too old – and Sarah herself was barren – because he considered him faithful who had promised. Therefore from one person, and this one as good as dead, descendants were born, 'as many as the stars of heaven and as the innumerable grains of sand by the seashore.'   →

All of these died in faith without having received the promises, but from a distance they saw and greeted them. They confessed that they were strangers and foreigners on the earth, for people who speak in this way make it clear that they are seeking a homeland. If they had been thinking of the land that they had left behind, they would have had opportunity to return. But as it is, they desire a better country, that is, a heavenly one. Therefore God is not ashamed to be called their God; indeed, he has prepared a city for them.

By faith Abraham, when put to the test, offered up Isaac. He who had received the promises was ready to offer up his only son, of whom he had been told, 'It is through Isaac that descendants shall be named after you.' He considered the fact that God is able even to raise someone from the dead – and figuratively speaking, he did receive him back.

This is the word of the Lord.   Hebrews 11.1–2, 8–19

Canticle

R **Blessed be the Lord the God of Israel,**
   who has come to his people and set them free.   Luke 1.68

Blessed be the Lord the God of Israel,
who has come to his people and set them free.
He has raised up for us a mighty saviour
born of the house of his servant David.   **R**

Through his holy prophets God promised of old
to save us from our enemies,
from the hand of all that hate us,
to show mercy to our ancestors,
and to remember his holy covenant.   **R**

This was the oath God swore to our father Abraham:
to set us free from the hands of our enemies,
free to worship him without fear,
holy and righteous in his sight
all the days of our life.   **R**   Luke 1.68–73

Year 2

A reading from the Second Book of Samuel.

The LORD sent Nathan to David. He came to him, and said to him, 'There were two men in a certain city, one rich and the other poor. The rich man had very many flocks and herds; but the poor man had nothing but one little ewe lamb, which he had bought. He brought it up, and it grew up with him and with his children; it used to eat of his meagre fare, and drink from his cup, and lie in his bosom, and it was like a daughter to him. Now there came a traveller to the rich man, and he was loath to take one of his own flock or herd to prepare for the wayfarer who had come to him, but he took the poor man's lamb, and prepared that for the guest who had come to him.' Then David's anger was greatly kindled against the man. He said to Nathan, 'As the LORD lives, the man who has done this deserves to die; he shall restore the lamb fourfold, because he did this thing, and because he had no pity.'

Nathan said to David, 'You are the man! Thus says the LORD, the God of Israel: I anointed you king over Israel, and I rescued you from the hand of Saul; Now therefore the sword shall never depart from your house, for you have despised me, and have taken the wife of Uriah the Hittite to be your wife. Thus says the LORD: I will raise up trouble against you from within your own house; and I will take your wives before your eyes, and give them to your neighbour, and he shall lie with your wives in the sight of this very sun. For you did it secretly; but I will do this thing before all Israel, and before the sun.' David said to Nathan, 'I have sinned against the LORD.' Nathan said to David, 'Now the LORD has put away your sin; you shall not die. Nevertheless, because by this deed you have utterly scorned the LORD, the child that is born to you shall die.' Then Nathan went to his house.

The LORD struck the child that Uriah's wife bore to David, and it became very ill. David therefore pleaded with God for the child; David fasted, and went in and lay all night on the ground. The elders of his house stood beside him, urging him to rise from the ground; but he would not, nor did he eat food with them.

This is the word of the Lord.   2 Samuel 12.1–7, 10–17

Responsorial Psalm

R **Make me a clean heart, O God,
[and renew a right spirit within me].**   Psalm 51.11

Make me a clean heart, O God,
and renew a right spirit within me.
Cast me not away from your presence
and take not your holy spirit from me. R

Give me again the joy of your salvation
and sustain me with your gracious spirit;
then shall I teach your ways to the wicked
and sinners shall return to you. R

Deliver me from my guilt, O God,
the God of my salvation,
and my tongue shall sing of your righteousness.
O Lord, open my lips
and my mouth shall proclaim your praise. R   Psalm 51.11–16

Year 1 and Year 2

Hear the Gospel of our Lord Jesus Christ according to Mark.

When evening had come, Jesus said to his disciples, 'Let us go across to the
other side.' And leaving the crowd behind, they took him with them in the
boat, just as he was. Other boats were with him. A great gale arose, and the
waves beat into the boat, so that the boat was already being swamped. But
he was in the stern, asleep on the cushion; and they woke him up and said
to him, 'Teacher, do you not care that we are perishing?' He woke up and
rebuked the wind, and said to the sea, 'Peace! Be still!' Then the wind ceased,
and there was a dead calm. He said to them, 'Why are you afraid? Have you
still no faith?' And they were filled with great awe and said to one another,
'Who then is this, that even the wind and the sea obey him?'

This is the Gospel of the Lord.   Mark 4.35–end

Week 4: Monday between 29 January and 4 February

Year I

A reading from the Letter to the Hebrews.

What more should I say? For time would fail me to tell of Gideon, Barak, Samson, Jephthah, of David and Samuel and the prophets – who through faith conquered kingdoms, administered justice, obtained promises, shut the mouths of lions, quenched raging fire, escaped the edge of the sword, won strength out of weakness, became mighty in war, put foreign armies to flight. Women received their dead by resurrection. Others were tortured, refusing to accept release, in order to obtain a better resurrection. Others suffered mocking and flogging, and even chains and imprisonment. They were stoned to death, they were sawn in two, they were killed by the sword; they went about in skins of sheep and goats, destitute, persecuted, tormented – of whom the world was not worthy. They wandered in deserts and mountains, and in caves and holes in the ground.

Yet all these, though they were commended for their faith, did not receive what was promised, since God had provided something better so that they would not, without us, be made perfect.

This is the word of the Lord.   Hebrews 11.32–end

Responsorial Psalm

R* **Be strong and let your heart take courage,**
   [all who wait in hope for the Lord].   cf Psalm 31.24

How abundant is your goodness, O Lord,
which you have laid up for those who fear you;
which you have prepared in the sight of all
for those who put their trust in you.   **R**

You hide them in the shelter of your presence
from those who slander them;
you keep them safe in your refuge from the strife of tongues.   **R**

Blessed be the Lord!
For he has shown me his steadfast love
when I was as a city besieged.
I had said in my alarm,
'I have been cut off from the sight of your eyes.'   **R**

Nevertheless, you heard the voice of my prayer
when I cried out to you.
Love the Lord, all you his servants;
for the Lord protects the faithful,
but repays to the full the proud.   **R***   Psalm 31.19–end

A reading from the Second Book of Samuel.

A messenger came to David, saying, 'The hearts of the Israelites have gone after Absalom.' Then David said to all his officials who were with him at Jerusalem, 'Get up! Let us flee, or there will be no escape for us from Absalom. Hurry, or he will soon overtake us, and bring disaster down upon us, and attack the city with the edge of the sword.'

But David went up the ascent of the Mount of Olives, weeping as he went, with his head covered and walking barefoot; and all the people who were with him covered their heads and went up, weeping as they went.

When King David came to Bahurim, a man of the family of the house of Saul came out whose name was Shimei son of Gera; he came out cursing. He threw stones at David and at all the servants of King David; now all the people and all the warriors were on his right and on his left. Shimei shouted while he cursed, 'Out! Out! Murderer! Scoundrel! The LORD has avenged on all of you the blood of the house of Saul, in whose place you have reigned; and the LORD has given the kingdom into the hand of your son Absalom. See, disaster has overtaken you; for you are a man of blood.'

Then Abishai son of Zeruiah said to the king, 'Why should this dead dog curse my lord the king? Let me go over and take off his head.' But the king said, 'What have I to do with you, you sons of Zeruiah? If he is cursing because the LORD has said to him, "Curse David", who then shall say, "Why have you done so?"' David said to Abishai and to all his servants, 'My own son seeks my life; how much more now may this Benjaminite! Let him alone, and let him curse; for the LORD has bidden him. It may be that the LORD will look on my distress, and the LORD will repay me with good for this cursing of me today.' So David and his men went on the road, while Shimei went along on the hillside opposite him and cursed as he went, throwing stones and flinging dust at him.

This is the word of the Lord.   *2 Samuel 15.13–14, 30, 16.5–13*

Responsorial Psalm

R **Rise up, O Lord, and deliver me, O my God.**   *Psalm 3.7a*

Lord, how many are my adversaries;
many are they who rise up against me.
Many are they who say to my soul,
'There is no help for you in your God.'   R

But you, Lord, are a shield about me;
you are my glory, and the lifter up of my head.
When I cry aloud to the Lord,
he will answer me from his holy hill.   R

I lie down and sleep and rise again,
because the Lord sustains me.
I will not be afraid of hordes of the peoples
that have set themselves against me all around. R

Rise up, O Lord, and deliver me, O my God,
for you strike all my enemies on the cheek
and break the teeth of the wicked.
Salvation belongs to the Lord:
may your blessing be upon your people. R   *Psalm 3*

Year 1 and Year 2

Hear the Gospel of our Lord Jesus Christ according to Mark.

Jesus and his disciples came to the other side of the lake, to the country of
the Gerasenes. And when he had stepped out of the boat, immediately a man
out of the tombs with an unclean spirit met him. He lived among the tombs;
and no one could restrain him any more, even with a chain; for he had often
been restrained with shackles and chains, but the chains he wrenched apart,
and the shackles he broke in pieces; and no one had the strength to subdue
him. Night and day among the tombs and on the mountains he was always
howling and bruising himself with stones.

When he saw Jesus from a distance, he ran and bowed down before him;
and he shouted at the top of his voice, 'What have you to do with me, Jesus,
Son of the Most High God? I adjure you by God, do not torment me.' For
he had said to him, 'Come out of the man, you unclean spirit!' Then Jesus
asked him, 'What is your name?' He replied, 'My name is Legion; for we are
many.' He begged him earnestly not to send them out of the country. Now
there on the hillside a great herd of swine was feeding; and the unclean
spirits begged him, 'Send us into the swine; let us enter them.' So he gave
them permission. And the unclean spirits came out and entered the swine;
and the herd, numbering about two thousand, rushed down the steep bank
into the lake, and were drowned in the lake.

The swineherds ran off and told it in the city and in the country. Then
people came to see what it was that had happened. They came to Jesus and
saw the demoniac sitting there, clothed and in his right mind, the very man
who had had the legion; and they were afraid. Those who had seen what had
happened to the demoniac and to the swine reported it. Then they began to
beg Jesus to leave their neighbourhood. As he was getting into the boat, the
man who had been possessed by demons begged him that he might be with
him. But Jesus refused, and said to him, 'Go home to your friends, and tell
them how much the Lord has done for you, and what mercy he has shown
you.' And he went away and began to proclaim in the Decapolis how much
Jesus had done for him; and everyone was amazed.

This is the Gospel of the Lord.   Mark 5.1–20

Week 4: Tuesday between 30 January and 5 February

Year I

A reading from the Letter to the Hebrews.

Since we are surrounded by so great a cloud of witnesses, let us also lay aside every weight and the sin that clings so closely, and let us run with perseverance the race that is set before us, looking to Jesus the pioneer and perfecter of our faith, who for the sake of the joy that was set before him endured the cross, disregarding its shame, and has taken his seat at the right hand of the throne of God.

Consider him who endured such hostility against himself from sinners, so that you may not grow weary or lose heart. In your struggle against sin you have not yet resisted to the point of shedding your blood.

This is the word of the Lord. *Hebrews 12.1–4*

Responsorial Psalm

R **I will proclaim your name among the people:**
[and praise you in the midst of the congregation]. *cf Psalm 22.22*

I will perform my vows in the presence of those that fear you.
The poor shall eat and be satisfied;
those who seek the Lord shall praise him;
their hearts shall live for ever. **R**

All the ends of the earth shall remember and turn to the Lord,
and all the families of the nations shall bow before him.
For the kingdom is the Lord's
and he rules over the nations. **R**

How can those who sleep in the earth bow down in worship,
or those who go down to the dust kneel before him?
He has saved my life for himself;
my descendants shall serve him. **R**

This shall be told of the Lord for generations to come,
they shall come and make known his salvation,
to a people yet unborn,
declaring that he, the Lord, has done it. **R** *Psalm 22.25b–end*

Year 2

A reading from the Second Book of Samuel.

Absalom happened to meet the servants of David. Absalom was riding on his mule, and the mule went under the thick branches of a great oak. His head caught fast in the oak, and he was left hanging between heaven and earth, while the mule that was under him went on. A man saw it, and told Joab, 'I saw Absalom hanging in an oak.' Joab said, 'I will not waste time like this with you.' He took three spears in his hand, and thrust them into the heart of Absalom, while he was still alive in the oak.

Now David was sitting between the two gates. The sentinel went up to the roof of the gate by the wall, and when he looked up, he saw a man running alone. The sentinel shouted and told the king. The king said, 'If he is alone, there are tidings in his mouth.' He kept coming, and drew near. The king said, 'Turn aside, and stand here.' So he turned aside, and stood still.

Then the Cushite came; and the Cushite said, 'Good tidings for my lord the king! For the LORD has vindicated you this day, delivering you from the power of all who rose up against you.' The king said to the Cushite, 'Is it well with the young man Absalom?' The Cushite answered, 'May the enemies of my lord the king, and all who rise up to do you harm, be like that young man.'

The king was deeply moved, and went up to the chamber over the gate, and wept; and as he went, he said, 'O my son Absalom, my son, my son Absalom! Would that I had died instead of you, O Absalom, my son, my son!'

It was told Joab, 'The king is weeping and mourning for Absalom.' So the victory that day was turned into mourning for all the troops; for the troops heard that day, 'The king is grieving for his son.' The troops stole into the city that day as soldiers steal in who are ashamed when they flee in battle.

This is the word of the Lord.   2 Samuel 18.9–10, 14, 24–25, 30 – 19.3

Responsorial Psalm

R **Teach me your way, O Lord,
and I will walk in your truth.**   Psalm 86.11a

Incline your ear, O Lord, and answer me,
for I am poor and in misery.
Preserve my soul, for I am faithful;
save your servant, for I put my trust in you.   **R**

Be merciful to me, O Lord, for you are my God;
I call upon you all the day long.
Gladden the soul of your servant,
for to you, O Lord, I lift up my soul.   **R**

For you, Lord, are good and forgiving,
abounding in steadfast love to all who call upon you.
Give ear, O Lord, to my prayer
and listen to the voice of my supplication.   **R**   Psalm 86.1–6

Hear the Gospel of our Lord Jesus Christ according to Mark.

When Jesus had crossed again in the boat to the other side, a great crowd gathered round him; and he was by the lake. Then one of the leaders of the synagogue named Jairus came and, when he saw him, fell at his feet and begged him repeatedly, 'My little daughter is at the point of death. Come and lay your hands on her, so that she may be made well, and live.' So he went with him.

And a large crowd followed him and pressed in on him. Now there was a woman who had been suffering from haemorrhages for twelve years. She had endured much under many physicians, and had spent all that she had; and she was no better, but rather grew worse. She had heard about Jesus, and came up behind him in the crowd and touched his cloak, for she said, 'If I but touch his clothes, I will be made well.' Immediately her haemorrhage stopped; and she felt in her body that she was healed of her disease. Immediately aware that power had gone forth from him, Jesus turned about in the crowd and said, 'Who touched my clothes?' And his disciples said to him, 'You see the crowd pressing in on you; how can you say, "Who touched me?" ' He looked all round to see who had done it. But the woman, knowing what had happened to her, came in fear and trembling, fell down before him, and told him the whole truth. He said to her, 'Daughter, your faith has made you well; go in peace, and be healed of your disease.'

While he was still speaking, some people came from the leader's house to say, 'Your daughter is dead. Why trouble the teacher any further?' But overhearing what they said, Jesus said to the leader of the synagogue, 'Do not fear, only believe.' He allowed no one to follow him except Peter, James, and John, the brother of James. When they came to the house of the leader of the synagogue, he saw a commotion, people weeping and wailing loudly. When he had entered, he said to them, 'Why do you make a commotion and weep? The child is not dead but sleeping.' And they laughed at him. Then he put them all outside, and took the child's father and mother and those who were with him, and went in where the child was. He took her by the hand and said to her, 'Talitha cum', which means, 'Little girl, get up!' And immediately the girl got up and began to walk about (she was twelve years of age). At this they were overcome with amazement. He strictly ordered them that no one should know this, and told them to give her something to eat.

This is the Gospel of the Lord.   Mark 5.21–end

Week 4: Wednesday between 31 January and 6 February *(if before Lent)*

Year 1

A reading from the Letter to the Hebrews.

In your struggle against sin you have not yet resisted to the point of shedding your blood. And you have forgotten the exhortation that addresses you as children –

'My child, do not regard lightly the discipline of the Lord,
> or lose heart when you are punished by him;
for the Lord disciplines those whom he loves,
> and chastises every child whom he accepts.'

Endure trials for the sake of discipline. God is treating you as children; for what child is there whom a parent does not discipline? Now, discipline always seems painful rather than pleasant at the time, but later it yields the peaceful fruit of righteousness to those who have been trained by it.

Therefore lift your drooping hands and strengthen your weak knees, and make straight paths for your feet, so that what is lame may not be put out of joint, but rather be healed. Pursue peace with everyone, and the holiness without which no one will see the Lord. See to it that no one fails to obtain the grace of God; that no root of bitterness springs up and causes trouble, and through it many become defiled.

This is the word of the Lord.   *Hebrews 12.4–7, 11–15*

Responsorial Psalm

R   **Bless the Lord, O my soul,**
   [and bless his holy name].   *cf Psalm 103.1*

Bless the Lord, O my soul,
and all that is within me bless his holy name.
Bless the Lord, O my soul,
and forget not all his benefits.   **R**

As a father has compassion on his children,
so is the Lord merciful towards those who fear him.
For he knows of what we are made;
he remembers that we are but dust.   **R**

Our days are but as grass;
we flourish as a flower of the field;
for as soon as the wind goes over it, it is gone,
and its place shall know it no more.   **R**

But the merciful goodness of the Lord is from of old
and endures for ever on those who fear him,
and his righteousness on children's children;
on those who keep his covenant
and remember his commandments to do them.   **R**   *Psalm 103.1–2, 13–18*

A reading from the Second Book of Samuel.

King David said to Joab and the commanders of the army, who were with him, 'Go through all the tribes of Israel, from Dan to Beer-sheba, and take a census of the people, so that I may know how many there are.' Joab reported to the king the number of those who had been recorded: in Israel there were eight hundred thousand soldiers able to draw the sword, and those of Judah were five hundred thousand.

But afterwards, David was stricken to the heart because he had numbered the people. David said to the LORD, 'I have sinned greatly in what I have done. But now, O LORD, I pray you, take away the guilt of your servant; for I have done very foolishly.' When David rose in the morning, the word of the LORD came to the prophet Gad, David's seer, saying, 'Go and say to David: Thus says the LORD: Three things I offer you; choose one of them, and I will do it to you.' So Gad came to David and told him; he asked him, 'Shall three years of famine come to you on your land? Or will you flee for three months before your foes while they pursue you? Or shall there be three days' pestilence in your land? Now consider, and decide what answer I shall return to the one who sent me.' Then David said to Gad, 'I am in great distress; let us fall into the hand of the LORD, for his mercy is great; but let me not fall into human hands.'

So the LORD sent a pestilence on Israel from that morning until the appointed time; and seventy thousand of the people died, from Dan to Beer-sheba. But when the angel stretched out his hand towards Jerusalem to destroy it, the LORD relented concerning the evil, and said to the angel who was bringing destruction among the people, 'It is enough; now stay your hand.' The angel of the LORD was then by the threshing-floor of Araunah the Jebusite. When David saw the angel who was destroying the people, he said to the LORD, 'I alone have sinned, and I alone have done wickedly; but these sheep, what have they done? Let your hand, I pray, be against me and against my father's house.'

This is the word of the Lord.   2 Samuel 24.2, 9–17

Responsorial Psalm

R **Be glad, you righteous, and rejoice in the Lord;**
   [shout for joy, all who are true of heart].   Psalm 32.12

Happy the one whose transgression is forgiven,
and whose sin is covered.
Happy the one to whom the Lord imputes no guilt,
and in whose spirit there is no guile.   **R**

For I held my tongue;
my bones wasted away
through my groaning all the day long.   **R**

Your hand was heavy upon me day and night;
my moisture was dried up like the drought in summer.
Then I acknowledged my sin to you
and my iniquity I did not hide. R

I said, 'I will confess my transgressions to the Lord,'
and you forgave the guilt of my sin.
Therefore let all the faithful make their prayers to you
in time of trouble;
in the great water flood, it shall not reach them. R

You are a place for me to hide in;
you preserve me from trouble;
you surround me with songs of deliverance. R   Psalm 32.1–8

Year 1 and Year 2

Hear the Gospel of our Lord Jesus Christ according to Mark.

Jesus came to his home town, and his disciples followed him. On the sabbath
he began to teach in the synagogue, and many who heard him were astounded.
They said, 'Where did this man get all this? What is this wisdom that has
been given to him? What deeds of power are being done by his hands! Is not
this the carpenter, the son of Mary and brother of James and Joses and Judas
and Simon, and are not his sisters here with us?' And they took offence at
him. Then Jesus said to them, 'Prophets are not without honour, except in
their home town, and among their own kin, and in their own house.' And
he could do no deed of power there, except that he laid his hands on a few
sick people and cured them. And he was amazed at their unbelief. Then he
went about among the villages teaching.

This is the Gospel of the Lord.   Mark 6.1–6a

Week 4: Thursday between 1 and 7 February *(if before Lent)*

Year 1

A reading from the Letter to the Hebrews.

You have not come to something that can be touched, a blazing fire, and
darkness, and gloom, and a tempest, and the sound of a trumpet, and a
voice whose words made the hearers beg that not another word be spoken
to them. (Indeed, so terrifying was the sight that Moses said, 'I tremble with
fear.') But you have come to Mount Zion and to the city of the living God,
the heavenly Jerusalem, and to innumerable angels in festal gathering, and
to the assembly of the firstborn who are enrolled in heaven, and to God the
judge of all, and to the spirits of the righteous made perfect, and to Jesus, the
mediator of a new covenant, and to the sprinkled blood that speaks a better
word than the blood of Abel.

This is the word of the Lord.   Hebrews 12.18–19, 21–24

Responsorial Psalm

R **Let Mount Zion rejoice in your judgements, O Lord
[and the daughters of Judah be glad].** *cf Psalm* 48.11

Great is the Lord and highly to be praised,
in the city of our God.
His holy mountain is fair and lifted high,
the joy of all the earth. **R**

On Mount Zion, the divine dwelling place,
stands the city of the great king.
As we had heard, so have we seen
in the city of the Lord of hosts, the city of our God:
God has established her for ever. **R**

We have waited on your loving-kindness, O God,
in the midst of your temple.
As with your name, O God,
so your praise reaches to the ends of the earth;
your right hand is full of justice. **R** *Psalm* 48.1–3, 8–10

Year 2

A reading from the First Book of the Kings.

When David's time to die drew near, he charged his son Solomon, saying: 'I am about to go the way of all the earth. Be strong, be courageous, and keep the charge of the LORD your God, walking in his ways and keeping his statutes, his commandments, his ordinances, and his testimonies, as it is written in the law of Moses, so that you may prosper in all that you do and wherever you turn. Then the LORD will establish his word that he spoke concerning me: "If your heirs take heed to their way, to walk before me in faithfulness with all their heart and with all their soul, there shall not fail you a successor on the throne of Israel." '

Then David slept with his ancestors, and was buried in the city of David. The time that David reigned over Israel was forty years; he reigned for seven years in Hebron, and thirty-three years in Jerusalem. So Solomon sat on the throne of his father David; and his kingdom was firmly established.

This is the word of the Lord. 1 Kings 2.1–4, 10–12

Either

Canticle

R **Blessed are you, God of Israel, for ever and ever.**   1 *Chronicles* 29.10b

Blessed are you, God of Israel, for ever and ever,
for yours is the greatness, the power,
the glory, the splendour and the majesty.   R

Everything in heaven and on earth is yours;
yours is the kingdom, O Lord,
and you are exalted as head over all.   R

Riches and honour come from you
and you rule over all.
In your hand are power and might;
yours it is to give power and strength to all.   R   1 *Chronicles* 29.10b–12

or

Responsorial Psalm

R* **I will exalt you, O God my King,**
     [and bless your name for ever].   cf *Psalm* 145.1

Every day will I bless you
and praise your name for ever and ever.
Great is the Lord and highly to be praised;
his greatness is beyond all searching out.   R

One generation shall praise your works to another
and declare your mighty acts.
They shall speak of the majesty of your glory,
and I will tell of all your wonderful deeds.   R   *Psalm* 145.1–5

Year 1 and Year 2

Hear the Gospel of our Lord Jesus Christ according to Mark.

Jesus called the twelve and began to send them out two by two, and gave them
authority over the unclean spirits. He ordered them to take nothing for their
journey except a staff; no bread, no bag, no money in their belts; but to wear
sandals and not to put on two tunics. He said to them, 'Wherever you enter
a house, stay there until you leave the place. If any place will not welcome
you and they refuse to hear you, as you leave, shake off the dust that is on
your feet as a testimony against them.' So they went out and proclaimed that
all should repent. They cast out many demons, and anointed with oil many
who were sick and cured them.

This is the Gospel of the Lord.   *Mark* 6.7–13

Week 4: Friday between 2 and 8 February *(if before Lent)*

Year I

A reading from the Letter to the Hebrews.

Let mutual love continue. Do not neglect to show hospitality to strangers, for by doing that some have entertained angels without knowing it. Remember those who are in prison, as though you were in prison with them; those who are being tortured, as though you yourselves were being tortured. Let marriage be held in honour by all, and let the marriage bed be kept undefiled; for God will judge fornicators and adulterers. Keep your lives free from the love of money, and be content with what you have; for he has said, 'I will never leave you or forsake you.' So we can say with confidence,

'The Lord is my helper;
I will not be afraid.
What can anyone do to me?'

Remember your leaders, those who spoke the word of God to you; consider the outcome of their way of life, and imitate their faith. Jesus Christ is the same yesterday and today and for ever.

This is the word of the Lord. Hebrews 13.1–8

Responsorial Psalm

R **The Lord is my light and my salvation:
[he is the strength of my life].** cf Psalm 27.1

The Lord is my light and my salvation;
whom then shall I fear?
The Lord is the strength of my life;
of whom then shall I be afraid? **R**

When the wicked,
even my enemies and my foes,
came upon me to eat up my flesh,
they stumbled and fell. **R**

Though a host encamp against me,
my heart shall not be afraid,
and though there rise up war against me,
yet will I put my trust in him. **R**

One thing have I asked of the Lord and that alone I seek:
that I may dwell in the house of the Lord
all the days of my life,
to behold the fair beauty of the Lord
and to seek his will in his temple. **R**

For in the day of trouble
he shall hide me in his shelter;
in the secret place of his dwelling shall he hide me
and set me high upon a rock.   R

Hear my voice, O Lord, when I call;
have mercy upon me and answer me.
My heart tells of your word, 'Seek my face.'
Your face, Lord, will I seek.   R

Hide not your face from me,
nor cast your servant away in displeasure.
You have been my helper;
leave me not, neither forsake me, O God of my salvation.   R

Psalm 27.1–6, 9–12

Year 2

A reading from the book Ecclesiasticus.

As the fat is set apart from the offering of well-being,
　　so David was set apart from the Israelites.
He played with lions as though they were young goats,
　　and with bears as though they were lambs of the flock.
In his youth did he not kill a giant,
　　and take away the people's disgrace,
when he whirled the stone in the sling
　　and struck down the boasting Goliath?
For he called on the Lord, the Most High,
　　and he gave strength to his right arm
to strike down a mighty warrior,
　　and to exalt the power of his people.
So they glorified him for the tens of thousands he conquered,
　　and praised him for the blessings bestowed by the Lord,
　　when the glorious diadem was given to him.
For he wiped out his enemies on every side,
　　and annihilated his adversaries the Philistines;
　　he crushed their power to our own day.
In all that he did he gave thanks
　　to the Holy One, the Most High, proclaiming his glory;
he sang praise with all his heart,
　　and he loved his Maker.
He placed singers before the altar,
　　to make sweet melody with their voices.
He gave beauty to the festivals,
　　and arranged their times throughout the year,
while they praised God's holy name,
　　and the sanctuary resounded from early morning.   →

The Lord took away his sins,
and exalted his power for ever;
he gave him a covenant of kingship
and a glorious throne in Israel.

This is the word of the Lord.   Ecclesiasticus 47.2–11

Responsorial Psalm

R   **O God, you are my rock and my refuge,
[you are my shield and strong defence].**   cf Psalm 18.2

As for God, his way is perfect;
the word of the Lord is tried in the fire;
he is a shield to all who trust in him.
For who is God but the Lord,
and who is the rock except our God?   R

It is God who girds me about with strength
and makes my way perfect.
He makes my feet like hinds' feet
so that I tread surely on the heights.   R

He teaches my hands to fight
and my arms to bend a bow of bronze.
You have given me the shield of your salvation;
your right hand upholds me
and your grace has made me great.   R

Therefore will I give you thanks, O Lord, among the nations
and sing praises to your name,
to the one who gives great victory to his king
and shows faithful love to his anointed,
to David and his seed for ever.   R   Psalm 18.31–36, 50–end

Year 1 and Year 2

Hear the Gospel of our Lord Jesus Christ according to Mark.

King Herod heard of the healings and other miracles, for Jesus' name had become known. Some were saying, 'John the baptizer has been raised from the dead; and for this reason these powers are at work in him.' But others said, 'It is Elijah.' And others said, 'It is a prophet, like one of the prophets of old.' But when Herod heard of it, he said, 'John, whom I beheaded, has been raised.'

For Herod himself had sent men who arrested John, bound him, and put him in prison on account of Herodias, his brother Philip's wife, because Herod had married her. For John had been telling Herod, 'It is not lawful for you to have your brother's wife.' And Herodias had a grudge against him, and wanted to kill him. But she could not, for Herod feared John, knowing that he was a righteous and holy man, and he protected him. When he heard him, he was greatly perplexed; and yet he liked to listen to him. But an opportunity came when Herod on his birthday gave a banquet for his courtiers and officers and for the leaders of Galilee. When his daughter Herodias came in and danced, she pleased Herod and his guests; and the king said to the girl, 'Ask me for whatever you wish, and I will give it.' And he solemnly swore to her, 'Whatever you ask me, I will give you, even half of my kingdom.' She went out and said to her mother, 'What should I ask for?' She replied, 'The head of John the baptizer.' Immediately she rushed back to the king and requested, 'I want you to give me at once the head of John the Baptist on a platter.'

The king was deeply grieved; yet out of regard for his oaths and for the guests, he did not want to refuse her. Immediately the king sent a soldier of the guard with orders to bring John's head. He went and beheaded him in the prison, brought his head on a platter, and gave it to the girl. Then the girl gave it to her mother. When his disciples heard about it, they came and took his body, and laid it in a tomb.

This is the Gospel of the Lord. Mark 6.14–29

Week 4: Saturday between 3 and 9 February *(if before Lent)*

Year 1

A reading from the Letter to the Hebrews.

Through Jesus let us continually offer a sacrifice of praise to God, that is, the fruit of lips that confess his name. Do not neglect to do good and to share what you have, for such sacrifices are pleasing to God.

Obey your leaders and submit to them, for they are keeping watch over your souls and will give an account. Let them do this with joy and not with sighing – for that would be harmful to you.

Now may the God of peace, who brought back from the dead our Lord Jesus, the great shepherd of the sheep, by the blood of the eternal covenant, make you complete in everything good so that you may do his will, working among us that which is pleasing in his sight, through Jesus Christ, to whom be the glory for ever and ever. Amen.

This is the word of the Lord. Hebrews 13.15–17, 20–21

R **I will search for my sheep, says the Lord,**
[and I will seek them out].
Ezekiel 34.11

The Lord is my shepherd;
therefore can I lack nothing.
He makes me lie down in green pastures
and leads me beside still waters. R

He shall refresh my soul
and guide me in the paths of righteousness
for his name's sake. R

Though I walk through the valley of the shadow of death,
I will fear no evil;
for you are with me;
your rod and your staff, they comfort me. R

You spread a table before me
in the presence of those who trouble me;
you have anointed my head with oil
and my cup shall be full. R

Surely goodness and loving mercy shall follow me
all the days of my life,
and I will dwell in the house of the Lord for ever. R
Psalm 23

Year 2

A reading from the First Book of the Kings.

King Solomon went to Gibeon to sacrifice there, for that was the principal high place; Solomon used to offer a thousand burnt-offerings on that altar. At Gibeon the LORD appeared to Solomon in a dream by night; and God said, 'Ask what I should give you.' And Solomon said, 'You have shown great and steadfast love to your servant my father David, because he walked before you in faithfulness, in righteousness, and in uprightness of heart towards you; and you have kept for him this great and steadfast love, and have given him a son to sit on his throne today. And now, O LORD my God, you have made your servant king in place of my father David, although I am only a little child; I do not know how to go out or come in. And your servant is in the midst of the people whom you have chosen, a great people, so numerous they cannot be numbered or counted. Give your servant therefore an understanding mind to govern your people, able to discern between good and evil; for who can govern this your great people?'

It pleased the Lord that Solomon had asked this. God said to him, 'Because you have asked this, and have not asked for yourself long life or riches, or for the life of your enemies, but have asked for yourself understanding to discern what is right, I now do according to your word. Indeed I give you a wise and discerning mind; no one like you has been before you and no one like you shall arise after you. I give you also what you have not asked, both riches and honour all your life; no other king shall compare with you.'

This is the word of the Lord. 1 Kings 3.4–13

Responsorial Psalm

R **Blessed are they who fear the Lord,**
 [and walk in the ways of God]. cf Psalm 128.1

How shall young people cleanse their way
to keep themselves according to your word?
With my whole heart have I sought you;
O let me not go astray from your commandments. **R**

Your words have I hidden within my heart,
that I should not sin against you.
Blessed are you, O Lord;
O teach me your statutes. **R**

With my lips have I been telling
of all the judgements of your mouth.
I have taken greater delight in the way of your testimonies
than in all manner of riches. **R**

I will meditate on your commandments
and contemplate your ways.
My delight shall be in your statutes
and I will not forget your word. **R** Psalm 119.9–16

Year 1 and Year 2

Hear the Gospel of our Lord Jesus Christ according to Mark.

The apostles gathered around Jesus, and told him all that they had done and taught. He said to them, 'Come away to a deserted place all by yourselves and rest a while.' For many were coming and going, and they had no leisure even to eat. And they went away in the boat to a deserted place by themselves. Now many saw them going and recognized them, and they hurried there on foot from all the towns and arrived ahead of them. As he went ashore, he saw a great crowd; and he had compassion for them, because they were like sheep without a shepherd; and he began to teach them many things.

This is the Gospel of the Lord. Mark 6.30–34

Week 5: Monday between 5 and 11 February *(if before Lent)*

Year 1

A reading from the book Genesis.

In the beginning when God created the heavens and the earth, the earth was a formless void and darkness covered the face of the deep, while a wind from God swept over the face of the waters. Then God said, 'Let there be light'; and there was light. And God saw that the light was good; and God separated the light from the darkness. God called the light Day, and the darkness he called Night. And there was evening and there was morning, the first day.

And God said, 'Let there be a dome in the midst of the waters, and let it separate the waters from the waters.' So God made the dome and separated the waters that were under the dome from the waters that were above the dome. And it was so. God called the dome Sky. And there was evening and there was morning, the second day.

And God said, 'Let the waters under the sky be gathered together into one place, and let the dry land appear.' And it was so. God called the dry land Earth, and the waters that were gathered together he called Seas. And God saw that it was good. Then God said, 'Let the earth put forth vegetation: plants yielding seed, and fruit trees of every kind on earth that bear fruit with the seed in it.' And it was so. The earth brought forth vegetation: plants yielding seed of every kind, and trees of every kind bearing fruit with the seed in it. And God saw that it was good. And there was evening and there was morning, the third day.

And God said, 'Let there be lights in the dome of the sky to separate the day from the night; and let them be for signs and for seasons and for days and years, and let them be lights in the dome of the sky to give light upon the earth.' And it was so. God made the two great lights – the greater light to rule the day and the lesser light to rule the night – and the stars. God set them in the dome of the sky to give light upon the earth, to rule over the day and over the night, and to separate the light from the darkness. And God saw that it was good. And there was evening and there was morning, the fourth day.

This is the word of the Lord.   *Genesis 1.1–19*

Responsorial Psalm

R **I shall sing to the Lord as long as I live:**
   [and praise him while I have my being].   cf Psalm 104.35

Bless the Lord, O my soul.
O Lord my God, how excellent is your greatness!
You are clothed with majesty and honour,
wrapped in light as in a garment. **R**

You laid the foundations of the earth,
that it never should move at any time.
You covered it with the deep like a garment;
the waters stood high above the hills. **R**

At your rebuke they fled;
at the voice of your thunder they hastened away.
They rose up to the hills and flowed down to the valleys beneath,
to the place which you had appointed for them. **R**

You have set them their bounds that they should not pass,
nor turn again to cover the earth.
You send the springs into the brooks,
which run among the hills. **R**

They give drink to every beast of the field,
and the wild asses quench their thirst.
Beside them the birds of the air make their nests
and sing among the branches. **R**

O Lord, how manifold are your works!
In wisdom you have made them all;
the earth is full of your creatures. **R**   Psalm 104.1–2, 6–13, 26

Year 2

A reading from the First Book of the Kings.

Solomon assembled the elders of Israel and all the heads of the tribes, the leaders of the ancestral houses of the Israelites, before King Solomon in Jerusalem, to bring up the ark of the covenant of the LORD out of the city of David, which is Zion. All the people of Israel assembled to King Solomon at the festival in the month Ethanim, which is the seventh month. And all the elders of Israel came, and the priests carried the ark. So they brought up the ark of the LORD, the tent of meeting, and all the holy vessels that were in the tent; the priests and the Levites brought them up. King Solomon and all the congregation of Israel, who had assembled before him, were with him before the ark, sacrificing so many sheep and oxen that they could not be counted or numbered. Then the priests brought the ark of the covenant of the LORD to its place, in the inner sanctuary of the house, in the most holy place, underneath the wings of the cherubim. For the cherubim spread out their wings over the place of the ark, so that the cherubim made a covering above →

the ark and its poles. There was nothing in the ark except the two tablets of stone that Moses had placed there at Horeb, where the LORD made a covenant with the Israelites, when they came out of the land of Egypt. And when the priests came out of the holy place, a cloud filled the house of the LORD, so that the priests could not stand to minister because of the cloud; for the glory of the LORD filled the house of the LORD. Then Solomon said,
'The LORD has said that he would dwell in thick darkness.
I have built you an exalted house,
a place for you to dwell in for ever.'

This is the word of the Lord.   1 Kings 8.1–7, 9–13

Responsorial Psalm

R **Let us enter the dwelling place of the Lord
[and fall low before his footstool].**   cf Psalm 132.7

Lord, remember for David
all the hardships he endured;
how he swore an oath to the Lord
and vowed a vow to the Mighty One of Jacob.   **R**

'I will not come within the shelter of my house,
nor climb up into my bed;
I will not allow my eyes to sleep,
nor let my eyelids slumber,
until I find a place for the Lord,
a dwelling for the Mighty One of Jacob.'   **R**

Now, we heard of the ark in Ephrathah
and found it in the fields of Ja-ar.
Let us enter his dwelling place
and fall low before his footstool.   **R**

Arise, O Lord, into your resting place,
you and the ark of your strength.
Let your priests be clothed with righteousness
and your faithful ones sing with joy.   **R**   Psalm 132.1–9

Year 1 and Year 2

Hear the Gospel of our Lord Jesus Christ according to Mark.

When Jesus and his disciples had crossed over the lake, they came to land at Gennesaret and moored the boat. When they got out of the boat, people at once recognized him, and rushed about that whole region and began to bring the sick on mats to wherever they heard he was. And wherever he went, into villages or cities or farms, they laid the sick in the market-places, and begged him that they might touch even the fringe of his cloak; and all who touched it were healed.

This is the Gospel of the Lord.   Mark 6.53–end

Year I

A reading from the book Genesis.

God said, 'Let the waters bring forth swarms of living creatures, and let birds fly above the earth across the dome of the sky.' So God created the great sea monsters and every living creature that moves, of every kind, with which the waters swarm, and every winged bird of every kind. And God saw that it was good. God blessed them, saying, 'Be fruitful and multiply and fill the waters in the seas, and let birds multiply on the earth.' And there was evening and there was morning, the fifth day.

And God said, 'Let the earth bring forth living creatures of every kind: cattle and creeping things and wild animals of the earth of every kind.' And it was so. God made the wild animals of the earth of every kind, and the cattle of every kind, and everything that creeps upon the ground of every kind. And God saw that it was good.

Then God said, 'Let us make humankind in our image, according to our likeness; and let them have dominion over the fish of the sea, and over the birds of the air, and over the cattle, and over all the wild animals of the earth, and over every creeping thing that creeps upon the earth.'

So God created humankind in his image,
 in the image of God he created them;
 male and female he created them.

God blessed them, and God said to them, 'Be fruitful and multiply, and fill the earth and subdue it; and have dominion over the fish of the sea and over the birds of the air and over every living thing that moves upon the earth.' God said, 'See, I have given you every plant yielding seed that is upon the face of all the earth, and every tree with seed in its fruit; you shall have them for food. And to every beast of the earth, and to every bird of the air, and to everything that creeps on the earth, everything that has the breath of life, I have given every green plant for food.' And it was so. God saw everything that he had made, and indeed, it was very good. And there was evening and there was morning, the sixth day.

Thus the heavens and the earth were finished, and all their multitude. And on the seventh day God finished the work that he had done, and he rested on the seventh day from all the work that he had done. So God blessed the seventh day and hallowed it, because on it God rested from all the work that he had done in creation. These are the generations of the heavens and the earth when they were created.

This is the word of the Lord.   Genesis 1.20 – 2.4a

Responsorial Psalm

R* **O Lord our governor,**
 how glorious is your name in all the world!   *Psalm 8.1*

Your majesty above the heavens is praised
out of the mouths of babes at the breast.
You have founded a stronghold against your foes,
that you might still the enemy and the avenger.   **R**

When I consider your heavens, the work of your fingers,
the moon and the stars that you have ordained,
what is man, that you should be mindful of him;
the son of man, that you should seek him out?   **R**

You have made him little lower than the angels
and crown him with glory and honour.
You have given him dominion over the works of your hands
and put all things under his feet.   **R**

All sheep and oxen,
even the wild beasts of the field,
the birds of the air, the fish of the sea
and whatsoever moves in the paths of the sea.   **R**   *Psalm 8*

Year 2

A reading from the First Book of the Kings.

Solomon stood before the altar of the LORD in the presence of all the assembly of Israel, and spread out his hands to heaven. He said, 'O LORD, God of Israel, there is no God like you in heaven above or on earth beneath, keeping covenant and steadfast love for your servants who walk before you with all their heart.

'But will God indeed dwell on the earth? Even heaven and the highest heaven cannot contain you, much less this house that I have built! Have regard to your servant's prayer and his plea, O LORD my God, heeding the cry and the prayer that your servant prays to you today; that your eyes may be open night and day towards this house, the place of which you said, "My name shall be there", that you may heed the prayer that your servant prays towards this place. Hear the plea of your servant and of your people Israel when they pray towards this place; O hear in heaven your dwelling-place; heed and forgive.'

This is the word of the Lord.   1 Kings 8.22–23, 27–30

Responsorial Psalm

R   **How lovely is your dwelling place, O Lord of hosts!**   *Psalm 84.1*

How lovely is your dwelling place, O Lord of hosts!
My soul has a desire and longing
to enter the courts of the Lord;
my heart and my flesh rejoice in the living God.   **R**

The sparrow has found her a house
and the swallow a nest where she may lay her young:
at your altars, O Lord of hosts,
my King and my God.   **R**

Blessed are they who dwell in your house:
they will always be praising you.
Blessed are those whose strength is in you,
in whose heart are the highways to Zion.   **R**

Who going through the barren valley find there a spring,
and the early rains will clothe it with blessing.
They will go from strength to strength
and appear before God in Zion.   **R**

O Lord God of hosts, hear my prayer;
listen, O God of Jacob.
Behold our defender, O God,
and look upon the face of your anointed.   **R**

For one day in your courts
is better than a thousand.
I would rather be a doorkeeper in the house of my God
than dwell in the tents of ungodliness.   **R**   *Psalm 84.1–10*

Year 1 and Year 2

Hear the Gospel of our Lord Jesus Christ according to Mark.

When the Pharisees and some of the scribes who had come from Jerusalem gathered around Jesus, they noticed that some of his disciples were eating with defiled hands, that is, without washing them. (For the Pharisees, and all the Jews, do not eat unless they thoroughly wash their hands, thus observing the tradition of the elders; and they do not eat anything from the market unless they wash it; and there are also many other traditions that they observe, the washing of cups, pots, and bronze kettles.) So the Pharisees and the scribes asked him, 'Why do your disciples not live according to the tradition of the elders, but eat with defiled hands?' He said to them, 'Isaiah prophesied rightly about you hypocrites, as it is written,
     "This people honours me with their lips,
          but their hearts are far from me;   →

in vain do they worship me,
teaching human precepts as doctrines."
You abandon the commandment of God and hold to human tradition.'

Then he said to them, 'You have a fine way of rejecting the commandment of God in order to keep your tradition! For Moses said, "Honour your father and your mother"; and, "Whoever speaks evil of father or mother must surely die." But you say that if anyone tells father or mother, "Whatever support you might have had from me is Corban" (that is, an offering to God) – then you no longer permit doing anything for a father or mother, thus making void the word of God through your tradition that you have handed on. And you do many things like this.'

This is the Gospel of the Lord.   Mark 7.1–13

Week 5: Wednesday between 7 and 13 February *(if before Lent)*

Year 1

A reading from the book Genesis.

In the day that the LORD God made the earth and the heavens, when no plant of the field was yet in the earth and no herb of the field had yet sprung up – for the LORD God had not caused it to rain upon the earth, and there was no one to till the ground; but a stream would rise from the earth, and water the whole face of the ground – then the LORD God formed man from the dust of the ground, and breathed into his nostrils the breath of life; and the man became a living being. And the LORD God planted a garden in Eden, in the east; and there he put the man whom he had formed. Out of the ground the LORD God made to grow every tree that is pleasant to the sight and good for food, the tree of life also in the midst of the garden, and the tree of the knowledge of good and evil.

The LORD God took the man and put him in the garden of Eden to till it and keep it. And the LORD God commanded the man, 'You may freely eat of every tree of the garden; but of the tree of the knowledge of good and evil you shall not eat, for in the day that you eat of it you shall die.'

This is the word of the Lord.   Genesis 2.4b–9, 15–17

Responsorial Psalm

R **Send forth your spirit, O Lord:**
   and renew the face of the earth!   cf *Psalm* 104.32

You send the springs into the brooks,
which run among the hills.
They give drink to every beast of the field,
and the wild asses quench their thirst. **R**

All of these look to you
to give them their food in due season.
When you give it them, they gather it;
you open your hand and they are filled with good. **R**

When you hide your face they are troubled;
when you take away their breath,
they die and return again to the dust.
When you send forth your spirit, they are created,
and you renew the face of the earth. **R**   *Psalm* 104.11–12, 29–32

Year 2

A reading from the First Book of the Kings.

When the queen of Sheba heard of the fame of Solomon, (fame due to the
name of the LORD), she came to test him with hard questions. She came to
Jerusalem with a very great retinue, with camels bearing spices, and very much
gold, and precious stones; and when she came to Solomon, she told him all
that was on her mind. Solomon answered all her questions; there was nothing
hidden from the king that he could not explain to her. When the queen of
Sheba had observed all the wisdom of Solomon, the house that he had built,
the food of his table, the seating of his officials, and the attendance of his
servants, their clothing, his valets, and his burnt-offerings that he offered at
the house of the LORD, there was no more spirit in her.

So she said to the king, 'The report was true that I heard in my own land
of your accomplishments and of your wisdom, but I did not believe the reports
until I came and my own eyes had seen it. Not even half had been told me;
your wisdom and prosperity far surpass the report that I had heard. Happy
are your wives! Happy are these your servants, who continually attend you
and hear your wisdom! Blessed be the LORD your God, who has delighted in
you and set you on the throne of Israel! Because the LORD loved Israel for ever,
he has made you king to execute justice and righteousness.' Then she gave the
king one hundred and twenty talents of gold, a great quantity of spices, and
precious stones; never again did spices come in such quantity as that which
the queen of Sheba gave to King Solomon.

This is the word of the Lord.   1 *Kings* 10.1–10

Responsorial Psalm

R* **The mouth of the righteous utters wisdom
[and their tongue speaks what is right].** *Psalm 37.31*

Trust in the Lord and be doing good;
dwell in the land and be nourished with truth.
Let your delight be in the Lord
and he will give you your heart's desire.   R

Commit your way to the Lord and put your trust in him,
and he will bring it to pass.
He will make your righteousness as clear as the light
and your just dealing as the noonday.   R

The righteous shall possess the land
and dwell in it for ever.*
The law of their God is in their heart
and their footsteps shall not slide.   R   *Psalm 37.3–6, 30–32*

Year 1 and Year 2

Hear the Gospel of our Lord Jesus Christ according to Mark.

Jesus called the crowd again and said to them, 'Listen to me, all of you, and understand: there is nothing outside a person that by going in can defile, but the things that come out are what defile.'

When he had left the crowd and entered the house, his disciples asked him about the parable. He said to them, 'Then do you also fail to understand? Do you not see that whatever goes into a person from outside cannot defile, since it enters, not the heart but the stomach, and goes out into the sewer?' (Thus he declared all foods clean.) And he said, 'It is what comes out of a person that defiles. For it is from within, from the human heart, that evil intentions come: fornication, theft, murder, adultery, avarice, wickedness, deceit, licentiousness, envy, slander, pride, folly. All these evil things come from within, and they defile a person.'

This is the Gospel of the Lord.   Mark 7.14–23

Week 5: Thursday between 8 and 14 February *(if before Lent)*

Year 1

A reading from the book Genesis.

The LORD God said, 'It is not good that the man should be alone; I will make him a helper as his partner.' So out of the ground the LORD God formed every animal of the field and every bird of the air, and brought them to the man to see what he would call them; and whatever the man called each living creature, that was its name. The man gave names to all cattle, and to the birds of the air, and to every animal of the field; but for the man there was not found a helper as his partner. So the LORD God caused a deep sleep to fall upon the man, and he slept; then he took one of his ribs and closed up its place with flesh. And the rib that the LORD God had taken from the man he made into a woman and brought her to the man. Then the man said,

'This at last is bone of my bones
and flesh of my flesh;
this one shall be called Woman,
for out of Man this one was taken.'

Therefore a man leaves his father and his mother and clings to his wife, and they become one flesh. And the man and his wife were both naked, and were not ashamed.

This is the word of the Lord.   *Genesis 2.18–end*

Responsorial Psalm

R **Blessed are those who fear the Lord,
[and walk in the ways of God].**   *cf Psalm 128.1*

Blessed are all those who fear the Lord,
and walk in his ways.
You shall eat the fruit of the toil of your hands;
it shall go well with you,
and happy shall you be.   **R**

Your wife within your house
shall be like a fruitful vine;
your children round your table,
like fresh olive branches.
Thus shall the one be blest who fears the Lord.   **R**

The Lord from out of Zion bless you,
that you may see Jerusalem in prosperity
all the days of your life.
May you see your children's children,
and may there be peace upon Israel.   **R**   *Psalm 128*

A reading from the First Book of the Kings.

When Solomon was old, his wives turned away his heart after other gods; and his heart was not true to the LORD his God, as was the heart of his father David. For Solomon followed Astarte the goddess of the Sidonians, and Milcom the abomination of the Ammonites. So Solomon did what was evil in the sight of the LORD, and did not completely follow the LORD, as his father David had done. Then Solomon built a high place for Chemosh the abomination of Moab, and for Molech the abomination of the Ammonites, on the mountain east of Jerusalem. He did the same for all his foreign wives, who offered incense and sacrificed to their gods.

Then the LORD was angry with Solomon, because his heart had turned away from the LORD, the God of Israel, who had appeared to him twice, and had commanded him concerning this matter, that he should not follow other gods; but he did not observe what the LORD commanded. Therefore the LORD said to Solomon, 'Since this has been your mind and you have not kept my covenant and my statutes that I have commanded you, I will surely tear the kingdom from you and give it to your servant. Yet for the sake of your father David I will not do it in your lifetime; I will tear it out of the hand of your son. I will not, however, tear away the entire kingdom; I will give one tribe to your son, for the sake of my servant David and for the sake of Jerusalem, which I have chosen.'

This is the word of the Lord. 1 Kings 11.4–13

Responsorial Psalm

R **Remember me, Lord,**
   when you show favour to your people. cf Psalm 106.4a

Blessed are those who observe what is right
and always do what is just. **R**

They mingled with the nations
and learned to follow their ways,
so that they worshipped their idols,
which became to them a snare. **R**

Their own sons and daughters
they sacrificed to evil spirits.
They shed innocent blood,
the blood of their sons and daughters,
which they offered to the idols of Canaan,
and the land was defiled with blood. **R**

Thus were they polluted by their actions,
and in their wanton deeds went whoring after other gods.
Therefore was the wrath of the Lord
kindled against his people,
and he abhorred his inheritance. **R**   *Psalm 106.3, 35–41*

Year 1 and Year 2

Hear the Gospel of our Lord Jesus Christ according to Mark.

Jesus set out and went away to the region of Tyre. He entered a house and did not want anyone to know he was there. Yet he could not escape notice, but a woman whose little daughter had an unclean spirit immediately heard about him, and she came and bowed down at his feet. Now the woman was a Gentile, of Syrophoenician origin. She begged him to cast the demon out of her daughter. He said to her, 'Let the children be fed first, for it is not fair to take the children's food and throw it to the dogs.' But she answered him, 'Sir, even the dogs under the table eat the children's crumbs.' Then he said to her, 'For saying that, you may go – the demon has left your daughter.' So she went home, found the child lying on the bed, and the demon gone.

This is the Gospel of the Lord.   *Mark 7.24–30*

Week 5: Friday between 9 and 15 February *(if before Lent)*

Year 1

A reading from the book Genesis.

The serpent was more crafty than any other wild animal that the Lord God had made. He said to the woman, 'Did God say, "You shall not eat from any tree in the garden"?' The woman said to the serpent, 'We may eat of the fruit of the trees in the garden; but God said, "You shall not eat of the fruit of the tree that is in the middle of the garden, nor shall you touch it, or you shall die." ' But the serpent said to the woman, 'You will not die; for God knows that when you eat of it your eyes will be opened, and you will be like God, knowing good and evil.' So when the woman saw that the tree was good for food, and that it was a delight to the eyes, and that the tree was to be desired to make one wise, she took of its fruit and ate; and she also gave some to her husband, who was with her, and he ate. Then the eyes of both were opened, and they knew that they were naked; and they sewed fig leaves together and made loincloths for themselves.

They heard the sound of the Lord God walking in the garden at the time of the evening breeze, and the man and his wife hid themselves from the presence of the Lord God among the trees of the garden.

This is the word of the Lord.   *Genesis 3.1–8*

Responsorial Psalm

R **Be glad, you righteous, and rejoice in the Lord;
[shout for joy, all who are true of heart].**   Psalm 32.12

Happy the one whose transgression is forgiven,
and whose sin is covered.
Happy the one to whom the Lord imputes no guilt,
and in whose spirit there is no guile. **R**

For I held my tongue;
my bones wasted away
through my groaning all the day long. **R**

Your hand was heavy upon me day and night;
my moisture was dried up like the drought in summer.
Then I acknowledged my sin to you
and my iniquity I did not hide. **R**

I said, 'I will confess my transgressions to the Lord,'
and you forgave the guilt of my sin.
Therefore let all the faithful make their prayers to you
     in time of trouble;
in the great water flood, it shall not reach them. **R**

You are a place for me to hide in;
you preserve me from trouble;
you surround me with songs of deliverance. **R**   Psalm 32.1–8

Year 2

A reading from the First Book of the Kings.

When Jeroboam was leaving Jerusalem, the prophet Ahijah the Shilonite found
him on the road. Ahijah had clothed himself with a new garment. The two of
them were alone in the open country when Ahijah laid hold of the new garment he was wearing and tore it into twelve pieces. He then said to Jeroboam:
Take for yourself ten pieces; for thus says the LORD, the God of Israel, 'See, I
am about to tear the kingdom from the hand of Solomon, and will give you
ten tribes. One tribe will remain his, for the sake of my servant David and for
the sake of Jerusalem, the city that I have chosen out of all the tribes of Israel.'
So Israel has been in rebellion against the house of David to this day.

This is the word of the Lord.   1 Kings 11.29–32, 12.19

Responsorial Psalm

R **Sing merrily to God our strength,
[shout for joy to the God of Jacob].**   Psalm 81.1

'Hear, O my people, and I will admonish you:
O Israel, if you would but listen to me!
There shall be no strange god among you;
you shall not worship a foreign god. R

'I am the Lord your God,
who brought you up from the land of Egypt;
open your mouth wide and I shall fill it.' R

But my people would not hear my voice
and Israel would not obey me.
So I sent them away in the stubbornness of their hearts,
and let them walk after their own counsels. R

O that my people would listen to me,
that Israel would walk in my ways!
Then I should soon put down their enemies
and turn my hand against their adversaries. R   Psalm 81.8–14

Year 1 and Year 2

Hear the Gospel of our Lord Jesus Christ according to Mark.

Jesus returned from the region of Tyre, and went by way of Sidon towards
the Sea of Galilee, in the region of the Decapolis. They brought to him a deaf
man who had an impediment in his speech; and they begged him to lay his
hand on him. He took him aside in private, away from the crowd, and put
his fingers into his ears, and he spat and touched his tongue. Then looking up
to heaven, he sighed and said to him, 'Ephphatha', that is, 'Be opened.' And
immediately his ears were opened, his tongue was released, and he spoke
plainly. Then Jesus ordered them to tell no one; but the more he ordered
them, the more zealously they proclaimed it. They were astounded beyond
measure, saying, 'He has done everything well; he even makes the deaf to
hear and the mute to speak.'

This is the Gospel of the Lord.   Mark 7.31–end

Week 5: Saturday between 10 and 16 February *(if before Lent)*

Year 1

A reading from the book Genesis.

The LORD God called to the man, and said to him, 'Where are you?' He said, 'I heard the sound of you in the garden, and I was afraid, because I was naked; and I hid myself.' He said, 'Who told you that you were naked? Have you eaten from the tree of which I commanded you not to eat?' The man said, 'The woman whom you gave to be with me, she gave me fruit from the tree, and I ate.' Then the LORD God said to the woman, 'What is this that you have done?' The woman said, 'The serpent tricked me, and I ate.' The LORD God said to the serpent,

'Because you have done this,
 cursed are you among all animals
 and among all wild creatures;
upon your belly you shall go,
 and dust you shall eat
 all the days of your life.
I will put enmity between you and the woman,
 and between your offspring and hers;
he will strike your head,
 and you will strike his heel.'

To the woman he said,

'I will greatly increase your pangs in childbearing;
 in pain you shall bring forth children,
yet your desire shall be for your husband,
 and he shall rule over you.'

And to the man he said,

'Because you have listened to the voice of your wife,
 and have eaten of the tree
about which I commanded you,
 "You shall not eat of it",
cursed is the ground because of you;
 in toil you shall eat of it all the days of your life;
thorns and thistles it shall bring forth for you;
 and you shall eat the plants of the field.
By the sweat of your face
 you shall eat bread
until you return to the ground,
 for out of it you were taken;
you are dust,
 and to dust you shall return.'

The man named his wife Eve, because she was the mother of all who live. And the Lord God made garments of skins for the man and for his wife, and clothed them.

Then the Lord God said, 'See, the man has become like one of us, knowing good and evil; and now, he might reach out his hand and take also from the tree of life, and eat, and live for ever' – therefore the Lord God sent him forth from the garden of Eden, to till the ground from which he was taken. He drove out the man; and at the east of the garden of Eden he placed the cherubim, and a sword flaming and turning to guard the way to the tree of life.

This is the word of the Lord. *Genesis 3.9–end*

Responsorial Psalm

R* **O Lord, you have been our refuge from one generation to another.** *Psalm 90.1*

Before the mountains were brought forth,
or the earth and the world were formed,
from everlasting to everlasting
you are God.   **R**

You turn us back to dust and say:
'Turn back, O children of earth.'
For a thousand years in your sight are but as yesterday,
which passes like a watch in the night.   **R**

You sweep them away like a dream;
they fade away suddenly like the grass.
In the morning it is green and flourishes;
in the evening it is dried up and withered.   **R**

For we consume away in your displeasure;
we are afraid at your wrathful indignation.
You have set our misdeeds before you
and our secret sins in the light of your countenance.   **R**

When you are angry, all our days are gone;
our years come to an end like a sigh.
The days of our life are three score years and ten,
or if our strength endures, even four score;
yet the sum of them is but labour and sorrow,
for they soon pass away and we are gone.   **R**

Who regards the power of your wrath
and your indignation like those who fear you?
So teach us to number our days
that we may apply our hearts to wisdom.   **R** *Psalm 90.1–12*

A reading from the First Book of the Kings.

Jeroboam said to himself, 'Now the kingdom may well revert to the house of David. If this people continues to go up to offer sacrifices in the house of the LORD at Jerusalem, the heart of this people will turn again to their master, King Rehoboam of Judah; they will kill me and return to King Rehoboam of Judah.' So the king took counsel, and made two calves of gold. He said to the people, 'You have gone up to Jerusalem long enough. Here are your gods, O Israel, who brought you up out of the land of Egypt.' He set one in Bethel, and the other he put in Dan. And this thing became a sin, for the people went to worship before the one at Bethel and before the other as far as Dan. He also made houses on high places, and appointed priests from among all the people, who were not Levites. Jeroboam appointed a festival on the fifteenth day of the eighth month like the festival that was in Judah, and he offered sacrifices on the altar; so he did in Bethel, sacrificing to the calves that he had made. And he placed in Bethel the priests of the high places that he had made.

Jeroboam did not turn from his evil way, but made priests for the high places again from among all the people; any who wanted to be priests he consecrated for the high places. This matter became sin to the house of Jeroboam, so as to cut it off and to destroy it from the face of the earth.

This is the word of the Lord.   1 Kings 12.26–32, 13.33–end

Responsorial Psalm

R **Remember me, Lord,
   when you show favour to your people.**   cf Psalm 106.4a

We have sinned like our forebears;
we have done wrong and dealt wickedly.
In Egypt they did not consider your wonders,
nor remember the abundance of your faithful love;
they rebelled against the Most High at the Red Sea.   **R**

Thus they exchanged their glory
for the image of an ox that feeds on hay.
They forgot God their saviour,
who had done such great things in Egypt.   **R**

Wonderful deeds in the land of Ham
and fearful things at the Red Sea.
So he would have destroyed them,
had not Moses his chosen stood before him in the breach,
to turn away his wrath from consuming them.   **R**

                                        Psalm 106.6–7, 20–23

Year 1 and Year 2

Hear the Gospel of our Lord Jesus Christ according to Mark.

There was a great crowd without anything to eat, so Jesus called his disciples and said to them, 'I have compassion for the crowd, because they have been with me now for three days and have nothing to eat. If I send them away hungry to their homes, they will faint on the way – and some of them have come from a great distance.' His disciples replied, 'How can one feed these people with bread here in the desert?' He asked them, 'How many loaves do you have?' They said, 'Seven.' Then he ordered the crowd to sit down on the ground; and he took the seven loaves, and after giving thanks he broke them and gave them to his disciples to distribute; and they distributed them to the crowd. They had also a few small fish; and after blessing them, he ordered that these too should be distributed. They ate and were filled; and they took up the broken pieces left over, seven baskets full. Now there were about four thousand people. And he sent them away. And immediately he got into the boat with his disciples and went to the district of Dalmanutha.

This is the Gospel of the Lord. Mark 8.1–10

Week 6: Monday

between 12 and 18 February *(if before Lent)*
between 11 and 15 May *(if after Pentecost)*

Year 1

A reading from the book Genesis.

The man knew his wife Eve, and she conceived and bore Cain, saying, 'I have produced a man with the help of the LORD.' Next she bore his brother Abel. Now Abel was a keeper of sheep, and Cain a tiller of the ground. In the course of time Cain brought to the LORD an offering of the fruit of the ground, and Abel for his part brought of the firstlings of his flock, their fat portions. And the LORD had regard for Abel and his offering, but for Cain and his offering he had no regard. So Cain was very angry, and his countenance fell. The LORD said to Cain, 'Why are you angry, and why has your countenance fallen? If you do well, will you not be accepted? And if you do not do well, sin is lurking at the door; its desire is for you, but you must master it.'

Cain said to his brother Abel, 'Let us go out to the field.' And when they were in the field, Cain rose up against his brother Abel and killed him. Then the LORD said to Cain, 'Where is your brother Abel?' He said, 'I do not know; am I my brother's keeper?' And the LORD said, 'What have you done? Listen; your brother's blood is crying out to me from the ground! And now you are cursed from the ground, which has opened its mouth to receive your brother's blood from your hand. When you till the ground, it will no longer yield to you its strength; you will be a fugitive and a wanderer on the earth.' Cain said to the LORD, 'My punishment is greater than I can bear! Today you have driven me away from the soil, and I shall be hidden from your face; I shall be a fugitive and a wanderer on the earth, and anyone who meets me may kill me.' Then the LORD said to him, 'Not so! Whoever kills Cain will suffer a sevenfold vengeance.' And the LORD put a mark on Cain, so that no one who came upon him would kill him.

Adam knew his wife again, and she bore a son and named him Seth, for she said, 'God has appointed for me another child instead of Abel, because Cain killed him.'

This is the word of the Lord.   Genesis 4.1–15, 25

Responsorial Psalm

R   **I will show my salvation
to those who keep my way.**   *cf Psalm 50.24b*

The Lord, the most mighty God, has spoken
and called the world from the rising of the sun to its setting.
'I will not reprove you for your sacrifices,
for your burnt offerings are always before me.'   **R**

But to the wicked, says God:
'Why do you recite my statutes
and take my covenant upon your lips,
since you refuse to be disciplined
and have cast my words behind you?   **R**

'When you saw a thief, you made friends with him
and you threw in your lot with adulterers.
You have loosed your lips for evil
and harnessed your tongue to deceit.   **R**

'You sit and speak evil of your brother;
you slander your own mother's son.
These things have you done, and should I keep silence?
Did you think that I am even such a one as yourself?   **R**

'But no, I must reprove you,
and set before your eyes the things that you have done.
You that forget God, consider this well,
lest I tear you apart and there is none to deliver you.   **R**

'Whoever offers me the sacrifice of thanksgiving honours me
and to those who keep my way
will I show the salvation of God.'   **R**   *Psalm 50.1, 8, 16–end*

Year 2

A reading from the Letter of James.

James, a servant of God and of the Lord Jesus Christ, to the twelve tribes in the Dispersion: Greetings.

My brothers and sisters, whenever you face trials of any kind, consider it nothing but joy, because you know that the testing of your faith produces endurance; and let endurance have its full effect, so that you may be mature and complete, lacking in nothing.

If any of you is lacking in wisdom, ask God, who gives to all generously and ungrudgingly, and it will be given you. But ask in faith, never doubting, for the one who doubts is like a wave of the sea, driven and tossed by the wind; for the doubter, being double-minded and unstable in every way, must not expect to receive anything from the Lord.

Let the believer who is lowly boast in being raised up, and the rich in being brought low, because the rich will disappear like a flower in the field. For the sun rises with its scorching heat and withers the field; its flower falls, and its beauty perishes. It is the same with the rich; in the midst of a busy life, they will wither away.

This is the word of the Lord.   *James 1.1–11*

R **Blessed are those who walk in the law of the Lord.** cf *Psalm* 119.1

You have dealt graciously with your servant,
according to your word, O Lord.
O teach me true understanding and knowledge,
for I have trusted in your commandments. R

Before I was afflicted I went astray,
but now I keep your word.
You are gracious and do good;
O Lord, teach me your statutes. R

The proud have smeared me with lies,
but I will keep your commandments with my whole heart.
Their heart has become gross with fat,
but my delight is in your law. R

It is good for me that I have been afflicted,
that I may learn your statutes.
The law of your mouth is dearer to me
than a hoard of gold and silver. R *Psalm* 119.65–72

Year 1 and Year 2

Hear the Gospel of our Lord Jesus Christ according to Mark.

The Pharisees came and began to argue with Jesus, asking him for a sign
from heaven, to test him. And he sighed deeply in his spirit and said, 'Why
does this generation ask for a sign? Truly I tell you, no sign will be given to
this generation.' And he left them, and getting into the boat again, he went
across to the other side.

This is the Gospel of the Lord. Mark 8.11–13

Week 6: Tuesday

between 13 and 19 February *(if before Lent)*
between 12 and 16 May *(if after Pentecost)*

Year 1

A reading from the book Genesis.

The LORD saw that the wickedness of humankind was great in the earth, and
that every inclination of the thoughts of their hearts was only evil continually.
And the LORD was sorry that he had made humankind on the earth, and it
grieved him to his heart. So the LORD said, 'I will blot out from the earth the
human beings I have created – people together with animals and creeping

things and birds of the air, for I am sorry that I have made them.' But Noah found favour in the sight of the LORD.

Then the LORD said to Noah, 'Go into the ark, you and all your household, for I have seen that you alone are righteous before me in this generation. Take with you seven pairs of all clean animals, the male and its mate; and a pair of the animals that are not clean, the male and its mate; and seven pairs of the birds of the air also, male and female, to keep their kind alive on the face of all the earth. For in seven days I will send rain on the earth for forty days and forty nights; and every living thing that I have made I will blot out from the face of the ground.' And Noah did all that the LORD had commanded him. And after seven days the waters of the flood came on the earth.

This is the word of the Lord. *Genesis 6.5–8, 7.1–5, 10*

Responsorial Psalm

R **The Lord gives strength to his people;**
   [and gives them the blessing of peace]. *cf Psalm 29.10*

Ascribe to the Lord, you powers of heaven,
ascribe to the Lord glory and strength.
Ascribe to the Lord the honour due to his name;
worship the Lord in the beauty of holiness.   **R**

The voice of the Lord is upon the waters;
the God of glory thunders;
the Lord is upon the mighty waters.
The voice of the Lord is mighty in operation;
the voice of the Lord is a glorious voice.   **R**

The voice of the Lord breaks the cedar trees;
the Lord breaks the cedars of Lebanon;
he makes Lebanon skip like a calf
and Sirion like a young wild ox.   **R**

The voice of the Lord splits the flash of lightning;
the voice of the Lord shakes the wilderness;
the Lord shakes the wilderness of Kadesh.
The voice of the Lord makes the oak trees writhe
      and strips the forests bare;
in his temple all cry, 'Glory!'   **R**

The Lord sits enthroned above the water flood;
the Lord sits enthroned as king for evermore.
The Lord shall give strength to his people;
the Lord shall give his people the blessing of peace.   **R**   *Psalm 29*

A reading from the Letter of James.

Blessed is anyone who endures temptation. Such a one has stood the test and will receive the crown of life that the Lord has promised to those who love him. No one, when tempted, should say, 'I am being tempted by God'; for God cannot be tempted by evil and he himself tempts no one. But one is tempted by one's own desire, being lured and enticed by it; then, when that desire has conceived, it gives birth to sin, and that sin, when it is fully grown, gives birth to death. Do not be deceived, my beloved.

Every generous act of giving, with every perfect gift, is from above, coming down from the Father of lights, with whom there is no variation or shadow due to change. In fulfilment of his own purpose he gave us birth by the word of truth, so that we would become a kind of first fruits of his creatures.

This is the word of the Lord. *James 1.12–18*

Responsorial Psalm

R **Justice shall return to the righteous,**
   [and the true of heart shall follow it]. *cf Psalm 94.15*

Blessed are those whom you chasten, O Lord,
whom you instruct from your law;
that you may give them rest in days of adversity,
until a pit is dug for the wicked.   R

For the Lord will not fail his people,
neither will he forsake his inheritance.
For justice shall return to the righteous,
and all that are true of heart shall follow it.   R

Who will rise up for me against the wicked?
Who will take my part against the evildoers?
If the Lord had not helped me,
my soul would soon have been put to silence.
And when I said, 'My foot has slipped',
your loving mercy, O Lord, upheld me.   R   *Psalm 94.12–18*

Year 1 and Year 2

Hear the Gospel of our Lord Jesus Christ according to Mark.

The disciples had forgotten to bring any bread; and they had only one loaf with them in the boat. And Jesus cautioned them, saying, 'Watch out – beware of the yeast of the Pharisees and the yeast of Herod.' They said to one another, 'It is because we have no bread.' And becoming aware of it, Jesus said to them, 'Why are you talking about having no bread? Do you still not perceive or understand? Are your hearts hardened? Do you have eyes, and fail to see? Do you have ears, and fail to hear? And do you not remember? When I broke the five loaves for the five thousand, how many baskets full of broken pieces did you collect?' They said to him, 'Twelve.' 'And the seven for the four thousand, how many baskets full of broken pieces did you collect?' And they said to him, 'Seven.' Then he said to them, 'Do you not yet understand?'

This is the Gospel of the Lord.   Mark 8.14–21

Week 6: Wednesday

between 14 and 20 February *(if before Lent)*
between 13 and 17 May *(if after Pentecost)*

Year 1

A reading from the book Genesis.

At the end of forty days Noah opened the window of the ark that he had made and sent out the raven; and it went to and fro until the waters were dried up from the earth. Then he sent out the dove from him, to see if the waters had subsided from the face of the ground; but the dove found no place to set its foot, and it returned to him to the ark, for the waters were still on the face of the whole earth. So he put out his hand and took it and brought it into the ark with him. He waited another seven days, and again he sent out the dove from the ark; and the dove came back to him in the evening, and there in its beak was a freshly plucked olive leaf; so Noah knew that the waters had subsided from the earth. Then he waited another seven days, and sent out the dove; and it did not return to him any more.

In the six hundred and first year, in the first month, on the first day of the month, the waters were dried up from the earth; and Noah removed the covering of the ark, and looked, and saw that the face of the ground was drying.

Then Noah built an altar to the LORD, and took of every clean animal and of every clean bird, and offered burnt-offerings on the altar. And when the LORD smelt the pleasing odour, the LORD said in his heart, 'I will never again curse the ground because of humankind, for the inclination of the human heart is evil from youth; nor will I ever again destroy every living creature as I have done.

As long as the earth endures,
    seedtime and harvest, cold and heat,
summer and winter, day and night,
    shall not cease.'

This is the word of the Lord.   Genesis 8.6–13, 20–end

Responsorial Psalm

R   **I will offer to you a sacrifice of thanksgiving:**
   [and call upon the name of the Lord].   Psalm 116.15

   or

R   **Alleluia!**

How shall I repay the Lord
for all the benefits he has given to me?
I will lift up the cup of salvation
and call upon the name of the Lord.   R

I will fulfil my vows to the Lord
in the presence of all his people.
Precious in the sight of the Lord
is the death of his faithful servants.   R

O Lord, I am your servant,
your servant, the child of your handmaid;
you have freed me from my bonds.
I will offer to you a sacrifice of thanksgiving
and call upon the name of the Lord.   R

I will fulfil my vows to the Lord
in the presence of all his people,
in the courts of the house of the Lord,
in the midst of you, O Jerusalem.   R   Psalm 116.10–end

Year 2

A reading from the Letter of James.

You must understand this, my beloved: let everyone be quick to listen, slow
to speak, slow to anger; for your anger does not produce God's righteousness.
Therefore rid yourselves of all sordidness and rank growth of wickedness,
and welcome with meekness the implanted word that has the power to save
your souls.

   But be doers of the word, and not merely hearers who deceive themselves.
For if any are hearers of the word and not doers, they are like those who look
at themselves in a mirror; for they look at themselves and, on going away,
immediately forget what they were like. But those who look into the perfect
law, the law of liberty, and persevere, being not hearers who forget but doers
who act – they will be blessed in their doing.

   If any think they are religious, and do not bridle their tongues but deceive
their hearts, their religion is worthless. Religion that is pure and undefiled
before God, the Father, is this: to care for orphans and widows in their distress,
and to keep oneself unstained by the world.

This is the word of the Lord.   James 1.19–end

Responsorial Psalm

R **Blessed are those who persevere in the law,
[the law that makes us free].**   cf James 1.25

Lord, who may dwell in your tabernacle?
Who may rest upon your holy hill?
Whoever leads an uncorrupt life
and does the thing that is right.   R

Who speaks the truth from the heart
and bears no deceit on the tongue;
who does no evil to a friend
and pours no scorn on a neighbour.   R

In whose sight the wicked are not esteemed,
but who honours those who fear the Lord.
Whoever has sworn to a neighbour
and never goes back on that word.   R

Who does not lend money in hope of gain,
nor takes a bribe against the innocent;
whoever does these things
shall never fall.   R   Psalm 15

Year 1 and Year 2

Hear the Gospel of our Lord Jesus Christ according to Mark.

Jesus and his disciples came to Bethsaida. Some people brought a blind man
to him and begged him to touch him. He took the blind man by the hand
and led him out of the village; and when he had put saliva on his eyes and
laid his hands on him, he asked him, 'Can you see anything?' And the man
looked up and said, 'I can see people, but they look like trees, walking.' Then
Jesus laid his hands on his eyes again; and he looked intently and his sight
was restored, and he saw everything clearly. Then he sent him away to his
home, saying, 'Do not even go into the village.'

This is the Gospel of the Lord.   Mark 8.22–26

Week 6: Thursday

between 15 and 21 February *(if before Lent)*
between 14 and 18 May *(if after Pentecost)*

Year 1

A reading from the book Genesis.

God blessed Noah and his sons, and said to them, 'Be fruitful and multiply, and fill the earth. The fear and dread of you shall rest on every animal of the earth, and on every bird of the air, on everything that creeps on the ground, and on all the fish of the sea; into your hand they are delivered. Every moving thing that lives shall be food for you; and just as I gave you the green plants, I give you everything. Only, you shall not eat flesh with its life, that is, its blood. For your own lifeblood I will surely require a reckoning: from every animal I will require it and from human beings, each one for the blood of another, I will require a reckoning for human life.

> Whoever sheds the blood of a human,
>> by a human shall that person's blood be shed;
> for in his own image
>> God made humankind.

And you, be fruitful and multiply, abound on the earth and multiply in it.'

Then God said to Noah and to his sons with him, 'As for me, I am establishing my covenant with you and your descendants after you, and with every living creature that is with you, the birds, the domestic animals, and every animal of the earth with you, as many as came out of the ark. I establish my covenant with you, that never again shall all flesh be cut off by the waters of a flood, and never again shall there be a flood to destroy the earth.' God said, 'This is the sign of the covenant that I make between me and you and every living creature that is with you, for all future generations: I have set my bow in the clouds, and it shall be a sign of the covenant between me and the earth.'

This is the word of the Lord.   Genesis 9.1–13

R **O Lord, hear my prayer**
   and let my crying come before you.   Psalm 102.1

Then shall the nations fear your name, O Lord,
and all the kings of the earth your glory,
when the Lord has built up Zion
and shown himself in glory. R

When he has turned to the prayer of the destitute
and has not despised their plea.
This shall be written for those that come after,
and a people yet unborn shall praise the Lord. R

For he has looked down from his holy height;
from the heavens he beheld the earth,
that he might hear the sighings of the prisoner
and set free those condemned to die. R

That the name of the Lord may be proclaimed in Zion
and his praises in Jerusalem,
when peoples are gathered together
and kingdoms also, to serve the Lord. R   Psalm 102.16–23

Year 2

A reading from the Letter of James.

My brothers and sisters, do you with your acts of favouritism really believe
in our glorious Lord Jesus Christ? For if a person with gold rings and in fine
clothes comes into your assembly, and if a poor person in dirty clothes also
comes in, and if you take notice of the one wearing the fine clothes and say,
'Have a seat here, please', while to the one who is poor you say, 'Stand there',
or, 'Sit at my feet', have you not made distinctions among yourselves, and
become judges with evil thoughts? Listen, my beloved brothers and sisters.
Has not God chosen the poor in the world to be rich in faith and to be heirs
of the kingdom that he has promised to those who love him? But you have
dishonoured the poor. Is it not the rich who oppress you? Is it not they who
drag you into court? Is it not they who blaspheme the excellent name that
was invoked over you?

You do well if you really fulfil the royal law according to the scripture, 'You
shall love your neighbour as yourself.' But if you show partiality, you commit
sin and are convicted by the law as transgressors.

This is the word of the Lord.   James 2.1–9

R   **I sought the Lord and he answered me;**
   [and delivered me from all my fears].   *Psalm* 34.4

I will bless the Lord at all times;
his praise shall ever be in my mouth.
My soul shall glory in the Lord;
let the humble hear and be glad.   R

O magnify the Lord with me;
let us exalt his name together.
I sought the Lord and he answered me
and delivered me from all my fears.   R

Look upon him and be radiant
and your faces shall not be ashamed.
This poor soul cried, and the Lord heard me
and saved me from all my troubles.   R

The angel of the Lord
encamps around those who fear him
and delivers them.   R   *Psalm* 34.1–7

Year 1 and Year 2

Hear the Gospel of our Lord Jesus Christ according to Mark.

Jesus went on with his disciples to the villages of Caesarea Philippi; and on the way he asked his disciples, 'Who do people say that I am?' And they answered him, 'John the Baptist; and others, Elijah; and still others, one of the prophets.' He asked them, 'But who do you say that I am?' Peter answered him, 'You are the Messiah.' And he sternly ordered them not to tell anyone about him.

Then he began to teach them that the Son of Man must undergo great suffering, and be rejected by the elders, the chief priests, and the scribes, and be killed, and after three days rise again. He said all this quite openly. And Peter took him aside and began to rebuke him. But turning and looking at his disciples, he rebuked Peter and said, 'Get behind me, Satan! For you are setting your mind not on divine things but on human things.'

This is the Gospel of the Lord.   *Mark* 8.27–33

Week 6: Friday

between 16 and 22 February *(if before Lent)*
between 15 and 19 May *(if after Pentecost)*

Year 1

A reading from the book Genesis.

The whole earth had one language and the same words. And as they migrated from the east, they came upon a plain in the land of Shinar and settled there. And they said to one another, 'Come, let us make bricks, and burn them thoroughly.' And they had brick for stone, and bitumen for mortar. Then they said, 'Come, let us build ourselves a city, and a tower with its top in the heavens, and let us make a name for ourselves; otherwise we shall be scattered abroad upon the face of the whole earth.'

The LORD came down to see the city and the tower, which mortals had built. And the LORD said, 'Look, they are one people, and they have all one language; and this is only the beginning of what they will do; nothing that they propose to do will now be impossible for them. Come, let us go down, and confuse their language there, so that they will not understand one another's speech.' So the LORD scattered them abroad from there over the face of all the earth, and they left off building the city. Therefore it was called Babel, because there the LORD confused the language of all the earth; and from there the LORD scattered them abroad over the face of all the earth.

This is the word of the Lord.   *Genesis 11.1–9*

Responsorial Psalm

R   Happy the people God has chosen for his own.   cf *Psalm 33.12*

The Lord brings the counsel of the nations to naught;
he frustrates the designs of the peoples.
But the counsel of the Lord shall endure for ever
and the designs of his heart from generation to generation.   **R**

Happy the nation whose God is the Lord
and the people he has chosen for his own.
The Lord looks down from heaven
and beholds all the children of earth.   **R**

From where he sits enthroned he turns his gaze
on all who dwell on the earth.
He fashions all the hearts of them
and understands all their works.   **R**   *Psalm 33.10–15*

A reading from the Letter of James.

What good is it, my brothers and sisters, if you say you have faith but do not have works? Can faith save you? If a brother or sister is naked and lacks daily food, and one of you says to them, 'Go in peace; keep warm and eat your fill', and yet you do not supply their bodily needs, what is the good of that? So faith by itself, if it has no works, is dead.

But someone will say, 'You have faith and I have works.' Show me your faith without works, and I by my works will show you my faith. You believe that God is one; you do well. Even the demons believe – and shudder. Do you want to be shown, you senseless person, that faith without works is barren? Was not our ancestor Abraham justified by works when he offered his son Isaac on the altar? You see that faith was active along with his works, and faith was brought to completion by the works. Thus the scripture was fulfilled that says, 'Abraham believed God, and it was reckoned to him as righteousness', and he was called the friend of God. You see that a person is justified by works and not by faith alone. For just as the body without the spirit is dead, so faith without works is also dead.

This is the word of the Lord.   James 2.14–24, 26

Responsorial Psalm

R   **Blessed are those
    who delight in the commandments of the Lord.**   cf Psalm 112.1

Blessed are those who fear the Lord
and have great delight in his commandments.
Their descendants will be mighty in the land,
a generation of the faithful that will be blest.   **R**

Wealth and riches will be in their house,
and their righteousness endures for ever.
Light shines in the darkness for the upright;
gracious and full of compassion are the righteous.   **R**

It goes well with those who are generous in lending
and order their affairs with justice,
for they will never be shaken;
the righteous will be held in everlasting remembrance.   **R**

They will not be afraid of any evil tidings;
their heart is steadfast, trusting in the Lord.
Their heart is sustained and will not fear,
until they see the downfall of their foes.   **R**

They have given freely to the poor;
their righteousness stands fast for ever;
their head will be exalted with honour.   **R**

The wicked shall see it and be angry;
they shall gnash their teeth in despair;
the desire of the wicked shall perish.   **R**   *Psalm 112*

Year 1 and Year 2

Hear the Gospel of our Lord Jesus Christ according to Mark.

Jesus called the crowd with his disciples, and said to them, 'If any want to
become my followers, let them deny themselves and take up their cross and
follow me. For those who want to save their life will lose it, and those who
lose their life for my sake, and for the sake of the gospel, will save it. For what
will it profit them to gain the whole world and forfeit their life? Indeed, what
can they give in return for their life? Those who are ashamed of me and of
my words in this adulterous and sinful generation, of them the Son of Man
will also be ashamed when he comes in the glory of his Father with the holy
angels.' And he said to them, 'Truly I tell you, there are some standing here
who will not taste death until they see that the kingdom of God has come
with power.'

This is the Gospel of the Lord.   *Mark 8.34 – 9.1*

Week 6: Saturday

between 17 and 23 February *(if before Lent)*
between 16 and 20 May *(if after Pentecost)*

Year 1

A reading from the Letter to the Hebrews.

Faith is the assurance of things hoped for, the conviction of things not seen.
Indeed, by faith our ancestors received approval. By faith we understand that
the worlds were prepared by the word of God, so that what is seen was made
from things that are not visible.

By faith Abel offered to God a more acceptable sacrifice than Cain's. Through
this he received approval as righteous, God himself giving approval to his gifts;
he died, but through his faith he still speaks. By faith Enoch was taken so that
he did not experience death; and 'he was not found, because God had taken
him.' For it was attested before he was taken away that 'he had pleased God.'
And without faith it is impossible to please God, for whoever would approach
him must believe that he exists and that he rewards those who seek him. By
faith Noah, warned by God about events as yet unseen, respected the warning
and built an ark to save his household; by this he condemned the world and
became an heir to the righteousness that is in accordance with faith.

This is the word of the Lord.   *Hebrews 11.1–7*

Responsorial Psalm

R   **I will exalt you, O God my King,**
    [and bless your name for ever].   cf *Psalm* 145.1

I will exalt you, O God my King,
and bless your name for ever and ever.
Every day will I bless you
and praise your name for ever and ever.   **R**

Great is the Lord and highly to be praised;
his greatness is beyond all searching out.
One generation shall praise your works to another
and declare your mighty acts.   **R**

They shall speak of the majesty of your glory,
and I will tell of all your wonderful deeds.
They shall speak of the might of your marvellous acts,
and I will also tell of your greatness.   **R**

They shall pour forth the story of your abundant kindness
and joyfully sing of your righteousness.
The Lord is gracious and merciful,
long-suffering and of great goodness.   **R**

The Lord is loving to everyone
and his mercy is over all his creatures.
All your works praise you, O Lord,
and your faithful servants bless you.   **R**   *Psalm* 145.1–10

Year 2

A reading from the Letter of James.

Not many of you should become teachers, my brothers and sisters, for you
know that we who teach will be judged with greater strictness. For all of us
make many mistakes. Anyone who makes no mistakes in speaking is perfect,
able to keep the whole body in check with a bridle. If we put bits into the
mouths of horses to make them obey us, we guide their whole bodies. Or look
at ships: though they are so large that it takes strong winds to drive them, yet
they are guided by a very small rudder wherever the will of the pilot directs.
So also the tongue is a small member, yet it boasts of great exploits.

How great a forest is set ablaze by a small fire! And the tongue is a fire. The
tongue is placed among our members as a world of iniquity; it stains the whole
body, sets on fire the cycle of nature, and is itself set on fire by hell. For every
species of beast and bird, of reptile and sea creature, can be tamed and has
been tamed by the human species, but no one can tame the tongue – a restless
evil, full of deadly poison. With it we bless the Lord and Father, and with it we
curse those who are made in the likeness of God. From the same mouth come
blessing and cursing. My brothers and sisters, this ought not to be so.

This is the word of the Lord.   *James* 3.1–10

Responsorial Psalm

R **You, O Lord, will watch over us**
  [from this generation for ever]. cf Psalm 12.7

Help me, Lord, for no one godly is left;
the faithful have vanished from the whole human race.
They all speak falsely with their neighbour;
they flatter with their lips, but speak from a double heart. **R**

O that the Lord would cut off all flattering lips
and the tongue that speaks proud boasts!
Those who say, 'With our tongue will we prevail;
our lips we will use; who is lord over us?' **R**

'Because of the oppression of the needy,
and the groaning of the poor,
I will rise up now,' says the Lord,
'and set them in the safety that they long for.' **R**

The words of the Lord are pure words,
like silver refined in the furnace
and purified seven times in the fire.
You, O Lord, will watch over us
and guard us from this generation for ever. **R** Psalm 12.1–7

Year I and Year 2

Hear the Gospel of our Lord Jesus Christ according to Mark.

Jesus took with him Peter and James and John, and led them up a high mountain apart, by themselves. And he was transfigured before them, and his clothes became dazzling white, such as no one on earth could bleach them. And there appeared to them Elijah with Moses, who were talking with Jesus. Then Peter said to Jesus, 'Rabbi, it is good for us to be here; let us make three dwellings, one for you, one for Moses, and one for Elijah.' He did not know what to say, for they were terrified. Then a cloud overshadowed them, and from the cloud there came a voice, 'This is my Son, the Beloved; listen to him!' Suddenly when they looked around, they saw no one with them any more, but only Jesus.

As they were coming down the mountain, he ordered them to tell no one about what they had seen, until after the Son of Man had risen from the dead. So they kept the matter to themselves, questioning what this rising from the dead could mean. Then they asked him, 'Why do the scribes say that Elijah must come first?' He said to them, 'Elijah is indeed coming first to restore all things. How then is it written about the Son of Man, that he is to go through many sufferings and be treated with contempt? But I tell you that Elijah has come, and they did to him whatever they pleased, as it is written about him.'

This is the Gospel of the Lord. Mark 9.2–13

Week 7: Monday
between 19 and 25 February *(if before Lent)*
between 16 and 22 May *(if after Pentecost)*

Year I

Either

A reading from the book Ecclesiasticus.

All wisdom is from the Lord,
  and with him it remains for ever.
The sand of the sea, the drops of rain,
  and the days of eternity – who can count them?
The height of heaven, the breadth of the earth,
  the abyss, and wisdom – who can search them out?
Wisdom was created before all other things,
  and prudent understanding from eternity.
The root of wisdom – to whom has it been revealed?
  Her subtleties – who knows them?
There is but one who is wise, greatly to be feared,
  seated upon his throne – the Lord.
It is he who created her;
  he saw her and took her measure;
  he poured her out upon all his works,
upon all the living according to his gift;
  he lavished her upon those who love him.

This is the word of the Lord.   *Ecclesiasticus 1.1–10*

Responsorial Psalm

R **The Lord has put on his glory
   and girded himself with strength.**   *Psalm 93.1b*

The Lord is king and has put on glorious apparel;
the Lord has put on his glory
and girded himself with strength.

He has made the whole world so sure
that it cannot be moved.
Your throne has been established from of old;
you are from everlasting.

The floods have lifted up, O Lord,
the floods have lifted up their voice;
the floods lift up their pounding waves.

Mightier than the thunder of many waters,
mightier than the breakers of the sea,
the Lord on high is mightier.
Your testimonies are very sure;
holiness adorns your house, O Lord, for ever.   R   *Psalm 93*

or James 1.1–11; Psalm 119.65–72 (page 331 ff).

Year 2

A reading from the Letter of James.

Who is wise and understanding among you? Show by your good life that your works are done with gentleness born of wisdom. But if you have bitter envy and selfish ambition in your hearts, do not be boastful and false to the truth. Such wisdom does not come down from above, but is earthly, unspiritual, devilish. For where there is envy and selfish ambition, there will also be disorder and wickedness of every kind. But the wisdom from above is first pure, then peaceable, gentle, willing to yield, full of mercy and good fruits, without a trace of partiality or hypocrisy. And a harvest of righteousness is sown in peace for those who make peace.

This is the word of the Lord.   James 3.13–end

Responsorial Psalm

R **The judgements of the Lord are true:**
    more to be desired than gold.   cf Psalm 19.9b, 10a

The law of the Lord is perfect, reviving the soul;
the testimony of the Lord is sure
and gives wisdom to the simple.   R

The statutes of the Lord are right and rejoice the heart;
the commandment of the Lord is pure
and gives light to the eyes.   R

The fear of the Lord is clean and endures for ever;
the judgements of the Lord are true
and righteous altogether.   R

More to be desired are they than gold,
more than much fine gold,
sweeter also than honey,
dripping from the honeycomb.   R

By them also is your servant taught
and in keeping them there is great reward.
Who can tell how often they offend?
O cleanse me from my secret faults!   R

Keep your servant also from presumptuous sins
lest they get dominion over me;
so shall I be undefiled,
and innocent of great offence.   R

Let the words of my mouth
and the meditation of my heart
be acceptable in your sight,
O Lord, my strength and my redeemer.   R   Psalm 19.7–end

Hear the Gospel of our Lord Jesus Christ according to Mark.

When Jesus, with Peter and James and John, came to the disciples, they saw a great crowd around them, and some scribes arguing with them. When the whole crowd saw him, they were immediately overcome with awe, and they ran forward to greet him. He asked them, 'What are you arguing about with them?' Someone from the crowd answered him, 'Teacher, I brought you my son; he has a spirit that makes him unable to speak; and whenever it seizes him, it dashes him down; and he foams and grinds his teeth and becomes rigid; and I asked your disciples to cast it out, but they could not do so.' He answered them, 'You faithless generation, how much longer must I be among you? How much longer must I put up with you? Bring him to me.' And they brought the boy to him. When the spirit saw him, immediately it threw the boy into convulsions, and he fell on the ground and rolled about, foaming at the mouth.

Jesus asked the father, 'How long has this been happening to him?' And he said, 'From childhood. It has often cast him into the fire and into the water, to destroy him; but if you are able to do anything, have pity on us and help us.' Jesus said to him, 'If you are able! – All things can be done for the one who believes.' Immediately the father of the child cried out, 'I believe; help my unbelief!' When Jesus saw that a crowd came running together, he rebuked the unclean spirit, saying to it, 'You spirit that keep this boy from speaking and hearing, I command you, come out of him, and never enter him again!' After crying out and convulsing him terribly, it came out, and the boy was like a corpse, so that most of them said, 'He is dead.' But Jesus took him by the hand and lifted him up, and he was able to stand. When he had entered the house, his disciples asked him privately, 'Why could we not cast it out?' He said to them, 'This kind can come out only through prayer.'

This is the Gospel of the Lord.   Mark 9.14–29

Week 7: Tuesday
between 20 and 26 February *(if before Lent)*
between 17 and 23 May *(if after Pentecost)*

Year 1

Either

A reading from the book Ecclesiasticus.

My child, when you come to serve the Lord,
    prepare yourself for testing.
Set your heart right and be steadfast,
    and do not be impetuous in time of calamity.

Cling to him and do not depart,
  so that your last days may be prosperous.
Accept whatever befalls you,
  and in times of humiliation be patient.
For gold is tested in the fire,
  and those found acceptable, in the furnace of humiliation.
Trust in him, and he will help you;
  make your ways straight, and hope in him.

You who fear the Lord, wait for his mercy;
  do not stray, or else you may fall.
You who fear the Lord, trust in him,
  and your reward will not be lost.
You who fear the Lord, hope for good things,
  for lasting joy and mercy.
Consider the generations of old and see:
  has anyone trusted in the Lord and been disappointed?
Or has anyone persevered in the fear of the Lord and been forsaken?
  Or has anyone called upon him and been neglected?
For the Lord is compassionate and merciful;
  he forgives sins and saves in time of distress.

This is the word of the Lord.   *Ecclesiasticus* 2.1–11

Responsorial Psalm

R **Commit your way to the Lord**
   and put your trust in him.   *Psalm* 37.5a

Trust in the Lord and be doing good;
dwell in the land and be nourished with truth.
Let your delight be in the Lord
and he will give you your heart's desire. **R**

Commit your way to the Lord and put your trust in him,
and he will bring it to pass.
He will make your righteousness as clear as the light
and your just dealing as the noonday. **R**

Depart from evil and do good
and you shall abide for ever.
For the Lord loves the thing that is right
and will not forsake his faithful ones. **R**   *Psalm* 37.3–6, 27–28

or James 1.12–18; Psalm 94.12–18 (page 334 ff).

A reading from the Letter of James.

Those conflicts and disputes among you, where do they come from? Do they not come from your cravings that are at war within you? You want something and do not have it; so you commit murder. And you covet something and cannot obtain it; so you engage in disputes and conflicts. You do not have, because you do not ask. You ask and do not receive, because you ask wrongly, in order to spend what you get on your pleasures. Adulterers! Do you not know that friendship with the world is enmity with God? Therefore whoever wishes to be a friend of the world becomes an enemy of God. Or do you suppose that it is for nothing that the scripture says, 'God yearns jealously for the spirit that he has made to dwell in us'? But he gives all the more grace; therefore it says,

> 'God opposes the proud,
> > but gives grace to the humble.'

Submit yourselves therefore to God. Resist the devil, and he will flee from you. Draw near to God, and he will draw near to you. Cleanse your hands, you sinners, and purify your hearts, you double-minded. Lament and mourn and weep. Let your laughter be turned into mourning and your joy into dejection. Humble yourselves before the Lord, and he will exalt you.

This is the word of the Lord.   James 4.1–10

Responsorial Psalm

R **Cast your burden upon the Lord**
   and he will sustain you.   Psalm 55.24a

O that I had wings like a dove,
for then would I fly away and be at rest.
Then would I flee far away
and make my lodging in the wilderness. **R**

I would make haste to escape
from the stormy wind and tempest.
Cast your burden upon the Lord and he will sustain you,
and will not let the righteous fall for ever. **R**   Psalm 55.7–9, 24

Year 1 and Year 2

Hear the Gospel of our Lord Jesus Christ according to Mark.

Jesus and his disciples passed through Galilee. He did not want anyone to know it; for he was teaching his disciples, saying to them, 'The Son of Man is to be betrayed into human hands, and they will kill him, and three days after being killed, he will rise again.' But they did not understand what he was saying and were afraid to ask him.

Then they came to Capernaum; and when he was in the house he asked them, 'What were you arguing about on the way?' But they were silent, for on the way they had argued with one another about who was the greatest. He sat down, called the twelve, and said to them, 'Whoever wants to be first must be last of all and servant of all.' Then he took a little child and put it among them; and taking it in his arms, he said to them, 'Whoever welcomes one such child in my name welcomes me, and whoever welcomes me welcomes not me but the one who sent me.'

This is the Gospel of the Lord.   Mark 9.30–37

Week 7: Wednesday

between 21 and 27 February *(if before Lent)*
between 18 and 24 May *(if after Pentecost)*

Year I

Either

A reading from the book Ecclesiasticus.

Wisdom teaches her children
    and gives help to those who seek her.
Whoever loves her loves life,
    and those who seek her from early morning are filled with joy.
Whoever holds her fast inherits glory,
    and the Lord blesses the place she enters.
Those who serve her minister to the Holy One;
    the Lord loves those who love her.
Those who obey her will judge the nations,
    and all who listen to her will live secure.
If they remain faithful, they will inherit her;
    their descendants will also obtain her.
For at first she will walk with them on tortuous paths;
    she will bring fear and dread upon them,
and will torment them by her discipline
    until she trusts them,
and she will test them with her ordinances.
Then she will come straight back to them again and gladden them,
    and will reveal her secrets to them.
If they go astray she will forsake them,
    and hand them over to their ruin.

This is the word of the Lord.   Ecclesiasticus 4.11–19

R **Great peace have they who love your law;**
   [nothing shall make them stumble].   Psalm 119.165

Princes have persecuted me without a cause,
but my heart stands in awe of your word.
I am as glad of your word
as one who finds great spoils. **R**

As for lies, I hate and abhor them,
but your law do I love.
Seven times a day do I praise you,
because of your righteous judgements. **R**

Great peace have they who love your law;
nothing shall make them stumble.
Lord, I have looked for your salvation
and I have fulfilled your commandments. **R**

My soul has kept your testimonies
and greatly have I loved them.
I have kept your commandments and testimonies,
for all my ways are before you. **R**   Psalm 119.161–168

or James 1.19–end; Psalm 15 (page 336 ff).

Year 2

A reading from the Letter of James.

Come now, you who say, 'Today or tomorrow we will go to such and such
a town and spend a year there, doing business and making money.' Yet you
do not even know what tomorrow will bring. What is your life? For you are
a mist that appears for a little while and then vanishes. Instead you ought to
say, 'If the Lord wishes, we will live and do this or that.' As it is, you boast in
your arrogance; all such boasting is evil. Anyone, then, who knows the right
thing to do and fails to do it, commits sin.

This is the word of the Lord.   James 4.13–end

Responsorial Psalm

R **God shall ransom my soul;**
    from the grasp of death will he take me.   Psalm 49.16

Hear this, all you peoples;
listen, all you that dwell in the world,
you of low or high degree,
both rich and poor together. R

Why should I fear in evil days,
when the malice of my foes surrounds me,
such as trust in their goods
and glory in the abundance of their riches? R

For no one can indeed ransom another
or pay to God the price of deliverance.
To ransom a soul is too costly;
there is no price one could pay for it,
so that they might live for ever,
and never see the grave. R

For we see that the wise die also;
with the foolish and ignorant they perish
and leave their riches to others. R   Psalm 49.1–2, 5–10

Year 1 and Year 2

Hear the Gospel of our Lord Jesus Christ according to Mark.

John said to Jesus, 'Teacher, we saw someone casting out demons in your name, and we tried to stop him, because he was not following us.' But Jesus said, 'Do not stop him; for no one who does a deed of power in my name will be able soon afterwards to speak evil of me. Whoever is not against us is for us.'

This is the Gospel of the Lord.   Mark 9.38–40

Week 7: Thursday

between 22 and 28 February *(if before Lent)*
between 19 and 25 May *(if after Pentecost)*

Year 1

Either

A reading from the book Ecclesiasticus.

Do not rely on your wealth,
    or say, 'I have enough.'
Do not follow your inclination and strength
    in pursuing the desires of your heart.
Do not say, 'Who can have power over me?'
    for the Lord will surely punish you.
Do not say, 'I sinned, yet what has happened to me?'
    for the Lord is slow to anger.
Do not be so confident of forgiveness
    that you add sin to sin.
Do not say, 'His mercy is great,
    he will forgive the multitude of my sins',
for both mercy and wrath are with him,
    and his anger will rest on sinners.
Do not delay to turn back to the Lord,
    and do not postpone it from day to day;
for suddenly the wrath of the Lord will come upon you,
    and at the time of punishment you will perish.
Do not depend on dishonest wealth,
    for it will not benefit you on the day of calamity.

This is the word of the Lord.   *Ecclesiasticus 5.1–8*

Responsorial Psalm

R **The Lord knows the way of the righteous;**
    [who delight in his law].   *cf Psalm 1.6a, 2a*

Blessed are they who have not walked
in the counsel of the wicked,
nor lingered in the way of sinners,
nor sat in the assembly of the scornful.
Their delight is in the law of the Lord
and they meditate on his law day and night.   **R**

Like a tree planted by streams of water
bearing fruit in due season,
with leaves that do not wither,
whatever they do, it shall prosper.   **R**

As for the wicked, it is not so with them;
they are like chaff which the wind blows away.
Therefore the wicked shall not be able to stand in the judgement,
nor the sinner in the congregation of the righteous.
For the Lord knows the way of the righteous,
but the way of the wicked shall perish.   R   *Psalm 1*

or James 2.1–9; Psalm 34.1–7 (page 339 ff).

Year 2

A reading from the Letter of James.

Come now, you rich people, weep and wail for the miseries that are coming
to you. Your riches have rotted, and your clothes are moth-eaten. Your gold
and silver have rusted, and their rust will be evidence against you, and it will
eat your flesh like fire. You have laid up treasure for the last days. Listen! The
wages of the labourers who mowed your fields, which you kept back by fraud,
cry out, and the cries of the harvesters have reached the ears of the Lord of
hosts. You have lived on the earth in luxury and in pleasure; you have fattened
your hearts on a day of slaughter. You have condemned and murdered the
righteous one, who does not resist you.

This is the word of the Lord.   *James 5.1–6*

Responsorial Psalm

R   **God shall ransom my soul;**
[from the grasp of death will he take me].   *Psalm 49.16*

Those who have honour, but lack understanding,
are like the beasts that perish.
Such is the way of those who boast in themselves,
the end of those who delight in their own words.   R

Like a flock of sheep they are destined to die;
death is their shepherd;
they go down straight to the Pit.   R

Their beauty shall waste away,
and the land of the dead shall be their dwelling.
But God shall ransom my soul;
from the grasp of death will he take me.   R

Be not afraid if some grow rich
and the glory of their house increases,
for they will carry nothing away when they die,
nor will their glory follow after them.   R

Though they count themselves happy while they live
and praise you for your success,
they shall enter the company of their ancestors
who will nevermore see the light.   R   *Psalm 49.12–20*

Hear the Gospel of our Lord Jesus Christ according to Mark.

Jesus said to his disciples, 'Truly I tell you, whoever gives you a cup of water to drink because you bear the name of Christ will by no means lose the reward.

'If any of you put a stumbling-block before one of these little ones who believe in me, it would be better for you if a great millstone were hung around your neck and you were thrown into the sea. If your hand causes you to stumble, cut it off; it is better for you to enter life maimed than to have two hands and to go to hell, to the unquenchable fire. And if your foot causes you to stumble, cut it off; it is better for you to enter life lame than to have two feet and to be thrown into hell., And if your eye causes you to stumble, tear it out; it is better for you to enter the kingdom of God with one eye than to have two eyes and to be thrown into hell, where their worm never dies, and the fire is never quenched.

'For everyone will be salted with fire. Salt is good; but if salt has lost its saltiness, how can you season it? Have salt in yourselves, and be at peace with one another.'

This is the Gospel of the Lord.   Mark 9.41—end

Week 7: Friday

> **between 23 February and 1 March** *(if before Lent and not a leap year)*
> **between 23 and 29 February** *(if before Lent in a leap year)*
> **between 20 and 26 May** *(if after Pentecost)*

Year 1

Either

A reading from the book Ecclesiasticus.

Pleasant speech multiplies friends,
    and a gracious tongue multiplies courtesies.
Let those who are friendly with you be many,
    but let your advisers be one in a thousand.
When you gain friends, gain them through testing,
    and do not trust them hastily.
For there are friends who are such when it suits them,
    but they will not stand by you in time of trouble.
And there are friends who change into enemies,
    and tell of the quarrel to your disgrace.
And there are friends who sit at your table,
    but they will not stand by you in time of trouble.
When you are prosperous, they become your second self,
    and lord it over your servants;

but if you are brought low, they turn against you,
　　and hide themselves from you.
Keep away from your enemies,
　　and be on guard with your friends.
Faithful friends are a sturdy shelter:
　　whoever finds one has found a treasure.
Faithful friends are beyond price;
　　no amount can balance their worth.
Faithful friends are life-saving medicine;
　　and those who fear the Lord will find them.
Those who fear the Lord direct their friendship aright,
　　for as they are, so are their neighbours also.

This is the word of the Lord.　　　　　　　　　　*Ecclesiasticus 6.5–17*

Responsorial Psalm

R　**My soul is longing for your judgements, O Lord,**
　　[and I meditate on your statutes].　　　　　*cf Psalm 119.20, 23b*

I am a stranger upon earth;
hide not your commandments from me.
My soul is consumed at all times
with fervent longing for your judgements.　　**R**

You have rebuked the arrogant;
cursed are those who stray from your commandments.
Turn from me shame and rebuke,
for I have kept your testimonies.　　**R**

Rulers also sit and speak against me,
but your servant meditates on your statutes.
For your testimonies are my delight;
they are my faithful counsellors.　　**R**　　　　　*Psalm 119.19–24*

or James 2.14–24, 26; Psalm 112 (page 342 ff).

Year 2

A reading from the Letter of James.

Beloved, do not grumble against one another, so that you may not be judged.
See, the Judge is standing at the doors! As an example of suffering and
patience, beloved, take the prophets who spoke in the name of the Lord.
Indeed we call blessed those who showed endurance. You have heard of the
endurance of Job, and you have seen the purpose of the Lord, how the Lord
is compassionate and merciful.

　　Above all, my beloved, do not swear, either by heaven or by earth or by
any other oath, but let your 'Yes' be yes and your 'No' be no, so that you may
not fall under condemnation.

This is the word of the Lord.　　　　　　　　　　*James 5.9–12*

Responsorial Psalm

R **Bless the Lord, O my soul,**
   [and bless his holy name].   cf Psalm 103.1

Bless the Lord, O my soul,
and all that is within me bless his holy name.
Bless the Lord, O my soul,
and forget not all his benefits.   **R**

Who forgives all your sins
and heals all your infirmities;
who redeems your life from the Pit
and crowns you with faithful love and compassion.   **R**

The Lord is full of compassion and mercy,
slow to anger and of great kindness.
He will not always accuse us,
neither will he keep his anger for ever.   **R**

He has not dealt with us according to our sins,
nor rewarded us according to our wickedness.
For as the heavens are high above the earth,
so great is his mercy upon those who fear him.   **R**

As far as the east is from the west,
so far has he set our sins from us.
As a father has compassion on his children,
so is the Lord merciful towards those who fear him.   **R**

Psalm 103.1–4, 8–13

Year 1 and Year 2

Hear the Gospel of our Lord Jesus Christ according to Mark.

Jesus went to the region of Judea and beyond the Jordan. And crowds again gathered around him; and, as was his custom, he again taught them.

Some Pharisees came, and to test him they asked, 'Is it lawful for a man to divorce his wife?' He answered them, 'What did Moses command you?' They said, 'Moses allowed a man to write a certificate of dismissal and to divorce her.' But Jesus said to them, 'Because of your hardness of heart he wrote this commandment for you. But from the beginning of creation, "God made them male and female." "For this reason a man shall leave his father and mother and be joined to his wife, and the two shall become one flesh." So they are no longer two, but one flesh. Therefore what God has joined together, let no one separate.'

Then in the house the disciples asked him again about this matter. He said to them, 'Whoever divorces his wife and marries another commits adultery against her; and if she divorces her husband and marries another, she commits adultery.'

This is the Gospel of the Lord.   Mark 10.1–12

Week 7: Saturday

between 24 February and 2 March *(if before Lent and not a leap year)*
between 24 February and 1 March *(if before Lent in a leap year)*
between 21 and 27 May *(if after Pentecost)*

Year 1

Either

A reading from the book Ecclesiasticus.

The Lord created human beings out of earth,
    and makes them return to it again.
He gave them a fixed number of days,
    but granted them authority over everything on the earth.
He endowed them with strength like his own,
    and made them in his own image.
He put the fear of them in all living beings,
    and gave them dominion over beasts and birds.
Discretion and tongue and eyes,
    ears and a mind for thinking he gave them.
He filled them with knowledge and understanding,
    and showed them good and evil.
He put the fear of him into their hearts
    to show them the majesty of his works.
And they will praise his holy name,
    to proclaim the grandeur of his works.
He bestowed knowledge upon them,
    and allotted to them the law of life.
He established with them an eternal covenant,
    and revealed to them his decrees.
Their eyes saw his glorious majesty,
    and their ears heard the glory of his voice.
He said to them, 'Beware of all evil.'
    And he gave commandment to each of them concerning a neighbour.
Their ways are always known to him;
    they will not be hid from his eyes.

This is the word of the Lord.   *Ecclesiasticus 17.1–15*

Responsorial Psalm

R **Bless the Lord, O my soul,
[and bless his holy name].** *cf Psalm 103.1*

As a father has compassion on his children,
so is the Lord merciful towards those who fear him.
For he knows of what we are made;
he remembers that we are but dust.   R

Our days are but as grass;
we flourish as a flower of the field;
for as soon as the wind goes over it, it is gone,
and its place shall know it no more.   R

But the merciful goodness of the Lord is from of old
and endures for ever on those who fear him,
and his righteousness on children's children;
on those who keep his covenant
and remember his commandments to do them.   R *Psalm 103.13–18*

or James 3.1–10; Psalm 12.1–7 (page 344 ff).

Year 2

A reading from the Letter of James.

Are any among you suffering? They should pray. Are any cheerful? They should sing songs of praise. Are any among you sick? They should call for the elders of the church and have them pray over them, anointing them with oil in the name of the Lord. The prayer of faith will save the sick, and the Lord will raise them up; and anyone who has committed sins will be forgiven. Therefore confess your sins to one another, and pray for one another, so that you may be healed. The prayer of the righteous is powerful and effective. Elijah was a human being like us, and he prayed fervently that it might not rain, and for three years and six months it did not rain on the earth. Then he prayed again, and the heaven gave rain and the earth yielded its harvest.

My brothers and sisters, if anyone among you wanders from the truth and is brought back by another, you should know that whoever brings back a sinner from wandering will save the sinner's soul from death and will cover a multitude of sins.

This is the word of the Lord. *James 5.13–end*

Responsorial Psalm

R **Let my prayer rise before you as incense, O Lord.** cf Psalm 141.2a

O Lord, I call to you; come to me quickly;
hear my voice when I cry to you.
Let my prayer rise before you as incense,
the lifting up of my hands as the evening sacrifice. **R**

Set a watch before my mouth, O Lord,
and guard the door of my lips;
let not my heart incline to any evil thing;
let me not be occupied in wickedness with evildoers,
nor taste the pleasures of their table. **R** Psalm 141.1–4

Year 1 and Year 2

Hear the Gospel of our Lord Jesus Christ according to Mark.

People were bringing little children to Jesus in order that he might touch
them; and the disciples spoke sternly to them. But when Jesus saw this, he
was indignant and said to them, 'Let the little children come to me; do not
stop them; for it is to such as these that the kingdom of God belongs. Truly
I tell you, whoever does not receive the kingdom of God as a little child will
never enter it.' And he took them up in his arms, laid his hands on them,
and blessed them.

This is the Gospel of the Lord. Mark 10.13–16

Week 8: Monday

between 26 February and 4 March *(if before Lent and not a leap year)*
between 26 February and 3 March *(if before Lent in a leap year)*
between 23 and 29 May *(if after Pentecost)*

Year 1

Either

A reading from the book Ecclesiasticus.

To those who repent the Lord grants a return,
  and he encourages those who are losing hope.
Turn back to the Lord and forsake your sins;
  pray in his presence and lessen your offence.
Return to the Most High and turn away from iniquity,
  and hate intensely what he abhors.
Who will sing praises to the Most High in Hades
  in place of the living who give thanks?
From the dead, as from one who does not exist, thanksgiving has ceased;
  those who are alive and well sing the Lord's praises.
How great is the mercy of the Lord,
  and his forgiveness for those who return to him!

This is the word of the Lord.   *Ecclesiasticus 17.24–29*

Responsorial Psalm

R **Be glad, you righteous, and rejoice in the Lord;**
   [shout for joy, all who are true of heart].   *Psalm 32.12*

Happy the one whose transgression is forgiven,
and whose sin is covered.
Happy the one to whom the Lord imputes no guilt,
and in whose spirit there is no guile.   **R**

For I held my tongue;
my bones wasted away
    through my groaning all the day long.
Your hand was heavy upon me day and night;
my moisture was dried up like the drought in summer.   **R**

Then I acknowledged my sin to you
and my iniquity I did not hide.
I said, 'I will confess my transgressions to the Lord,'
and you forgave the guilt of my sin.   **R**

Therefore let all the faithful make their prayers to you
   in time of trouble;
in the great water flood, it shall not reach them.
You are a place for me to hide in;
you preserve me from trouble;
you surround me with songs of deliverance.   R   Psalm 32.1–8

or James 3.13–end; Psalm 19.7–end (page 347 ff).

Year 2

A reading from the First Letter of Peter.

Blessed be the God and Father of our Lord Jesus Christ! By his great mercy he
has given us a new birth into a living hope through the resurrection of Jesus
Christ from the dead, and into an inheritance that is imperishable, undefiled,
and unfading, kept in heaven for you, who are being protected by the power
of God through faith for a salvation ready to be revealed in the last time. In
this you rejoice, even if now for a little while you have had to suffer various
trials, so that the genuineness of your faith – being more precious than gold
that, though perishable, is tested by fire – may be found to result in praise and
glory and honour when Jesus Christ is revealed. Although you have not seen
him, you love him; and even though you do not see him now, you believe in
him and rejoice with an indescribable and glorious joy, for you are receiving
the outcome of your faith, the salvation of your souls.

This is the word of the Lord.   1 Peter 1.3–9

Responsorial Psalm

R **The works of God are truth and justice:**
   [he is gracious and full of compassion].   cf Psalm 111.7a, 4b
   or

R **Alleluia!**

I will give thanks to the Lord with my whole heart,
in the company of the faithful and in the congregation.
The works of the Lord are great,
sought out by all who delight in them.   R

His work is full of majesty and honour
and his righteousness endures for ever.
He appointed a memorial for his marvellous deeds;
the Lord is gracious and full of compassion.   R   →

He gave food to those who feared him;
he is ever mindful of his covenant.
He showed his people the power of his works
in giving them the heritage of the nations.   R

R   **The works of God are truth and justice:
[he is gracious and full of compassion].**

or

R   **Alleluia!**

The works of his hands are truth and justice;
all his commandments are sure.
They stand fast for ever and ever;
they are done in truth and equity.   R

He sent redemption to his people;
he commanded his covenant for ever;
holy and awesome is his name.   R

The fear of the Lord is the beginning of wisdom;
a good understanding have those who live by it;
his praise endures for ever.   R   *Psalm* 111

Year 1 and Year 2

Hear the Gospel of our Lord Jesus Christ according to Mark.

As Jesus was setting out on a journey, a man ran up and knelt before him, and
asked him, 'Good Teacher, what must I do to inherit eternal life?' Jesus said
to him, 'Why do you call me good? No one is good but God alone. You know
the commandments: "You shall not murder; You shall not commit adultery;
You shall not steal; You shall not bear false witness; You shall not defraud;
Honour your father and mother." ' He said to him, 'Teacher, I have kept all
these since my youth.' Jesus, looking at him, loved him and said, 'You lack
one thing; go, sell what you own, and give the money to the poor, and you
will have treasure in heaven; then come, follow me.' When he heard this, he
was shocked and went away grieving, for he had many possessions.

Then Jesus looked around and said to his disciples, 'How hard it will be
for those who have wealth to enter the kingdom of God!' And the disciples
were perplexed at these words. But Jesus said to them again, 'Children, how
hard it is to enter the kingdom of God! It is easier for a camel to go through
the eye of a needle than for someone who is rich to enter the kingdom of
God.' They were greatly astounded and said to one another, 'Then who can
be saved?' Jesus looked at them and said, 'For mortals it is impossible, but
not for God; for God all things are possible.'

This is the Gospel of the Lord.   *Mark* 10.17–27

Week 8: Tuesday

between 27 February and 5 March *(if before Lent and not a leap year)*
between 27 February and 4 March *(if before Lent in a leap year)*
between 24 and 30 May *(if after Pentecost)*

Year 1

Either

A reading from the book Ecclesiasticus.

One who keeps the law makes many offerings;
    one who heeds the commandments makes an offering of well-being.
One who returns a kindness offers choice flour,
    and one who gives alms sacrifices a thank-offering.
To keep from wickedness is pleasing to the Lord,
    and to forsake unrighteousness is an atonement.
Do not appear before the Lord empty-handed,
    for all that you offer is in fulfilment of the commandment.
The offering of the righteous enriches the altar,
    and its pleasing odour rises before the Most High.
The sacrifice of the righteous is acceptable,
    and it will never be forgotten.
Be generous when you worship the Lord,
    and do not stint the first fruits of your hands.
With every gift show a cheerful face,
    and dedicate your tithe with gladness.
Give to the Most High as he has given to you,
    and as generously as you can afford.

This is the word of the Lord. *Ecclesiasticus 35.1–12*

Responsorial Psalm

R **I will show my salvation
to those who keep my way.** *cf Psalm 50.24b*

The Lord, the most mighty God, has spoken
and called the world from the rising of the sun to its setting.
Out of Zion, perfect in beauty, God shines forth;
our God comes and will not keep silence. **R**

Consuming fire goes out before him
and a mighty tempest stirs about him.
He calls the heaven above,
and the earth, that he may judge his people. **R**

'Gather to me my faithful,
who have sealed my covenant with sacrifice.'
Let the heavens declare his righteousness,
for God himself is judge. **R** *Psalm 50.1–6*

or James 4.1–10; Psalm 55.7–9, 24 (page 350ff).

Year 2

A reading from the First Letter of Peter.

Concerning this salvation, the prophets who prophesied of the grace that was to be yours made careful search and inquiry, inquiring about the person or time that the Spirit of Christ within them indicated, when it testified in advance to the sufferings destined for Christ and the subsequent glory. It was revealed to them that they were serving not themselves but you, in regard to the things that have now been announced to you through those who brought you good news by the Holy Spirit sent from heaven – things into which angels long to look!

Therefore prepare your minds for action; discipline yourselves; set all your hope on the grace that Jesus Christ will bring you when he is revealed. Like obedient children, do not be conformed to the desires that you formerly had in ignorance. Instead, as he who called you is holy, be holy yourselves in all your conduct; for it is written, 'You shall be holy, for I am holy.'

This is the word of the Lord.   1 Peter 1.10–16

Responsorial Psalm

R* **Sound praises to the Lord, all the earth;**
   [break into song and make music].   cf Psalm 98.5

Sing to the Lord a new song,
for he has done marvellous things.
His own right hand and his holy arm
have won for him the victory.   **R**

The Lord has made known his salvation;
his deliverance has he openly shown
in the sight of the nations.   **R**

He has remembered his mercy and faithfulness
towards the house of Israel,
and all the ends of the earth have seen
the salvation of our God.   **R***   Psalm 98.1–5

Year 1 and Year 2

Hear the Gospel of our Lord Jesus Christ according to Mark.

Peter began to say to Jesus, 'Look, we have left everything and followed you.' Jesus said, 'Truly I tell you, there is no one who has left house or brothers or sisters or mother or father or children or fields, for my sake and for the sake of the good news, who will not receive a hundredfold now in this age – houses, brothers and sisters, mothers and children, and fields, with persecutions – and in the age to come eternal life. But many who are first will be last, and the last will be first.'

This is the Gospel of the Lord.   Mark 10.28–31

Week 8: Wednesday
between 28 February and 3 March *(if before Lent)*
between 25 and 31 May *(if after Pentecost)*

Year 1

Either

A reading from the book Ecclesiasticus.

Have mercy upon us, O God of all,
    and put all the nations in fear of you.
As you have used us to show your holiness to them,
    so use them to show your glory to us.
Then they will know, as we have known,
    that there is no God but you, O Lord.
Hasten the day, and remember the appointed time,
    and let people recount your mighty deeds.
Let survivors be consumed in the fiery wrath,
    and may those who harm your people meet destruction.
Crush the heads of hostile rulers
    who say, 'There is no one but ourselves.'
Gather all the tribes of Jacob,
    and give them their inheritance, as at the beginning.
Have mercy, O Lord, on the people called by your name,
    on Israel, whom you have named your firstborn.

This is the word of the Lord.   *Ecclesiasticus 36.1–2, 4–5, 10–17*

Responsorial Psalm

R **Have mercy upon us, O Lord:**
    [there is no God but you].   *cf Ecclesiasticus 36.1a, 5b*

Remember not against us our former sins;
let your compassion make haste to meet us,
for we are brought very low.   **R**

Help us, O God of our salvation,
for the glory of your name;
deliver us, and wipe away our sins
for your name's sake.   **R**

Let the sorrowful sighing of the prisoners
come before you,
and by your mighty arm
preserve those who are condemned to die.   **R**

But we that are your people
and the sheep of your pasture
will give you thanks for ever,
and tell of your praise from generation to generation.   **R**

       Psalm 79.8–9, 12, 14

or James 4.13—end; Psalm 49.1—2, 5—10 (page 352 ff).

A reading from the First Letter of Peter.

You know that you were ransomed from the futile ways inherited from your ancestors, not with perishable things like silver or gold, but with the precious blood of Christ, like that of a lamb without defect or blemish. He was destined before the foundation of the world, but was revealed at the end of the ages for your sake. Through him you have come to trust in God, who raised him from the dead and gave him glory, so that your faith and hope are set on God.

Now that you have purified your souls by your obedience to the truth so that you have genuine mutual love, love one another deeply from the heart. You have been born anew, not of perishable but of imperishable seed, through the living and enduring word of God. For

'All flesh is like grass
    and all its glory like the flower of grass.
The grass withers,
    and the flower falls,
but the word of the Lord endures for ever.'
That word is the good news that was announced to you.

This is the word of the Lord.   1 Peter 1.18—end

Responsorial Psalm

R* **Sing praise to the Lord, O Jerusalem:**
[praise your God, O Zion].   Psalm 147.13

The Lord has strengthened the bars of your gates
and has blest your children within you.
He has established peace in your borders
and satisfies you with the finest wheat.   **R**

He sends forth his command to the earth
and his word runs very swiftly.
He gives snow like wool
and scatters the hoarfrost like ashes.   **R**

He casts down his hailstones like morsels of bread;
who can endure his frost?
He sends forth his word and melts them;
he blows with his wind and the waters flow.   **R**

He declares his word to Jacob,
his statutes and judgements to Israel.
He has not dealt so with any other nation;
they do not know his laws.   **R**   Psalm 147.13—end

368 *Week 8: Wednesday*

Hear the Gospel of our Lord Jesus Christ according to Mark.

The disciples were on the road, going up to Jerusalem, and Jesus was walking ahead of them; they were amazed, and those who followed were afraid. He took the twelve aside again and began to tell them what was to happen to him, saying, 'See, we are going up to Jerusalem, and the Son of Man will be handed over to the chief priests and the scribes, and they will condemn him to death; then they will hand him over to the Gentiles; they will mock him, and spit upon him, and flog him, and kill him; and after three days he will rise again.'

James and John, the sons of Zebedee, came forward to him and said to him, 'Teacher, we want you to do for us whatever we ask of you.' And he said to them, 'What is it you want me to do for you?' And they said to him, 'Grant us to sit, one at your right hand and one at your left, in your glory.' But Jesus said to them, 'You do not know what you are asking. Are you able to drink the cup that I drink, or be baptized with the baptism that I am baptized with?' They replied, 'We are able.' Then Jesus said to them, 'The cup that I drink you will drink; and with the baptism with which I am baptized, you will be baptized; but to sit at my right hand or at my left is not mine to grant, but it is for those for whom it has been prepared.'

When the ten heard this, they began to be angry with James and John. So Jesus called them and said to them, 'You know that among the Gentiles those whom they recognize as their rulers lord it over them, and their great ones are tyrants over them. But it is not so among you; but whoever wishes to become great among you must be your servant, and whoever wishes to be first among you must be slave of all. For the Son of Man came not to be served but to serve, and to give his life a ransom for many.'

This is the Gospel of the Lord.   Mark 10.32–45

Week 8: Thursday

between 1 and 4 March *(if before Lent and not a leap year)*

between 29 February and 4 March *(if before Lent in a leap year)*

between 26 May and 1 June *(if after Pentecost)*

Year 1

Either

A reading from the book Ecclesiasticus.

I will now call to mind the works of the Lord,
    and will declare what I have seen.
By the word of the Lord his works are made;
    and all his creatures do his will.   →

The sun looks down on everything with its light,
and the work of the Lord is full of his glory.
The Lord has not empowered even his holy ones
to recount all his marvellous works,
which the Lord the Almighty has established
so that the universe may stand firm in his glory.
He searches out the abyss and the human heart;
he understands their innermost secrets.
For the Most High knows all that may be known;
he sees from of old the things that are to come.
He discloses what has been and what is to be,
and he reveals the traces of hidden things.
No thought escapes him,
and nothing is hidden from him.
He has set in order the splendours of his wisdom;
he is from all eternity one and the same.
Nothing can be added or taken away,
and he needs no one to be his counsellor.
How desirable are all his works,
and how sparkling they are to see!
All these things live and remain for ever;
each creature is preserved to meet a particular need.
All things come in pairs, one opposite to the other,
and he has made nothing incomplete.
Each supplements the virtues of the other.
Who could ever tire of seeing his glory?

This is the word of the Lord.   Ecclesiasticus 42.15–25

Responsorial Psalm

R* **The Lord loves righteousness and justice;**
[the earth is full of his loving-kindness].   cf Psalm 33.5

Rejoice in the Lord, O you righteous,
for it is good for the just to sing praises.
Praise the Lord with the lyre;
on the ten-stringed harp sing his praise.   **R**

Sing for him a new song;
play skilfully, with shouts of praise.
For the word of the Lord is true
and all his works are sure.   **R***

By the word of the Lord were the heavens made
and all their host by the breath of his mouth.
He gathers up the waters of the sea as in a waterskin
and lays up the deep in his treasury.   **R**

Let all the earth fear the Lord;
stand in awe of him, all who dwell in the world.
For he spoke, and it was done;
he commanded, and it stood fast.   **R**   Psalm 33.1–9

or James 5.1–6; Psalm 49.12–20 (page 355 ff).

Year 2

A reading from the First Letter of Peter.

Like newborn infants, long for the pure, spiritual milk, so that by it you may
grow into salvation – if indeed you have tasted that the Lord is good.
    Come to him, a living stone, though rejected by mortals yet chosen and
precious in God's sight, and like living stones, let yourselves be built into a
spiritual house, to be a holy priesthood, to offer spiritual sacrifices acceptable
to God through Jesus Christ. But you are a chosen race, a royal priesthood, a
holy nation, God's own people, in order that you may proclaim the mighty
acts of him who called you out of darkness into his marvellous light.
    Once you were not a people,
        but now you are God's people;
    once you had not received mercy,
        but now you have received mercy.
Beloved, I urge you as aliens and exiles to abstain from the desires of the
flesh that wage war against the soul. Conduct yourselves honourably among
the Gentiles, so that, though they malign you as evildoers, they may see your
honourable deeds and glorify God when he comes to judge.

This is the word of the Lord.   1 Peter 2.2–5, 9–12

Responsorial Psalm

**R Be joyful in the Lord, all the earth:
   [give thanks and bless his name].**   cf Psalm 100.1a, 3b

O be joyful in the Lord, all the earth;
serve the Lord with gladness
and come before his presence with a song.   **R**

Know that the Lord is God;
it is he that has made us and we are his;
we are his people and the sheep of his pasture.   **R**

Enter his gates with thanksgiving
and his courts with praise;
give thanks to him and bless his name.   **R**

For the Lord is gracious;
his steadfast love is everlasting,
and his faithfulness endures from generation to generation.   **R**

Psalm 100

Hear the Gospel of our Lord Jesus Christ according to Mark.

As Jesus and his disciples and a large crowd were leaving Jericho, Bartimaeus son of Timaeus, a blind beggar, was sitting by the roadside. When he heard that it was Jesus of Nazareth, he began to shout out and say, 'Jesus, Son of David, have mercy on me!' Many sternly ordered him to be quiet, but he cried out even more loudly, 'Son of David, have mercy on me!' Jesus stood still and said, 'Call him here.' And they called the blind man, saying to him, 'Take heart; get up, he is calling you.' So throwing off his cloak, he sprang up and came to Jesus. Then Jesus said to him, 'What do you want me to do for you?' The blind man said to him, 'My teacher, let me see again.' Jesus said to him, 'Go; your faith has made you well.' Immediately he regained his sight and followed him on the way.

This is the Gospel of the Lord.   Mark 10.46–end

Week 8: Friday

between 2 and 5 March *(if before Lent and not a leap year)*
between 1 and 5 March *(if before Lent in a leap year)*
between 27 May and 2 June *(if after Pentecost)*

Year 1

Either

A reading from the book Ecclesiasticus.

Let us now sing the praises of famous men,
    our ancestors in their generations.
But of others there is no memory;
    they have perished as though they had never existed;
they have become as though they had never been born,
    they and their children after them.
But these also were godly men,
    whose righteous deeds have not been forgotten;
their wealth will remain with their descendants,
    and their inheritance with their children's children.
Their descendants stand by the covenants;
    their children also, for their sake.
Their offspring will continue for ever,
    and their glory will never be blotted out.

This is the word of the Lord.   *Ecclesiasticus 44.1, 9–13*

Responsorial Psalm

R* **Sing to the Lord a new song:**
   [sing his praise in the congregation of the faithful].   Psalm 149.1

Let Israel rejoice in their maker;
let the children of Zion be joyful in their king.
Let them praise his name in the dance;
let them sing praise to him with timbrel and lyre.   **R**

For the Lord has pleasure in his people
and adorns the poor with salvation.
Let the faithful be joyful in glory;
let them rejoice in their ranks.   **R**   Psalm 149.1–5

or James 5.9–12; Psalm 103.1–4, 8–13 (page 357 ff).

Year 2

A reading from the First Letter of Peter.

The end of all things is near; therefore be serious and discipline yourselves
for the sake of your prayers. Above all, maintain constant love for one another,
for love covers a multitude of sins. Be hospitable to one another without
complaining. Like good stewards of the manifold grace of God, serve one
another with whatever gift each of you has received. Whoever speaks must
do so as one speaking the very words of God; whoever serves must do so
with the strength that God supplies, so that God may be glorified in all things
through Jesus Christ. To him belong the glory and the power for ever and
ever. Amen.
   Beloved, do not be surprised at the fiery ordeal that is taking place among
you to test you, as though something strange were happening to you. But
rejoice in so far as you are sharing Christ's sufferings, so that you may also
be glad and shout for joy when his glory is revealed.

This is the word of the Lord.   1 Peter 4.7–13

Responsorial Psalm

R **The Lord is king;**
   he comes to judge the earth.   cf Psalm 96.10a, 13a

Tell it out among the nations that the Lord is king.
He has made the world so firm that it cannot be moved;
he will judge the peoples with equity.   **R**

Let the heavens rejoice and let the earth be glad;
let the sea thunder and all that is in it;
let the fields be joyful and all that is in them;
let all the trees of the wood shout for joy before the Lord.   **R**   →

For he comes,
he comes to judge the earth;
with righteousness he will judge the world
and the peoples with his truth. R   Psalm 96.10–end

R   **The Lord is king;**
    he comes to judge the earth.

Year 1 and Year 2

Hear the Gospel of our Lord Jesus Christ according to Mark.

Jesus entered Jerusalem and went into the temple; and when he had looked
around at everything, as it was already late, he went out to Bethany with the
twelve.

On the following day, when they came from Bethany, he was hungry.
Seeing in the distance a fig tree in leaf, he went to see whether perhaps he
would find anything on it. When he came to it, he found nothing but leaves,
for it was not the season for figs. He said to it, 'May no one ever eat fruit
from you again.' And his disciples heard it.

Then they came to Jerusalem. And he entered the temple and began to
drive out those who were selling and those who were buying in the temple,
and he overturned the tables of the money-changers and the seats of those
who sold doves; and he would not allow anyone to carry anything through
the temple. He was teaching and saying, 'Is it not written,
"My house shall be called a house of prayer for all the nations"?
But you have made it a den of robbers.'

And when the chief priests and the scribes heard it, they kept looking for
a way to kill him; for they were afraid of him, because the whole crowd was
spellbound by his teaching. And when evening came, Jesus and his disciples
went out of the city.

In the morning as they passed by, they saw the fig tree withered away to
its roots. Then Peter remembered and said to him, 'Rabbi, look! The fig tree
that you cursed has withered.' Jesus answered them, 'Have faith in God. Truly
I tell you, if you say to this mountain, "Be taken up and thrown into the sea",
and if you do not doubt in your heart, but believe that what you say will come
to pass, it will be done for you. So I tell you, whatever you ask for in prayer,
believe that you have received it, and it will be yours.

'Whenever you stand praying, forgive, if you have anything against anyone;
so that your Father in heaven may also forgive you your trespasses.'

This is the Gospel of the Lord.   Mark 11.11–26

Week 8: Saturday
between 3 and 6 March *(if before Lent and not a leap year)*
between 2 and 6 March *(if before Lent in a leap year)*
between 28 May and 3 June *(if after Pentecost)*

Year I

Either

A reading from the book Ecclesiasticus.

I thank you and praise you,
    and I bless the name of the Lord.
While I was still young, before I went on my travels,
    I sought wisdom openly in my prayer.
Before the temple I asked for her,
    and I will search for her until the end.
From the first blossom to the ripening grape
    my heart delighted in her;
my foot walked on the straight path;
    from my youth I followed her steps.
I inclined my ear a little and received her,
    and I found for myself much instruction.
I made progress in her;
    to him who gives wisdom I will give glory.
For I resolved to live according to wisdom,
    and I was zealous for the good,
    and I shall never be disappointed.
My soul grappled with wisdom,
    and in my conduct I was strict;
I spread out my hands to the heavens,
    and lamented my ignorance of her.
I directed my soul to her,
    and in purity I found her.

This is the word of the Lord.
Ecclesiasticus 51.12b–20a

Responsorial Psalm

R **The judgements of the Lord are true:**
   more to be desired than gold.   cf Psalm 19.9b, 10a

The law of the Lord is perfect, reviving the soul;
the testimony of the Lord is sure
and gives wisdom to the simple.
The statutes of the Lord are right and rejoice the heart;
the commandment of the Lord is pure
and gives light to the eyes.   R

The fear of the Lord is clean and endures for ever;
the judgements of the Lord are true
and righteous altogether;
more to be desired are they than gold,
more than much fine gold,
sweeter also than honey,
dripping from the honeycomb.   R

By them also is your servant taught
and in keeping them there is great reward.
Who can tell how often they offend?
O cleanse me from my secret faults!   R

Keep your servant also from presumptuous sins
lest they get dominion over me;
so shall I be undefiled,
and innocent of great offence.
Let the words of my mouth and the meditation of my heart
be acceptable in your sight,
O Lord, my strength and my redeemer.   R   Psalm 19.7–end

or James 5.13–end; Psalm 141.1–4 (page 360 ff).

Year 2

A reading from the Letter of Jude.

You, beloved, must remember the predictions of the apostles of our Lord
Jesus Christ; build yourselves up on your most holy faith; pray in the Holy
Spirit; keep yourselves in the love of God; look forward to the mercy of our
Lord Jesus Christ that leads to eternal life. And have mercy on some who are
wavering; save others by snatching them out of the fire; and have mercy on
still others with fear, hating even the tunic defiled by their bodies.

   Now to him who is able to keep you from falling, and to make you stand
without blemish in the presence of his glory with rejoicing, to the only God
our Saviour, through Jesus Christ our Lord, be glory, majesty, power, and
authority, before all time and now and for ever. Amen.

This is the word of the Lord.   Jude 17, 20–end

Responsorial Psalm

R **My soul is athirst for you,
O God, my God.** cf Psalm 63.1

O God, you are my God; eagerly I seek you;
my soul is athirst for you.
My flesh also faints for you,
as in a dry and thirsty land where there is no water.

So would I gaze upon you in your holy place,
that I might behold your power and your glory.
Your loving-kindness is better than life itself
and so my lips shall praise you.

I will bless you as long as I live
and lift up my hands in your name.
My soul shall be satisfied, as with marrow and fatness,
and my mouth shall praise you with joyful lips. Psalm 63.1–6

Year 1 and Year 2

Hear the Gospel of our Lord Jesus Christ according to Mark.

Jesus and his disciples came to Jerusalem. As he was walking in the temple, the chief priests, the scribes, and the elders came to him and said, 'By what authority are you doing these things? Who gave you this authority to do them?' Jesus said to them, 'I will ask you one question; answer me, and I will tell you by what authority I do these things. Did the baptism of John come from heaven, or was it of human origin? Answer me.' They argued with one another, 'If we say, "From heaven", he will say, "Why then did you not believe him?" But shall we say, "Of human origin"?' – they were afraid of the crowd, for all regarded John as truly a prophet. So they answered Jesus, 'We do not know.' And Jesus said to them, 'Neither will I tell you by what authority I am doing these things.'

This is the Gospel of the Lord. Mark 11.27–end

Week 9: Monday

> **between 5 and 8 March** *(if before Lent and not a leap year)*
> **between 4 and 8 March** *(if before Lent in a leap year)*
> **between 30 May and 5 June** *(if after Pentecost)*

Year 1

Either

A reading from the Book of Tobit.

This book tells the story of Tobit son of Tobiel son of Hananiel son of Aduel son of Gabael son of Raphael of the descendants of Asiel, of the tribe of Naphtali, who in the days of King Shalmaneser of the Assyrians was taken into captivity from Thisbe, which is to the south of Kedesh Naphtali in Upper Galilee, above Asher towards the west, and north of Phogor.

During the reign of Esar-haddon I returned home, and my wife Anna and my son Tobias were restored to me. At our festival of Pentecost, which is the sacred festival of weeks, a good dinner was prepared for me and I reclined to eat. When the table was set for me and an abundance of food placed before me, I said to my son Tobias, 'Go, my child, and bring whatever poor person you may find of our people among the exiles in Nineveh, who is wholeheartedly mindful of God, and he shall eat together with me. I will wait for you, until you come back.' So Tobias went to look for some poor person of our people. When he had returned he said, 'Father!' And I replied, 'Here I am, my child.' Then he went on to say, 'Look, father, one of our own people has been murdered and thrown into the market-place, and now he lies there strangled.' Then I sprang up, left the dinner before even tasting it, and removed the body from the square and laid it in one of the rooms until sunset when I might bury it. When I returned, I washed myself and ate my food in sorrow. Then I remembered the prophecy of Amos, how he said against Bethel,

> 'Your festivals shall be turned into mourning,
>> and all your songs into lamentation.'

And I wept.

When the sun had set, I went and dug a grave and buried him. And my neighbours laughed and said, 'Is he still not afraid? He has already been hunted down to be put to death for doing this, and he ran away; yet here he is again burying the dead!'

This is the word of the Lord.   Tobit 1.1–2, 2.1–8

Responsorial Psalm

R **They shall dwell in your tabernacle, O Lord:**
    [those who do what is right].   *cf Psalm 15.1a, 2b*

Lord, who may dwell in your tabernacle?
Who may rest upon your holy hill?
Whoever leads an uncorrupt life
and does the thing that is right. R

Who speaks the truth from the heart
and bears no deceit on the tongue;
who does no evil to a friend
and pours no scorn on a neighbour. R

In whose sight the wicked are not esteemed,
but who honours those who fear the Lord.
Whoever has sworn to a neighbour
and never goes back on that word. R

Who does not lend money in hope of gain,
nor takes a bribe against the innocent;
whoever does these things
shall never fall. R   *Psalm 15*

or 1 Peter 1.3–9; Psalm 111 (page 363 ff).

Year 2

A reading from the Second Letter of Peter.

May grace and peace be yours in abundance in the knowledge of God and of Jesus our Lord.

His divine power has given us everything needed for life and godliness, through the knowledge of him who called us by his own glory and goodness. Thus he has given us, through these things, his precious and very great promises, so that through them you may escape from the corruption that is in the world because of lust, and may become participants in the divine nature. For this very reason, you must make every effort to support your faith with goodness, and goodness with knowledge, and knowledge with self-control, and self-control with endurance, and endurance with godliness, and godliness with mutual affection, and mutual affection with love.

This is the word of the Lord.   *2 Peter 1.2–7*

R   **I have made the Lord my refuge,**
     [and the Most High my stronghold].   *cf Psalm 91.9*

Whoever dwells in the shelter of the Most High
and abides under the shadow of the Almighty,
shall say to the Lord, 'My refuge and my stronghold,
my God, in whom I put my trust.'   R

Because they have set their love upon me,
therefore will I deliver them;
I will lift them up, because they know my name.
They will call upon me and I will answer them.   R

I am with them in trouble,
I will deliver them and bring them to honour.
With long life will I satisfy them
and show them my salvation.   R   *Psalm 91.1–2, 14–end*

Year 1 and Year 2

Hear the Gospel of our Lord Jesus Christ according to Mark.

Jesus began to speak to the chief priests, the scribes, and the elders in parables.
'A man planted a vineyard, put a fence around it, dug a pit for the wine press,
and built a watch-tower; then he leased it to tenants and went to another
country. When the season came, he sent a slave to the tenants to collect from
them his share of the produce of the vineyard. But they seized him, and beat
him, and sent him away empty-handed. And again he sent another slave to
them; this one they beat over the head and insulted. Then he sent another,
and that one they killed. And so it was with many others; some they beat,
and others they killed. He had still one other, a beloved son. Finally he sent
him to them, saying, "They will respect my son." But those tenants said to
one another, "This is the heir; come, let us kill him, and the inheritance will
be ours." So they seized him, killed him, and threw him out of the vineyard.
What then will the owner of the vineyard do? He will come and destroy the
tenants and give the vineyard to others. Have you not read this scripture:
   "The stone that the builders rejected
      has become the cornerstone;
   this was the Lord's doing,
      and it is amazing in our eyes"?'

When they realized that he had told this parable against them, they wanted to
arrest him, but they feared the crowd. So they left him and went away.

This is the Gospel of the Lord.   *Mark 12.1–12*

Week 9: Tuesday

between 6 and 9 March *(if before Lent and not a leap year)*
between 5 and 9 March *(if before Lent in a leap year)*
between 31 May and 6 June *(if after Pentecost)*

Year I

Either

A reading from the Book of Tobit.

That night I washed myself and went into my courtyard and slept by the wall of the courtyard; and my face was uncovered because of the heat. I did not know that there were sparrows on the wall; their fresh droppings fell into my eyes and produced white films. I went to physicians to be healed, but the more they treated me with ointments the more my vision was obscured by the white films, until I became completely blind. For four years I remained unable to see. All my kindred were sorry for me, and Ahikar took care of me for two years before he went to Elymais.

At that time, also, my wife Anna earned money at women's work. She used to send what she made to the owners and they would pay wages to her. One day, the seventh of Dystrus, when she cut off a piece she had woven and sent it to the owners, they paid her full wages and also gave her a kid for a meal. When she returned to me, the kid began to bleat. So I called her and said, 'Where did you get this kid? It is surely not stolen, is it? Return it to the owners; for we have no right to eat anything stolen.' But she said to me, 'It was given to me as a gift in addition to my wages.' But I did not believe her, and told her to return it to the owners. I became flushed with anger against her over this. Then she replied to me, 'Where are your acts of charity? Where are your righteous deeds? These things are known about you!'

This is the word of the Lord. Tobit 2.9–end

Responsorial Psalm

R **Blessed are those
who delight in the commandments of the Lord.** cf Psalm 112.1

Blessed are those who fear the Lord
and have great delight in his commandments.
Their descendants will be mighty in the land,
a generation of the faithful that will be blest. **R**

Wealth and riches will be in their house,
and their righteousness endures for ever.
Light shines in the darkness for the upright;
gracious and full of compassion are the righteous. **R** →

It goes well with those who are generous in lending
and order their affairs with justice,
for they will never be shaken;
the righteous will be held in everlasting remembrance.   R

R   **Blessed are those
who delight in the commandments of the Lord.**

They will not be afraid of any evil tidings;
their heart is steadfast, trusting in the Lord.
Their heart is sustained and will not fear,
until they see the downfall of their foes.   R

They have given freely to the poor;
their righteousness stands fast for ever;
their head will be exalted with honour.   R

The wicked shall see it and be angry;
they shall gnash their teeth in despair;
the desire of the wicked shall perish.   R   *Psalm* 112

or 1 Peter 1.10–16; Psalm 98.1–5 (page 366 ff).

Year 2

A reading from the Second Letter of Peter.

What sort of people ought you to be in leading lives of holiness and godliness,
waiting for and hastening the coming of the day of God, because of which
the heavens will be set ablaze and dissolved, and the elements will melt with
fire? But, in accordance with his promise, we wait for new heavens and a
new earth, where righteousness is at home. Therefore, beloved, while you are
waiting for these things, strive to be found by him at peace, without spot or
blemish; and regard the patience of our Lord as salvation.
    You therefore, beloved, since you are forewarned, beware that you are not
carried away with the error of the lawless and lose your own stability. But
grow in the grace and knowledge of our Lord and Saviour Jesus Christ. To
him be the glory both now and to the day of eternity. Amen.

This is the word of the Lord.   2 Peter 3.11–15a, 17–end

Responsorial Psalm

R* **O Lord, you have been our refuge
from one generation to another.** Psalm 90.1

Before the mountains were brought forth,
or the earth and the world were formed,
from everlasting to everlasting
you are God. R

You turn us back to dust and say:
'Turn back, O children of earth.'
For a thousand years in your sight are but as yesterday,
which passes like a watch in the night. R

The days of our life are three score years and ten,
or if our strength endures, even four score;
yet the sum of them is but labour and sorrow,
for they soon pass away and we are gone. R

Satisfy us with your loving-kindness in the morning,
that we may rejoice and be glad all our days.
Show your servants your works,
and let your glory be over their children. R Psalm 90.1–4, 10, 14, 16

Year I and Year 2

Hear the Gospel of our Lord Jesus Christ according to Mark.

The chief priests, the scribes, and the elders sent to Jesus some Pharisees
and some Herodians to trap him in what he said. And they came and said
to him, 'Teacher, we know that you are sincere, and show deference to no
one; for you do not regard people with partiality, but teach the way of God
in accordance with truth. Is it lawful to pay taxes to the emperor, or not?
Should we pay them, or should we not?' But knowing their hypocrisy, he said
to them, 'Why are you putting me to the test? Bring me a denarius and let
me see it.' And they brought one. Then he said to them, 'Whose head is this,
and whose title?' They answered, 'The emperor's.' Jesus said to them, 'Give
to the emperor the things that are the emperor's, and to God the things that
are God's.' And they were utterly amazed at him.

This is the Gospel of the Lord. Mark 12.13–17

Week 9: Wednesday between 1 and 7 June *(if after Pentecost)*

Year 1

Either

A reading from the Book of Tobit.

With much grief and anguish of heart I wept, and with groaning began to pray:

'You are righteous, O Lord,
    and all your deeds are just;
all your ways are mercy and truth;
    you judge the world.
And now, O Lord, remember me
    and look favourably upon me.
Do not punish me for my sins
    and for my unwitting offences
    and those that my ancestors committed before you.
They sinned against you,
    and disobeyed your commandments.
So you gave us over to plunder, exile, and death,
    to become the talk, the byword, and an object of reproach,
    among all the nations among whom you have dispersed us.
And now your many judgements are true
    in exacting penalty from me for my sins.
For we have not kept your commandments
    and have not walked in accordance with truth before you.
So now deal with me as you will;
    command my spirit to be taken from me,
    so that I may be released from the face of the earth
        and become dust.
For it is better for me to die than to live,
    because I have had to listen to undeserved insults,
    and great is the sorrow within me.
Command, O Lord, that I be released from this distress;
    release me to go to the eternal home,
    and do not, O Lord, turn your face away from me.
For it is better for me to die
    than to see so much distress in my life
    and to listen to insults.'

On the same day, at Ecbatana in Media, it also happened that Sarah, the daughter of Raguel, was reproached by one of her father's maids. For she had been married to seven husbands, and the wicked demon Asmodeus had killed each of them before they had been with her as is customary for wives. So the maid said to her, 'You are the one who kills your husbands! See, you have already been married to seven husbands and have not borne the name of a single one of them. Why do you beat us? Because your husbands are dead? Go with them! May we never see a son or daughter of yours!'

On that day she was grieved in spirit and wept. When she had gone up to her father's upper room, she intended to hang herself. But she thought it over and said, 'Never shall they reproach my father, saying to him, "You had only one beloved daughter but she hanged herself because of her distress." And I shall bring my father in his old age down in sorrow to Hades. It is better for me not to hang myself, but to pray the Lord that I may die and not listen to these reproaches any more.' At that same time, with hands outstretched towards the window, she prayed and said,

'Blessed are you, merciful God!

Blessed is your name for ever;

let all your works praise you for ever.'

At that very moment, the prayers of both of them were heard in the glorious presence of God. So Raphael was sent to heal both of them: Tobit, by removing the white films from his eyes, so that he might see God's light with his eyes; and Sarah daughter of Raguel, by giving her in marriage to Tobias son of Tobit, and by setting her free from the wicked demon Asmodeus. For Tobias was entitled to have her before all others who had desired to marry her. At the same time that Tobit returned from the courtyard into his house, Sarah daughter of Raguel came down from her upper room.

This is the word of the Lord. Tobit 3.1–11, 16–end

Responsorial Psalm

R* **To you, O Lord, I lift up my soul;**
[My God, in you I trust]. cf Psalm 25.1a

Let me not be put to shame;
let not my enemies triumph over me.
Let none who look to you be put to shame,
but let the treacherous be shamed and frustrated. R

Make me to know your ways, O Lord,
and teach me your paths.
Lead me in your truth and teach me,
for you are the God of my salvation;
for you have I hoped all the day long. R

Remember, Lord, your compassion and love,
for they are from everlasting.
Remember not the sins of my youth or my transgressions,
but think on me in your goodness, O Lord,
according to your steadfast love. R

Gracious and upright is the Lord;
therefore shall he teach sinners in the way.
He will guide the humble in doing right
and teach his way to the lowly. R Psalm 25.1–8

or 1 Peter 1.18–end; Psalm 147.13–end (page 368 ff).

Year 2

A reading from the Second Letter of Paul to Timothy.

Paul, an apostle of Christ Jesus by the will of God, for the sake of the promise of life that is in Christ Jesus, to Timothy, my beloved child: Grace, mercy, and peace from God the Father and Christ Jesus our Lord.

I am grateful to God – whom I worship with a clear conscience, as my ancestors did – when I remember you constantly in my prayers night and day. For this reason I remind you to rekindle the gift of God that is within you through the laying on of my hands; for God did not give us a spirit of cowardice, but rather a spirit of power and of love and of self-discipline.

Do not be ashamed, then, of the testimony about our Lord or of me his prisoner, but join with me in suffering for the gospel, relying on the power of God, who saved us and called us with a holy calling, not according to our works but according to his own purpose and grace. This grace was given to us in Christ Jesus before the ages began, but it has now been revealed through the appearing of our Saviour Christ Jesus, who abolished death and brought life and immortality to light through the gospel. For this gospel I was appointed a herald and an apostle and a teacher, and for this reason I suffer as I do. But I am not ashamed, for I know the one in whom I have put my trust, and I am sure that he is able to guard until that day what I have entrusted to him.

This is the word of the Lord.   2 Timothy 1.1–3, 6–12

Responsorial Psalm

R* **To you, O Lord, I lift up my eyes,**
   to you that are enthroned in the heavens.   cf Psalm 123.1

As the eyes of servants look to the hand of their master,
or the eyes of a maid to the hand of her mistress,
so our eyes wait upon the Lord our God,
until he have mercy upon us.   **R**

Have mercy upon us, O Lord, have mercy upon us,
for we have had more than enough of contempt.
Our soul has had more than enough of the scorn of the arrogant,
and of the contempt of the proud.   **R**   Psalm 123

Hear the Gospel of our Lord Jesus Christ according to Mark.

Some Sadducees, who say there is no resurrection, came to Jesus and asked him a question, saying, 'Teacher, Moses wrote for us that if a man's brother dies, leaving a wife but no child, the man shall marry the widow and raise up children for his brother. There were seven brothers; the first married and, when he died, left no children; and the second married her and died, leaving no children; and the third likewise; none of the seven left children. Last of all the woman herself died. In the resurrection whose wife will she be? For the seven had married her.'

Jesus said to them, 'Is not this the reason you are wrong, that you know neither the scriptures nor the power of God? For when they rise from the dead, they neither marry nor are given in marriage, but are like angels in heaven. And as for the dead being raised, have you not read in the book of Moses, in the story about the bush, how God said to him, "I am the God of Abraham, the God of Isaac, and the God of Jacob"? He is God not of the dead, but of the living; you are quite wrong.'

This is the Gospel of the Lord.   Mark 12.18–27

Week 9: Thursday between 2 and 8 June *(if after Pentecost)*

Year I

Either

A reading from the Book of Tobit.

When Raphael and Tobias were approaching Ecbatana, Raphael said to the young man, 'Brother Tobias.' 'Here I am,' he answered. Then Raphael said to him, 'We must stay this night in the home of Raguel. He is your relative, and he has a daughter named Sarah.

Now when they entered Ecbatana, Tobias said to him, 'Brother Azariah, take me straight to our brother Raguel.' So he took him to Raguel's house, where they found him sitting beside the courtyard door. They greeted him first, and he replied, 'Joyous greetings, brothers; welcome and good health!' Then he brought them into his house. He said to his wife Edna, 'How much the young man resembles my kinsman Tobit!' Then Edna questioned them, saying, 'Where are you from, brothers?' They answered, 'We belong to the descendants of Naphtali who are exiles in Nineveh.' She said to them, 'Do you know our kinsman Tobit?' And they replied, 'Yes, we know him.' Then she asked them, 'Is he in good health?' They replied, 'He is alive and in good health.' And Tobias added, 'He is my father!' At that Raguel jumped up and kissed him and wept. He also spoke to him as follows, 'Blessings on you, my child, son of a good and noble father! O most miserable of calamities that such an upright and beneficent man has become blind!' He then embraced his kinsman Tobias and wept. His wife Edna also wept for him, and their →

daughter Sarah likewise wept. Then Raguel slaughtered a ram from the flock and received them very warmly.

When they had bathed and washed themselves and had reclined to dine, Tobias said to Raphael, 'Brother Azariah, ask Raguel to give me my kinswoman Sarah.' But Raguel overheard it and said to the lad, 'Eat and drink, and be merry tonight. For no one except you, brother, has the right to marry my daughter Sarah. Likewise I am not at liberty to give her to any other man than yourself, because you are my nearest relative. But let me explain to you the true situation more fully, my child. I have given her to seven men of our kinsmen, and all died on the night when they went in to her. But now, my child, eat and drink, and the Lord will act on behalf of you both.' But Tobias said, 'I will neither eat nor drink anything until you settle the things that pertain to me.' So Raguel said, 'I will do so. She is given to you in accordance with the decree in the book of Moses, and it has been decreed from heaven that she should be given to you. Take your kinswoman; from now on you are her brother and she is your sister. She is given to you from today and for ever. May the Lord of heaven, my child, guide and prosper you both this night and grant you mercy and peace.' Then Raguel summoned his daughter Sarah. When she came to him he took her by the hand and gave her to Tobias, saying, 'Take her to be your wife in accordance with the law and decree written in the book of Moses. Take her and bring her safely to your father. And may the God of heaven prosper your journey with his peace.' Then he called her mother and told her to bring writing material; and he wrote out a copy of a marriage contract, to the effect that he gave her to him as wife according to the decree of the law of Moses. Then they began to eat and drink.

Raguel called his wife Edna and said to her, 'Sister, get the other room ready, and take her there.'

When the parents had gone out and shut the door of the room, Tobias got out of bed and said to Sarah, 'Sister, get up, and let us pray and implore our Lord that he grant us mercy and safety.' So she got up, and they began to pray and implore that they might be kept safe. Tobias began by saying,

'Blessed are you, O God of our ancestors,
     and blessed is your name in all generations for ever.
Let the heavens and the whole creation bless you for ever.
You made Adam, and for him you made his wife Eve
     as a helper and support.
From the two of them the human race has sprung.
You said, "It is not good that the man should be alone;
     let us make a helper for him like himself."
I now am taking this kinswoman of mine,
     not because of lust,
     but with sincerity.
Grant that she and I may find mercy
     and that we may grow old together.'
And they both said, 'Amen, Amen.'

This is the word of the Lord.   Tobit 6.10–11, 7.1–15, 8.4–8

Responsorial Psalm

R **Blessed are those who fear the Lord,**
   [and walk in the ways of God].   *cf Psalm 128.1*

Blessed are all those who fear the Lord,
and walk in his ways.
You shall eat the fruit of the toil of your hands;
it shall go well with you,
and happy shall you be. R

Your wife within your house
shall be like a fruitful vine;
your children round your table,
like fresh olive branches.
Thus shall the one be blest who fears the Lord. R

The Lord from out of Zion bless you,
that you may see Jerusalem in prosperity
all the days of your life.
May you see your children's children,
and may there be peace upon Israel. R   *Psalm 128*

or I Peter 2.2–5, 9–12; Psalm 100 (page 371 ff).

Year 2

A reading from the Second Letter of Paul to Timothy.

Remember Jesus Christ, raised from the dead, a descendant of David – that is
my gospel, for which I suffer hardship, even to the point of being chained like
a criminal. But the word of God is not chained. Therefore I endure everything
for the sake of the elect, so that they may also obtain the salvation that is in
Christ Jesus, with eternal glory. The saying is sure:
    If we have died with him, we will also live with him;
    if we endure, we will also reign with him;
    if we deny him, he will also deny us;
    if we are faithless, he remains faithful –
    for he cannot deny himself.

Remind them of this, and warn them before God that they are to avoid wrangling over words, which does no good but only ruins those who are listening.
Do your best to present yourself to God as one approved by him, a worker
who has no need to be ashamed, rightly explaining the word of truth.

This is the word of the Lord.   2 Timothy 2.8–15

Responsorial Psalm

R **To you, O Lord, I lift up my soul;**
   [My God, in you I trust].   *cf Psalm 25.1a*

Lead me in your truth and teach me,
for you are the God of my salvation;
for you have I hoped all the day long.   R

Remember, Lord, your compassion and love,
for they are from everlasting.
Remember not the sins of my youth or my transgressions,
but think on me in your goodness, O Lord,
according to your steadfast love.   R

Gracious and upright is the Lord;
therefore shall he teach sinners in the way.
He will guide the humble in doing right
and teach his way to the lowly.   R

All the paths of the Lord are mercy and truth
to those who keep his covenant and his testimonies.
For your name's sake, O Lord,
be merciful to my sin, for it is great.   R

Who are those who fear the Lord?
Them will he teach in the way that they should choose.
Their soul shall dwell at ease
and their offspring shall inherit the land.   R   *Psalm 25.4–12*

Year 1 and Year 2

Hear the Gospel of our Lord Jesus Christ according to Mark.

One of the scribes came near and asked Jesus, 'Which commandment is the
first of all?' Jesus answered, 'The first is, "Hear, O Israel: the Lord our God,
the Lord is one; you shall love the Lord your God with all your heart, and
with all your soul, and with all your mind, and with all your strength." The
second is this, "You shall love your neighbour as yourself." There is no other
commandment greater than these.' Then the scribe said to him, 'You are
right, Teacher; you have truly said that "he is one, and besides him there is
no other"; and "to love him with all the heart, and with all the understanding,
and with all the strength", and "to love one's neighbour as oneself", – this is
much more important than all whole burnt-offerings and sacrifices.' When
Jesus saw that he answered wisely, he said to him, 'You are not far from the
kingdom of God.' After that no one dared to ask him any question.

This is the Gospel of the Lord.   *Mark 12.28–34*

Week 9: Friday between 3 and 9 June *(if after Pentecost)*

Year I

Either

A reading from the Book of Tobit.

Anna sat looking intently down the road by which her son would come. When she caught sight of him coming, she said to his father, 'Look, your son is coming, and the man who went with him!'

Raphael said to Tobias, before he had approached his father, 'I know that his eyes will be opened. Smear the gall of the fish on his eyes; the medicine will make the white films shrink and peel off from his eyes, and your father will regain his sight and see the light.'

Then Anna ran up to her son and threw her arms around him, saying, 'Now that I have seen you, my child, I am ready to die.' And she wept. Then Tobit got up and came stumbling out through the courtyard door. Tobias went up to him, with the gall of the fish in his hand, and holding him firmly, he blew into his eyes, saying, 'Take courage, father.' With this he applied the medicine on his eyes, and it made them smart. Next, with both his hands he peeled off the white films from the corners of his eyes. Then Tobit saw his son and threw his arms around him, and he wept and said to him, 'I see you, my son, the light of my eyes!' Then he said,

'Blessed be God,
    and blessed be his great name,
    and blessed be all his holy angels.
May his holy name be blessed
    throughout all the ages.
Though he afflicted me,
    he has had mercy upon me.
Now I see my son Tobias!'

So Tobit went in rejoicing and praising God at the top of his voice. Tobias reported to his father that his journey had been successful, that he had brought the money, that he had married Raguel's daughter Sarah, and that she was, indeed, on her way there, very near to the gate of Nineveh.

This is the word of the Lord.   Tobit 11.5–15

Responsorial Psalm

R* **The Lord shall reign for ever,**
  [your God, O Zion, throughout all generations].   Psalm 146.10

Praise the Lord, O my soul:
while I live will I praise the Lord;
as long as I have any being,
I will sing praises to my God.   R

Put not your trust in princes, nor in any human power,
for there is no help in them.
When their breath goes forth, they return to the earth;
on that day all their thoughts perish.   R

Happy are those who have the God of Jacob for their help,
whose hope is in the Lord their God;
who made heaven and earth, the sea and all that is in them;
who keeps his promise for ever.   R

Who gives justice to those that suffer wrong
and bread to those who hunger.
The Lord looses those that are bound;
the Lord opens the eyes of the blind;
the Lord lifts up those who are bowed down.   R

The Lord loves the righteous;
the Lord watches over the stranger in the land;
he upholds the orphan and widow;
but the way of the wicked he turns upside down.   R*   Psalm 146

or 1 Peter 4.7–13; Psalm 96.10–end (page 373 ff).

Year 2

A reading from the Second Letter of Paul to Timothy.

You have observed my teaching, my conduct, my aim in life, my faith, my
patience, my love, my steadfastness, my persecutions, and my suffering the
things that happened to me in Antioch, Iconium, and Lystra. What persecutions
I endured! Yet the Lord rescued me from all of them. Indeed, all who want
to live a godly life in Christ Jesus will be persecuted. But wicked people and
impostors will go from bad to worse, deceiving others and being deceived.
But as for you, continue in what you have learned and firmly believed, knowing from whom you learned it, and how from childhood you have known
the sacred writings that are able to instruct you for salvation through faith in
Christ Jesus. All scripture is inspired by God and is useful for teaching, for
reproof, for correction, and for training in righteousness, so that everyone
who belongs to God may be proficient, equipped for every good work.

This is the word of the Lord.   2 Timothy 3.10–end

Responsorial Psalm

R **Great peace have they who love your law;**
  [nothing shall make them stumble].   *Psalm 119.165*

Princes have persecuted me without a cause,
but my heart stands in awe of your word.
I am as glad of your word
as one who finds great spoils. R

As for lies, I hate and abhor them,
but your law do I love.
Seven times a day do I praise you,
because of your righteous judgements. R

Great peace have they who love your law;
nothing shall make them stumble.
Lord, I have looked for your salvation
and I have fulfilled your commandments. R

My soul has kept your testimonies
and greatly have I loved them.
I have kept your commandments and testimonies,
for all my ways are before you. R   *Psalm 119.161–168*

Year 1 and Year 2

Hear the Gospel of our Lord Jesus Christ according to Mark.

While Jesus was teaching in the temple, he said, 'How can the scribes say that the Messiah is the son of David? David himself, by the Holy Spirit, declared,
  "The Lord said to my Lord,
   'Sit at my right hand,
     until I put your enemies under your feet.' "
David himself calls him Lord; so how can he be his son?' And the large crowd was listening to him with delight.

This is the Gospel of the Lord.   *Mark 12.35–37*

Week 9: Saturday between 4 and 10 June *(if after Pentecost)*

Year 1

Either

A reading from the Book of Tobit.

When the wedding celebration was ended, Tobit called his son Tobias and said to him, 'My child, see to paying the wages of the man who went with you, and give him a bonus as well.' So Tobias called him and said, 'Take for your wages half of all that you brought back, and farewell.'

Then Raphael called the two of them privately and said to them, 'Bless God and acknowledge him in the presence of all the living for the good things he has done for you. Bless and sing praise to his name. With fitting honour declare to all people the deeds of God. Do not be slow to acknowledge him. It is good to conceal the secret of a king, but to acknowledge and reveal the works of God, and with fitting honour to acknowledge him. Do good, and evil will not overtake you. Prayer with fasting is good, but better than both is almsgiving with righteousness. A little with righteousness is better than wealth with wrongdoing. It is better to give alms than to lay up gold. For almsgiving saves from death and purges away every sin. Those who give alms will enjoy a full life, but those who commit sin and do wrong are their own worst enemies.

'I will now declare the whole truth to you and will conceal nothing from you. Already I have declared it to you when I said, "It is good to conceal the secret of a king, but to reveal with due honour the works of God." So now, when you and Sarah prayed, it was I who brought and read the record of your prayer before the glory of the Lord, and likewise whenever you buried the dead. And that time when you did not hesitate to get up and leave your dinner to go and bury the dead, I was sent to you to test you. And at the same time God sent me to heal you and Sarah your daughter-in-law. I am Raphael, one of the seven angels who stand ready and enter before the glory of the Lord.

'So now get up from the ground, and acknowledge God. See, I am ascending to him who sent me.'

This is the word of the Lord.   Tobit 12.1, 5–15, 20a

Responsorial Psalm

R* **Bless the Lord, O my soul,**
[all that is within me bless his holy name].   *Psalm 103.1*

The Lord is full of compassion and mercy,
slow to anger and of great kindness.
He will not always accuse us,
neither will he keep his anger for ever.   **R**

He has not dealt with us according to our sins,
nor rewarded us according to our wickedness.
For as the heavens are high above the earth,
so great is his mercy upon those who fear him.   **R**

As far as the east is from the west,
so far has he set our sins from us.
As a father has compassion on his children,
so is the Lord merciful towards those who fear him.   **R**   *Psalm 103.1, 8–13*

or Jude 17, 20–end; Psalm 63.1–6 (page 376 ff).

Year 2

A reading from the Second Letter of Paul to Timothy.

In the presence of God and of Christ Jesus, who is to judge the living and
the dead, and in view of his appearing and his kingdom, I solemnly urge
you: proclaim the message; be persistent whether the time is favourable or
unfavourable; convince, rebuke, and encourage, with the utmost patience in
teaching. For the time is coming when people will not put up with sound
doctrine, but having itching ears, they will accumulate for themselves teachers
to suit their own desires, and will turn away from listening to the truth and
wander away to myths. As for you, always be sober, endure suffering, do the
work of an evangelist, carry out your ministry fully.

As for me, I am already being poured out as a libation, and the time of
my departure has come. I have fought the good fight, I have finished the race,
I have kept the faith. From now on there is reserved for me the crown of
righteousness, which the Lord, the righteous judge, will give to me on that
day, and not only to me but also to all who have longed for his appearing.

This is the word of the Lord.   2 Timothy 4.1–8

R   **O Lord, you are my refuge and my strength,**
    [let my mouth be full of your praise].   cf Psalm 71.7b, 8a

I have become a portent to many,
but you are my refuge and my strength.
Let my mouth be full of your praise
and your glory all the day long.   R

Do not cast me away in the time of old age;
forsake me not when my strength fails.
For my enemies are talking against me,
and those who lie in wait for my life take counsel together.   R

They say, 'God has forsaken him;
pursue him and take him,
because there is none to deliver him.'
O God, be not far from me;
come quickly to help me, O my God.   R

Let those who are against me
be put to shame and disgrace;
let those who seek to do me evil
be covered with scorn and reproach.
But as for me I will hope continually
and will praise you more and more.   R

My mouth shall tell of your righteousness
and salvation all the day long,
for I know no end of the telling.
I will begin with the mighty works of the Lord God;
I will recall your righteousness, yours alone.   R   Psalm 71.7–16

Year 1 and Year 2

Hear the Gospel of our Lord Jesus Christ according to Mark.

As Jesus taught, he said, 'Beware of the scribes, who like to walk around in
long robes, and to be greeted with respect in the market-places, and to have
the best seats in the synagogues and places of honour at banquets! They devour
widows' houses and for the sake of appearance say long prayers. They will
receive the greater condemnation.'

He sat down opposite the treasury, and watched the crowd putting money
into the treasury. Many rich people put in large sums. A poor widow came
and put in two small copper coins, which are worth a penny. Then he called
his disciples and said to them, 'Truly I tell you, this poor widow has put in
more than all those who are contributing to the treasury. For all of them
have contributed out of their abundance; but she out of her poverty has put
in everything she had, all she had to live on.'

This is the Gospel of the Lord.   Mark 12.38–end

Week 10: Monday between 6 and 12 June *(if after Pentecost)*

Year I

A reading from the Second Letter of Paul to the Corinthians.

Paul, an apostle of Christ Jesus by the will of God, and Timothy our brother, to the church of God that is in Corinth, including all the saints throughout Achaia: Grace to you and peace from God our Father and the Lord Jesus Christ.

Blessed be the God and Father of our Lord Jesus Christ, the Father of mercies and the God of all consolation, who consoles us in all our affliction, so that we may be able to console those who are in any affliction with the consolation with which we ourselves are consoled by God. For just as the sufferings of Christ are abundant for us, so also our consolation is abundant through Christ. If we are being afflicted, it is for your consolation and salvation; if we are being consoled, it is for your consolation, which you experience when you patiently endure the same sufferings that we are also suffering. Our hope for you is unshaken; for we know that as you share in our sufferings, so also you share in our consolation.

This is the word of the Lord.   2 Corinthians 1.1–7

Responsorial Psalm

R **Taste and see that the Lord is good:**
   [happy are all who trust in him].   cf Psalm 34.8

I will bless the Lord at all times;
his praise shall ever be in my mouth.
My soul shall glory in the Lord;
let the humble hear and be glad. **R**

O magnify the Lord with me;
let us exalt his name together.
I sought the Lord and he answered me
and delivered me from all my fears. **R**

Look upon him and be radiant
and your faces shall not be ashamed.
This poor soul cried, and the Lord heard me
and saved me from all my troubles. **R**

The angel of the Lord encamps around those who fear him
and delivers them.
O taste and see that the Lord is gracious;
blessed is the one who trusts in him. **R**   Psalm 34.1–8

A reading from the First Book of the Kings.

Elijah the Tishbite, of Tishbe in Gilead, said to Ahab, 'As the LORD the God of Israel lives, before whom I stand, there shall be neither dew nor rain these years, except by my word.' The word of the LORD came to him, saying, 'Go from here and turn eastwards, and hide yourself by the Wadi Cherith, which is east of the Jordan. You shall drink from the wadi, and I have commanded the ravens to feed you there.' So he went and did according to the word of the LORD; he went and lived by the Wadi Cherith, which is east of the Jordan. The ravens brought him bread and meat in the morning, and bread and meat in the evening; and he drank from the wadi.

This is the word of the Lord.   1 Kings 17.1–6

Responsorial Psalm

R **My help comes from the Lord,**
  [the maker of heaven and earth].   Psalm 121.2

I lift up my eyes to the hills;
from where is my help to come?
My help comes from the Lord,
the maker of heaven and earth. **R**

He will not suffer your foot to stumble;
he who watches over you will not sleep.
Behold, he who keeps watch over Israel
shall neither slumber nor sleep. **R**

The Lord himself watches over you;
the Lord is your shade at your right hand,
so that the sun shall not strike you by day,
neither the moon by night. **R**

The Lord shall keep you from all evil;
it is he who shall keep your soul.
The Lord shall keep watch over your going out
and your coming in,
from this time forth for evermore. **R**   Psalm 121

Year 1 and Year 2

Hear the Gospel of our Lord Jesus Christ according to Matthew.

When Jesus saw the crowds, he went up the mountain; and after he sat down, his disciples came to him. Then he began to speak, and taught them, saying:
'Blessed are the poor in spirit,
for theirs is the kingdom of heaven.
Blessed are those who mourn,
for they will be comforted.
Blessed are the meek,
for they will inherit the earth.
Blessed are those who hunger and thirst for righteousness,
for they will be filled.
Blessed are the merciful,
for they will receive mercy.
Blessed are the pure in heart,
for they will see God.
Blessed are the peacemakers,
for they will be called children of God.
Blessed are those who are persecuted for righteousness' sake,
for theirs is the kingdom of heaven.
'Blessed are you when people revile you and persecute you and utter all kinds of evil against you falsely on my account. Rejoice and be glad, for your reward is great in heaven, for in the same way they persecuted the prophets who were before you.'

This is the Gospel of the Lord. Matthew 5.1–12

Week 10: Tuesday between 7 and 13 June *(if after Pentecost)*

Year 1

A reading from the Second Letter of Paul to the Corinthians.

As surely as God is faithful, our word to you has not been 'Yes and No.' For the Son of God, Jesus Christ, whom we proclaimed among you, Silvanus and Timothy and I, was not 'Yes and No'; but in him it is always 'Yes.' For in him every one of God's promises is a 'Yes.' For this reason it is through him that we say the 'Amen', to the glory of God. But it is God who establishes us with you in Christ and has anointed us, by putting his seal on us and giving us his Spirit in our hearts as a first instalment.

This is the word of the Lord. 2 Corinthians 1.18–22

Responsorial Psalm

R **Let your face shine upon me, O Lord,
   [and teach me your statutes].**   cf Psalm 119.135

Your testimonies are wonderful;
therefore my soul keeps them.
The opening of your word gives light;
it gives understanding to the simple. R

I open my mouth and draw in my breath,
as I long for your commandments.
Turn to me and be gracious to me,
as is your way with those who love your name. R

Order my steps by your word,
and let no wickedness have dominion over me.
Redeem me from earthly oppressors
so that I may keep your commandments. R

Show the light of your countenance upon your servant
and teach me your statutes.
My eyes run down with streams of water,
because the wicked do not keep your law. R   Psalm 119.129–136

Year 2

A reading from the First Book of the Kings.

The wadi where Elijah was hiding dried up, because there was no rain in the
land. Then the word of the LORD came to him, saying, 'Go now to Zarephath,
which belongs to Sidon, and live there; for I have commanded a widow there
to feed you.' So he set out and went to Zarephath. When he came to the gate
of the town, a widow was there gathering sticks; he called to her and said,
'Bring me a little water in a vessel, so that I may drink.' As she was going to
bring it, he called to her and said, 'Bring me a morsel of bread in your hand.'
But she said, 'As the LORD your God lives, I have nothing baked, only a handful
of meal in a jar, and a little oil in a jug; I am now gathering a couple of sticks,
so that I may go home and prepare it for myself and my son, that we may eat
it, and die.'

Elijah said to her, 'Do not be afraid; go and do as you have said; but first
make me a little cake of it and bring it to me, and afterwards make something
for yourself and your son. For thus says the LORD the God of Israel: The jar
of meal will not be emptied and the jug of oil will not fail until the day that
the LORD sends rain on the earth.' She went and did as Elijah said, so that she
as well as he and her household ate for many days. The jar of meal was not
emptied, neither did the jug of oil fail, according to the word of the LORD
that he spoke by Elijah.

This is the word of the Lord.   1 Kings 17.7–16

Responsorial Psalm

R **The Lord has shown me marvellous kindness;**
[when I call, he will hear me].   cf Psalm 4.3

Answer me when I call, O God of my righteousness;
you set me at liberty when I was in trouble;
have mercy on me and hear my prayer.
How long will you nobles dishonour my glory;
how long will you love vain things and seek after falsehood? R

But know that the Lord has shown me his marvellous kindness;
when I call upon the Lord, he will hear me.
Stand in awe, and sin not;
commune with your own heart upon your bed, and be still. R

Offer the sacrifices of righteousness
and put your trust in the Lord.
There are many that say, 'Who will show us any good?'
Lord, lift up the light of your countenance upon us. R

You have put gladness in my heart,
more than when their corn and wine and oil increase.
In peace I will lie down and sleep,
for it is you Lord, only, who make me dwell in safety. R   Psalm 4

Year 1 and Year 2

Hear the Gospel of our Lord Jesus Christ according to Matthew.

Jesus said to his disciples, 'You are the salt of the earth; but if salt has lost its
taste, how can its saltiness be restored? It is no longer good for anything, but
is thrown out and trampled under foot.
  'You are the light of the world. A city built on a hill cannot be hidden. No
one after lighting a lamp puts it under the bushel basket, but on the lampstand,
and it gives light to all in the house. In the same way, let your light shine
before others, so that they may see your good works and give glory to your
Father in heaven.'

This is the Gospel of the Lord.   Matthew 5.13–16

Week 10: Wednesday between 8 and 14 June *(if after Pentecost)*

Year 1

A reading from the Second Letter of Paul to the Corinthians.

Such is the confidence that we have through Christ towards God. Not that we are competent of ourselves to claim anything as coming from us; our competence is from God, who has made us competent to be ministers of a new covenant, not of letter but of spirit; for the letter kills, but the Spirit gives life.

Now if the ministry of death, chiselled in letters on stone tablets, came in glory so that the people of Israel could not gaze at Moses' face because of the glory of his face, a glory now set aside, how much more will the ministry of the Spirit come in glory? For if there was glory in the ministry of condemnation, much more does the ministry of justification abound in glory! Indeed, what once had glory has lost its glory because of the greater glory; for if what was set aside came through glory, much more has the permanent come in glory!

This is the word of the Lord.   2 Corinthians 3.4–11

Responsorial Psalm

R **We will recount the praises of the Lord,**
   [and the wonderful works he has done].   cf Psalm 78.4

Hear my teaching, O my people;
incline your ears to the words of my mouth.
I will open my mouth in a parable;
I will pour forth mysteries from of old,
such as we have heard and known,
which our forebears have told us.   R

We will not hide from their children,
but will recount to generations to come,
the praises of the Lord and his power
and the wonderful works he has done.   R   Psalm 78.1–4

Year 2

A reading from the First Book of the Kings.

Ahab sent to all the Israelites, and assembled the prophets at Mount Carmel. Elijah then came near to all the people, and said, 'How long will you go limping with two different opinions? If the LORD is God, follow him; but if Baal, then follow him.' The people did not answer him a word. Then Elijah said to the people, 'I, even I only, am left a prophet of the LORD; but Baal's prophets number four hundred and fifty. Let two bulls be given to us; let them choose one bull for themselves, cut it in pieces, and lay it on the wood, but put no fire to it; I will prepare the other bull and lay it on the wood, but put no fire to it. Then you call on the name of your god and I will call on the name of the LORD; the god who answers by fire is indeed God.' All the people answered, 'Well spoken!'

Then Elijah said to the prophets of Baal, 'Choose for yourselves one bull and prepare it first, for you are many; then call on the name of your god, but put no fire to it.' So they took the bull that was given them, prepared it, and called on the name of Baal from morning until noon, crying, 'O Baal, answer us!' But there was no voice, and no answer. They limped about the altar that they had made. At noon Elijah mocked them, saying, 'Cry aloud! Surely he is a god; either he is meditating, or he has wandered away, or he is on a journey, or perhaps he is asleep and must be awakened.' Then they cried aloud and, as was their custom, they cut themselves with swords and lances until the blood gushed out over them. As midday passed, they raved on until the time of the offering of the oblation, but there was no voice, no answer, and no response.

Then Elijah said to all the people, 'Come closer to me'; and all the people came closer to him. First he repaired the altar of the LORD that had been thrown down; Elijah took twelve stones, according to the number of the tribes of the sons of Jacob, to whom the word of the LORD came, saying, 'Israel shall be your name'; with the stones he built an altar in the name of the LORD. Then he made a trench around the altar, large enough to contain two measures of seed. Next he put the wood in order, cut the bull in pieces, and laid it on the wood. He said, 'Fill four jars with water and pour it on the burnt-offering and on the wood.' Then he said, 'Do it a second time'; and they did it a second time. Again he said, 'Do it a third time'; and they did it a third time, so that the water ran all round the altar, and filled the trench also with water.

At the time of the offering of the oblation, the prophet Elijah came near and said, 'O LORD, God of Abraham, Isaac, and Israel, let it be known this day that you are God in Israel, that I am your servant, and that I have done all these things at your bidding. Answer me, O LORD, answer me, so that this people may know that you, O LORD, are God, and that you have turned their hearts back.' Then the fire of the LORD fell and consumed the burnt-offering, the wood, the stones, and the dust, and even licked up the water that was in the trench. When all the people saw it, they fell on their faces and said, 'The LORD indeed is God; the LORD indeed is God.'

This is the word of the Lord.   1 Kings 18.20–39

Responsorial Psalm

R **Preserve me, O God,**
   for in you have I taken refuge. Psalm 16.1

Preserve me, O God, for in you have I taken refuge;
I have said to the Lord, 'You are my lord,
all my good depends on you.'
I will bless the Lord who has given me counsel,
and in the night watches he instructs my heart. **R**

I have set the Lord always before me;
he is at my right hand; I shall not fall.
Wherefore my heart is glad and my spirit rejoices;
my flesh also shall rest secure. **R**

For you will not abandon my soul to Death,
nor suffer your faithful one to see the Pit;
you will show me the path of life.
In your presence is the fullness of joy
and in your right hand are pleasures for evermore. **R** Psalm 16.1, 6–end

Year 1 and Year 2

Hear the Gospel of our Lord Jesus Christ according to Matthew.

Jesus said to his disciples, 'Do not think that I have come to abolish the law or the prophets; I have come not to abolish but to fulfil. For truly I tell you, until heaven and earth pass away, not one letter, not one stroke of a letter, will pass from the law until all is accomplished. Therefore, whoever breaks one of the least of these commandments, and teaches others to do the same, will be called least in the kingdom of heaven; but whoever does them and teaches them will be called great in the kingdom of heaven.'

This is the Gospel of the Lord. Matthew 5.17–19

Week 10: Thursday between 9 and 15 June *(if after Pentecost)*

Year 1

A reading from the Second Letter of Paul to the Corinthians.

To this very day whenever Moses is read, a veil lies over the minds of the people of Israel; but when one turns to the Lord, the veil is removed. Now the Lord is the Spirit, and where the Spirit of the Lord is, there is freedom. And all of us, with unveiled faces, seeing the glory of the Lord as though reflected in a mirror, are being transformed into the same image from one degree of glory to another; for this comes from the Lord, the Spirit.

Therefore, since it is by God's mercy that we are engaged in this ministry, we do not lose heart. And even if our gospel is veiled, it is veiled to those who are perishing. In their case the god of this world has blinded the minds of the unbelievers, to keep them from seeing the light of the gospel of the glory of Christ, who is the image of God. For we do not proclaim ourselves; we proclaim Jesus Christ as Lord and ourselves as your slaves for Jesus' sake. For it is the God who said, 'Let light shine out of darkness', who has shone in our hearts to give the light of the knowledge of the glory of God in the face of Jesus Christ.

This is the word of the Lord.   2 Corinthians 3.15 – 4.1, 3–6

Responsorial Psalm

R **They remembered that God was their rock**
   [and the Most High God their redeemer].   Psalm 78.35

Yet they did but flatter him with their mouth
and dissembled with their tongue.
Their heart was not steadfast towards him,
neither were they faithful to his covenant. R

But he was so merciful that he forgave their misdeeds
and did not destroy them;
many a time he turned back his wrath
and did not suffer his whole displeasure to be roused. R

For he remembered that they were but flesh,
a wind that passes by and does not return.
How often they rebelled against him in the wilderness
and grieved him in the desert! R   Psalm 78.36–40

Year 2

A reading from the First Book of the Kings.

Elijah said to Ahab, 'Go up, eat and drink; for there is a sound of rushing rain.' So Ahab went up to eat and to drink. Elijah went up to the top of Carmel; there he bowed himself down upon the earth and put his face between his knees. He said to his servant, 'Go up now, look towards the sea.' He went up and looked, and said, 'There is nothing.' Then he said, 'Go again seven times.' At the seventh time he said, 'Look, a little cloud no bigger than a person's hand is rising out of the sea.' Then he said, 'Go and say to Ahab, "Harness your chariot and go down before the rain stops you."' In a little while the heavens grew black with clouds and wind; there was heavy rain. Ahab rode off and went to Jezreel. But the hand of the LORD was on Elijah; he girded up his loins and ran in front of Ahab to the entrance of Jezreel.

This is the word of the Lord.   1 Kings 18.41–end

Responsorial Psalm

R **You visit the earth and water it;**
   you make it very plenteous.   *Psalm 65.8*

You visit the earth and water it;
you make it very plenteous.
The river of God is full of water;
you prepare grain for your people,
for so you provide for the earth.   R

You drench the furrows and smooth out the ridges;
you soften the ground with showers and bless its increase.
You crown the year with your goodness,
and your paths overflow with plenty.   R

May the pastures of the wilderness flow with goodness
and the hills be girded with joy.
May the meadows be clothed with flocks of sheep
and the valleys stand so thick with corn
that they shall laugh and sing.   R   *Psalm 65.8–end*

Year 1 and Year 2

Hear the Gospel of our Lord Jesus Christ according to Matthew.

Jesus said to his disciples, 'For I tell you, unless your righteousness exceeds that
of the scribes and Pharisees, you will never enter the kingdom of heaven.
   'You have heard that it was said to those of ancient times, "You shall not
murder"; and "whoever murders shall be liable to judgement." But I say to you
that if you are angry with a brother or sister, you will be liable to judgement;
and if you insult a brother or sister, you will be liable to the council; and
if you say, "You fool", you will be liable to the hell of fire. So when you are
offering your gift at the altar, if you remember that your brother or sister has
something against you, leave your gift there before the altar and go; first be
reconciled to your brother or sister, and then come and offer your gift. Come
to terms quickly with your accuser while you are on the way to court with
him, or your accuser may hand you over to the judge, and the judge to the
guard, and you will be thrown into prison. Truly I tell you, you will never get
out until you have paid the last penny.'

This is the Gospel of the Lord.   *Matthew 5.20–26*

Week 10: Friday between 10 and 16 June *(if after Pentecost)*

Year 1

A reading from the Second Letter of Paul to the Corinthians.

We have this treasure in clay jars, so that it may be made clear that this extraordinary power belongs to God and does not come from us. We are afflicted in every way, but not crushed; perplexed, but not driven to despair; persecuted, but not forsaken; struck down, but not destroyed; always carrying in the body the death of Jesus, so that the life of Jesus may also be made visible in our bodies. For while we live, we are always being given up to death for Jesus' sake, so that the life of Jesus may be made visible in our mortal flesh. So death is at work in us, but life in you.

But just as we have the same spirit of faith that is in accordance with scripture – 'I believed, and so I spoke' – we also believe, and so we speak, because we know that the one who raised the Lord Jesus will raise us also with Jesus, and will bring us with you into his presence. Yes, everything is for your sake, so that grace, as it extends to more and more people, may increase thanksgiving, to the glory of God.

This is the word of the Lord.   2 Corinthians 4.7–15

Responsorial Psalm

R **Exalt the Lord our God:**
   for holy is his name.   cf Psalm 99.3, 5, 9

The Lord is king: let the peoples tremble;
he is enthroned above the cherubim:
let the earth shake.
The Lord is great in Zion
and high above all peoples.   **R**

Let them praise your name, which is great and awesome;
the Lord our God is holy.
Mighty king, who loves justice,
you have established equity;
you have executed justice and righteousness in Jacob.   **R**

Exalt the Lord our God;
bow down before his footstool, for he is holy.
Moses and Aaron among his priests
and Samuel among those who call upon his name;
they called upon the Lord and he answered them.   **R**   →

He spoke to them out of the pillar of cloud;
they kept his testimonies and the law that he gave them.
You answered them, O Lord our God;
you were a God who forgave them
and pardoned them for their offences. R

R **Exalt the Lord our God:
for holy is his name.**

Exalt the Lord our God
and worship him upon his holy hill,
for the Lord our God is holy. R   *Psalm 99*

Year 2

A reading from the First Book of the Kings.

Elijah came to a cave, and spent the night there. Then the word of the LORD
came to him, saying, 'What are you doing here, Elijah? Go out and stand on
the mountain before the LORD, for the LORD is about to pass by.'

Now there was a great wind, so strong that it was splitting mountains and
breaking rocks in pieces before the LORD, but the LORD was not in the wind;
and after the wind an earthquake, but the LORD was not in the earthquake;
and after the earthquake a fire, but the LORD was not in the fire; and after the
fire a sound of sheer silence. When Elijah heard it, he wrapped his face in his
mantle and went out and stood at the entrance of the cave. Then there came
a voice to him that said, 'What are you doing here, Elijah?' He answered, 'I
have been very zealous for the LORD, the God of hosts; for the Israelites have
forsaken your covenant, thrown down your altars, and killed your prophets with
the sword. I alone am left, and they are seeking my life, to take it away.'

Then the LORD said to him, 'Go, return on your way to the wilderness of
Damascus; when you arrive, you shall anoint Hazael as king over Aram. Also
you shall anoint Jehu son of Nimshi as king over Israel; and you shall anoint
Elisha son of Shaphat of Abel-meholah as prophet in your place.'

This is the word of the Lord.   1 Kings 19.9, 11–16

Responsorial Psalm

R   **I shall see the goodness of the Lord
    in the land of the living.**   Psalm 27.16

Therefore will I offer in his dwelling an oblation
with great gladness;
I will sing and make music to the Lord.
Hear my voice, O Lord, when I call;
have mercy upon me and answer me.   R

My heart tells of your word, 'Seek my face.'
Your face, Lord, will I seek.
Hide not your face from me,
nor cast your servant away in displeasure.   R

You have been my helper;
leave me not, neither forsake me, O God of my salvation.
Though my father and my mother forsake me,
the Lord will take me up.   R

Teach me your way, O Lord;
lead me on a level path,
because of those who lie in wait for me.   R

Deliver me not into the will of my adversaries,
for false witnesses have risen up against me,
and those who breathe out violence.
I believe that I shall see the goodness of the Lord
in the land of the living.   R   Psalm 27.8–16

Year 1 and Year 2

Hear the Gospel of our Lord Jesus Christ according to Matthew.

Jesus said to his disciples, 'You have heard that it was said, "You shall not
commit adultery." But I say to you that everyone who looks at a woman with
lust has already committed adultery with her in his heart. If your right eye
causes you to sin, tear it out and throw it away; it is better for you to lose one
of your members than for your whole body to be thrown into hell. And if your
right hand causes you to sin, cut it off and throw it away; it is better for you
to lose one of your members than for your whole body to go into hell.

   'It was also said, "Whoever divorces his wife, let him give her a certificate
of divorce." But I say to you that anyone who divorces his wife, except on the
ground of unchastity, causes her to commit adultery; and whoever marries
a divorced woman commits adultery.'

This is the Gospel of the Lord.   Matthew 5.27–32

Week 10: Saturday between 11 and 17 June *(if after Pentecost)*

Year 1

A reading from the Second Letter of Paul to the Corinthians.

The love of Christ urges us on, because we are convinced that one has died for all; therefore all have died. And he died for all, so that those who live might live no longer for themselves, but for him who died and was raised for them.

From now on, therefore, we regard no one from a human point of view; even though we once knew Christ from a human point of view, we know him no longer in that way. So if anyone is in Christ, there is a new creation: everything old has passed away; see, everything has become new! All this is from God, who reconciled us to himself through Christ, and has given us the ministry of reconciliation; that is, in Christ God was reconciling the world to himself, not counting their trespasses against them, and entrusting the message of reconciliation to us. So we are ambassadors for Christ, since God is making his appeal through us; we entreat you on behalf of Christ, be reconciled to God. For our sake he made him to be sin who knew no sin, so that in him we might become the righteousness of God.

This is the word of the Lord.   2 Corinthians 5.14–end

Responsorial Psalm

R **Bless the Lord, O my soul,
   [and bless his holy name].**   cf Psalm 103.1

Bless the Lord, O my soul,
and all that is within me bless his holy name.
Bless the Lord, O my soul,
and forget not all his benefits. R

Who forgives all your sins
and heals all your infirmities;
who redeems your life from the Pit
and crowns you with faithful love and compassion. R

Who satisfies you with good things,
so that your youth is renewed like an eagle's.
The Lord executes righteousness
and judgement for all who are oppressed. R

He made his ways known to Moses
and his works to the children of Israel.
The Lord is full of compassion and mercy,
slow to anger and of great kindness. R

He will not always accuse us,
neither will he keep his anger for ever.
He has not dealt with us according to our sins,
nor rewarded us according to our wickedness. R

For as the heavens are high above the earth,
so great is his mercy upon those who fear him.
As far as the east is from the west,
so far has he set our sins from us. R

Psalm 103.1–12

Year 2

A reading from the First Book of the Kings.

Elijah set out, and found Elisha son of Shaphat, who was ploughing. There were twelve yoke of oxen ahead of him, and he was with the twelfth. Elijah passed by him and threw his mantle over him. He left the oxen, ran after Elijah, and said, 'Let me kiss my father and my mother, and then I will follow you.' Then Elijah said to him, 'Go back again; for what have I done to you?' He returned from following him, took the yoke of oxen, and slaughtered them; using the equipment from the oxen, he boiled their flesh, and gave it to the people, and they ate. Then he set out and followed Elijah, and became his servant.

This is the word of the Lord.   1 Kings 19.19–end

Responsorial Psalm

R* **Preserve me, O God,**
   for in you have I taken refuge.   Psalm 16.1a

I have said to the Lord, 'You are my lord,
all my good depends on you.'
All my delight is upon the godly that are in the land,
upon those who are noble in heart. R

Though the idols are legion
that many run after,
their drink offerings of blood I will not offer,
neither make mention of their names upon my lips. R

The Lord himself is my portion and my cup;
in your hands alone is my fortune.
My share has fallen in a fair land;
indeed, I have a goodly heritage. R

I will bless the Lord who has given me counsel,
and in the night watches he instructs my heart.
I have set the Lord always before me;
he is at my right hand; I shall not fall. R   Psalm 16.1–7

Hear the Gospel of our Lord Jesus Christ according to Matthew.

Jesus said to his disciples, 'Again, you have heard that it was said to those of ancient times, "You shall not swear falsely, but carry out the vows you have made to the Lord." But I say to you, Do not swear at all, either by heaven, for it is the throne of God, or by the earth, for it is his footstool, or by Jerusalem, for it is the city of the great King. And do not swear by your head, for you cannot make one hair white or black. Let your word be "Yes, Yes" or "No, No"; anything more than this comes from the evil one.'

This is the Gospel of the Lord.   Matthew 5.33–37

Week 11: Monday between 13 and 19 June

Year 1

A reading from the Second Letter of Paul to the Corinthians.

As we work together with Christ, we urge you also not to accept the grace of God in vain. For he says,

'At an acceptable time I have listened to you,
and on a day of salvation I have helped you.'

See, now is the acceptable time; see, now is the day of salvation! We are putting no obstacle in anyone's way, so that no fault may be found with our ministry, but as servants of God we have commended ourselves in every way: through great endurance, in afflictions, hardships, calamities, beatings, imprisonments, riots, labours, sleepless nights, hunger; by purity, knowledge, patience, kindness, holiness of spirit, genuine love, truthful speech, and the power of God; with the weapons of righteousness for the right hand and for the left; in honour and dishonour, in ill repute and good repute. We are treated as impostors, and yet are true; as unknown, and yet are well known; as dying, and see — we are alive; as punished, and yet not killed; as sorrowful, yet always rejoicing; as poor, yet making many rich; as having nothing, and yet possessing everything.

This is the word of the Lord.   2 Corinthians 6.1–10

Responsorial Psalm

R* **Sound praises to the Lord, all the earth;
[break into song and make music].**   *cf Psalm 98.5*

Sing to the Lord a new song,
for he has done marvellous things.
His own right hand and his holy arm
have won for him the victory.   **R**

The Lord has made known his salvation;
his deliverance has he openly shown
in the sight of the nations.   **R**

He has remembered his mercy and faithfulness
towards the house of Israel,
and all the ends of the earth have seen
the salvation of our God.   **R***

Make music to the Lord with the lyre,
with the lyre and the voice of melody.
With trumpets and the sound of the horn
sound praises before the Lord, the King.   **R**   →

Let the sea thunder and all that fills it,
the world and all that dwell upon it.
Let the rivers clap their hands
and let the hills ring out together before the Lord. R

R* **Sound praises to the Lord, all the earth;**
[break into song and make music].

For he comes to judge the earth:
in righteousness shall he judge the world
and the peoples with equity. R   Psalm 98

Year 2

A reading from the First Book of the Kings.

Naboth the Jezreelite had a vineyard in Jezreel, beside the palace of King Ahab
of Samaria. And Ahab said to Naboth, 'Give me your vineyard, so that I may
have it for a vegetable garden, because it is near my house; I will give you
a better vineyard for it; or, if it seems good to you, I will give you its value
in money.' But Naboth said to Ahab, 'The LORD forbid that I should give you
my ancestral inheritance.' Ahab went home resentful and sullen because of
what Naboth the Jezreelite had said to him; for he had said, 'I will not give
you my ancestral inheritance.' He lay down on his bed, turned away his face,
and would not eat.

His wife Jezebel came to him and said, 'Why are you so depressed that
you will not eat?' He said to her, 'Because I spoke to Naboth the Jezreelite
and said to him, "Give me your vineyard for money; or else, if you prefer, I
will give you another vineyard for it"; but he answered, "I will not give you
my vineyard." ' His wife Jezebel said to him, 'Do you now govern Israel? Get
up, eat some food, and be cheerful; I will give you the vineyard of Naboth
the Jezreelite.'

So she wrote letters in Ahab's name and sealed them with his seal; she
sent the letters to the elders and the nobles who lived with Naboth in his
city. She wrote in the letters, 'Proclaim a fast, and seat Naboth at the head
of the assembly; seat two scoundrels opposite him, and have them bring a
charge against him, saying, "You have cursed God and the king." Then take
him out, and stone him to death.' The men of his city, the elders and the
nobles who lived in his city, did as Jezebel had sent word to them. Just as it
was written in the letters that she had sent to them, they proclaimed a fast
and seated Naboth at the head of the assembly. The two scoundrels came in
and sat opposite him; and the scoundrels brought a charge against Naboth,
in the presence of the people, saying, 'Naboth cursed God and the king.' So
they took him outside the city, and stoned him to death. Then they sent to
Jezebel, saying, 'Naboth has been stoned; he is dead.'

As soon as Jezebel heard that Naboth had been stoned and was dead, Jezebel
said to Ahab, 'Go, take possession of the vineyard of Naboth the Jezreelite,

which he refused to give you for money; for Naboth is not alive, but dead.'
As soon as Ahab heard that Naboth was dead, Ahab set out to go down to the
vineyard of Naboth the Jezreelite, to take possession of it.

This is the word of the Lord. 1 Kings 21.1–16

Responsorial Psalm

R **Lead me, Lord, in your righteousness,**
   [make straight your way before me]. cf Psalm 5.8

Give ear to my words, O Lord;
consider my lamentation.
Hearken to the voice of my crying, my King and my God,
for to you I make my prayer. **R**

In the morning, Lord,
you will hear my voice;
early in the morning I make my appeal to you,
and look up. **R**

For you are the God who takes no pleasure in wickedness;
no evil can dwell with you.
The boastful cannot stand in your sight;
you hate all those that work wickedness. **R** Psalm 5.1–5

Year 1 and Year 2

Hear the Gospel of our Lord Jesus Christ according to Matthew.

Jesus said to his disciples, 'You have heard that it was said, "An eye for an
eye and a tooth for a tooth." But I say to you, Do not resist an evildoer. But
if anyone strikes you on the right cheek, turn the other also; and if anyone
wants to sue you and take your coat, give your cloak as well; and if anyone
forces you to go one mile, go also the second mile. Give to everyone who begs
from you, and do not refuse anyone who wants to borrow from you.'

This is the Gospel of the Lord. Matthew 5.38–42

Week 11: Tuesday between 14 and 20 June

Year 1

A reading from the Second Letter of Paul to the Corinthians.

We want you to know, brothers and sisters, about the grace of God that has been granted to the churches of Macedonia; for during a severe ordeal of affliction, their abundant joy and their extreme poverty have overflowed in a wealth of generosity on their part. For, as I can testify, they voluntarily gave according to their means, and even beyond their means, begging us earnestly for the privilege of sharing in this ministry to the saints – and this, not merely as we expected; they gave themselves first to the Lord and, by the will of God, to us, so that we might urge Titus that, as he had already made a beginning, so he should also complete this generous undertaking among you. Now as you excel in everything – in faith, in speech, in knowledge, in utmost eagerness, and in our love for you – so we want you to excel also in this generous undertaking.

I do not say this as a command, but I am testing the genuineness of your love against the earnestness of others. For you know the generous act of our Lord Jesus Christ, that though he was rich, yet for your sakes he became poor, so that by his poverty you might become rich.

This is the word of the Lord.   2 Corinthians 8.1–9

Responsorial Psalm

R* **The Lord shall reign for ever,**
     [your God, O Zion, throughout all generations].   Psalm 146.10

Praise the Lord, O my soul:
while I live will I praise the Lord;
as long as I have any being,
I will sing praises to my God.   **R**

Put not your trust in princes, nor in any human power,
for there is no help in them.
When their breath goes forth, they return to the earth;
on that day all their thoughts perish.   **R**

Happy are those who have the God of Jacob for their help,
whose hope is in the Lord their God;
who made heaven and earth, the sea and all that is in them;
who keeps his promise for ever.   **R**

Who gives justice to those that suffer wrong
and bread to those who hunger.
The Lord looses those that are bound;
the Lord opens the eyes of the blind;
the Lord lifts up those who are bowed down.   **R**

The Lord loves the righteous;
the Lord watches over the stranger in the land;
he upholds the orphan and widow;
but the way of the wicked he turns upside down. R*   *Psalm* 146

Year 2

A reading from the First Book of the Kings.

The word of the LORD came to Elijah the Tishbite, saying: Go down to meet
King Ahab of Israel, who rules in Samaria; he is now in the vineyard of Naboth,
where he has gone to take possession. You shall say to him, 'Thus says the
LORD: Have you killed, and also taken possession?' You shall say to him, 'Thus
says the LORD: In the place where dogs licked up the blood of Naboth, dogs
will also lick up your blood.'

Ahab said to Elijah, 'Have you found me, O my enemy?' He answered, 'I
have found you. Because you have sold yourself to do what is evil in the sight
of the LORD, I will bring disaster on you; I will consume you, and will cut
off from Ahab every male, bond or free, in Israel; and I will make your house
like the house of Jeroboam son of Nebat, and like the house of Baasha son
of Ahijah, because you have provoked me to anger and have caused Israel to
sin. Also concerning Jezebel the LORD said, "The dogs shall eat Jezebel within
the bounds of Jezreel." Anyone belonging to Ahab who dies in the city the
dogs shall eat; and anyone of his who dies in the open country the birds of
the air shall eat.'

(Indeed, there was no one like Ahab, who sold himself to do what was
evil in the sight of the LORD, urged on by his wife Jezebel. He acted most
abominably in going after idols, as the Amorites had done, whom the LORD
drove out before the Israelites.)

When Ahab heard those words, he tore his clothes and put sackcloth over
his bare flesh; he fasted, lay in the sackcloth, and went about dejectedly. Then
the word of the LORD came to Elijah the Tishbite: 'Have you seen how Ahab
has humbled himself before me? Because he has humbled himself before me,
I will not bring the disaster in his days; but in his son's days I will bring the
disaster on his house.'

This is the word of the Lord.   1 *Kings* 21.17–*end*

Responsorial Psalm

R **Make me a clean heart, O God,**
   [and renew a right spirit within me]. *Psalm 51.11*

Have mercy on me, O God,
in your great goodness;
according to the abundance of your compassion
blot out my offences. R

Wash me thoroughly from my wickedness
and cleanse me from my sin.
For I acknowledge my faults
and my sin is ever before me. R

Against you only have I sinned
and done what is evil in your sight,
so that you are justified in your sentence
and righteous in your judgement. R

I have been wicked even from my birth,
a sinner when my mother conceived me.
Behold, you desire truth deep within me
and shall make me understand wisdom
     in the depths of my heart. R

Purge me with hyssop and I shall be clean;
wash me and I shall be whiter than snow.
Make me hear of joy and gladness,
that the bones you have broken may rejoice. R *Psalm 51.1–9*

Year 1 and Year 2

Hear the Gospel of our Lord Jesus Christ according to Matthew.

Jesus said to his disciples, 'You have heard that it was said, "You shall love your neighbour and hate your enemy." But I say to you, Love your enemies and pray for those who persecute you, so that you may be children of your Father in heaven; for he makes his sun rise on the evil and on the good, and sends rain on the righteous and on the unrighteous. For if you love those who love you, what reward do you have? Do not even the tax-collectors do the same? And if you greet only your brothers and sisters, what more are you doing than others? Do not even the Gentiles do the same? Be perfect, therefore, as your heavenly Father is perfect.'

This is the Gospel of the Lord. *Matthew 5.43–end*

Week 11: Wednesday between 15 and 21 June

Year 1

A reading from the Second Letter of Paul to the Corinthians.

The point is this: the one who sows sparingly will also reap sparingly, and the one who sows bountifully will also reap bountifully. Each of you must give as you have made up your mind, not reluctantly or under compulsion, for God loves a cheerful giver. And God is able to provide you with every blessing in abundance, so that by always having enough of everything, you may share abundantly in every good work. As it is written,
'He scatters abroad, he gives to the poor;
    his righteousness endures for ever.'
He who supplies seed to the sower and bread for food will supply and multiply your seed for sowing and increase the harvest of your righteousness. You will be enriched in every way for your great generosity, which will produce thanksgiving to God through us.

This is the word of the Lord.   2 Corinthians 9.6–11

Responsorial Psalm

R **Blessed are those**
   who delight in the commandments of the Lord.   cf Psalm 112.1

Blessed are those who fear the Lord
and have great delight in his commandments.
Their descendants will be mighty in the land,
a generation of the faithful that will be blest. **R**

Wealth and riches will be in their house,
and their righteousness endures for ever.
Light shines in the darkness for the upright;
gracious and full of compassion are the righteous. **R**

It goes well with those who are generous in lending
and order their affairs with justice,
for they will never be shaken;
the righteous will be held in everlasting remembrance. **R**

They will not be afraid of any evil tidings;
their heart is steadfast, trusting in the Lord.
Their heart is sustained and will not fear,
until they see the downfall of their foes. **R**

They have given freely to the poor;
their righteousness stands fast for ever;
their head will be exalted with honour. **R**

The wicked shall see it and be angry;
they shall gnash their teeth in despair;
the desire of the wicked shall perish. **R**   Psalm 112

Year 2

A reading from the Second Book of the Kings.

When the LORD was about to take Elijah up to heaven by a whirlwind, Elijah and Elisha were on their way from Gilgal. Then Elijah said to him, 'Stay here; for the LORD has sent me to the Jordan.' But he said, 'As the LORD lives, and as you yourself live, I will not leave you.' So the two of them went on. Fifty men of the company of prophets also went, and stood at some distance from them, as they both were standing by the Jordan. Then Elijah took his mantle and rolled it up, and struck the water; the water was parted to the one side and to the other, until the two of them crossed on dry ground.

When they had crossed, Elijah said to Elisha, 'Tell me what I may do for you, before I am taken from you.' Elisha said, 'Please let me inherit a double share of your spirit.' He responded, 'You have asked a hard thing; yet, if you see me as I am being taken from you, it will be granted you; if not, it will not.' As they continued walking and talking, a chariot of fire and horses of fire separated the two of them, and Elijah ascended in a whirlwind into heaven. Elisha kept watching and crying out, 'Father, father! The chariots of Israel and its horsemen!' But when he could no longer see him, he grasped his own clothes and tore them in two pieces.

He picked up the mantle of Elijah that had fallen from him, and went back and stood on the bank of the Jordan. He took the mantle of Elijah that had fallen from him, and struck the water, saying, 'Where is the LORD, the God of Elijah?' When he had struck the water, the water was parted to the one side and to the other, and Elisha went over.

This is the word of the Lord. 2 Kings 2.1, 6–14

Responsorial Psalm

R* **Be strong and let your heart take courage,**
  [all who wait in hope for the Lord]. cf Psalm 31.24

Blessed be the Lord!
For he has shown me his steadfast love
when I was as a city besieged.
I had said in my alarm,
'I have been cut off from the sight of your eyes.' **R**

Nevertheless, you heard the voice of my prayer
when I cried out to you.
Love the Lord, all you his servants;
for the Lord protects the faithful,
but repays to the full the proud. **R*** Psalm 31.21–end

Hear the Gospel of our Lord Jesus Christ according to Matthew.

Jesus said to his disciples, 'Beware of practising your piety before others in order to be seen by them; for then you have no reward from your Father in heaven.

'So whenever you give alms, do not sound a trumpet before you, as the hypocrites do in the synagogues and in the streets, so that they may be praised by others. Truly I tell you, they have received their reward. But when you give alms, do not let your left hand know what your right hand is doing, so that your alms may be done in secret; and your Father who sees in secret will reward you.

'And whenever you pray, do not be like the hypocrites; for they love to stand and pray in the synagogues and at the street corners, so that they may be seen by others. Truly I tell you, they have received their reward. But whenever you pray, go into your room and shut the door and pray to your Father who is in secret; and your Father who sees in secret will reward you.

'And whenever you fast, do not look dismal, like the hypocrites, for they disfigure their faces so as to show others that they are fasting. Truly I tell you, they have received their reward. But when you fast, put oil on your head and wash your face, so that your fasting may be seen not by others but by your Father who is in secret; and your Father who sees in secret will reward you.'

This is the Gospel of the Lord.   Matthew 6.1–6, 16–18

Week 11: Thursday between 16 and 22 June

Year 1

A reading from the Second Letter of Paul to the Corinthians.

I wish you would bear with me in a little foolishness. Do bear with me! I feel a divine jealousy for you, for I promised you in marriage to one husband, to present you as a chaste virgin to Christ. But I am afraid that as the serpent deceived Eve by its cunning, your thoughts will be led astray from a sincere and pure devotion to Christ. For if someone comes and proclaims another Jesus than the one we proclaimed, or if you receive a different spirit from the one you received, or a different gospel from the one you accepted, you submit to it readily enough. I think that I am not in the least inferior to these super-apostles. I may be untrained in speech, but not in knowledge; certainly in every way and in all things we have made this evident to you.

Did I commit a sin by humbling myself so that you might be exalted, because I proclaimed God's good news to you free of charge? I robbed other churches by accepting support from them in order to serve you. And when I was with you and was in need, I did not burden anyone, for my needs were supplied by the friends who came from Macedonia. So I refrained and will   →

continue to refrain from burdening you in any way. As the truth of Christ is in me, this boast of mine will not be silenced in the regions of Achaia. And why? Because I do not love you? God knows I do!

This is the word of the Lord. 2 Corinthians 11.1–11

Responsorial Psalm

R **The works of God are truth and justice:
[he is gracious and full of compassion].** cf Psalm 111.7a, 4b

I will give thanks to the Lord with my whole heart,
in the company of the faithful and in the congregation.
The works of the Lord are great,
sought out by all who delight in them. **R**

His work is full of majesty and honour
and his righteousness endures for ever.
He appointed a memorial for his marvellous deeds;
the Lord is gracious and full of compassion. **R**

He gave food to those who feared him;
he is ever mindful of his covenant.
He showed his people the power of his works
in giving them the heritage of the nations. **R**

The works of his hands are truth and justice;
all his commandments are sure.
They stand fast for ever and ever;
they are done in truth and equity. **R**

He sent redemption to his people;
he commanded his covenant for ever;
holy and awesome is his name. **R**

The fear of the Lord is the beginning of wisdom;
a good understanding have those who live by it;
his praise endures for ever. **R** *Psalm 111*

Either

A reading from the book Ecclesiasticus.

Elijah arose, a prophet like fire,
    and his word burned like a torch.
He brought a famine upon them,
    and by his zeal he made them few in number.
By the word of the Lord he shut up the heavens,
    and also three times brought down fire.
How glorious you were, Elijah, in your wondrous deeds!
    Whose glory is equal to yours?
You raised a corpse from death
    and from Hades, by the word of the Most High.
You sent kings down to destruction,
    and famous men, from their sickbeds.
You heard rebuke at Sinai
    and judgements of vengeance at Horeb.
You anointed kings to inflict retribution,
    and prophets to succeed you.
You were taken up by a whirlwind of fire,
    in a chariot with horses of fire.
At the appointed time, it is written, you are destined
    to calm the wrath of God before it breaks out in fury,
to turn the hearts of parents to their children,
    and to restore the tribes of Jacob.
Happy are those who saw you
    and were adorned with your love!
    For we also shall surely live.

When Elijah was enveloped in the whirlwind,
    Elisha was filled with his spirit.
He performed twice as many signs,
    and marvels with every utterance of his mouth.
Never in his lifetime did he tremble before any ruler,
    nor could anyone intimidate him at all.
Nothing was too hard for him,
    and when he was dead, his body prophesied.
In his life he did wonders,
    and in death his deeds were marvellous.

This is the word of the Lord.   *Ecclesiasticus* 48.1–14

or

A reading from the prophecy of Isaiah

I will recount the gracious deeds of the LORD,
 the praiseworthy acts of the LORD,
because of all that the LORD has done for us,
 and the great favour to the house of Israel
that he has shown them according to his mercy,
 according to the abundance of his steadfast love.
For he said, 'Surely they are my people,
 children who will not deal falsely';
and he became their saviour
 in all their distress.
It was no messenger or angel
 but his presence that saved them;
in his love and in his pity he redeemed them;
 he lifted them up and carried them all the days of old.

This is the word of the Lord. Isaiah 63.7–9

Responsorial Psalm

R **The Lord is king: let the earth rejoice;**
 [let the multitude of the isles be glad]. Psalm 97.1

The Lord is king: let the earth rejoice;
let the multitude of the isles be glad.
Clouds and darkness are round about him;
righteousness and justice are the foundation of his throne. **R**

Fire goes before him
and burns up his enemies on every side.
His lightnings lit up the world;
the earth saw it and trembled. **R**

The mountains melted like wax at the presence of the Lord,
at the presence of the Lord of the whole earth.
The heavens declared his righteousness,
and all the peoples have seen his glory. **R**

Confounded be all who worship carved images
and delight in mere idols.
Bow down before him, all you gods.
Zion heard and was glad, and the daughters of Judah rejoiced,
because of your judgements, O Lord. **R** Psalm 97.1–8

Hear the Gospel of our Lord Jesus Christ according to Matthew.

Jesus said to his disciples, 'When you are praying, do not heap up empty phrases as the Gentiles do; for they think that they will be heard because of their many words. Do not be like them, for your Father knows what you need before you ask him.

'Pray then in this way:
Our Father in heaven,
hallowed be your name.
Your kingdom come.
Your will be done,
on earth as it is in heaven.
Give us this day our daily bread.
And forgive us our debts,
as we also have forgiven our debtors.
And do not bring us to the time of trial,
but rescue us from the evil one.

'For if you forgive others their trespasses, your heavenly Father will also forgive you; but if you do not forgive others, neither will your Father forgive your trespasses.'

This is the Gospel of the Lord. Matthew 6.7–15

Week 11: Friday between 17 and 23 June

Year 1

A reading from the Second Letter of Paul to the Corinthians.

Since many boast according to human standards, I will also boast. But whatever anyone dares to boast of – I am speaking as a fool – I also dare to boast of that. Are they Hebrews? So am I. Are they Israelites? So am I. Are they descendants of Abraham? So am I. Are they ministers of Christ? I am talking like a madman – I am a better one: with far greater labours, far more imprisonments, with countless floggings, and often near death. Five times I have received from the Jews the forty lashes minus one. Three times I was beaten with rods. Once I received a stoning. Three times I was shipwrecked; for a night and a day I was adrift at sea; on frequent journeys, in danger from rivers, danger from bandits, danger from my own people, danger from Gentiles, danger in the city, danger in the wilderness, danger at sea, danger from false brothers and sisters; in toil and hardship, through many a sleepless night, hungry and thirsty, often without food, cold and naked. And, besides other things, I am under daily pressure because of my anxiety for all the churches. Who is weak, and I am not weak? Who is made to stumble, and I am not indignant? If I must boast, I will boast of the things that show my weakness.

This is the word of the Lord. 2 Corinthians 11.18, 21b–30

R **Taste and see that the Lord is good:
   [happy are all who trust in him].**   cf Psalm 34.8

I will bless the Lord at all times;
his praise shall ever be in my mouth.
My soul shall glory in the Lord;
let the humble hear and be glad.   R

O magnify the Lord with me;
let us exalt his name together.
I sought the Lord and he answered me
and delivered me from all my fears.   R

Look upon him and be radiant
and your faces shall not be ashamed.
This poor soul cried, and the Lord heard me
and saved me from all my troubles.   R   Psalm 34.1–6

Year 2

A reading from the Second Book of the Kings.

When Athaliah, Ahaziah's mother, saw that her son was dead, she set about to destroy all the royal family. But Jehosheba, King Joram's daughter, Ahaziah's sister, took Joash son of Ahaziah, and stole him away from among the king's children who were about to be killed; she put him and his nurse in a bedroom. Thus she hid him from Athaliah, so that he was not killed; he remained with her for six years, hidden in the house of the LORD, while Athaliah reigned over the land.

But in the seventh year Jehoiada summoned the captains of the Carites and of the guards and had them come to him in the house of the LORD. He made a covenant with them and put them under oath in the house of the LORD; then he showed them the king's son.

The captains did according to all that the priest Jehoiada commanded; each brought his men who were to go off duty on the sabbath, with those who were to come on duty on the sabbath, and came to the priest Jehoiada. The priest delivered to the captains the spears and shields that had been King David's, which were in the house of the LORD; the guards stood, every man with his weapons in his hand, from the south side of the house to the north side of the house, around the altar and the house, to guard the king on every side. Then he brought out the king's son, put the crown on him, and gave him the covenant; they proclaimed him king, and anointed him; they clapped their hands and shouted, 'Long live the king!'

When Athaliah heard the noise of the guard and of the people, she went into the house of the LORD to the people; when she looked, there was the king standing by the pillar, according to custom, with the captains and the trumpeters beside the king, and all the people of the land rejoicing and blowing trumpets. Athaliah tore her clothes and cried, 'Treason! Treason!' Then the priest Jehoiada commanded the captains who were set over the army, 'Bring her out between the ranks, and kill with the sword anyone who follows her.' For the priest said, 'Let her not be killed in the house of the LORD.' So they laid hands on her; she went through the horses' entrance to the king's house, and there she was put to death.

Jehoiada made a covenant between the LORD and the king and people, that they should be the LORD's people; also between the king and the people. Then all the people of the land went to the house of Baal, and tore it down; his altars and his images they broke in pieces, and they killed Mattan, the priest of Baal, before the altars. The priest posted guards over the house of the LORD. So all the people of the land rejoiced; and the city was quiet after Athaliah had been killed with the sword at the king's house.

This is the word of the Lord.   2 Kings 11.1–4, 9–18, 20

Responsorial Psalm

R **Let us enter the dwelling place of the Lord
[and fall low before his footstool].**   cf Psalm 132.7

Lord, remember for David
all the hardships he endured;
how he swore an oath to the Lord
and vowed a vow to the Mighty One of Jacob. **R**

'I will not come within the shelter of my house,
nor climb up into my bed;
I will not allow my eyes to sleep,
nor let my eyelids slumber,
until I find a place for the Lord,
a dwelling for the Mighty One of Jacob.' **R**

The Lord has sworn an oath to David,
a promise from which he will not shrink:
'Of the fruit of your body
shall I set upon your throne. **R**

'If your children keep my covenant
and my testimonies that I shall teach them,
their children also shall sit
upon your throne for evermore.' **R**   Psalm 132.1–5, 11–13

Year I and Year 2

Hear the Gospel of our Lord Jesus Christ according to Matthew.

Jesus said to his disciples, 'Do not store up for yourselves treasures on earth, where moth and rust consume and where thieves break in and steal; but store up for yourselves treasures in heaven, where neither moth nor rust consumes and where thieves do not break in and steal. For where your treasure is, there your heart will be also.

'The eye is the lamp of the body. So, if your eye is healthy, your whole body will be full of light; but if your eye is unhealthy, your whole body will be full of darkness. If then the light in you is darkness, how great is the darkness!'

This is the Gospel of the Lord.   Matthew 6.19–23

Week 11: Saturday between 18 and 24 June

Year I

A reading from the Second Letter of Paul to the Corinthians.

It is necessary to boast; nothing is to be gained by it, but I will go on to visions and revelations of the Lord. I know a person in Christ who fourteen years ago was caught up to the third heaven – whether in the body or out of the body I do not know; God knows. And I know that such a person – whether in the body or out of the body I do not know; God knows – was caught up into Paradise and heard things that are not to be told, that no mortal is permitted to repeat. On behalf of such a one I will boast, but on my own behalf I will not boast, except of my weaknesses. But if I wish to boast, I will not be a fool, for I will be speaking the truth. But I refrain from it, so that no one may think better of me than what is seen in me or heard from me, even considering the exceptional character of the revelations. Therefore, to keep me from being too elated, a thorn was given to me in the flesh, a messenger of Satan to torment me, to keep me from being too elated. Three times I appealed to the Lord about this, that it would leave me, but he said to me, 'My grace is sufficient for you, for power is made perfect in weakness.' So, I will boast all the more gladly of my weaknesses, so that the power of Christ may dwell in me. Therefore I am content with weaknesses, insults, hardships, persecutions, and calamities for the sake of Christ; for whenever I am weak, then I am strong.

This is the word of the Lord.   2 Corinthians 12.1–10

Responsorial Psalm

R* **The Lord will keep David in his steadfast love
and not betray his faithfulness.** *cf Psalm 89.33*

I have found David my servant;
with my holy oil have I anointed him.
My hand shall hold him fast
and my arm shall strengthen him. R

No enemy shall deceive him,
nor any wicked person afflict him.
I will strike down his foes before his face
and beat down those that hate him. R

My truth also and my steadfast love shall be with him,
and in my name shall his head be exalted.
I will set his dominion upon the sea
and his right hand upon the rivers. R

He shall call to me, 'You are my Father,
my God, and the rock of my salvation.'
And I will make him my firstborn,
the most high above the kings of the earth. R

The love I have pledged to him will I keep for ever,
and my covenant will stand fast with him.
His seed also will I make to endure for ever
and his throne as the days of heaven. R

But if his children forsake my law
and cease to walk in my judgements,
if they break my statutes
and do not keep my commandments,
I will punish their offences with a rod
and their sin with scourges. R* *Psalm 89.20–33*

Year 2

A reading from the Second Book of the Chronicles.

After the death of Jehoiada the officials of Judah came and did obeisance to the king; then the king listened to them. They abandoned the house of the LORD, the God of their ancestors, and served the sacred poles and the idols. And wrath came upon Judah and Jerusalem for this guilt of theirs. Yet he sent prophets among them to bring them back to the LORD; they testified against them, but they would not listen.

Then the spirit of God took possession of Zechariah son of the priest Jehoiada; he stood above the people and said to them, 'Thus says God: Why do you transgress the commandments of the LORD, so that you cannot prosper? →

Because you have forsaken the LORD, he has also forsaken you.' But they conspired against him, and by command of the king they stoned him to death in the court of the house of the LORD. King Joash did not remember the kindness that Jehoiada, Zechariah's father, had shown him, but killed his son. As he was dying, he said, 'May the LORD see and avenge!'

At the end of the year the army of Aram came up against Joash. They came to Judah and Jerusalem, and destroyed all the officials of the people from among them, and sent all the booty they took to the king of Damascus. Although the army of Aram had come with few men, the LORD delivered into their hand a very great army, because they had abandoned the LORD, the God of their ancestors. Thus they executed judgement on Joash.

When they had withdrawn, leaving him severely wounded, his servants conspired against him because of the blood of the son of the priest Jehoiada, and they killed him on his bed. So he died; and they buried him in the city of David, but they did not bury him in the tombs of the kings.

This is the word of the Lord. 2 Chronicles 24.17–25

Responsorial Psalm

R* **The Lord will keep David in his steadfast love
and not betray his faithfulness.** cf Psalm 89.33

I will set his dominion upon the sea
and his right hand upon the rivers.
He shall call to me, 'You are my Father,
my God, and the rock of my salvation.' **R**

And I will make him my firstborn,
the most high above the kings of the earth.
The love I have pledged to him will I keep for ever,
and my covenant will stand fast with him.
His seed also will I make to endure for ever
and his throne as the days of heaven. **R**

But if his children forsake my law
and cease to walk in my judgements,
if they break my statutes
and do not keep my commandments,
I will punish their offences with a rod
and their sin with scourges. **R*** Psalm 89.25–33

Hear the Gospel of our Lord Jesus Christ according to Matthew.

Jesus said to his disciples, 'No one can serve two masters; for a slave will either hate the one and love the other, or be devoted to the one and despise the other. You cannot serve God and wealth.

'Therefore I tell you, do not worry about your life, what you will eat or what you will drink, or about your body, what you will wear. Is not life more than food, and the body more than clothing? Look at the birds of the air; they neither sow nor reap nor gather into barns, and yet your heavenly Father feeds them. Are you not of more value than they? And can any of you by worrying add a single hour to your span of life? And why do you worry about clothing? Consider the lilies of the field, how they grow; they neither toil nor spin, yet I tell you, even Solomon in all his glory was not clothed like one of these. But if God so clothes the grass of the field, which is alive today and tomorrow is thrown into the oven, will he not much more clothe you – you of little faith?

'Therefore do not worry, saying, "What will we eat?" or "What will we drink?" or "What will we wear?" For it is the Gentiles who strive for all these things; and indeed your heavenly Father knows that you need all these things. But strive first for the kingdom of God and his righteousness, and all these things will be given to you as well. So do not worry about tomorrow, for tomorrow will bring worries of its own. Today's trouble is enough for today.'

This is the Gospel of the Lord.   *Matthew 6.24–end*

Week 12: Monday between 20 and 26 June

Year 1

A reading from the book Genesis.

The LORD said to Abram, 'Go from your country and your kindred and your father's house to the land that I will show you. I will make of you a great nation, and I will bless you, and make your name great, so that you will be a blessing. I will bless those who bless you, and the one who curses you I will curse; and in you all the families of the earth shall be blessed.'

So Abram went, as the LORD had told him; and Lot went with him. Abram was seventy-five years old when he departed from Haran. Abram took his wife Sarai and his brother's son Lot, and all the possessions that they had gathered, and the persons whom they had acquired in Haran; and they set forth to go to the land of Canaan. When they had come to the land of Canaan, Abram passed through the land to the place at Shechem, to the oak of Moreh. At that time the Canaanites were in the land. Then the LORD appeared to Abram, and said, 'To your offspring I will give this land.' So he built there an altar to the LORD, who had appeared to him. From there he moved on to the hill country on the east of Bethel, and pitched his tent, with Bethel on the west and Ai on the east; and there he built an altar to the LORD and invoked the name of the LORD. And Abram journeyed on by stages towards the Negeb.

This is the word of the Lord. *Genesis 12.1–9*

Responsorial Psalm

R* **Let your loving-kindness, O Lord, be upon us,**
   [as we have set our hope on you]. *Psalm 33.22*

Happy the nation whose God is the Lord
and the people he has chosen for his own.
The Lord looks down from heaven
and beholds all the children of earth.   **R**

From where he sits enthroned he turns his gaze
on all who dwell on the earth.
He fashions all the hearts of them
and understands all their works.   **R**

No king is saved by the might of his host;
no warrior delivered by his great strength.
A horse is a vain hope for deliverance;
for all its strength it cannot save.   **R**

Behold, the eye of the Lord
is upon those who fear him,
on those who wait in hope for his steadfast love,
to deliver their soul from death
and to feed them in time of famine. **R**

Our soul waits longingly for the Lord;
he is our help and our shield.
Indeed, our heart rejoices in him;
in his holy name have we put our trust. **R***   *Psalm 33.12–end*

Year 2

A reading from the Second Book of the Kings.

The king of Assyria invaded all the land and came to Samaria; for three years
he besieged it. In the ninth year of Hoshea, the king of Assyria captured
Samaria; he carried the Israelites away to Assyria. He placed them in Halah,
on the Habor, the river of Gozan, and in the cities of the Medes.

This occurred because the people of Israel had sinned against the LORD
their God, who had brought them up out of the land of Egypt from under the
hand of Pharaoh king of Egypt. They had worshipped other gods and walked
in the customs of the nations whom the LORD drove out before the people
of Israel, and in the customs that the kings of Israel had introduced.

Yet the LORD warned Israel and Judah by every prophet and every seer,
saying, 'Turn from your evil ways and keep my commandments and my statutes,
in accordance with all the law that I commanded your ancestors and that I
sent to you by my servants the prophets.' They would not listen but were
stubborn, as their ancestors had been, who did not believe in the LORD their
God. They despised his statutes, and his covenant that he made with their
ancestors, and the warnings that he gave them. They went after false idols and
became false; they followed the nations that were around them, concerning
whom the LORD had commanded them that they should not do as they did.
Therefore the LORD was very angry with Israel and removed them out of his
sight; none was left but the tribe of Judah alone.

This is the word of the Lord.   *2 Kings 17.5–8, 13–15, 18*

R* **Set free, O Lord, those that you love**
   [save us by your right hand and answer us].   cf Psalm 60.5

O God, you have cast us off and broken us;
you have been angry; restore us to yourself again.
You have shaken the earth and torn it apart;
heal its wounds, for it trembles.   **R**

You have made your people drink bitter things;
we reel from the deadly wine you have given us.
You have made those who fear you to flee,
to escape from the range of the bow.   **R***

Grant us your help against the enemy,
for earthly help is in vain.
Through God will we do great acts,
for it is he that shall tread down our enemies.   **R**   Psalm 60.1–5, 11–end

Year 1 and Year 2

Hear the Gospel of our Lord Jesus Christ according to Matthew.

Jesus said to his disciples, 'Do not judge, so that you may not be judged. For
with the judgement you make you will be judged, and the measure you give
will be the measure you get. Why do you see the speck in your neighbour's
eye, but do not notice the log in your own eye? Or how can you say to your
neighbour, "Let me take the speck out of your eye", while the log is in your
own eye? You hypocrite, first take the log out of your own eye, and then you
will see clearly to take the speck out of your neighbour's eye.'

This is the Gospel of the Lord.   Matthew 7.1–5

Week 12: Tuesday between 21 and 27 June

Year 1

A reading from the book Genesis.

Abram was very rich in livestock, in silver, and in gold. Lot, who went with
Abram, also had flocks and herds and tents, so that the land could not support
both of them living together; for their possessions were so great that they
could not live together, and there was strife between the herders of Abram's
livestock and the herders of Lot's livestock. At that time the Canaanites and
the Perizzites lived in the land.

Then Abram said to Lot, 'Let there be no strife between you and me, and
between your herders and my herders; for we are kindred. Is not the whole
land before you? Separate yourself from me. If you take the left hand, then
I will go to the right; or if you take the right hand, then I will go to the

left.' Lot looked about him, and saw that the plain of the Jordan was well watered everywhere like the garden of the LORD, like the land of Egypt, in the direction of Zoar; this was before the LORD had destroyed Sodom and Gomorrah. So Lot chose for himself all the plain of the Jordan, and Lot journeyed eastwards; thus they separated from each other. Abram settled in the land of Canaan, while Lot settled among the cities of the Plain and moved his tent as far as Sodom. Now the people of Sodom were wicked, great sinners against the LORD.

The LORD said to Abram, after Lot had separated from him, 'Raise your eyes now, and look from the place where you are, northwards and southwards and eastwards and westwards; for all the land that you see I will give to you and to your offspring for ever. I will make your offspring like the dust of the earth; so that if one can count the dust of the earth, your offspring also can be counted. Rise up, walk through the length and the breadth of the land, for I will give it to you.' So Abram moved his tent, and came and settled by the oaks of Mamre, which are at Hebron; and there he built an altar to the LORD.

This is the word of the Lord.   *Genesis 13.2, 5–end*

Responsorial Psalm

R **They shall dwell in your tabernacle, O Lord:**
   [those who do what is right].   *cf Psalm 15.1a, 2b*

Lord, who may dwell in your tabernacle?
Who may rest upon your holy hill?
Whoever leads an uncorrupt life
and does the thing that is right. **R**

Who speaks the truth from the heart
and bears no deceit on the tongue;
who does no evil to a friend
and pours no scorn on a neighbour. **R**

In whose sight the wicked are not esteemed,
but who honours those who fear the Lord.
Whoever has sworn to a neighbour
and never goes back on that word. **R**

Who does not lend money in hope of gain,
nor takes a bribe against the innocent;
whoever does these things
shall never fall. **R**   *Psalm 15*

A reading from the Second Book of the Kings.

King Sennacherib of Assyria sent messengers to Hezekiah, saying, 'Thus shall you speak to King Hezekiah of Judah: Do not let your God on whom you rely deceive you by promising that Jerusalem will not be given into the hand of the king of Assyria. See, you have heard what the kings of Assyria have done to all lands, destroying them utterly. Shall you be delivered?'

Hezekiah received the letter from the hand of the messengers and read it; then Hezekiah went up to the house of the LORD and spread it before the LORD. And Hezekiah prayed before the LORD, and said: 'O LORD the God of Israel, who are enthroned above the cherubim, you are God, you alone, of all the kingdoms of the earth; you have made heaven and earth. Incline your ear, O LORD, and hear; open your eyes, O LORD, and see; hear the words of Sennacherib, which he has sent to mock the living God. Truly, O LORD, the kings of Assyria have laid waste the nations and their lands, and have hurled their gods into the fire, though they were no gods but the work of human hands – wood and stone – and so they were destroyed. So now, O LORD our God, save us, I pray you, from his hand, so that all the kingdoms of the earth may know that you, O LORD, are God alone.'

Then Isaiah son of Amoz sent to Hezekiah, saying, 'Thus says the LORD, the God of Israel: I have heard your prayer to me about King Sennacherib of Assyria. This is the word that the LORD has spoken concerning him:
She despises you, she scorns you –
    virgin daughter Zion;
she tosses her head – behind your back,
    daughter Jerusalem.

'For from Jerusalem a remnant shall go out, and from Mount Zion a band of survivors. The zeal of the LORD of hosts will do this.

'Therefore thus says the LORD concerning the king of Assyria: He shall not come into this city, shoot an arrow there, come before it with a shield, or cast up a siege-ramp against it. By the way that he came, by the same he shall return; he shall not come into this city, says the LORD. For I will defend this city to save it, for my own sake and for the sake of my servant David.'

That very night the angel of the LORD set out and struck down one hundred and eighty-five thousand in the camp of the Assyrians; when morning dawned, they were all dead bodies. Then King Sennacherib of Assyria left, went home, and lived at Nineveh.

This is the word of the Lord.   2 Kings 19.9b–11, 14–21, 31–36

Responsorial Psalm

R* **Let Mount Zion rejoice in your judgements, O Lord
[and the daughters of Judah be glad].**   cf Psalm 48.11

Great is the Lord and highly to be praised,
in the city of our God.
His holy mountain is fair and lifted high,
the joy of all the earth.   **R**

As we had heard, so have we seen
in the city of the Lord of hosts, the city of our God:
God has established her for ever.
We have waited on your loving-kindness, O God,
in the midst of your temple.   **R**

As with your name, O God,
so your praise reaches to the ends of the earth;
your right hand is full of justice.   **R***

Walk about Zion and go round about her;
count all her towers;
consider well her bulwarks; pass through her citadels,
that you may tell those who come after
that such is our God for ever and ever.
It is he that shall be our guide for evermore.   **R**   *Psalm 48.1–2, 8–end*

Year 1 and Year 2

Hear the Gospel of our Lord Jesus Christ according to Matthew.

Jesus said to his disciples, 'Do not give what is holy to dogs; and do not throw your pearls before swine, or they will trample them under foot and turn and maul you.

'In everything do to others as you would have them do to you; for this is the law and the prophets.

'Enter through the narrow gate; for the gate is wide and the road is easy that leads to destruction, and there are many who take it. For the gate is narrow and the road is hard that leads to life, and there are few who find it.'

This is the Gospel of the Lord.   *Matthew 7.6, 12–14*

Week 12: Wednesday between 22 and 28 June

Year I

A reading from the book Genesis.

The word of the LORD came to Abram in a vision, 'Do not be afraid, Abram, I am your shield; your reward shall be very great.' But Abram said, 'O Lord GOD, what will you give me, for I continue childless, and the heir of my house is Eliezer of Damascus?' And Abram said, 'You have given me no offspring, and so a slave born in my house is to be my heir.' But the word of the LORD came to him, 'This man shall not be your heir; no one but your very own issue shall be your heir.' He brought him outside and said, 'Look towards heaven and count the stars, if you are able to count them.' Then he said to him, 'So shall your descendants be.' And he believed the LORD; and the LORD reckoned it to him as righteousness.

Then he said to him, 'I am the LORD who brought you from Ur of the Chaldeans, to give you this land to possess.' But he said, 'O Lord GOD, how am I to know that I shall possess it?' He said to him, 'Bring me a heifer three years old, a female goat three years old, a ram three years old, a turtle-dove, and a young pigeon.' He brought him all these and cut them in two, laying each half over against the other; but he did not cut the birds in two. And when birds of prey came down on the carcasses, Abram drove them away.

As the sun was going down, a deep sleep fell upon Abram, and a deep and terrifying darkness descended upon him. When the sun had gone down and it was dark, a smoking fire-pot and a flaming torch passed between these pieces. On that day the LORD made a covenant with Abram, saying, 'To your descendants I give this land, from the river of Egypt to the great river, the river Euphrates.'

This is the word of the Lord.   Genesis 15.1–12, 17–18

Responsorial Psalm

R* **Sing to the Lord, sing praises,
[and tell of his marvellous works].**   cf Psalm 105.2

O give thanks to the Lord and call upon his name;
make known his deeds among the peoples.*
Rejoice in the praise of his holy name;
let the hearts of them rejoice who seek the Lord.   **R**

Seek the Lord and his strength;
seek his face continually.
Remember the marvels he has done,
his wonders and the judgements of his mouth.   **R**

O seed of Abraham his servant,
O children of Jacob his chosen:
he is the Lord our God;
his judgements are in all the earth.   R

He has always been mindful of his covenant,
the promise that he made for a thousand generations:
the covenant he made with Abraham,
the oath that he swore to Isaac.   R   *Psalm* 105.1–9

Year 2

A reading from the Second Book of the Kings.

The high priest Hilkiah said to Shaphan the secretary, 'I have found the book
of the law in the house of the LORD.' When Hilkiah gave the book to Shaphan,
he read it. Then Shaphan the secretary came to the king, and reported to the
king, 'Your servants have emptied out the money that was found in the house,
and have delivered it into the hand of the workers who have oversight of the
house of the LORD.' Shaphan the secretary informed the king, 'The priest
Hilkiah has given me a book.' Shaphan then read it aloud to the king.

When the king heard the words of the book of the law, he tore his clothes.
Then the king commanded the priest Hilkiah, Ahikam son of Shaphan, Achbor
son of Micaiah, Shaphan the secretary, and the king's servant Asaiah, saying,
'Go, inquire of the LORD for me, for the people, and for all Judah, concerning
the words of this book that has been found; for great is the wrath of the LORD
that is kindled against us, because our ancestors did not obey the words of
this book, to do according to all that is written concerning us.'

Then the king directed that all the elders of Judah and Jerusalem should
be gathered to him. The king went up to the house of the LORD, and with him
went all the people of Judah, all the inhabitants of Jerusalem, the priests, the
prophets, and all the people, both small and great; he read in their hearing all
the words of the book of the covenant that had been found in the house of
the LORD. The king stood by the pillar and made a covenant before the LORD,
to follow the LORD, keeping his commandments, his decrees, and his statutes,
with all his heart and all his soul, to perform the words of this covenant that
were written in this book. All the people joined in the covenant.

This is the word of the Lord.   2 *Kings* 22.8–13, 23.1–3

Responsorial Psalm

R **Teach me, O Lord, the way of your statutes:**
   [lead me in the path of your commandments].   Psalm 119.33a, 35a

Teach me, O Lord, the way of your statutes
and I shall keep it to the end.
Give me understanding and I shall keep your law;
I shall keep it with my whole heart. **R**

Lead me in the path of your commandments,
for therein is my delight.
Incline my heart to your testimonies
and not to unjust gain. **R**

Turn away my eyes lest they gaze on vanities;
O give me life in your ways.
Confirm to your servant your promise,
which stands for all who fear you. **R**

Turn away the reproach which I dread,
because your judgements are good.
Behold, I long for your commandments;
in your righteousness give me life. **R**   Psalm 119.33–40

Year 1 and Year 2

Hear the Gospel of our Lord Jesus Christ according to Matthew.

Jesus said to his disciples, 'Beware of false prophets, who come to you in sheep's clothing but inwardly are ravenous wolves. You will know them by their fruits. Are grapes gathered from thorns, or figs from thistles? In the same way, every good tree bears good fruit, but the bad tree bears bad fruit. A good tree cannot bear bad fruit, nor can a bad tree bear good fruit. Every tree that does not bear good fruit is cut down and thrown into the fire. Thus you will know them by their fruits.'

This is the Gospel of the Lord.   Matthew 7.15–20

Week 12: Thursday between 23 and 29 June

Year 1

A reading from the book Genesis.

Sarai, Abram's wife, bore him no children. She had an Egyptian slave-girl whose name was Hagar, and Sarai said to Abram, 'You see that the Lord has prevented me from bearing children; go in to my slave-girl; it may be that I shall obtain children by her.' And Abram listened to the voice of Sarai. So, after Abram had lived for ten years in the land of Canaan, Sarai, Abram's wife, took Hagar the Egyptian, her slave-girl, and gave her to her husband Abram as a wife. He went in to Hagar, and she conceived; and when she saw that she had conceived, she looked with contempt on her mistress. Then Sarai said to Abram, 'May the wrong done to me be on you! I gave my slave-girl to your embrace, and when she saw that she had conceived, she looked on me with contempt. May the LORD judge between you and me!' But Abram said to Sarai, 'Your slave-girl is in your power; do to her as you please.' Then Sarai dealt harshly with her, and she ran away from her.

The angel of the LORD found her by a spring of water in the wilderness, the spring on the way to Shur. And he said, 'Hagar, slave-girl of Sarai, where have you come from and where are you going?' She said, 'I am running away from my mistress Sarai.' The angel of the LORD said to her, 'Return to your mistress, and submit to her.' The angel of the LORD also said to her, 'I will so greatly multiply your offspring that they cannot be counted for multitude.' And the angel of the LORD said to her,

'Now you have conceived and shall bear a son;
    you shall call him Ishmael,
    for the LORD has given heed to your affliction.
He shall be a wild ass of a man,
with his hand against everyone,
    and everyone's hand against him;
and he shall live at odds with all his kin.'

Hagar bore Abram a son; and Abram named his son, whom Hagar bore, Ishmael. Abram was eighty-six years old when Hagar bore him Ishmael.

This is the word of the Lord. Genesis 16.1–12, 15–16

Responsorial Psalm

R **Give thanks to the Lord, for he is gracious:**
   [his faithfulness endures for ever]. cf Psalm 106.1

   or

R **Alleluia!**

Give thanks to the Lord, for he is gracious,
for his faithfulness endures for ever.
Who can express the mighty acts of the Lord
or show forth all his praise? **R**

Blessed are those who observe what is right
and always do what is just.
Remember me, O Lord,
in the favour you bear for your people. **R**

Visit me in the day of your salvation,
that I may see the prosperity of your chosen;
and rejoice in the gladness of your people,
and exult with your inheritance. **R** Psalm 106.1–5

A reading from the Second Book of the Kings.

Jehoiachin was eighteen years old when he began to reign; he reigned for three months in Jerusalem. His mother's name was Nehushta daughter of Elnathan of Jerusalem. He did what was evil in the sight of the LORD, just as his father had done.

At that time the servants of King Nebuchadnezzar of Babylon came up to Jerusalem, and the city was besieged. King Nebuchadnezzar of Babylon came to the city, while his servants were besieging it; King Jehoiachin of Judah gave himself up to the king of Babylon, himself, his mother, his servants, his officers, and his palace officials. The king of Babylon took him prisoner in the eighth year of his reign. He carried off all the treasures of the house of the LORD, and the treasures of the king's house; he cut in pieces all the vessels of gold in the temple of the LORD, which King Solomon of Israel had made, all this as the LORD had foretold. He carried away all Jerusalem, all the officials, all the warriors, ten thousand captives, all the artisans and the smiths; no one remained, except the poorest people of the land. He carried away Jehoiachin to Babylon; the king's mother, the king's wives, his officials, and the elite of the land, he took into captivity from Jerusalem to Babylon. The king of Babylon brought captive to Babylon all the men of valour, seven thousand, the artisans and the smiths, one thousand, all of them strong and fit for war. The king of Babylon made Mattaniah, Jehoiachin's uncle, king in his place, and changed his name to Zedekiah.

This is the word of the Lord.   2 Kings 24.8–17

Responsorial Psalm

R **Help us, O God, for the glory of your name;**
   [deliver us, and wipe away our sins].   *cf Psalm 79.9*

O God, the heathen have come into your heritage;
your holy temple have they defiled
and made Jerusalem a heap of stones.
The dead bodies of your servants they have given
to be food for the birds of the air,
and the flesh of your faithful to the beasts of the field. **R**

Their blood have they shed like water
on every side of Jerusalem,
and there was no one to bury them.
We have become the taunt of our neighbours,
the scorn and derision of those that are round about us. **R**

Lord, how long will you be angry, for ever?
How long will your jealous fury blaze like fire?
Pour out your wrath upon the nations that have not known you,
and upon the kingdoms that have not called upon your name. **R**

For they have devoured Jacob
and laid waste his dwelling place.
Remember not against us our former sins;
let your compassion make haste to meet us,
for we are brought very low. R

Help us, O God of our salvation, for the glory of your name;
deliver us, and wipe away our sins for your name's sake.
Let the sorrowful sighing of the prisoners come before you,
and by your mighty arm
preserve those who are condemned to die. R   *Psalm 79.1–9, 12*

Year 1 and Year 2

Hear the Gospel of our Lord Jesus Christ according to Matthew.

Jesus said to his disciples, 'Not everyone who says to me, "Lord, Lord", will
enter the kingdom of heaven, but only one who does the will of my Father in
heaven. On that day many will say to me, "Lord, Lord, did we not prophesy
in your name, and cast out demons in your name, and do many deeds of
power in your name?" Then I will declare to them, "I never knew you; go
away from me, you evildoers."

'Everyone then who hears these words of mine and acts on them will be
like a wise man who built his house on rock. The rain fell, the floods came,
and the winds blew and beat on that house, but it did not fall, because it had
been founded on rock. And everyone who hears these words of mine and
does not act on them will be like a foolish man who built his house on sand.
The rain fell, and the floods came, and the winds blew and beat against that
house, and it fell – and great was its fall!'

Now when Jesus had finished saying these things, the crowds were
astounded at his teaching, for he taught them as one having authority, and
not as their scribes.

This is the Gospel of the Lord.   *Matthew 7.21–end*

Week 12: Friday between 24 and 30 June

Year 1

A reading from the book Genesis.

When Abram was ninety-nine years old, the LORD appeared to Abram, and
said to him, 'I am God Almighty; walk before me, and be blameless.

'You shall keep my covenant, you and your offspring after you throughout
their generations. This is my covenant, which you shall keep, between me
and you and your offspring after you: Every male among you shall be
circumcised.   →

'As for Sarai your wife, you shall not call her Sarai, but Sarah shall be her name. I will bless her, and moreover I will give you a son by her. I will bless her, and she shall give rise to nations; kings of peoples shall come from her.' Then Abraham fell on his face and laughed, and said to himself, 'Can a child be born to a man who is a hundred years old? Can Sarah, who is ninety years old, bear a child?' And Abraham said to God, 'O that Ishmael might live in your sight!' God said, 'No, but your wife Sarah shall bear you a son, and you shall name him Isaac. I will establish my covenant with him as an everlasting covenant for his offspring after him. As for Ishmael, I have heard you; I will bless him and make him fruitful and exceedingly numerous; he shall be the father of twelve princes, and I will make him a great nation. But my covenant I will establish with Isaac, whom Sarah shall bear to you at this season next year.' And when he had finished talking with him, God went up from Abraham.

This is the word of the Lord. Genesis 17.1, 9–10, 15–22

Responsorial Psalm

R **Blessed are those who fear the Lord,**
   [and walk in the ways of God]. cf Psalm 128.1

Blessed are all those who fear the Lord,
and walk in his ways.
You shall eat the fruit of the toil of your hands;
it shall go well with you,
and happy shall you be.   **R**

Your wife within your house
shall be like a fruitful vine;
your children round your table,
like fresh olive branches.
Thus shall the one be blest who fears the Lord.   **R**

The Lord from out of Zion bless you,
that you may see Jerusalem in prosperity
all the days of your life.
May you see your children's children,
and may there be peace upon Israel.   **R** Psalm 128

Year 2

A reading from the Second Book of the Kings.

In the ninth year of the reign of Zedekiah, in the tenth month, on the tenth day of the month, King Nebuchadnezzar of Babylon came with all his army against Jerusalem, and laid siege to it; they built siege-works against it all round. So the city was besieged until the eleventh year of King Zedekiah. On the ninth day of the fourth month the famine became so severe in the city that there was no food for the people of the land. Then a breach was made in the city wall; the king with all the soldiers fled by night by the way of the gate between the two walls, by the king's garden, though the Chaldeans were all round the city. They went in the direction of the Arabah. But the army of the Chaldeans pursued the king, and overtook him in the plains of Jericho; all his army was scattered, deserting him. Then they captured the king and brought him up to the king of Babylon at Riblah, who passed sentence on him. They slaughtered the sons of Zedekiah before his eyes, then put out the eyes of Zedekiah; they bound him in fetters and took him to Babylon.

In the fifth month, on the seventh day of the month – which was the nineteenth year of King Nebuchadnezzar, king of Babylon – Nebuzaradan, the captain of the bodyguard, a servant of the king of Babylon, came to Jerusalem. He burned the house of the LORD, the king's house, and all the houses of Jerusalem; every great house he burned down. All the army of the Chaldeans who were with the captain of the guard broke down the walls around Jerusalem. Nebuzaradan the captain of the guard carried into exile the rest of the people who were left in the city and the deserters who had defected to the king of Babylon – all the rest of the population. But the captain of the guard left some of the poorest people of the land to be vine-dressers and tillers of the soil.

This is the word of the Lord. 2 *Kings* 25.1–12

Responsorial Psalm

R **By the waters of Babylon we sat down and wept,
when we remembered Zion.** *Psalm* 137.1

By the waters of Babylon we sat down and wept,
when we remembered Zion.
As for our lyres, we hung them up
on the willows that grow in that land. R

For there our captors asked for a song,
our tormentors called for mirth:
'Sing us one of the songs of Zion.'
How shall we sing the Lord's song
in a strange land? R

If I forget you, O Jerusalem,
let my right hand forget its skill.
Let my tongue cleave to the roof of my mouth
if I do not remember you,
if I set not Jerusalem above my highest joy. R *Psalm* 137.1–6

Hear the Gospel of our Lord Jesus Christ according to Matthew.

When Jesus had come down from the mountain, great crowds followed him; and there was a leper who came to him and knelt before him, saying, 'Lord, if you choose, you can make me clean.' He stretched out his hand and touched him, saying, 'I do choose. Be made clean!' Immediately his leprosy was cleansed. Then Jesus said to him, 'See that you say nothing to anyone; but go, show yourself to the priest, and offer the gift that Moses commanded, as a testimony to them.'

This is the Gospel of the Lord.   Matthew 8.1–4

Week 12: Saturday between 25 June and 1 July

Year 1

A reading from the book Genesis.

The Lord appeared to Abraham by the oaks of Mamre, as he sat at the entrance of his tent in the heat of the day. He looked up and saw three men standing near him. When he saw them, he ran from the tent entrance to meet them, and bowed down to the ground. He said, 'My lord, if I find favour with you, do not pass by your servant. Let a little water be brought, and wash your feet, and rest yourselves under the tree. Let me bring a little bread, that you may refresh yourselves, and after that you may pass on – since you have come to your servant.' So they said, 'Do as you have said.' And Abraham hastened into the tent to Sarah, and said, 'Make ready quickly three measures of choice flour, knead it, and make cakes.' Abraham ran to the herd, and took a calf, tender and good, and gave it to the servant, who hastened to prepare it. Then he took curds and milk and the calf that he had prepared, and set it before them; and he stood by them under the tree while they ate.

They said to him, 'Where is your wife Sarah?' And he said, 'There, in the tent.' Then one said, 'I will surely return to you in due season, and your wife Sarah shall have a son.' And Sarah was listening at the tent entrance behind him. Now Abraham and Sarah were old, advanced in age; it had ceased to be with Sarah after the manner of women. So Sarah laughed to herself, saying, 'After I have grown old, and my husband is old, shall I have pleasure?' The Lord said to Abraham, 'Why did Sarah laugh, and say, "Shall I indeed bear a child, now that I am old?" Is anything too wonderful for the Lord? At the set time I will return to you, in due season, and Sarah shall have a son.' But Sarah denied, saying, 'I did not laugh'; for she was afraid. He said, 'Oh yes, you did laugh.'

This is the word of the Lord.   Genesis 18.1–15

Canticle

R **The Almighty has done great things for me
[and holy is his name].** Luke 1.49

My soul proclaims the greatness of the Lord,
my spirit rejoices in God my Saviour;
he has looked with favour on his lowly servant.
From this day all generations will call me blessed. R

The Almighty has done great things for me
and holy is his name.
He has mercy on those who fear him,
from generation to generation. R

He has shown strength with his arm
and has scattered the proud in their conceit,
casting down the mighty from their thrones
and lifting up the lowly. R

He has filled the hungry with good things
and sent the rich away empty.
He has come to the aid of his servant Israel,
to remember his promise of mercy,
the promise made to our ancestors,
to Abraham and his children for ever. R Luke 1.46b–55

Year 2

A reading from the book of Lamentations.

The Lord has destroyed without mercy
    all the dwellings of Jacob;
in his wrath he has broken down
    the strongholds of daughter Judah;
he has brought down to the ground in dishonour
    the kingdom and its rulers.

The elders of daughter Zion
    sit on the ground in silence;
they have thrown dust on their heads
    and put on sackcloth;
the young girls of Jerusalem
    have bowed their heads to the ground.

My eyes are spent with weeping;
    my stomach churns;
my bile is poured out on the ground
    because of the destruction of my people,
because infants and babes faint
    in the streets of the city. →

They cry to their mothers,
    'Where is bread and wine?'
as they faint like the wounded
    in the streets of the city,
as their life is poured out
    on their mothers' bosom.

What can I say for you, to what compare you,
    O daughter Jerusalem?
To what can I liken you, that I may comfort you,
    O virgin daughter Zion?
For vast as the sea is your ruin;
    who can heal you?

Your prophets have seen for you
    false and deceptive visions;
they have not exposed your iniquity
    to restore your fortunes,
but have seen oracles for you
    that are false and misleading.

Cry aloud to the Lord!
    O wall of daughter Zion!
Let tears stream down like a torrent
    day and night!
Give yourself no rest,
    your eyes no respite!

Arise, cry out in the night,
    at the beginning of the watches!
Pour out your heart like water
    before the presence of the Lord!
Lift your hands to him
    for the lives of your children,
who faint for hunger
    at the head of every street.

This is the word of the Lord.　　　　　　Lamentations 2.2, 10–14, 18–19

R **Do not forget the lives of your poor for ever:**
   [arise, O God, and maintain your cause].   *cf Psalm 74.18b, 21a*

O God, why have you utterly disowned us?
Why does your anger burn
against the sheep of your pasture?   R

Remember your congregation that you purchased of old,
the tribe you redeemed for your own possession,
and Mount Zion where you dwelt.
Hasten your steps towards the endless ruins,
where the enemy has laid waste all your sanctuary.   R

Arise, O God, maintain your own cause;
remember how fools revile you all the day long.
Forget not the clamour of your adversaries,
the tumult of your enemies that ascends continually.   R

       Psalm 74.1–3, 21–end

Year 1 and Year 2

Hear the Gospel of our Lord Jesus Christ according to Matthew.

When Jesus entered Capernaum, a centurion came to him, appealing to him and saying, 'Lord, my servant is lying at home paralysed, in terrible distress.' And he said to him, 'I will come and cure him.' The centurion answered, 'Lord, I am not worthy to have you come under my roof; but only speak the word, and my servant will be healed. For I also am a man under authority, with soldiers under me; and I say to one, "Go", and he goes, and to another, "Come", and he comes, and to my slave, "Do this", and the slave does it.' When Jesus heard him, he was amazed and said to those who followed him, 'Truly I tell you, in no one in Israel have I found such faith. I tell you, many will come from east and west and will eat with Abraham and Isaac and Jacob in the kingdom of heaven, while the heirs of the kingdom will be thrown into the outer darkness, where there will be weeping and gnashing of teeth.' And to the centurion Jesus said, 'Go; let it be done for you according to your faith.' And the servant was healed in that hour.

When Jesus entered Peter's house, he saw his mother-in-law lying in bed with a fever; he touched her hand, and the fever left her, and she got up and began to serve him. That evening they brought to him many who were possessed by demons; and he cast out the spirits with a word, and cured all who were sick. This was to fulfil what had been spoken through the prophet Isaiah, 'He took our infirmities and bore our diseases.'

This is the Gospel of the Lord.   *Matthew 8.5–17*

Week 13: Monday between 27 June and 3 July

Year 1

A reading from the book Genesis.

The men set out from Mamre, and they looked towards Sodom; and Abraham went with them to set them on their way. The LORD said, 'Shall I hide from Abraham what I am about to do, seeing that Abraham shall become a great and mighty nation, and all the nations of the earth shall be blessed in him? No, for I have chosen him, that he may charge his children and his household after him to keep the way of the LORD by doing righteousness and justice; so that the LORD may bring about for Abraham what he has promised him.' Then the LORD said, 'How great is the outcry against Sodom and Gomorrah and how very grave their sin! I must go down and see whether they have done altogether according to the outcry that has come to me; and if not, I will know.'

So the men turned from there, and went towards Sodom, while Abraham remained standing before the LORD. Then Abraham came near and said, 'Will you indeed sweep away the righteous with the wicked? Suppose there are fifty righteous within the city; will you then sweep away the place and not forgive it for the fifty righteous who are in it? Far be it from you to do such a thing, to slay the righteous with the wicked, so that the righteous fare as the wicked! Far be that from you! Shall not the Judge of all the earth do what is just?' And the LORD said, 'If I find at Sodom fifty righteous in the city, I will forgive the whole place for their sake.' Abraham answered, 'Let me take it upon myself to speak to the Lord, I who am but dust and ashes. Suppose five of the fifty righteous are lacking? Will you destroy the whole city for lack of five?' And he said, 'I will not destroy it if I find forty-five there.' Again he spoke to him, 'Suppose forty are found there.' He answered, 'For the sake of forty I will not do it.' Then he said, 'Oh do not let the Lord be angry if I speak. Suppose thirty are found there.' He answered, 'I will not do it, if I find thirty there.' He said, 'Let me take it upon myself to speak to the Lord. Suppose twenty are found there.' He answered, 'For the sake of twenty I will not destroy it.' Then he said, 'Oh do not let the Lord be angry if I speak just once more. Suppose ten are found there.' He answered, 'For the sake of ten I will not destroy it.' And the LORD went his way, when he had finished speaking to Abraham; and Abraham returned to his place.

This is the word of the Lord.   *Genesis 18.16—end*

Responsorial Psalm

R **The Lord is full of compassion and mercy:**
   [his goodness endures for ever].   cf Psalm 103.8a, 17a

The Lord executes righteousness
and judgement for all who are oppressed.
He made his ways known to Moses
and his works to the children of Israel.   R

The Lord is full of compassion and mercy,
slow to anger and of great kindness.
He will not always accuse us,
neither will he keep his anger for ever.   R

He has not dealt with us according to our sins,
nor rewarded us according to our wickedness.
For as the heavens are high above the earth,
so great is his mercy upon those who fear him.   R

As far as the east is from the west,
so far has he set our sins from us.
As a father has compassion on his children,
so is the Lord merciful towards those who fear him.   R

For he knows of what we are made;
he remembers that we are but dust.
Our days are but as grass;
we flourish as a flower of the field;
for as soon as the wind goes over it, it is gone,
and its place shall know it no more.   R

But the merciful goodness of the Lord is from of old
and endures for ever on those who fear him,
and his righteousness on children's children.   R   Psalm 103.6–17

Week 13: Monday 451

A reading from the prophecy of Amos.

Thus says the LORD:
For three transgressions of Israel,
    and for four, I will not revoke the punishment;
because they sell the righteous for silver,
    and the needy for a pair of sandals –
they who trample the head of the poor into the dust of the earth,
    and push the afflicted out of the way;
father and son go in to the same girl,
    so that my holy name is profaned;
they lay themselves down beside every altar
    on garments taken in pledge;
and in the house of their God they drink
    wine bought with fines they imposed.

Yet I destroyed the Amorite before them,
    whose height was like the height of cedars,
    and who was as strong as oaks;
I destroyed his fruit above,
    and his roots beneath.
Also I brought you up out of the land of Egypt,
    and led you for forty years in the wilderness,
    to possess the land of the Amorite.
So, I will press you down in your place,
    just as a cart presses down
    when it is full of sheaves.
Flight shall perish from the swift,
    and the strong shall not retain their strength,
    nor shall the mighty save their lives;
those who handle the bow shall not stand,
    and those who are swift of foot shall not save themselves,
    nor shall those who ride horses save their lives;
and those who are stout of heart among the mighty
    shall flee away naked on that day,
                  says the LORD.

This is the word of the Lord.   Amos 2.6–10, 13–end

Responsorial Psalm

R **The Lord will show salvation**
  to those who keep his way.   *cf Psalm 50.24b*

Why do you recite my statutes
and take my covenant upon your lips,
since you refuse to be disciplined
and have cast my words behind you?   R

When you saw a thief, you made friends with him
and you threw in your lot with adulterers.
You have loosed your lips for evil
and harnessed your tongue to deceit.   R

You sit and speak evil of your brother;
you slander your own mother's son.
These things have you done, and should I keep silence?
Did you think that I am even such a one as yourself?   R

But no, I must reprove you,
and set before your eyes the things that you have done.
You that forget God, consider this well,
lest I tear you apart and there is none to deliver you.   R   *Psalm 50.16–23*

Year 1 and Year 2

Hear the Gospel of our Lord Jesus Christ according to Matthew.

When Jesus saw great crowds around him, he gave orders to go over to the other side. A scribe then approached and said, 'Teacher, I will follow you wherever you go.' And Jesus said to him, 'Foxes have holes, and birds of the air have nests; but the Son of Man has nowhere to lay his head.' Another of his disciples said to him, 'Lord, first let me go and bury my father.' But Jesus said to him, 'Follow me, and let the dead bury their own dead.'

This is the Gospel of the Lord.   *Matthew 8.18–22*

Week 13: Tuesday between 28 June and 4 July

Year I

A reading from the book Genesis.

When morning dawned, the angels urged Lot, saying, 'Get up, take your wife and your two daughters who are here, or else you will be consumed in the punishment of the city.' But he lingered; so the men seized him and his wife and his two daughters by the hand, the LORD being merciful to him, and they brought him out and left him outside the city. When they had brought them outside, they said, 'Flee for your life; do not look back or stop anywhere in the Plain; flee to the hills, or else you will be consumed.' And Lot said to them, 'Oh, no, my lords; your servant has found favour with you, and you have shown me great kindness in saving my life; but I cannot flee to the hills, for fear the disaster will overtake me and I die. Look, that city is near enough to flee to, and it is a little one. Let me escape there – is it not a little one? – and my life will be saved!' He said to him, 'Very well, I grant you this favour too, and will not overthrow the city of which you have spoken. Hurry, escape there, for I can do nothing until you arrive there.' Therefore the city was called Zoar. The sun had risen on the earth when Lot came to Zoar.

Then the LORD rained on Sodom and Gomorrah sulphur and fire from the LORD out of heaven; and he overthrew those cities, and all the Plain, and all the inhabitants of the cities, and what grew on the ground. But Lot's wife, behind him, looked back, and she became a pillar of salt.

Abraham went early in the morning to the place where he had stood before the LORD; and he looked down towards Sodom and Gomorrah and towards all the land of the Plain, and saw the smoke of the land going up like the smoke of a furnace.

So it was that, when God destroyed the cities of the Plain, God remembered Abraham, and sent Lot out of the midst of the overthrow, when he overthrew the cities in which Lot had settled.

This is the word of the Lord.   *Genesis* 19.15–29

Responsorial Psalm

R **Your love, O Lord, is before my eyes.**   cf *Psalm* 26.3

Give judgement for me, O Lord,
for I have walked with integrity;
I have trusted in the Lord and have not faltered.
Test me, O Lord, and try me;
examine my heart and my mind.   **R**

For your love is before my eyes;
I have walked in your truth.
I have not joined the company of the false,
nor consorted with the deceitful.
I hate the gathering of evildoers
and I will not sit down with the wicked.   R

I will wash my hands in innocence, O Lord,
that I may go about your altar,
to make heard the voice of thanksgiving
and tell of all your wonderful deeds.
Lord, I love the house of your habitation
and the place where your glory abides.   R

Sweep me not away with sinners,
nor my life with the bloodthirsty,
whose hands are full of wicked schemes
and their right hand full of bribes.   R

As for me, I will walk with integrity;
redeem me, Lord, and be merciful to me.
My foot stands firm;
in the great congregation I will bless the Lord.   R   Psalm 26

Year 2

A reading from the prophecy of Amos.

Hear this word that the LORD has spoken against you, O people of Israel, against
the whole family that I brought up out of the land of Egypt:
    You only have I known
        of all the families of the earth;
    therefore I will punish you
        for all your iniquities.

    Do two walk together
        unless they have made an appointment?
    Does a lion roar in the forest,
        when it has no prey?
    Does a young lion cry out from its den,
        if it has caught nothing?
    Does a bird fall into a snare on the earth,
        when there is no trap for it?
    Does a snare spring up from the ground,
        when it has taken nothing?
    Is a trumpet blown in a city,
        and the people are not afraid?
    Does disaster befall a city,
        unless the LORD has done it?   →

Surely the Lord GOD does nothing,
   without revealing his secret
   to his servants the prophets.
The lion has roared;
   who will not fear?
The Lord GOD has spoken;
   who can but prophesy?

I overthrew some of you,
   as when God overthrew Sodom and Gomorrah,
   and you were like a brand snatched from the fire;
yet you did not return to me,
                              says the LORD.

Therefore, thus I will do to you, O Israel;
   because I will do this to you,
   prepare to meet your God, O Israel!

This is the word of the Lord.   Amos 3.1–8, 4.11–12

Responsorial Psalm

R* **You bless the righteous, O Lord:**
   [your favour defends them like a shield].   cf Psalm 5.14

Lead me, Lord, in your righteousness,
because of my enemies;
make your way straight before my face.   **R**

For there is no truth in their mouth,
in their heart is destruction,
their throat is an open sepulchre,
and they flatter with their tongue.   **R**

Punish them, O God;
let them fall through their own devices.
Because of their many transgressions cast them out,
for they have rebelled against you.   **R**

But let all who take refuge in you be glad;
let them sing out their joy for ever.
You will shelter them,
so that those who love your name may exult in you.   **R***   *Psalm 5.8–end*

Year 1 and Year 2

Hear the Gospel of our Lord Jesus Christ according to Matthew.

When Jesus got into the boat, his disciples followed him. A gale arose on the lake, so great that the boat was being swamped by the waves; but he was asleep. And they went and woke him up, saying, 'Lord, save us! We are perishing!' And he said to them, 'Why are you afraid, you of little faith?' Then he got up and rebuked the winds and the sea; and there was a dead calm. They were amazed, saying, 'What sort of man is this, that even the winds and the sea obey him?'

This is the Gospel of the Lord. *Matthew 8.23–27*

Week 13: Wednesday between 29 June and 5 July

Year 1

A reading from the book Genesis.

Abraham was a hundred years old when his son Isaac was born to him. The child grew, and was weaned; and Abraham made a great feast on the day that Isaac was weaned. But Sarah saw the son of Hagar the Egyptian, whom she had borne to Abraham, playing with her son Isaac. So she said to Abraham, 'Cast out this slave woman with her son; for the son of this slave woman shall not inherit along with my son Isaac.' The matter was very distressing to Abraham on account of his son. But God said to Abraham, 'Do not be distressed because of the boy and because of your slave woman; whatever Sarah says to you, do as she tells you, for it is through Isaac that offspring shall be named after you. As for the son of the slave woman, I will make a nation of him also, because he is your offspring.' So Abraham rose early in the morning, and took bread and a skin of water, and gave it to Hagar, putting it on her shoulder, along with the child, and sent her away. And she departed, and wandered about in the wilderness of Beer-sheba.

When the water in the skin was gone, she cast the child under one of the bushes. Then she went and sat down opposite him a good way off, about the distance of a bowshot; for she said, 'Do not let me look on the death of the child.' And as she sat opposite him, she lifted up her voice and wept. And God heard the voice of the boy; and the angel of God called to Hagar from heaven, and said to her, 'What troubles you, Hagar? Do not be afraid; for God has heard the voice of the boy where he is. Come, lift up the boy and hold him fast with your hand, for I will make a great nation of him.' Then God opened her eyes, and she saw a well of water. She went, and filled the skin with water, and gave the boy a drink.

God was with the boy, and he grew up; he lived in the wilderness, and became an expert with the bow.

This is the word of the Lord. *Genesis 21.5, 8–20*

Responsorial Psalm

R **Taste and see that the Lord is good:**
    [happy are all who trust in him].   cf Psalm 34.8

I will bless the Lord at all times;
his praise shall ever be in my mouth.
My soul shall glory in the Lord;
let the humble hear and be glad.   R

O magnify the Lord with me;
let us exalt his name together.
I sought the Lord and he answered me
and delivered me from all my fears.   R

Look upon him and be radiant
and your faces shall not be ashamed.
This poor soul cried, and the Lord heard me
and saved me from all my troubles.   R

The angel of the Lord encamps around those who fear him
and delivers them.
O taste and see that the Lord is gracious;
blessed is the one who trusts in him.   R

Fear the Lord, all you his holy ones,
for those who fear him lack nothing.
Lions may lack and suffer hunger,
but those who seek the Lord lack nothing that is good.   R

Come, my children, and listen to me;
I will teach you the fear of the Lord.
Who is there who delights in life
and longs for days to enjoy good things?   R   Psalm 34.1–12

Year 2

A reading from the prophecy of Amos.

Seek good and not evil,
    that you may live;
and so the Lord, the God of hosts, will be with you,
    just as you have said.
Hate evil and love good,
    and establish justice in the gate;
it may be that the Lord, the God of hosts,
    will be gracious to the remnant of Joseph.

I hate, I despise your festivals,
    and I take no delight in your solemn assemblies.
Even though you offer me your burnt-offerings and grain-offerings,

I will not accept them;
and the offerings of well-being of your fatted animals
    I will not look upon.
Take away from me the noise of your songs;
    I will not listen to the melody of your harps.
But let justice roll down like waters,
    and righteousness like an ever-flowing stream.

This is the word of the Lord.   Amos 5.14–15, 21–24

Responsorial Psalm

R* **Let us offer to God a sacrifice of thanksgiving:**
   [and fulfil our vows to the Most High].   cf Psalm 50.14

Hear, O my people, and I will speak:
I will testify against you, O Israel;
for I am God, your God.   **R**

I will not reprove you for your sacrifices,
for your burnt offerings are always before me.
I will take no bull out of your house,
nor he-goat out of your folds.   **R**

For all the beasts of the forest are mine,
the cattle upon a thousand hills.
I know every bird of the mountains
and the insect of the field is mine.   **R**

If I were hungry, I would not tell you,
for the whole world is mine and all that fills it.
Do you think I eat the flesh of bulls,
or drink the blood of goats?   **R***   Psalm 50.7–14

Year I and Year 2

Hear the Gospel of our Lord Jesus Christ according to Matthew.

When Jesus came to the country of the Gadarenes, two demoniacs coming out
of the tombs met him. They were so fierce that no one could pass that way.
Suddenly they shouted, 'What have you to do with us, Son of God? Have you
come here to torment us before the time?' Now a large herd of swine was
feeding at some distance from them. The demons begged him, 'If you cast us
out, send us into the herd of swine.' And he said to them, 'Go!' So they came
out and entered the swine; and suddenly, the whole herd rushed down the
steep bank into the lake and perished in the water. The swineherds ran off, and
on going into the town, they told the whole story about what had happened
to the demoniacs. Then the whole town came out to meet Jesus; and when
they saw him, they begged him to leave their neighbourhood.

This is the Gospel of the Lord.   Matthew 8.28–end

Week 13: Thursday between 30 June and 6 July

Year 1

A reading from the book Genesis.

God tested Abraham. He said to him, 'Abraham!' And he said, 'Here I am.' He said, 'Take your son, your only son Isaac, whom you love, and go to the land of Moriah, and offer him there as a burnt-offering on one of the mountains that I shall show you.' So Abraham rose early in the morning, saddled his donkey, and took two of his young men with him, and his son Isaac; he cut the wood for the burnt-offering, and set out and went to the place in the distance that God had shown him. On the third day Abraham looked up and saw the place far away. Then Abraham said to his young men, 'Stay here with the donkey; the boy and I will go over there; we will worship, and then we will come back to you.' Abraham took the wood of the burnt-offering and laid it on his son Isaac, and he himself carried the fire and the knife. So the two of them walked on together. Isaac said to his father Abraham, 'Father!' And he said, 'Here I am, my son.' He said, 'The fire and the wood are here, but where is the lamb for a burnt-offering?' Abraham said, 'God himself will provide the lamb for a burnt-offering, my son.' So the two of them walked on together.

When they came to the place that God had shown him, Abraham built an altar there and laid the wood in order. He bound his son Isaac, and laid him on the altar, on top of the wood. Then Abraham reached out his hand and took the knife to kill his son. But the angel of the LORD called to him from heaven, and said, 'Abraham, Abraham!' And he said, 'Here I am.' He said, 'Do not lay your hand on the boy or do anything to him; for now I know that you fear God, since you have not withheld your son, your only son, from me.' And Abraham looked up and saw a ram, caught in a thicket by its horns. Abraham went and took the ram and offered it up as a burnt-offering instead of his son. So Abraham called that place 'The LORD will provide'; as it is said to this day, 'On the mount of the LORD it shall be provided.'

The angel of the LORD called to Abraham a second time from heaven, and said, 'By myself I have sworn, says the LORD: Because you have done this, and have not withheld your son, your only son, I will indeed bless you, and I will make your offspring as numerous as the stars of heaven and as the sand that is on the seashore. And your offspring shall possess the gate of their enemies, and by your offspring shall all the nations of the earth gain blessing for themselves, because you have obeyed my voice.' So Abraham returned to his young men, and they arose and went together to Beer-sheba; and Abraham lived at Beer-sheba.

This is the word of the Lord.   *Genesis 22.1–19*

R* **[I called upon the name of the Lord:]**
  O Lord, deliver my soul.   cf Psalm 116.3

I love the Lord,
for he has heard the voice of my supplication;
because he inclined his ear to me
on the day I called to him.   **R**

The snares of death encompassed me;
the pains of hell took hold of me;
by grief and sorrow was I held.   **R***

Gracious is the Lord and righteous;
our God is full of compassion.
The Lord watches over the simple;
I was brought very low and he saved me.   **R**

Turn again to your rest, O my soul,
for the Lord has been gracious to you.
For you have delivered my soul from death,
my eyes from tears and my feet from falling.   **R**   Psalm 116.1–7

Year 2

A reading from the prophecy of Amos.

Amaziah, the priest of Bethel, sent to King Jeroboam of Israel, saying, 'Amos
has conspired against you in the very centre of the house of Israel; the land
is not able to bear all his words. For thus Amos has said,
  "Jeroboam shall die by the sword,
      and Israel must go into exile away from his land." '
And Amaziah said to Amos, 'O seer, go, flee away to the land of Judah, earn
your bread there, and prophesy there; but never again prophesy at Bethel, for
it is the king's sanctuary, and it is a temple of the kingdom.'
  Then Amos answered Amaziah, 'I am no prophet, nor a prophet's son;
but I am a herdsman, and a dresser of sycomore trees, and the LORD took
me from following the flock, and the LORD said to me, "Go, prophesy to my
people Israel."
  'Now therefore hear the word of the LORD.
  You say, "Do not prophesy against Israel,
      and do not preach against the house of Isaac."
  Therefore, thus says the LORD:
  "Your wife shall become a prostitute in the city,
      and your sons and your daughters shall fall by the sword,
      and your land shall be parcelled out by line;
  you yourself shall die in an unclean land,
      and Israel shall surely go into exile away from its land." '

This is the word of the Lord.   Amos 7.10–end

R **The judgements of the Lord are true:**
   more to be desired than gold.   *cf Psalm* 19.9b, 10a

The law of the Lord is perfect, reviving the soul;
the testimony of the Lord is sure
and gives wisdom to the simple.   **R**

The statutes of the Lord are right and rejoice the heart;
the commandment of the Lord is pure
and gives light to the eyes.   **R**

The fear of the Lord is clean and endures for ever;
the judgements of the Lord are true
and righteous altogether.   **R**

More to be desired are they than gold,
more than much fine gold,
sweeter also than honey,
dripping from the honeycomb.   **R**   *Psalm* 19.7–10

Year 1 and Year 2

Hear the Gospel of our Lord Jesus Christ according to Matthew.

And after getting into a boat Jesus crossed the water and came to his own town. And just then some people were carrying a paralysed man lying on a bed. When Jesus saw their faith, he said to the paralytic, 'Take heart, son; your sins are forgiven.' Then some of the scribes said to themselves, 'This man is blaspheming.' But Jesus, perceiving their thoughts, said, 'Why do you think evil in your hearts? For which is easier, to say, "Your sins are forgiven", or to say, "Stand up and walk"? But so that you may know that the Son of Man has authority on earth to forgive sins' – he then said to the paralytic – 'Stand up, take your bed and go to your home.' And he stood up and went to his home. When the crowds saw it, they were filled with awe, and they glorified God, who had given such authority to human beings.

This is the Gospel of the Lord.   *Matthew* 9.1–8

Week 13: Friday between 1 and 7 July

Year 1

A reading from the book Genesis.

Sarah lived for one hundred and twenty-seven years; this was the length of Sarah's life. And Sarah died at Kiriath-arba (that is, Hebron) in the land of Canaan; and Abraham went in to mourn for Sarah and to weep for her. Abraham rose up from beside his dead, and said to the Hittites, 'I am a stranger and an alien residing among you; give me property among you for a burying-place, so that I may bury my dead out of my sight.'

After this, Abraham buried Sarah his wife in the cave of the field of Machpelah facing Mamre (that is, Hebron) in the land of Canaan.

Now Abraham was old, well advanced in years; and the LORD had blessed Abraham in all things. Abraham said to his servant, the oldest of his house, who had charge of all that he had, 'Put your hand under my thigh and I will make you swear by the LORD, the God of heaven and earth, that you will not get a wife for my son from the daughters of the Canaanites, among whom I live, but will go to my country and to my kindred and get a wife for my son Isaac.' The servant said to him, 'Perhaps the woman may not be willing to follow me to this land; must I then take your son back to the land from which you came?' Abraham said to him, 'See to it that you do not take my son back there. The LORD, the God of heaven, who took me from my father's house and from the land of my birth, and who spoke to me and swore to me, "To your offspring I will give this land", he will send his angel before you; you shall take a wife for my son from there. But if the woman is not willing to follow you, then you will be free from this oath of mine; only you must not take my son back there.'

Now Isaac had come from Beer-lahai-roi, and was settled in the Negeb. Isaac went out in the evening to walk in the field; and looking up, he saw camels coming. And Rebekah looked up, and when she saw Isaac, she slipped quickly from the camel, and said to the servant, 'Who is the man over there, walking in the field to meet us?' The servant said, 'It is my master.' So she took her veil and covered herself. And the servant told Isaac all the things that he had done. Then Isaac brought her into his mother Sarah's tent. He took Rebekah, and she became his wife; and he loved her. So Isaac was comforted after his mother's death.

This is the word of the Lord.   *Genesis 23.1–4, 19, 24.1–8, 62–end*

R **Give thanks to the Lord, for he is gracious:**
   [his faithfulness endures for ever].   cf *Psalm* 106.1

   or

R **Alleluia!**

Give thanks to the Lord, for he is gracious,
for his faithfulness endures for ever.
Who can express the mighty acts of the Lord
or show forth all his praise?   R

Blessed are those who observe what is right
and always do what is just.
Remember me, O Lord,
in the favour you bear for your people.   R

Visit me in the day of your salvation,
that I may see the prosperity of your chosen;
and rejoice in the gladness of your people,
and exult with your inheritance.   R   *Psalm* 106.1–5

Year 2

A reading from the prophecy of Amos.

Hear this, you that trample on the needy,
   and bring to ruin the poor of the land,
saying, 'When will the new moon be over
   so that we may sell grain;
and the sabbath,
   so that we may offer wheat for sale?
We will make the ephah small and the shekel great,
   and practise deceit with false balances,
buying the poor for silver
   and the needy for a pair of sandals,
   and selling the sweepings of the wheat.'

On that day, says the Lord GOD,
   I will make the sun go down at noon,
   and darken the earth in broad daylight.
I will turn your feasts into mourning,
   and all your songs into lamentation;
I will bring sackcloth on all loins,
   and baldness on every head;
I will make it like the mourning for an only son,
   and the end of it like a bitter day.

The time is surely coming, says the Lord GOD,
  when I will send a famine on the land;
not a famine of bread, or a thirst for water,
  but of hearing the words of the LORD.
They shall wander from sea to sea,
  and from north to east;
they shall run to and fro, seeking the word of the LORD,
  but they shall not find it.

This is the word of the Lord.   *Amos 8.4–6, 9–12*

Responsorial Psalm

R **Blessed are they who fear the Lord,**
  [and walk in the ways of God].   *cf Psalm 128.1*

Blessed are those whose way is pure,
who walk in the law of the Lord.
Blessed are those who keep his testimonies
and seek him with their whole heart. **R**

Those who do no wickedness,
but walk in his ways.
You, O Lord, have charged
that we should diligently keep your commandments. **R**

O that my ways were made so direct
that I might keep your statutes.
Then should I not be put to shame,
because I have regard for all your commandments. **R**

I will thank you with an unfeigned heart,
when I have learned your righteous judgements.
I will keep your statutes;
O forsake me not utterly. **R**   *Psalm 119.1–8*

Year 1 and Year 2

Hear the Gospel of our Lord Jesus Christ according to Matthew.

As Jesus was walking along, he saw a man called Matthew sitting at the tax
booth; and he said to him, 'Follow me.' And he got up and followed him.
    And as he sat at dinner in the house, many tax-collectors and sinners
came and were sitting with him and his disciples. When the Pharisees saw
this, they said to his disciples, 'Why does your teacher eat with tax-collectors
and sinners?' But when he heard this, he said, 'Those who are well have no
need of a physician, but those who are sick. Go and learn what this means,
"I desire mercy, not sacrifice." For I have come to call not the righteous but
sinners.'

This is the Gospel of the Lord.   *Matthew 9.9–13*

Week 13: Saturday between 2 and 8 July

Year 1

A reading from the book Genesis.

When Isaac was old and his eyes were dim so that he could not see, he called his elder son Esau and said to him, 'My son'; and he answered, 'Here I am.' He said, 'See, I am old; I do not know the day of my death. Now then, take your weapons, your quiver and your bow, and go out to the field, and hunt game for me. Then prepare for me savoury food, such as I like, and bring it to me to eat, so that I may bless you before I die.'

Now Rebekah was listening when Isaac spoke to his son Esau. Then Rebekah took the best garments of her elder son Esau, which were with her in the house, and put them on her younger son Jacob; and she put the skins of the kids on his hands and on the smooth part of his neck. Then she handed the savoury food, and the bread that she had prepared, to her son Jacob.

So he went in to his father, and said, 'My father'; and he said, 'Here I am; who are you, my son?' Jacob said to his father, 'I am Esau your firstborn. I have done as you told me; now sit up and eat of my game, so that you may bless me.' But Isaac said to his son, 'How is it that you have found it so quickly, my son?' He answered, 'Because the LORD your God granted me success.' Then Isaac said to Jacob, 'Come near, that I may feel you, my son, to know whether you are really my son Esau or not.' So Jacob went up to his father Isaac, who felt him and said, 'The voice is Jacob's voice, but the hands are the hands of Esau.' He did not recognize him, because his hands were hairy like his brother Esau's hands; so he blessed him. He said, 'Are you really my son Esau?' He answered, 'I am.' Then he said, 'Bring it to me, that I may eat of my son's game and bless you.' So he brought it to him, and he ate; and he brought him wine, and he drank. Then his father Isaac said to him, 'Come near and kiss me, my son.' So he came near and kissed him; and he smelled the smell of his garments, and blessed him, and said,

'Ah, the smell of my son
    is like the smell of a field that the LORD has blessed.
May God give you of the dew of heaven,
    and of the fatness of the earth,
    and plenty of grain and wine.
Let peoples serve you,
    and nations bow down to you.
Be lord over your brothers,
    and may your mother's sons bow down to you.
Cursed be everyone who curses you,
    and blessed be everyone who blesses you!'

This is the word of the Lord.   Genesis 27.1–5a, 15–29

Responsorial Psalm

R **Praise the Lord, for he is good.**

or

R **Alleluia!**

Praise the name of the Lord;
give praise, you servants of the Lord,
you that stand in the house of the Lord,
in the courts of the house of our God. R

Praise the Lord, for the Lord is good;
make music to his name, for it is lovely.
For the Lord has chosen Jacob for himself
and Israel for his own possession. R

For I know that the Lord is great
and that our Lord is above all gods.
The Lord does whatever he pleases
in heaven and on earth,
in the seas and in all the deeps. R

cf Psalm 135.3a

Psalm 135.1–6

Year 2

A reading from the prophecy of Amos.

On that day I will raise up
    the booth of David that is fallen,
and repair its breaches,
    and raise up its ruins,
    and rebuild it as in the days of old;
in order that they may possess the remnant of Edom
    and all the nations who are called by my name,
    says the LORD who does this.

The time is surely coming, says the LORD,
    when the one who ploughs shall overtake the one who reaps,
    and the treader of grapes the one who sows the seed;
the mountains shall drip sweet wine,
    and all the hills shall flow with it.
I will restore the fortunes of my people Israel,
    and they shall rebuild the ruined cities and inhabit them;
they shall plant vineyards and drink their wine,
    and they shall make gardens and eat their fruit.
I will plant them upon their land,
    and they shall never again be plucked up
    out of the land that I have given them,
                    says the LORD your God.

This is the word of the Lord.

Amos 9.11–end

R **The Lord shall speak peace to the faithful;**
 [that his glory may dwell in our land]. *cf Psalm 85.8b, 9b*

I will listen to what the Lord God will say.
For he shall speak peace to his people and to the faithful,
that they turn not again to folly.
Truly, his salvation is near to those who fear him,
that his glory may dwell in our land. **R**

Mercy and truth are met together,
righteousness and peace have kissed each other.
Truth shall spring up from the earth
and righteousness look down from heaven. **R**

The Lord will indeed give all that is good,
and our land will yield its increase.
Righteousness shall go before him
and direct his steps in the way. **R** *Psalm 85.8–end*

Year 1 and Year 2

Hear the Gospel of our Lord Jesus Christ according to Matthew.

The disciples of John came to Jesus, saying, 'Why do we and the Pharisees fast often, but your disciples do not fast?' And Jesus said to them, 'The wedding-guests cannot mourn as long as the bridegroom is with them, can they? The days will come when the bridegroom is taken away from them, and then they will fast. No one sews a piece of unshrunk cloth on an old cloak, for the patch pulls away from the cloak, and a worse tear is made. Neither is new wine put into old wineskins; otherwise, the skins burst, and the wine is spilled, and the skins are destroyed; but new wine is put into fresh wineskins, and so both are preserved.'

This is the Gospel of the Lord. *Matthew 9.14–17*

Week 14: Monday between 4 and 10 July

Year 1

A reading from the book Genesis.

Jacob left Beer-sheba and went towards Haran. He came to a certain place and stayed there for the night, because the sun had set. Taking one of the stones of the place, he put it under his head and lay down in that place. And he dreamed that there was a ladder set up on the earth, the top of it reaching to heaven; and the angels of God were ascending and descending on it. And the Lord stood beside him and said, 'I am the Lord, the God of Abraham your father and the God of Isaac; the land on which you lie I will give to you and to your offspring; and your offspring shall be like the dust of the earth, and you shall spread abroad to the west and to the east and to the north and to the south; and all the families of the earth shall be blessed in you and in your offspring. Know that I am with you and will keep you wherever you go, and will bring you back to this land; for I will not leave you until I have done what I have promised you.' Then Jacob woke from his sleep and said, 'Surely the Lord is in this place – and I did not know it!' And he was afraid, and said, 'How awesome is this place! This is none other than the house of God, and this is the gate of heaven.'

So Jacob rose early in the morning, and he took the stone that he had put under his head and set it up for a pillar and poured oil on the top of it. He called that place Bethel; but the name of the city was Luz at the first. Then Jacob made a vow, saying, 'If God will be with me, and will keep me in this way that I go, and will give me bread to eat and clothing to wear, so that I come again to my father's house in peace, then the Lord shall be my God, and this stone, which I have set up for a pillar, shall be God's house; and of all that you give me I will surely give one-tenth to you.'

This is the word of the Lord.   *Genesis 28.10–end*

Responsorial Psalm

R **I have made the Lord my refuge,**
   [and the Most High my stronghold].   *cf Psalm 91.9*

Whoever dwells in the shelter of the Most High
and abides under the shadow of the Almighty,
shall say to the Lord, 'My refuge and my stronghold,
my God, in whom I put my trust.'   **R**

For he shall deliver you from the snare of the fowler
and from the deadly pestilence.
He shall cover you with his wings
and you shall be safe under his feathers;
his faithfulness shall be your shield and buckler.   **R**   →

You shall not be afraid of any terror by night,
nor of the arrow that flies by day;
of the pestilence that stalks in darkness,
nor of the sickness that destroys at noonday.   R

R   **I have made the Lord my refuge,
[and the Most High my stronghold].**

Though a thousand fall at your side
and ten thousand at your right hand,
yet it shall not come near you.
Your eyes have only to behold
to see the reward of the wicked.   R

Because you have made the Lord your refuge
and the Most High your stronghold,
there shall no evil happen to you,
neither shall any plague come near your tent.   R   Psalm 91.1–10

Year 2

A reading from the prophecy of Hosea.

The LORD said to Hosea:
　　I will persuade her,
　　　　and bring her into the wilderness,
　　　　and speak tenderly to her.
　　There she shall respond as in the days of her youth,
　　　　as at the time when she came out of the land of Egypt.
On that day, says the LORD, you will call me, 'My husband', and no longer will
you call me, 'My Baal'. And I will take you for my wife for ever; I will take you
for my wife in righteousness and in justice, in steadfast love, and in mercy. I
will take you for my wife in faithfulness; and you shall know the LORD.

This is the word of the Lord.   Hosea 2.14–16, 19–20

Responsorial Psalm

R   **I will bless the Lord every day,
and praise his name for ever.**   cf Psalm 145.2

Every day will I bless you
and praise your name for ever and ever.
Great is the Lord and highly to be praised;
his greatness is beyond all searching out.   R

One generation shall praise your works to another
and declare your mighty acts.
They shall speak of the majesty of your glory,
and I will tell of all your wonderful deeds.   R

They shall speak of the might of your marvellous acts,
and I will also tell of your greatness.
They shall pour forth the story of your abundant kindness
and joyfully sing of your righteousness. R

The Lord is gracious and merciful,
long-suffering and of great goodness.
The Lord is loving to everyone
and his mercy is over all his creatures. R   Psalm 145.2–9

Year 1 and Year 2

Hear the Gospel of our Lord Jesus Christ according to Matthew.

While Jesus was speaking, suddenly a leader of the synagogue came in and
knelt before him, saying, 'My daughter has just died; but come and lay your
hand on her, and she will live.' And Jesus got up and followed him, with his
disciples.

Then suddenly a woman who had been suffering from haemorrhages for
twelve years came up behind him and touched the fringe of his cloak, for she
said to herself, 'If I only touch his cloak, I will be made well.' Jesus turned,
and seeing her he said, 'Take heart, daughter; your faith has made you well.'
And instantly the woman was made well.

When Jesus came to the leader's house and saw the flute-players and the
crowd making a commotion, he said, 'Go away; for the girl is not dead but
sleeping.' And they laughed at him. But when the crowd had been put outside,
he went in and took her by the hand, and the girl got up. And the report of
this spread throughout that district.

This is the Gospel of the Lord.   Matthew 9.18–26

Week 14: Tuesday between 5 and 11 July

Year 1

A reading from the book Genesis.

Jacob got up and took his two wives, his two maids, and his eleven children,
and crossed the ford of the Jabbok. He took them and sent them across the
stream, and likewise everything that he had. Jacob was left alone; and a man
wrestled with him until daybreak. When the man saw that he did not prevail
against Jacob, he struck him on the hip socket; and Jacob's hip was put out of
joint as he wrestled with him. Then he said, 'Let me go, for the day is breaking.' But Jacob said, 'I will not let you go, unless you bless me.' So he said
to him, 'What is your name?' And he said, 'Jacob.' Then the man said, 'You
shall no longer be called Jacob, but Israel, for you have striven with God and
with humans, and have prevailed.' Then Jacob asked him, 'Please tell me your
name.' But he said, 'Why is it that you ask my name?' And there he blessed   →

him. So Jacob called the place Peniel, saying, 'For I have seen God face to face, and yet my life is preserved.' The sun rose upon him as he passed Penuel, limping because of his hip. Therefore to this day the Israelites do not eat the thigh muscle that is on the hip socket, because he struck Jacob on the hip socket at the thigh muscle.

This is the word of the Lord.   Genesis 32.22—end

Responsorial Psalm

R* **Keep me as the apple of your eye;**
    [hide me under the shadow of your wings].   Psalm 17.8

Hear my just cause, O Lord; consider my complaint;
listen to my prayer, which comes not from lying lips.
Let my vindication come forth from your presence;
let your eyes behold what is right.   R

Weigh my heart, examine me by night,
refine me, and you will find no impurity in me.
My mouth does not trespass for earthly rewards;
I have heeded the words of your lips.   R

My footsteps hold fast in the ways of your commandments;
my feet have not stumbled in your paths.
I call upon you, O God, for you will answer me;
incline your ear to me, and listen to my words.   R

Show me your marvellous loving-kindness,
O Saviour of those who take refuge at your right hand
from those who rise up against them.   R*   Psalm 17.1—8

Year 2

A reading from the prophecy of Hosea.

They made kings, but not through me;
    they set up princes, but without my knowledge.
With their silver and gold they made idols
    for their own destruction.
Your calf is rejected, O Samaria.
    My anger burns against them.
How long will they be incapable of innocence?
    For it is from Israel,
an artisan made it;
    it is not God.
The calf of Samaria
    shall be broken to pieces.
For they sow the wind,
    and they shall reap the whirlwind.

The standing grain has no heads,
  it shall yield no meal;
if it were to yield,
  foreigners would devour it.
When Ephraim multiplied altars to expiate sin,
  they became to him altars for sinning.
Though I write for him the multitude of my instructions,
  they are regarded as a strange thing.
Though they offer choice sacrifices,
  though they eat flesh,
  the LORD does not accept them.
Now he will remember their iniquity,
  and punish their sins;
  they shall return to Egypt.

This is the word of the Lord. *Hosea 8.4–7, 11–13*

Responsorial Psalm

R* **The Lord is full of compassion and mercy,
  [slow to anger and of great kindness].** *cf Psalm 103.8*

He will not always accuse us,
neither will he keep his anger for ever.
He has not dealt with us according to our sins,
nor rewarded us according to our wickedness. **R**

For as the heavens are high above the earth,
so great is his mercy upon those who fear him.
As far as the east is from the west,
so far has he set our sins from us. **R** *Psalm 103.8–12*

Year 1 and Year 2

Hear the Gospel of our Lord Jesus Christ according to Matthew.

A demoniac who was mute was brought to Jesus. And when the demon had been cast out, the one who had been mute spoke; and the crowds were amazed and said, 'Never has anything like this been seen in Israel.' But the Pharisees said, 'By the ruler of the demons he casts out the demons.'

Then Jesus went about all the cities and villages, teaching in their synagogues, and proclaiming the good news of the kingdom, and curing every disease and every sickness. When he saw the crowds, he had compassion for them, because they were harassed and helpless, like sheep without a shepherd. Then he said to his disciples, 'The harvest is plentiful, but the labourers are few; therefore ask the Lord of the harvest to send out labourers into his harvest.'

This is the Gospel of the Lord. *Matthew 9.32–end*

Year 1

A reading from the book Genesis.

When all the land of Egypt was famished, the people cried to Pharaoh for bread. Pharaoh said to all the Egyptians, 'Go to Joseph; what he says to you, do.' And since the famine had spread over all the land, Joseph opened all the storehouses, and sold to the Egyptians, for the famine was severe in the land of Egypt. Moreover, all the world came to Joseph in Egypt to buy grain, because the famine became severe throughout the world.

The sons of Israel were among the other people who came to buy grain, for the famine had reached the land of Canaan. Now Joseph was governor over the land; it was he who sold to all the people of the land. And Joseph's brothers came and bowed themselves before him with their faces to the ground. When Joseph saw his brothers, he recognized them, but he treated them like strangers and spoke harshly to them. 'Where do you come from?' he said. They said, 'From the land of Canaan, to buy food.' And he put them all together in prison for three days.

On the third day Joseph said to them, 'Do this and you will live, for I fear God: if you are honest men, let one of your brothers stay here where you are imprisoned. The rest of you shall go and carry grain for the famine of your households, and bring your youngest brother to me. Thus your words will be verified, and you shall not die.' And they agreed to do so. They said to one another, 'Alas, we are paying the penalty for what we did to our brother; we saw his anguish when he pleaded with us, but we would not listen. That is why this anguish has come upon us.' Then Reuben answered them, 'Did I not tell you not to wrong the boy? But you would not listen. So now there comes a reckoning for his blood.' They did not know that Joseph understood them, since he spoke with them through an interpreter. He turned away from them and wept; then he returned and spoke to them. And he picked out Simeon and had him bound before their eyes. Joseph then gave orders to fill their bags with grain, to return every man's money to his sack, and to give them provisions for their journey. This was done for them.

They loaded their donkeys with their grain, and departed. When one of them opened his sack to give his donkey fodder at the lodging-place, he saw his money at the top of the sack. He said to his brothers, 'My money has been put back; here it is in my sack!' At this they lost heart and turned trembling to one another, saying, 'What is this that God has done to us?'

When they came to their father Jacob in the land of Canaan, they told him all that had happened to them, saying, 'The man, the lord of the land, spoke harshly to us, and charged us with spying on the land. But we said to him, "We are honest men, we are not spies. We are twelve brothers, sons of our father; one is no more, and the youngest is now with our father in the land of Canaan." Then the man, the lord of the land, said to us, "By this I shall know that you are honest men: leave one of your brothers with me, take grain for the famine of your households, and go your way. Bring your youngest brother to me, and I shall know that you are not spies but honest men. Then I will release your brother to you, and you may trade in the land." '

As they were emptying their sacks, there in each one's sack was his bag of money. When they and their father saw their bundles of money, they were dismayed. And their father Jacob said to them, 'I am the one you have bereaved of children: Joseph is no more, and Simeon is no more, and now you would take Benjamin. All this has happened to me!' Then Reuben said to his father, 'You may kill my two sons if I do not bring him back to you. Put him in my hands, and I will bring him back to you.' But he said, 'My son shall not go down with you, for his brother is dead, and he alone is left. If harm should come to him on the journey that you are to make, you would bring down my grey hairs with sorrow to Sheol.'

This is the word of the Lord.　　　　　　　*Genesis 41.55–end, 42.5–7, 17–end*

Responsorial Psalm

R* **Let your loving-kindness, O Lord, be upon us,**
　　[as we have set our hope on you].　　　　　　*Psalm 33.22*

Rejoice in the Lord, O you righteous,
for it is good for the just to sing praises.
Praise the Lord with the lyre;
on the ten-stringed harp sing his praise.　**R**

Sing for him a new song;
play skilfully, with shouts of praise.
For the word of the Lord is true
and all his works are sure.　**R**

Behold, the eye of the Lord
is upon those who fear him,
on those who wait in hope for his steadfast love,
to deliver their soul from death
and to feed them in time of famine.　**R**

Our soul waits longingly for the Lord;
he is our help and our shield.
Indeed, our heart rejoices in him;
in his holy name have we put our trust.　**R***　　　*Psalm 33.1–4, 18–end*

A reading from the prophecy of Hosea.

Israel is a luxuriant vine
    that yields its fruit.
The more his fruit increased
    the more altars he built;
as his country improved,
    he improved his pillars.
Their heart is false;
    now they must bear their guilt.
The LORD will break down their altars,
    and destroy their pillars.

For now they will say:
    'We have no king,
for we do not fear the LORD,
    and a king – what could he do for us?'
Samaria's king shall perish
    like a splinter on the face of the waters.
The high places of Aven, the sin of Israel,
    shall be destroyed.
Thorn and thistle shall grow up
    on their altars.
They shall say to the mountains, Cover us,
    and to the hills, Fall on us.

Sow for yourselves righteousness;
    reap steadfast love;
    break up your fallow ground;
for it is time to seek the LORD,
    that he may come and rain righteousness upon you.

This is the word of the Lord.   Hosea 10.1–3, 7–8, 12

Responsorial Psalm

R **To your name, Lord, be the glory
    [for you are loving and faithful].**   cf Psalm 115.1

As for our God, he is in heaven;
he does whatever he pleases.
Their idols are silver and gold,
the work of human hands.   **R**

They have mouths, but cannot speak;
eyes have they, but cannot see;
they have ears, but cannot hear;
noses have they, but cannot smell. **R**

They have hands, but cannot feel;
feet have they, but cannot walk;
not a whisper do they make from their throats.
Those who make them shall become like them
and so will all who put their trust in them. **R**

But you, Israel, put your trust in the Lord;
he is their help and their shield.
House of Aaron, trust in the Lord;
he is their help and their shield. **R**   *Psalm 115.3–10*

Year 1 and Year 2

Hear the Gospel of our Lord Jesus Christ according to Matthew.

Jesus summoned his twelve disciples and gave them authority over unclean
spirits, to cast them out, and to cure every disease and every sickness. These
are the names of the twelve apostles: first, Simon, also known as Peter, and
his brother Andrew; James son of Zebedee, and his brother John; Philip
and Bartholomew; Thomas and Matthew the tax-collector; James son of
Alphaeus, and Thaddaeus; Simon the Cananaean, and Judas Iscariot, the one
who betrayed him.

These twelve Jesus sent out with the following instructions: 'Go nowhere
among the Gentiles, and enter no town of the Samaritans, but go rather to
the lost sheep of the house of Israel. As you go, proclaim the good news, "The
kingdom of heaven has come near." '

This is the Gospel of the Lord.   *Matthew 10.1–7*

Week 14: Thursday between 7 and 13 July

Year 1

A reading from the book Genesis.

Judah stepped up to Joseph and said, 'O my lord, let your servant please
speak a word in my lord's ears, and do not be angry with your servant; for
you are like Pharaoh himself. My lord asked his servants, saying, "Have you
a father or a brother?" And we said to my lord, "We have a father, an old
man, and a young brother, the child of his old age. His brother is dead; he
alone is left of his mother's children, and his father loves him." Then you
said to your servants, "Bring him down to me, so that I may set my eyes on
him." Then you said to your servants, "Unless your youngest brother comes →

down with you, you shall see my face no more." When we went back to your servant my father we told him the words of my lord. And when our father said, "Go again, buy us a little food", we said, "We cannot go down. Only if our youngest brother goes with us, will we go down; for we cannot see the man's face unless our youngest brother is with us." Then your servant my father said to us, "You know that my wife bore me two sons; one left me, and I said, Surely he has been torn to pieces; and I have never seen him since. If you take this one also from me, and harm comes to him, you will bring down my grey hairs in sorrow to Sheol." '

Then Joseph could no longer control himself before all those who stood by him, and he cried out, 'Send everyone away from me.' So no one stayed with him when Joseph made himself known to his brothers. And he wept so loudly that the Egyptians heard it, and the household of Pharaoh heard it. Joseph said to his brothers, 'I am Joseph. Is my father still alive?' But his brothers could not answer him, so dismayed were they at his presence.

Then Joseph said to his brothers, 'Come closer to me.' And they came closer. He said, 'I am your brother Joseph, whom you sold into Egypt. And now do not be distressed, or angry with yourselves, because you sold me here; for God sent me before you to preserve life.'

This is the word of the Lord. Genesis 44.18–21, 23–29, 45.1–5

Responsorial Psalm

R* **To you will I give the land of Canaan
[to be the portion of your inheritance].** Psalm 105.11

When they were but few in number,
of little account, and sojourners in the land,
wandering from nation to nation,
from one kingdom to another people.   R

He suffered no one to do them wrong
and rebuked even kings for their sake,
saying, 'Touch not my anointed
and do my prophets no harm.'   R

Then he called down famine over the land
and broke every staff of bread.
But he had sent a man before them,
Joseph, who was sold as a slave.   R Psalm 105.11–17

A reading from the prophecy of Hosea.

When Israel was a child, I loved him,
    and out of Egypt I called my son.
Yet it was I who taught Ephraim to walk,
    I took them up in my arms;
    but they did not know that I healed them.
I led them with cords of human kindness,
    with bands of love.
I was to them like those
    who lift infants to their cheeks.
    I bent down to them and fed them.

How can I give you up, Ephraim?
    How can I hand you over, O Israel?
How can I make you like Admah?
    How can I treat you like Zeboiim?
My heart recoils within me;
    my compassion grows warm and tender.
I will not execute my fierce anger;
    I will not again destroy Ephraim;
for I am God and no mortal,
    the Holy One in your midst,
    and I will not come in wrath.

This is the word of the Lord.   *Hosea* 11.1, 3–4, 8–9

Responsorial Psalm

R* Remember the marvels the Lord has done:
    [his wonders and the judgements he has given].   *cf Psalm* 105.5

O give thanks to the Lord and call upon his name;
make known his deeds among the peoples.
Sing to him, sing praises,
and tell of all his marvellous works.   **R**

Rejoice in the praise of his holy name;
let the hearts of them rejoice who seek the Lord.
Seek the Lord and his strength;
seek his face continually.   **R***

O seed of Abraham his servant,
O children of Jacob his chosen.
He is the Lord our God;
his judgements are in all the earth.   **R**   *Psalm* 105.1–7

Hear the Gospel of our Lord Jesus Christ according to Matthew.

Jesus said to the twelve, 'As you go, proclaim the good news, "The kingdom of heaven has come near." Cure the sick, raise the dead, cleanse the lepers, cast out demons. You received without payment; give without payment. Take no gold, or silver, or copper in your belts, no bag for your journey, or two tunics, or sandals, or a staff; for labourers deserve their food. Whatever town or village you enter, find out who in it is worthy, and stay there until you leave. As you enter the house, greet it. If the house is worthy, let your peace come upon it; but if it is not worthy, let your peace return to you. If anyone will not welcome you or listen to your words, shake off the dust from your feet as you leave that house or town. Truly I tell you, it will be more tolerable for the land of Sodom and Gomorrah on the day of judgement than for that town.'

This is the Gospel of the Lord.   Matthew 10.7–15

Week 14: Friday between 8 and 14 July

Year I

A reading from the book Genesis.

When Israel set out for Egypt with all that he had and came to Beer-sheba, he offered sacrifices to the God of his father Isaac. God spoke to Israel in visions of the night, and said, 'Jacob, Jacob.' And he said, 'Here I am.' Then he said, 'I am God, the God of your father; do not be afraid to go down to Egypt, for I will make of you a great nation there. I myself will go down with you to Egypt, and I will also bring you up again; and Joseph's own hand shall close your eyes.'

Then Jacob set out from Beer-sheba; and the sons of Israel carried their father Jacob, their little ones, and their wives, in the wagons that Pharaoh had sent to carry him. They also took their livestock and the goods that they had acquired in the land of Canaan, and they came into Egypt, Jacob and all his offspring with him, his sons, and his sons' sons with him, his daughters, and his sons' daughters; all his offspring he brought with him into Egypt.

Israel sent Judah ahead to Joseph to lead the way before him into Goshen. When they came to the land of Goshen, Joseph made ready his chariot and went up to meet his father Israel in Goshen. He presented himself to him, fell on his neck, and wept on his neck a good while. Israel said to Joseph, 'I can die now, having seen for myself that you are still alive.'

This is the word of the Lord.   Genesis 46.1–7, 28–30

R **Commit your way to the Lord
and put your trust in him.**   Psalm 37.5*a*

Trust in the Lord and be doing good;
dwell in the land and be nourished with truth.
Let your delight be in the Lord
and he will give you your heart's desire.   R

Commit your way to the Lord and put your trust in him,
and he will bring it to pass.
He will make your righteousness as clear as the light
and your just dealing as the noonday.   R

Depart from evil and do good
and you shall abide for ever.
For the Lord loves the thing that is right
and will not forsake his faithful ones.   R   Psalm 37.3–6, 27–28

Year 2

A reading from the prophecy of Hosea.

Take words with you
        and return to the LORD;
say to him,
        'Take away all guilt;
accept that which is good,
        and we will offer
        the fruit of our lips.
Assyria shall not save us;
        we will not ride upon horses;
we will say no more, "Our God",
        to the work of our hands.
In you the orphan finds mercy.'

I will heal their disloyalty;
        I will love them freely,
        for my anger has turned from them.
I will be like the dew to Israel;
        he shall blossom like the lily,
        he shall strike root like the forests of Lebanon.
His shoots shall spread out;
        his beauty shall be like the olive tree,
        and his fragrance like that of Lebanon.
They shall again live beneath my shadow,
        they shall flourish as a garden;
they shall blossom like the vine,
        their fragrance shall be like the wine of Lebanon.   →

O Ephraim, what have I to do with idols?
  It is I who answer and look after you.
I am like an evergreen cypress;
  your faithfulness comes from me.
Those who are wise understand these things;
  those who are discerning know them.
For the ways of the LORD are right,
  and the upright walk in them,
  but transgressors stumble in them.

This is the word of the Lord.   *Hosea 14.2—end*

Responsorial Psalm

R* **Make your face shine upon us, O Lord:**
  [restore us, and we shall be saved].   *cf Psalm 80.4, 8, 20*

Hear, O Shepherd of Israel,
you that led Joseph like a flock;
shine forth, you that are enthroned upon the cherubim,
before Ephraim, Benjamin and Manasseh.   **R**

Stir up your mighty strength
and come to our salvation.*
O Lord God of hosts,
how long will you be angry at your people's prayer?

You feed them with the bread of tears;
you give them abundance of tears to drink.
You have made us the derision of our neighbours,
and our enemies laugh us to scorn.   **R**   *Psalm 80.1—7*

Year 1 and Year 2

Hear the Gospel of our Lord Jesus Christ according to Matthew.

Jesus said to the twelve, 'I am sending you out like sheep into the midst of wolves; so be wise as serpents and innocent as doves. Beware of them, for they will hand you over to councils and flog you in their synagogues; and you will be dragged before governors and kings because of me, as a testimony to them and the Gentiles. When they hand you over, do not worry about how you are to speak or what you are to say; for what you are to say will be given to you at that time; for it is not you who speak, but the Spirit of your Father speaking through you. Brother will betray brother to death, and a father his child, and children will rise against parents and have them put to death; and you will be hated by all because of my name. But the one who endures to the end will be saved. When they persecute you in one town, flee to the next; for truly I tell you, you will not have gone through all the towns of Israel before the Son of Man comes.'

This is the Gospel of the Lord.   *Matthew 10.16—23*

Week 14: Saturday between 9 and 15 July

Year 1

A reading from the book Genesis.

Jacob charged his sons, saying to them, 'I am about to be gathered to my people. Bury me with my ancestors – in the cave in the field of Ephron the Hittite, in the cave in the field at Machpelah, near Mamre, in the land of Canaan, in the field that Abraham bought from Ephron the Hittite as a burial site. There Abraham and his wife Sarah were buried; there Isaac and his wife Rebekah were buried; and there I buried Leah – the field and the cave that is in it were purchased from the Hittites.' When Jacob ended his charge to his sons, he drew up his feet into the bed, breathed his last, and was gathered to his people.

Realizing that their father was dead, Joseph's brothers said, 'What if Joseph still bears a grudge against us and pays us back in full for all the wrong that we did to him?' So they approached Joseph, saying, 'Your father gave this instruction before he died, "Say to Joseph: I beg you, forgive the crime of your brothers and the wrong they did in harming you." Now therefore please forgive the crime of the servants of the God of your father.' Joseph wept when they spoke to him. Then his brothers also wept, fell down before him, and said, 'We are here as your slaves.' But Joseph said to them, 'Do not be afraid! Am I in the place of God? Even though you intended to do harm to me, God intended it for good, in order to preserve a numerous people, as he is doing today. So have no fear; I myself will provide for you and your little ones.' In this way he reassured them, speaking kindly to them.

So Joseph remained in Egypt, he and his father's household; and Joseph lived for one hundred and ten years. Joseph saw Ephraim's children of the third generation; the children of Machir son of Manasseh were also born on Joseph's knees.

Then Joseph said to his brothers, 'I am about to die; but God will surely come to you, and bring you up out of this land to the land that he swore to Abraham, to Isaac, and to Jacob.' So Joseph made the Israelites swear, saying, 'When God comes to you, you shall carry up my bones from here.'

This is the word of the Lord.   Genesis 49.29–end, 50.15–25

R* **Remember the marvels the Lord has done:**
   [his wonders and the judgements he has given].   *cf Psalm* 105.5

O give thanks to the Lord and call upon his name;
make known his deeds among the peoples.
Sing to him, sing praises,
and tell of all his marvellous works. **R**

Rejoice in the praise of his holy name;
let the hearts of them rejoice who seek the Lord.
Seek the Lord and his strength;
seek his face continually. **R***

O seed of Abraham his servant,
O children of Jacob his chosen.
He is the Lord our God;
his judgements are in all the earth. **R**   *Psalm* 105.1–7

Year 2

A reading from the prophecy of Isaiah.

In the year that King Uzziah died, I saw the Lord sitting on a throne, high and lofty; and the hem of his robe filled the temple. Seraphs were in attendance above him; each had six wings: with two they covered their faces, and with two they covered their feet, and with two they flew. And one called to another and said:
    'Holy, holy, holy is the Lord of hosts;
    the whole earth is full of his glory.'
The pivots on the thresholds shook at the voices of those who called, and the house filled with smoke. And I said: 'Woe is me! I am lost, for I am a man of unclean lips, and I live among a people of unclean lips; yet my eyes have seen the King, the Lord of hosts!'
    Then one of the seraphs flew to me, holding a live coal that had been taken from the altar with a pair of tongs. The seraph touched my mouth with it and said: 'Now that this has touched your lips, your guilt has departed and your sin is blotted out.' Then I heard the voice of the Lord saying, 'Whom shall I send, and who will go for us?' And I said, 'Here am I; send me!'

This is the word of the Lord.   *Isaiah* 6.1–8

Responsorial Psalm

R **Make me a clean heart, O God,
[and renew a right spirit within me].**   Psalm 51.11

Have mercy on me, O God,
in your great goodness;
according to the abundance of your compassion
blot out my offences. **R**

Wash me thoroughly from my wickedness
and cleanse me from my sin.
For I acknowledge my faults
and my sin is ever before me. **R**

Against you only have I sinned
and done what is evil in your sight,
so that you are justified in your sentence
and righteous in your judgement. **R**

I have been wicked even from my birth,
a sinner when my mother conceived me.
Behold, you desire truth deep within me
and shall make me understand wisdom
in the depths of my heart. **R**   Psalm 51.1–7

Year 1 and Year 2

Hear the Gospel of our Lord Jesus Christ according to Matthew.

Jesus said to the twelve, 'A disciple is not above the teacher, nor a slave above
the master; it is enough for the disciple to be like the teacher, and the slave
like the master. If they have called the master of the house Beelzebul, how
much more will they malign those of his household!

'So have no fear of them; for nothing is covered up that will not be
uncovered, and nothing secret that will not become known. What I say to you
in the dark, tell in the light; and what you hear whispered, proclaim from the
housetops. Do not fear those who kill the body but cannot kill the soul; rather
fear him who can destroy both soul and body in hell. Are not two sparrows
sold for a penny? Yet not one of them will fall to the ground unperceived by
your Father. And even the hairs of your head are all counted. So do not be
afraid; you are of more value than many sparrows.

'Everyone therefore who acknowledges me before others, I also will
acknowledge before my Father in heaven; but whoever denies me before
others, I also will deny before my Father in heaven.'

This is the Gospel of the Lord.   Matthew 10.24–33

Week 15: Monday between 11 and 17 July

Year 1

A reading from the Book of the Exodus.

A new king arose over Egypt, who did not know Joseph. He said to his people, 'Look, the Israelite people are more numerous and more powerful than we. Come, let us deal shrewdly with them, or they will increase and, in the event of war, join our enemies and fight against us and escape from the land.' Therefore they set taskmasters over them to oppress them with forced labour. They built supply cities, Pithom and Rameses, for Pharaoh. But the more they were oppressed, the more they multiplied and spread, so that the Egyptians came to dread the Israelites. The Egyptians became ruthless in imposing tasks on the Israelites, and made their lives bitter with hard service in mortar and brick and in every kind of field labour. They were ruthless in all the tasks that they imposed on them. Then Pharaoh commanded all his people, 'Every boy that is born to the Hebrews you shall throw into the Nile, but you shall let every girl live.'

This is the word of the Lord.   *Exodus 1.8–14, 22*

Responsorial Psalm

R* **Our help is in the name of the Lord,**
   [who has made heaven and earth].   *Psalm 124.7*

If the Lord himself had not been on our side,
now may Israel say;
if the Lord had not been on our side,
when enemies rose up against us.   **R**

Then would they have swallowed us alive
when their anger burned against us;
then would the waters have overwhelmed us
and the torrent gone over our soul;
over our soul would have swept the raging waters.   **R**

But blessed be the Lord
who has not given us over to be a prey for their teeth.
Our soul has escaped
as a bird from the snare of the fowler;
the snare is broken and we are delivered.   **R***   *Psalm 124*

Year 2

A reading from the prophecy of Isaiah.

What to me is the multitude of your sacrifices?
    says the LORD;
I have had enough of burnt-offerings of rams
    and the fat of fed beasts;
I do not delight in the blood of bulls,
    or of lambs, or of goats.

When you come to appear before me,
    who asked this from your hand?
Trample my courts no more;
bringing offerings is futile;
    incense is an abomination to me.
New moon and sabbath and calling of convocation –
    I cannot endure solemn assemblies with iniquity.
Your new moons and your appointed festivals
    my soul hates;
they have become a burden to me,
    I am weary of bearing them.
When you stretch out your hands,
    I will hide my eyes from you;
even though you make many prayers,
    I will not listen;
        your hands are full of blood.
Wash yourselves; make yourselves clean;
    remove the evil of your doings
        from before my eyes;
cease to do evil,
    learn to do good;
seek justice,
    rescue the oppressed,
defend the orphan,
    plead for the widow.

This is the word of the Lord.   *Isaiah* 1.11–17

Responsorial Psalm

R **Let us offer to God a sacrifice of thanksgiving:**
   [and fulfil our vows to the Most High].   *cf Psalm 50.14*

Hear, O my people, and I will speak:
I will testify against you, O Israel;
for I am God, your God.   R

I will not reprove you for your sacrifices,
for your burnt offerings are always before me.
I will take no bull out of your house,
nor he-goat out of your folds.   R

For all the beasts of the forest are mine,
the cattle upon a thousand hills.
I know every bird of the mountains
and the insect of the field is mine.   R

If I were hungry, I would not tell you,
for the whole world is mine and all that fills it.
Do you think I eat the flesh of bulls,
or drink the blood of goats?   R

Offer to God a sacrifice of thanksgiving
and fulfil your vows to God Most High.
Call upon me in the day of trouble;
I will deliver you and you shall honour me.   R   *Psalm 50.7–15*

Year 1 and Year 2

Hear the Gospel of our Lord Jesus Christ according to Matthew.

Jesus said to the twelve, 'Do not think that I have come to bring peace to the
earth; I have not come to bring peace, but a sword.
      For I have come to set a man against his father,
      and a daughter against her mother,
      and a daughter-in-law against her mother-in-law;
      and one's foes will be members of one's own household.
Whoever loves father or mother more than me is not worthy of me; and
whoever loves son or daughter more than me is not worthy of me; and whoever
does not take up the cross and follow me is not worthy of me. Those who find
their life will lose it, and those who lose their life for my sake will find it.
      'Whoever welcomes you welcomes me, and whoever welcomes me welcomes
the one who sent me. Whoever welcomes a prophet in the name of a prophet
will receive a prophet's reward; and whoever welcomes a righteous person in
the name of a righteous person will receive the reward of the righteous; and
whoever gives even a cup of cold water to one of these little ones in the name
of a disciple – truly I tell you, none of these will lose their reward.'
      Now when Jesus had finished instructing his twelve disciples, he went on
from there to teach and proclaim his message in their cities.

This is the Gospel of the Lord.   *Matthew 10.34 – 11.1*

Week 15: Tuesday between 12 and 18 July

Year I

A reading from the Book of the Exodus.

A man from the house of Levi went and married a Levite woman. The woman conceived and bore a son; and when she saw that he was a fine baby, she hid him for three months. When she could hide him no longer she got a papyrus basket for him, and plastered it with bitumen and pitch; she put the child in it and placed it among the reeds on the bank of the river. His sister stood at a distance, to see what would happen to him.

The daughter of Pharaoh came down to bathe at the river, while her attendants walked beside the river. She saw the basket among the reeds and sent her maid to bring it. When she opened it, she saw the child. He was crying, and she took pity on him. 'This must be one of the Hebrews' children,' she said. Then his sister said to Pharaoh's daughter, 'Shall I go and get you a nurse from the Hebrew women to nurse the child for you?' Pharaoh's daughter said to her, 'Yes.' So the girl went and called the child's mother. Pharaoh's daughter said to her, 'Take this child and nurse it for me, and I will give you your wages.' So the woman took the child and nursed it. When the child grew up, she brought him to Pharaoh's daughter, and she took him as her son. She named him Moses, 'because', she said, 'I drew him out of the water.'

One day, after Moses had grown up, he went out to his people and saw their forced labour. He saw an Egyptian beating a Hebrew, one of his kinsfolk. He looked this way and that, and seeing no one he killed the Egyptian and hid him in the sand. When he went out the next day, he saw two Hebrews fighting; and he said to the one who was in the wrong, 'Why do you strike your fellow Hebrew?' He answered, 'Who made you a ruler and judge over us? Do you mean to kill me as you killed the Egyptian?' Then Moses was afraid and thought, 'Surely the thing is known.' When Pharaoh heard of it, he sought to kill Moses. But Moses fled from Pharaoh and settled in the land of Midian.

This is the word of the Lord.   Exodus 2.1–15

Responsorial Psalm

R **Your saving help will lift me up:**
   I will praise your name in song.   *cf Psalm 69.31b, 32a*

Save me, O God,
  for the waters have come up, even to my neck.
I sink in deep mire where there is no foothold;
  I have come into deep waters and the flood sweeps over me.   **R**

As for me, I am poor and in misery;
  your saving help, O God, will lift me up.
I will praise the name of God with a song;
  I will proclaim his greatness with thanksgiving.   **R**

This will please the Lord more than an offering of oxen,
more than bulls with horns and hooves.
The humble shall see and be glad;
you who seek God, your heart shall live.   R

R **Your saving help will lift me up:**
   I will praise your name in song.

For the Lord listens to the needy,
and his own who are imprisoned he does not despise.
Let the heavens and the earth praise him,
the seas and all that moves in them.   R

For God will save Zion and rebuild the cities of Judah;
they shall live there and have it in possession.
The children of his servants shall inherit it,
and they that love his name shall dwell therein.   R   *Psalm 69.1–2, 31–end*

Year 2

A reading from the prophecy of Isaiah.

In the days of Ahaz son of Jotham son of Uzziah, king of Judah, King Rezin of
Aram and King Pekah son of Remaliah of Israel went up to attack Jerusalem,
but could not mount an attack against it. When the house of David heard that
Aram had allied itself with Ephraim, the heart of Ahaz and the heart of his
people shook as the trees of the forest shake before the wind.

Then the LORD said to Isaiah, Go out to meet Ahaz, you and your son
Shear-jashub, at the end of the conduit of the upper pool on the highway
to the Fuller's Field, and say to him, Take heed, be quiet, do not fear, and
do not let your heart be faint because of these two smouldering stumps of
firebrands, because of the fierce anger of Rezin and Aram and the son of
Remaliah. Because Aram – with Ephraim and the son of Remaliah – has plotted
evil against you, saying, Let us go up against Judah and cut off Jerusalem and
conquer it for ourselves and make the son of Tabeel king in it; therefore thus
says the Lord GOD:
   It shall not stand,
      and it shall not come to pass.
   For the head of Aram is Damascus,
      and the head of Damascus is Rezin.
   (Within sixty-five years Ephraim will be shattered,
      no longer a people.)
   The head of Ephraim is Samaria,
      and the head of Samaria is the son of Remaliah.
   If you do not stand firm in faith,
      you shall not stand at all.

This is the word of the Lord.   *Isaiah 7.1–9*

R **Great is the Lord and highly to be praised;**
   [our God is a sure refuge].   *Psalm* 48.1*a*, 4*b*

Great is the Lord and highly to be praised,
in the city of our God.
His holy mountain is fair and lifted high,
the joy of all the earth. R

On Mount Zion, the divine dwelling place,
stands the city of the great king.
In her palaces God has shown himself
to be a sure refuge. R

For behold, the kings of the earth assembled
and swept forward together.
They saw, and were dumbfounded;
dismayed, they fled in terror. R

Trembling seized them there;
they writhed like a woman in labour,
as when the east wind shatters the ships of Tarshish. R   *Psalm* 48.1–7

Year 1 and Year 2

Hear the Gospel of our Lord Jesus Christ according to Matthew.

Jesus began to reproach the cities in which most of his deeds of power had been done, because they did not repent. 'Woe to you, Chorazin! Woe to you, Bethsaida! For if the deeds of power done in you had been done in Tyre and Sidon, they would have repented long ago in sackcloth and ashes. But I tell you, on the day of judgement it will be more tolerable for Tyre and Sidon than for you. And you, Capernaum,
    will you be exalted to heaven?
    No, you will be brought down to Hades.
For if the deeds of power done in you had been done in Sodom, it would have remained until this day. But I tell you that on the day of judgement it will be more tolerable for the land of Sodom than for you.'

This is the Gospel of the Lord.   *Matthew* 11.20–24

Week 15: Wednesday between 13 and 19 July

Year 1

A reading from the Book of the Exodus.

Moses was keeping the flock of his father-in-law Jethro, the priest of Midian; he led his flock beyond the wilderness, and came to Horeb, the mountain of God. There the angel of the LORD appeared to him in a flame of fire out of a bush; he looked, and the bush was blazing, yet it was not consumed. Then Moses said, 'I must turn aside and look at this great sight, and see why the bush is not burned up.' When the LORD saw that he had turned aside to see, God called to him out of the bush, 'Moses, Moses!' And he said, 'Here I am.' Then he said, 'Come no closer! Remove the sandals from your feet, for the place on which you are standing is holy ground.' He said further, 'I am the God of your father, the God of Abraham, the God of Isaac, and the God of Jacob.' And Moses hid his face, for he was afraid to look at God.

Then the LORD said, 'The cry of the Israelites has now come to me; I have also seen how the Egyptians oppress them. So come, I will send you to Pharaoh to bring my people, the Israelites, out of Egypt.' But Moses said to God, 'Who am I that I should go to Pharaoh, and bring the Israelites out of Egypt?' He said, 'I will be with you; and this shall be the sign for you that it is I who sent you: when you have brought the people out of Egypt, you shall worship God on this mountain.'

This is the word of the Lord.   Exodus 3.1–6, 9–12

Responsorial Psalm

R* **Bless the Lord, O my soul,**
   [all that is within me bless his holy name].   cf Psalm 103.1

Bless the Lord, O my soul,
and forget not all his benefits.
Who forgives all your sins
and heals all your infirmities.   **R**

Who redeems your life from the Pit
and crowns you with faithful love and compassion;
who satisfies you with good things,
so that your youth is renewed like an eagle's.   **R**

The Lord executes righteousness
and judgement for all who are oppressed.
He made his ways known to Moses
and his works to the children of Israel.   **R**   Psalm 103.1–7

A reading from the prophecy of Isaiah.

Ah, Assyria, the rod of my anger –
    the club in their hands is my fury!
Against a godless nation I send him,
    and against the people of my wrath I command him,
to take spoil and seize plunder,
    and to tread them down like the mire of the streets.
But this is not what he intends,
    nor does he have this in mind;
but it is in his heart to destroy,
    and to cut off nations not a few. For he says:
'By the strength of my hand I have done it,
    and by my wisdom, for I have understanding;
I have removed the boundaries of peoples,
    and have plundered their treasures;
    like a bull I have brought down those who sat on thrones.
My hand has found, like a nest,
    the wealth of the peoples;
and as one gathers eggs that have been forsaken,
    so I have gathered all the earth;
and there was none that moved a wing,
    or opened its mouth, or chirped.'

Shall the axe vaunt itself over the one who wields it,
    or the saw magnify itself against the one who handles it?
As if a rod should raise the one who lifts it up,
    or as if a staff should lift the one who is not wood!
Therefore the Sovereign, the Lord of hosts,
    will send wasting sickness among his stout warriors,
and under his glory a burning will be kindled,
    like the burning of fire.

This is the word of the Lord.   *Isaiah 10.5–7, 13–16*

Responsorial Psalm

R* **The Lord knows every human thought,**
   [they are but an empty breath].   *cf Psalm 94.11*

They crush your people, O Lord,
and afflict your heritage.
They murder the widow and the stranger;
the orphans they put to death. **R**

And yet they say, 'The Lord will not see,
neither shall the God of Jacob regard it.'
Consider, most stupid of people;
you fools, when will you understand? **R**   →

He that planted the ear, shall he not hear?
He that formed the eye, shall he not see?
He who corrects the nations, shall he not punish?
He who teaches the peoples, does he lack knowledge?   R*   Psalm 94.5–11

R* **The Lord knows every human thought,**
   [they are but an empty breath].

Year 1 and Year 2

Hear the Gospel of our Lord Jesus Christ according to Matthew.

Jesus said, 'I thank you, Father, Lord of heaven and earth, because you have
hidden these things from the wise and the intelligent and have revealed them
to infants; yes, Father, for such was your gracious will. All things have been
handed over to me by my Father; and no one knows the Son except the Father,
and no one knows the Father except the Son and anyone to whom the Son
chooses to reveal him.'

This is the Gospel of the Lord.   Matthew 11.25–27

Week 15: Thursday between 14 and 20 July

Year 1

A reading from the Book of the Exodus.

Moses said to God, 'If I come to the Israelites and say to them, "The God of
your ancestors has sent me to you", and they ask me, "What is his name?"
what shall I say to them?' God said to Moses, 'I AM WHO I AM.' He said further,
'Thus you shall say to the Israelites, "I AM has sent me to you." ' God also said
to Moses, 'Thus you shall say to the Israelites, "The LORD, the God of your
ancestors, the God of Abraham, the God of Isaac, and the God of Jacob, has
sent me to you":
   This is my name for ever,
   and this my title for all generations.
Go and assemble the elders of Israel, and say to them, "The LORD, the God
of your ancestors, the God of Abraham, of Isaac, and of Jacob, has appeared
to me, saying: I have given heed to you and to what has been done to you in
Egypt. I declare that I will bring you up out of the misery of Egypt, to the land
of the Canaanites, the Hittites, the Amorites, the Perizzites, the Hivites, and
the Jebusites, a land flowing with milk and honey." They will listen to your
voice; and you and the elders of Israel shall go to the king of Egypt and say to
him, "The LORD, the God of the Hebrews, has met with us; let us now go a
three days' journey into the wilderness, so that we may sacrifice to the LORD
our God." I know, however, that the king of Egypt will not let you go unless
compelled by a mighty hand. So I will stretch out my hand and strike Egypt
with all my wonders that I will perform in it; after that he will let you go.'

This is the word of the Lord.   Exodus 3.13–20

Responsorial Psalm

R* **Sing to the Lord, sing praises,
[and tell of his marvellous works].** cf Psalm 105.2

O give thanks to the Lord and call upon his name;
make known his deeds among the peoples.   R*

Then Israel came into Egypt;
Jacob sojourned in the land of Ham.   R Psalm 105.1–2, 23

Year 2

A reading from the prophecy of Isaiah.

The way of the righteous is level;
  O Just One, you make smooth the path of the righteous.
In the path of your judgements,
  O LORD, we wait for you;
your name and your renown
  are the soul's desire.
My soul yearns for you in the night,
  my spirit within me earnestly seeks you.
For when your judgements are in the earth,
  the inhabitants of the world learn righteousness.
O LORD, in distress they sought you,
  they poured out a prayer
  when your chastening was on them.
Like a woman with child,
  who writhes and cries out in her pangs
  when she is near her time,
so were we because of you, O LORD;
  we were with child, we writhed,
  but we gave birth only to wind.
We have won no victories on earth,
  and no one is born to inhabit the world.
Your dead shall live, their corpses shall rise.
  O dwellers in the dust, awake and sing for joy!
For your dew is a radiant dew,
  and the earth will give birth to those long dead.

This is the word of the Lord. Isaiah 26.7–9, 16–19

R **O Lord, hear my prayer
and let my crying come before you.** *Psalm* 102.1

You will arise and have pity on Zion;
it is time to have mercy upon her;
surely the time has come.
For your servants love her very stones
and feel compassion for her dust.   R

Then shall the nations fear your name, O Lord,
and all the kings of the earth your glory,
when the Lord has built up Zion
and shown himself in glory.   R

When he has turned to the prayer of the destitute
and has not despised their plea.
This shall be written for those that come after,
and a people yet unborn shall praise the Lord.   R

For he has looked down from his holy height;
from the heavens he beheld the earth,
that he might hear the sighings of the prisoner
and set free those condemned to die.   R *Psalm* 102.14–21

Year 1 and Year 2

Hear the Gospel of our Lord Jesus Christ according to Matthew.

Jesus said, 'Come to me, all you that are weary and are carrying heavy burdens,
and I will give you rest. Take my yoke upon you, and learn from me; for I
am gentle and humble in heart, and you will find rest for your souls. For my
yoke is easy, and my burden is light.'

This is the Gospel of the Lord. *Matthew* 11.28–end

Week 15: Friday between 15 and 21 July

Year 1

A reading from the Book of the Exodus.

Moses and Aaron performed all these wonders before Pharaoh; but the LORD hardened Pharaoh's heart, and he did not let the people of Israel go out of his land.

The LORD said to Moses and Aaron in the land of Egypt: 'This month shall mark for you the beginning of months; it shall be the first month of the year for you. Tell the whole congregation of Israel that on the tenth of this month they are to take a lamb for each family, a lamb for each household. If a household is too small for a whole lamb, it shall join its closest neighbour in obtaining one; the lamb shall be divided in proportion to the number of people who eat of it. Your lamb shall be without blemish, a year-old male; you may take it from the sheep or from the goats. You shall keep it until the fourteenth day of this month; then the whole assembled congregation of Israel shall slaughter it at twilight.

'They shall take some of the blood and put it on the two doorposts and the lintel of the houses in which they eat it. They shall eat the lamb that same night; they shall eat it roasted over the fire with unleavened bread and bitter herbs. Do not eat any of it raw or boiled in water, but roasted over the fire, with its head, legs, and inner organs. You shall let none of it remain until the morning; anything that remains until the morning you shall burn. This is how you shall eat it: your loins girded, your sandals on your feet, and your staff in your hand; and you shall eat it hurriedly. It is the passover of the LORD. For I will pass through the land of Egypt that night, and I will strike down every firstborn in the land of Egypt, both human beings and animals; on all the gods of Egypt I will execute judgements: I am the LORD. The blood shall be a sign for you on the houses where you live: when I see the blood, I will pass over you, and no plague shall destroy you when I strike the land of Egypt.

'This day shall be a day of remembrance for you. You shall celebrate it as a festival to the LORD; throughout your generations you shall observe it as a perpetual ordinance.'

This is the word of the Lord.   *Exodus 11.10 – 12.14*

Responsorial Psalm

R **I will offer to you a sacrifice of thanksgiving:**
   [and call upon the name of the Lord].   *Psalm 116.15*

   or

R **Alleluia!**

How shall I repay the Lord
for all the benefits he has given to me?
I will lift up the cup of salvation
and call upon the name of the Lord.   **R**

I will fulfil my vows to the Lord
in the presence of all his people.
Precious in the sight of the Lord
is the death of his faithful servants.   **R**

O Lord, I am your servant,
your servant, the child of your handmaid;
you have freed me from my bonds.
I will offer to you a sacrifice of thanksgiving
and call upon the name of the Lord.   **R**

I will fulfil my vows to the Lord
in the presence of all his people,
in the courts of the house of the Lord,
in the midst of you, O Jerusalem.   **R**   *Psalm 116.10–end*

Year 2

A reading from the prophecy of Isaiah.

Hezekiah became sick and was at the point of death. The prophet Isaiah son of Amoz came to him, and said to him, 'Thus says the LORD: Set your house in order, for you shall die; you shall not recover.' Then Hezekiah turned his face to the wall, and prayed to the LORD: 'Remember now, O LORD, I implore you, how I have walked before you in faithfulness with a whole heart, and have done what is good in your sight.' And Hezekiah wept bitterly.

Then the word of the LORD came to Isaiah: 'Go and say to Hezekiah, Thus says the LORD, the God of your ancestor David: I have heard your prayer, I have seen your tears; I will add fifteen years to your life. I will deliver you and this city out of the hand of the king of Assyria, and defend this city.'

Now Isaiah had said, 'Let them take a lump of figs, and apply it to the boil, so that he may recover.' Hezekiah also had said, 'What is the sign that I shall go up to the house of the LORD?'

Isaiah said, 'This is the sign to you from the LORD, that the LORD will do this thing that he has promised: See, I will make the shadow cast by the declining sun on the dial of Ahaz turn back ten steps.' So the sun turned back on the dial the ten steps by which it had declined.

This is the word of the Lord.   *Isaiah 38.1–6, 21–22, 7–8 [sic]*

Either

Canticle

R **Your love, O Lord, has saved me from death:**
   [and my sins you have set aside].   cf *Isaiah* 38.17b

In the noontide of my days I must pass away;
I am consigned to the underworld
for the rest of my years.
I shall not see the Lord in the land of the living;
I shall look no more upon mortals,
upon the inhabitants of the world.   R

My dwelling is plucked up
and removed from me like a shepherd's tent;
you have rolled up my life,
like a weaver who cuts me from the loom.
Day and night I am tormented,
I cry for help until morning.   R

All my bones are broken as if by a lion.
Like a swallow or a crane I twitter,
I moan like a dove.
My eyes are weary with looking upwards.
O Lord, I am oppressed;
be my safeguard.   R

But what can I say? For he has spoken to me,
and he himself has done this.
All my sleep has fled because of the bitterness of my soul.
O Lord, because of you my spirit will live,
give rest to my spirit;
O restore me to health and give me life!   R   *Isaiah* 38.10–16

or

Responsorial Psalm

R **Your love, O Lord, has saved me from death:**
   [and my sins you have set aside].   *cf Isaiah 38.17b*

Happy the one whose transgression is forgiven,
and whose sin is covered.
Happy the one to whom the Lord imputes no guilt,
and in whose spirit there is no guile.   R

For I held my tongue;
my bones wasted away
through my groaning all the day long.   R

Your hand was heavy upon me day and night;
my moisture was dried up like the drought in summer.
Then I acknowledged my sin to you
and my iniquity I did not hide.   R

I said, 'I will confess my transgressions to the Lord,'
and you forgave the guilt of my sin.
Therefore let all the faithful make their prayers to you
    in time of trouble;
in the great water flood, it shall not reach them.   R

You are a place for me to hide in;
you preserve me from trouble;
you surround me with songs of deliverance.   R   *Psalm 32.1–8*

Year 1 and Year 2

Hear the Gospel of our Lord Jesus Christ according to Matthew.

Jesus went through the cornfields on the sabbath; his disciples were hungry,
and they began to pluck heads of grain and to eat. When the Pharisees saw it,
they said to him, 'Look, your disciples are doing what is not lawful to do on
the sabbath.' He said to them, 'Have you not read what David did when he
and his companions were hungry? He entered the house of God and ate the
bread of the Presence, which it was not lawful for him or his companions
to eat, but only for the priests. Or have you not read in the law that on the
sabbath the priests in the temple break the sabbath and yet are guiltless? I tell
you, something greater than the temple is here. But if you had known what
this means, "I desire mercy and not sacrifice", you would not have condemned
the guiltless. For the Son of Man is lord of the sabbath.'

This is the Gospel of the Lord.   *Matthew 12.1–8*

Week 15: Saturday between 16 and 22 July

Year 1

A reading from the Book of the Exodus.

The Israelites journeyed from Rameses to Succoth, about six hundred thousand men on foot, besides children. A mixed crowd also went up with them, and livestock in great numbers, both flocks and herds. They baked unleavened cakes of the dough that they had brought out of Egypt; it was not leavened, because they were driven out of Egypt and could not wait, nor had they prepared any provisions for themselves.

The time that the Israelites had lived in Egypt was four hundred and thirty years. At the end of four hundred and thirty years, on that very day, all the companies of the LORD went out from the land of Egypt. That was for the LORD a night of vigil, to bring them out of the land of Egypt. That same night is a vigil to be kept for the LORD by all the Israelites throughout their generations.

This is the word of the Lord.   Exodus 12.37–42

Responsorial Psalm

R **His mercy endures for ever.**

Give thanks to the Lord, for he is gracious: [R]
Give thanks to the God of gods: R

Give thanks to the Lord of lords: [R]
Who alone does great wonders: R

Who smote the firstborn of Egypt: [R]
and brought out Israel from among them: [R]
with a mighty hand and outstretched arm: R

Who divided the Red Sea in two: [R]
and made Israel to pass through the midst of it: [R]
But Pharaoh and his host he overthrew in the Red Sea: R
                                        Psalm 136.1–4, 10–15

A reading from the prophecy of Micah.

Alas for those who devise wickedness
    and evil deeds on their beds!
When the morning dawns, they perform it,
    because it is in their power.
They covet fields, and seize them;
    houses, and take them away;
they oppress householder and house,
    people and their inheritance.
Therefore, thus says the LORD:
Now, I am devising against this family an evil
    from which you cannot remove your necks;
and you shall not walk haughtily,
    for it will be an evil time.
On that day they shall take up a taunt-song against you,
    and wail with bitter lamentation,
and say, 'We are utterly ruined;
    the LORD alters the inheritance of my people;
how he removes it from me!
    Among our captors he parcels out our fields.'
Therefore you will have no one to cast the line by lot
    in the assembly of the LORD.

This is the word of the Lord.   Micah 2.1–5

Responsorial Psalm

R **The Lord hears the desire of the poor;**
   [he gives justice to the orphan and the oppressed]. cf Psalm 10.18a, 19a

Why stand so far off, O Lord?
Why hide yourself in time of trouble?
The wicked in their pride persecute the poor;
let them be caught in the schemes they have devised. **R**

The wicked boast of their heart's desire;
the covetous curse and revile the Lord.
The wicked in their arrogance say, 'God will not avenge it';
in all their scheming God counts for nothing. **R**

They are stubborn in all their ways,
for your judgements are far above out of their sight;
arise, O Lord God, and lift up your hand;
forget not the poor. **R**   Psalm 10.1–5a, 12

Hear the Gospel of our Lord Jesus Christ according to Matthew.

The Pharisees went out and conspired against Jesus, how to destroy him. When Jesus became aware of this, he departed. Many crowds followed him, and he cured all of them, and he ordered them not to make him known. This was to fulfil what had been spoken through the prophet Isaiah:
    'Here is my servant, whom I have chosen,
        my beloved, with whom my soul is well pleased.
    I will put my Spirit upon him,
        and he will proclaim justice to the Gentiles.
    He will not wrangle or cry aloud,
        nor will anyone hear his voice in the streets.
    He will not break a bruised reed
        or quench a smouldering wick
    until he brings justice to victory.
        And in his name the Gentiles will hope.'

This is the Gospel of the Lord. Matthew 12.14–21

Week 16: Monday between 18 and 24 July

Year 1

A reading from the Book of the Exodus.

When the king of Egypt was told that the Israelites had fled, the minds of Pharaoh and his officials were changed towards the people, and they said, 'What have we done, letting Israel leave our service?' So he had his chariot made ready, and took his army with him; he took six hundred picked chariots and all the other chariots of Egypt with officers over all of them. The LORD hardened the heart of Pharaoh king of Egypt and he pursued the Israelites, who were going out boldly. The Egyptians pursued them, all Pharaoh's horses and chariots, his chariot drivers and his army; they overtook them camped by the sea, by Pi-hahiroth, in front of Baal-zephon.

As Pharaoh drew near, the Israelites looked back, and there were the Egyptians advancing on them. In great fear the Israelites cried out to the LORD. They said to Moses, 'Was it because there were no graves in Egypt that you have taken us away to die in the wilderness? What have you done to us, bringing us out of Egypt? Is this not the very thing we told you in Egypt, "Let us alone and let us serve the Egyptians"? For it would have been better for us to serve the Egyptians than to die in the wilderness.' But Moses said to the people, 'Do not be afraid, stand firm, and see the deliverance that the LORD will accomplish for you today; for the Egyptians whom you see today you shall never see again. The LORD will fight for you, and you have only to keep still.'

Then the LORD said to Moses, 'Why do you cry out to me? Tell the Israelites to go forward. But you lift up your staff, and stretch out your hand over the sea and divide it, that the Israelites may go into the sea on dry ground. Then I will harden the hearts of the Egyptians so that they will go in after them; and so I will gain glory for myself over Pharaoh and all his army, his chariots, and his chariot drivers. And the Egyptians shall know that I am the LORD, when I have gained glory for myself over Pharaoh, his chariots, and his chariot drivers.'

This is the word of the Lord.   *Exodus 14.5–18*

Either

Canticle

R **I will sing to the Lord: glorious his triumph!**   *cf Exodus 15.1b*

I will sing to the Lord, who has triumphed gloriously,
the horse and his rider he has thrown into the sea.
The Lord is my strength and my song
and has become my salvation.   **R**

This is my God whom I will praise,
the God of my forebears whom I will exalt.
The Lord is a warrior;
the Lord is his name.   R

Pharaoh's chariots and his army he cast into the sea;
his picked officers were sunk in the Red Sea.
The floods covered them;
they sank into the depths like a stone.   R

Your right hand, O Lord, is glorious in power:
your right hand, O Lord, shatters the enemy.   R   Exodus 15.1–6

or

Responsorial Psalm

R **His mercy endures for ever.**

Give thanks to the Lord, for he is gracious: [R]
Give thanks to the God of gods: R

Give thanks to the Lord of lords: [R]
Who alone does great wonders: R

Who smote the firstborn of Egypt: [R]
and brought out Israel from among them: [R]
with a mighty hand and outstretched arm: R

Who divided the Red Sea in two: [R]
and made Israel to pass through the midst of it: [R]
But Pharaoh and his host he overthrew in the Red Sea: R
                                                    Psalm 136.1–4, 10–15

Year 2

A reading from the prophecy of Micah.

Hear what the LORD says:
    Rise, plead your case before the mountains,
        and let the hills hear your voice.
Hear, you mountains, the controversy of the LORD,
        and you enduring foundations of the earth;
for the LORD has a controversy with his people,
        and he will contend with Israel.

'O my people, what have I done to you?
    In what have I wearied you? Answer me!
For I brought you up from the land of Egypt,
        and redeemed you from the house of slavery;
and I sent before you Moses,
        Aaron, and Miriam.   →

'With what shall I come before the LORD,
　　and bow myself before God on high?
Shall I come before him with burnt-offerings,
　　with calves a year old?
Will the LORD be pleased with thousands of rams,
　　with tens of thousands of rivers of oil?
Shall I give my firstborn for my transgression,
　　the fruit of my body for the sin of my soul?'
He has told you, O mortal, what is good;
　　and what does the LORD require of you
but to do justice, and to love kindness,
　　and to walk humbly with your God?

This is the word of the Lord.　　　　　　　　　　　　Micah 6.1–4, 6–8

Responsorial Psalm

R* **Let us offer to God a sacrifice of thanksgiving:**
　　[and fulfil our vows to the Most High].　　　　cf Psalm 50.14

Consuming fire goes out before him
and a mighty tempest stirs about him.
He calls the heaven above,
and the earth, that he may judge his people.　**R**

'Gather to me my faithful,
who have sealed my covenant with sacrifice.'
Let the heavens declare his righteousness,
for God himself is judge.　**R**

Hear, O my people, and I will speak:
'I will testify against you, O Israel;
for I am God, your God.'　**R***　　　　　　　　　Psalm 50.3–7, 14

Year 1 and Year 2

Hear the Gospel of our Lord Jesus Christ according to Matthew.

Some of the scribes and Pharisees said to Jesus, 'Teacher, we wish to see a
sign from you.' But he answered them, 'An evil and adulterous generation
asks for a sign, but no sign will be given to it except the sign of the prophet
Jonah. For just as Jonah was for three days and three nights in the belly of
the sea monster, so for three days and three nights the Son of Man will be in
the heart of the earth. The people of Nineveh will rise up at the judgement
with this generation and condemn it, because they repented at the proclamation of Jonah, and see, something greater than Jonah is here! The queen of
the South will rise up at the judgement with this generation and condemn
it, because she came from the ends of the earth to listen to the wisdom of
Solomon, and see, something greater than Solomon is here!'

This is the Gospel of the Lord.　　　　　　　　　　Matthew 12.38–42

Week 16: Tuesday between 19 and 25 July

Year 1

A reading from the Book of the Exodus.

Moses stretched out his hand over the sea. The LORD drove the sea back by a strong east wind all night, and turned the sea into dry land; and the waters were divided. The Israelites went into the sea on dry ground, the waters forming a wall for them on their right and on their left. The Egyptians pursued, and went into the sea after them, all of Pharaoh's horses, chariots, and chariot drivers. At the morning watch the LORD in the pillar of fire and cloud looked down upon the Egyptian army, and threw the Egyptian army into panic. He clogged their chariot wheels so that they turned with difficulty. The Egyptians said, 'Let us flee from the Israelites, for the LORD is fighting for them against Egypt.'

Then the LORD said to Moses, 'Stretch out your hand over the sea, so that the water may come back upon the Egyptians, upon their chariots and chariot drivers.' So Moses stretched out his hand over the sea, and at dawn the sea returned to its normal depth. As the Egyptians fled before it, the LORD tossed the Egyptians into the sea. The waters returned and covered the chariots and the chariot drivers, the entire army of Pharaoh that had followed them into the sea; not one of them remained. But the Israelites walked on dry ground through the sea, the waters forming a wall for them on their right and on their left.

Thus the LORD saved Israel that day from the Egyptians; and Israel saw the Egyptians dead on the seashore. Israel saw the great work that the LORD did against the Egyptians. So the people feared the LORD and believed in the LORD and in his servant Moses. Then Moses and the Israelites sang this song to the LORD.

If the Canticle (Exodus 15.8–10, 12, 17) is used it may follow immediately; otherwise the reader may say:

This is the word of the Lord.　　　　　　　　　　　　　　Exodus 14.21 – 15.1a

Either

Canticle

R　**I will sing to the Lord: glorious his triumph!**　　　　cf Exodus 15.1b

At the blast of your anger, the sea piled high;
the floods stood up like a bank;
the deeps turned solid in the heart of the sea.
The enemy boasted, 'I shall pursue, I shall overtake,
I shall divide the spoil, my desire shall have its fill of them.　**R**　→

I shall draw my sword, my hand shall destroy them.'
You blew with your breath, the sea covered them;
they sank like lead in the mighty waters.
You will bring your people in and plant them, O Lord,
on the mountain that you have made your home,
in the sanctuary which your hands have established.   R

Exodus 15.8–10, 12, 17

R   I will sing to the Lord: glorious his triumph!

or

Responsorial Psalm

**R   Sing to the Lord, sing praises,
      [and tell of his marvellous works].**

cf Psalm 105.2

He brought them out with silver and gold;
there was not one among their tribes that stumbled.
Egypt was glad at their departing,
for a dread of them had fallen upon them.   R

He spread out a cloud for a covering
and a fire to light up the night.
They asked and he brought them quails;
he satisfied them with the bread of heaven.
He opened the rock, and the waters gushed out
and ran in the dry places like a river.   R

For he remembered his holy word
and Abraham, his servant.
So he brought forth his people with joy,
his chosen ones with singing.
He gave them the lands of the nations
and they took possession of the fruit of their toil.   R   Psalm 105.37–44

Year 2

A reading from the prophecy of Micah.

Shepherd your people with your staff,
    the flock that belongs to you,
which lives alone in a forest
    in the midst of a garden land;
let them feed in Bashan and Gilead
    as in the days of old.
As in the days when you came out of the land of Egypt,
    show us marvellous things.

Who is a God like you, pardoning iniquity
    and passing over the transgression
    of the remnant of your possession?
He does not retain his anger for ever,
    because he delights in showing clemency.
He will again have compassion upon us;
    he will tread our iniquities under foot.
You will cast all our sins
    into the depths of the sea.
You will show faithfulness to Jacob
    and unswerving loyalty to Abraham,
as you have sworn to our ancestors
    from the days of old.

This is the word of the Lord.   Micah 7.14–15, 18–20

Responsorial Psalm

R* **Show us your mercy, O Lord,**
    [and grant us your salvation].   Psalm 85.7

Lord, you were gracious to your land;
you restored the fortunes of Jacob.
You forgave the offence of your people
and covered all their sins.   **R**

You laid aside all your fury
and turned from your wrathful indignation.
Restore us again, O God our Saviour,
and let your anger cease from us.   **R**

Will you be displeased with us for ever?
Will you stretch out your wrath from one generation to another?
Will you not give us life again,
that your people may rejoice in you?   **R***   Psalm 85.1–7

Year 1 and Year 2

Hear the Gospel of our Lord Jesus Christ according to Matthew.

While Jesus was still speaking to the crowds, his mother and his brothers
were standing outside, wanting to speak to him. Someone told him, 'Look,
your mother and your brothers are standing outside, wanting to speak to you.'
But to the one who had told him this, Jesus replied, 'Who is my mother, and
who are my brothers?' And pointing to his disciples, he said, 'Here are my
mother and my brothers! For whoever does the will of my Father in heaven
is my brother and sister and mother.'

This is the Gospel of the Lord.   Matthew 12.46–end

Week 16: Wednesday between 20 and 26 July

Year 1

A reading from the Book of the Exodus.

The whole congregation of the Israelites set out from Elim; and Israel came to the wilderness of Sin, which is between Elim and Sinai, on the fifteenth day of the second month after they had departed from the land of Egypt. The whole congregation of the Israelites complained against Moses and Aaron in the wilderness. The Israelites said to them, 'If only we had died by the hand of the LORD in the land of Egypt, when we sat by the fleshpots and ate our fill of bread; for you have brought us out into this wilderness to kill this whole assembly with hunger.'

Then the LORD said to Moses, 'I am going to rain bread from heaven for you, and each day the people shall go out and gather enough for that day. In that way I will test them, whether they will follow my instruction or not. On the sixth day, when they prepare what they bring in, it will be twice as much as they gather on other days.'

Then Moses said to Aaron, 'Say to the whole congregation of the Israelites, "Draw near to the LORD, for he has heard your complaining." ' And as Aaron spoke to the whole congregation of the Israelites, they looked towards the wilderness, and the glory of the LORD appeared in the cloud. The LORD spoke to Moses and said, 'I have heard the complaining of the Israelites; say to them, "At twilight you shall eat meat, and in the morning you shall have your fill of bread; then you shall know that I am the LORD your God." '

In the evening quails came up and covered the camp; and in the morning there was a layer of dew around the camp. When the layer of dew lifted, there on the surface of the wilderness was a fine flaky substance, as fine as frost on the ground. When the Israelites saw it, they said to one another, 'What is it?' For they did not know what it was. Moses said to them, 'It is the bread that the LORD has given you to eat.'

This is the word of the Lord.   Exodus 16.1–5, 9–15

Responsorial Psalm

R **The Lord gave them the grain of heaven,
[they ate the bread of angels].**   Psalm 78.24b, 25a

Yet for all this they sinned more against him
and defied the Most High in the wilderness.
They tested God in their hearts
and demanded food for their craving. **R**

They spoke against God and said,
'Can God prepare a table in the wilderness?
He struck the rock indeed, so that the waters gushed out
and the streams overflowed,
but can he give bread or provide meat for his people?' **R**

When the Lord heard this, he was full of wrath;
a fire was kindled against Jacob
and his anger went out against Israel,
for they had no faith in God
and put no trust in his saving help. R

So he commanded the clouds above
and opened the doors of heaven.
He rained down upon them manna to eat
and gave them the grain of heaven.
So mortals ate the bread of angels;
he sent them food in plenty. R

He caused the east wind to blow in the heavens
and led out the south wind by his might.
He rained flesh upon them as thick as dust
and winged fowl like the sand of the sea. R

He let it fall in the midst of their camp
and round about their tents.
So they ate and were well filled,
for he gave them what they desired. R

But they did not stop their craving;
their food was still in their mouths,
when the anger of God rose against them,
and slew their strongest men
and felled the flower of Israel. R   *Psalm* 78.17–31

Year 2

A reading from the prophecy of Jeremiah.

The words of Jeremiah son of Hilkiah, of the priests who were in Anathoth
in the land of Benjamin. Now the word of the LORD came to me saying,
     'Before I formed you in the womb I knew you,
          and before you were born I consecrated you;
          I appointed you a prophet to the nations.'

Then I said, 'Ah, Lord GOD! Truly I do not know how to speak, for I am
only a boy.' But the LORD said to me,
     'Do not say, "I am only a boy";
          for you shall go to all to whom I send you,
          and you shall speak whatever I command you.
          Do not be afraid of them,
               for I am with you to deliver you,
                         says the LORD.'   →

Then the LORD put out his hand and touched my mouth; and the LORD said to me,

'Now I have put my words in your mouth.
See, today I appoint you over nations and over kingdoms,
to pluck up and to pull down,
to destroy and to overthrow,
to build and to plant.'

This is the word of the Lord. *Jeremiah 1.1, 4–10*

Responsorial Psalm

R* **O God, make speed to save me;**
[O Lord, make haste to help me]. *Psalm 70.1*

Let those who seek my life
be put to shame and confusion;
let them be turned back and disgraced
who wish me evil.   **R**

Let those who mock and deride me
turn back because of their shame.
But let all who seek you rejoice and be glad in you;
let those who love your salvation say always,
'Great is the Lord!'   **R**

As for me, I am poor and needy;
come to me quickly, O God.
You are my help and my deliverer;
O Lord, do not delay.   **R** *Psalm 70*

Year 1 and Year 2

Hear the Gospel of our Lord Jesus Christ according to Matthew.

Jesus went out of the house and sat beside the lake. Such great crowds gathered around him that he got into a boat and sat there, while the whole crowd stood on the beach. And he told them many things in parables, saying: 'Listen! A sower went out to sow. And as he sowed, some seeds fell on the path, and the birds came and ate them up. Other seeds fell on rocky ground, where they did not have much soil, and they sprang up quickly, since they had no depth of soil. But when the sun rose, they were scorched; and since they had no root, they withered away. Other seeds fell among thorns, and the thorns grew up and choked them. Other seeds fell on good soil and brought forth grain, some a hundredfold, some sixty, some thirty. Let anyone with ears listen!'

This is the Gospel of the Lord. *Matthew 13.1–9*

Week 16: Thursday between 21 and 27 July

Year 1

A reading from the Book of the Exodus.

At the third new moon after the Israelites had gone out of the land of Egypt, on that very day, they came into the wilderness of Sinai. They had journeyed from Rephidim, entered the wilderness of Sinai, and camped in the wilderness; Israel camped there in front of the mountain. Then the LORD said to Moses, 'I am going to come to you in a dense cloud, in order that the people may hear when I speak with you and so trust you ever after.'

When Moses had told the words of the people to the LORD, the LORD said to Moses: 'Go to the people and consecrate them today and tomorrow. Have them wash their clothes and prepare for the third day, because on the third day the LORD will come down upon Mount Sinai in the sight of all the people.'

On the morning of the third day there was thunder and lightning, as well as a thick cloud on the mountain, and a blast of a trumpet so loud that all the people who were in the camp trembled. Moses brought the people out of the camp to meet God. They took their stand at the foot of the mountain. Now Mount Sinai was wrapped in smoke, because the LORD had descended upon it in fire; the smoke went up like the smoke of a kiln, while the whole mountain shook violently. As the blast of the trumpet grew louder and louder, Moses would speak and God would answer him in thunder. When the LORD descended upon Mount Sinai, to the top of the mountain, the LORD summoned Moses to the top of the mountain, and Moses went up.

This is the word of the Lord.   Exodus 19.1–2, 9–11, 16–20

Canticle

R **You are worthy to be praised and exalted for ever.**

Blessed are you, the God of our ancestors.   [R]
Blessed is your holy and glorious name.   [R]
Blessed are you, in your holy and glorious temple.   R

Blessed are you who look into the depths.   [R]
Blessed are you, enthroned on the cherubim.   [R]
Blessed are you on the throne of your kingdom.   [R]
Blessed are you in the heights of heaven.   R   *Song of the Three* 29–34

A reading from the prophecy of Jeremiah.

The word of the LORD came to me, saying: Go and proclaim in the hearing of Jerusalem, Thus says the LORD:
>I remember the devotion of your youth,
>>your love as a bride,
>how you followed me in the wilderness,
>>in a land not sown.
>Israel was holy to the LORD,
>>the first fruits of his harvest.
>All who ate of it were held guilty;
>>disaster came upon them,
>>>says the LORD.

>I brought you into a plentiful land
>>to eat its fruits and its good things.
>But when you entered you defiled my land,
>>and made my heritage an abomination.
>The priests did not say, 'Where is the LORD?'
>>Those who handle the law did not know me;
>the rulers transgressed against me;
>>the prophets prophesied by Baal,
>>and went after things that do not profit.

>Be appalled, O heavens, at this,
>>be shocked, be utterly desolate,
>>>says the LORD,
>for my people have committed two evils:
>>they have forsaken me,
>the fountain of living water,
>>and dug out cisterns for themselves,
>cracked cisterns
>>that can hold no water.

This is the word of the Lord.   Jeremiah 2.1–3, 7–8, 12–13

Responsorial Psalm

R **Your love, O Lord, reaches to the heavens:**
[and your faithfulness to the clouds]. Psalm 36.5

Your love, O Lord, reaches to the heavens
and your faithfulness to the clouds.
Your righteousness stands like the strong mountains,
your justice like the great deep;
you, Lord, shall save both man and beast. **R**

How precious is your loving mercy, O God!
All mortal flesh shall take refuge
under the shadow of your wings.
They shall be satisfied with the abundance of your house;
they shall drink from the river of your delights. **R**

For with you is the well of life
and in your light shall we see light.
O continue your loving-kindness to those who know you
and your righteousness to those who are true of heart. **R**

Psalm 36.5–10

Year 1 and Year 2

Hear the Gospel of our Lord Jesus Christ according to Matthew.

The disciples came and asked Jesus, 'Why do you speak to the crowds in parables?' He answered, 'To you it has been given to know the secrets of the kingdom of heaven, but to them it has not been given. For to those who have, more will be given, and they will have an abundance; but from those who have nothing, even what they have will be taken away. The reason I speak to them in parables is that "seeing they do not perceive, and hearing they do not listen, nor do they understand." With them indeed is fulfilled the prophecy of Isaiah that says:
"You will indeed listen, but never understand,
    and you will indeed look, but never perceive.
For this people's heart has grown dull,
    and their ears are hard of hearing,
        and they have shut their eyes;
            so that they might not look with their eyes,
        and listen with their ears,
    and understand with their heart and turn –
    and I would heal them."
But blessed are your eyes, for they see, and your ears, for they hear. Truly I tell you, many prophets and righteous people longed to see what you see, but did not see it, and to hear what you hear, but did not hear it.'

This is the Gospel of the Lord. Matthew 13.10–17

Week 16: Friday between 22 and 28 July

Year 1

A reading from the Book of the Exodus.

Then God spoke all these words:

I am the LORD your God, who brought you out of the land of Egypt, out of the house of slavery; you shall have no other gods before me.

You shall not make for yourself an idol, whether in the form of anything that is in heaven above, or that is on the earth beneath, or that is in the water under the earth. You shall not bow down to them or worship them; for I the LORD your God am a jealous God, punishing children for the iniquity of parents, to the third and the fourth generation of those who reject me, but showing steadfast love to the thousandth generation of those who love me and keep my commandments.

You shall not make wrongful use of the name of the LORD your God, for the LORD will not acquit anyone who misuses his name.

Remember the sabbath day, and keep it holy. For six days you shall labour and do all your work. But the seventh day is a sabbath to the LORD your God; you shall not do any work – you, your son or your daughter, your male or female slave, your livestock, or the alien resident in your towns. For in six days the LORD made heaven and earth, the sea, and all that is in them, but rested the seventh day; therefore the LORD blessed the sabbath day and consecrated it.

Honour your father and your mother, so that your days may be long in the land that the LORD your God is giving you.

You shall not murder.

You shall not commit adultery.

You shall not steal.

You shall not bear false witness against your neighbour.

You shall not covet your neighbour's house; you shall not covet your neighbour's wife, or male or female slave, or ox, or donkey, or anything that belongs to your neighbour.

This is the word of the Lord.   Exodus 20.1–17

Responsorial Psalm

R **The law of the Lord is perfect:
more to be desired than gold.** *cf Psalm 19.7a, 10a*

The law of the Lord is perfect, reviving the soul;
the testimony of the Lord is sure
and gives wisdom to the simple.
The statutes of the Lord are right
and rejoice the heart.   R

The commandment of the Lord is pure
and gives light to the eyes.
The fear of the Lord is clean and endures for ever;
the judgements of the Lord are true
and righteous altogether.   R

More to be desired are they than gold,
more than much fine gold,
sweeter also than honey,
dripping from the honeycomb.
By them also is your servant taught
and in keeping them there is great reward.   R *Psalm 19.7–11*

Year 2

A reading from the prophecy of Jeremiah.

The Lord said to me:
Return, O faithless children,
says the LORD,
for I am your master;
I will take you, one from a city and two from a family,
and I will bring you to Zion.

I will give you shepherds after my own heart, who will feed you with knowledge
and understanding. And when you have multiplied and increased in the land,
in those days, says the LORD, they shall no longer say, 'The ark of the covenant
of the LORD.' It shall not come to mind, or be remembered, or missed; nor
shall another one be made. At that time Jerusalem shall be called the throne
of the LORD, and all nations shall gather to it, to the presence of the LORD in
Jerusalem, and they shall no longer stubbornly follow their own evil will.

This is the word of the Lord. *Jeremiah 3.14–17*

Either

Canticle

R   **The Lord will watch over us**
  as a shepherd watches the flock.   cf Jeremiah 31.10b

Hear the word of the Lord, O nations,
and declare it in the coastlands far away;
say, 'He who scattered Israel will gather him,
and will watch over him as a shepherd watches the flock.'   R

For the Lord has ransomed Jacob,
and redeemed him from hands too strong for him.
They shall come and sing aloud on the height of Zion,
and they shall be radiant at the goodness of the Lord.   R

They shall be radiant over the grain, the wine, and the oil,
and over the young of the flock and the herd;
their life shall be like a watered garden,
and they shall never languish again.   R

Then shall young women rejoice in the dance,
and young men and old shall be glad together.
I will turn their mourning into joy,
I will comfort them, and give them gladness for sorrow.   R

                                                        Jeremiah 31.10–13

or

Responsorial Psalm

R   **The Lord will watch over us**
  as a shepherd watches the flock.   cf Jeremiah 31.10b

The Lord is my shepherd;
therefore can I lack nothing.
He makes me lie down in green pastures
and leads me beside still waters.   R

He shall refresh my soul
and guide me in the paths of righteousness
for his name's sake.   R

Though I walk through the valley of the shadow of death,
I will fear no evil;
for you are with me;
your rod and your staff, they comfort me.   R

You spread a table before me
in the presence of those who trouble me;
you have anointed my head with oil
and my cup shall be full. **R**

Surely goodness and loving mercy shall follow me
all the days of my life,
and I will dwell in the house of the Lord for ever. **R**   *Psalm 23*

Year 1 and Year 2

Hear the Gospel of our Lord Jesus Christ according to Matthew.

Jesus said to his disciples, 'Hear then the parable of the sower. When anyone
hears the word of the kingdom and does not understand it, the evil one
comes and snatches away what is sown in the heart; this is what was sown
on the path. As for what was sown on rocky ground, this is the one who
hears the word and immediately receives it with joy; yet such a person has
no root, but endures only for a while, and when trouble or persecution arises
on account of the word, that person immediately falls away. As for what was
sown among thorns, this is the one who hears the word, but the cares of
the world and the lure of wealth choke the word, and it yields nothing. But
as for what was sown on good soil, this is the one who hears the word and
understands it, who indeed bears fruit and yields, in one case a hundredfold,
in another sixty, and in another thirty.'

This is the Gospel of the Lord.   *Matthew 13.18–23*

Week 16: Saturday between 23 and 29 July

Year 1

A reading from the Book of the Exodus.

Moses came and told the people all the words of the LORD and all the ordinances; and all the people answered with one voice, and said, 'All the words
that the LORD has spoken we will do.' And Moses wrote down all the words
of the LORD. He rose early in the morning, and built an altar at the foot of
the mountain, and set up twelve pillars, corresponding to the twelve tribes of
Israel. He sent young men of the people of Israel, who offered burnt-offerings
and sacrificed oxen as offerings of well-being to the LORD. Moses took half
of the blood and put it in basins, and half of the blood he dashed against the
altar. Then he took the book of the covenant, and read it in the hearing of
the people; and they said, 'All that the LORD has spoken we will do, and we
will be obedient.' Moses took the blood and dashed it on the people, and said,
'See the blood of the covenant that the LORD has made with you in accordance
with all these words.'

This is the word of the Lord.   *Exodus 24.3–8*

Responsorial Psalm

R   **Let us offer to God a sacrifice of thanksgiving:**
    [and fulfil our vows to the Most High].   cf Psalm 50.14

The Lord, the most mighty God, has spoken
and called the world from the rising of the sun to its setting.
Out of Zion, perfect in beauty, God shines forth;
our God comes and will not keep silence.   R

Consuming fire goes out before him
and a mighty tempest stirs about him.
He calls the heaven above,
and the earth, that he may judge his people.   R

'Gather to me my faithful,
who have sealed my covenant with sacrifice.'
Let the heavens declare his righteousness,
for God himself is judge.   R

'Offer to God a sacrifice of thanksgiving
and fulfil your vows to God Most High.
Call upon me in the day of trouble;
I will deliver you and you shall honour me.'   R   Psalm 50.1–6, 14–15

Year 2

A reading from the prophecy of Jeremiah.

The word that came to Jeremiah from the LORD:
Stand in the gate of the LORD's house, and proclaim there this word, and
say, Hear the word of the LORD, all you people of Judah, you that enter these
gates to worship the LORD. Thus says the LORD of hosts, the God of Israel:
Amend your ways and your doings, and let me dwell with you in this place.
Do not trust in these deceptive words: 'This is the temple of the LORD, the
temple of the LORD, the temple of the LORD.'
For if you truly amend your ways and your doings, if you truly act justly
one with another, if you do not oppress the alien, the orphan, and the widow,
or shed innocent blood in this place, and if you do not go after other gods
to your own hurt, then I will dwell with you in this place, in the land that I
gave of old to your ancestors for ever and ever.
Here you are, trusting in deceptive words to no avail. Will you steal, murder,
commit adultery, swear falsely, make offerings to Baal, and go after other gods
that you have not known, and then come and stand before me in this house,
which is called by my name, and say, 'We are safe!' – only to go on doing all
these abominations? Has this house, which is called by my name, become a
den of robbers in your sight? You know, I too am watching, says the LORD.

This is the word of the Lord.   Jeremiah 7.1–11

Responsorial Psalm

R **How lovely is your dwelling place, O Lord of hosts!**   Psalm 84.1

How lovely is your dwelling place, O Lord of hosts!
My soul has a desire and longing
to enter the courts of the Lord;
my heart and my flesh rejoice in the living God. **R**

The sparrow has found her a house
and the swallow a nest where she may lay her young:
at your altars, O Lord of hosts,
my King and my God. **R**

Blessed are they who dwell in your house:
they will always be praising you.
Blessed are those whose strength is in you,
in whose heart are the highways to Zion. **R**

Who going through the barren valley find there a spring,
and the early rains will clothe it with blessing.
They will go from strength to strength
and appear before God in Zion. **R**   Psalm 84.1–6

Year I and Year 2

Hear the Gospel of our Lord Jesus Christ according to Matthew.

Jesus put before the crowds another parable: 'The kingdom of heaven may
be compared to someone who sowed good seed in his field; but while eve-
rybody was asleep, an enemy came and sowed weeds among the wheat, and
then went away. So when the plants came up and bore grain, then the weeds
appeared as well. And the slaves of the householder came and said to him,
"Master, did you not sow good seed in your field? Where, then, did these
weeds come from?" He answered, "An enemy has done this." The slaves said
to him, "Then do you want us to go and gather them?" But he replied, "No;
for in gathering the weeds you would uproot the wheat along with them. Let
both of them grow together until the harvest; and at harvest time I will tell
the reapers, Collect the weeds first and bind them in bundles to be burned,
but gather the wheat into my barn." '

This is the Gospel of the Lord.   Matthew 13.24–30

Week 17: Monday between 25 and 31 July

Year 1

A reading from the Book of the Exodus.

Moses turned and went down from the mountain, carrying the two tablets of the covenant in his hands, tablets that were written on both sides, written on the front and on the back. The tablets were the work of God, and the writing was the writing of God, engraved upon the tablets. When Joshua heard the noise of the people as they shouted, he said to Moses, 'There is a noise of war in the camp.' But he said,

'It is not the sound made by victors,
or the sound made by losers;
it is the sound of revellers that I hear.'

As soon as he came near the camp and saw the calf and the dancing, Moses' anger burned hot, and he threw the tablets from his hands and broke them at the foot of the mountain. He took the calf that they had made, burned it with fire, ground it to powder, scattered it on the water, and made the Israelites drink it.

Moses said to Aaron, 'What did this people do to you that you have brought so great a sin upon them?' And Aaron said, 'Do not let the anger of my lord burn hot; you know the people, that they are bent on evil. They said to me, "Make us gods, who shall go before us; as for this Moses, the man who brought us up out of the land of Egypt, we do not know what has become of him." So I said to them, "Whoever has gold, take it off"; so they gave it to me, and I threw it into the fire, and out came this calf!'

On the next day Moses said to the people, 'You have sinned a great sin. But now I will go up to the LORD; perhaps I can make atonement for your sin.' So Moses returned to the LORD and said, 'Alas, this people has sinned a great sin; they have made for themselves gods of gold. But now, if you will only forgive their sin – but if not, blot me out of the book that you have written.' But the LORD said to Moses, 'Whoever has sinned against me I will blot out of my book. But now go, lead the people to the place about which I have spoken to you; see, my angel shall go in front of you. Nevertheless, when the day comes for punishment, I will punish them for their sin.'

This is the word of the Lord. Exodus 32.15–24, 30–34

Responsorial Psalm

R **Give thanks to the Lord, for he is gracious:**
   [his faithfulness endures for ever].   cf Psalm 106.1

They made a calf at Horeb
and worshipped the molten image;
thus they exchanged their glory
for the image of an ox that feeds on hay.   R

They forgot God their saviour,
who had done such great things in Egypt,
wonderful deeds in the land of Ham
and fearful things at the Red Sea.   R

So he would have destroyed them,
had not Moses his chosen
stood before him in the breach,
to turn away his wrath from consuming them.   R   Psalm 106.19–23

Year 2

A reading from the prophecy of Jeremiah.

Thus said the LORD to me, 'Go and buy yourself a linen loincloth, and put it
on your loins, but do not dip it in water.' So I bought a loincloth according
to the word of the LORD, and put it on my loins. And the word of the LORD
came to me a second time, saying, 'Take the loincloth that you bought and
are wearing, and go now to the Euphrates, and hide it there in a cleft of the
rock.' So I went, and hid it by the Euphrates, as the LORD commanded me.
And after many days the LORD said to me, 'Go now to the Euphrates, and take
from there the loincloth that I commanded you to hide there.' Then I went to
the Euphrates, and dug, and I took the loincloth from the place where I had
hidden it. But now the loincloth was ruined; it was good for nothing.

Then the word of the LORD came to me: Thus says the LORD: Just so I will
ruin the pride of Judah and the great pride of Jerusalem. This evil people, who
refuse to hear my words, who stubbornly follow their own will and have gone
after other gods to serve them and worship them, shall be like this loincloth,
which is good for nothing. For as the loincloth clings to one's loins, so I made
the whole house of Israel and the whole house of Judah cling to me, says the
LORD, in order that they might be for me a people, a name, a praise, and a
glory. But they would not listen.

This is the word of the Lord.   Jeremiah 13.1–11

Either

Canticle

R **Arise, O God and judge the earth,**
[and take the nations for your possession].   cf Psalm 82.8

You forgot the Rock that conceived you;
you were unmindful of the God who gave you birth.
The Lord saw it, and was jealous;
and spurned his sons and daughters.   **R**

God said: I will hide my face from them,
I will see what their end shall be;
for they are a perverse generation,
children in whom there is no faithfulness.   **R**

They have moved me to jealousy with what is no god,
and provoked me with their idols.
So I will move them to jealousy with what is no people,
and provoke them with a foolish nation.   **R**   Deuteronomy 32.18–21

or

Responsorial Psalm

R* **Arise, O God and judge the earth,**
[and take the nations for your possession].   cf Psalm 82.8

God has taken his stand in the council of heaven;
in the midst of the gods he gives judgement:
how long will you judge unjustly
and show such favour to the wicked?   **R**

You were to judge the weak and the orphan;
defend the right of the humble and needy;
rescue the weak and the poor;
deliver them from the hand of the wicked.   **R**

They have no knowledge or wisdom;
they walk on still in darkness:
all the foundations of the earth are shaken.   **R**

Therefore I say that though you are gods
and all of you children of the Most High,
nevertheless, you shall die like mortals
and fall like one of their princes.   **R***   Psalm 82

Year 1 and Year 2

Hear the Gospel of our Lord Jesus Christ according to Matthew.

Jesus put before the crowds another parable: 'The kingdom of heaven is like a mustard seed that someone took and sowed in his field; it is the smallest of all the seeds, but when it has grown it is the greatest of shrubs and becomes a tree, so that the birds of the air come and make nests in its branches.'

He told them another parable: 'The kingdom of heaven is like yeast that a woman took and mixed in with three measures of flour until all of it was leavened.'

Jesus told the crowds all these things in parables; without a parable he told them nothing. This was to fulfil what had been spoken through the prophet:

'I will open my mouth to speak in parables;
   I will proclaim what has been hidden
      from the foundation of the world.'

This is the Gospel of the Lord.   Matthew 13.31–35

Week 17: Tuesday between 26 July and 1 August

Year 1

A reading from the Book of the Exodus.

Moses used to take the tent and pitch it outside the camp, far off from the camp; he called it the tent of meeting. And everyone who sought the LORD would go out to the tent of meeting, which was outside the camp. Whenever Moses went out to the tent, all the people would rise and stand, each of them, at the entrance of their tents and watch Moses until he had gone into the tent. When Moses entered the tent, the pillar of cloud would descend and stand at the entrance of the tent, and the LORD would speak with Moses. When all the people saw the pillar of cloud standing at the entrance of the tent, all the people would rise and bow down, all of them, at the entrance of their tents. Thus the LORD used to speak to Moses face to face, as one speaks to a friend. Then he would return to the camp; but his young assistant, Joshua son of Nun, would not leave the tent.

The LORD descended in the cloud and stood with Moses there, and proclaimed the name, 'The LORD.' The LORD passed before him, and proclaimed,

'The LORD, the LORD,
a God merciful and gracious,
slow to anger,
and abounding in steadfast love and faithfulness,
keeping steadfast love for the thousandth generation,
forgiving iniquity and transgression and sin,
yet by no means clearing the guilty,   →

but visiting the iniquity of the parents
upon the children
and the children's children,
to the third and the fourth generation.'
And Moses quickly bowed his head towards the earth, and worshipped. He
said, 'If now I have found favour in your sight, O Lord, I pray, let the Lord go
with us. Although this is a stiff-necked people, pardon our iniquity and our
sin, and take us for your inheritance.'

He was there with the LORD for forty days and forty nights; he neither ate
bread nor drank water. And he wrote on the tablets the words of the covenant,
the ten commandments.

This is the word of the Lord.   Exodus 33.7–11, 34.5–9, 28

Responsorial Psalm

R* **The Lord is full of compassion and mercy,
[slow to anger and of great kindness].**   cf Psalm 103.8

He will not always accuse us,
neither will he keep his anger for ever.
He has not dealt with us according to our sins,
nor rewarded us according to our wickedness.   **R**

For as the heavens are high above the earth,
so great is his mercy upon those who fear him.
As far as the east is from the west,
so far has he set our sins from us.   **R**   Psalm 103.8–12

Year 2

A reading from the prophecy of Jeremiah.

You shall say to them this word:
Let my eyes run down with tears night and day,
    and let them not cease,
for the virgin daughter – my people –
        is struck down with a crushing blow,
    with a very grievous wound.
If I go out into the field,
    look – those killed by the sword!
And if I enter the city,
    look – those sick with famine!
For both prophet and priest ply their trade throughout the land,
    and have no knowledge.

Have you completely rejected Judah?
    Does your heart loathe Zion?
Why have you struck us down

so that there is no healing for us?
We look for peace, but find no good;
    for a time of healing, but there is terror instead.
We acknowledge our wickedness, O Lord,
    the iniquity of our ancestors,
    for we have sinned against you.
Do not spurn us, for your name's sake;
    do not dishonour your glorious throne;
    remember and do not break your covenant with us.
Can any idols of the nations bring rain?
    Or can the heavens give showers?
Is it not you, O Lord our God?
    We set our hope on you,
    for it is you who do all this.

This is the word of the Lord.   *Jeremiah* 14.17–end

Responsorial Psalm

R **Help us, O God, for the glory of your name;**
    [deliver us, and wipe away our sins].   *cf Psalm* 79.9

Remember not against us our former sins;
let your compassion make haste to meet us,
for we are brought very low. **R**

Help us, O God of our salvation,
for the glory of your name;
deliver us, and wipe away our sins
for your name's sake. **R**

Why should the heathen say,
'Where is now their God?'
Let vengeance for your servants' blood that is shed
be known among the nations in our sight. **R**

Let the sorrowful sighing of the prisoners come before you,
and by your mighty arm preserve those who are condemned to die.
May the taunts with which our neighbours taunted you, Lord,
return sevenfold into their bosom. **R**

But we that are your people
and the sheep of your pasture
will give you thanks for ever,
and tell of your praise from generation to generation. **R**   *Psalm* 79.8–end

Hear the Gospel of our Lord Jesus Christ according to Matthew.

Jesus left the crowds and went into the house. And his disciples approached him, saying, 'Explain to us the parable of the weeds of the field.' He answered, 'The one who sows the good seed is the Son of Man; the field is the world, and the good seed are the children of the kingdom; the weeds are the children of the evil one, and the enemy who sowed them is the devil; the harvest is the end of the age, and the reapers are angels. Just as the weeds are collected and burned up with fire, so will it be at the end of the age. The Son of Man will send his angels, and they will collect out of his kingdom all causes of sin and all evildoers, and they will throw them into the furnace of fire, where there will be weeping and gnashing of teeth. Then the righteous will shine like the sun in the kingdom of their Father. Let anyone with ears listen!'

This is the Gospel of the Lord.   Matthew 13.36–43

Week 17: Wednesday between 27 July and 2 August

Year 1

A reading from the Book of the Exodus.

Moses came down from Mount Sinai. As he came down from the mountain with the two tablets of the covenant in his hand, Moses did not know that the skin of his face shone because he had been talking with God. When Aaron and all the Israelites saw Moses, the skin of his face was shining, and they were afraid to come near him. But Moses called to them; and Aaron and all the leaders of the congregation returned to him, and Moses spoke with them. Afterwards all the Israelites came near, and he gave them in commandment all that the LORD had spoken with him on Mount Sinai. When Moses had finished speaking with them, he put a veil on his face; but whenever Moses went in before the LORD to speak with him, he would take the veil off, until he came out; and when he came out, and told the Israelites what he had been commanded, the Israelites would see the face of Moses, that the skin of his face was shining; and Moses would put the veil on his face again, until he went in to speak with him.

This is the word of the Lord.   Exodus 34.29–end

Responsorial Psalm

R **Exalt the Lord our God:**
  for holy is his name.   *cf Psalm 99.3, 5, 9*

The Lord is king: let the peoples tremble;
he is enthroned above the cherubim:
let the earth shake.
The Lord is great in Zion
and high above all peoples.   **R**

Let them praise your name, which is great and awesome;
the Lord our God is holy.
Mighty king, who loves justice,
you have established equity;
you have executed justice and righteousness in Jacob.   **R**

Exalt the Lord our God;
bow down before his footstool, for he is holy.
Moses and Aaron among his priests
and Samuel among those who call upon his name;
they called upon the Lord and he answered them.   **R**

He spoke to them out of the pillar of cloud;
they kept his testimonies and the law that he gave them.
You answered them, O Lord our God;
you were a God who forgave them
and pardoned them for their offences.   **R**

Exalt the Lord our God
and worship him upon his holy hill,
for the Lord our God is holy.   **R**   *Psalm 99*

Year 2

A reading from the prophecy of Jeremiah.

Woe is me, my mother, that you ever bore me, a man of strife and conten-
tion to the whole land! I have not lent, nor have I borrowed, yet all of them
curse me.
> Your words were found, and I ate them,
>   and your words became to me a joy
>   and the delight of my heart;
> for I am called by your name,
>   O LORD, God of hosts.
> I did not sit in the company of merrymakers,
>   nor did I rejoice;
> under the weight of your hand I sat alone,
>   for you had filled me with indignation.   →

Why is my pain unceasing,
    my wound incurable,
    refusing to be healed?
Truly, you are to me like a deceitful brook,
    like waters that fail.

Therefore, thus says the LORD:
If you turn back, I will take you back,
    and you shall stand before me.
If you utter what is precious, and not what is worthless,
    you shall serve as my mouth.
It is they who will turn to you,
    not you who will turn to them.
And I will make you to this people
    a fortified wall of bronze;
they will fight against you,
    but they shall not prevail over you,
for I am with you
    to save you and deliver you,
                    says the LORD.
I will deliver you out of the hand of the wicked,
    and redeem you from the grasp of the ruthless.

This is the word of the Lord.   *Jeremiah 15.10, 16–end*

Responsorial Psalm

R **I will sing, O God, of your strength:**
    [my refuge in the day of my trouble].   *cf Psalm 59.18a, 19b*

Rescue me from my enemies, O my God;
set me high above those that rise up against me.
Save me from the evildoers
and from murderous foes deliver me.   **R**

For see how they lie in wait for my soul
and the mighty stir up trouble against me.
Not for any fault or sin of mine, O Lord;
for no offence, they run and prepare themselves for war.   **R**

Yet will I sing of your strength
and every morning praise your steadfast love;
for you have been my stronghold,
my refuge in the day of my trouble.   **R**

To you, O my strength, will I sing;
for you, O God, are my refuge,
my God of steadfast love.   **R**   *Psalm 59.1–4, 18–end*

Hear the Gospel of our Lord Jesus Christ according to Matthew.

Jesus said to his disciples, 'The kingdom of heaven is like treasure hidden in a field, which someone found and hid; then in his joy he goes and sells all that he has and buys that field.

'Again, the kingdom of heaven is like a merchant in search of fine pearls; on finding one pearl of great value, he went and sold all that he had and bought it.'

This is the Gospel of the Lord. Matthew 13.44–46

Week 17: Thursday between 28 July and 3 August

Year 1

A reading from the Book of the Exodus.

Moses did everything just as the LORD had commanded him. In the first month in the second year, on the first day of the month, the tabernacle was set up. Moses set up the tabernacle; he laid its bases, and set up its frames, and put in its poles, and raised up its pillars; and he spread the tent over the tabernacle, and put the covering of the tent over it; as the LORD had commanded Moses. He took the covenant and put it into the ark, and put the poles on the ark, and set the mercy-seat above the ark; and he brought the ark into the tabernacle, and set up the curtain for screening, and screened the ark of the covenant; as the LORD had commanded Moses.

Then the cloud covered the tent of meeting, and the glory of the LORD filled the tabernacle. Moses was not able to enter the tent of meeting because the cloud settled upon it, and the glory of the LORD filled the tabernacle. Whenever the cloud was taken up from the tabernacle, the Israelites would set out on each stage of their journey; but if the cloud was not taken up, then they did not set out until the day that it was taken up. For the cloud of the LORD was on the tabernacle by day, and fire was in the cloud by night, before the eyes of all the house of Israel at each stage of their journey.

This is the word of the Lord. Exodus 40.16–21, 34–end

R **How lovely is your dwelling place, O Lord of hosts!**   Psalm 84.1

How lovely is your dwelling place, O Lord of hosts!
My soul has a desire and longing
to enter the courts of the Lord;
my heart and my flesh rejoice in the living God.   R

The sparrow has found her a house
and the swallow a nest where she may lay her young:
at your altars, O Lord of hosts,
my King and my God.   R

Blessed are they who dwell in your house:
they will always be praising you.
Blessed are those whose strength is in you,
in whose heart are the highways to Zion.   R

Who going through the barren valley find there a spring,
and the early rains will clothe it with blessing.
They will go from strength to strength
and appear before God in Zion.   R   Psalm 84.1–6

Year 2

A reading from the prophecy of Jeremiah.

The word that came to Jeremiah from the LORD: 'Come, go down to the potter's house, and there I will let you hear my words.' So I went down to the potter's house, and there he was working at his wheel. The vessel he was making of clay was spoiled in the potter's hand, and he reworked it into another vessel, as seemed good to him.

Then the word of the LORD came to me: Can I not do with you, O house of Israel, just as this potter has done? says the LORD. Just like the clay in the potter's hand, so are you in my hand, O house of Israel.

This is the word of the Lord.   Jeremiah 18.1–6

Responsorial Psalm

R **The Lord shall reign for ever,
     [your God, O Zion, throughout all generations].**   Psalm 146.10

Praise the Lord, O my soul:
while I live will I praise the Lord;
as long as I have any being,
I will sing praises to my God.   R

Put not your trust in princes, nor in any human power,
for there is no help in them.
When their breath goes forth, they return to the earth;
on that day all their thoughts perish. R

Happy are those who have the God of Jacob for their help,
whose hope is in the Lord their God;
who made heaven and earth, the sea and all that is in them;
who keeps his promise for ever. R   *Psalm 146.1–5*

Year 1 and Year 2

Hear the Gospel of our Lord Jesus Christ according to Matthew.

Jesus said to his disciples, 'Again, the kingdom of heaven is like a net that
was thrown into the sea and caught fish of every kind; when it was full, they
drew it ashore, sat down, and put the good into baskets but threw out the
bad. So it will be at the end of the age. The angels will come out and separate
the evil from the righteous and throw them into the furnace of fire, where
there will be weeping and gnashing of teeth.
   'Have you understood all this?' They answered, 'Yes.' And he said to them,
'Therefore every scribe who has been trained for the kingdom of heaven is
like the master of a household who brings out of his treasure what is new and
what is old.' When Jesus had finished these parables, he left that place.

This is the Gospel of the Lord.   *Matthew 13.47–53*

Week 17: Friday between 29 July and 4 August

Year 1

A reading from the book Leviticus.

The Lord spoke to Moses, saying:
   These are the appointed festivals of the Lord, the holy convocations, which
you shall celebrate at the time appointed for them. In the first month, on the
fourteenth day of the month, at twilight, there shall be a passover-offering
to the Lord, and on the fifteenth day of the same month is the festival of
unleavened bread to the Lord; for seven days you shall eat unleavened bread.
On the first day you shall have a holy convocation; you shall not work at your
occupations. For seven days you shall present the Lord's offerings by fire; on
the seventh day there shall be a holy convocation: you shall not work at your
occupations.
   The Lord spoke to Moses: Speak to the people of Israel and say to them:
When you enter the land that I am giving you and you reap its harvest, you
shall bring the sheaf of the first fruits of your harvest to the priest. He shall
raise the sheaf before the Lord, so that you may find acceptance; on the day
after the sabbath the priest shall raise it. →

And from the day after the sabbath, from the day on which you bring the sheaf of the elevation-offering, you shall count off seven weeks; they shall be complete. You shall count until the day after the seventh sabbath, fifty days; then you shall present an offering of new grain to the LORD.

The tenth day of the seventh month is the day of atonement; it shall be a holy convocation for you: you shall deny yourselves and present the LORD's offering by fire.

Speak to the people of Israel, saying: On the fifteenth day of this seventh month, and lasting seven days, there shall be the festival of booths to the LORD. The first day shall be a holy convocation; you shall not work at your occupations. For seven days you shall present the LORD's offerings by fire; on the eighth day you shall observe a holy convocation and present the LORD's offerings by fire; it is a solemn assembly; you shall not work at your occupations.

These are the appointed festivals of the LORD, which you shall celebrate as times of holy convocation, for presenting to the LORD offerings by fire – burnt-offerings and grain-offerings, sacrifices and drink-offerings, each on its proper day.

This is the word of the Lord.   *Leviticus 23.1, 4–11, 15–16, 27, 34–37*

Responsorial Psalm

R **Sing merrily to God our strength,**
   [shout for joy to the God of Jacob].   *Psalm 81.1*

Sing merrily to God our strength,
shout for joy to the God of Jacob.
Take up the song and sound the timbrel,
the tuneful lyre with the harp. **R**

Blow the trumpet at the new moon,
as at the full moon, upon our solemn feast day.
For this is a statute for Israel, a law of the God of Jacob,
the charge he laid on the people of Joseph,
when they came out of the land of Egypt. **R**

I heard a voice I did not know, that said:
'I eased their shoulder from the burden;
their hands were set free from bearing the load.
You called upon me in trouble and I delivered you. **R**

'I answered you from the secret place of thunder
and proved you at the waters of Meribah.
Hear, O my people, and I will admonish you:
O Israel, if you would but listen to me!' **R**   *Psalm 81.1–8*

A reading from the prophecy of Jeremiah.

At the beginning of the reign of King Jehoiakim son of Josiah of Judah, this word came from the LORD: Thus says the LORD: Stand in the court of the LORD's house, and speak to all the cities of Judah that come to worship in the house of the LORD; speak to them all the words that I command you; do not hold back a word. It may be that they will listen, all of them, and will turn from their evil way, that I may change my mind about the disaster that I intend to bring on them because of their evil doings. You shall say to them: Thus says the LORD: If you will not listen to me, to walk in my law that I have set before you, and to heed the words of my servants the prophets whom I send to you urgently – though you have not heeded – then I will make this house like Shiloh, and I will make this city a curse for all the nations of the earth.

The priests and the prophets and all the people heard Jeremiah speaking these words in the house of the LORD. And when Jeremiah had finished speaking all that the LORD had commanded him to speak to all the people, then the priests and the prophets and all the people laid hold of him, saying, 'You shall die! Why have you prophesied in the name of the LORD, saying, "This house shall be like Shiloh, and this city shall be desolate, without inhabitant"?' And all the people gathered around Jeremiah in the house of the LORD.

This is the word of the Lord.   Jeremiah 26.1–9

Responsorial Psalm

R **To you, O Lord, I make my prayer;**
    [answer me with your sure salvation].   *cf Psalm 69.14a, 15b*

Those who hate me without any cause
are more than the hairs of my head;
those who would destroy me are mighty;
my enemies accuse me falsely:
must I now give back what I never stole? **R**

O God, you know my foolishness,
and my faults are not hidden from you.
Let not those who hope in you
be put to shame through me, Lord God of hosts;
let not those who seek you be disgraced because of me,
O God of Israel. **R**

For your sake have I suffered reproach;
shame has covered my face.
I have become a stranger to my kindred,
an alien to my mother's children.
Zeal for your house has eaten me up;
the scorn of those who scorn you has fallen upon me. **R**   *Psalm 69.4–10*

Hear the Gospel of our Lord Jesus Christ according to Matthew.

Jesus came to his home town and began to teach the people in their synagogue, so that they were astounded and said, 'Where did this man get this wisdom and these deeds of power? Is not this the carpenter's son? Is not his mother called Mary? And are not his brothers James and Joseph and Simon and Judas? And are not all his sisters with us? Where then did this man get all this?' And they took offence at him. But Jesus said to them, 'Prophets are not without honour except in their own country and in their own house.' And he did not do many deeds of power there, because of their unbelief.

This is the Gospel of the Lord.   *Matthew* 13.54–end

Week 17: Saturday between 30 July and 5 August

Year 1

A reading from the book Leviticus.

The LORD spoke to Moses on Mount Sinai, saying:
      You shall count off seven weeks of years, seven times seven years, so that the period of seven weeks of years gives forty-nine years. Then you shall have the trumpet sounded loud; on the tenth day of the seventh month – on the day of atonement – you shall have the trumpet sounded throughout all your land. And you shall hallow the fiftieth year and you shall proclaim liberty throughout the land to all its inhabitants. It shall be a jubilee for you: you shall return, every one of you, to your property and every one of you to your family. That fiftieth year shall be a jubilee for you: you shall not sow, or reap the aftergrowth, or harvest the unpruned vines. For it is a jubilee; it shall be holy to you: you shall eat only what the field itself produces.
      In this year of jubilee you shall return, every one of you, to your property. When you make a sale to your neighbour or buy from your neighbour, you shall not cheat one another. When you buy from your neighbour, you shall pay only for the number of years since the jubilee; the seller shall charge you only for the remaining crop-years. If the years are more, you shall increase the price, and if the years are fewer, you shall diminish the price; for it is a certain number of harvests that are being sold to you. You shall not cheat one another, but you shall fear your God; for I am the LORD your God.

This is the word of the Lord.   *Leviticus* 25.1, 8–17

Responsorial Psalm

R* **Let the peoples praise you, O God,**
   [let all the peoples praise you]. *Psalm 67.3, 5*

God be gracious to us and bless us
and make his face to shine upon us,
that your way may be known upon earth,
your saving power among all nations.   R*

O let the nations rejoice and be glad,
for you will judge the peoples righteously
and govern the nations upon earth.   R*

Then shall the earth bring forth her increase,
and God, our own God, will bless us.
God will bless us,
and all the ends of the earth shall fear him.   R   *Psalm 67*

Year 2

A reading from the prophecy of Jeremiah.

The priests and the prophets said to the officials and to all the people, 'This
man deserves the sentence of death because he has prophesied against this
city, as you have heard with your own ears.'

Then Jeremiah spoke to all the officials and all the people, saying, 'It is
the LORD who sent me to prophesy against this house and this city all the
words you have heard. Now therefore amend your ways and your doings, and
obey the voice of the LORD your God, and the LORD will change his mind
about the disaster that he has pronounced against you. But as for me, here I
am in your hands. Do with me as seems good and right to you. Only know
for certain that if you put me to death, you will be bringing innocent blood
upon yourselves and upon this city and its inhabitants, for in truth the LORD
sent me to you to speak all these words in your ears.'

Then the officials and all the people said to the priests and the prophets,
'This man does not deserve the sentence of death, for he has spoken to us
in the name of the LORD our God.' And the hand of Ahikam son of Shaphan
was with Jeremiah so that he was not given over into the hands of the people
to be put to death.

This is the word of the Lord.   *Jeremiah 26.11–16, 24*

Responsorial Psalm

R **To you, O Lord, I make my prayer;**
   [answer me with your sure salvation].   cf Psalm 69.14a, 15b

But as for me, I make my prayer to you, O Lord;
at an acceptable time, O God.
Answer me, O God, in the abundance of your mercy
and with your sure salvation. R

Draw me out of the mire,
that I sink not;
let me be rescued from those who hate me
and out of the deep waters. R

Let not the water flood drown me,
neither the deep swallow me up;
let not the Pit shut its mouth upon me.
Answer me, Lord, for your loving-kindness is good;
turn to me in the multitude of your mercies. R

Hide not your face from your servant;
be swift to answer me, for I am in trouble.
Draw near to my soul and redeem me;
deliver me because of my enemies. R   Psalm 69.14–20

Year 1 and Year 2

Hear the Gospel of our Lord Jesus Christ according to Matthew.

Herod the ruler heard reports about Jesus; and he said to his servants, 'This is John the Baptist; he has been raised from the dead, and for this reason these powers are at work in him.' For Herod had arrested John, bound him, and put him in prison on account of Herodias, his brother Philip's wife, because John had been telling him, 'It is not lawful for you to have her.' Though Herod wanted to put him to death, he feared the crowd, because they regarded him as a prophet. But when Herod's birthday came, the daughter of Herodias danced before the company, and she pleased Herod so much that he promised on oath to grant her whatever she might ask. Prompted by her mother, she said, 'Give me the head of John the Baptist here on a platter.' The king was grieved, yet out of regard for his oaths and for the guests, he commanded it to be given; he sent and had John beheaded in the prison. The head was brought on a platter and given to the girl, who brought it to her mother. His disciples came and took the body and buried it; then they went and told Jesus.

This is the Gospel of the Lord.   Matthew 14.1–12

Week 18: Monday between 1 and 7 August

Year 1

A reading from the book Numbers.

The Israelites wept, and said, 'If only we had meat to eat! We remember the fish we used to eat in Egypt for nothing, the cucumbers, the melons, the leeks, the onions, and the garlic; but now our strength is dried up, and there is nothing at all but this manna to look at.'

Now the manna was like coriander seed, and its colour was like the colour of gum resin. The people went around and gathered it, ground it in mills or beat it in mortars, then boiled it in pots and made cakes of it; and the taste of it was like the taste of cakes baked with oil. When the dew fell on the camp in the night, the manna would fall with it.

Moses heard the people weeping throughout their families, all at the entrances of their tents. Then the LORD became very angry, and Moses was displeased. So Moses said to the LORD, 'Why have you treated your servant so badly? Why have I not found favour in your sight, that you lay the burden of all this people on me? Did I conceive all this people? Did I give birth to them, that you should say to me, "Carry them in your bosom, as a nurse carries a sucking child", to the land that you promised on oath to their ancestors? Where am I to get meat to give to all this people? For they come weeping to me and say, "Give us meat to eat!" I am not able to carry all this people alone, for they are too heavy for me. If this is the way you are going to treat me, put me to death at once — if I have found favour in your sight — and do not let me see my misery.'

This is the word of the Lord. Numbers 11.4–15

Responsorial Psalm

R **Sing merrily to God our strength,**
  [shout for joy to the God of Jacob]. Psalm 81.1

My people would not hear my voice
and Israel would not obey me.
So I sent them away in the stubbornness of their hearts,
and let them walk after their own counsels. R

O that my people would listen to me,
that Israel would walk in my ways!
Then I should soon put down their enemies
and turn my hand against their adversaries. R

Those who hate the Lord would be humbled before him,
and their punishment would last for ever.
But Israel would I feed with the finest wheat
and with honey from the rock would I satisfy them. R   Psalm 81.11–end

A reading from the prophecy of Jeremiah.

At the beginning of the reign of King Zedekiah of Judah, in the fifth month of the fourth year, the prophet Hananiah son of Azzur, from Gibeon, spoke to me in the house of the LORD, in the presence of the priests and all the people, saying, 'Thus says the LORD of hosts, the God of Israel: I have broken the yoke of the king of Babylon. Within two years I will bring back to this place all the vessels of the LORD's house, which King Nebuchadnezzar of Babylon took away from this place and carried to Babylon. I will also bring back to this place King Jeconiah son of Jehoiakim of Judah, and all the exiles from Judah who went to Babylon, says the LORD, for I will break the yoke of the king of Babylon.'

Then the prophet Jeremiah spoke to the prophet Hananiah in the presence of the priests and all the people who were standing in the house of the LORD; and the prophet Jeremiah said, 'Amen! May the LORD do so; may the LORD fulfil the words that you have prophesied, and bring back to this place from Babylon the vessels of the house of the LORD, and all the exiles. But listen now to this word that I speak in your hearing and in the hearing of all the people. The prophets who preceded you and me from ancient times prophesied war, famine, and pestilence against many countries and great kingdoms. As for the prophet who prophesies peace, when the word of that prophet comes true, then it will be known that the LORD has truly sent the prophet.'

Then the prophet Hananiah took the yoke from the neck of the prophet Jeremiah, and broke it. And Hananiah spoke in the presence of all the people, saying, 'Thus says the LORD: This is how I will break the yoke of King Nebuchadnezzar of Babylon from the neck of all the nations within two years.' At this, the prophet Jeremiah went his way.

Some time after the prophet Hananiah had broken the yoke from the neck of the prophet Jeremiah, the word of the LORD came to Jeremiah: Go, tell Hananiah, Thus says the LORD: You have broken wooden bars only to forge iron bars in place of them! For thus says the LORD of hosts, the God of Israel: I have put an iron yoke on the neck of all these nations so that they may serve King Nebuchadnezzar of Babylon, and they shall indeed serve him; I have even given him the wild animals. And the prophet Jeremiah said to the prophet Hananiah, 'Listen, Hananiah, the LORD has not sent you, and you made this people trust in a lie. Therefore thus says the LORD: I am going to send you off the face of the earth. Within this year you will be dead, because you have spoken rebellion against the LORD.'

In that same year, in the seventh month, the prophet Hananiah died.

This is the word of the Lord. *Jeremiah 28*

Responsorial Psalm

R **Teach me, O Lord, the way of your statutes:**
   [lead me in the path of your commandments].   *Psalm 119.33a, 35a*

O Lord, your word is everlasting;
it ever stands firm in the heavens.
Your faithfulness also remains from one generation to another;
you have established the earth and it abides. R

So also your judgements stand firm this day,
for all things are your servants.
If your law had not been my delight,
I should have perished in my trouble. R

I will never forget your commandments,
for by them you have given me life.
I am yours, O save me!
For I have sought your commandments. R

The wicked have waited for me to destroy me,
but I will meditate on your testimonies.
I have seen an end of all perfection,
but your commandment knows no bounds. R   *Psalm 119.89–96*

Year B and Year C

Hear the Gospel of our Lord Jesus Christ according to Matthew.

When Jesus heard that John the Baptist had been killed, he withdrew from
there in a boat to a deserted place by himself. But when the crowds heard it,
they followed him on foot from the towns. When he went ashore, he saw a
great crowd; and he had compassion for them and cured their sick. When
it was evening, the disciples came to him and said, 'This is a deserted place,
and the hour is now late; send the crowds away so that they may go into the
villages and buy food for themselves.' Jesus said to them, 'They need not go
away; you give them something to eat.' They replied, 'We have nothing here
but five loaves and two fish.' And he said, 'Bring them here to me.' Then he
ordered the crowds to sit down on the grass. Taking the five loaves and the
two fish, he looked up to heaven, and blessed and broke the loaves, and gave
them to the disciples, and the disciples gave them to the crowds. And all ate
and were filled; and they took up what was left over of the broken pieces,
twelve baskets full. And those who ate were about five thousand men, besides
women and children.

This is the Gospel of the Lord.   *Matthew 14.13–21*

Hear the Gospel of our Lord Jesus Christ according to Matthew.

Immediately Jesus had fed the crowd, he made the disciples get into the boat and go on ahead to the other side, while he dismissed the crowds. And after he had dismissed the crowds, he went up the mountain by himself to pray. When evening came, he was there alone, but by this time the boat, battered by the waves, was far from the land, for the wind was against them. And early in the morning he came walking towards them on the lake. But when the disciples saw him walking on the lake, they were terrified, saying, 'It is a ghost!' And they cried out in fear. But immediately Jesus spoke to them and said, 'Take heart, it is I; do not be afraid.'

Peter answered him, 'Lord, if it is you, command me to come to you on the water.' He said, 'Come.' So Peter got out of the boat, started walking on the water, and came towards Jesus. But when he noticed the strong wind, he became frightened, and beginning to sink, he cried out, 'Lord, save me!' Jesus immediately reached out his hand and caught him, saying to him, 'You of little faith, why did you doubt?' When they got into the boat, the wind ceased. And those in the boat worshipped him, saying, 'Truly you are the Son of God.'

When they had crossed over, they came to land at Gennesaret. After the people of that place recognized him, they sent word throughout the region and brought all who were sick to him, and begged him that they might touch even the fringe of his cloak; and all who touched it were healed.

This is the Gospel of the Lord.   Matthew 14.22–end

Week 18: Tuesday between 2 and 8 August

Year 1

A reading from the book Numbers.

Miriam and Aaron spoke against Moses because of the Cushite woman whom he had married (for he had indeed married a Cushite woman); and they said, 'Has the LORD spoken only through Moses? Has he not spoken through us also?' And the LORD heard it. Now the man Moses was very humble, more so than anyone else on the face of the earth. Suddenly the LORD said to Moses, Aaron, and Miriam, 'Come out, you three, to the tent of meeting.' So the three of them came out. Then the LORD came down in a pillar of cloud, and stood at the entrance of the tent, and called Aaron and Miriam; and they both came forward. And he said, 'Hear my words:

When there are prophets among you,
    I the LORD make myself known to them in visions;
    I speak to them in dreams.
Not so with my servant Moses;
    he is entrusted with all my house.

With him I speak face to face – clearly, not in riddles;
and he beholds the form of the LORD.
Why then were you not afraid to speak against my servant Moses?' And the
anger of the LORD was kindled against them, and he departed.
When the cloud went away from over the tent, Miriam had become
leprous, as white as snow. And Aaron turned towards Miriam and saw that she
was leprous. Then Aaron said to Moses, 'Oh, my lord, do not punish us for a
sin that we have so foolishly committed. Do not let her be like one stillborn,
whose flesh is half consumed when it comes out of its mother's womb.' And
Moses cried to the LORD, 'O God, please heal her.'

This is the word of the Lord.   Numbers 12.1–13

Responsorial Psalm

R* **Purge me with hyssop and I shall be clean;**
[wash me and I shall be whiter than snow].   Psalm 51.8

Have mercy on me, O God,
in your great goodness;
according to the abundance of your compassion
blot out my offences. **R**

Wash me thoroughly from my wickedness
and cleanse me from my sin.
For I acknowledge my faults
and my sin is ever before me. **R**

Against you only have I sinned
and done what is evil in your sight,
so that you are justified in your sentence
and righteous in your judgement. **R**

I have been wicked even from my birth,
a sinner when my mother conceived me.
Behold, you desire truth deep within me
and shall make me understand wisdom
in the depths of my heart. **R***   Psalm 51.1–8

Year 2

A reading from the prophecy of Jeremiah.

The word that came to Jeremiah from the Lord: Thus says the Lord, the God
of Israel: Write in a book all the words that I have spoken to you.
  For thus says the Lord:
  Your hurt is incurable,
      your wound is grievous.
  There is no one to uphold your cause,
      no medicine for your wound,
      no healing for you.
  All your lovers have forgotten you;
      they care nothing for you;
  for I have dealt you the blow of an enemy,
      the punishment of a merciless foe,
  because your guilt is great,
      because your sins are so numerous.
  Why do you cry out over your hurt?
      Your pain is incurable.
  Because your guilt is great,
      because your sins are so numerous,
      I have done these things to you.

  Thus says the Lord:
  I am going to restore the fortunes of the tents of Jacob,
      and have compassion on his dwellings;
  the city shall be rebuilt upon its mound,
      and the citadel set on its rightful site.
  Out of them shall come thanksgiving,
      and the sound of merrymakers.
  I will make them many, and they shall not be few;
      I will make them honoured, and they shall not be disdained.
  Their children shall be as of old,
      their congregation shall be established before me;
      and I will punish all who oppress them.
  Their prince shall be one of their own,
      their ruler shall come from their midst;
  I will bring him near, and he shall approach me,
      for who would otherwise dare to approach me?
                    says the Lord.
  And you shall be my people,
      and I will be your God.

This is the word of the Lord.   Jeremiah 30.1–2, 12–15, 18–22

R **The Lord has built up Zion
and shown himself in glory.**   cf Psalm 102.17

Then shall the nations fear your name, O Lord,
and all the kings of the earth your glory,
when the Lord has built up Zion
and shown himself in glory. R

When he has turned to the prayer of the destitute
and has not despised their plea.
This shall be written for those that come after,
and a people yet unborn shall praise the Lord. R

For he has looked down from his holy height;
from the heavens he beheld the earth,
that he might hear the sighings of the prisoner
and set free those condemned to die. R   Psalm 102.16–21

Year B and Year C

Hear the Gospel of our Lord Jesus Christ according to Matthew.

Immediately Jesus had fed the crowd he made the disciples get into the boat
and go on ahead to the other side, while he dismissed the crowds. And after
he had dismissed the crowds, he went up the mountain by himself to pray.
When evening came, he was there alone, but by this time the boat, battered
by the waves, was far from the land, for the wind was against them. And
early in the morning he came walking towards them on the lake. But when
the disciples saw him walking on the lake, they were terrified, saying, 'It is a
ghost!' And they cried out in fear. But immediately Jesus spoke to them and
said, 'Take heart, it is I; do not be afraid.'

Peter answered him, 'Lord, if it is you, command me to come to you on
the water.' He said, 'Come.' So Peter got out of the boat, started walking on
the water, and came towards Jesus. But when he noticed the strong wind, he
became frightened, and beginning to sink, he cried out, 'Lord, save me!' Jesus
immediately reached out his hand and caught him, saying to him, 'You of little
faith, why did you doubt?' When they got into the boat, the wind ceased. And
those in the boat worshipped him, saying, 'Truly you are the Son of God.'

When they had crossed over, they came to land at Gennesaret. After the
people of that place recognized him, they sent word throughout the region
and brought all who were sick to him, and begged him that they might touch
even the fringe of his cloak; and all who touched it were healed.

This is the Gospel of the Lord.   Matthew 14.22–end

Hear the Gospel of our Lord Jesus Christ according to Matthew.

Pharisees and scribes came to Jesus from Jerusalem and said, 'Why do your disciples break the tradition of the elders? For they do not wash their hands before they eat.'

Then he called the crowd to him and said to them, 'Listen and understand: it is not what goes into the mouth that defiles a person, but it is what comes out of the mouth that defiles.' Then the disciples approached and said to him, 'Do you know that the Pharisees took offence when they heard what you said?' He answered, 'Every plant that my heavenly Father has not planted will be uprooted. Let them alone; they are blind guides of the blind. And if one blind person guides another, both will fall into a pit.'

This is the Gospel of the Lord.   Matthew 15.1–2, 10–14

Week 18: Wednesday between 3 and 9 August

Year I

A reading from the book Numbers.

The LORD said to Moses, 'Send men to spy out the land of Canaan, which I am giving to the Israelites; from each of their ancestral tribes you shall send a man, every one a leader among them.'

At the end of forty days they returned from spying out the land. And they came to Moses and Aaron and to all the congregation of the Israelites in the wilderness of Paran, at Kadesh; they brought back word to them and to all the congregation, and showed them the fruit of the land. And they told him, 'We came to the land to which you sent us; it flows with milk and honey, and this is its fruit. Yet the people who live in the land are strong, and the towns are fortified and very large; and besides, we saw the descendants of Anak there. The Amalekites live in the land of the Negeb; the Hittites, the Jebusites, and the Amorites live in the hill country; and the Canaanites live by the sea, and along the Jordan.'

But Caleb quieted the people before Moses, and said, 'Let us go up at once and occupy it, for we are well able to overcome it.' Then the men who had gone up with him said, 'We are not able to go up against this people, for they are stronger than we are.' So they brought to the Israelites an unfavourable report of the land that they had spied out, saying, 'The land that we have gone through as spies is a land that devours its inhabitants; and all the people that we saw in it are of great size. There we saw the Nephilim (the Anakites come from the Nephilim); and to ourselves we seemed like grasshoppers, and so we seemed to them.'

Then all the congregation raised a loud cry, and the people wept that night. And the LORD spoke to Moses and to Aaron, saying: How long shall this wicked congregation complain against me? I have heard the complaints of the

Israelites, which they complain against me. Say to them, 'As I live', says the LORD, 'I will do to you the very things I heard you say: your dead bodies shall fall in this very wilderness; and of all your number, included in the census, from twenty years old and upwards, who have complained against me, not one of you shall come into the land in which I swore to settle you, except Caleb son of Jephunneh and Joshua son of Nun. But your little ones, who you said would become booty, I will bring in, and they shall know the land that you have despised. But as for you, your dead bodies shall fall in this wilderness. And your children shall be shepherds in the wilderness for forty years, and shall suffer for your faithlessness, until the last of your dead bodies lies in the wilderness. According to the number of the days in which you spied out the land, forty days, for every day a year, you shall bear your iniquity, forty years, and you shall know my displeasure.' I the LORD have spoken; surely I will do thus to all this wicked congregation gathered together against me: in this wilderness they shall come to a full end, and there they shall die.

This is the word of the Lord.   Numbers 13.1–2, 25 – 14.1, 26–35

Responsorial Psalm

R **Remember me, Lord,**
   when you show favour to your people.   cf Psalm 106.4a

A craving seized them in the wilderness,
and they put God to the test in the desert.
He gave them their desire,
but sent a wasting sickness among them. **R**

They grew jealous of Moses in the camp
and of Aaron, the holy one of the Lord.
So the earth opened and swallowed up Dathan
and covered the company of Abiram. **R**

A fire was kindled in their company;
the flame burnt up the wicked.
They made a calf at Horeb
and worshipped the molten image;
thus they exchanged their glory
for the image of an ox that feeds on hay. **R**

They forgot God their saviour,
who had done such great things in Egypt,
wonderful deeds in the land of Ham
and fearful things at the Red Sea. **R**

So he would have destroyed them,
had not Moses his chosen stood before him in the breach,
to turn away his wrath from consuming them.
Then they scorned the Promised Land
and would not believe his word. **R**   Psalm 106.14–24

A reading from the prophecy of Jeremiah.

At that time, says the LORD, I will be the God of all the families of Israel, and they shall be my people.

Thus says the LORD:
The people who survived the sword
found grace in the wilderness;
when Israel sought for rest,
the LORD appeared to him from far away.
I have loved you with an everlasting love;
therefore I have continued my faithfulness to you.
Again I will build you, and you shall be built,
O virgin Israel!
Again you shall take your tambourines,
and go forth in the dance of the merrymakers.
Again you shall plant vineyards
on the mountains of Samaria;
the planters shall plant,
and shall enjoy the fruit.
For there shall be a day when sentinels will call
in the hill country of Ephraim:
'Come, let us go up to Zion,
to the LORD our God.'

For thus says the LORD:
Sing aloud with gladness for Jacob,
and raise shouts for the chief of the nations;
proclaim, give praise, and say,
'Save, O LORD, your people,
the remnant of Israel.'

This is the word of the Lord.   Jeremiah 31.1–7

Responsorial Psalm

R **My help comes from the Lord,**
   [the maker of heaven and earth].   Psalm 121.2

I lift up my eyes to the hills;
from where is my help to come?
My help comes from the Lord,
the maker of heaven and earth. **R**

He will not suffer your foot to stumble;
he who watches over you will not sleep.
Behold, he who keeps watch over Israel
shall neither slumber nor sleep. **R**

The Lord himself watches over you;
the Lord is your shade at your right hand,
so that the sun shall not strike you by day,
neither the moon by night. **R**

The Lord shall keep you from all evil;
it is he who shall keep your soul.
The Lord shall keep watch over your going out
	and your coming in,
from this time forth for evermore. **R** *Psalm* 121

Year 1 and Year 2

Hear the Gospel of our Lord Jesus Christ according to Matthew.

Jesus went away to the district of Tyre and Sidon. Just then a Canaanite woman
from that region came out and started shouting, 'Have mercy on me, Lord,
Son of David; my daughter is tormented by a demon.' But he did not answer
her at all. And his disciples came and urged him, saying, 'Send her away, for
she keeps shouting after us.' He answered, 'I was sent only to the lost sheep
of the house of Israel.' But she came and knelt before him, saying, 'Lord, help
me.' He answered, 'It is not fair to take the children's food and throw it to
the dogs.' She said, 'Yes, Lord, yet even the dogs eat the crumbs that fall from
their masters' table.' Then Jesus answered her, 'Woman, great is your faith! Let
it be done for you as you wish.' And her daughter was healed instantly.

This is the Gospel of the Lord. *Matthew* 15.21–28

Week 18: Thursday between 4 and 10 August

Year 1

A reading from the book Numbers.

The Israelites, the whole congregation, came into the wilderness of Zin in
the first month, and the people stayed in Kadesh. Miriam died there, and
was buried there.

Now there was no water for the congregation; so they gathered together
against Moses and against Aaron. The people quarrelled with Moses and said,
'Would that we had died when our kindred died before the Lord! Why have
you brought the assembly of the Lord into this wilderness for us and our
livestock to die here? Why have you brought us up out of Egypt, to bring us to
this wretched place? It is no place for grain, or figs, or vines, or pomegranates;
and there is no water to drink.' Then Moses and Aaron went away from the
assembly to the entrance of the tent of meeting; they fell on their faces, and
the glory of the Lord appeared to them. The Lord spoke to Moses, saying:
Take the staff, and assemble the congregation, you and your brother Aaron,
and command the rock before their eyes to yield its water. Thus you shall →

bring water out of the rock for them; thus you shall provide drink for the congregation and their livestock.

So Moses took the staff from before the LORD, as he had commanded him. Moses and Aaron gathered the assembly together before the rock, and he said to them, 'Listen, you rebels, shall we bring water for you out of this rock?' Then Moses lifted up his hand and struck the rock twice with his staff; water came out abundantly, and the congregation and their livestock drank. But the LORD said to Moses and Aaron, 'Because you did not trust in me, to show my holiness before the eyes of the Israelites, therefore you shall not bring this assembly into the land that I have given them.' These are the waters of Meribah, where the people of Israel quarrelled with the LORD, and by which he showed his holiness.

This is the word of the Lord. Numbers 20.1–13

Responsorial Psalm

R* **Come, let us sing to the Lord;**
    and rejoice in the rock of our salvation. cf Psalm 95.1

O that today you would listen to his voice:
Harden not your hearts as at Meribah,
on that day at Massah in the wilderness,
when your forebears tested me, and put me to the proof,
though they had seen my works.   **R**

Forty years long I detested that generation and said,
'This people are wayward in their hearts;
they do not know my ways.'
So I swore in my wrath,
'They shall not enter into my rest.'   **R** Psalm 95.1, 8–end

Year 2

A reading from the prophecy of Jeremiah.

The days are surely coming, says the LORD, when I will make a new covenant with the house of Israel and the house of Judah. It will not be like the covenant that I made with their ancestors when I took them by the hand to bring them out of the land of Egypt – a covenant that they broke, though I was their husband, says the LORD. But this is the covenant that I will make with the house of Israel after those days, says the LORD: I will put my law within them, and I will write it on their hearts; and I will be their God, and they shall be my people. No longer shall they teach one another, or say to each other, 'Know the LORD', for they shall all know me, from the least of them to the greatest, says the LORD; for I will forgive their iniquity, and remember their sin no more.

This is the word of the Lord. Jeremiah 31.31–34

Responsorial Psalm

R **Make me a clean heart, O God,**
[and renew a right spirit within me]. Psalm 51.11

Make me a clean heart, O God,
and renew a right spirit within me.
Cast me not away from your presence
and take not your holy spirit from me. **R**

Give me again the joy of your salvation
and sustain me with your gracious spirit;
then shall I teach your ways to the wicked
and sinners shall return to you. **R**

Deliver me from my guilt, O God,
the God of my salvation,
and my tongue shall sing of your righteousness.
O Lord, open my lips
and my mouth shall proclaim your praise. **R**

For you desire no sacrifice, else I would give it;
you take no delight in burnt offerings.
The sacrifice of God is a broken spirit;
a broken and contrite heart, O God, you will not despise. **R**

Psalm 51.11–18

Year 1 and Year 2

Hear the Gospel of our Lord Jesus Christ according to Matthew.

When Jesus came into the district of Caesarea Philippi, he asked his disciples, 'Who do people say that the Son of Man is?' And they said, 'Some say John the Baptist, but others Elijah, and still others Jeremiah or one of the prophets.' He said to them, 'But who do you say that I am?' Simon Peter answered, 'You are the Messiah, the Son of the living God.' And Jesus answered him, 'Blessed are you, Simon son of Jonah! For flesh and blood has not revealed this to you, but my Father in heaven. And I tell you, you are Peter, and on this rock I will build my church, and the gates of Hades will not prevail against it. I will give you the keys of the kingdom of heaven, and whatever you bind on earth will be bound in heaven, and whatever you loose on earth will be loosed in heaven.' Then he sternly ordered the disciples not to tell anyone that he was the Messiah.

From that time on, Jesus began to show his disciples that he must go to Jerusalem and undergo great suffering at the hands of the elders and chief priests and scribes, and be killed, and on the third day be raised. And Peter took him aside and began to rebuke him, saying, 'God forbid it, Lord! This must never happen to you.' But he turned and said to Peter, 'Get behind me, Satan! You are a stumbling-block to me; for you are setting your mind not on divine things but on human things.'

This is the Gospel of the Lord. Matthew 16.13–23

Week 18: Friday between 5 and 11 August

Year 1

A reading from the book Deuteronomy.

Moses said to the people, 'Ask now about former ages, long before your own, ever since the day that God created human beings on the earth; ask from one end of heaven to the other: has anything so great as this ever happened or has its like ever been heard of? Has any people ever heard the voice of a god speaking out of a fire, as you have heard, and lived? Or has any god ever attempted to go and take a nation for himself from the midst of another nation, by trials, by signs and wonders, by war, by a mighty hand and an outstretched arm, and by terrifying displays of power, as the LORD your God did for you in Egypt before your very eyes? To you it was shown so that you would acknowledge that the LORD is God; there is no other besides him. From heaven he made you hear his voice to discipline you. On earth he showed you his great fire, while you heard his words coming out of the fire. And because he loved your ancestors, he chose their descendants after them. He brought you out of Egypt with his own presence, by his great power, driving out before you nations greater and mightier than yourselves, to bring you in, giving you their land for a possession, as it is still today. So acknowledge today and take to heart that the LORD is God in heaven above and on the earth beneath; there is no other. Keep his statutes and his commandments, which I am commanding you today for your own well-being and that of your descendants after you, so that you may long remain in the land that the LORD your God is giving you for all time.'

This is the word of the Lord.   Deuteronomy 4.32–40

Responsorial Psalm

R   **I will remember the works of the Lord
    [and call to mind your wonders].**   cf Psalm 77.11

I will remember the works of the Lord
and call to mind your wonders of old time.
I will meditate on all your works
and ponder your mighty deeds.   **R**

Your way, O God, is holy;
who is so great a god as our God?
You are the God who worked wonders
and declared your power among the peoples.   **R**

With a mighty arm you redeemed your people,
the children of Jacob and Joseph.
The waters saw you, O God;
the waters saw you and were afraid;
the depths also were troubled.   **R**

The clouds poured out water; the skies thundered;
your arrows flashed on every side;
the voice of your thunder was in the whirlwind;
your lightnings lit up the ground;
the earth trembled and shook. R

Your way was in the sea,
and your paths in the great waters,
but your footsteps were not known.
You led your people like sheep
by the hand of Moses and Aaron. R   *Psalm 77.11–end*

Year 2

A reading from the prophecy of Nahum.

A shatterer has come up against you.
    Guard the ramparts;
    watch the road;
gird your loins;
    collect all your strength.

The shields of his warriors are red;
    his soldiers are clothed in crimson.
The metal on the chariots flashes
    on the day when he musters them;
    the chargers prance.

Ah! City of bloodshed,
    utterly deceitful, full of booty –
    no end to the plunder!
The crack of whip and rumble of wheel,
    galloping horse and bounding chariot!
Horsemen charging,
    flashing sword and glittering spear,
piles of dead,
    heaps of corpses,
dead bodies without end –
    they stumble over the bodies!
I will throw filth at you
    and treat you with contempt,
    and make you a spectacle.
Then all who see you will shrink from you and say,
'Nineveh is devastated; who will bemoan her?'
    Where shall I seek comforters for you?

This is the word of the Lord.   *Nahum 2.1, 3, 3.1–3, 6–7*

Either

Canticle

R **The Lord will vindicate his people;**
[he puts to death and he keeps alive]. *cf Deuteronomy 32.36a, 39b*

The day of their downfall is at hand,
their doom is fast approaching.
For the Lord will vindicate his people,
and have compassion on his servants;
when he sees that their power is gone,
and neither slave nor free remains. **R**

See now that I, I am he:
there is no god but me.
I put to death and I keep alive;
it is I who strike and I who heal;
and there is no deliverance from my hand. **R**

When I whet my flashing sword,
and my hand takes hold on judgement,
then I will take vengeance on my adversaries,
and will repay those who hate me. **R** *Deuteronomy 32.35–36, 39, 41*

or

Responsorial Psalm

R **By the waters of Babylon we sat down and wept,**
when we remembered Zion. *Psalm 137.1*

By the waters of Babylon we sat down and wept,
when we remembered Zion.
As for our lyres, we hung them up
on the willows that grow in that land. **R**

For there our captors asked for a song,
our tormentors called for mirth:
'Sing us one of the songs of Zion.'
How shall we sing the Lord's song
in a strange land? **R**

If I forget you, O Jerusalem,
let my right hand forget its skill.
Let my tongue cleave to the roof of my mouth
if I do not remember you,
if I set not Jerusalem above my highest joy. **R** *Psalm 137.1–6*

Hear the Gospel of our Lord Jesus Christ according to Matthew.

Jesus told his disciples, 'If any want to become my followers, let them deny themselves and take up their cross and follow me. For those who want to save their life will lose it, and those who lose their life for my sake will find it. For what will it profit them if they gain the whole world but forfeit their life? Or what will they give in return for their life?

'For the Son of Man is to come with his angels in the glory of his Father, and then he will repay everyone for what has been done. Truly I tell you, there are some standing here who will not taste death before they see the Son of Man coming in his kingdom.'

This is the Gospel of the Lord. Matthew 16.24–28

Week 18: Saturday between 6 and 12 August

Year 1

A reading from the book Deuteronomy.

Moses said to the people, 'Hear, O Israel: The LORD is our God, the LORD alone. You shall love the LORD your God with all your heart, and with all your soul, and with all your might. Keep these words that I am commanding you today in your heart. Recite them to your children and talk about them when you are at home and when you are away, when you lie down and when you rise. Bind them as a sign on your hand, fix them as an emblem on your forehead, and write them on the doorposts of your house and on your gates.

'When the LORD your God has brought you into the land that he swore to your ancestors, to Abraham, to Isaac, and to Jacob, to give you – a land with fine, large cities that you did not build, houses filled with all sorts of goods that you did not fill, hewn cisterns that you did not hew, vineyards and olive groves that you did not plant – and when you have eaten your fill, take care that you do not forget the LORD, who brought you out of the land of Egypt, out of the house of slavery. The LORD your God you shall fear; him you shall serve, and by his name alone you shall swear.'

This is the word of the Lord. Deuteronomy 6.4–13

Responsorial Psalm

R **O God, you are my rock and my refuge,**
   [you are my shield and strong defence].   cf *Psalm* 18.2

I love you, O Lord my strength.
The Lord is my crag, my fortress and my deliverer,
my God, my rock in whom I take refuge,
my shield, the horn of my salvation and my stronghold. **R**

Even the God who vindicates me
and subdues the peoples under me!
You that deliver me from my enemies,
you will set me up above my foes;
from the violent you will deliver me. **R**

Therefore will I give you thanks, O Lord, among the nations
and sing praises to your name,
to the one who gives great victory to his king
and shows faithful love to his anointed,
to David and his seed for ever. **R**   *Psalm* 18.1–2, 48–end

Year 2

A reading from the prophecy of Habakkuk.

Are you not from of old,
    O Lord my God, my Holy One?
    You shall not die.
O Lord, you have marked them for judgement;
    and you, O Rock, have established them for punishment.
Your eyes are too pure to behold evil,
    and you cannot look on wrongdoing;
why do you look on the treacherous,
    and are silent when the wicked swallow
    those more righteous than they?
You have made people like the fish of the sea,
    like crawling things that have no ruler.

The enemy brings all of them up with a hook;
    he drags them out with his net,
he gathers them in his seine;
    so he rejoices and exults.
Therefore he sacrifices to his net
    and makes offerings to his seine;
for by them his portion is lavish,
    and his food is rich.
Is he then to keep on emptying his net,
    and destroying nations without mercy?

I will stand at my watch-post,
    and station myself on the rampart;
I will keep watch to see what he will say to me,
    and what he will answer concerning my complaint.
Then the LORD answered me and said:
Write the vision;
    make it plain on tablets,
    so that a runner may read it.
For there is still a vision for the appointed time;
    it speaks of the end, and does not lie.
If it seems to tarry, wait for it;
    it will surely come, it will not delay.
Look at the proud!
    Their spirit is not right in them,
    but the righteous live by their faith.

This is the word of the Lord.   Habakkuk 1.12 − 2.4

Responsorial Psalm

R* **Sing praises to the Lord who dwells in Zion;**
    [declare among the peoples the things he has done].   Psalm 9.11

But the Lord shall endure for ever;
he has made fast his throne for judgement.
For he shall rule the world with righteousness
and govern the peoples with equity.   **R**

Then will the Lord be a refuge for the oppressed,
a refuge in the time of trouble.
And those who know your name will put their trust in you,
for you, Lord, have never failed those who seek you.   **R***   Psalm 9.7–11

Year 1 and Year 2

Hear the Gospel of our Lord Jesus Christ according to Matthew.

A man came to Jesus, knelt before him, and said, 'Lord, have mercy on my son, for he is an epileptic and he suffers terribly; he often falls into the fire and often into the water. And I brought him to your disciples, but they could not cure him.' Jesus answered, 'You faithless and perverse generation, how much longer must I be with you? How much longer must I put up with you? Bring him here to me.' And Jesus rebuked the demon, and it came out of him, and the boy was cured instantly.

    Then the disciples came to Jesus privately and said, 'Why could we not cast it out?' He said to them, 'Because of your little faith. For truly I tell you, if you have faith the size of a mustard seed, you will say to this mountain, "Move from here to there", and it will move; and nothing will be impossible for you.'

This is the Gospel of the Lord.   Matthew 17.14–20

Week 19: Monday between 8 and 14 August

Year 1

A reading from the book Deuteronomy.

Moses said to the people, 'What does the LORD your God require of you? Only to fear the LORD your God, to walk in all his ways, to love him, to serve the LORD your God with all your heart and with all your soul, and to keep the commandments of the LORD your God and his decrees that I am commanding you today, for your own well-being.

'Although heaven and the heaven of heavens belong to the LORD your God, the earth with all that is in it, yet the LORD set his heart in love on your ancestors alone and chose you, their descendants after them, out of all the peoples, as it is today. Circumcise, then, the foreskin of your heart, and do not be stubborn any longer. For the LORD your God is God of gods and Lord of lords, the great God, mighty and awesome, who is not partial and takes no bribe, who executes justice for the orphan and the widow, and who loves the strangers, providing them with food and clothing. You shall also love the stranger, for you were strangers in the land of Egypt. You shall fear the LORD your God; him alone you shall worship; to him you shall hold fast, and by his name you shall swear. He is your praise; he is your God, who has done for you these great and awesome things that your own eyes have seen. Your ancestors went down to Egypt seventy persons; and now the LORD your God has made you as numerous as the stars in heaven.'

This is the word of the Lord.   Deuteronomy 10.12–end

Responsorial Psalm

R* **Sing praise to the Lord, O Jerusalem:**
   [praise your God, O Zion].   Psalm 147.13

The Lord has strengthened the bars of your gates
and has blest your children within you.
He has established peace in your borders
and satisfies you with the finest wheat.   **R**

He sends forth his command to the earth
and his word runs very swiftly.
He gives snow like wool
and scatters the hoarfrost like ashes.   **R**

He casts down his hailstones like morsels of bread;
who can endure his frost?
He sends forth his word and melts them;
he blows with his wind and the waters flow.   **R**

He declares his word to Jacob,
his statutes and judgements to Israel.
He has not dealt so with any other nation;
they do not know his laws.   **R**   Psalm 147.13–end

A reading from the prophecy of Ezekiel.

On the fifth day of the month (it was the fifth year of the exile of King Jehoiachin), the word of the LORD came to the priest Ezekiel son of Buzi, in the land of the Chaldeans by the river Chebar; and the hand of the LORD was on him there.

As I looked, a stormy wind came out of the north: a great cloud with brightness around it and fire flashing forth continually, and in the middle of the fire, something like gleaming amber. In the middle of it was something like four living creatures. This was their appearance: they were of human form. When they moved, I heard the sound of their wings like the sound of mighty waters, like the thunder of the Almighty, a sound of tumult like the sound of an army; when they stopped, they let down their wings. And there came a voice from above the dome over their heads; when they stopped, they let down their wings.

And above the dome over their heads there was something like a throne, in appearance like sapphire; and seated above the likeness of a throne was something that seemed like a human form. Upwards from what appeared like the loins I saw something like gleaming amber, something that looked like fire enclosed all round; and downwards from what looked like the loins I saw something that looked like fire, and there was a splendour all round. Like the bow in a cloud on a rainy day, such was the appearance of the splendour all round. This was the appearance of the likeness of the glory of the LORD. When I saw it, I fell on my face.

This is the word of the Lord.   Ezekiel 1.2–5, 24–end

Responsorial Psalm

R **The name of the Lord is exalted,**
   [his splendour above earth and heaven].   cf Psalm 148.13

Praise the Lord from the heavens;
praise him in the heights.
Praise him, all you his angels;
praise him, all his host.   **R**

Praise him, sun and moon;
praise him, all you stars of light.
Praise him, heaven of heavens,
and you waters above the heavens.   **R**

Young men and women,
old and young together;
let them praise the name of the Lord.
For his name only is exalted,
his splendour above earth and heaven.   **R**   Psalm 148.1–4, 12–13

Hear the Gospel of our Lord Jesus Christ according to Matthew.

As they were gathering in Galilee, Jesus said to his disciples, 'The Son of Man is going to be betrayed into human hands, and they will kill him, and on the third day he will be raised.' And they were greatly distressed.

When they reached Capernaum, the collectors of the temple tax came to Peter and said, 'Does your teacher not pay the temple tax?' He said, 'Yes, he does.' And when he came home, Jesus spoke of it first, asking, 'What do you think, Simon? From whom do kings of the earth take toll or tribute? From their children or from others?' When Peter said, 'From others', Jesus said to him, 'Then the children are free. However, so that we do not give offence to them, go to the lake and cast a hook; take the first fish that comes up; and when you open its mouth, you will find a coin; take that and give it to them for you and me.'

This is the Gospel of the Lord.   Matthew 17.22–end

Week 19: Tuesday between 9 and 15 August

Year 1

A reading from the book Deuteronomy.

Moses said these words to all Israel, 'I am now a hundred and twenty years old. I am no longer able to get about, and the LORD has told me, "You shall not cross over this Jordan." The LORD your God himself will cross over before you. He will destroy these nations before you, and you shall dispossess them. Joshua also will cross over before you, as the LORD promised. The LORD will do to them as he did to Sihon and Og, the kings of the Amorites, and to their land, when he destroyed them. The LORD will give them over to you and you shall deal with them in full accord with the command that I have given to you. Be strong and bold; have no fear or dread of them, because it is the LORD your God who goes with you; he will not fail you or forsake you.'

Then Moses summoned Joshua and said to him in the sight of all Israel: 'Be strong and bold, for you are the one who will go with this people into the land that the LORD has sworn to their ancestors to give them; and you will put them in possession of it. It is the LORD who goes before you. He will be with you; he will not fail you or forsake you. Do not fear or be dismayed.'

This is the word of the Lord.   Deuteronomy 31.1–8

Either

Canticle

**R* I will proclaim the name of the Lord,
[and tell of the greatness of God].** cf Deuteronomy 32.3

The Rock, his work is perfect; for all his ways are just:
a faithful God, without deceit, just and upright is he.
Remember the days of old, consider the years long past;
ask your father, and he will show you,
your elders, and they will tell you. **R**

When the Most High gave the nations their inheritance,
when he divided the children of the earth,
he fixed the bounds of the peoples
according to the number of the children of God.
For the Lord's own portion is his people,
Jacob his allotted heritage. **R** Deuteronomy 32.3–4, 7–9

or

Responsorial Psalm

**R* Give thanks to the Lord, for he is gracious;
[his steadfast love endures for ever].** Psalm 107.1

Let the redeemed of the Lord say this,
those he redeemed from the hand of the enemy,
and gathered out of the lands
from the east and from the west,
from the north and from the south. **R**

The upright will see this and rejoice,
but all wickedness will shut its mouth.
Whoever is wise will ponder these things
and consider the loving-kindness of the Lord. **R** Psalm 107.1–3, 42–end

Year 2

A reading from the prophecy of Ezekiel.

I heard the voice of someone speaking: You, mortal, hear what I say to you; do not be rebellious like that rebellious house; open your mouth and eat what I give you.

I looked, and a hand was stretched out to me, and a written scroll was in it. He spread it before me; it had writing on the front and on the back, and written on it were words of lamentation and mourning and woe.

He said to me, O mortal, eat what is offered to you; eat this scroll, and go, speak to the house of Israel. So I opened my mouth, and he gave me the scroll to eat. He said to me, Mortal, eat this scroll that I give you and fill your →

stomach with it. Then I ate it; and in my mouth it was as sweet as honey. He said to me: Mortal, go to the house of Israel and speak my very words to them.

This is the word of the Lord. Ezekiel 2.8 – 3.4

Responsorial Psalm

R **Blessed are those who walk in the law of the Lord.** cf Psalm 119.1

You have dealt graciously with your servant,
according to your word, O Lord.
O teach me true understanding and knowledge,
for I have trusted in your commandments.   R

Before I was afflicted I went astray,
but now I keep your word.
You are gracious and do good;
O Lord, teach me your statutes.   R

The proud have smeared me with lies,
but I will keep your commandments with my whole heart.
Their heart has become gross with fat,
but my delight is in your law.   R

It is good for me that I have been afflicted,
that I may learn your statutes.
The law of your mouth is dearer to me
than a hoard of gold and silver.   R Psalm 119.65–72

Year 1 and Year 2

Hear the Gospel of our Lord Jesus Christ according to Matthew.

The disciples came to Jesus and asked, 'Who is the greatest in the kingdom of heaven?' He called a child, whom he put among them, and said, 'Truly I tell you, unless you change and become like children, you will never enter the kingdom of heaven. Whoever becomes humble like this child is the greatest in the kingdom of heaven. Whoever welcomes one such child in my name welcomes me.

'Take care that you do not despise one of these little ones; for, I tell you, in heaven their angels continually see the face of my Father in heaven. What do you think? If a shepherd has a hundred sheep, and one of them has gone astray, does he not leave the ninety-nine on the mountains and go in search of the one that went astray? And if he finds it, truly I tell you, he rejoices over it more than over the ninety-nine that never went astray. So it is not the will of your Father in heaven that one of these little ones should be lost.'

This is the Gospel of the Lord. Matthew 18.1–5, 10, 12–14

Week 19: Wednesday between 10 and 16 August

Year 1

A reading from the book Deuteronomy.

Moses went up from the plains of Moab to Mount Nebo, to the top of Pisgah, which is opposite Jericho, and the LORD showed him the whole land: Gilead as far as Dan, all Naphtali, the land of Ephraim and Manasseh, all the land of Judah as far as the Western Sea, the Negeb, and the Plain – that is, the valley of Jericho, the city of palm trees – as far as Zoar. The LORD said to him, 'This is the land of which I swore to Abraham, to Isaac, and to Jacob, saying, "I will give it to your descendants"; I have let you see it with your eyes, but you shall not cross over there.' Then Moses, the servant of the LORD, died there in the land of Moab, at the LORD's command. He was buried in a valley in the land of Moab, opposite Beth-peor, but no one knows his burial place to this day. Moses was one hundred and twenty years old when he died; his sight was unimpaired and his vigour had not abated. The Israelites wept for Moses in the plains of Moab for thirty days; then the period of mourning for Moses was ended.

Joshua son of Nun was full of the spirit of wisdom, because Moses had laid his hands on him; and the Israelites obeyed him, doing as the LORD had commanded Moses.

Never since has there arisen a prophet in Israel like Moses, whom the LORD knew face to face. He was unequalled for all the signs and wonders that the LORD sent him to perform in the land of Egypt, against Pharaoh and all his servants and his entire land, and for all the mighty deeds and all the terrifying displays of power that Moses performed in the sight of all Israel.

This is the word of the Lord. Deuteronomy 34

Responsorial Psalm

R* **Blessed be God, who has not rejected my prayer;
[nor withheld his loving mercy].** cf Psalm 66.18

Come and listen, all you who fear God,
and I will tell you what he has done for my soul.
I called out to him with my mouth
and his praise was on my tongue.   R

If I had nursed evil in my heart,
the Lord would not have heard me,
but in truth God has heard me;
he has heeded the voice of my prayer.   R* Psalm 66.14–end

A reading from the prophecy of Ezekiel.

The LORD cried in my hearing with a loud voice, saying, 'Draw near, you executioners of the city, each with his destroying weapon in his hand.' And six men came from the direction of the upper gate, which faces north, each with his weapon for slaughter in his hand; among them was a man clothed in linen, with a writing-case at his side. They went in and stood beside the bronze altar.

Now the glory of the God of Israel had gone up, from the cherub on which it rested, to the threshold of the house. The LORD called to the man clothed in linen, who had the writing-case at his side, and said to him, 'Go through the city, through Jerusalem, and put a mark on the foreheads of those who sigh and groan over all the abominations that are committed in it.' To the others he said in my hearing, 'Pass through the city after him, and kill; your eye shall not spare, and you shall show no pity. Cut down old men, young men and young women, little children and women, but touch no one who has the mark. And begin at my sanctuary.' So they began with the elders who were in front of the house. Then he said to them, 'Defile the house, and fill the courts with the slain. Go!' So they went out and killed in the city.

Then the glory of the LORD went out from the threshold of the house and stopped above the cherubim. The cherubim lifted up their wings and rose up from the earth in my sight as they went out with the wheels beside them. They stopped at the entrance of the east gate of the house of the LORD; and the glory of the God of Israel was above them.

These were the living creatures that I saw underneath the God of Israel by the river Chebar; and I knew that they were cherubim. Each had four faces, each four wings, and underneath their wings something like human hands. As for what their faces were like, they were the same faces whose appearance I had seen by the river Chebar. Each one moved straight ahead.

This is the word of the Lord. Ezekiel 9.1–7, 10.18–end

Responsorial Psalm

R **Blessed be the name of the Lord:
[from this time forth and for evermore].** Psalm 113.2

Give praise, you servants of the Lord,
O praise the name of the Lord.
Blessed be the name of the Lord,
from this time forth and for evermore.   **R**

From the rising of the sun to its setting
let the name of the Lord be praised.
The Lord is high above all nations
and his glory above the heavens.   **R**

Who is like the Lord our God,
that has his throne so high,
yet humbles himself to behold
the things of heaven and earth?   R

He raises the poor from the dust
and lifts the needy from the ashes,
to set them with princes,
with the princes of his people.
He gives the barren woman a place in the house
and makes her a joyful mother of children.   R   Psalm 113

Year 1 and Year 2

Hear the Gospel of our Lord Jesus Christ according to Matthew.

Jesus said to his disciples, 'If another member of the church sins against you,
go and point out the fault when the two of you are alone. If the member listens
to you, you have regained that one. But if you are not listened to, take one
or two others along with you, so that every word may be confirmed by the
evidence of two or three witnesses. If the member refuses to listen to them,
tell it to the church; and if the offender refuses to listen even to the church, let
such a one be to you as a Gentile and a tax-collector. Truly I tell you, whatever
you bind on earth will be bound in heaven, and whatever you loose on earth
will be loosed in heaven. Again, truly I tell you, if two of you agree on earth
about anything you ask, it will be done for you by my Father in heaven. For
where two or three are gathered in my name, I am there among them.'

This is the Gospel of the Lord.   Matthew 18.15–20

Week 19: Thursday between 11 and 17 August

Year 1

A reading from the Book of Joshua.

The LORD said to Joshua, 'This day I will begin to exalt you in the sight of all
Israel, so that they may know that I will be with you as I was with Moses. You
are the one who shall command the priests who bear the ark of the covenant,
"When you come to the edge of the waters of the Jordan, you shall stand still in
the Jordan." ' Joshua then said to the Israelites, 'Draw near and hear the words
of the LORD your God.' Joshua said, 'By this you shall know that among you is
the living God who without fail will drive out from before you the Canaanites,
Hittites, Hivites, Perizzites, Girgashites, Amorites, and Jebusites: the ark of the
covenant of the Lord of all the earth is going to pass before you into the Jordan.
When the soles of the feet of the priests who bear the ark of the LORD, the
Lord of all the earth, rest in the waters of the Jordan, the waters of the Jordan
flowing from above shall be cut off; they shall stand in a single heap.'   →

When the people set out from their tents to cross over the Jordan, the priests bearing the ark of the covenant were in front of the people. Now the Jordan overflows all its banks throughout the time of harvest. So when those who bore the ark had come to the Jordan, and the feet of the priests bearing the ark were dipped in the edge of the water, the waters flowing from above stood still, rising up in a single heap far off at Adam, the city that is beside Zarethan, while those flowing towards the sea of the Arabah, the Dead Sea, were wholly cut off. Then the people crossed over opposite Jericho. While all Israel were crossing over on dry ground, the priests who bore the ark of the covenant of the LORD stood on dry ground in the middle of the Jordan, until the entire nation finished crossing over the Jordan.

This is the word of the Lord. *Joshua 3.7–11, 13–end*

Responsorial Psalm

R **The earth shall tremble at the presence of the Lord:**
  [at the presence of the God of Jacob]. *cf Psalm 114.7*

When Israel came out of Egypt,
the house of Jacob from a people of a strange tongue,
Judah became his sanctuary,
Israel his dominion. R

The sea saw that, and fled;
Jordan was driven back.
The mountains skipped like rams,
the little hills like young sheep. R

What ailed you, O sea, that you fled?
O Jordan, that you were driven back?
You mountains, that you skipped like rams,
you little hills like young sheep? R

Tremble, O earth, at the presence of the Lord,
at the presence of the God of Jacob,
who turns the hard rock into a pool of water,
the flint-stone into a springing well. R   *Psalm 114*

Year 2

A reading from the prophecy of Ezekiel.

The word of the LORD came to me: Mortal, you are living in the midst of a rebellious house, who have eyes to see but do not see, who have ears to hear but do not hear; for they are a rebellious house. Therefore, mortal, prepare for yourself an exile's baggage, and go into exile by day in their sight; you shall go like an exile from your place to another place in their sight. Perhaps they will understand, though they are a rebellious house. You shall bring out your baggage by day in their sight, as baggage for exile; and you shall go out yourself at evening in their sight, as those do who go into exile. Dig through the wall in their sight, and carry the baggage through it. In their sight you shall lift the baggage on your shoulder, and carry it out in the dark; you shall cover your face, so that you may not see the land; for I have made you a sign for the house of Israel.

I did just as I was commanded. I brought out my baggage by day, as baggage for exile, and in the evening I dug through the wall with my own hands; I brought it out in the dark, carrying it on my shoulder in their sight.

In the morning the word of the LORD came to me: Mortal, has not the house of Israel, the rebellious house, said to you, 'What are you doing?' Say to them, 'Thus says the Lord GOD: This oracle concerns the prince in Jerusalem and all the house of Israel in it.' Say, 'I am a sign for you: as I have done, so shall it be done to them; they shall go into exile, into captivity.' And the prince who is among them shall lift his baggage on his shoulder in the dark, and shall go out; he shall dig through the wall and carry it through; he shall cover his face, so that he may not see the land with his eyes.

This is the word of the Lord.   Ezekiel 12.1–12

Responsorial Psalm

R **Forget not the deeds of the Lord:**
   [trust him and keep his commandments].   cf *Psalm* 78.7

They grieved him with their hill altars
and provoked him to displeasure with their idols.
God heard and was greatly angered,
and utterly rejected Israel.   **R**

He forsook the tabernacle at Shiloh,
the tent of his presence on earth.
He gave the ark of his strength into captivity,
his splendour into the adversary's hand.   **R**

He delivered his people to the sword
and raged against his inheritance.
The fire consumed their young men;
there was no one to lament their maidens.
Their priests fell by the sword,
and their widows made no lamentation.   **R**   *Psalm* 78.58–64

Year 1 and Year 2

Hear the Gospel of our Lord Jesus Christ according to Matthew.

Peter came and said to Jesus, 'Lord, if another member of the church sins against me, how often should I forgive? As many as seven times?' Jesus said to him, 'Not seven times, but, I tell you, seventy-seven times.

'For this reason the kingdom of heaven may be compared to a king who wished to settle accounts with his slaves. When he began the reckoning, one who owed him ten thousand talents was brought to him; and, as he could not pay, his lord ordered him to be sold, together with his wife and children and all his possessions, and payment to be made. So the slave fell on his knees before him, saying, "Have patience with me, and I will pay you everything." And out of pity for him, the lord of that slave released him and forgave him the debt. But that same slave, as he went out, came upon one of his fellow-slaves who owed him a hundred denarii; and seizing him by the throat, he said, "Pay what you owe." Then his fellow-slave fell down and pleaded with him, "Have patience with me, and I will pay you." But he refused; then he went and threw him into prison until he should pay the debt. When his fellow-slaves saw what had happened, they were greatly distressed, and they went and reported to their lord all that had taken place. Then his lord summoned him and said to him, "You wicked slave! I forgave you all that debt because you pleaded with me. Should you not have had mercy on your fellow-slave, as I had mercy on you?" And in anger his lord handed him over to be tortured until he should pay his entire debt. So my heavenly Father will also do to every one of you, if you do not forgive your brother or sister from your heart.'

When Jesus had finished saying these things, he left Galilee and went to the region of Judea beyond the Jordan.

This is the Gospel of the Lord.   Matthew 18.21 − 19.1

Week 19: Friday between 12 and 18 August

Year 1

A reading from the Book of Joshua.

Joshua gathered all the tribes of Israel to Shechem, and summoned the elders, the heads, the judges, and the officers of Israel; and they presented themselves before God. And Joshua said to all the people, 'Thus says the LORD, the God of Israel: Long ago your ancestors – Terah and his sons Abraham and Nahor – lived beyond the Euphrates and served other gods. Then I took your father Abraham from beyond the River and led him through all the land of Canaan and made his offspring many. I gave him Isaac; and to Isaac I gave Jacob and Esau. I gave Esau the hill country of Seir to possess, but Jacob and his children went down to Egypt. Then I sent Moses and Aaron, and I plagued Egypt with what I did in its midst; and afterwards I brought you out. When I brought your ancestors out of Egypt, you came to the sea; and the Egyptians pursued your ancestors with chariots and horsemen to the Red Sea. When they cried out to the Lord, he put darkness between you and the Egyptians, and made the sea come upon them and cover them; and your eyes saw what I did to Egypt. Afterwards you lived in the wilderness for a long time. Then I brought you to the land of the Amorites, who lived on the other side of the Jordan; they fought with you, and I handed them over to you, and you took possession of their land, and I destroyed them before you. Then King Balak, son of Zippor of Moab, set out to fight against Israel. He sent and invited Balaam son of Beor to curse you, but I would not listen to Balaam; therefore he blessed you; so I rescued you out of his hand.

'When you went over the Jordan and came to Jericho, the citizens of Jericho fought against you, and also the Amorites, the Perizzites, the Canaanites, the Hittites, the Girgashites, the Hivites, and the Jebusites; and I handed them over to you. I sent the hornet ahead of you, which drove out before you the two kings of the Amorites; it was not by your sword or by your bow. I gave you a land on which you had not laboured, and towns that you had not built, and you live in them; you eat the fruit of vineyards and olive groves that you did not plant.'

This is the word of the Lord. *Joshua 24.1–13*

Either

Canticle

R* **With joy you will draw water**
   from the wells of salvation. *Isaiah 12.3*

'Behold, God is my salvation;
I will trust, and will not be afraid;
for the Lord God is my strength and my song,
and has become my salvation.' **R***

On that day you will say,
'Give thanks to the Lord, call on his name;
make known his deeds among the nations;
proclaim that his name is exalted. **R**

'Sing praises to the Lord, who has triumphed gloriously;
let this be known in all the world.
Shout and sing for joy, you that dwell in Zion,
for great in your midst is the Holy One of Israel.' **R** *Isaiah 12.2–6*

or

Responsorial Psalm

R **His mercy endures for ever.**

Give thanks to the Lord, for he is gracious: [R]
Give thanks to the God of gods: [R]
Give thanks to the Lord of lords: [R]
Who led his people through the wilderness: R

Who smote great kings: [R]
And slew mighty kings: [R]
Sihon, king of the Amorites: [R]
And Og, the king of Bashan: R

And gave away their land for a heritage: [R]
A heritage for Israel his servant: R   Psalm 136.1–3, 16–22

Year 2

A reading from the prophecy of Ezekiel.

The word of the LORD came to me: Mortal, make known to Jerusalem her abominations, and say, Thus says the Lord GOD to Jerusalem: Your origin and your birth were in the land of the Canaanites; your father was an Amorite, and your mother a Hittite. As for your birth, on the day you were born your navel cord was not cut, nor were you washed with water to cleanse you, nor rubbed with salt, nor wrapped in cloths. No eye pitied you, to do any of these things for you out of compassion for you; but you were thrown out in the open field, for you were abhorred on the day you were born.

I passed by you, and saw you flailing about in your blood. As you lay in your blood, I said to you, 'Live! and grow up like a plant of the field.' You grew up and became tall and arrived at full womanhood; your breasts were formed, and your hair had grown; yet you were naked and bare.

I passed by you again and looked on you; you were at the age for love. I spread the edge of my cloak over you, and covered your nakedness: I pledged myself to you and entered into a covenant with you, says the Lord GOD, and you became mine. Then I bathed you with water and washed off the blood from you, and anointed you with oil. I clothed you with embroidered cloth and with sandals of fine leather; I bound you in fine linen and covered you with rich fabric. I adorned you with ornaments: I put bracelets on your arms, a chain on your neck, a ring on your nose, ear-rings in your ears, and a beautiful crown upon your head. You were adorned with gold and silver, while your clothing was of fine linen, rich fabric, and embroidered cloth. You had choice flour and honey and oil for food. You grew exceedingly beautiful, fit to be a queen. Your fame spread among the nations on account of your beauty, for it was perfect because of my splendour that I had bestowed on you, says the Lord GOD.

But you trusted in your beauty, and played the whore because of your fame, and lavished your whorings on any passer-by. yet I will remember my covenant with you in the days of your youth, and I will establish with you an everlasting covenant. Then you will remember your ways, and be ashamed when I take your sisters, both your elder and your younger, and give them to you as daughters, but not on account of my covenant with you. I will establish my covenant with you, and you shall know that I am the LORD, in order that you may remember and be confounded, and never open your mouth again because of your shame, when I forgive you all that you have done, says the Lord GOD.

This is the word of the Lord. *Ezekiel 16.1–15, 60–end*

Responsorial Psalm

R* **The right hand of the Lord does mighty deeds,**
the right hand of the Lord is exalted. *cf Psalm 118.16*

The Lord is my strength and my song,
and he has become my salvation.
Joyful shouts of salvation
sound from the tents of the righteous. **R***

I shall not die, but live
and declare the works of the Lord.
The Lord has punished me sorely,
but he has not given me over to death. **R** *Psalm 118.14–18*

Year 1 and Year 2

Hear the Gospel of our Lord Jesus Christ according to Matthew.

Some Pharisees came to Jesus, and to test him they asked, 'Is it lawful for a man to divorce his wife for any cause?' He answered, 'Have you not read that the one who made them at the beginning "made them male and female", and said, "For this reason a man shall leave his father and mother and be joined to his wife, and the two shall become one flesh"? So they are no longer two, but one flesh. Therefore what God has joined together, let no one separate.' They said to him, 'Why then did Moses command us to give a certificate of dismissal and to divorce her?' He said to them, 'It was because you were so hard-hearted that Moses allowed you to divorce your wives, but at the beginning it was not so. And I say to you, whoever divorces his wife, except for unchastity, and marries another commits adultery.'

His disciples said to him, 'If such is the case of a man with his wife, it is better not to marry.' But he said to them, 'Not everyone can accept this teaching, but only those to whom it is given. For there are eunuchs who have been so from birth, and there are eunuchs who have been made eunuchs by others, and there are eunuchs who have made themselves eunuchs for the sake of the kingdom of heaven. Let anyone accept this who can.'

This is the Gospel of the Lord. *Matthew 19.3–12*

Week 19: Saturday between 13 and 19 August

Year 1

A reading from the Book of Joshua.

Joshua said to all the people, 'Now therefore revere the LORD, and serve him in sincerity and in faithfulness; put away the gods that your ancestors served beyond the River and in Egypt, and serve the LORD. Now if you are unwilling to serve the LORD, choose this day whom you will serve, whether the gods your ancestors served in the region beyond the River or the gods of the Amorites in whose land you are living; but as for me and my household, we will serve the LORD.'

Then the people answered, 'Far be it from us that we should forsake the LORD to serve other gods; for it is the LORD our God who brought us and our ancestors up from the land of Egypt, out of the house of slavery, and who did those great signs in our sight. He protected us along all the way that we went, and among all the peoples through whom we passed; and the LORD drove out before us all the peoples, the Amorites who lived in the land. Therefore we also will serve the LORD, for he is our God.'

But Joshua said to the people, 'You cannot serve the LORD, for he is a holy God. He is a jealous God; he will not forgive your transgressions or your sins. If you forsake the LORD and serve foreign gods, then he will turn and do you harm, and consume you, after having done you good.' And the people said to Joshua, 'No, we will serve the LORD!' Then Joshua said to the people, 'You are witnesses against yourselves that you have chosen the LORD, to serve him.' And they said, 'We are witnesses.' He said, 'Then put away the foreign gods that are among you, and incline your hearts to the LORD, the God of Israel.' The people said to Joshua, 'The LORD our God we will serve, and him we will obey.' So Joshua made a covenant with the people that day, and made statutes and ordinances for them at Shechem. Joshua wrote these words in the book of the law of God; and he took a large stone, and set it up there under the oak in the sanctuary of the LORD. Joshua said to all the people, 'See, this stone shall be a witness against us; for it has heard all the words of the LORD that he spoke to us; therefore it shall be a witness against you, if you deal falsely with your God.' So Joshua sent the people away to their inheritances.

After these things Joshua son of Nun, the servant of the LORD, died, being one hundred and ten years old.

This is the word of the Lord.   Joshua 24.14–29

Responsorial Psalm

R **Preserve me, O God,
   for in you have I taken refuge.**   Psalm 16.1a

Preserve me, O God,
for in you have I taken refuge;
I have said to the Lord, 'You are my lord,
all my good depends on you.'   **R**

My share has fallen in a fair land;
indeed, I have a goodly heritage.
I will bless the Lord who has given me counsel,
and in the night watches he instructs my heart. **R**

I have set the Lord always before me;
he is at my right hand; I shall not fall.
Wherefore my heart is glad and my spirit rejoices;
my flesh also shall rest secure. **R**

For you will not abandon my soul to Death,
nor suffer your faithful one to see the Pit;
you will show me the path of life.
In your presence is the fullness of joy
and in your right hand are pleasures for evermore. **R**   *Psalm 16.1, 5–end*

Year 2

A reading from the prophecy of Ezekiel.

The word of the LORD came to me: What do you mean by repeating this proverb concerning the land of Israel, 'The parents have eaten sour grapes, and the children's teeth are set on edge'? As I live, says the Lord GOD, this proverb shall no more be used by you in Israel. Know that all lives are mine; the life of the parent as well as the life of the child is mine: it is only the person who sins that shall die.

If a man is righteous and does what is lawful and right – if he does not eat upon the mountains or lift up his eyes to the idols of the house of Israel, does not defile his neighbour's wife or approach a woman during her menstrual period, does not oppress anyone, but restores to the debtor his pledge, commits no robbery, gives his bread to the hungry and covers the naked with a garment, does not take advance or accrued interest, withholds his hand from iniquity, executes true justice between contending parties, follows my statutes, and is careful to observe my ordinances, acting faithfully – such a one is righteous; he shall surely live, says the Lord GOD.

If he has a son who is violent, a shedder of blood, who does any of these things, shall he then live? He shall not. He has done all these abominable things; he shall surely die; his blood shall be upon himself.

Therefore I will judge you, O house of Israel, all of you according to your ways, says the Lord GOD. Repent and turn from all your transgressions; otherwise iniquity will be your ruin. For I have no pleasure in the death of anyone, says the Lord GOD. Turn, then, and live.

This is the word of the Lord.   *Ezekiel 18.1–11a, 13b, 30, 32*

R **Make me a clean heart, O God,**
   [and renew a right spirit within me].   *Psalm 51.11*

Have mercy on me, O God,
in your great goodness;
according to the abundance of your compassion
blot out my offences.   R

Wash me thoroughly from my wickedness
and cleanse me from my sin.
For I acknowledge my faults
and my sin is ever before me.   R

Deliver me from my guilt, O God,
the God of my salvation,
and my tongue shall sing of your righteousness.   R

O Lord, open my lips
and my mouth shall proclaim your praise.
For you desire no sacrifice, else I would give it;
you take no delight in burnt offerings.   R   *Psalm 51.1–3, 15–17*

Year 1 and Year 2

Hear the Gospel of our Lord Jesus Christ according to Matthew.

Little children were being brought to Jesus in order that he might lay his
hands on them and pray. The disciples spoke sternly to those who brought
them; but Jesus said, 'Let the little children come to me, and do not stop
them; for it is to such as these that the kingdom of heaven belongs.' And he
laid his hands on them and went on his way.

This is the Gospel of the Lord.   *Matthew 19.13–15*

Week 20: Monday between 15 and 21 August

Year I

A reading from the book Judges.

The Israelites did what was evil in the sight of the Lord and worshipped the Baals; and they abandoned the Lord, the God of their ancestors, who had brought them out of the land of Egypt; they followed other gods, from among the gods of the peoples who were all around them, and bowed down to them; and they provoked the Lord to anger. They abandoned the Lord, and worshipped Baal and the Astartes. So the anger of the Lord was kindled against Israel, and he gave them over to plunderers who plundered them, and he sold them into the power of their enemies all around, so that they could no longer withstand their enemies. Whenever they marched out, the hand of the Lord was against them to bring misfortune, as the Lord had warned them and sworn to them; and they were in great distress.

Then the Lord raised up judges, who delivered them out of the power of those who plundered them. Yet they did not listen even to their judges; for they lusted after other gods and bowed down to them. They soon turned aside from the way in which their ancestors had walked, who had obeyed the commandments of the Lord; they did not follow their example. Whenever the Lord raised up judges for them, the Lord was with the judge, and he delivered them from the hand of their enemies all the days of the judge; for the Lord would be moved to pity by their groaning because of those who persecuted and oppressed them. But whenever the judge died, they would relapse and behave worse than their ancestors, following other gods, worshipping them and bowing down to them. They would not drop any of their practices or their stubborn ways.

This is the word of the Lord.   Judges 2.11–19

Responsorial Psalm

R **Remember me, Lord,
    when you show favour to your people.**   cf Psalm 106.4a

They did not destroy the peoples
as the Lord had commanded them.
They mingled with the nations
and learned to follow their ways,
so that they worshipped their idols,
which became to them a snare. **R**   →

Their own sons and daughters
they sacrificed to evil spirits.
They shed innocent blood,
the blood of their sons and daughters,
which they offered to the idols of Canaan,
and the land was defiled with blood.   R

R   **Remember me, Lord,
      when you show favour to your people.**

Thus were they polluted by their actions,
and in their wanton deeds went whoring after other gods.
Therefore was the wrath of the Lord kindled against his people,
and he abhorred his inheritance.
He gave them over to the hand of the nations,
and those who hated them ruled over them.   R   *Psalm* 106.34–42

Year 2

A reading from the prophecy of Ezekiel.

The word of the LORD came to me: Mortal, with one blow I am about to take
away from you the delight of your eyes; yet you shall not mourn or weep, nor
shall your tears run down. Sigh, but not aloud; make no mourning for the
dead. Bind on your turban, and put your sandals on your feet; do not cover
your upper lip or eat the bread of mourners. So I spoke to the people in the
morning, and at evening my wife died. And on the next morning I did as I
was commanded.

   Then the people said to me, 'Will you not tell us what these things mean
for us, that you are acting in this way?' Then I said to them: The word of the
LORD came to me: Say to the house of Israel, Thus says the Lord GOD: I will
profane my sanctuary, the pride of your power, the delight of your eyes, and
your heart's desire; and your sons and your daughters whom you left behind
shall fall by the sword. And you shall do as I have done; you shall not cover
your upper lip or eat the bread of mourners. Your turbans shall be on your
heads and your sandals on your feet; you shall not mourn or weep, but you
shall pine away in your iniquities and groan to one another. Thus Ezekiel shall
be a sign to you; you shall do just as he has done. When this comes, then you
shall know that I am the Lord GOD.

This is the word of the Lord.   *Ezekiel* 24.15–24

Responsorial Psalm

R **We will recount the praises of the Lord,
[and the wonderful works he has done].** cf Psalm 78.4

Hear my teaching, O my people;
incline your ears to the words of my mouth.
I will open my mouth in a parable;
I will pour forth mysteries from of old,
such as we have heard and known,
which our forebears have told us. R

We will not hide from their children,
but will recount to generations to come,
the praises of the Lord and his power
and the wonderful works he has done. R

He laid a solemn charge on Jacob
and made it a law in Israel,
which he commanded them to teach their children,
that the generations to come might know,
and the children yet unborn. R

That they in turn might tell it to their children;
so that they might put their trust in God
and not forget the deeds of God,
but keep his commandments. R

And not be like their forebears,
a stubborn and rebellious generation,
a generation whose heart was not steadfast,
and whose spirit was not faithful to God. R Psalm 78.1–8

Year 1 and Year 2

Hear the Gospel of our Lord Jesus Christ according to Matthew.

Someone came to Jesus and said, 'Teacher, what good deed must I do to
have eternal life?' And he said to him, 'Why do you ask me about what is
good? There is only one who is good. If you wish to enter into life, keep the
commandments.' He said to him, 'Which ones?' And Jesus said, 'You shall
not murder; You shall not commit adultery; You shall not steal; You shall not
bear false witness; Honour your father and mother; also, You shall love your
neighbour as yourself.' The young man said to him, 'I have kept all these;
what do I still lack?' Jesus said to him, 'If you wish to be perfect, go, sell your
possessions, and give the money to the poor, and you will have treasure in
heaven; then come, follow me.' When the young man heard this word, he
went away grieving, for he had many possessions.

This is the Gospel of the Lord. Matthew 19.16–22

Week 20: Tuesday between 16 and 22 August

Year 1

A reading from the book Judges.

The angel of the LORD came and sat under the oak at Ophrah, which belonged to Joash the Abiezrite, as his son Gideon was beating out wheat in the wine press, to hide it from the Midianites. The angel of the LORD appeared to him and said to him, 'The LORD is with you, you mighty warrior.' Gideon answered him, 'But sir, if the LORD is with us, why then has all this happened to us? And where are all his wonderful deeds that our ancestors recounted to us, saying, "Did not the LORD bring us up from Egypt?" But now the LORD has cast us off, and given us into the hand of Midian.' Then the LORD turned to him and said, 'Go in this might of yours and deliver Israel from the hand of Midian; I hereby commission you.' He responded, 'But sir, how can I deliver Israel? My clan is the weakest in Manasseh, and I am the least in my family.' The LORD said to him, 'But I will be with you, and you shall strike down the Midianites, every one of them.' Then he said to him, 'If now I have found favour with you, then show me a sign that it is you who speak with me. Do not depart from here until I come to you, and bring out my present, and set it before you.' And he said, 'I will stay until you return.'

So Gideon went into his house and prepared a kid, and unleavened cakes from an ephah of flour; the meat he put in a basket, and the broth he put in a pot, and brought them to him under the oak and presented them. The angel of God said to him, 'Take the meat and the unleavened cakes, and put them on this rock, and pour out the broth.' And he did so. Then the angel of the LORD reached out the tip of the staff that was in his hand, and touched the meat and the unleavened cakes; and fire sprang up from the rock and consumed the meat and the unleavened cakes; and the angel of the LORD vanished from his sight. Then Gideon perceived that it was the angel of the LORD; and Gideon said, 'Help me, Lord GOD! For I have seen the angel of the LORD face to face.' But the LORD said to him, 'Peace be to you; do not fear, you shall not die.' Then Gideon built an altar there to the LORD, and called it, The LORD is peace. To this day it still stands at Ophrah, which belongs to the Abiezrites.

This is the word of the Lord.   Judges 6.11–24

Responsorial Psalm

R **The Lord shall speak peace to the faithful;**
   [that his glory may dwell in our land].   cf *Psalm* 85.8b, 9b

I will listen to what the Lord God will say.
For he shall speak peace to his people and to the faithful,
that they turn not again to folly.
Truly, his salvation is near to those who fear him,
that his glory may dwell in our land. **R**

Mercy and truth are met together,
righteousness and peace have kissed each other.
Truth shall spring up from the earth
and righteousness look down from heaven. **R**

The Lord will indeed give all that is good,
and our land will yield its increase.
Righteousness shall go before him
and direct his steps in the way. **R**   *Psalm* 85.8–*end*

Year 2

A reading from the prophecy of Ezekiel.

The word of the Lᴏʀᴅ came to me: Mortal, say to the prince of Tyre, Thus
says the Lord Gᴏᴅ:
    Because your heart is proud
        and you have said, 'I am a god;
    I sit in the seat of the gods,
        in the heart of the seas',
    yet you are but a mortal, and no god,
        though you compare your mind
        with the mind of a god.
    You are indeed wiser than Daniel;
        no secret is hidden from you;
    by your wisdom and your understanding
        you have amassed wealth for yourself,
    and have gathered gold and silver
        into your treasuries.
    By your great wisdom in trade
        you have increased your wealth,
        and your heart has become proud in your wealth.
    Therefore, thus says the Lord Gᴏᴅ:
    Because you compare your mind
        with the mind of a god,
    therefore, I will bring strangers against you,
        the most terrible of the nations;
    they shall draw their swords against the beauty of your wisdom
        and defile your splendour. →

They shall thrust you down to the Pit,
  and you shall die a violent death
  in the heart of the seas.
Will you still say, 'I am a god',
  in the presence of those who kill you,
though you are but a mortal, and no god,
  in the hands of those who wound you?
You shall die the death of the uncircumcised
  by the hand of foreigners;
  for I have spoken, says the Lord GOD.

This is the word of the Lord.   *Ezekiel 28.1–10*

Responsorial Psalm

R* **Give thanks to the Lord, for he is gracious;**
  [his steadfast love endures for ever].   *Psalm 107.1*

Let the redeemed of the Lord say this,
those he redeemed from the hand of the enemy,
and gathered out of the lands
from the east and from the west,
from the north and from the south. **R**

They are diminished and brought low,
through stress of misfortune and sorrow.
Whoever is wise will ponder these things
and consider the loving-kindness of the Lord. **R**   *Psalm 107.1–3, 40, 43*

Year 1 and Year 2

Hear the Gospel of our Lord Jesus Christ according to Matthew.

Jesus said to his disciples, 'Truly I tell you, it will be hard for a rich person
to enter the kingdom of heaven. Again I tell you, it is easier for a camel to
go through the eye of a needle than for someone who is rich to enter the
kingdom of God.' When the disciples heard this, they were greatly astounded
and said, 'Then who can be saved?' But Jesus looked at them and said, 'For
mortals it is impossible, but for God all things are possible.'

Then Peter said in reply, 'Look, we have left everything and followed you.
What then will we have?' Jesus said to them, 'Truly I tell you, at the renewal
of all things, when the Son of Man is seated on the throne of his glory, you
who have followed me will also sit on twelve thrones, judging the twelve
tribes of Israel. And everyone who has left houses or brothers or sisters or
father or mother or children or fields, for my name's sake, will receive a
hundredfold, and will inherit eternal life. But many who are first will be last,
and the last will be first.'

This is the Gospel of the Lord.   *Matthew 19.23–end*

A reading from the book Judges.

All the lords of Shechem and all Beth-millo came together, and they went and made Abimelech king, by the oak of the pillar at Shechem.

When it was told to Jotham, he went and stood on the top of Mount Gerizim, and cried aloud and said to them, 'Listen to me, you lords of Shechem, so that God may listen to you.

The trees once went out
> to anoint a king over themselves.
So they said to the olive tree,
> "Reign over us."
The olive tree answered them,
> "Shall I stop producing my rich oil
>> by which gods and mortals are honoured,
>> and go to sway over the trees?"
Then the trees said to the fig tree,
> "You come and reign over us."
But the fig tree answered them,
> "Shall I stop producing my sweetness
>> and my delicious fruit,
>> and go to sway over the trees?"
Then the trees said to the vine,
> "You come and reign over us."
But the vine said to them,
> "Shall I stop producing my wine
>> that cheers gods and mortals,
>> and go to sway over the trees?"
So all the trees said to the bramble,
> "You come and reign over us."
And the bramble said to the trees,
> "If in good faith you are anointing me king over you,
>> then come and take refuge in my shade;
> but if not, let fire come out of the bramble
>> and devour the cedars of Lebanon."'

This is the word of the Lord.

Judges 9.6–15

R **Be exalted, O Lord, in your might;**
   [we will make music and sing of your power].   *Psalm 21.13*

The king shall rejoice in your strength, O Lord;
how greatly shall he rejoice in your salvation!
You have given him his heart's desire
and have not denied the request of his lips.   **R**

For you come to meet him with blessings of goodness
and set a crown of pure gold upon his head.
He asked of you life and you gave it him,
length of days, for ever and ever.   **R**

His honour is great because of your salvation;
glory and majesty have you laid upon him.
You have granted him everlasting felicity
and will make him glad with joy in your presence.   **R**   *Psalm 21.1–6*

Year 2

A reading from the prophecy of Ezekiel.

The word of the LORD came to me: Mortal, prophesy against the shepherds of Israel: prophesy, and say to them – to the shepherds: Thus says the Lord GOD: Ah, you shepherds of Israel who have been feeding yourselves! Should not shepherds feed the sheep? You eat the fat, you clothe yourselves with the wool, you slaughter the fatlings; but you do not feed the sheep. You have not strengthened the weak, you have not healed the sick, you have not bound up the injured, you have not brought back the strayed, you have not sought the lost, but with force and harshness you have ruled them. So they were scattered, because there was no shepherd; and scattered, they became food for all the wild animals. My sheep were scattered, they wandered over all the mountains and on every high hill; my sheep were scattered over all the face of the earth, with no one to search or seek for them.

Therefore, you shepherds, hear the word of the LORD: As I live, says the Lord GOD, because my sheep have become a prey, and my sheep have become food for all the wild animals, since there was no shepherd; and because my shepherds have not searched for my sheep, but the shepherds have fed themselves, and have not fed my sheep; therefore, you shepherds, hear the word of the LORD: Thus says the Lord GOD, I am against the shepherds; and I will demand my sheep at their hand, and put a stop to their feeding the sheep; no longer shall the shepherds feed themselves. I will rescue my sheep from their mouths, so that they may not be food for them.

For thus says the Lord GOD: I myself will search for my sheep, and will seek them out.

This is the word of the Lord.   *Ezekiel 34.1–11*

Responsorial Psalm

R **I will search for my sheep, says the Lord,
[and I will seek them out].** cf Ezekiel 34.11

The Lord is my shepherd;
therefore can I lack nothing.
He makes me lie down in green pastures
and leads me beside still waters. R

He shall refresh my soul
and guide me in the paths of righteousness
for his name's sake. R

Though I walk through the valley of the shadow of death,
I will fear no evil;
for you are with me;
your rod and your staff, they comfort me. R

You spread a table before me
in the presence of those who trouble me;
you have anointed my head with oil
and my cup shall be full. R

Surely goodness and loving mercy shall follow me
all the days of my life,
and I will dwell in the house of the Lord for ever. R Psalm 23

Year 1 and Year 2

Hear the Gospel of our Lord Jesus Christ according to Matthew.

Jesus said to his disciples, 'For the kingdom of heaven is like a landowner
who went out early in the morning to hire labourers for his vineyard. After
agreeing with the labourers for the usual daily wage, he sent them into his
vineyard. When he went out about nine o'clock, he saw others standing idle
in the market-place; and he said to them, "You also go into the vineyard, and
I will pay you whatever is right." So they went. When he went out again about
noon and about three o'clock, he did the same. And about five o'clock he
went out and found others standing around; and he said to them, "Why are
you standing here idle all day?" They said to him, "Because no one has hired
us." He said to them, "You also go into the vineyard."

'When evening came, the owner of the vineyard said to his manager,
"Call the labourers and give them their pay, beginning with the last and then
going to the first." When those hired about five o'clock came, each of them
received the usual daily wage. Now when the first came, they thought they
would receive more; but each of them also received the usual daily wage. And
when they received it, they grumbled against the landowner, saying, "These
last worked only one hour, and you have made them equal to us who have
borne the burden of the day and the scorching heat." But he replied to one →

of them, "Friend, I am doing you no wrong; did you not agree with me for the usual daily wage? Take what belongs to you and go; I choose to give to this last the same as I give to you. Am I not allowed to do what I choose with what belongs to me? Or are you envious because I am generous?" So the last will be first, and the first will be last.'

This is the Gospel of the Lord. *Matthew* 20.1–16

Week 20: Thursday between 18 and 24 August

Year 1

A reading from the book Judges.

The spirit of the LORD came upon Jephthah, and he passed through Gilead and Manasseh. He passed on to Mizpah of Gilead, and from Mizpah of Gilead he passed on to the Ammonites. And Jephthah made a vow to the LORD, and said, 'If you will give the Ammonites into my hand, then whoever comes out of the doors of my house to meet me, when I return victorious from the Ammonites, shall be the LORD's, to be offered up by me as a burnt-offering.' So Jephthah crossed over to the Ammonites to fight against them; and the LORD gave them into his hand. He inflicted a massive defeat on them from Aroer to the neighbourhood of Minnith, twenty towns, and as far as Abel-keramim. So the Ammonites were subdued before the people of Israel.

Then Jephthah came to his home at Mizpah; and there was his daughter coming out to meet him with timbrels and with dancing. She was his only child; he had no son or daughter except her. When he saw her, he tore his clothes, and said, 'Alas, my daughter! You have brought me very low; you have become the cause of great trouble to me. For I have opened my mouth to the LORD, and I cannot take back my vow.' She said to him, 'My father, if you have opened your mouth to the LORD, do to me according to what has gone out of your mouth, now that the LORD has given you vengeance against your enemies, the Ammonites.' And she said to her father, 'Let this thing be done for me: Grant me two months, so that I may go and wander on the mountains, and bewail my virginity, my companions and I.' 'Go,' he said and sent her away for two months. So she departed, she and her companions, and bewailed her virginity on the mountains. At the end of two months, she returned to her father, who did with her according to the vow he had made. She had never slept with a man. So there arose an Israelite custom that for four days every year the daughters of Israel would go out to lament the daughter of Jephthah the Gileadite.

This is the word of the Lord. *Judges* 11.29–end

**R* Blessed is the one who trusts in the Lord,
[and does not turn to the proud that follow false gods].** *Psalm* 40.4

Great are the wonders you have done, O Lord my God.
How great your designs for us!
There is none that can be compared with you.
If I were to proclaim them and tell of them
they would be more than I am able to express. **R**

Sacrifice and offering you do not desire
but my ears you have opened;
burnt offering and sacrifice for sin
you have not required. **R**

Then said I: 'Lo, I come.
In the scroll of the book it is written of me
that I should do your will, O my God;
I delight to do it: your law is within my heart.' **R**

I have declared your righteousness
in the great congregation;
behold, I did not restrain my lips,
and that, O Lord, you know. **R**

Your righteousness I have not hidden in my heart;
I have spoken of your faithfulness and your salvation;
I have not concealed your loving-kindness and truth
from the great congregation. **R** *Psalm* 40.4–11

Year 2

A reading from the prophecy of Ezekiel.

The word of the Lord came to me: I will sanctify my great name, which has been profaned among the nations, and which you have profaned among them; and the nations shall know that I am the LORD, says the Lord GOD, when through you I display my holiness before their eyes. I will take you from the nations, and gather you from all the countries, and bring you into your own land. I will sprinkle clean water upon you, and you shall be clean from all your uncleannesses, and from all your idols I will cleanse you. A new heart I will give you, and a new spirit I will put within you; and I will remove from your body the heart of stone and give you a heart of flesh. I will put my spirit within you, and make you follow my statutes and be careful to observe my ordinances. Then you shall live in the land that I gave to your ancestors; and you shall be my people, and I will be your God.

This is the word of the Lord. *Ezekiel* 36.23–28

R* **Purge me with hyssop and I shall be clean;**
[wash me and I shall be whiter than snow].   *Psalm* 51.8

Behold, you desire truth deep within me
and shall make me understand wisdom
in the depths of my heart.   R*

Make me hear of joy and gladness,
that the bones you have broken may rejoice.
Turn your face from my sins
and blot out all my misdeeds.   R

Make me a clean heart, O God,
and renew a right spirit within me.
Cast me not away from your presence
and take not your holy spirit from me.   R   *Psalm* 51.7–12

Year 1 and Year 2

Hear the Gospel of our Lord Jesus Christ according to Matthew.

Jesus spoke to the chief priests and the Pharisees in parables, saying: 'The kingdom of heaven may be compared to a king who gave a wedding banquet for his son. He sent his slaves to call those who had been invited to the wedding banquet, but they would not come. Again he sent other slaves, saying, "Tell those who have been invited: Look, I have prepared my dinner, my oxen and my fat calves have been slaughtered, and everything is ready; come to the wedding banquet." But they made light of it and went away, one to his farm, another to his business, while the rest seized his slaves, maltreated them, and killed them. The king was enraged. He sent his troops, destroyed those murderers, and burned their city. Then he said to his slaves, "The wedding is ready, but those invited were not worthy. Go therefore into the main streets, and invite everyone you find to the wedding banquet." Those slaves went out into the streets and gathered all whom they found, both good and bad; so the wedding hall was filled with guests.

'But when the king came in to see the guests, he noticed a man there who was not wearing a wedding robe, and he said to him, "Friend, how did you get in here without a wedding robe?" And he was speechless. Then the king said to the attendants, "Bind him hand and foot, and throw him into the outer darkness, where there will be weeping and gnashing of teeth." For many are called, but few are chosen.'

This is the Gospel of the Lord.   *Matthew* 22.1–14

Week 20: Friday between 19 and 25 August

Year 1

A reading from the Book of Ruth.

In the days when the judges ruled, there was a famine in the land, and a certain man of Bethlehem in Judah went to live in the country of Moab, he and his wife and two sons. Elimelech, the husband of Naomi, died, and she was left with her two sons. These took Moabite wives; the name of one was Orpah and the name of the other Ruth. When they had lived there for about ten years, both Mahlon and Chilion also died, so that the woman was left without her two sons or her husband.

Then she started to return with her daughters-in-law from the country of Moab, for she had heard in the country of Moab that the LORD had had consideration for his people and given them food. Orpah kissed her mother-in-law and went back to her people, but Ruth clung to her.

So she said, 'See, your sister-in-law has gone back to her people and to her gods; return after your sister-in-law.' But Ruth said,

'Do not press me to leave you
    or to turn back from following you!
Where you go, I will go;
    where you lodge, I will lodge;
your people shall be my people,
    and your God my God.'

So Naomi returned together with Ruth the Moabite, her daughter-in-law, who came back with her from the country of Moab. They came to Bethlehem at the beginning of the barley harvest.

This is the word of the Lord.   Ruth 1.1, 3–6, 14–16, 22

Responsorial Psalm

R* **The Lord shall reign for ever,**
    [your God, O Zion, throughout all generations].   Psalm 146.10

Praise the Lord, O my soul:
while I live will I praise the Lord;
as long as I have any being,
I will sing praises to my God.   **R**

Put not your trust in princes, nor in any human power,
for there is no help in them.
When their breath goes forth, they return to the earth;
on that day all their thoughts perish.   **R**

Happy are those who have the God of Jacob for their help,
whose hope is in the Lord their God;
who made heaven and earth, the sea and all that is in them;
who keeps his promise for ever.   **R**   →

Who gives justice to those that suffer wrong
and bread to those who hunger.
The Lord looses those that are bound;
the Lord opens the eyes of the blind;
the Lord lifts up those who are bowed down.   R

R* **The Lord shall reign for ever,**
  [your God, O Zion, throughout all generations].

The Lord loves the righteous;
the Lord watches over the stranger in the land;
he upholds the orphan and widow;
but the way of the wicked he turns upside down.   R*   *Psalm* 146

Year 2

A reading from the prophecy of Ezekiel.

The hand of the LORD came upon me, and he brought me out by the spirit
of the LORD and set me down in the middle of a valley; it was full of bones.
He led me all round them; there were very many lying in the valley, and they
were very dry. He said to me, 'Mortal, can these bones live?' I answered, 'O
Lord GOD, you know.' Then he said to me, 'Prophesy to these bones, and say
to them: O dry bones, hear the word of the LORD. Thus says the Lord GOD
to these bones: I will cause breath to enter you, and you shall live. I will lay
sinews on you, and will cause flesh to come upon you, and cover you with
skin, and put breath in you, and you shall live; and you shall know that I am
the LORD.'

So I prophesied as I had been commanded; and as I prophesied, suddenly
there was a noise, a rattling, and the bones came together, bone to its bone. I
looked, and there were sinews on them, and flesh had come upon them, and
skin had covered them; but there was no breath in them. Then he said to me,
'Prophesy to the breath, prophesy, mortal, and say to the breath: Thus says the
Lord GOD: Come from the four winds, O breath, and breathe upon these slain,
that they may live.' I prophesied as he commanded me, and the breath came
into them, and they lived, and stood on their feet, a vast multitude.

Then he said to me, 'Mortal, these bones are the whole house of Israel. They
say, "Our bones are dried up, and our hope is lost; we are cut off completely."
Therefore prophesy, and say to them, Thus says the Lord GOD: I am going
to open your graves, and bring you up from your graves, O my people; and
I will bring you back to the land of Israel. And you shall know that I am the
LORD, when I open your graves, and bring you up from your graves, O my
people. I will put my spirit within you, and you shall live, and I will place
you on your own soil; then you shall know that I, the LORD, have spoken and
will act, says the LORD.'

This is the word of the Lord.   *Ezekiel* 37.1–14

Responsorial Psalm

R* **Give thanks to the Lord, for he is gracious;**
   [his steadfast love endures for ever].   Psalm 107.1

Let the redeemed of the Lord say this,
those he redeemed from the hand of the enemy,
and gathered out of the lands
from the east and from the west,
from the north and from the south.   **R**

Some went astray in desert wastes
and found no path to a city to dwell in.
Hungry and thirsty,
their soul was fainting within them.
So they cried to the Lord in their trouble
and he delivered them from their distress.   **R**

He set their feet on the right way
till they came to a city to dwell in.
Let them give thanks to the Lord for his goodness
and the wonders he does for his children.   **R**   Psalm 107.1–8

Year 1 and Year 2

Hear the Gospel of our Lord Jesus Christ according to Matthew.

When the Pharisees heard that Jesus had silenced the Sadducees, they gathered together, and one of them, a lawyer, asked him a question to test him. 'Teacher, which commandment in the law is the greatest?' He said to him, ' "You shall love the Lord your God with all your heart, and with all your soul, and with all your mind." This is the greatest and first commandment. And a second is like it: "You shall love your neighbour as yourself." On these two commandments hang all the law and the prophets.'

This is the Gospel of the Lord.   Matthew 22.34–40

Week 20: Saturday between 20 and 26 August

Year I

A reading from the Book of Ruth.

Naomi had a kinsman on her husband's side, a prominent rich man, of the family of Elimelech, whose name was Boaz. And Ruth the Moabite said to Naomi, 'Let me go to the field and glean among the ears of grain, behind someone in whose sight I may find favour.' She said to her, 'Go, my daughter.' So she went. She came and gleaned in the field behind the reapers. As it happened, she came to the part of the field belonging to Boaz, who was of the family of Elimelech.

Then Boaz said to Ruth, 'Now listen, my daughter, do not go to glean in another field or leave this one, but keep close to my young women. Keep your eyes on the field that is being reaped, and follow behind them. I have ordered the young men not to bother you. If you get thirsty, go to the vessels and drink from what the young men have drawn.' Then she fell prostrate, with her face to the ground, and said to him, 'Why have I found favour in your sight, that you should take notice of me, when I am a foreigner?' But Boaz answered her, 'All that you have done for your mother-in-law since the death of your husband has been fully told me, and how you left your father and mother and your native land and came to a people that you did not know before.'

So Boaz took Ruth and she became his wife. When they came together, the Lord made her conceive, and she bore a son. Then the women said to Naomi, 'Blessed be the Lord, who has not left you this day without next-of-kin; and may his name be renowned in Israel! He shall be to you a restorer of life and a nourisher of your old age; for your daughter-in-law who loves you, who is more to you than seven sons, has borne him.' Then Naomi took the child and laid him in her bosom, and became his nurse. The women of the neighbourhood gave him a name, saying, 'A son has been born to Naomi.' They named him Obed; he became the father of Jesse, the father of David.

This is the word of the Lord. Ruth 2.1–3, 8–11, 4.13–17

Responsorial Psalm

R **Blessed are those who fear the Lord,**
    [and walk in the ways of God].   cf *Psalm* 128.1

Blessed are all those who fear the Lord,
and walk in his ways.
You shall eat the fruit of the toil of your hands;
it shall go well with you,
and happy shall you be. R

Your wife within your house
shall be like a fruitful vine;
your children round your table,
like fresh olive branches.
Thus shall the one be blest who fears the Lord. R

The Lord from out of Zion bless you,
that you may see Jerusalem in prosperity
all the days of your life.
May you see your children's children,
and may there be peace upon Israel. R   *Psalm* 128

Year 2

A reading from the prophecy of Ezekiel.

In my vision the man brought me to the gate, the gate facing east. And there, the glory of the God of Israel was coming from the east; the sound was like the sound of mighty waters; and the earth shone with his glory. The vision I saw was like the vision that I had seen when he came to destroy the city, and like the vision that I had seen by the river Chebar; and I fell upon my face. As the glory of the Lord entered the temple by the gate facing east, the spirit lifted me up, and brought me into the inner court; and the glory of the Lord filled the temple.

While the man was standing beside me, I heard someone speaking to me out of the temple. He said to me: Mortal, this is the place of my throne and the place for the soles of my feet, where I will reside among the people of Israel for ever. The house of Israel shall no more defile my holy name, neither they nor their kings, by their whoring, and by the corpses of their kings at their death.

This is the word of the Lord.   *Ezekiel* 43.1–7

R **The Lord was gracious to his land;
and restored the fortunes of Jacob.**   *cf Psalm 85.1*

Show us your mercy, O Lord,
and grant us your salvation.
I will listen
to what the Lord God will say.   **R**

For he shall speak peace to his people and to the faithful,
that they turn not again to folly.
Truly, his salvation is near to those who fear him,
that his glory may dwell in our land.   **R**

Mercy and truth are met together,
righteousness and peace have kissed each other.
Truth shall spring up from the earth
and righteousness look down from heaven.   **R**

The Lord will indeed give all that is good,
and our land will yield its increase.
Righteousness shall go before him
and direct his steps in the way.   **R**   *Psalm 85.7–end*

Year 1 and Year 2

Hear the Gospel of our Lord Jesus Christ according to Matthew.

Jesus said to the crowds and to his disciples, 'The scribes and the Pharisees sit on Moses' seat; therefore, do whatever they teach you and follow it; but do not do as they do, for they do not practise what they teach. They tie up heavy burdens, hard to bear, and lay them on the shoulders of others; but they themselves are unwilling to lift a finger to move them. They do all their deeds to be seen by others; for they make their phylacteries broad and their fringes long. They love to have the place of honour at banquets and the best seats in the synagogues, and to be greeted with respect in the market-places, and to have people call them rabbi. But you are not to be called rabbi, for you have one teacher, and you are all students. And call no one your father on earth, for you have one Father – the one in heaven. Nor are you to be called instructors, for you have one instructor, the Messiah. The greatest among you will be your servant. All who exalt themselves will be humbled, and all who humble themselves will be exalted.'

This is the Gospel of the Lord.   *Matthew 23.1–12*

Week 21: Monday between 22 and 28 August

Year 1

A reading from the First Letter of Paul to the Thessalonians.

Paul, Silvanus, and Timothy, to the church of the Thessalonians in God the Father and the Lord Jesus Christ: Grace to you and peace.

We always give thanks to God for all of you and mention you in our prayers, constantly remembering before our God and Father your work of faith and labour of love and steadfastness of hope in our Lord Jesus Christ. For we know, brothers and sisters beloved by God, that he has chosen you, because our message of the gospel came to you not in word only, but also in power and in the Holy Spirit and with full conviction; just as you know what kind of people we proved to be among you for your sake. For the word of the Lord has sounded forth from you not only in Macedonia and Achaia, but in every place where your faith in God has become known, so that we have no need to speak about it. For the people of those regions report about us what kind of welcome we had among you, and how you turned to God from idols, to serve a living and true God, and to wait for his Son from heaven, whom he raised from the dead – Jesus, who rescues us from the wrath that is coming.

This is the word of the Lord.   1 Thessalonians 1.1–5, 8–end

Responsorial Psalm

R* **Sing to the Lord a new song:**
   [sing his praise in the congregation of the faithful].   Psalm 149.1

Let Israel rejoice in their maker;
let the children of Zion be joyful in their king.
Let them praise his name in the dance;
let them sing praise to him with timbrel and lyre.   **R**

For the Lord has pleasure in his people
and adorns the poor with salvation.
Let the faithful be joyful in glory;
let them rejoice in their ranks.   **R**   Psalm 149.1–5

A reading from the Second Letter of Paul to the Thessalonians.

Paul, Silvanus, and Timothy, to the church of the Thessalonians in God our Father and the Lord Jesus Christ: Grace to you and peace from God our Father and the Lord Jesus Christ.

We must always give thanks to God for you, brothers and sisters, as is right, because your faith is growing abundantly, and the love of every one of you for one another is increasing. Therefore we ourselves boast of you among the churches of God for your steadfastness and faith during all your persecutions and the afflictions that you are enduring.

This is evidence of the righteous judgement of God, and is intended to make you worthy of the kingdom of God, for which you are also suffering. To this end we always pray for you, asking that our God will make you worthy of his call and will fulfil by his power every good resolve and work of faith, so that the name of our Lord Jesus may be glorified in you, and you in him, according to the grace of our God and the Lord Jesus Christ.

This is the word of the Lord.   2 Thessalonians 1.1–5, 11–end

Responsorial Psalm

R **Hear my prayer, O Lord,
    and listen to my cry.**   cf Psalm 39.13a

I said, 'I will keep watch over my ways,
so that I offend not with my tongue.
I will guard my mouth with a muzzle,
while the wicked are in my sight.'
So I held my tongue and said nothing;
I kept silent but to no avail.   R

My distress increased, my heart grew hot within me;
while I mused, the fire was kindled
and I spoke out with my tongue:
'Lord, let me know my end and the number of my days,
that I may know how short my time is.   R

'You have made my days but a handsbreadth,
and my lifetime is as nothing in your sight;
truly, even those who stand upright are but a breath.
We walk about like a shadow
and in vain we are in turmoil;
we heap up riches and cannot tell who will gather them.   R

'And now, what is my hope?
Truly my hope is even in you.
Deliver me from all my transgressions
and do not make me the taunt of the fool.'   R   Psalm 39.1–9

Year 1 and Year 2

Hear the Gospel of our Lord Jesus Christ according to Matthew.

Jesus said, 'Woe to you, scribes and Pharisees, hypocrites! For you lock people out of the kingdom of heaven. For you do not go in yourselves, and when others are going in, you stop them. Woe to you, scribes and Pharisees, hypocrites! For you cross sea and land to make a single convert, and you make the new convert twice as much a child of hell as yourselves.

'Woe to you, blind guides, who say, "Whoever swears by the sanctuary is bound by nothing, but whoever swears by the gold of the sanctuary is bound by the oath." You blind fools! For which is greater, the gold or the sanctuary that has made the gold sacred? And you say, "Whoever swears by the altar is bound by nothing, but whoever swears by the gift that is on the altar is bound by the oath." How blind you are! For which is greater, the gift or the altar that makes the gift sacred? So whoever swears by the altar, swears by it and by everything on it; and whoever swears by the sanctuary, swears by it and by the one who dwells in it; and whoever swears by heaven, swears by the throne of God and by the one who is seated upon it.'

This is the Gospel of the Lord. *Matthew 23.13–22*

Week 21: Tuesday between 23 and 29 August

Year 1

A reading from the First Letter of Paul to the Thessalonians.

You yourselves know, brothers and sisters, that our coming to you was not in vain, but though we had already suffered and been shamefully maltreated at Philippi, as you know, we had courage in our God to declare to you the gospel of God in spite of great opposition. For our appeal does not spring from deceit or impure motives or trickery, but just as we have been approved by God to be entrusted with the message of the gospel, even so we speak, not to please mortals, but to please God who tests our hearts. As you know and as God is our witness, we never came with words of flattery or with a pretext for greed; nor did we seek praise from mortals, whether from you or from others, though we might have made demands as apostles of Christ. But we were gentle among you, like a nurse tenderly caring for her own children. So deeply do we care for you that we are determined to share with you not only the gospel of God but also our own selves, because you have become very dear to us.

This is the word of the Lord. *1 Thessalonians 2.1–8*

Responsorial Psalm

R **O Lord, you have searched me out and known me.**   Psalm 139.1a

O Lord, you have searched me out and known me;
you know my sitting down and my rising up;
you discern my thoughts from afar.   **R**

You mark out my journeys and my resting place
and are acquainted with all my ways.
For there is not a word on my tongue,
but you, O Lord, know it altogether.   **R**

You encompass me behind and before
and lay your hand upon me.
Such knowledge is too wonderful for me,
so high that I cannot attain it.   **R**

Where can I go then from your spirit?
Or where can I flee from your presence?
If I climb up to heaven, you are there;
if I make the grave my bed, you are there also.   **R**

If I take the wings of the morning
and dwell in the uttermost parts of the sea,
even there your hand shall lead me,
your right hand hold me fast.   **R**   Psalm 139.1–9

Year 2

A reading from the Second Letter of Paul to the Thessalonians.

As to the coming of our Lord Jesus Christ and our being gathered together
to him, we beg you, brothers and sisters, not to be quickly shaken in mind
or alarmed, either by spirit or by word or by letter, as though from us, to
the effect that the day of the Lord is already here. Let no one deceive you in
any way.

   For this purpose he called you through our proclamation of the good news,
so that you may obtain the glory of our Lord Jesus Christ. So then, brothers
and sisters, stand firm and hold fast to the traditions that you were taught by
us, either by word of mouth or by our letter.

   Now may our Lord Jesus Christ himself and God our Father, who loved
us and through grace gave us eternal comfort and good hope, comfort your
hearts and strengthen them in every good work and word.

This is the word of the Lord.   *2 Thessalonians 2.1–3a, 14–end*

Responsorial Psalm

R* **Sound praises to the Lord, all the earth;**
[break into song and make music].   cf Psalm 98.5

Sing to the Lord a new song,
for he has done marvellous things.
His own right hand and his holy arm
have won for him the victory.   R

The Lord has made known his salvation;
his deliverance has he openly shown
in the sight of the nations.   R

He has remembered his mercy and faithfulness
towards the house of Israel,
and all the ends of the earth have seen
the salvation of our God.   R*

Make music to the Lord with the lyre,
with the lyre and the voice of melody.
With trumpets and the sound of the horn
sound praises before the Lord, the King.   R

Let the sea thunder and all that fills it,
the world and all that dwell upon it.
Let the rivers clap their hands
and let the hills ring out together before the Lord.   R

For he comes to judge the earth:
in righteousness shall he judge the world
and the peoples with equity.   R   Psalm 98

Year 1 and Year 2

Hear the Gospel of our Lord Jesus Christ according to Matthew.

Jesus said, 'Woe to you, scribes and Pharisees, hypocrites! For you tithe mint,
dill, and cummin, and have neglected the weightier matters of the law: justice
and mercy and faith. It is these you ought to have practised without neglecting
the others. You blind guides! You strain out a gnat but swallow a camel!

'Woe to you, scribes and Pharisees, hypocrites! For you clean the outside of
the cup and of the plate, but inside they are full of greed and self-indulgence.
You blind Pharisee! First clean the inside of the cup, so that the outside also
may become clean.'

This is the Gospel of the Lord.   Matthew 23.23–26

Week 21: Wednesday between 24 and 30 August

Year 1

A reading from the First Letter of Paul to the Thessalonians.

You remember our labour and toil, brothers and sisters; we worked night and day, so that we might not burden any of you while we proclaimed to you the gospel of God. You are witnesses, and God also, how pure, upright, and blameless our conduct was towards you believers. As you know, we dealt with each one of you like a father with his children, urging and encouraging you and pleading that you should lead a life worthy of God, who calls you into his own kingdom and glory.

We also constantly give thanks to God for this, that when you received the word of God that you heard from us, you accepted it not as a human word but as what it really is, God's word, which is also at work in you believers.

This is the word of the Lord.   1 Thessalonians 2.9–13

Responsorial Psalm

R **Those who sow in tears
shall reap with songs of joy.**   Psalm 126.6

When the Lord restored the fortunes of Zion,
then were we like those who dream.
Then was our mouth filled with laughter
and our tongue with songs of joy. **R**

Then said they among the nations,
'The Lord has done great things for them.'
The Lord has indeed done great things for us,
and therefore we rejoiced. **R**

Restore again our fortunes, O Lord,
as the river beds of the desert.
Those who sow in tears
shall reap with songs of joy. **R**

Those who go out weeping,
bearing the seed,
will come back with shouts of joy,
bearing their sheaves with them. **R**   Psalm 126

Year 2

A reading from the Second Letter of Paul to the Thessalonians.

We command you, beloved, in the name of our Lord Jesus Christ, to keep away from believers who are living in idleness and not according to the tradition that they received from us. For you yourselves know how you ought to imitate us; we were not idle when we were with you, and we did not eat anyone's bread without paying for it; but with toil and labour we worked night and day, so that we might not burden any of you. This was not because we do not have that right, but in order to give you an example to imitate. For even when we were with you, we gave you this command: Anyone unwilling to work should not eat.

Now may the Lord of peace himself give you peace at all times in all ways. The Lord be with all of you.

I, Paul, write this greeting with my own hand. This is the mark in every letter of mine; it is the way I write. The grace of our Lord Jesus Christ be with all of you.

This is the word of the Lord.   *2 Thessalonians 3.6–10, 16–end*

Responsorial Psalm

R **Blessed are those who fear the Lord,**
    [and walk in the ways of God].   *cf Psalm 128.1*

Blessed are all those who fear the Lord,
and walk in his ways.
You shall eat the fruit of the toil of your hands;
it shall go well with you,
and happy shall you be.   **R**

Your wife within your house
shall be like a fruitful vine;
your children round your table,
like fresh olive branches.
Thus shall the one be blest who fears the Lord.   **R**

The Lord from out of Zion bless you,
that you may see Jerusalem in prosperity
all the days of your life.
May you see your children's children,
and may there be peace upon Israel.   **R**   *Psalm 128*

Hear the Gospel of our Lord Jesus Christ according to Matthew.

Jesus said, 'Woe to you, scribes and Pharisees, hypocrites! For you are like whitewashed tombs, which on the outside look beautiful, but inside they are full of the bones of the dead and of all kinds of filth. So you also on the outside look righteous to others, but inside you are full of hypocrisy and lawlessness.

'Woe to you, scribes and Pharisees, hypocrites! For you build the tombs of the prophets and decorate the graves of the righteous, and you say, "If we had lived in the days of our ancestors, we would not have taken part with them in shedding the blood of the prophets." Thus you testify against yourselves that you are descendants of those who murdered the prophets. Fill up, then, the measure of your ancestors.'

This is the Gospel of the Lord.   Matthew 23.27–32

Week 21: Thursday between 25 and 31 August

Year 1

A reading from the First Letter of Paul to the Thessalonians.

Brothers and sisters, during all our distress and persecution we have been encouraged about you through your faith. For we now live, if you continue to stand firm in the Lord. How can we thank God enough for you in return for all the joy that we feel before our God because of you? Night and day we pray most earnestly that we may see you face to face and restore whatever is lacking in your faith.

Now may our God and Father himself and our Lord Jesus direct our way to you. And may the Lord make you increase and abound in love for one another and for all, just as we abound in love for you. And may he so strengthen your hearts in holiness that you may be blameless before our God and Father at the coming of our Lord Jesus with all his saints.

This is the word of the Lord.   1 Thessalonians 3.7–end

Responsorial Psalm

R **Fill us with your love that we may rejoice.**   cf Psalm 90.14

Turn again, O Lord; how long will you delay?
Have compassion on your servants.
Satisfy us with your loving-kindness in the morning,
that we may rejoice and be glad all our days.   R

Give us gladness for the days you have afflicted us,
and for the years in which we have seen adversity.
Show your servants your works,
and let your glory be over their children. R

May the gracious favour of the Lord our God be upon us;
prosper our handiwork;
O prosper the work of our hands. R *Psalm 90.13–end*

Year 2

A reading from the First Letter of Paul to the Corinthians.

Paul, called to be an apostle of Christ Jesus by the will of God, and our brother
Sosthenes, to the church of God that is in Corinth, to those who are sanctified
in Christ Jesus, called to be saints, together with all those who in every place
call on the name of our Lord Jesus Christ, both their Lord and ours: Grace to
you and peace from God our Father and the Lord Jesus Christ.

I give thanks to my God always for you because of the grace of God that
has been given you in Christ Jesus, for in every way you have been enriched
in him, in speech and knowledge of every kind – just as the testimony of
Christ has been strengthened among you – so that you are not lacking in any
spiritual gift as you wait for the revealing of our Lord Jesus Christ. He will also
strengthen you to the end, so that you may be blameless on the day of our
Lord Jesus Christ. God is faithful; by him you were called into the fellowship
of his Son, Jesus Christ our Lord.

This is the word of the Lord. *1 Corinthians 1.1–9*

Responsorial Psalm

**R* I will exalt you, O God my King,
[and bless your name for ever].** *cf Psalm 145.1*

Every day will I bless you
and praise your name for ever and ever.
Great is the Lord and highly to be praised;
his greatness is beyond all searching out. R

One generation shall praise your works to another
and declare your mighty acts.
They shall speak of the majesty of your glory,
and I will tell of all your wonderful deeds. R

They shall speak of the might of your marvellous acts,
and I will also tell of your greatness.
They shall pour forth the story of your abundant kindness
and joyfully sing of your righteousness. R *Psalm 145.1–7*

Year I and Year 2

Hear the Gospel of our Lord Jesus Christ according to Matthew.

Jesus said to his disciples, 'Keep awake therefore, for you do not know on what day your Lord is coming. But understand this: if the owner of the house had known in what part of the night the thief was coming, he would have stayed awake and would not have let his house be broken into. Therefore you also must be ready, for the Son of Man is coming at an unexpected hour.

'Who then is the faithful and wise slave, whom his master has put in charge of his household, to give the other slaves their allowance of food at the proper time? Blessed is that slave whom his master will find at work when he arrives. Truly I tell you, he will put that one in charge of all his possessions. But if that wicked slave says to himself, "My master is delayed", and he begins to beat his fellow-slaves, and eats and drinks with drunkards, the master of that slave will come on a day when he does not expect him and at an hour that he does not know. He will cut him in pieces and put him with the hypocrites, where there will be weeping and gnashing of teeth.'

This is the Gospel of the Lord. Matthew 24.42—end

Week 21: Friday between 26 August and 1 September

Year I

A reading from the First Letter of Paul to the Thessalonians.

Brothers and sisters, we ask and urge you in the Lord Jesus that, as you learned from us how you ought to live and to please God (as, in fact, you are doing), you should do so more and more. For you know what instructions we gave you through the Lord Jesus. For this is the will of God, your sanctification: that you abstain from fornication; that each one of you knows how to control your own body in holiness and honour, not with lustful passion, like the Gentiles who do not know God; that no one wrongs or exploits a brother or sister in this matter, because the Lord is an avenger in all these things, just as we have already told you beforehand and solemnly warned you. For God did not call us to impurity but in holiness. Therefore whoever rejects this rejects not human authority but God, who also gives his Holy Spirit to you.

This is the word of the Lord. 1 Thessalonians 4.1—8

Responsorial Psalm

R* **The Lord is king: let the earth rejoice;**
   [let the multitude of the isles be glad]. Psalm 97.1

Clouds and darkness are round about him;
righteousness and justice are the foundation of his throne.
Fire goes before him
and burns up his enemies on every side. **R**

His lightnings lit up the world;
the earth saw it and trembled.
The mountains melted like wax at the presence of the Lord,
at the presence of the Lord of the whole earth. **R**

The heavens declared his righteousness,
and all the peoples have seen his glory.
Confounded be all who worship carved images
  and delight in mere idols.
Bow down before him, all you gods. **R**

Zion heard and was glad, and the daughters of Judah rejoiced,
because of your judgements, O Lord.
For you, Lord, are most high over all the earth;
you are exalted far above all gods. **R**

The Lord loves those who hate evil;
he preserves the lives of his faithful
and delivers them from the hand of the wicked. **R**

Light has sprung up for the righteous
and joy for the true of heart.
Rejoice in the Lord, you righteous,
and give thanks to his holy name. **R**   *Psalm 97*

Year 2

A reading from the First Letter of Paul to the Corinthians.

Christ did not send me to baptize but to proclaim the gospel, and not with
eloquent wisdom, so that the cross of Christ might not be emptied of its power.
For the message about the cross is foolishness to those who are perishing, but
to us who are being saved it is the power of God. For it is written,
    'I will destroy the wisdom of the wise,
        and the discernment of the discerning I will thwart.'
Where is the one who is wise? Where is the scribe? Where is the debater
of this age? Has not God made foolish the wisdom of the world? For since,
in the wisdom of God, the world did not know God through wisdom, God
decided, through the foolishness of our proclamation, to save those who
believe. For Jews demand signs and Greeks desire wisdom, but we proclaim
Christ crucified, a stumbling-block to Jews and foolishness to Gentiles, but
to those who are the called, both Jews and Greeks, Christ the power of God
and the wisdom of God. For God's foolishness is wiser than human wisdom,
and God's weakness is stronger than human strength.

This is the word of the Lord.   *1 Corinthians 1.17–25*

Responsorial Psalm

R* **Happy the nation whose God is the Lord:**
[the people he has chosen for his own]. *cf Psalm 33.12*

By the word of the Lord were the heavens made
and all their host by the breath of his mouth.
He gathers up the waters of the sea as in a waterskin
and lays up the deep in his treasury. **R**

Let all the earth fear the Lord;
stand in awe of him, all who dwell in the world.
For he spoke, and it was done;
he commanded, and it stood fast. **R**

The Lord brings the counsel of the nations to naught;
he frustrates the designs of the peoples.
But the counsel of the Lord shall endure for ever
and the designs of his heart from generation to generation. **R***

Psalm 33.6–12

Year 1 and Year 2

Hear the Gospel of our Lord Jesus Christ according to Matthew.

Jesus said to his disciples, 'The kingdom of heaven will be like this. Ten bridesmaids took their lamps and went to meet the bridegroom. Five of them were foolish, and five were wise. When the foolish took their lamps, they took no oil with them; but the wise took flasks of oil with their lamps. As the bridegroom was delayed, all of them became drowsy and slept. But at midnight there was a shout, "Look! Here is the bridegroom! Come out to meet him." Then all those bridesmaids got up and trimmed their lamps. The foolish said to the wise, "Give us some of your oil, for our lamps are going out." But the wise replied, "No! there will not be enough for you and for us; you had better go to the dealers and buy some for yourselves." And while they went to buy it, the bridegroom came, and those who were ready went with him into the wedding banquet; and the door was shut. Later the other bridesmaids came also, saying, "Lord, lord, open to us." But he replied, "Truly I tell you, I do not know you." Keep awake therefore, for you know neither the day nor the hour.'

This is the Gospel of the Lord. *Matthew 25.1–13*

Week 21: Saturday between 27 August and 2 September

Year 1

A reading from the First Letter of Paul to the Thessalonians.

Concerning love of the brothers and sisters, you do not need to have anyone write to you, for you yourselves have been taught by God to love one another; and indeed you do love all the brothers and sisters throughout Macedonia. But we urge you, beloved, to do so more and more, to aspire to live quietly, to mind your own affairs, and to work with your hands, as we directed you, so that you may behave properly towards outsiders and be dependent on no one.

This is the word of the Lord. *1 Thessalonians 4.9–12*

Responsorial Psalm

R   The Lord has come to judge the earth;
   [and the peoples with equity]. *cf Psalm 98.9b, 10b*

Sing to the Lord a new song,
for he has done marvellous things.
His own right hand and his holy arm
have won for him the victory.   **R**

Let the sea thunder and all that fills it,
the world and all that dwell upon it.
Let the rivers clap their hands
and let the hills ring out together before the Lord.   **R**

For he comes to judge the earth:
in righteousness shall he judge the world
and the peoples with equity.   **R** *Psalm 98.1–2, 8–end*

Year 2

A reading from the First Letter of Paul to the Corinthians.

Consider your own call, brothers and sisters: not many of you were wise by human standards, not many were powerful, not many were of noble birth. But God chose what is foolish in the world to shame the wise; God chose what is weak in the world to shame the strong; God chose what is low and despised in the world, things that are not, to reduce to nothing things that are, so that no one might boast in the presence of God. He is the source of your life in Christ Jesus, who became for us wisdom from God, and righteousness and sanctification and redemption, in order that, as it is written, 'Let the one who boasts, boast in the Lord.'

This is the word of the Lord. *1 Corinthians 1.26–end*

Responsorial Psalm

R* **Let your loving-kindness, O Lord, be upon us,**
   [as we have set our hope on you]. *Psalm 33.22*

Happy the nation whose God is the Lord
and the people he has chosen for his own.
The Lord looks down from heaven
and beholds all the children of earth. **R**

From where he sits enthroned he turns his gaze
on all who dwell on the earth.
He fashions all the hearts of them
and understands all their works. **R**

Our soul waits longingly for the Lord;
he is our help and our shield.
Indeed, our heart rejoices in him;
in his holy name have we put our trust. **R*** *Psalm 33.12–15, 20–end*

Year 1 and Year 2

Hear the Gospel of our Lord Jesus Christ according to Matthew.

Jesus told his disciples this parable: 'A man, going on a journey, summoned his slaves and entrusted his property to them; to one he gave five talents, to another two, to another one, to each according to his ability. Then he went away. The one who had received the five talents went off at once and traded with them, and made five more talents. In the same way, the one who had the two talents made two more talents. But the one who had received the one talent went off and dug a hole in the ground and hid his master's money.

'After a long time the master of those slaves came and settled accounts with them. Then the one who had received the five talents came forward, bringing five more talents, saying, "Master, you handed over to me five talents; see, I have made five more talents." His master said to him, "Well done, good and trustworthy slave; you have been trustworthy in a few things, I will put you in charge of many things; enter into the joy of your master."

'And the one with the two talents also came forward, saying, "Master, you handed over to me two talents; see, I have made two more talents." His master said to him, "Well done, good and trustworthy slave; you have been trustworthy in a few things, I will put you in charge of many things; enter into the joy of your master."

'Then the one who had received the one talent also came forward, saying, "Master, I knew that you were a harsh man, reaping where you did not sow, and gathering where you did not scatter seed; so I was afraid, and I went and hid your talent in the ground. Here you have what is yours."

'But his master replied, "You wicked and lazy slave! You knew, did you, that I reap where I did not sow, and gather where I did not scatter? Then you ought to have invested my money with the bankers, and on my return I would have received what was my own with interest. So take the talent from him, and give it to the one with the ten talents. For to all those who have, more will be given, and they will have an abundance; but from those who have nothing, even what they have will be taken away. As for this worthless slave, throw him into the outer darkness, where there will be weeping and gnashing of teeth." '

This is the Gospel of the Lord.   *Matthew 25.14–30*

Week 22: Monday between 29 August and 4 September

Year 1

A reading from the First Letter of Paul to the Thessalonians.

We do not want you to be uninformed, brothers and sisters, about those who have died, so that you may not grieve as others do who have no hope. For since we believe that Jesus died and rose again, even so, through Jesus, God will bring with him those who have died. For this we declare to you by the word of the Lord, that we who are alive, who are left until the coming of the Lord, will by no means precede those who have died. For the Lord himself, with a cry of command, with the archangel's call and with the sound of God's trumpet, will descend from heaven, and the dead in Christ will rise first. Then we who are alive, who are left, will be caught up in the clouds together with them to meet the Lord in the air; and so we will be with the Lord for ever. Therefore encourage one another with these words.

This is the word of the Lord. 1 Thessalonians 4.13–end

Responsorial Psalm

R **Sing to the Lord a new song;**
  [sing to the Lord, all the earth]. Psalm 96.1

Sing to the Lord and bless his name;
tell out his salvation from day to day.
Declare his glory among the nations
and his wonders among all peoples. R

For great is the Lord and greatly to be praised;
he is more to be feared than all gods.
For all the gods of the nations are but idols;
it is the Lord who made the heavens. R

Honour and majesty are before him;
power and splendour are in his sanctuary.
Ascribe to the Lord, you families of the peoples;
ascribe to the Lord honour and strength. R

Ascribe to the Lord the honour due to his name;
bring offerings and come into his courts.
O worship the Lord in the beauty of holiness;
let the whole earth tremble before him. R

Tell it out among the nations
that the Lord is king.
He has made the world so firm that it cannot be moved;
he will judge the peoples with equity. R

Let the heavens rejoice and let the earth be glad;
let the sea thunder and all that is in it;
let the fields be joyful and all that is in them;
let all the trees of the wood shout for joy before the Lord.   R

For he comes, he comes to judge the earth;
with righteousness he will judge the world
and the peoples with his truth.   R   Psalm 96

Year 2

A reading from the First Letter of Paul to the Corinthians.

When I came to you, brothers and sisters, I did not come proclaiming the
mystery of God to you in lofty words or wisdom. For I decided to know nothing among you except Jesus Christ, and him crucified. And I came to you in
weakness and in fear and in much trembling. My speech and my proclamation were not with plausible words of wisdom, but with a demonstration of
the Spirit and of power, so that your faith might rest not on human wisdom
but on the power of God.

This is the word of the Lord.   1 Corinthians 2.1–5

Responsorial Psalm

R **Let your loving-kindness, O Lord, be upon us,
[as we have set our hope on you].**   Psalm 33.22

Happy the nation whose God is the Lord
and the people he has chosen for his own.
The Lord looks down from heaven
and beholds all the children of earth.   R

From where he sits enthroned he turns his gaze
on all who dwell on the earth.
He fashions all the hearts of them
and understands all their works.   R

No king is saved by the might of his host;
no warrior delivered by his great strength.
A horse is a vain hope for deliverance;
for all its strength it cannot save.   R

Behold, the eye of the Lord
is upon those who fear him,
on those who wait in hope for his steadfast love,
to deliver their soul from death
and to feed them in time of famine.   R

Our soul waits longingly for the Lord;
he is our help and our shield.
Indeed, our heart rejoices in him;
in his holy name have we put our trust.   R   Psalm 33.12–21

Hear the Gospel of our Lord Jesus Christ according to Luke.

When Jesus came to Nazareth, where he had been brought up, he went to the synagogue on the sabbath day, as was his custom. He stood up to read, and the scroll of the prophet Isaiah was given to him. He unrolled the scroll and found the place where it was written:
> 'The Spirit of the Lord is upon me,
>> because he has anointed me
>>> to bring good news to the poor.
> He has sent me to proclaim release to the captives
>> and recovery of sight to the blind,
>>> to let the oppressed go free,
> to proclaim the year of the Lord's favour.'

And he rolled up the scroll, gave it back to the attendant, and sat down. The eyes of all in the synagogue were fixed on him. Then he began to say to them, 'Today this scripture has been fulfilled in your hearing.' All spoke well of him and were amazed at the gracious words that came from his mouth. They said, 'Is not this Joseph's son?' He said to them, 'Doubtless you will quote to me this proverb, "Doctor, cure yourself!" And you will say, "Do here also in your home town the things that we have heard you did at Capernaum." ' And he said, 'Truly I tell you, no prophet is accepted in the prophet's home town. But the truth is, there were many widows in Israel in the time of Elijah, when the heaven was shut up for three years and six months, and there was a severe famine over all the land; yet Elijah was sent to none of them except to a widow at Zarephath in Sidon. There were also many lepers in Israel in the time of the prophet Elisha, and none of them was cleansed except Naaman the Syrian.' When they heard this, all in the synagogue were filled with rage. They got up, drove him out of the town, and led him to the brow of the hill on which their town was built, so that they might hurl him off the cliff. But he passed through the midst of them and went on his way.

This is the Gospel of the Lord.   Luke 4.16–30

Week 22: Tuesday between 30 August and 5 September

Year 1

A reading from the First Letter of Paul to the Thessalonians.

Concerning the times and the seasons, brothers and sisters, you do not need to have anything written to you. For you yourselves know very well that the day of the Lord will come like a thief in the night. When they say, 'There is peace and security', then sudden destruction will come upon them, as labour pains come upon a pregnant woman, and there will be no escape! But you, beloved, are not in darkness, for that day to surprise you like a thief; for you are all children of light and children of the day; we are not of the night or of darkness. So then, let us not fall asleep as others do, but let us keep awake and be sober. For God has destined us not for wrath but for obtaining salvation through our Lord Jesus Christ, who died for us, so that whether we are awake or asleep we may live with him. Therefore encourage one another and build up each other, as indeed you are doing.

This is the word of the Lord. 1 Thessalonians 5.1–6, 9–11

Responsorial Psalm

R **The Lord is my light and my salvation:
[he is the strength of my life].** cf Psalm 27.1

The Lord is my light and my salvation;
whom then shall I fear?
The Lord is the strength of my life;
of whom then shall I be afraid? R

When the wicked,
even my enemies and my foes,
came upon me to eat up my flesh,
they stumbled and fell. R

Though a host encamp against me,
my heart shall not be afraid,
and though there rise up war against me,
yet will I put my trust in him. R

One thing have I asked of the Lord and that alone I seek:
that I may dwell in the house of the Lord
    all the days of my life,
to behold the fair beauty of the Lord
and to seek his will in his temple. R

For in the day of trouble
he shall hide me in his shelter;
in the secret place of his dwelling shall he hide me
and set me high upon a rock. R

And now shall he lift up my head
above my enemies round about me;
therefore will I offer in his dwelling an oblation
    with great gladness;
I will sing and make music to the Lord. R Psalm 27.1–8

A reading from the First Letter of Paul to the Corinthians.

The Spirit searches everything, even the depths of God. For what human being knows what is truly human except the human spirit that is within? So also no one comprehends what is truly God's except the Spirit of God. Now we have received not the spirit of the world, but the Spirit that is from God, so that we may understand the gifts bestowed on us by God. And we speak of these things in words not taught by human wisdom but taught by the Spirit, interpreting spiritual things to those who are spiritual.

Those who are unspiritual do not receive the gifts of God's Spirit, for they are foolishness to them, and they are unable to understand them because they are discerned spiritually. Those who are spiritual discern all things, and they are themselves subject to no one else's scrutiny.

'For who has known the mind of the Lord
    so as to instruct him?'
But we have the mind of Christ.

This is the word of the Lord.   1 Corinthians 2.10b–end

Responsorial Psalm

R **The Lord is righteous in all his ways**
    and loving in all his works.   Psalm 145.18

All your works praise you, O Lord,
and your faithful servants bless you.
They tell of the glory of your kingdom
and speak of your mighty power.   **R**

To make known to all peoples your mighty acts
and the glorious splendour of your kingdom.
Your kingdom is an everlasting kingdom;
your dominion endures throughout all ages.   **R**

The Lord is sure in all his words
and faithful in all his deeds.
The Lord upholds all those who fall
and lifts up all those who are bowed down.   **R**

The eyes of all wait upon you, O Lord,
and you give them their food in due season.
You open wide your hand
and fill all things living with plenty.   **R**   Psalm 145.10–17

Hear the Gospel of our Lord Jesus Christ according to Luke.

Jesus went down to Capernaum, a city in Galilee, and was teaching them on the sabbath. They were astounded at his teaching, because he spoke with authority. In the synagogue there was a man who had the spirit of an unclean demon, and he cried out with a loud voice, 'Let us alone! What have you to do with us, Jesus of Nazareth? Have you come to destroy us? I know who you are, the Holy One of God.' But Jesus rebuked him, saying, 'Be silent, and come out of him!' When the demon had thrown him down before them, he came out of him without having done him any harm. They were all amazed and kept saying to one another, 'What kind of utterance is this? For with authority and power he commands the unclean spirits, and out they come!' And a report about him began to reach every place in the region.

This is the Gospel of the Lord. *Luke 4.31–37*

Week 22: Wednesday between 31 August and 6 September

Year 1

A reading from the Letter of Paul to the Colossians.

Paul, an apostle of Christ Jesus by the will of God, and Timothy our brother, to the saints and faithful brothers and sisters in Christ in Colossae: Grace to you and peace from God our Father.

In our prayers for you we always thank God, the Father of our Lord Jesus Christ, for we have heard of your faith in Christ Jesus and of the love that you have for all the saints, because of the hope laid up for you in heaven. You have heard of this hope before in the word of the truth, the gospel that has come to you. Just as it is bearing fruit and growing in the whole world, so it has been bearing fruit among yourselves from the day you heard it and truly comprehended the grace of God. This you learned from Epaphras, our beloved fellow-servant. He is a faithful minister of Christ on your behalf, and he has made known to us your love in the Spirit.

This is the word of the Lord. *Colossians 1.1–8*

R   **Taste and see that the Lord is good:**
    [happy are all who trust in him].   cf Psalm 34.8

Come, my children, and listen to me;
I will teach you the fear of the Lord.
Who is there who delights in life
and longs for days to enjoy good things?   **R**

Keep your tongue from evil
and your lips from lying words.
Turn from evil and do good;
seek peace and pursue it.   **R**

The eyes of the Lord are upon the righteous
and his ears are open to their cry.
The face of the Lord is against those who do evil,
to root out the remembrance of them from the earth.   **R**

The righteous cry and the Lord hears them
and delivers them out of all their troubles.
The Lord is near to the brokenhearted
and will save those who are crushed in spirit.   **R**   Psalm 34.11–18

Year 2

A reading from the First Letter of Paul to the Corinthians.

Brothers and sisters, I could not speak to you as spiritual people, but rather
as people of the flesh, as infants in Christ. I fed you with milk, not solid food,
for you were not ready for solid food. Even now you are still not ready, for
you are still of the flesh. For as long as there is jealousy and quarrelling among
you, are you not of the flesh, and behaving according to human inclinations?
For when one says, 'I belong to Paul', and another, 'I belong to Apollos', are
you not merely human?

What then is Apollos? What is Paul? Servants through whom you came
to believe, as the Lord assigned to each. I planted, Apollos watered, but God
gave the growth. So neither the one who plants nor the one who waters is
anything, but only God who gives the growth. The one who plants and the one
who waters have a common purpose, and each will receive wages according
to the labour of each. For we are God's servants, working together; you are
God's field, God's building.

This is the word of the Lord.   1 Corinthians 3.1–9

Responsorial Psalm

R **God alone is my rock and my salvation**
[my stronghold, so I shall not be shaken]. Psalm 62.2, 6

On God alone my soul in stillness waits;
from him comes my salvation.
He alone is my rock and my salvation,
my stronghold, so that I shall never be shaken. **R**

How long will all of you assail me to destroy me,
as you would a tottering wall or a leaning fence?
They plot only to thrust me down from my place of honour;
lies are their chief delight;
they bless with their mouth, but in their heart they curse. **R**

Wait on God alone in stillness, O my soul;
for in him is my hope.
He alone is my rock and my salvation,
my stronghold, so that I shall not be shaken. **R**

In God is my strength and my glory;
God is my strong rock; in him is my refuge.
Put your trust in him always, my people;
pour out your hearts before him, for God is our refuge. **R**

The peoples are but a breath,
the whole human race a deceit;
on the scales they are altogether lighter than air.
Put no trust in oppression; in robbery take no empty pride;
though wealth increase, set not your heart upon it. **R**

God spoke once, and twice have I heard the same,
that power belongs to God.
Steadfast love belongs to you, O Lord,
for you repay everyone according to their deeds. **R** Psalm 62

Hear the Gospel of our Lord Jesus Christ according to Luke.

After leaving the synagogue Jesus entered Simon's house. Now Simon's mother-in-law was suffering from a high fever, and they asked him about her. Then he stood over her and rebuked the fever, and it left her. Immediately she got up and began to serve them.

As the sun was setting, all those who had any who were sick with various kinds of diseases brought them to him; and he laid his hands on each of them and cured them. Demons also came out of many, shouting, 'You are the Son of God!' But he rebuked them and would not allow them to speak, because they knew that he was the Messiah.

At daybreak he departed and went into a deserted place. And the crowds were looking for him; and when they reached him, they wanted to prevent him from leaving them. But he said to them, 'I must proclaim the good news of the kingdom of God to the other cities also; for I was sent for this purpose.' So he continued proclaiming the message in the synagogues of Judea.

This is the Gospel of the Lord.   *Luke 4.38–end*

Week 22: Thursday between 1 and 7 September

Year 1

A reading from the Letter of Paul to the Colossians.

Since the day we heard it, we have not ceased praying for you and asking that you may be filled with the knowledge of God's will in all spiritual wisdom and understanding, so that you may lead lives worthy of the Lord, fully pleasing to him, as you bear fruit in every good work and as you grow in the knowledge of God. May you be made strong with all the strength that comes from his glorious power, and may you be prepared to endure everything with patience, while joyfully giving thanks to the Father, who has enabled you to share in the inheritance of the saints in the light. He has rescued us from the power of darkness and transferred us into the kingdom of his beloved Son, in whom we have redemption, the forgiveness of sins.

This is the word of the Lord.   *Colossians 1.9–14*

Responsorial Psalm

R* **Sound praises to the Lord, all the earth;**
   [break into song and make music].   *cf Psalm 98.5*

Sing to the Lord a new song,
for he has done marvellous things.
His own right hand and his holy arm
have won for him the victory.   **R**

The Lord has made known his salvation;
his deliverance has he openly shown
in the sight of the nations. **R**

He has remembered his mercy and faithfulness
towards the house of Israel,
and all the ends of the earth have seen
the salvation of our God. **R***   *Psalm 98.1–5*

Year 2

A reading from the First Letter of Paul to the Corinthians.

Do not deceive yourselves. If you think that you are wise in this age, you
should become fools so that you may become wise. For the wisdom of this
world is foolishness with God. For it is written,
    'He catches the wise in their craftiness',
and again,
    'The Lord knows the thoughts of the wise,
        that they are futile.'
So let no one boast about human leaders. For all things are yours, whether
Paul or Apollos or Cephas or the world or life or death or the present or
the future – all belong to you, and you belong to Christ, and Christ belongs
to God.

This is the word of the Lord.   *1 Corinthians 3.18–end*

Responsorial Psalm

R The earth is the Lord's, and all who dwell therein.   *cf Psalm 24.1*

The earth is the Lord's and all that fills it,
the compass of the world and all who dwell therein.
For he has founded it upon the seas
and set it firm upon the rivers of the deep. **R**

'Who shall ascend the hill of the Lord,
or who can rise up in his holy place?
Those who have clean hands and a pure heart,
who have not lifted up their soul to an idol,
nor sworn an oath to a lie. **R**

'They shall receive a blessing from the Lord,
a just reward from the God of their salvation.'
Such is the company of those who seek him,
of those who seek your face, O God of Jacob. **R**   *Psalm 24.1–6*

Year 1 and Year 2

Hear the Gospel of our Lord Jesus Christ according to Luke.

Once while Jesus was standing beside the lake of Gennesaret, and the crowd was pressing in on him to hear the word of God, he saw two boats there at the shore of the lake; the fishermen had gone out of them and were washing their nets. He got into one of the boats, the one belonging to Simon, and asked him to put out a little way from the shore. Then he sat down and taught the crowds from the boat.

When he had finished speaking, he said to Simon, 'Put out into the deep water and let down your nets for a catch.' Simon answered, 'Master, we have worked all night long but have caught nothing. Yet if you say so, I will let down the nets.' When they had done this, they caught so many fish that their nets were beginning to break. So they signalled to their partners in the other boat to come and help them. And they came and filled both boats, so that they began to sink.

But when Simon Peter saw it, he fell down at Jesus' knees, saying, 'Go away from me, Lord, for I am a sinful man!' For he and all who were with him were amazed at the catch of fish that they had taken; and so also were James and John, sons of Zebedee, who were partners with Simon. Then Jesus said to Simon, 'Do not be afraid; from now on you will be catching people.' When they had brought their boats to shore, they left everything and followed him.

This is the Gospel of the Lord.   Luke 5.1–11

Week 22: Friday between 2 and 8 September

Year 1

A reading from the Letter of Paul to the Colossians.

Christ is the image of the invisible God, the firstborn of all creation; for in him all things in heaven and on earth were created, things visible and invisible, whether thrones or dominions or rulers or powers – all things have been created through him and for him. He himself is before all things, and in him all things hold together. He is the head of the body, the church; he is the beginning, the firstborn from the dead, so that he might come to have first place in everything. For in him all the fullness of God was pleased to dwell, and through him God was pleased to reconcile to himself all things, whether on earth or in heaven, by making peace through the blood of his cross.

This is the word of the Lord.   Colossians 1.15–20

R **The Lord made a covenant with David,
[and anointed him with holy oil].** *cf Psalm 89.3a, 20b*

I have set a youth above the mighty;
I have raised a young man over the people.
I have found David my servant;
with my holy oil have I anointed him. R

My hand shall hold him fast
and my arm shall strengthen him.
No enemy shall deceive him,
nor any wicked person afflict him. R

I will strike down his foes before his face
and beat down those that hate him.
My truth also and my steadfast love shall be with him,
and in my name shall his head be exalted. R

I will set his dominion upon the sea
and his right hand upon the rivers.
He shall call to me, 'You are my Father,
my God, and the rock of my salvation.' R

And I will make him my firstborn,
the most high above the kings of the earth.
The love I have pledged to him will I keep for ever,
and my covenant will stand fast with him. R *Psalm 89.19b–28*

Year 2

A reading from the First Letter of Paul to the Corinthians.

Think of us in this way, as servants of Christ and stewards of God's mysteries. Moreover, it is required of stewards that they should be found trustworthy. But with me it is a very small thing that I should be judged by you or by any human court. I do not even judge myself. I am not aware of anything against myself, but I am not thereby acquitted. It is the Lord who judges me. Therefore do not pronounce judgement before the time, before the Lord comes, who will bring to light the things now hidden in darkness and will disclose the purposes of the heart. Then each one will receive commendation from God.

This is the word of the Lord. *1 Corinthians 4.1–5*

R **The salvation of the righteous comes from the Lord;**
   [he is their stronghold in the time of trouble].   *Psalm 37.40*

Trust in the Lord and be doing good;
dwell in the land and be nourished with truth.
Let your delight be in the Lord
and he will give you your heart's desire.   **R**

Commit your way to the Lord and put your trust in him,
and he will bring it to pass.
He will make your righteousness as clear as the light
and your just dealing as the noonday.   **R**

Be still before the Lord and wait for him;
do not fret over those that prosper
as they follow their evil schemes.
Refrain from anger and abandon wrath;
do not fret, lest you be moved to do evil.   **R**   *Psalm 37.3–8*

Year 1 and Year 2

Hear the Gospel of our Lord Jesus Christ according to Luke.

The Pharisees and their scribes said to Jesus, 'John's disciples, like the disciples of the Pharisees, frequently fast and pray, but your disciples eat and drink.' Jesus said to them, 'You cannot make wedding-guests fast while the bridegroom is with them, can you? The days will come when the bridegroom will be taken away from them, and then they will fast in those days.'

He also told them a parable: 'No one tears a piece from a new garment and sews it on an old garment; otherwise the new will be torn, and the piece from the new will not match the old. And no one puts new wine into old wineskins; otherwise the new wine will burst the skins and will be spilled, and the skins will be destroyed. But new wine must be put into fresh wineskins. And no one after drinking old wine desires new wine, but says, "The old is good." '

This is the Gospel of the Lord.   *Luke 5.33–end*

Week 22: Saturday between 3 and 9 September

Year 1

A reading from the Letter of Paul to the Colossians.

You who were once estranged and hostile in mind, doing evil deeds, God has now reconciled in Christ's fleshly body through death, so as to present you holy and blameless and irreproachable before him – provided that you continue securely established and steadfast in the faith, without shifting from the hope promised by the gospel that you heard, which has been proclaimed to every creature under heaven. I, Paul, became a servant of this gospel.

This is the word of the Lord.   *Colossians* 1.21–23

Responsorial Psalm

R **Alleluia!**

O praise the Lord, all you nations;
praise him, all you peoples. R

For great is his steadfast love towards us,
and the faithfulness of the Lord endures for ever. R   *Psalm* 117

Year 2

A reading from the First Letter of Paul to the Corinthians.

I have applied all this to Apollos and myself for your benefit, brothers and sisters, so that you may learn through us the meaning of the saying, 'Nothing beyond what is written', so that none of you will be puffed up in favour of one against another. For who sees anything different in you? What do you have that you did not receive? And if you received it, why do you boast as if it were not a gift?

Already you have all you want! Already you have become rich! Quite apart from us you have become kings! Indeed, I wish that you had become kings, so that we might be kings with you! For I think that God has exhibited us apostles as last of all, as though sentenced to death, because we have become a spectacle to the world, to angels and to mortals. We are fools for the sake of Christ, but you are wise in Christ. We are weak, but you are strong. You are held in honour, but we in disrepute. To the present hour we are hungry and thirsty, we are poorly clothed and beaten and homeless, and we grow weary from the work of our own hands. When reviled, we bless; when persecuted, we endure; when slandered, we speak kindly. We have become like the rubbish of the world, the dregs of all things, to this very day.

I am not writing this to make you ashamed, but to admonish you as my beloved children. For though you might have ten thousand guardians in Christ, you do not have many fathers. Indeed, in Christ Jesus I became your father through the gospel.

This is the word of the Lord.   *1 Corinthians* 4.6–15

Responsorial Psalm

R* **The Lord is righteous in all his ways
and loving in all his works.**   Psalm 145.18

The Lord is near to those who call upon him,
to all who call upon him faithfully.
He fulfils the desire of those who fear him;
he hears their cry and saves them.   R

The Lord watches over those who love him,
but all the wicked shall he destroy.
My mouth shall speak the praise of the Lord,
and let all flesh bless his holy name for ever and ever.   R

Psalm 145.18–end

Year 1 and Year 2

Hear the Gospel of our Lord Jesus Christ according to Luke.

One sabbath while Jesus was going through the cornfields, his disciples
plucked some heads of grain, rubbed them in their hands, and ate them. But
some of the Pharisees said, 'Why are you doing what is not lawful on the
sabbath?' Jesus answered, 'Have you not read what David did when he and
his companions were hungry? He entered the house of God and took and
ate the bread of the Presence, which it is not lawful for any but the priests
to eat, and gave some to his companions?' Then he said to them, 'The Son
of Man is lord of the sabbath.'

This is the Gospel of the Lord.   Luke 6.1–5

Week 23: Monday between 5 and 11 September

Year 1

A reading from the Letter of Paul to the Colossians.

I am now rejoicing in my sufferings for your sake, and in my flesh I am completing what is lacking in Christ's afflictions for the sake of his body, that is, the church. I became its servant according to God's commission that was given to me for you, to make the word of God fully known, the mystery that has been hidden throughout the ages and generations but has now been revealed to his saints. To them God chose to make known how great among the Gentiles are the riches of the glory of this mystery, which is Christ in you, the hope of glory. It is he whom we proclaim, warning everyone and teaching everyone in all wisdom, so that we may present everyone mature in Christ. For this I toil and struggle with all the energy that he powerfully inspires within me.

For I want you to know how much I am struggling for you, and for those in Laodicea, and for all who have not seen me face to face. I want their hearts to be encouraged and united in love, so that they may have all the riches of assured understanding and have the knowledge of God's mystery, that is, Christ himself, in whom are hidden all the treasures of wisdom and knowledge.

This is the word of the Lord.   Colossians 1.24 – 2.3

Responsorial Psalm

R* **God is my strength and glory;**
  [my strong rock and my refuge].   cf Psalm 62.7

On God alone my soul in stillness waits;
from him comes my salvation.
He alone is my rock and my salvation,
my stronghold, so that I shall never be shaken.   **R**

How long will all of you assail me to destroy me,
as you would a tottering wall or a leaning fence?
They plot only to thrust me down from my place of honour;
lies are their chief delight;
they bless with their mouth, but in their heart they curse.   **R**

Wait on God alone in stillness, O my soul;
for in him is my hope.
He alone is my rock and my salvation,
my stronghold, so that I shall not be shaken.   **R***   Psalm 62.1–7

A reading from the First Letter of Paul to the Corinthians.

It is actually reported that there is sexual immorality among you, and of a kind that is not found even among pagans; for a man is living with his father's wife. And you are arrogant! Should you not rather have mourned, so that he who has done this would have been removed from among you?

For though absent in body, I am present in spirit; and as if present I have already pronounced judgement in the name of the Lord Jesus on the man who has done such a thing. When you are assembled, and my spirit is present with the power of our Lord Jesus, you are to hand this man over to Satan for the destruction of the flesh, so that his spirit may be saved on the day of the Lord.

Your boasting is not a good thing. Do you not know that a little yeast leavens the whole batch of dough? Clean out the old yeast so that you may be a new batch, as you really are unleavened. For our paschal lamb, Christ, has been sacrificed. Therefore, let us celebrate the festival, not with the old yeast, the yeast of malice and evil, but with the unleavened bread of sincerity and truth.

This is the word of the Lord.   1 Corinthians 5.1–8

Responsorial Psalm

R   **Lead me, Lord, in your righteousness,**
    [make straight your way before me].   cf Psalm 5.8

The boastful cannot stand in your sight;
you hate all those that work wickedness.
You destroy those who speak lies;
the bloodthirsty and deceitful the Lord will abhor.   **R**

But as for me, through the greatness of your mercy,
I will come into your house;
I will bow down towards your holy temple
in awe of you.   **R**

Lead me, Lord, in your righteousness,
because of my enemies;
make your way straight before my face.
For there is no truth in their mouth,
in their heart is destruction.   **R**   Psalm 5.5–9a

Hear the Gospel of our Lord Jesus Christ according to Luke.

On the sabbath Jesus entered the synagogue and taught, and there was a man there whose right hand was withered. The scribes and the Pharisees watched him to see whether he would cure on the sabbath, so that they might find an accusation against him. Even though he knew what they were thinking, he said to the man who had the withered hand, 'Come and stand here.' He got up and stood there. Then Jesus said to them, 'I ask you, is it lawful to do good or to do harm on the sabbath, to save life or to destroy it?' After looking around at all of them, he said to him, 'Stretch out your hand.' He did so, and his hand was restored. But they were filled with fury and discussed with one another what they might do to Jesus.

This is the Gospel of the Lord.   Luke 6.6–11

Week 23: Tuesday between 6 and 12 September

Year 1

A reading from the Letter of Paul to the Colossians.

As you have received Christ Jesus the Lord, continue to live your lives in him, rooted and built up in him and established in the faith, just as you were taught, abounding in thanksgiving.

See to it that no one takes you captive through philosophy and empty deceit, according to human tradition, according to the elemental spirits of the universe, and not according to Christ. For in him the whole fullness of deity dwells bodily, and you have come to fullness in him, who is the head of every ruler and authority. In him also you were circumcised with a spiritual circumcision, by putting off the body of the flesh in the circumcision of Christ; when you were buried with him in baptism, you were also raised with him through faith in the power of God, who raised him from the dead. And when you were dead in trespasses and the uncircumcision of your flesh, God made you alive together with him, when he forgave us all our trespasses, erasing the record that stood against us with its legal demands. He set this aside, nailing it to the cross. He disarmed the rulers and authorities and made a public example of them, triumphing over them in it.

This is the word of the Lord.   Colossians 2.6–15

Responsorial Psalm

R* **O Lord our governor,**
   how glorious is your name in all the world!   *Psalm 8.1*

Your majesty above the heavens is praised
out of the mouths of babes at the breast.
You have founded a stronghold against your foes,
that you might still the enemy and the avenger. **R**

When I consider your heavens, the work of your fingers,
the moon and the stars that you have ordained,
what is man, that you should be mindful of him;
the son of man, that you should seek him out? **R**

You have made him little lower than the angels
and crown him with glory and honour.
You have given him dominion over the works of your hands
and put all things under his feet. **R**

All sheep and oxen,
even the wild beasts of the field,
the birds of the air, the fish of the sea
and whatsoever moves in the paths of the sea. **R**   *Psalm 8*

Year 2

A reading from the First Letter of Paul to the Corinthians.

When any of you has a grievance against another, do you dare to take it to
court before the unrighteous, instead of taking it before the saints? Do you
not know that the saints will judge the world? And if the world is to be
judged by you, are you incompetent to try trivial cases? Do you not know
that we are to judge angels – to say nothing of ordinary matters? If you have
ordinary cases, then, do you appoint as judges those who have no standing
in the church? I say this to your shame. Can it be that there is no one among
you wise enough to decide between one believer and another, but a believer
goes to court against a believer – and before unbelievers at that?

In fact, to have lawsuits at all with one another is already a defeat for you.
Why not rather be wronged? Why not rather be defrauded? But you yourselves
wrong and defraud – and believers at that.

Do you not know that wrongdoers will not inherit the kingdom of God? Do
not be deceived! Fornicators, idolaters, adulterers, male prostitutes, sodomites,
thieves, the greedy, drunkards, revilers, robbers – none of these will inherit
the kingdom of God. And this is what some of you used to be. But you were
washed, you were sanctified, you were justified in the name of the Lord Jesus
Christ and in the Spirit of our God.

This is the word of the Lord.   *1 Corinthians 6.1–11*

Responsorial Psalm

R* **Sing to the Lord a new song:**
[sing his praise in the congregation of the faithful].   Psalm 149.1

Let Israel rejoice in their maker;
let the children of Zion be joyful in their king.
Let them praise his name in the dance;
let them sing praise to him with timbrel and lyre.   **R**

For the Lord has pleasure in his people
and adorns the poor with salvation.
Let the faithful be joyful in glory;
let them rejoice in their ranks.   **R**   Psalm 149.1–5

Year 1 and Year 2

Hear the Gospel of our Lord Jesus Christ according to Luke.

Jesus went out to the mountain to pray; and he spent the night in prayer to
God. And when day came, he called his disciples and chose twelve of them,
whom he also named apostles: Simon, whom he named Peter, and his brother
Andrew, and James, and John, and Philip, and Bartholomew, and Matthew, and
Thomas, and James son of Alphaeus, and Simon, who was called the Zealot,
and Judas son of James, and Judas Iscariot, who became a traitor.

He came down with them and stood on a level place, with a great crowd
of his disciples and a great multitude of people from all Judea, Jerusalem, and
the coast of Tyre and Sidon. They had come to hear him and to be healed of
their diseases; and those who were troubled with unclean spirits were cured.
And all in the crowd were trying to touch him, for power came out from
him and healed all of them.

This is the Gospel of the Lord.   Luke 6.12–19

Week 23: Wednesday between 7 and 13 September

Year I

A reading from the Letter of Paul to the Colossians.

If you have been raised with Christ, seek the things that are above, where Christ is, seated at the right hand of God. Set your minds on things that are above, not on things that are on earth, for you have died, and your life is hidden with Christ in God. When Christ who is your life is revealed, then you also will be revealed with him in glory.

Put to death, therefore, whatever in you is earthly: fornication, impurity, passion, evil desire, and greed (which is idolatry). On account of these the wrath of God is coming on those who are disobedient. These are the ways you also once followed, when you were living that life. But now you must get rid of all such things – anger, wrath, malice, slander, and abusive language from your mouth. Do not lie to one another, seeing that you have stripped off the old self with its practices and have clothed yourselves with the new self, which is being renewed in knowledge according to the image of its creator. In that renewal there is no longer Greek and Jew, circumcised and uncircumcised, barbarian, Scythian, slave and free; but Christ is all and in all!

This is the word of the Lord.   *Colossians 3.1–11*

Responsorial Psalm

R **They shall dwell in your tabernacle, O Lord:**
   [those who do what is right].   *cf Psalm 15.1a, 2b*

Lord, who may dwell in your tabernacle?
Who may rest upon your holy hill?
Whoever leads an uncorrupt life
and does the thing that is right.   R

Who speaks the truth from the heart
and bears no deceit on the tongue;
who does no evil to a friend
and pours no scorn on a neighbour.   R

In whose sight the wicked are not esteemed,
but who honours those who fear the Lord.
Whoever has sworn to a neighbour
and never goes back on that word.   R

Who does not lend money in hope of gain,
nor takes a bribe against the innocent;
whoever does these things
shall never fall.   R   *Psalm 15*

A reading from the First Letter of Paul to the Corinthians.

Concerning virgins, I have no command of the Lord, but I give my opinion as one who by the Lord's mercy is trustworthy. I think that, in view of the impending crisis, it is well for you to remain as you are. Are you bound to a wife? Do not seek to be free. Are you free from a wife? Do not seek a wife. But if you marry, you do not sin, and if a virgin marries, she does not sin. Yet those who marry will experience distress in this life, and I would spare you that. I mean, brothers and sisters, the appointed time has grown short; from now on, let even those who have wives be as though they had none, and those who mourn as though they were not mourning, and those who rejoice as though they were not rejoicing, and those who buy as though they had no possessions, and those who deal with the world as though they had no dealings with it. For the present form of this world is passing away.

This is the word of the Lord.   1 Corinthians 7.25–31

Responsorial Psalm

R* **Your name shall be remembered through all generations;**
   [the peoples shall praise you for ever and ever].   cf Psalm 45.17

So shall the king have pleasure in your beauty;
he is your lord, so do him honour.
The people of Tyre shall bring you gifts;
the richest of the people shall seek your favour.   **R**

The king's daughter is all glorious within;
her clothing is embroidered cloth of gold.
She shall be brought to the king in raiment of needlework;
after her the virgins that are her companions.   **R**

With joy and gladness shall they be brought
and enter into the palace of the king.
'Instead of your fathers you shall have sons,
whom you shall make princes over all the land.   **R***   Psalm 45.11–end

Hear the Gospel of our Lord Jesus Christ according to Luke.

Jesus looked up at his disciples and said:
'Blessed are you who are poor,
for yours is the kingdom of God.
Blessed are you who are hungry now,
for you will be filled.
Blessed are you who weep now,
for you will laugh.

'Blessed are you when people hate you, and when they exclude you, revile you, and defame you on account of the Son of Man. Rejoice on that day and leap for joy, for surely your reward is great in heaven; for that is what their ancestors did to the prophets.
'But woe to you who are rich,
for you have received your consolation.
Woe to you who are full now,
for you will be hungry.
Woe to you who are laughing now,
for you will mourn and weep.

'Woe to you when all speak well of you, for that is what their ancestors did to the false prophets.'

This is the Gospel of the Lord.   Luke 6.20–26

Week 23: Thursday between 8 and 14 September

Year 1

A reading from the Letter of Paul to the Colossians.

As God's chosen ones, holy and beloved, clothe yourselves with compassion, kindness, humility, meekness, and patience. Bear with one another and, if anyone has a complaint against another, forgive each other; just as the Lord has forgiven you, so you also must forgive. Above all, clothe yourselves with love, which binds everything together in perfect harmony. And let the peace of Christ rule in your hearts, to which indeed you were called in the one body. And be thankful. Let the word of Christ dwell in you richly; teach and admonish one another in all wisdom; and with gratitude in your hearts sing psalms, hymns, and spiritual songs to God. And whatever you do, in word or deed, do everything in the name of the Lord Jesus, giving thanks to God the Father through him.

This is the word of the Lord.   Colossians 3.12–17

Responsorial Psalm

R* **Sing to the Lord a new song:**
   [sing his praise in the congregation of the faithful].   *Psalm 149.1*

Let Israel rejoice in their maker;
let the children of Zion be joyful in their king.
Let them praise his name in the dance;
let them sing praise to him with timbrel and lyre.   **R**

For the Lord has pleasure in his people
and adorns the poor with salvation.
Let the faithful be joyful in glory;
let them rejoice in their ranks.   **R**   *Psalm 149.1–5*

Year 2

A reading from the First Letter of Paul to the Corinthians.

Concerning food sacrificed to idols: we know that 'all of us possess knowledge.' Knowledge puffs up, but love builds up. Anyone who claims to know something does not yet have the necessary knowledge; but anyone who loves God is known by him.

Hence, as to the eating of food offered to idols, we know that 'no idol in the world really exists', and that 'there is no God but one.' Indeed, even though there may be so-called gods in heaven or on earth – as in fact there are many gods and many lords – yet for us there is one God, the Father, from whom are all things and for whom we exist, and one Lord, Jesus Christ, through whom are all things and through whom we exist.

It is not everyone, however, who has this knowledge. Since some have become so accustomed to idols until now, they still think of the food they eat as food offered to an idol; and their conscience, being weak, is defiled. So by your knowledge those weak believers for whom Christ died are destroyed. But when you thus sin against members of your family, and wound their conscience when it is weak, you sin against Christ. Therefore, if food is a cause of their falling, I will never eat meat, so that I may not cause one of them to fall.

This is the word of the Lord.   *1 Corinthians 8.1–7, 11–end*

Responsorial Psalm

R **O Lord, you have searched me out and known me.**   Psalm 139.1a

O Lord, you have searched me out and known me;
you know my sitting down and my rising up;
you discern my thoughts from afar.   R

You mark out my journeys and my resting place
and are acquainted with all my ways.
For there is not a word on my tongue,
but you, O Lord, know it altogether.   R

You encompass me behind and before
and lay your hand upon me.
Such knowledge is too wonderful for me,
so high that I cannot attain it.   R

Where can I go then from your spirit?
Or where can I flee from your presence?
If I climb up to heaven, you are there;
if I make the grave my bed, you are there also.   R

If I take the wings of the morning
and dwell in the uttermost parts of the sea,
even there your hand shall lead me,
your right hand hold me fast.   R   Psalm 139.1–9

Year 1 and Year 2

Hear the Gospel of our Lord Jesus Christ according to Luke.

Jesus said to his disciples, 'I say to you that listen, Love your enemies, do
good to those who hate you, bless those who curse you, pray for those who
abuse you. If anyone strikes you on the cheek, offer the other also; and from
anyone who takes away your coat do not withhold even your shirt. Give to
everyone who begs from you; and if anyone takes away your goods, do not
ask for them again. Do to others as you would have them do to you.

'If you love those who love you, what credit is that to you? For even sinners
love those who love them. If you do good to those who do good to you, what
credit is that to you? For even sinners do the same. If you lend to those from
whom you hope to receive, what credit is that to you? Even sinners lend
to sinners, to receive as much again. But love your enemies, do good, and
lend, expecting nothing in return. Your reward will be great, and you will be
children of the Most High; for he is kind to the ungrateful and the wicked.
Be merciful, just as your Father is merciful. Do not judge, and you will not be
judged; do not condemn, and you will not be condemned. Forgive, and you will
be forgiven; give, and it will be given to you. A good measure, pressed down,
shaken together, running over, will be put into your lap; for the measure you
give will be the measure you get back.'

This is the Gospel of the Lord.   Luke 6.27–38

Week 23: Friday between 9 and 15 September

Year 1

A reading from the First Letter of Paul to Timothy.

Paul, an apostle of Christ Jesus by the command of God our Saviour and of Christ Jesus our hope, to Timothy, my loyal child in the faith: Grace, mercy, and peace from God the Father and Christ Jesus our Lord.

I am grateful to Christ Jesus our Lord, who has strengthened me, because he judged me faithful and appointed me to his service, even though I was formerly a blasphemer, a persecutor, and a man of violence. But I received mercy because I had acted ignorantly in unbelief, and the grace of our Lord overflowed for me with the faith and love that are in Christ Jesus.

This is the word of the Lord.   1 Timothy 1.1–2, 12–14

Responsorial Psalm

R **You are my lord,
my good depends on you.**   Psalm 16.1b

Preserve me, O God, for in you have I taken refuge;
I have said to the Lord, 'You are my lord,
all my good depends on you.'
All my delight is upon the godly that are in the land,
upon those who are noble in heart.   **R**

Though the idols are legion that many run after,
their drink offerings of blood I will not offer,
neither make mention of their names upon my lips.
The Lord himself is my portion and my cup;
in your hands alone is my fortune.   **R**

My share has fallen in a fair land;
indeed, I have a goodly heritage.
I will bless the Lord
who has given me counsel,
and in the night watches he instructs my heart.   **R**

I have set the Lord always before me;
he is at my right hand; I shall not fall.
Wherefore my heart is glad
and my spirit rejoices;
my flesh also shall rest secure.   **R**

For you will not abandon my soul to Death,
nor suffer your faithful one to see the Pit;
you will show me the path of life.
In your presence is the fullness of joy
and in your right hand are pleasures for evermore.   **R**   Psalm 16

Year 2

A reading from the First Letter of Paul to the Corinthians.

If I proclaim the gospel, this gives me no ground for boasting, for an obligation is laid on me, and woe betide me if I do not proclaim the gospel! For if I do this of my own will, I have a reward; but if not of my own will, I am entrusted with a commission. What then is my reward? Just this: that in my proclamation I may make the gospel free of charge, so as not to make full use of my rights in the gospel.

For though I am free with respect to all, I have made myself a slave to all, so that I might win more of them. To the weak I became weak, so that I might win the weak. I have become all things to all people, so that I might by any means save some. I do it all for the sake of the gospel, so that I may share in its blessings.

Do you not know that in a race the runners all compete, but only one receives the prize? Run in such a way that you may win it. Athletes exercise self-control in all things; they do it to receive a perishable garland, but we an imperishable one. So I do not run aimlessly, nor do I box as though beating the air; but I punish my body and enslave it, so that after proclaiming to others I myself should not be disqualified.

This is the word of the Lord.   1 Corinthians 9.16–19, 22–end

Responsorial Psalm

R   **How lovely is your dwelling place, O Lord of hosts!**   Psalm 84.1
    or

R   **Alleluia!**

How lovely is your dwelling place, O Lord of hosts!
My soul has a desire and longing
to enter the courts of the Lord;
my heart and my flesh rejoice in the living God.   **R**

The sparrow has found her a house
and the swallow a nest where she may lay her young:
at your altars, O Lord of hosts,
my King and my God.   **R**

Blessed are they who dwell in your house:
they will always be praising you.
Blessed are those whose strength is in you,
in whose heart are the highways to Zion.   **R**

Who going through the barren valley find there a spring,
and the early rains will clothe it with blessing.
They will go from strength to strength
and appear before God in Zion.   **R**   Psalm 84.1–6

Hear the Gospel of our Lord Jesus Christ according to Luke.

Jesus told his disciples a parable: 'Can a blind person guide a blind person? Will not both fall into a pit? A disciple is not above the teacher, but everyone who is fully qualified will be like the teacher. Why do you see the speck in your neighbour's eye, but do not notice the log in your own eye? Or how can you say to your neighbour, "Friend, let me take out the speck in your eye", when you yourself do not see the log in your own eye? You hypocrite, first take the log out of your own eye, and then you will see clearly to take the speck out of your neighbour's eye.'

This is the Gospel of the Lord.   Luke 6.39–42

Week 23: Saturday between 10 and 16 September

Year 1

A reading from the First Letter of Paul to Timothy.

The saying is sure and worthy of full acceptance, that Christ Jesus came into the world to save sinners – of whom I am the foremost. But for that very reason I received mercy, so that in me, as the foremost, Jesus Christ might display the utmost patience, making me an example to those who would come to believe in him for eternal life. To the King of the ages, immortal, invisible, the only God, be honour and glory for ever and ever. Amen.

This is the word of the Lord.   1 Timothy 1.15–17

Responsorial Psalm

R   **Blessed be the name of the Lord:**
    [from this time forth and for evermore].   Psalm 113.2

Give praise, you servants of the Lord,
O praise the name of the Lord.
Blessed be the name of the Lord,
from this time forth and for evermore.   **R**

From the rising of the sun to its setting
let the name of the Lord be praised.
The Lord is high above all nations
and his glory above the heavens.   **R**

Who is like the Lord our God,
that has his throne so high,
yet humbles himself to behold
the things of heaven and earth?   **R**   →

He raises the poor from the dust
and lifts the needy from the ashes,
to set them with princes,
with the princes of his people.
He gives the barren woman a place in the house
and makes her a joyful mother of children. R   *Psalm 113*

R **Blessed be the name of the Lord:**
   [from this time forth and for evermore].

Year 2

A reading from the First Letter of Paul to the Corinthians.

My dear friends, flee from the worship of idols. I speak as to sensible people;
judge for yourselves what I say. The cup of blessing that we bless, is it not a
sharing in the blood of Christ? The bread that we break, is it not a sharing
in the body of Christ? Because there is one bread, we who are many are one
body, for we all partake of the one bread. Consider the people of Israel; are
not those who eat the sacrifices partners in the altar? What do I imply then?
That food sacrificed to idols is anything, or that an idol is anything? No, I
imply that what pagans sacrifice, they sacrifice to demons and not to God. I
do not want you to be partners with demons. You cannot drink the cup of
the Lord and the cup of demons. You cannot partake of the table of the Lord
and the table of demons. Or are we provoking the Lord to jealousy? Are we
stronger than he?

This is the word of the Lord.   1 Corinthians 10.14–22

Responsorial Psalm

R **I will offer to you a sacrifice of thanksgiving:**
   [and call upon the name of the Lord].   *Psalm 116.15*
   or

R **Alleluia!**

How shall I repay the Lord
for all the benefits he has given to me?
I will lift up the cup of salvation
and call upon the name of the Lord.   R

I will fulfil my vows to the Lord
in the presence of all his people.
Precious in the sight of the Lord
is the death of his faithful servants.   R

O Lord, I am your servant,
your servant, the child of your handmaid;
you have freed me from my bonds.
I will offer to you a sacrifice of thanksgiving
and call upon the name of the Lord.   R

I will fulfil my vows to the Lord
in the presence of all his people,
in the courts of the house of the Lord,
in the midst of you, O Jerusalem.   R   Psalm 116.10–end

Year 1 and Year 2

Hear the Gospel of our Lord Jesus Christ according to Luke.

Jesus said to his disciples, 'No good tree bears bad fruit, nor again does a
bad tree bear good fruit; for each tree is known by its own fruit. Figs are
not gathered from thorns, nor are grapes picked from a bramble bush. The
good person out of the good treasure of the heart produces good, and the
evil person out of evil treasure produces evil; for it is out of the abundance
of the heart that the mouth speaks.

'Why do you call me "Lord, Lord", and do not do what I tell you? I will
show you what someone is like who comes to me, hears my words, and acts
on them. That one is like a man building a house, who dug deeply and laid
the foundation on rock; when a flood arose, the river burst against that house
but could not shake it, because it had been well built. But the one who hears
and does not act is like a man who built a house on the ground without a
foundation. When the river burst against it, immediately it fell, and great was
the ruin of that house.'

This is the Gospel of the Lord.   Luke 6.43–end

Week 24: Monday between 12 and 18 September

Year I

A reading from the First Letter of Paul to Timothy.

First of all, I urge that supplications, prayers, intercessions, and thanksgivings should be made for everyone, for kings and all who are in high positions, so that we may lead a quiet and peaceable life in all godliness and dignity. This is right and is acceptable in the sight of God our Saviour, who desires everyone to be saved and to come to the knowledge of the truth. For

there is one God;
there is also one mediator between God and humankind,
Christ Jesus, himself human,
who gave himself a ransom for all

– this was attested at the right time. For this I was appointed a herald and an apostle (I am telling the truth, I am not lying), a teacher of the Gentiles in faith and truth.

I desire, then, that in every place the men should pray, lifting up holy hands without anger or argument.

This is the word of the Lord. 1 Timothy 2.1–8

Responsorial Psalm

R* Blessed be the Lord, for he has heard my prayer. cf Psalm 28.7

To you I call, O Lord my rock;
be not deaf to my cry,
lest, if you do not hear me,
I become like those who go down to the Pit.   **R**

Hear the voice of my prayer
when I cry out to you,
when I lift up my hands
to your holy of holies.   **R**

Do not snatch me away with the wicked,
with the evildoers,
who speak peaceably with their neighbours,
while malice is in their hearts.   **R**

Repay them according to their deeds
and according to the wickedness of their devices.
Reward them according to the work of their hands
and pay them their just deserts.   **R**

They take no heed of the Lord's doings,
nor of the works of his hands;
therefore shall he break them down
and not build them up. R*

The Lord is my strength and my shield;
my heart has trusted in him and I am helped;
therefore my heart dances for joy
and in my song will I praise him. R

The Lord is the strength of his people,
a safe refuge for his anointed.
Save your people and bless your inheritance;
shepherd them and carry them for ever. R   *Psalm 28*

Year 2

A reading from the First Letter of Paul to the Corinthians.

In the following instructions I do not commend you, because when you come together it is not for the better but for the worse. For, to begin with, when you come together as a church, I hear that there are divisions among you; and to some extent I believe it. Indeed, there have to be factions among you, for only so will it become clear who among you are genuine. When you come together, it is not really to eat the Lord's supper. For when the time comes to eat, each of you goes ahead with your own supper, and one goes hungry and another becomes drunk. What! Do you not have homes to eat and drink in? Or do you show contempt for the church of God and humiliate those who have nothing? What should I say to you? Should I commend you? In this matter I do not commend you!

For I received from the Lord what I also handed on to you, that the Lord Jesus on the night when he was betrayed took a loaf of bread, and when he had given thanks, he broke it and said, 'This is my body that is for you. Do this in remembrance of me.' In the same way he took the cup also, after supper, saying, 'This cup is the new covenant in my blood. Do this, as often as you drink it, in remembrance of me.' For as often as you eat this bread and drink the cup, you proclaim the Lord's death until he comes.

So then, my brothers and sisters, when you come together to eat, wait for one another.

This is the word of the Lord.   1 Corinthians 11.17–26, 33

Responsorial Psalm

R **I delight to do your will, O God;
[your law is in my heart].**   cf Psalm 40.9b

Sacrifice and offering you do not desire
but my ears you have opened;
burnt offering and sacrifice for sin
you have not required.   R

Then said I: 'Lo, I come.
In the scroll of the book it is written of me
that I should do your will, O my God;
I delight to do it: your law is within my heart.'   R

I have declared your righteousness
in the great congregation;
behold, I did not restrain my lips,
and that, O Lord, you know.   R

Your righteousness I have not hidden in my heart;
I have spoken of your faithfulness and your salvation;
I have not concealed your loving-kindness and truth
from the great congregation.   R   Psalm 40.7–11

Year 1 and Year 2

Hear the Gospel of our Lord Jesus Christ according to Luke.

After Jesus had finished all his sayings in the hearing of the people, he entered
Capernaum. A centurion there had a slave whom he valued highly, and who
was ill and close to death. When he heard about Jesus, he sent some Jewish
elders to him, asking him to come and heal his slave. When they came to
Jesus, they appealed to him earnestly, saying, 'He is worthy of having you do
this for him, for he loves our people, and it is he who built our synagogue
for us.' And Jesus went with them, but when he was not far from the house,
the centurion sent friends to say to him, 'Lord, do not trouble yourself, for I
am not worthy to have you come under my roof; therefore I did not presume
to come to you. But only speak the word, and let my servant be healed. For I
also am a man set under authority, with soldiers under me; and I say to one,
"Go", and he goes, and to another, "Come", and he comes, and to my slave,
"Do this", and the slave does it.' When Jesus heard this he was amazed at him,
and turning to the crowd that followed him, he said, 'I tell you, not even in
Israel have I found such faith.' When those who had been sent returned to
the house, they found the slave in good health.

This is the Gospel of the Lord.   Luke 7.1–10

Week 24: Tuesday between 13 and 19 September

Year I

A reading from the First Letter of Paul to Timothy.

The saying is sure: whoever aspires to the office of bishop desires a noble task. Now a bishop must be above reproach, married only once, temperate, sensible, respectable, hospitable, an apt teacher, not a drunkard, not violent but gentle, not quarrelsome, and not a lover of money. He must manage his own household well, keeping his children submissive and respectful in every way – for if someone does not know how to manage his own household, how can he take care of God's church? He must not be a recent convert, or he may be puffed up with conceit and fall into the condemnation of the devil. Moreover, he must be well thought of by outsiders, so that he may not fall into disgrace and the snare of the devil.

Deacons likewise must be serious, not double-tongued, not indulging in much wine, not greedy for money; they must hold fast to the mystery of the faith with a clear conscience. And let them first be tested; then, if they prove themselves blameless, let them serve as deacons. Women likewise must be serious, not slanderers, but temperate, faithful in all things. Let deacons be married only once, and let them manage their children and their households well; for those who serve well as deacons gain a good standing for themselves and great boldness in the faith that is in Christ Jesus.

This is the word of the Lord.   1 Timothy 3.1–13

Responsorial Psalm

R   **I will sing of faithfulness and justice;**
     [to you, O Lord, will I sing].   Psalm 101.1

I will sing of faithfulness and justice;
to you, O Lord, will I sing.
Let me be wise in the way that is perfect:
when will you come to me?   **R**

I will walk with purity of heart
within the walls of my house.
I will not set before my eyes
a counsel that is evil.   **R**

I abhor the deeds of unfaithfulness;
they shall not cling to me.
A crooked heart shall depart from me;
I will not know a wicked person.   **R**   →

One who slanders a neighbour in secret
I will quickly put to silence.
Haughty eyes and an arrogant heart
I will not endure. R

R **I will sing of faithfulness and justice;**
[to you, O Lord, will I sing].

My eyes are upon the faithful in the land,
that they may dwell with me.
One who walks in the way that is pure
shall be my servant. R

There shall not dwell in my house
one that practises deceit.
One who utters falsehood
shall not continue in my sight. R

Morning by morning will I put to silence
all the wicked in the land,
to cut off from the city of the Lord
all those who practise evil. R   *Psalm* 101

Year 2

A reading from the First Letter of Paul to the Corinthians.

Just as the body is one and has many members, and all the members of the
body, though many, are one body, so it is with Christ. For in the one Spirit
we were all baptized into one body – Jews or Greeks, slaves or free – and we
were all made to drink of one Spirit. Indeed, the body does not consist of
one member but of many.

Now you are the body of Christ and individually members of it. And God
has appointed in the church first apostles, second prophets, third teachers;
then deeds of power, then gifts of healing, forms of assistance, forms of
leadership, various kinds of tongues. Are all apostles? Are all prophets? Are all
teachers? Do all work miracles? Do all possess gifts of healing? Do all speak
in tongues? Do all interpret? But strive for the greater gifts. And I will show
you a still more excellent way.

This is the word of the Lord.   1 *Corinthians* 12.12–14, 27–end

Responsorial Psalm

R **Be joyful in the Lord, all the earth:**
[give thanks and bless his name]. *cf Psalm 100.1a, 3b*

O be joyful in the Lord, all the earth;
serve the Lord with gladness
and come before his presence with a song. **R**

Know that the Lord is God;
it is he that has made us and we are his;
we are his people and the sheep of his pasture. **R**

Enter his gates with thanksgiving
and his courts with praise;
give thanks to him and bless his name. **R**

For the Lord is gracious;
his steadfast love is everlasting,
and his faithfulness endures from generation to generation. **R**

Psalm 100

Year 1 and Year 2

Hear the Gospel of our Lord Jesus Christ according to Luke.

Jesus went to a town called Nain, and his disciples and a large crowd went
with him. As he approached the gate of the town, a man who had died was
being carried out. He was his mother's only son, and she was a widow; and
with her was a large crowd from the town. When the Lord saw her, he had
compassion for her and said to her, 'Do not weep.' Then he came forward
and touched the bier, and the bearers stood still. And he said, 'Young man,
I say to you, rise!' The dead man sat up and began to speak, and Jesus gave
him to his mother. Fear seized all of them; and they glorified God, saying, 'A
great prophet has risen among us!' and 'God has looked favourably on his
people!' This word about him spread throughout Judea and all the surrounding country.

This is the Gospel of the Lord. *Luke 7.11–17*

Week 24: Wednesday between 14 and 20 September

Year 1

A reading from the First Letter of Paul to Timothy.

I hope to come to you soon, but I am writing these instructions to you so that, if I am delayed, you may know how one ought to behave in the household of God, which is the church of the living God, the pillar and bulwark of the truth. Without any doubt, the mystery of our religion is great:

> He was revealed in flesh,
> > vindicated in spirit,
> > > seen by angels,
> > proclaimed among Gentiles,
> > > believed in throughout the world,
> > > > taken up in glory.

This is the word of the Lord.   1 Timothy 3.14–end

Responsorial Psalm

R* **The Lord is renowned for his marvellous deeds:**
   [he is gracious and full of compassion].   cf Psalm 111.4

I will give thanks to the Lord with my whole heart,
in the company of the faithful and in the congregation.
The works of the Lord are great,
sought out by all who delight in them.   **R**

His work is full of majesty and honour
and his righteousness endures for ever.*
He gave food to those who feared him;
he is ever mindful of his covenant.   **R**   Psalm 111.1–5

Year 2

A reading from the First Letter of Paul to the Corinthians.

I will show you a still more excellent way. If I speak in the tongues of mortals and of angels, but do not have love, I am a noisy gong or a clanging cymbal. And if I have prophetic powers, and understand all mysteries and all knowledge, and if I have all faith, so as to remove mountains, but do not have love, I am nothing. If I give away all my possessions, and if I hand over my body so that I may boast, but do not have love, I gain nothing.

Love is patient; love is kind; love is not envious or boastful or arrogant or rude. It does not insist on its own way; it is not irritable or resentful; it does not rejoice in wrongdoing, but rejoices in the truth. It bears all things, believes all things, hopes all things, endures all things.

Love never ends. But as for prophecies, they will come to an end; as for tongues, they will cease; as for knowledge, it will come to an end. For we know only in part, and we prophesy only in part; but when the complete comes, the partial will come to an end. When I was a child, I spoke like a child, I thought like a child, I reasoned like a child; when I became an adult, I put an end to childish ways. For now we see in a mirror, dimly, but then we will see face to face. Now I know only in part; then I will know fully, even as I have been fully known. And now faith, hope, and love abide, these three; and the greatest of these is love.

This is the word of the Lord. 1 Corinthians 12.31b – end of 13

Responsorial Psalm

R* **Rejoice in the Lord, O you righteous:**
   [it is good to sing his praises]. cf Psalm 33.1

Praise the Lord with the lyre;
on the ten-stringed harp sing his praise.
Sing for him a new song;
play skilfully, with shouts of praise.   **R**

For the word of the Lord is true
and all his works are sure.
He loves righteousness and justice;
the earth is full of the loving-kindness of the Lord.   **R**

By the word of the Lord were the heavens made
and all their host by the breath of his mouth.
He gathers up the waters of the sea as in a waterskin
and lays up the deep in his treasury.   **R**

Let all the earth fear the Lord;
stand in awe of him, all who dwell in the world.
For he spoke, and it was done;
he commanded, and it stood fast.   **R**

The Lord brings the counsel of the nations to naught;
he frustrates the designs of the peoples.
But the counsel of the Lord shall endure for ever
and the designs of his heart from generation to generation.
Happy the nation whose God is the Lord
and the people he has chosen for his own.   **R** Psalm 33.1–12

Hear the Gospel of our Lord Jesus Christ according to Luke.

Jesus said to the crowds, 'To what then will I compare the people of this generation, and what are they like? They are like children sitting in the market-place and calling to one another,

"We played the flute for you, and you did not dance;
    we wailed, and you did not weep."

For John the Baptist has come eating no bread and drinking no wine, and you say, "He has a demon"; the Son of Man has come eating and drinking, and you say, "Look, a glutton and a drunkard, a friend of tax-collectors and sinners!" Nevertheless, wisdom is vindicated by all her children.'

This is the Gospel of the Lord.   Luke 7.31–35

Week 24: Thursday between 15 and 21 September

Year 1

A reading from the First Letter of Paul to Timothy.

Let no one despise your youth, but set the believers an example in speech and conduct, in love, in faith, in purity. Until I arrive, give attention to the public reading of scripture, to exhorting, to teaching. Do not neglect the gift that is in you, which was given to you through prophecy with the laying on of hands by the council of elders. Put these things into practice, devote yourself to them, so that all may see your progress. Pay close attention to yourself and to your teaching; continue in these things, for in doing this you will save both yourself and your hearers.

This is the word of the Lord.   1 Timothy 4.12–end

Responsorial Psalm

R **The commandments of God stand firm for ever:
    [established in truth and equity].**   cf Psalm 111.8

He showed his people the power of his works
in giving them the heritage of the nations.
The works of his hands are truth and justice;
all his commandments are sure.   **R***

He sent redemption to his people;
he commanded his covenant for ever;
holy and awesome is his name.   **R**

The fear of the Lord is the beginning of wisdom;
a good understanding have those who live by it;
his praise endures for ever.   **R**   Psalm 111.6–end

A reading from the First Letter of Paul to the Corinthians.

I should remind you, brothers and sisters, of the good news that I proclaimed to you, which you in turn received, in which also you stand, through which also you are being saved, if you hold firmly to the message that I proclaimed to you – unless you have come to believe in vain.

For I handed on to you as of first importance what I in turn had received: that Christ died for our sins in accordance with the scriptures, and that he was buried, and that he was raised on the third day in accordance with the scriptures, and that he appeared to Cephas, then to the twelve. Then he appeared to more than five hundred brothers and sisters at one time, most of whom are still alive, though some have died. Then he appeared to James, then to all the apostles. Last of all, as to someone untimely born, he appeared also to me. For I am the least of the apostles, unfit to be called an apostle, because I persecuted the church of God. But by the grace of God I am what I am, and his grace towards me has not been in vain. On the contrary, I worked harder than any of them – though it was not I, but the grace of God that is with me. Whether then it was I or they, so we proclaim and so you have come to believe.

This is the word of the Lord.   1 Corinthians 15.1–11

Responsorial Psalm

R **Give thanks to the Lord, for he is good;
    [his mercy endures for ever].**   Psalm 118.1

O give thanks to the Lord, for he is good;
his mercy endures for ever.
Let Israel now proclaim,
'His mercy endures for ever.'   **R**

I shall not die, but live
and declare the works of the Lord.
The Lord has punished me sorely,
but he has not given me over to death.   **R**

Open to me the gates of righteousness,
that I may enter and give thanks to the Lord.
This is the gate of the Lord;
the righteous shall enter through it.   **R**   Psalm 118.1–2, 17–20

Hear the Gospel of our Lord Jesus Christ according to Luke.

One of the Pharisees asked Jesus to eat with him, and he went into the Pharisee's house and took his place at the table. And a woman in the city, who was a sinner, having learned that he was eating in the Pharisee's house, brought an alabaster jar of ointment. She stood behind him at his feet, weeping, and began to bathe his feet with her tears and to dry them with her hair. Then she continued kissing his feet and anointing them with the ointment.

Now when the Pharisee who had invited him saw it, he said to himself, 'If this man were a prophet, he would have known who and what kind of woman this is who is touching him – that she is a sinner.' Jesus spoke up and said to him, 'Simon, I have something to say to you.' 'Teacher,' he replied, 'speak.' 'A certain creditor had two debtors; one owed five hundred denarii, and the other fifty. When they could not pay, he cancelled the debts for both of them. Now which of them will love him more?' Simon answered, 'I suppose the one for whom he cancelled the greater debt.' And Jesus said to him, 'You have judged rightly.'

Then turning towards the woman, he said to Simon, 'Do you see this woman? I entered your house; you gave me no water for my feet, but she has bathed my feet with her tears and dried them with her hair. You gave me no kiss, but from the time I came in she has not stopped kissing my feet. You did not anoint my head with oil, but she has anointed my feet with ointment. Therefore, I tell you, her sins, which were many, have been forgiven; hence she has shown great love. But the one to whom little is forgiven, loves little.' Then he said to her, 'Your sins are forgiven.' But those who were at the table with him began to say among themselves, 'Who is this who even forgives sins?' And he said to the woman, 'Your faith has saved you; go in peace.'

This is the Gospel of the Lord.   Luke 7.36–end

Week 24: Friday between 16 and 22 September

Year 1

A reading from the First Letter of Paul to Timothy.

Teach and urge these duties. Whoever teaches otherwise and does not agree with the sound words of our Lord Jesus Christ and the teaching that is in accordance with godliness, is conceited, understanding nothing, and has a morbid craving for controversy and for disputes about words. From these come envy, dissension, slander, base suspicions, and wrangling among those who are depraved in mind and bereft of the truth, imagining that godliness is a means of gain. Of course, there is great gain in godliness combined with contentment; for we brought nothing into the world, so that we can take nothing out of it; but if we have food and clothing, we will be content with these. But those who want to be rich fall into temptation and are trapped by many senseless and harmful desires that plunge people into ruin and destruction. For the love of money is a root of all kinds of evil, and in their eagerness to be rich some have wandered away from the faith and pierced themselves with many pains.

But as for you, man of God, shun all this; pursue righteousness, godliness, faith, love, endurance, gentleness. Fight the good fight of the faith; take hold of the eternal life, to which you were called and for which you made the good confession in the presence of many witnesses.

This is the word of the Lord.   1 Timothy 6.2b–12

Responsorial Psalm

R **God shall ransom my soul;**
   from the grasp of death will he take me.   Psalm 49.16

Hear this, all you peoples;
listen, all you that dwell in the world,
you of low or high degree,
both rich and poor together.   **R**

My mouth shall speak of wisdom
and my heart shall meditate on understanding.
I will incline my ear to a parable;
I will unfold my riddle with the lyre.   **R**

Why should I fear in evil days,
when the malice of my foes surrounds me,
such as trust in their goods
and glory in the abundance of their riches?   **R**

For no one can indeed ransom another
or pay to God the price of deliverance.
To ransom a soul is too costly;
there is no price one could pay for it,
so that they might live for ever,
and never see the grave.   **R**   Psalm 49.1–9

A reading from the First Letter of Paul to the Corinthians.

If Christ is proclaimed as raised from the dead, how can some of you say there is no resurrection of the dead? If there is no resurrection of the dead, then Christ has not been raised; and if Christ has not been raised, then our proclamation has been in vain and your faith has been in vain. We are even found to be misrepresenting God, because we testified of God that he raised Christ – whom he did not raise if it is true that the dead are not raised. For if the dead are not raised, then Christ has not been raised. If Christ has not been raised, your faith is futile and you are still in your sins. Then those also who have died in Christ have perished. If for this life only we have hoped in Christ, we are of all people most to be pitied. But in fact Christ has been raised from the dead, the first fruits of those who have died.

This is the word of the Lord.   1 Corinthians 15.12–20

Responsorial Psalm

R* **Keep me as the apple of your eye;**
   [hide me under the shadow of your wings].   *Psalm* 17.8

Hear my just cause, O Lord; consider my complaint;
listen to my prayer, which comes not from lying lips.
Let my vindication come forth from your presence;
let your eyes behold what is right.   **R**

Weigh my heart, examine me by night,
refine me, and you will find no impurity in me.
My mouth does not trespass for earthly rewards;
I have heeded the words of your lips.   **R**

My footsteps hold fast in the ways of your commandments;
my feet have not stumbled in your paths.
I call upon you, O God, for you will answer me;
incline your ear to me, and listen to my words.   **R**

Show me your marvellous loving-kindness,
O Saviour of those who take refuge at your right hand
from those who rise up against them.   **R***   *Psalm* 17.1–8

Year 1 and Year 2

Hear the Gospel of our Lord Jesus Christ according to Luke.

Jesus went on through cities and villages, proclaiming and bringing the good news of the kingdom of God. The twelve were with him, as well as some women who had been cured of evil spirits and infirmities: Mary, called Magdalene, from whom seven demons had gone out, and Joanna, the wife of Herod's steward Chuza, and Susanna, and many others, who provided for them out of their resources.

This is the Gospel of the Lord.   Luke 8.1–3

Week 24: Saturday between 17 and 23 September

Year 1

A reading from the First Letter of Paul to Timothy.

In the presence of God, who gives life to all things, and of Christ Jesus, who in his testimony before Pontius Pilate made the good confession, I charge you to keep the commandment without spot or blame until the manifestation of our Lord Jesus Christ, which he will bring about at the right time – he who is the blessed and only Sovereign, the King of kings and Lord of lords. It is he alone who has immortality and dwells in unapproachable light, whom no one has ever seen or can see; to him be honour and eternal dominion. Amen.

This is the word of the Lord.   1 Timothy 6.13–16

Responsorial Psalm

R **Be joyful in the Lord, all the earth:**
    [give thanks and bless his name].   cf Psalm 100.1a, 3b

O be joyful in the Lord, all the earth;
serve the Lord with gladness
and come before his presence with a song. R

Know that the Lord is God;
it is he that has made us and we are his;
we are his people and the sheep of his pasture. R

Enter his gates with thanksgiving
and his courts with praise;
give thanks to him and bless his name. R

For the Lord is gracious;
his steadfast love is everlasting,
and his faithfulness endures from generation to generation. R

Psalm 100

A reading from the First Letter of Paul to the Corinthians.

Someone will ask, 'How are the dead raised? With what kind of body do they come?' Fool! What you sow does not come to life unless it dies. And as for what you sow, you do not sow the body that is to be, but a bare seed, perhaps of wheat or of some other grain.

So it is with the resurrection of the dead. What is sown is perishable, what is raised is imperishable. It is sown in dishonour, it is raised in glory. It is sown in weakness, it is raised in power. It is sown a physical body, it is raised a spiritual body. If there is a physical body, there is also a spiritual body. Thus it is written, 'The first man, Adam, became a living being'; the last Adam became a life-giving spirit. But it is not the spiritual that is first, but the physical, and then the spiritual. The first man was from the earth, a man of dust; the second man is from heaven. As was the man of dust, so are those who are of the dust; and as is the man of heaven, so are those who are of heaven. Just as we have borne the image of the man of dust, we will also bear the image of the man of heaven.

This is the word of the Lord. 1 Corinthians 15.35–37, 42–49

Responsorial Psalm

R   **I will exalt you, O Lord:**
   [because you have raised me up]. cf Psalm 30.1

I will exalt you, O Lord, because you have raised me up
and have not let my foes triumph over me.
O Lord my God, I cried out to you
and you have healed me.   **R**

You brought me up, O Lord, from the dead;
you restored me to life from among those that go down to the Pit.
Sing to the Lord, you servants of his;
give thanks to his holy name.   **R**

For his wrath endures but the twinkling of an eye,
his favour for a lifetime.
Heaviness may endure for a night,
but joy comes in the morning.   **R** Psalm 30.1–5

Hear the Gospel of our Lord Jesus Christ according to Luke.

When a great crowd gathered and people from town after town came to Jesus, he said in a parable: 'A sower went out to sow his seed; and as he sowed, some fell on the path and was trampled on, and the birds of the air ate it up. Some fell on the rock; and as it grew up, it withered for lack of moisture. Some fell among thorns, and the thorns grew with it and choked it. Some fell into good soil, and when it grew, it produced a hundredfold.' As he said this, he called out, 'Let anyone with ears to hear listen!'

Then his disciples asked him what this parable meant. He said, 'To you it has been given to know the secrets of the kingdom of God; but to others I speak in parables, so that

"looking they may not perceive,
    and listening they may not understand."

'Now the parable is this: The seed is the word of God. The ones on the path are those who have heard; then the devil comes and takes away the word from their hearts, so that they may not believe and be saved. The ones on the rock are those who, when they hear the word, receive it with joy. But these have no root; they believe only for a while and in a time of testing fall away. As for what fell among the thorns, these are the ones who hear; but as they go on their way, they are choked by the cares and riches and pleasures of life, and their fruit does not mature. But as for that in the good soil, these are the ones who, when they hear the word, hold it fast in an honest and good heart, and bear fruit with patient endurance.'

This is the Gospel of the Lord.   Luke 8.4–15

Week 25: Monday between 19 and 25 September

Year 1

A reading from the Book of Ezra.

In the first year of King Cyrus of Persia, in order that the word of the LORD by the mouth of Jeremiah might be accomplished, the LORD stirred up the spirit of King Cyrus of Persia so that he sent a herald throughout all his kingdom, and also in a written edict declared:

'Thus says King Cyrus of Persia: The LORD, the God of heaven, has given me all the kingdoms of the earth, and he has charged me to build him a house at Jerusalem in Judah. Any of those among you who are of his people – may their God be with them! – are now permitted to go up to Jerusalem in Judah, and rebuild the house of the LORD, the God of Israel – he is the God who is in Jerusalem; and let all survivors, in whatever place they reside, be assisted by the people of their place with silver and gold, with goods and with animals, besides freewill-offerings for the house of God in Jerusalem.'

The heads of the families of Judah and Benjamin, and the priests and the Levites – everyone whose spirit God had stirred – got ready to go up and rebuild the house of the LORD in Jerusalem. All their neighbours aided them with silver vessels, with gold, with goods, with animals, and with valuable gifts, besides all that was freely offered.

This is the word of the Lord.   Ezra 1.1–6

Responsorial Psalm

R   **Those who sow in tears
    shall reap with songs of joy.**   Psalm 126.6

When the Lord restored the fortunes of Zion,
then were we like those who dream.
Then was our mouth filled with laughter
and our tongue with songs of joy.   **R**

Then said they among the nations,
'The Lord has done great things for them.'
The Lord has indeed done great things for us,
and therefore we rejoiced.   **R**

Restore again our fortunes, O Lord,
as the river beds of the desert.
Those who sow in tears
shall reap with songs of joy.   **R**

Those who go out weeping, bearing the seed,
will come back with shouts of joy,
bearing their sheaves with them.   **R**   Psalm 126

Year 2

A reading from the book Proverbs.

Do not withhold good from those to whom it is due,
    when it is in your power to do it.
Do not say to your neighbour, 'Go, and come again;
    tomorrow I will give it' – when you have it with you.
Do not plan harm against your neighbour
    who lives trustingly beside you.
Do not quarrel with anyone without cause,
    when no harm has been done to you.
Do not envy the violent
    and do not choose any of their ways;
for the perverse are an abomination to the LORD,
    but the upright are in his confidence.
The LORD's curse is on the house of the wicked,
    but he blesses the abode of the righteous.
Towards the scorners he is scornful,
    but to the humble he shows favour.

This is the word of the Lord.   Proverbs 3.27–34

Responsorial Psalm

R **They shall dwell in your tabernacle, O Lord:**
   [those who do what is right].   *cf Psalm 15.1a, 2b*

Lord, who may dwell in your tabernacle?
Who may rest upon your holy hill?
Whoever leads an uncorrupt life
and does the thing that is right.   **R**

Who speaks the truth from the heart
and bears no deceit on the tongue;
who does no evil to a friend
and pours no scorn on a neighbour.   **R**

In whose sight the wicked are not esteemed,
but who honours those who fear the Lord.
Whoever has sworn to a neighbour
and never goes back on that word.   **R**

Who does not lend money in hope of gain,
nor takes a bribe against the innocent;
whoever does these things
shall never fall.   **R**   *Psalm 15*

Year 1 and Year 2

Hear the Gospel of our Lord Jesus Christ according to Luke.

Jesus said to his disciples, 'No one after lighting a lamp hides it under a jar, or puts it under a bed, but puts it on a lampstand, so that those who enter may see the light. For nothing is hidden that will not be disclosed, nor is anything secret that will not become known and come to light. Then pay attention to how you listen; for to those who have, more will be given; and from those who do not have, even what they seem to have will be taken away.'

This is the Gospel of the Lord.   Luke 8.16–18

Week 25: Tuesday between 20 and 26 September

Year 1

A reading from the Book of Ezra.

King Darius decreed: 'Let the work on this house of God alone; let the governor of the Jews and the elders of the Jews rebuild this house of God on its site. Moreover, I make a decree regarding what you shall do for these elders of the Jews for the rebuilding of this house of God: the cost is to be paid to these people, in full and without delay, from the royal revenue, the tribute of the province Beyond the River. May the God who has established his name there overthrow any king or people that shall put forth a hand to alter this, or to destroy this house of God in Jerusalem. I, Darius, make a decree; let it be done with all diligence.'

So the elders of the Jews built and prospered, through the prophesying of the prophet Haggai and Zechariah son of Iddo. They finished their building by command of the God of Israel and by decree of Cyrus, Darius, and King Artaxerxes of Persia; and this house was finished on the third day of the month of Adar, in the sixth year of the reign of King Darius.

The people of Israel, the priests and the Levites, and the rest of the returned exiles, celebrated the dedication of this house of God with joy. They offered at the dedication of this house of God one hundred bulls, two hundred rams, four hundred lambs, and as a sin-offering for all Israel twelve male goats, according to the number of the tribes of Israel. Then they set the priests in their divisions and the Levites in their courses for the service of God at Jerusalem, as it is written in the book of Moses.

On the fourteenth day of the first month the returned exiles kept the passover. For both the priests and the Levites had purified themselves; all of them were clean. So they killed the passover lamb for all the returned exiles, for their fellow-priests, and for themselves.

This is the word of the Lord.   Ezra 6.7–8, 12, 14–20

Responsorial Psalm

R* **Our help is in the name of the Lord,**
   [who has made heaven and earth].   *Psalm* 124.7

If the Lord himself had not been on our side,
now may Israel say;
if the Lord had not been on our side,
when enemies rose up against us.   R

Then would they have swallowed us alive
when their anger burned against us;
then would the waters have overwhelmed us
and the torrent gone over our soul;
over our soul would have swept the raging waters.   R

But blessed be the Lord
who has not given us over to be a prey for their teeth.
Our soul has escaped
as a bird from the snare of the fowler;
the snare is broken and we are delivered.   R*   *Psalm* 124

Year 2

A reading from the book Proverbs.

The king's heart is a stream of water in the hand of the LORD;
   he turns it wherever he will.
All deeds are right in the sight of the doer,
   but the LORD weighs the heart.
To do righteousness and justice
   is more acceptable to the LORD than sacrifice.
Haughty eyes and a proud heart –
   the lamp of the wicked – are sin.
The plans of the diligent lead surely to abundance,
   but everyone who is hasty comes only to want.
The getting of treasures by a lying tongue
   is a fleeting vapour and a snare of death.

The souls of the wicked desire evil;
   their neighbours find no mercy in their eyes.
When a scoffer is punished, the simple become wiser;
   when the wise are instructed, they increase in knowledge.
The Righteous One observes the house of the wicked;
   he casts the wicked down to ruin.
If you close your ear to the cry of the poor,
   you will cry out and not be heard.

This is the word of the Lord.   *Proverbs* 21.1–6, 10–13

Responsorial Psalm

R **Blessed are those who walk in the law of the Lord.**   *cf Psalm* 119.1

Blessed are those whose way is pure,
who walk in the law of the Lord.
Blessed are those who keep his testimonies
and seek him with their whole heart.   R

Those who do no wickedness,
but walk in his ways.
You, O Lord, have charged
that we should diligently keep your commandments.   R

O that my ways were made so direct
that I might keep your statutes.
Then should I not be put to shame,
because I have regard for all your commandments.   R

I will thank you with an unfeigned heart,
when I have learned your righteous judgements.
I will keep your statutes;
O forsake me not utterly.   R   *Psalm* 119.1–8

Year 1 and Year 2

Hear the Gospel of our Lord Jesus Christ according to Luke.

The mother of Jesus and his brothers came to him, but they could not reach him because of the crowd. And he was told, 'Your mother and your brothers are standing outside, wanting to see you.' But he said to them, 'My mother and my brothers are those who hear the word of God and do it.'

This is the Gospel of the Lord.   *Luke* 8.19–21

Week 25: Wednesday between 21 and 27 September

Year 1

A reading from the Book of Ezra.

At the evening sacrifice I got up from my fasting, with my garments and my mantle torn, and fell on my knees, spread out my hands to the LORD my God, and said, 'O my God, I am too ashamed and embarrassed to lift my face to you, my God, for our iniquities have risen higher than our heads, and our guilt has mounted up to the heavens. From the days of our ancestors to this day we have been deep in guilt, and for our iniquities we, our kings, and our priests have been handed over to the kings of the lands, to the sword, to captivity, to plundering, and to utter shame, as is now the case. But now for a brief moment favour has been shown by the LORD our God, who has left us a remnant, and given us a stake in his holy place, in order that he may brighten our eyes and grant us a little sustenance in our slavery. For we are slaves; yet our God has not forsaken us in our slavery, but has extended to us his steadfast love before the kings of Persia, to give us new life to set up the house of our God, to repair its ruins, and to give us a wall in Judea and Jerusalem.'

This is the word of the Lord.   *Ezra 9.5–9*

Either

Canticle

R* **Blessed be God, who lives for ever,**
    [whose reign endures throughout all ages].   *Tobit 13.1*

Declare God's praise before the nations,
you who are the children of Israel.
For if our God has scattered you among them,
there too has he shown you his greatness. **R**

Exalt him in the sight of the living,
because he is our Lord and God and our Father for ever.
Though God punishes you for your wickedness,
mercy will be shown to you all. **R**

God will gather you from every nation,
from wherever you have been scattered.
When you turn to the Lord with all your heart and soul,
God will hide his face from you no more. **R**

See what the Lord has done for you
and give thanks with a loud voice.
Praise the Lord of righteousness
and exalt the King of the ages. **R**   *Tobit 13.1, 3–6a*

or

Responsorial Psalm

R **Bless the Lord, O my soul,**
    [and bless his holy name].   *cf Psalm 103.1*

Bless the Lord, O my soul,
and all that is within me bless his holy name.
Bless the Lord, O my soul,
and forget not all his benefits. **R** →

Who forgives all your sins
and heals all your infirmities;
who redeems your life from the Pit
and crowns you with faithful love and compassion.   R

R   **Bless the Lord, O my soul,**
    [and bless his holy name].

Who satisfies you with good things,
so that your youth is renewed like an eagle's.
The Lord executes righteousness
and judgement for all who are oppressed.   R   Psalm 103.1–6

Year 2

A reading from the book Proverbs.

Every word of God proves true;
    he is a shield to those who take refuge in him.
Do not add to his words,
    or else he will rebuke you, and you will be found a liar.
Two things I ask of you;
    do not deny them to me before I die:
Remove far from me falsehood and lying;
    give me neither poverty nor riches;
    feed me with the food that I need,
or I shall be full, and deny you,
    and say, 'Who is the Lord?'
or I shall be poor, and steal,
    and profane the name of my God.

This is the word of the Lord.   Proverbs 30.5–9

Responsorial Psalm

R   **Your word, O Lord, is a lantern to my feet;**
    [and a light upon my path].   Psalm 119.105

Your word is a lantern to my feet
and a light upon my path.
I have sworn and will fulfil it,
to keep your righteous judgements.   R

I am troubled above measure;
give me life, O Lord, according to your word.
Accept the freewill offering of my mouth, O Lord,
and teach me your judgements.   R

My soul is ever in my hand,
yet I do not forget your law.
The wicked have laid a snare for me,
but I have not strayed from your commandments. **R**

Your testimonies have I claimed as my heritage for ever;
for they are the very joy of my heart.
I have applied my heart to fulfil your statutes:
always, even to the end. **R**   *Psalm 119.105–112*

Year 1 and Year 2

Hear the Gospel of our Lord Jesus Christ according to Luke.

Jesus called the twelve together and gave them power and authority over all
demons and to cure diseases, and he sent them out to proclaim the kingdom
of God and to heal. He said to them, 'Take nothing for your journey, no staff,
nor bag, nor bread, nor money – not even an extra tunic. Whatever house
you enter, stay there, and leave from there. Wherever they do not welcome
you, as you are leaving that town shake the dust off your feet as a testimony
against them.' They departed and went through the villages, bringing the good
news and curing diseases everywhere.

This is the Gospel of the Lord.   *Luke 9.1–6*

Week 25: Thursday between 22 and 28 September

Year 1

A reading from the Book of Haggai.

In the second year of King Darius, in the sixth month, on the first day of the
month, the word of the LORD came by the prophet Haggai to Zerubbabel son
of Shealtiel, governor of Judah, and to Joshua son of Jehozadak, the high priest:
Thus says the LORD of hosts: These people say the time has not yet come to
rebuild the LORD's house. Then the word of the LORD came by the prophet
Haggai, saying: Is it a time for you yourselves to live in your panelled houses,
while this house lies in ruins? Now therefore, thus says the LORD of hosts:
Consider how you have fared. You have sown much, and harvested little; you
eat, but you never have enough; you drink, but you never have your fill; you
clothe yourselves, but no one is warm; and you that earn wages earn wages
to put them into a bag with holes.

   Thus says the LORD of hosts: Consider how you have fared. Go up to the
hills and bring wood and build the house, so that I may take pleasure in it
and be honoured, says the LORD.

This is the word of the Lord.   *Haggai 1.1–8*

Responsorial Psalm

R* **Sing to the Lord a new song:**
[sing his praise in the congregation of the faithful]. Psalm 149.1

Let Israel rejoice in their maker;
let the children of Zion be joyful in their king.
Let them praise his name in the dance;
let them sing praise to him with timbrel and lyre. **R**

For the Lord has pleasure in his people
and adorns the poor with salvation.
Let the faithful be joyful in glory;
let them rejoice in their ranks. **R** Psalm 149.1–5

Year 2

A reading from the book Ecclesiastes.

Vanity of vanities, says the Teacher,
　vanity of vanities! All is vanity.
What do people gain from all the toil
　at which they toil under the sun?
A generation goes, and a generation comes,
　but the earth remains for ever.
The sun rises and the sun goes down,
　and hurries to the place where it rises.
The wind blows to the south,
　and goes round to the north;
round and round goes the wind,
　and on its circuits the wind returns.
All streams run to the sea,
　but the sea is not full;
to the place where the streams flow,
　there they continue to flow.
All things are wearisome;
　more than one can express;
the eye is not satisfied with seeing,
　or the ear filled with hearing.
What has been is what will be,
　and what has been done is what will be done;
　there is nothing new under the sun.
Is there a thing of which it is said, 'See, this is new'?
　It has already been, in the ages before us.
The people of long ago are not remembered,
　nor will there be any remembrance
of people yet to come
　by those who come after them.

This is the word of the Lord. Ecclesiastes 1.2–11

Responsorial Psalm

**R* O Lord, you have been our refuge
from one generation to another.**   Psalm 90.1

Before the mountains were brought forth,
or the earth and the world were formed,
from everlasting to everlasting
you are God. **R**

You turn us back to dust and say:
'Turn back, O children of earth.'
For a thousand years in your sight are but as yesterday,
which passes like a watch in the night. **R**

You sweep them away like a dream;
they fade away suddenly like the grass.
In the morning it is green and flourishes;
in the evening it is dried up and withered. **R**   Psalm 90.1–6

Year 1 and Year 2

Hear the Gospel of our Lord Jesus Christ according to Luke.

Herod the ruler heard about all that had taken place, and he was perplexed,
because it was said by some that John had been raised from the dead, by some
that Elijah had appeared, and by others that one of the ancient prophets had
arisen. Herod said, 'John I beheaded; but who is this about whom I hear such
things?' And he tried to see him.

This is the Gospel of the Lord.   Luke 9.7–9

Week 25: Friday between 23 and 29 September

Year 1

A reading from the Book of Haggai.

In the second year of King Darius, in the seventh month, on the twenty-first
day of the month, the word of the LORD came by the prophet Haggai, saying:
Speak now to Zerubbabel son of Shealtiel, governor of Judah, and to Joshua
son of Jehozadak, the high priest, and to the remnant of the people, and say,
Who is left among you that saw this house in its former glory? How does
it look to you now? Is it not in your sight as nothing? Yet now take courage,
O Zerubbabel, says the LORD; take courage, O Joshua, son of Jehozadak, the
high priest; take courage, all you people of the land, says the LORD; work, for
I am with you, says the LORD of hosts, according to the promise that I made
you when you came out of Egypt. My spirit abides among you; do not fear.
For thus says the LORD of hosts: Once again, in a little while, I will shake
the heavens and the earth and the sea and the dry land; and I will shake all →

the nations, so that the treasure of all nations shall come, and I will fill this house with splendour, says the LORD of hosts. The silver is mine, and the gold is mine, says the LORD of hosts. The latter splendour of this house shall be greater than the former, says the LORD of hosts; and in this place I will give prosperity, says the LORD of hosts.

This is the word of the Lord. *Haggai 1.15b – 2.9*

Responsorial Psalm

R **I will go to the altar of God
[to the God of my joy and gladness].** *Psalm 43.4a*

Give judgement for me, O God,
and defend my cause against an ungodly people;
deliver me from the deceitful and the wicked. R

For you are the God of my refuge;
why have you cast me from you,
and why go I so heavily, while the enemy oppresses me? R

O send out your light and your truth, that they may lead me,
and bring me to your holy hill and to your dwelling,
that I may go to the altar of God,
to the God of my joy and gladness;
and on the lyre I will give thanks to you, O God my God. R

Why are you so full of heaviness, O my soul,
and why are you so disquieted within me?
O put your trust in God;
for I will yet give him thanks,
who is the help of my countenance, and my God. R *Psalm 43*

Year 2

A reading from the book Ecclesiastes.

For everything there is a season, and a time for every matter under heaven:
    a time to be born, and a time to die;
    a time to plant, and a time to pluck up what is planted;
    a time to kill, and a time to heal;
    a time to break down, and a time to build up;
    a time to weep, and a time to laugh;
    a time to mourn, and a time to dance;
    a time to throw away stones, and a time to gather stones together;
    a time to embrace, and a time to refrain from embracing;
    a time to seek, and a time to lose;
    a time to keep, and a time to throw away;
    a time to tear, and a time to sew;

a time to keep silence, and a time to speak;
a time to love, and a time to hate;
a time for war, and a time for peace.

What gain have the workers from their toil? I have seen the business that God has given to everyone to be busy with. He has made everything suitable for its time; moreover, he has put a sense of past and future into their minds, yet they cannot find out what God has done from the beginning to the end.

This is the word of the Lord.   *Ecclesiastes 3.1–11*

Responsorial Psalm

R **Blessed be the Lord my rock,**
   [my stronghold and my deliverer].   *cf Psalm 144.1a, 2b*

Blessed be the Lord my rock,
who teaches my hands for war
and my fingers for battle. **R**

My steadfast help and my fortress,
my stronghold and my deliverer,
my shield in whom I trust,
who subdues the peoples under me. **R**

O Lord, what are mortals that you should consider them;
mere human beings, that you should take thought for them?
They are like a breath of wind;
their days pass away like a shadow. **R**   *Psalm 144.1–4*

Year 1 and Year 2

Hear the Gospel of our Lord Jesus Christ according to Luke.

Once when Jesus was praying alone, with only the disciples near him, he asked them, 'Who do the crowds say that I am?' They answered, 'John the Baptist; but others, Elijah; and still others, that one of the ancient prophets has arisen.' He said to them, 'But who do you say that I am?' Peter answered, 'The Messiah of God.'

He sternly ordered and commanded them not to tell anyone, saying, 'The Son of Man must undergo great suffering, and be rejected by the elders, chief priests, and scribes, and be killed, and on the third day be raised.'

This is the Gospel of the Lord.   *Luke 9.18–22*

Week 25: Saturday between 24 and 30 September

Year I

A reading from the prophecy of Zechariah.

I looked up and saw a man with a measuring line in his hand. Then I asked, 'Where are you going?' He answered me, 'To measure Jerusalem, to see what is its width and what is its length.' Then the angel who talked with me came forward, and another angel came forward to meet him, and said to him, 'Run, say to that young man: Jerusalem shall be inhabited like villages without walls, because of the multitude of people and animals in it. For I will be a wall of fire all round it, says the LORD, and I will be the glory within it.' Sing and rejoice, O daughter Zion! For lo, I will come and dwell in your midst, says the LORD. Many nations shall join themselves to the LORD on that day, and shall be my people; and I will dwell in your midst. And you shall know that the LORD of hosts has sent me to you.

This is the word of the Lord.   Zechariah 2.1–5, 10–11

Either

Canticle

R **The Lord will watch over us
   as a shepherd watches the flock.**   cf Jeremiah 31.10b

Hear the word of the Lord, O nations,
and declare it in the coastlands far away;
say, 'He who scattered Israel will gather him,
and will watch over him as a shepherd watches the flock.'   R

For the Lord has ransomed Jacob,
and redeemed him from hands too strong for him.
They shall come and sing aloud on the height of Zion,
and they shall be radiant at the goodness of the Lord.   R

They shall be radiant over the grain, the wine, and the oil,
and over the young of the flock and the herd;
their life shall be like a watered garden,
and they shall never languish again.   R

Then shall young women rejoice in the dance,
and young men and old shall be glad together.
I will turn their mourning into joy,
I will comfort them, and give them gladness for sorrow.   R

Jeremiah 31.10–13

or

Responsorial Psalm

R* **Do good, O Lord, to those who are good,
[and to the true of heart].** Psalm 125.4

Those who trust in the Lord are like Mount Zion,
which cannot be moved,
but stands fast for ever. R

As the hills stand about Jerusalem,
so the Lord stands round about his people,
from this time forth for evermore. R

The sceptre of wickedness shall not hold sway
over the land allotted to the righteous,
lest the righteous turn their hands to evil. R*

Those who turn aside to crooked ways
the Lord shall take away with the evildoers;
but let there be peace upon Israel. R Psalm 125

Year 2

A reading from the book Ecclesiastes.

Rejoice, young man, while you are young, and let your heart cheer you in the days of your youth. Follow the inclination of your heart and the desire of your eyes, but know that for all these things God will bring you into judgement.

Banish anxiety from your mind, and put away pain from your body; for youth and the dawn of life are vanity.

Remember your creator in the days of your youth, before the days of trouble come, and the years draw near when you will say, 'I have no pleasure in them'; before the sun and the light and the moon and the stars are darkened and the clouds return with the rain; on the day when the guards of the house tremble, and the strong men are bent, and the women who grind cease working because they are few, and those who look through the windows see dimly; when the doors on the street are shut, and the sound of the grinding is low, and one rises up at the sound of a bird, and all the daughters of song are brought low; when one is afraid of heights, and terrors are in the road; the almond tree blossoms, the grasshopper drags itself along and desire fails; because all must go to their eternal home, and the mourners will go about the streets; before the silver cord is snapped, and the golden bowl is broken, and the pitcher is broken at the fountain, and the wheel broken at the cistern, and the dust returns to the earth as it was, and the breath returns to God who gave it. Vanity of vanities, says the Teacher; all is vanity.

This is the word of the Lord. Ecclesiastes 11.9 – 12.8

Responsorial Psalm

R* **O Lord, you have been our refuge**
   from one generation to another.   Psalm 90.1

Before the mountains were brought forth,
or the earth and the world were formed,
from everlasting to everlasting
you are God.   R

So teach us to number our days
that we may apply our hearts to wisdom.
Turn again, O Lord; how long will you delay?
Have compassion on your servants.   R

Satisfy us with your loving-kindness in the morning,
that we may rejoice and be glad all our days.
Give us gladness for the days you have afflicted us,
and for the years in which we have seen adversity.   R

Show your servants your works,
and let your glory be over their children.
May the gracious favour of the Lord our God be upon us;
prosper our handiwork;
O prosper the work of our hands.   R   Psalm 90.1–2, 12–end

Year 1 and Year 2

Hear the Gospel of our Lord Jesus Christ according to Luke.

While everyone was amazed at all that Jesus was doing, he said to his disciples,
'Let these words sink into your ears: The Son of Man is going to be betrayed
into human hands.' But they did not understand this saying; its meaning was
concealed from them, so that they could not perceive it. And they were afraid
to ask him about this saying.

This is the Gospel of the Lord.   Luke 9.43b–45

Week 26: Monday between 26 September and 2 October

Year 1

A reading from the prophecy of Zechariah.

The word of the LORD of hosts came to me, saying: Thus says the LORD of hosts: I am jealous for Zion with great jealousy, and I am jealous for her with great wrath. Thus says the LORD: I will return to Zion, and will dwell in the midst of Jerusalem; Jerusalem shall be called the faithful city, and the mountain of the LORD of hosts shall be called the holy mountain. Thus says the LORD of hosts: Old men and old women shall again sit in the streets of Jerusalem, each with staff in hand because of their great age. And the streets of the city shall be full of boys and girls playing in its streets. Thus says the LORD of hosts: Even though it seems impossible to the remnant of this people in these days, should it also seem impossible to me, says the LORD of hosts? Thus says the LORD of hosts: I will save my people from the east country and from the west country; and I will bring them to live in Jerusalem. They shall be my people and I will be their God, in faithfulness and in righteousness.

This is the word of the Lord.   Zechariah 8.1–8

Responsorial Psalm

R **The Lord has built up Zion
   and shown himself in glory.**   cf Psalm 102.17

My days fade away like a shadow,
and I am withered like grass.
But you, O Lord, shall endure for ever
and your name through all generations.   **R**

You will arise and have pity on Zion;
it is time to have mercy upon her;
surely the time has come.
For your servants love her very stones
and feel compassion for her dust.   **R**

Then shall the nations fear your name, O Lord,
and all the kings of the earth your glory,
when the Lord has built up Zion
and shown himself in glory;
when he has turned to the prayer of the destitute
and has not despised their plea.   **R**

This shall be written for those that come after,
and a people yet unborn shall praise the Lord.
For he has looked down from his holy height;
from the heavens he beheld the earth.   **R**   →

That he might hear the sighings of the prisoner
and set free those condemned to die;
that the name of the Lord may be proclaimed in Zion
and his praises in Jerusalem.   R   Psalm 102.12–22

R   **The Lord has built up Zion
    and shown himself in glory.**

Year 2

A reading from the Book of Job.

One day the heavenly beings came to present themselves before the LORD,
and Satan also came among them. The LORD said to Satan, 'Where have
you come from?' Satan answered the LORD, 'From going to and fro on the
earth, and from walking up and down on it.' The LORD said to Satan, 'Have
you considered my servant Job? There is no one like him on the earth, a
blameless and upright man who fears God and turns away from evil.' Then
Satan answered the LORD, 'Does Job fear God for nothing? Have you not put a
fence around him and his house and all that he has, on every side? You have
blessed the work of his hands, and his possessions have increased in the land.
But stretch out your hand now, and touch all that he has, and he will curse
you to your face.' The LORD said to Satan, 'Very well, all that he has is in your
power; only do not stretch out your hand against him!' So Satan went out
from the presence of the LORD.

One day when his sons and daughters were eating and drinking wine in
the eldest brother's house, a messenger came to Job and said, 'The oxen were
ploughing and the donkeys were feeding beside them, and the Sabeans fell on
them and carried them off, and killed the servants with the edge of the sword;
I alone have escaped to tell you.' While he was still speaking, another came
and said, 'The fire of God fell from heaven and burned up the sheep and the
servants, and consumed them; I alone have escaped to tell you.' While he was
still speaking, another came and said, 'The Chaldeans formed three columns,
made a raid on the camels and carried them off, and killed the servants with
the edge of the sword; I alone have escaped to tell you.' While he was still
speaking, another came and said, 'Your sons and daughters were eating and
drinking wine in their eldest brother's house, and suddenly a great wind came
across the desert, struck the four corners of the house, and it fell on the young
people, and they are dead; I alone have escaped to tell you.'

Then Job arose, tore his robe, shaved his head, and fell on the ground
and worshipped. He said, 'Naked I came from my mother's womb, and naked
shall I return there; the LORD gave, and the LORD has taken away; blessed be
the name of the LORD.'

In all this Job did not sin or charge God with wrongdoing.

This is the word of the Lord.   Job 1.6–end

Responsorial Psalm

R **Keep me as the apple of your eye;
[hide me under the shadow of your wings].** *Psalm* 17.8

Hear my just cause, O Lord; consider my complaint;
listen to my prayer, which comes not from lying lips.
Let my vindication come forth from your presence;
let your eyes behold what is right. **R**

Weigh my heart, examine me by night,
refine me, and you will find no impurity in me.
My mouth does not trespass for earthly rewards;
I have heeded the words of your lips. **R**

My footsteps hold fast in the ways of your commandments;
my feet have not stumbled in your paths.
I call upon you, O God, for you will answer me;
incline your ear to me, and listen to my words. **R**

Show me your marvellous loving-kindness,
O Saviour of those who take refuge at your right hand
from those who rise up against them. **R**

Keep me as the apple of your eye;
hide me under the shadow of your wings,
from the wicked who assault me,
from my enemies who surround me to take away my life. **R**

They have closed their heart to pity
and their mouth speaks proud things.
They press me hard, they surround me on every side,
watching how they may cast me to the ground. **R** *Psalm* 17.1–11

Year 1 and Year 2

Hear the Gospel of our Lord Jesus Christ according to Luke.

An argument arose among the disciples as to which one of them was the
greatest. But Jesus, aware of their inner thoughts, took a little child and put
it by his side, and said to them, 'Whoever welcomes this child in my name
welcomes me, and whoever welcomes me welcomes the one who sent me;
for the least among all of you is the greatest.'

John answered, 'Master, we saw someone casting out demons in your name,
and we tried to stop him, because he does not follow with us.' But Jesus said
to him, 'Do not stop him; for whoever is not against you is for you.'

This is the Gospel of the Lord. Luke 9.46–50

Week 26: Tuesday between 27 September and 3 October

Year 1

A reading from the prophecy of Zechariah.

Thus says the LORD of hosts: Peoples shall yet come, the inhabitants of many cities; the inhabitants of one city shall go to another, saying, 'Come, let us go to entreat the favour of the LORD, and to seek the LORD of hosts; I myself am going.' Many peoples and strong nations shall come to seek the LORD of hosts in Jerusalem, and to entreat the favour of the LORD. Thus says the LORD of hosts: In those days ten men from nations of every language shall take hold of a Jew, grasping his garment and saying, 'Let us go with you, for we have heard that God is with you.'

This is the word of the Lord.   Zechariah 8.20–end

Responsorial Psalm

R **Glorious things are spoken of you,**
    Zion, city of our God.   Psalm 87.2

His foundation is on the holy mountains.
The Lord loves the gates of Zion
more than all the dwellings of Jacob.
Glorious things are spoken of you,
Zion, city of our God. **R**

I record Egypt and Babylon as those who know me;
behold Philistia, Tyre and Ethiopia:
in Zion were they born.
And of Zion it shall be said, 'Each one was born in her,
and the Most High himself has established her.' **R**

The Lord will record as he writes up the peoples,
'This one also was born there.'
And as they dance they shall sing,
'All my fresh springs are in you.' **R**   Psalm 87

Year 2

A reading from the Book of Job.

After this Job opened his mouth and cursed the day of his birth. Job said:
    'Let the day perish on which I was born,
        and the night that said,
        "A man-child is conceived."

    'Why did I not die at birth,
        come forth from the womb and expire?
    Why were there knees to receive me,

or breasts for me to suck?
Now I would be lying down and quiet;
 I would be asleep; then I would be at rest
with kings and counsellors of the earth
 who rebuild ruins for themselves,
or with princes who have gold,
 who fill their houses with silver.
Or why was I not buried like a stillborn child,
 like an infant that never sees the light?
There the wicked cease from troubling,
 and there the weary are at rest.

'Why is light given to one in misery,
 and life to the bitter in soul,
who long for death, but it does not come,
 and dig for it more than for hidden treasures;
who rejoice exceedingly,
 and are glad when they find the grave?
Why is light given to one who cannot see the way,
 whom God has fenced in?'

This is the word of the Lord.   Job 3.1–3, 11–17, 20–23

Responsorial Psalm

R **To you, O Lord, will I cry;**
   [my prayer shall come before you].   cf Psalm 88.15

Shall your wonders be known in the dark
or your righteous deeds in the land where all is forgotten?
But as for me, O Lord, I will cry to you;
early in the morning my prayer shall come before you. **R**

Lord, why have you rejected my soul?
Why have you hidden your face from me?
I have been wretched and at the point of death from my youth;
I suffer your terrors and am no more seen. **R**

Your wrath sweeps over me;
your horrors are come to destroy me;
all day long they come about me like water;
they close me in on every side. **R**   Psalm 88.14–19

Hear the Gospel of our Lord Jesus Christ according to Luke.

When the days drew near for Jesus to be taken up, he set his face to go to Jerusalem. And he sent messengers ahead of him. On their way they entered a village of the Samaritans to make ready for him; but they did not receive him, because his face was set towards Jerusalem. When his disciples James and John saw it, they said, 'Lord, do you want us to command fire to come down from heaven and consume them?' But he turned and rebuked them. Then they went on to another village.

This is the Gospel of the Lord.   Luke 9.51–56

Week 26: Wednesday between 28 September and 4 October

Year 1

A reading from the Book of Nehemiah.

In the month of Nisan, in the twentieth year of King Artaxerxes, when wine was served to him, I carried the wine and gave it to the king. Now, I had never been sad in his presence before. So the king said to me, 'Why is your face sad, since you are not sick? This can only be sadness of the heart.' Then I was very much afraid. I said to the king, 'May the king live for ever! Why should my face not be sad, when the city, the place of my ancestors' graves, lies waste, and its gates have been destroyed by fire?' Then the king said to me, 'What do you request?' So I prayed to the God of heaven. Then I said to the king, 'If it pleases the king, and if your servant has found favour with you, I ask that you send me to Judah, to the city of my ancestors' graves, so that I may rebuild it.' The king said to me (the queen also was sitting beside him), 'How long will you be gone, and when will you return?' So it pleased the king to send me, and I set him a date. Then I said to the king, 'If it pleases the king, let letters be given me to the governors of the province Beyond the River, that they may grant me passage until I arrive in Judah; and a letter to Asaph, the keeper of the king's forest, directing him to give me timber to make beams for the gates of the temple fortress, and for the wall of the city, and for the house that I shall occupy.' And the king granted me what I asked, for the gracious hand of my God was upon me.

This is the word of the Lord.   Nehemiah 2.1–8

Responsorial Psalm

R   **By the waters of Babylon we sat down and wept,
     when we remembered Zion.**   Psalm 137.1

By the waters of Babylon we sat down and wept,
when we remembered Zion.
As for our lyres, we hung them up
on the willows that grow in that land.   **R**

For there our captors asked for a song,
our tormentors called for mirth:
'Sing us one of the songs of Zion.'
How shall we sing the Lord's song
in a strange land?   R

If I forget you, O Jerusalem,
let my right hand forget its skill.
Let my tongue cleave to the roof of my mouth
if I do not remember you,
if I set not Jerusalem above my highest joy.   R   Psalm 137.1–6

Year 2

A reading from the Book of Job.

Job answered his friends:
   'Indeed I know that this is so;
      but how can a mortal be just before God?
   If one wished to contend with him,
      one could not answer him once in a thousand.
   He is wise in heart, and mighty in strength
    – who has resisted him, and succeeded? –
   he who removes mountains, and they do not know it,
      when he overturns them in his anger;
   who shakes the earth out of its place,
      and its pillars tremble;
   who commands the sun, and it does not rise;
      who seals up the stars;
   who alone stretched out the heavens
      and trampled the waves of the Sea;
   who made the Bear and Orion,
      the Pleiades and the chambers of the south;
   who does great things beyond understanding,
      and marvellous things without number.
   Look, he passes by me, and I do not see him;
      he moves on, but I do not perceive him.
   He snatches away; who can stop him?
      Who will say to him, "What are you doing?"

   'How then can I answer him,
      choosing my words with him?
   Though I am innocent, I cannot answer him;
      I must appeal for mercy to my accuser.
   If I summoned him and he answered me,
      I do not believe that he would listen to my voice.'

This is the word of the Lord.   Job 9.1–12, 14–16

R **To you, O Lord, will I cry;**
 [my prayer shall come before you]. *cf Psalm 88.15*

O Lord, God of my salvation,
I have cried day and night before you.
Let my prayer come into your presence;
incline your ear to my cry.   R

For my soul is full of troubles;
my life draws near to the land of death.
I am counted as one gone down to the Pit;
I am like one that has no strength.   R

Lost among the dead,
like the slain who lie in the grave,
whom you remember no more,
for they are cut off from your hand.
Lord, I have called daily upon you;
I have stretched out my hands to you.   R *Psalm 88.1–6, 11*

Year 1 and Year 2

Hear the Gospel of our Lord Jesus Christ according to Luke.

As Jesus and his disciples were going along the road, someone said to Jesus, 'I will follow you wherever you go.' And Jesus said to him, 'Foxes have holes, and birds of the air have nests; but the Son of Man has nowhere to lay his head.' To another he said, 'Follow me.' But he said, 'Lord, first let me go and bury my father.' But Jesus said to him, 'Let the dead bury their own dead; but as for you, go and proclaim the kingdom of God.' Another said, 'I will follow you, Lord; but let me first say farewell to those at my home.' Jesus said to him, 'No one who puts a hand to the plough and looks back is fit for the kingdom of God.'

This is the Gospel of the Lord. *Luke 9.57–end*

Week 26: Thursday between 29 September and 5 October

Year 1

A reading from the Book of Nehemiah.

When the seventh month came, all the people gathered together into the square before the Water Gate. They told the scribe Ezra to bring the book of the law of Moses, which the LORD had given to Israel. Accordingly, the priest Ezra brought the law before the assembly, both men and women and all who could hear with understanding. This was on the first day of the seventh month. He read from it facing the square before the Water Gate from early morning until midday, in the presence of the men and the women and those who could understand; and the ears of all the people were attentive to the book of the law.

The scribe Ezra stood on a wooden platform that had been made for the purpose; and beside him stood Mattithiah, Shema, Anaiah, Uriah, Hilkiah, and Maaseiah on his right hand; and Pedaiah, Mishael, Malchijah, Hashum, Hashbaddanah, Zechariah, and Meshullam on his left hand. And Ezra opened the book in the sight of all the people, for he was standing above all the people; and when he opened it, all the people stood up. Then Ezra blessed the LORD, the great God, and all the people answered, 'Amen, Amen', lifting up their hands. Then they bowed their heads and worshipped the LORD with their faces to the ground. Also Jeshua, Bani, Sherebiah, Jamin, Akkub, Shabbethai, Hodiah, Maaseiah, Kelita, Azariah, Jozabad, Hanan, Pelaiah, the Levites, helped the people to understand the law, while the people remained in their places. So they read from the book, from the law of God, with interpretation. They gave the sense, so that the people understood the reading.

And Nehemiah, who was the governor, and Ezra the priest and scribe, and the Levites who taught the people said to all the people, 'This day is holy to the LORD your God; do not mourn or weep.' For all the people wept when they heard the words of the law. Then he said to them, 'Go your way, eat the fat and drink sweet wine and send portions of them to those for whom nothing is prepared, for this day is holy to our LORD; and do not be grieved, for the joy of the LORD is your strength.' So the Levites stilled all the people, saying, 'Be quiet, for this day is holy; do not be grieved.' And all the people went their way to eat and drink and to send portions and to make great rejoicing, because they had understood the words that were declared to them.

This is the word of the Lord. Nehemiah 8.1–12

Responsorial Psalm

R **The judgements of the Lord are true:**
  more to be desired than gold. cf Psalm 19.9b, 10a

The law of the Lord is perfect, reviving the soul;
the testimony of the Lord is sure
and gives wisdom to the simple.
The statutes of the Lord are right
and rejoice the heart.   **R**

The commandment of the Lord is pure
and gives light to the eyes.
The fear of the Lord is clean and endures for ever;
the judgements of the Lord are true
and righteous altogether.   **R**   →

More to be desired are they than gold,
more than much fine gold,
sweeter also than honey,
dripping from the honeycomb.
By them also is your servant taught
and in keeping them there is great reward.   R

Psalm 19.7–11

R   **The judgements of the Lord are true:**
more to be desired than gold.

Year 2

A reading from the Book of Job.

Job said:
   'Have pity on me, have pity on me, O you my friends,
      for the hand of God has touched me!
   Why do you, like God, pursue me,
      never satisfied with my flesh?

   'O that my words were written down!
      O that they were inscribed in a book!
   O that with an iron pen and with lead
      they were engraved on a rock for ever!
   For I know that my Redeemer lives,
      and that at the last he will stand upon the earth;
   and after my skin has been thus destroyed,
      then in my flesh I shall see God,
   whom I shall see on my side,
      and my eyes shall behold, and not another.'

This is the word of the Lord.

Job 19.21–27a

Responsorial Psalm

R   **I shall see the goodness of the Lord**
in the land of the living.

Psalm 27.16

Though my father and my mother forsake me,
the Lord will take me up.
Teach me your way, O Lord;
lead me on a level path,
because of those who lie in wait for me.   R

Deliver me not into the will of my adversaries,
for false witnesses have risen up against me,
and those who breathe out violence.
I believe that I shall see the goodness of the Lord
in the land of the living.   R

Psalm 27.13–16

Year 1 and Year 2

Hear the Gospel of our Lord Jesus Christ according to Luke.

The Lord appointed seventy others and sent them on ahead of him in pairs to every town and place where he himself intended to go. He said to them, 'The harvest is plentiful, but the labourers are few; therefore ask the Lord of the harvest to send out labourers into his harvest. Go on your way. See, I am sending you out like lambs into the midst of wolves. Carry no purse, no bag, no sandals; and greet no one on the road. Whatever house you enter, first say, "Peace to this house!" And if anyone is there who shares in peace, your peace will rest on that person; but if not, it will return to you.

'Remain in the same house, eating and drinking whatever they provide, for the labourer deserves to be paid. Do not move about from house to house. Whenever you enter a town and its people welcome you, eat what is set before you; cure the sick who are there, and say to them, "The kingdom of God has come near to you." But whenever you enter a town and they do not welcome you, go out into its streets and say, "Even the dust of your town that clings to our feet, we wipe off in protest against you. Yet know this: the kingdom of God has come near." I tell you, on that day it will be more tolerable for Sodom than for that town.'

This is the Gospel of the Lord.   Luke 10.1–12

Week 26: Friday between 30 September and 6 October

Year 1

Either

A reading from the Book of Baruch.

The Lord our God is in the right, but there is open shame on us today, on the people of Judah, on the inhabitants of Jerusalem, and on our kings, our rulers, our priests, our prophets, and our ancestors, because we have sinned before the Lord. We have disobeyed him, and have not heeded the voice of the Lord our God, to walk in the statutes of the Lord that he set before us. From the time when the Lord brought our ancestors out of the land of Egypt until today, we have been disobedient to the Lord our God, and we have been negligent, in not heeding his voice. So to this day there have clung to us the calamities and the curse that the Lord declared through his servant Moses at the time when he brought our ancestors out of the land of Egypt to give to us a land flowing with milk and honey. We did not listen to the voice of the Lord our God in all the words of the prophets whom he sent to us, but all of us followed the intent of our own wicked hearts by serving other gods and doing what is evil in the sight of the Lord our God.

This is the word of the Lord.   Baruch 1.15–end

or

A reading from the book Deuteronomy.

Moses summoned Joshua and said to him in the sight of all Israel: 'Be strong and bold, for you are the one who will go with this people into the land that the LORD has sworn to their ancestors to give them; and you will put them in possession of it. It is the LORD who goes before you. He will be with you; he will not fail you or forsake you. Do not fear or be dismayed.'

Then Moses wrote down this law, and gave it to the priests, the sons of Levi, who carried the ark of the covenant of the LORD, and to all the elders of Israel. Moses commanded them: 'Every seventh year, in the scheduled year of remission, during the festival of booths, when all Israel comes to appear before the LORD your God at the place that he will choose, you shall read this law before all Israel in their hearing. Assemble the people – men, women, and children, as well as the aliens residing in your towns – so that they may hear and learn to fear the LORD your God and to observe diligently all the words of this law, and so that their children, who have not known it, may hear and learn to fear the LORD your God, as long as you live in the land that you are crossing over the Jordan to possess.'

This is the word of the Lord.   Deuteronomy 31.7–13

Responsorial Psalm

R **Help us, O God, for the glory of your name;**
   [deliver us, and wipe away our sins].   cf *Psalm* 79.9

O God, the heathen have come into your heritage;
your holy temple have they defiled
and made Jerusalem a heap of stones.
The dead bodies of your servants they have given
to be food for the birds of the air,
and the flesh of your faithful to the beasts of the field.   **R**

Their blood have they shed like water
on every side of Jerusalem,
and there was no one to bury them.
We have become the taunt of our neighbours,
the scorn and derision of those that are round about us.   **R**

Lord, how long will you be angry, for ever?
How long will your jealous fury blaze like fire?
Pour out your wrath upon the nations that have not known you,
and upon the kingdoms that have not called upon your name.
For they have devoured Jacob
and laid waste his dwelling place.   **R**

Remember not against us our former sins;
let your compassion make haste to meet us,
for we are brought very low.
Help us, O God of our salvation, for the glory of your name;
deliver us, and wipe away our sins for your name's sake. **R**

Psalm 79.1–9

Year 2

A reading from the Book of Job.

The LORD answered Job out of the whirlwind:
   'Have you commanded the morning since your days began,
     and caused the dawn to know its place,
so that it might take hold of the skirts of the earth,
     and the wicked be shaken out of it?
It is changed like clay under the seal,
     and it is dyed like a garment.
Light is withheld from the wicked,
     and their uplifted arm is broken.

'Have you entered into the springs of the sea,
     or walked in the recesses of the deep?
Have the gates of death been revealed to you,
     or have you seen the gates of deep darkness?
Have you comprehended the expanse of the earth?
     Declare, if you know all this.

'Where is the way to the dwelling of light,
     and where is the place of darkness,
that you may take it to its territory
     and that you may discern the paths to its home?
Surely you know, for you were born then,
     and the number of your days is great!'

Then Job answered the LORD:
   'See, I am of small account; what shall I answer you?
     I lay my hand on my mouth.
I have spoken once, and I will not answer;
     twice, but will proceed no further.'

This is the word of the Lord.   Job 38.1, 12–21, 40.3–5

R **O Lord, you have searched me out and known me.** *Psalm* 139.1a

Where can I go then from your spirit?
Or where can I flee from your presence?
If I climb up to heaven, you are there;
if I make the grave my bed, you are there also. R

If I take the wings of the morning
and dwell in the uttermost parts of the sea,
even there your hand shall lead me,
your right hand hold me fast. R

If I say, 'Surely the darkness will cover me
and the light around me turn to night,'
even darkness is no darkness with you;
the night is as clear as the day;
darkness and light to you are both alike. R *Psalm* 139.6–11

Year 1 and Year 2

Hear the Gospel of our Lord Jesus Christ according to Luke.

Jesus said to his disciples, 'Woe to you, Chorazin! Woe to you, Bethsaida! For if the deeds of power done in you had been done in Tyre and Sidon, they would have repented long ago, sitting in sackcloth and ashes. But at the judgement it will be more tolerable for Tyre and Sidon than for you. And you, Capernaum,

> will you be exalted to heaven?
>> No, you will be brought down to Hades.

Whoever listens to you listens to me, and whoever rejects you rejects me, and whoever rejects me rejects the one who sent me.'

This is the Gospel of the Lord. Luke 10.13–16

Week 26: Saturday between 1 and 7 October

Year 1

Either

A reading from the Book of Baruch.

Take courage, my people,
    who perpetuate Israel's name!
It was not for destruction
    that you were sold to the nations,
but you were handed over to your enemies
    because you angered God.

For you provoked the one who made you
   by sacrificing to demons and not to God.
You forgot the everlasting God, who brought you up,
   and you grieved Jerusalem, who reared you.
For she saw the wrath that came upon you from God,
   and she said:
Listen, you neighbours of Zion,
   God has brought great sorrow upon me;
for I have seen the exile of my sons and daughters,
   which the Everlasting brought upon them.
With joy I nurtured them,
   but I sent them away with weeping and sorrow.
Let no one rejoice over me, a widow
   and bereaved of many;
I was left desolate because of the sins of my children,
   because they turned away from the law of God.

Take courage, my children, and cry to God,
   for you will be remembered by the one who brought this upon you.
For just as you were disposed to go astray from God,
   return with tenfold zeal to seek him.
For the one who brought these calamities upon you
   will bring you everlasting joy with your salvation.

This is the word of the Lord.   Baruch 4.5–12, 27–29

or

A reading from the Book of Joshua.

Joshua summoned the Reubenites, the Gadites, and the half-tribe of Manasseh,
and said to them, 'You have observed all that Moses the servant of the LORD
commanded you, and have obeyed me in all that I have commanded you; you
have not forsaken your kindred these many days, down to this day, but have
been careful to keep the charge of the LORD your God. And now the LORD
your God has given rest to your kindred, as he promised them; therefore turn
and go to your tents in the land where your possession lies, which Moses the
servant of the LORD gave you on the other side of the Jordan. Take good care
to observe the commandment and instruction that Moses the servant of the
LORD commanded you, to love the LORD your God, to walk in all his ways,
to keep his commandments, and to hold fast to him, and to serve him with
all your heart and with all your soul.' So Joshua blessed them and sent them
away, and they went to their tents.

This is the word of the Lord.   Joshua 22.1–6

R* **The Lord listens to the needy,**
[he does not despise his captive people].   cf *Psalm* 69.35

This will please the Lord more than an offering of oxen,
more than bulls with horns and hooves.
The humble shall see and be glad;
you who seek God, your heart shall live.   R*

Let the heavens and the earth praise him,
the seas and all that moves in them;
for God will save Zion and rebuild the cities of Judah;
they shall live there and have it in possession.   R   *Psalm* 69.33–37

Year 2

A reading from the Book of Job.

Job answered the LORD:
'I know that you can do all things,
and that no purpose of yours can be thwarted.
"Who is this that hides counsel without knowledge?"
Therefore I have uttered what I did not understand,
things too wonderful for me, which I did not know.
therefore I despise myself,
and repent in dust and ashes.'

The LORD blessed the latter days of Job more than his beginning; and he had fourteen thousand sheep, six thousand camels, a thousand yoke of oxen, and a thousand donkeys. He also had seven sons and three daughters. He named the first Jemimah, the second Keziah, and the third Keren-happuch. In all the land there were no women so beautiful as Job's daughters; and their father gave them an inheritance along with their brothers. After this Job lived for one hundred and forty years, and saw his children, and his children's children, four generations. And Job died, old and full of days.

This is the word of the Lord.   *Job* 42.1–3, 6, 12–end

Responsorial Psalm

R **I have longed for your salvation, O Lord,
[and your law is my delight].**   Psalm 119.174

Let my cry come before you, O Lord;
give me understanding, according to your word.
Let my supplication come before you;
deliver me, according to your promise. **R**

My lips shall pour forth your praise,
when you have taught me your statutes.
My tongue shall sing of your word,
for all your commandments are righteous. **R**

Let your hand reach out to help me,
for I have chosen your commandments.
I have longed for your salvation, O Lord,
and your law is my delight. **R**

Let my soul live and it shall praise you,
and let your judgements be my help.
I have gone astray like a sheep that is lost;
O seek your servant, for I do not forget your commandments. **R**

                                                    Psalm 119.169–end

Year 1 and Year 2

Hear the Gospel of our Lord Jesus Christ according to Luke.

The seventy returned to Jesus with joy, saying, 'Lord, in your name even the
demons submit to us!' He said to them, 'I watched Satan fall from heaven
like a flash of lightning. See, I have given you authority to tread on snakes and
scorpions, and over all the power of the enemy; and nothing will hurt you.
Nevertheless, do not rejoice at this, that the spirits submit to you, but rejoice
that your names are written in heaven.'

At that same hour Jesus rejoiced in the Holy Spirit and said, 'I thank you,
Father, Lord of heaven and earth, because you have hidden these things from
the wise and the intelligent and have revealed them to infants; yes, Father, for
such was your gracious will. All things have been handed over to me by my
Father; and no one knows who the Son is except the Father, or who the Father
is except the Son and anyone to whom the Son chooses to reveal him.'

Then turning to the disciples, Jesus said to them privately, 'Blessed are
the eyes that see what you see! For I tell you that many prophets and kings
desired to see what you see, but did not see it, and to hear what you hear,
but did not hear it.'

This is the Gospel of the Lord.   Luke 10.17–24

Week 27: Monday between 3 and 9 October

Year 1

A reading from the Book of Jonah.

The word of the LORD came to Jonah son of Amittai, saying, 'Go at once to Nineveh, that great city, and cry out against it; for their wickedness has come up before me.' But Jonah set out to flee to Tarshish from the presence of the LORD. He went down to Joppa and found a ship going to Tarshish; so he paid his fare and went on board, to go with them to Tarshish, away from the presence of the LORD.

But the LORD hurled a great wind upon the sea, and such a mighty storm came upon the sea that the ship threatened to break up. Then the mariners were afraid, and each cried to his god. They threw the cargo that was in the ship into the sea, to lighten it for them. Jonah, meanwhile, had gone down into the hold of the ship and had lain down, and was fast asleep. The captain came and said to him, 'What are you doing sound asleep? Get up, call on your god! Perhaps the god will spare us a thought so that we do not perish.'

The sailors said to one another, 'Come, let us cast lots, so that we may know on whose account this calamity has come upon us.' So they cast lots, and the lot fell on Jonah. Then they said to him, 'Tell us why this calamity has come upon us. What is your occupation? Where do you come from? What is your country? And of what people are you?' 'I am a Hebrew,' he replied. 'I worship the LORD, the God of heaven, who made the sea and the dry land.' Then the men were even more afraid, and said to him, 'What is this that you have done!' For the men knew that he was fleeing from the presence of the LORD, because he had told them so.

Then they said to him, 'What shall we do to you, that the sea may quieten down for us?' For the sea was growing more and more tempestuous. He said to them, 'Pick me up and throw me into the sea; then the sea will quieten down for you; for I know it is because of me that this great storm has come upon you.' Nevertheless, the men rowed hard to bring the ship back to land, but they could not, for the sea grew more and more stormy against them. Then they cried out to the LORD, 'Please, O LORD, we pray, do not let us perish on account of this man's life. Do not make us guilty of innocent blood; for you, O LORD, have done as it pleased you.' So they picked Jonah up and threw him into the sea; and the sea ceased from its raging. Then the men feared the LORD even more, and they offered a sacrifice to the LORD and made vows.

But the LORD provided a large fish to swallow up Jonah; and Jonah was in the belly of the fish for three days and three nights. Then Jonah prayed to the LORD his God from the belly of the fish, saying,

'I called to the LORD out of my distress,
    and he answered me;
out of the belly of Sheol I cried,
    and you heard my voice.'

Then the LORD spoke to the fish, and it spewed Jonah out upon the dry land.

This is the word of the Lord.   Jonah 1.1 – 2.2, 10

Either

Canticle

R **My prayer came to you, O Lord,**
[and you brought me up from the depths]. cf Jonah 2.7b, 6b

I called to you, O God, out of my distress
and you answered me;
out of the belly of Sheol I cried,
and you heard my voice. R

You cast me into the deep,
into the heart of the seas,
and the flood surrounded me,
all your waves and billows passed over me. R

Then I said, I am driven away from your sight;
how shall I ever look again upon your holy temple?
As my life was ebbing away, I remembered you, O God,
and my prayer came to you, into your holy temple. R Jonah 2.2–4, 7

or

Responsorial Psalm

R **Your saving help will lift me up:**
I will praise your name in song. cf Psalm 69.31b, 32a

Save me, O God,
for the waters have come up, even to my neck.
I sink in deep mire where there is no foothold;
I have come into deep waters and the flood sweeps over me. R

I have grown weary with crying; my throat is raw;
my eyes have failed from looking so long for my God.
Those who hate me without any cause
are more than the hairs of my head. R

Those who would destroy me are mighty;
my enemies accuse me falsely:
must I now give back what I never stole?
O God, you know my foolishness,
and my faults are not hidden from you. R Psalm 69.1–6

A reading from the Letter of Paul to the Galatians.

I am astonished that you are so quickly deserting the one who called you in the grace of Christ and are turning to a different gospel – not that there is another gospel, but there are some who are confusing you and want to pervert the gospel of Christ. But even if we or an angel from heaven should proclaim to you a gospel contrary to what we proclaimed to you, let that one be accursed! As we have said before, so now I repeat, if anyone proclaims to you a gospel contrary to what you received, let that one be accursed!

Am I now seeking human approval, or God's approval? Or am I trying to please people? If I were still pleasing people, I would not be a servant of Christ. For I want you to know, brothers and sisters, that the gospel that was proclaimed by me is not of human origin; for I did not receive it from a human source, nor was I taught it, but I received it through a revelation of Jesus Christ.

This is the word of the Lord. *Galatians* 1.6–12

Responsorial Psalm

R **The Lord is ever mindful of his covenant;**
   [he is gracious and full of compassion]. *cf Psalm* 111.5b, 4b
   or

R **Alleluia!**

I will give thanks to the Lord with my whole heart,
in the company of the faithful and in the congregation.
The works of the Lord are great,
sought out by all who delight in them. **R**

His work is full of majesty and honour
and his righteousness endures for ever.
He appointed a memorial for his marvellous deeds;
the Lord is gracious and full of compassion. **R**

He gave food to those who feared him;
he is ever mindful of his covenant.
He showed his people the power of his works
in giving them the heritage of the nations. **R** *Psalm* 111.1–6

Year 1 and Year 2

Hear the Gospel of our Lord Jesus Christ according to Luke.

A lawyer stood up to test Jesus. 'Teacher,' he said, 'what must I do to inherit eternal life?' He said to him, 'What is written in the law? What do you read there?' He answered, 'You shall love the Lord your God with all your heart, and with all your soul, and with all your strength, and with all your mind;

and your neighbour as yourself.' And he said to him, 'You have given the right answer; do this, and you will live.'

But wanting to justify himself, he asked Jesus, 'And who is my neighbour?' Jesus replied, 'A man was going down from Jerusalem to Jericho, and fell into the hands of robbers, who stripped him, beat him, and went away, leaving him half dead. Now by chance a priest was going down that road; and when he saw him, he passed by on the other side. So likewise a Levite, when he came to the place and saw him, passed by on the other side. But a Samaritan while travelling came near him; and when he saw him, he was moved with pity. He went to him and bandaged his wounds, having poured oil and wine on them. Then he put him on his own animal, brought him to an inn, and took care of him. The next day he took out two denarii, gave them to the innkeeper, and said, "Take care of him; and when I come back, I will repay you whatever more you spend."

'Which of these three, do you think, was a neighbour to the man who fell into the hands of the robbers?' He said, 'The one who showed him mercy.' Jesus said to him, 'Go and do likewise.'

This is the Gospel of the Lord. Luke 10.25–37

Week 27: Tuesday between 4 and 10 October

Year I

A reading from the Book of Jonah.

The word of the LORD came to Jonah a second time, saying, 'Get up, go to Nineveh, that great city, and proclaim to it the message that I tell you.' So Jonah set out and went to Nineveh, according to the word of the LORD. Now Nineveh was an exceedingly large city, a three days' walk across. Jonah began to go into the city, going a day's walk. And he cried out, 'Forty days more, and Nineveh shall be overthrown!' And the people of Nineveh believed God; they proclaimed a fast, and everyone, great and small, put on sackcloth.

When the news reached the king of Nineveh, he rose from his throne, removed his robe, covered himself with sackcloth, and sat in ashes. Then he had a proclamation made in Nineveh: 'By the decree of the king and his nobles: No human being or animal, no herd or flock, shall taste anything. They shall not feed, nor shall they drink water. Human beings and animals shall be covered with sackcloth, and they shall cry mightily to God. All shall turn from their evil ways and from the violence that is in their hands. Who knows? God may relent and change his mind; he may turn from his fierce anger, so that we do not perish.'

When God saw what they did, how they turned from their evil ways, God changed his mind about the calamity that he had said he would bring upon them; and he did not do it.

This is the word of the Lord. Jonah 3

Responsorial Psalm

R **My soul waits for the Lord,**
   [more than the night watch for the morning].   Psalm 130.5

Out of the depths have I cried to you, O Lord;
Lord, hear my voice;
let your ears consider well the voice of my supplication. **R**

If you, Lord, were to mark what is done amiss,
O Lord, who could stand?
But there is forgiveness with you,
so that you shall be feared. **R**

I wait for the Lord; my soul waits for him;
in his word is my hope.
My soul waits for the Lord,
more than the night watch for the morning,
more than the night watch for the morning. **R**

O Israel, wait for the Lord,
for with the Lord there is mercy;
with him is plenteous redemption
and he shall redeem Israel from all their sins. **R**   Psalm 130

Year 2

A reading from the Letter of Paul to the Galatians.

You have heard, no doubt, of my earlier life in Judaism. I was violently
persecuting the church of God and was trying to destroy it. I advanced in
Judaism beyond many among my people of the same age, for I was far more
zealous for the traditions of my ancestors. But when God, who had set me
apart before I was born and called me through his grace, was pleased to reveal
his Son to me, so that I might proclaim him among the Gentiles, I did not
confer with any human being, nor did I go up to Jerusalem to those who
were already apostles before me, but I went away at once into Arabia, and
afterwards I returned to Damascus.

Then after three years I did go up to Jerusalem to visit Cephas and stayed
with him for fifteen days; but I did not see any other apostle except James the
Lord's brother. In what I am writing to you, before God, I do not lie! Then I
went into the regions of Syria and Cilicia, and I was still unknown by sight
to the churches of Judea that are in Christ; they only heard it said, 'The one
who formerly was persecuting us is now proclaiming the faith he once tried
to destroy.' And they glorified God because of me.

This is the word of the Lord.   *Galatians 1.13–end*

R **O Lord, you have searched me out and known me.**   *Psalm* 139.1a

O Lord, you have searched me out and known me;
you know my sitting down and my rising up;
you discern my thoughts from afar. R

You mark out my journeys and my resting place
and are acquainted with all my ways.
For there is not a word on my tongue,
but you, O Lord, know it altogether. R

You encompass me behind and before
and lay your hand upon me.
Such knowledge is too wonderful for me,
so high that I cannot attain it. R

Where can I go then from your spirit?
Or where can I flee from your presence?
If I climb up to heaven, you are there;
if I make the grave my bed, you are there also. R

If I take the wings of the morning
and dwell in the uttermost parts of the sea,
even there your hand shall lead me,
your right hand hold me fast. R   *Psalm* 139.1–9

Year 1 and Year 2

Hear the Gospel of our Lord Jesus Christ according to Luke.

Jesus entered a certain village, where a woman named Martha welcomed
him into her home. She had a sister named Mary, who sat at the Lord's feet
and listened to what he was saying. But Martha was distracted by her many
tasks; so she came to him and asked, 'Lord, do you not care that my sister
has left me to do all the work by myself? Tell her then to help me.' But the
Lord answered her, 'Martha, Martha, you are worried and distracted by many
things; there is need of only one thing. Mary has chosen the better part, which
will not be taken away from her.'

This is the Gospel of the Lord.   *Luke* 10.38–end

Week 27: Wednesday between 5 and 11 October

Year 1

A reading from the Book of Jonah.

Jonah was very displeased, and he became angry. He prayed to the LORD and said, 'O LORD! Is not this what I said while I was still in my own country? That is why I fled to Tarshish at the beginning; for I knew that you are a gracious God and merciful, slow to anger, and abounding in steadfast love, and ready to relent from punishing. And now, O LORD, please take my life from me, for it is better for me to die than to live.' And the LORD said, 'Is it right for you to be angry?' Then Jonah went out of the city and sat down east of the city, and made a booth for himself there. He sat under it in the shade, waiting to see what would become of the city.

The LORD God appointed a bush, and made it come up over Jonah, to give shade over his head, to save him from his discomfort; so Jonah was very happy about the bush. But when dawn came up the next day, God appointed a worm that attacked the bush, so that it withered. When the sun rose, God prepared a sultry east wind, and the sun beat down on the head of Jonah so that he was faint and asked that he might die. He said, 'It is better for me to die than to live.'

But God said to Jonah, 'Is it right for you to be angry about the bush?' And he said, 'Yes, angry enough to die.' Then the LORD said, 'You are concerned about the bush, for which you did not labour and which you did not grow; it came into being in a night and perished in a night. And should I not be concerned about Nineveh, that great city, in which there are more than a hundred and twenty thousand people who do not know their right hand from their left, and also many animals?'

This is the word of the Lord.   Jonah 4

Responsorial Psalm

**R* All nations shall come and worship you, O Lord,
[they shall glorify your name].**   *cf Psalm 86.9*

Incline your ear, O Lord, and answer me,
for I am poor and in misery.
Preserve my soul, for I am faithful;
save your servant, for I put my trust in you.   **R**

Be merciful to me, O Lord, for you are my God;
I call upon you all the day long.
Gladden the soul of your servant,
for to you, O Lord, I lift up my soul.   **R**

For you, Lord, are good and forgiving,
abounding in steadfast love to all who call upon you.
Give ear, O Lord, to my prayer
and listen to the voice of my supplication.   R

In the day of my distress I will call upon you,
for you will answer me.
Among the gods there is none like you, O Lord,
nor any works like yours.   R*   Psalm 86.1–9

Year 2

A reading from the Letter of Paul to the Galatians.

After fourteen years I went up again to Jerusalem with Barnabas, taking Titus
along with me. I went up in response to a revelation. Then I laid before them
(though only in a private meeting with the acknowledged leaders) the gospel
that I proclaim among the Gentiles, in order to make sure that I was not
running, or had not run, in vain. On the contrary, when they saw that I had
been entrusted with the gospel for the uncircumcised, just as Peter had been
entrusted with the gospel for the circumcised (for he who worked through
Peter making him an apostle to the circumcised also worked through me in
sending me to the Gentiles), and when James and Cephas and John, who were
acknowledged pillars, recognized the grace that had been given to me, they
gave to Barnabas and me the right hand of fellowship, agreeing that we should
go to the Gentiles and they to the circumcised. They asked only one thing, that
we remember the poor, which was actually what I was eager to do.

But when Cephas came to Antioch, I opposed him to his face, because
he stood self-condemned; for until certain people came from James, he used
to eat with the Gentiles. But after they came, he drew back and kept himself
separate for fear of the circumcision faction. And the other Jews joined him
in this hypocrisy, so that even Barnabas was led astray by their hypocrisy. But
when I saw that they were not acting consistently with the truth of the gospel,
I said to Cephas before them all, 'If you, though a Jew, live like a Gentile and
not like a Jew, how can you compel the Gentiles to live like Jews?'

This is the word of the Lord.   Galatians 2.1–2, 7–14

R **He will bring God's name to all the nations;
[to kings and to the people of Israel].**

cf Acts 9.15

or

R **Alleluia!**

O praise the Lord, all you nations;
praise him, all you peoples. **R**

For great is his steadfast love towards us,
and the faithfulness of the Lord endures for ever. **R**

Psalm 117

Year 1 and Year 2

Hear the Gospel of our Lord Jesus Christ according to Luke.

Jesus was praying in a certain place, and after he had finished, one of his
disciples said to him, 'Lord, teach us to pray, as John taught his disciples.' He
said to them, 'When you pray, say:
Father, hallowed be your name.
Your kingdom come.
Give us each day our daily bread.
And forgive us our sins,
for we ourselves forgive everyone indebted to us.
And do not bring us to the time of trial.'

This is the Gospel of the Lord.

Luke 11.1–4

Week 27: Thursday between 6 and 12 October

Year 1

A reading from the prophecy of Malachi.

You have spoken harsh words against me, says the LORD. Yet you say, 'How
have we spoken against you?' You have said, 'It is vain to serve God. What do
we profit by keeping his command or by going about as mourners before the
LORD of hosts? Now we count the arrogant happy; evildoers not only prosper,
but when they put God to the test they escape.'

Then those who revered the LORD spoke with one another. The LORD took
note and listened, and a book of remembrance was written before him of
those who revered the LORD and thought on his name. They shall be mine,
says the LORD of hosts, my special possession on the day when I act, and I will
spare them as parents spare their children who serve them. Then once more
you shall see the difference between the righteous and the wicked, between
one who serves God and one who does not serve him.

See, the day is coming, burning like an oven, when all the arrogant and all evildoers will be stubble; the day that comes shall burn them up, says the LORD of hosts, so that it will leave them neither root nor branch. But for you who revere my name the sun of righteousness shall rise, with healing in its wings.

This is the word of the Lord.   Malachi 3.13 – 4.2a

Responsorial Psalm

R **The Lord knows the way of the righteous;
[who delight in his law].**   cf Psalm 1.6a, 2a

Blessed are they who have not walked
in the counsel of the wicked,
nor lingered in the way of sinners,
nor sat in the assembly of the scornful.
Their delight is in the law of the Lord
and they meditate on his law day and night.   **R**

Like a tree planted by streams of water
bearing fruit in due season,
with leaves that do not wither,
whatever they do, it shall prosper.   **R**

As for the wicked, it is not so with them;
they are like chaff which the wind blows away.
Therefore the wicked shall not be able to stand in the judgement,
nor the sinner in the congregation of the righteous.
For the Lord knows the way of the righteous,
but the way of the wicked shall perish.   **R**   Psalm 1

Year 2

A reading from the Letter of Paul to the Galatians.

You foolish Galatians! Who has bewitched you? It was before your eyes that Jesus Christ was publicly exhibited as crucified! The only thing I want to learn from you is this: Did you receive the Spirit by doing the works of the law or by believing what you heard? Are you so foolish? Having started with the Spirit, are you now ending with the flesh? Did you experience so much for nothing? – if it really was for nothing. Well then, does God supply you with the Spirit and work miracles among you by your doing the works of the law, or by your believing what you heard?

This is the word of the Lord.   Galatians 3.1–5

Canticle

R **Blessed be the Lord the God of Israel,**
 who has come to his people and set them free. *Luke 1.68*

Blessed be the Lord the God of Israel,
who has come to his people and set them free.
He has raised up for us a mighty saviour
born of the house of his servant David. R

Through his holy prophets God promised of old
to save us from our enemies,
from the hand of all that hate us,
to show mercy to our ancestors,
and to remember his holy covenant. R

This was the oath God swore to our father Abraham:
to set us free from the hands of our enemies,
free to worship him without fear,
holy and righteous in his sight
all the days of our life. R *Luke 1.68–73*

Year 1 and Year 2

Hear the Gospel of our Lord Jesus Christ according to Luke.

Jesus said to them, 'Suppose one of you has a friend, and you go to him at midnight and say to him, "Friend, lend me three loaves of bread; for a friend of mine has arrived, and I have nothing to set before him." And he answers from within, "Do not bother me; the door has already been locked, and my children are with me in bed; I cannot get up and give you anything." I tell you, even though he will not get up and give him anything because he is his friend, at least because of his persistence he will get up and give him whatever he needs.

'So I say to you, Ask, and it will be given to you; search, and you will find; knock, and the door will be opened for you. For everyone who asks receives, and everyone who searches finds, and for everyone who knocks, the door will be opened. Is there anyone among you who, if your child asks for a fish, will give a snake instead of a fish? Or if the child asks for an egg, will give a scorpion? If you then, who are evil, know how to give good gifts to your children, how much more will the heavenly Father give the Holy Spirit to those who ask him!'

This is the Gospel of the Lord. *Luke 11.5–13*

Week 27: Friday between 7 and 13 October

Year 1

A reading from the prophecy of Joel.

Put on sackcloth and lament, you priests;
    wail, you ministers of the altar.
Come, pass the night in sackcloth,
    you ministers of my God!
Grain-offering and drink-offering
    are withheld from the house of your God.

Sanctify a fast,
    call a solemn assembly.
Gather the elders
    and all the inhabitants of the land
to the house of the LORD your God,
    and cry out to the LORD.

Alas for the day!
For the day of the LORD is near,
    and as destruction from the Almighty it comes.

Blow the trumpet in Zion;
    sound the alarm on my holy mountain!
Let all the inhabitants of the land tremble,
    for the day of the LORD is coming, it is near –
a day of darkness and gloom,
    a day of clouds and thick darkness!
Like blackness spread upon the mountains
    a great and powerful army comes;
their like has never been from of old,
    nor will be again after them
    in ages to come.

This is the word of the Lord.   Joel 1.13–15, 2.1–2

R* **I will give thanks to the Lord with my whole heart**
[and tell of his marvellous works].   *cf Psalm 9.1*

I will be glad and rejoice in you;
I will make music to your name, O Most High.
When my enemies are driven back,
they stumble and perish at your presence.   **R**

For you have maintained my right and my cause;
you sat on your throne giving righteous judgement.
You have rebuked the nations and destroyed the wicked;
you have blotted out their name for ever and ever.   **R**

The enemy was utterly laid waste.
You uprooted their cities;
their very memory has perished.
But the Lord shall endure for ever;
he has made fast his throne for judgement.   **R**   *Psalm 9.1–7*

Year 2

A reading from the Letter of Paul to the Galatians.

So, you see, those who believe are the descendants of Abraham. And the scripture, foreseeing that God would justify the Gentiles by faith, declared the gospel beforehand to Abraham, saying, 'All the Gentiles shall be blessed in you.' For this reason, those who believe are blessed with Abraham who believed.

For all who rely on the works of the law are under a curse; for it is written, 'Cursed is everyone who does not observe and obey all the things written in the book of the law.' Now it is evident that no one is justified before God by the law; for 'The one who is righteous will live by faith.' But the law does not rest on faith; on the contrary, 'Whoever does the works of the law will live by them.' Christ redeemed us from the curse of the law by becoming a curse for us – for it is written, 'Cursed is everyone who hangs on a tree' – in order that in Christ Jesus the blessing of Abraham might come to the Gentiles, so that we might receive the promise of the Spirit through faith.

This is the word of the Lord.   *Galatians 3.7–14*

Responsorial Psalm

R* **The Lord is renowned for his marvellous deeds:**
    [he is gracious and full of compassion].   cf Psalm 111.4

He gave food to those who feared him;
he is ever mindful of his covenant.
He showed his people the power of his works
in giving them the heritage of the nations. R

The works of his hands are truth and justice;
all his commandments are sure.
They stand fast for ever and ever;
they are done in truth and equity. R

He sent redemption to his people;
he commanded his covenant for ever;
holy and awesome is his name. R

The fear of the Lord is the beginning of wisdom;
a good understanding have those who live by it;
his praise endures for ever. R   Psalm 111.4–end

Year 1 and Year 2

Hear the Gospel of our Lord Jesus Christ according to Luke.

Some of the crowds said of Jesus, 'He casts out demons by Beelzebul, the ruler of the demons.' Others, to test him, kept demanding from him a sign from heaven. But he knew what they were thinking and said to them, 'Every kingdom divided against itself becomes a desert, and house falls on house. If Satan also is divided against himself, how will his kingdom stand? – for you say that I cast out the demons by Beelzebul. Now if I cast out the demons by Beelzebul, by whom do your exorcists cast them out? Therefore they will be your judges. But if it is by the finger of God that I cast out the demons, then the kingdom of God has come to you. When a strong man, fully armed, guards his castle, his property is safe. But when one stronger than he attacks him and overpowers him, he takes away his armour in which he trusted and divides his plunder. Whoever is not with me is against me, and whoever does not gather with me scatters.

'When the unclean spirit has gone out of a person, it wanders through waterless regions looking for a resting-place, but not finding any, it says, "I will return to my house from which I came." When it comes, it finds it swept and put in order. Then it goes and brings seven other spirits more evil than itself, and they enter and live there; and the last state of that person is worse than the first.'

This is the Gospel of the Lord.   Luke 11.15–26

Week 27: Saturday between 8 and 14 October

Year 1

A reading from the prophecy of Joel.

Let the nations rouse themselves,
    and come up to the valley of Jehoshaphat;
for there I will sit to judge
    all the neighbouring nations.

Put in the sickle,
    for the harvest is ripe.
Go in, tread,
    for the wine press is full.
The vats overflow,
    for their wickedness is great.

Multitudes, multitudes,
    in the valley of decision!
For the day of the LORD is near
    in the valley of decision.
The sun and the moon are darkened,
    and the stars withdraw their shining.
The LORD roars from Zion,
    and utters his voice from Jerusalem,
    and the heavens and the earth shake.
But the LORD is a refuge for his people,
    a stronghold for the people of Israel.
So you shall know that I, the LORD your God,
    dwell in Zion, my holy mountain.
And Jerusalem shall be holy,
    and strangers shall never again pass through it.

On that day the mountains shall drip sweet wine,
    the hills shall flow with milk,
and all the stream beds of Judah
    shall flow with water;
a fountain shall come forth from the house of the LORD
    and water the Wadi Shittim.

Egypt shall become a desolation
    and Edom a desolate wilderness,
because of the violence done to the people of Judah,
    in whose land they have shed innocent blood.
But Judah shall be inhabited for ever,
    and Jerusalem to all generations.
I will avenge their blood, and I will not clear the guilty,
    for the LORD dwells in Zion.

This is the word of the Lord.
Joel 3.12–end

Responsorial Psalm

R* **The Lord is king: let the earth rejoice;**
   [let the multitude of the isles be glad].   *Psalm 97.1*

Zion heard and was glad, and the daughters of Judah rejoiced,
because of your judgements, O Lord.
For you, Lord, are most high over all the earth;
you are exalted far above all gods. **R**

The Lord loves those who hate evil;
he preserves the lives of his faithful
and delivers them from the hand of the wicked. **R**

Light has sprung up for the righteous
and joy for the true of heart.
Rejoice in the Lord, you righteous,
and give thanks to his holy name. **R**   *Psalm 97.1, 8–end*

Year 2

A reading from the Letter of Paul to the Galatians.

The scripture has imprisoned all things under the power of sin, so that what
was promised through faith in Jesus Christ might be given to those who
believe.

Now before faith came, we were imprisoned and guarded under the law
until faith would be revealed. Therefore the law was our disciplinarian until
Christ came, so that we might be justified by faith. But now that faith has
come, we are no longer subject to a disciplinarian, for in Christ Jesus you are
all children of God through faith. As many of you as were baptized into Christ
have clothed yourselves with Christ. There is no longer Jew or Greek, there
is no longer slave or free, there is no longer male and female; for all of you
are one in Christ Jesus. And if you belong to Christ, then you are Abraham's
offspring, heirs according to the promise.

This is the word of the Lord.   *Galatians 3.22–end*

Responsorial Psalm

R* **Remember the marvels the Lord has done:
[his wonders and the judgements he has given].**   *cf Psalm 105.5*

O give thanks to the Lord and call upon his name;
make known his deeds among the peoples.
Sing to him, sing praises,
and tell of all his marvellous works.   R

Rejoice in the praise of his holy name;
let the hearts of them rejoice who seek the Lord.
Seek the Lord and his strength;
seek his face continually.   R*

O seed of Abraham his servant,
O children of Jacob his chosen.
He is the Lord our God;
his judgements are in all the earth.   R   *Psalm 105.1–7*

Year 1 and Year 2

Hear the Gospel of our Lord Jesus Christ according to Luke.

While Jesus was speaking, a woman in the crowd raised her voice and said to
him, 'Blessed is the womb that bore you and the breasts that nursed you!' But
he said, 'Blessed rather are those who hear the word of God and obey it!'

This is the Gospel of the Lord.   *Luke 11.27–28*

Week 28: Monday between 10 and 16 October

Year I

A reading from the Letter of Paul to the Romans.

Paul, a servant of Jesus Christ, called to be an apostle, set apart for the gospel of God, which he promised beforehand through his prophets in the holy scriptures, the gospel concerning his Son, who was descended from David according to the flesh and was declared to be Son of God with power according to the spirit of holiness by resurrection from the dead, Jesus Christ our Lord, through whom we have received grace and apostleship to bring about the obedience of faith among all the Gentiles for the sake of his name, including yourselves who are called to belong to Jesus Christ,

To all God's beloved in Rome, who are called to be saints: Grace to you and peace from God our Father and the Lord Jesus Christ.

This is the word of the Lord.   Romans 1.1–7

Responsorial Psalm

R* **Sound praises to the Lord, all the earth;**
   [break into song and make music].   cf Psalm 98.5

Sing to the Lord a new song,
for he has done marvellous things.
His own right hand and his holy arm
have won for him the victory.   **R**

The Lord has made known his salvation;
his deliverance has he openly shown
in the sight of the nations.   **R**

He has remembered his mercy and faithfulness
towards the house of Israel,
and all the ends of the earth have seen
the salvation of our God.   **R***

Make music to the Lord with the lyre,
with the lyre and the voice of melody.
With trumpets and the sound of the horn
sound praises before the Lord, the King.   **R**

Let the sea thunder and all that fills it,
the world and all that dwell upon it.
Let the rivers clap their hands
and let the hills ring out together before the Lord.   **R**

For he comes to judge the earth:
in righteousness shall he judge the world
and the peoples with equity.   **R**   Psalm 98

A reading from the Letter of Paul to the Galatians.

Tell me, you who desire to be subject to the law, will you not listen to the law? For it is written that Abraham had two sons, one by a slave woman and the other by a free woman. One, the child of the slave, was born according to the flesh; the other, the child of the free woman, was born through the promise. Now this is an allegory: these women are two covenants. One woman, in fact, is Hagar, from Mount Sinai, bearing children for slavery. But the other woman corresponds to the Jerusalem above; she is free, and she is our mother. For it is written,

'Rejoice, you childless one, you who bear no children,
  burst into song and shout, you who endure no birth pangs;
for the children of the desolate woman are more numerous
  than the children of the one who is married.'

So then, friends, we are children, not of the slave but of the free woman. For freedom Christ has set us free. Stand firm, therefore, and do not submit again to a yoke of slavery.

This is the word of the Lord.   *Galatians* 4.21–24, 26–27, 31 – 5.1

Responsorial Psalm

R **Blessed be the name of the Lord:**
   [from this time forth and for evermore].   *Psalm* 113.2

   or

R **Alleluia!**

Give praise, you servants of the Lord,
O praise the name of the Lord.
Blessed be the name of the Lord,
from this time forth and for evermore. **R**

From the rising of the sun to its setting
let the name of the Lord be praised.
The Lord is high above all nations
and his glory above the heavens. **R**

Who is like the Lord our God,
that has his throne so high,
yet humbles himself to behold
the things of heaven and earth? **R**

He raises the poor from the dust
and lifts the needy from the ashes,
to set them with princes,
with the princes of his people.
He gives the barren woman a place in the house
and makes her a joyful mother of children. **R**   *Psalm* 113

Hear the Gospel of our Lord Jesus Christ according to Luke.

When the crowds were increasing, Jesus began to say, 'This generation is an evil generation; it asks for a sign, but no sign will be given to it except the sign of Jonah. For just as Jonah became a sign to the people of Nineveh, so the Son of Man will be to this generation. The queen of the South will rise at the judgement with the people of this generation and condemn them, because she came from the ends of the earth to listen to the wisdom of Solomon, and see, something greater than Solomon is here! The people of Nineveh will rise up at the judgement with this generation and condemn it, because they repented at the proclamation of Jonah, and see, something greater than Jonah is here!'

This is the Gospel of the Lord.   Luke 11.29–32

Week 28: Tuesday between 11 and 17 October

Year 1

A reading from the Letter of Paul to the Romans.

I am not ashamed of the gospel; it is the power of God for salvation to everyone who has faith, to the Jew first and also to the Greek. For in it the righteousness of God is revealed through faith for faith; as it is written, 'The one who is righteous will live by faith.'

For the wrath of God is revealed from heaven against all ungodliness and wickedness of those who by their wickedness suppress the truth. For what can be known about God is plain to them, because God has shown it to them. Ever since the creation of the world his eternal power and divine nature, invisible though they are, have been understood and seen through the things he has made. So they are without excuse; for though they knew God, they did not honour him as God or give thanks to him, but they became futile in their thinking, and their senseless minds were darkened. Claiming to be wise, they became fools; and they exchanged the glory of the immortal God for images resembling a mortal human being or birds or four-footed animals or reptiles.

Therefore God gave them up in the lusts of their hearts to impurity, to the degrading of their bodies among themselves, because they exchanged the truth about God for a lie and worshipped and served the creature rather than the Creator, who is blessed for ever! Amen.

This is the word of the Lord.   Romans 1.16–25

R **The heavens proclaim the glory of God.**   *cf Psalm* 19.1a

The heavens are telling the glory of God
and the firmament proclaims his handiwork.
One day pours out its song to another
and one night unfolds knowledge to another. **R**

They have neither speech nor language
and their voices are not heard,
yet their sound has gone out into all lands
and their words to the ends of the world. **R**   *Psalm* 19.1–4

Year 2

A reading from the Letter of Paul to the Galatians.

For freedom Christ has set us free. Stand firm, therefore, and do not submit
again to a yoke of slavery.
 Listen! I, Paul, am telling you that if you let yourselves be circumcised,
Christ will be of no benefit to you. Once again I testify to every man who
lets himself be circumcised that he is obliged to obey the entire law. You
who want to be justified by the law have cut yourselves off from Christ;
you have fallen away from grace. For through the Spirit, by faith, we eagerly
wait for the hope of righteousness. For in Christ Jesus neither circumcision
nor uncircumcision counts for anything; the only thing that counts is faith
working through love.

This is the word of the Lord.   *Galatians* 5.1–6

Responsorial Psalm

R **O Lord, my delight is in your commandments,
   [I love them with all my heart].**   *cf Psalm* 119.47

Let your faithful love come unto me, O Lord,
even your salvation, according to your promise.
Then shall I answer those who taunt me,
for my trust is in your word. **R**

O take not the word of truth utterly out of my mouth,
for my hope is in your judgements.
So shall I always keep your law;
I shall keep it for ever and ever. **R**

I will walk at liberty,
because I study your commandments.
I will tell of your testimonies, even before kings,
and will not be ashamed. **R**

My delight shall be in your commandments,
which I have greatly loved.
My hands will I lift up to your commandments,
which I love,
and I will meditate on your statutes.   **R**   Psalm 119.41–48

Year 1 and Year 2

Hear the Gospel of our Lord Jesus Christ according to Luke.

While Jesus was speaking, a Pharisee invited him to dine with him; so he
went in and took his place at the table. The Pharisee was amazed to see that
he did not first wash before dinner. Then the Lord said to him, 'Now you
Pharisees clean the outside of the cup and of the dish, but inside you are full
of greed and wickedness. You fools! Did not the one who made the outside
make the inside also? So give for alms those things that are within; and see,
everything will be clean for you.'

This is the Gospel of the Lord.   Luke 11.37–41

Week 28: Wednesday between 12 and 18 October

Year 1

A reading from the Letter of Paul to the Romans.

You have no excuse, whoever you are, when you judge others; for in passing
judgement on another you condemn yourself, because you, the judge, are doing
the very same things. You say, 'We know that God's judgement on those who
do such things is in accordance with truth.' Do you imagine, whoever you
are, that when you judge those who do such things and yet do them yourself,
you will escape the judgement of God? Or do you despise the riches of his
kindness and forbearance and patience? Do you not realize that God's kindness is meant to lead you to repentance? But by your hard and impenitent
heart you are storing up wrath for yourself on the day of wrath, when God's
righteous judgement will be revealed. For he will repay according to each
one's deeds: to those who by patiently doing good seek for glory and honour
and immortality, he will give eternal life; while for those who are self-seeking
and who obey not the truth but wickedness, there will be wrath and fury.
There will be anguish and distress for everyone who does evil, the Jew first
and also the Greek, but glory and honour and peace for everyone who does
good, the Jew first and also the Greek. For God shows no partiality.

This is the word of the Lord.   Romans 2.1–11

Responsorial Psalm

R **God alone is my rock and my salvation
[my stronghold, so I shall not be shaken].**   Psalm 62.2, 6

On God alone my soul in stillness waits;
from him comes my salvation.
He alone is my rock and my salvation,
my stronghold, so that I shall never be shaken. **R**

How long will all of you assail me to destroy me,
as you would a tottering wall or a leaning fence?
They plot only to thrust me down from my place of honour;
lies are their chief delight;
they bless with their mouth, but in their heart they curse. **R**

Wait on God alone in stillness, O my soul;
for in him is my hope.
He alone is my rock and my salvation,
my stronghold, so that I shall not be shaken. **R**

In God is my strength and my glory;
God is my strong rock; in him is my refuge.
Put your trust in him always, my people;
pour out your hearts before him, for God is our refuge. **R**

Psalm 62.1–8

Year 2

A reading from the Letter of Paul to the Galatians.

If you are led by the Spirit, you are not subject to the law. Now the works of
the flesh are obvious: fornication, impurity, licentiousness, idolatry, sorcery,
enmities, strife, jealousy, anger, quarrels, dissensions, factions, envy, drunkenness, carousing, and things like these. I am warning you, as I warned you
before: those who do such things will not inherit the kingdom of God.

By contrast, the fruit of the Spirit is love, joy, peace, patience, kindness,
generosity, faithfulness, gentleness, and self-control. There is no law against
such things. And those who belong to Christ Jesus have crucified the flesh
with its passions and desires. If we live by the Spirit, let us also be guided
by the Spirit. Let us not become conceited, competing against one another,
envying one another.

This is the word of the Lord.   *Galatians 5.18–end*

Responsorial Psalm

R **The Lord knows the way of the righteous,**
    [who delight in his law].   cf Psalm 1.6a, 2a

Blessed are they who have not walked
in the counsel of the wicked,
nor lingered in the way of sinners,
nor sat in the assembly of the scornful.
Their delight is in the law of the Lord
and they meditate on his law day and night.   **R**

Like a tree planted by streams of water
bearing fruit in due season,
with leaves that do not wither,
whatever they do, it shall prosper.   **R**

As for the wicked, it is not so with them;
they are like chaff which the wind blows away.
Therefore the wicked shall not be able to stand in the judgement,
nor the sinner in the congregation of the righteous.
For the Lord knows the way of the righteous,
but the way of the wicked shall perish.   **R**   *Psalm 1*

Year 1 and Year 2

Hear the Gospel of our Lord Jesus Christ according to Luke.

Jesus said to the Pharisee, 'Woe to you Pharisees! For you tithe mint and rue
and herbs of all kinds, and neglect justice and the love of God; it is these you
ought to have practised, without neglecting the others. Woe to you Pharisees!
For you love to have the seat of honour in the synagogues and to be greeted
with respect in the market-places. Woe to you! For you are like unmarked
graves, and people walk over them without realizing it.'

    One of the lawyers answered him, 'Teacher, when you say these things, you
insult us too.' And he said, 'Woe also to you lawyers! For you load people with
burdens hard to bear, and you yourselves do not lift a finger to ease them.'

This is the Gospel of the Lord.   Luke 11.42–46

Week 28: Thursday between 13 and 19 October

Year 1

A reading from the Letter of Paul to the Romans.

Irrespective of law, the righteousness of God has been disclosed, and is attested by the law and the prophets, the righteousness of God through faith in Jesus Christ for all who believe. For there is no distinction, since all have sinned and fall short of the glory of God; they are now justified by his grace as a gift, through the redemption that is in Christ Jesus, whom God put forward as a sacrifice of atonement by his blood, effective through faith. He did this to show his righteousness, because in his divine forbearance he had passed over the sins previously committed; it was to prove at the present time that he himself is righteous and that he justifies the one who has faith in Jesus.

Then what becomes of boasting? It is excluded. By what law? By that of works? No, but by the law of faith. For we hold that a person is justified by faith apart from works prescribed by the law. Or is God the God of Jews only? Is he not the God of Gentiles also? Yes, of Gentiles also, since God is one; and he will justify the circumcised on the ground of faith and the uncircumcised through that same faith.

This is the word of the Lord.   Romans 3.21–30

Responsorial Psalm

R   **My soul waits for the Lord,
     [more than the night watch for the morning].**   *Psalm 130.5*

Out of the depths have I cried to you, O Lord;
Lord, hear my voice;
let your ears consider well
the voice of my supplication.   **R**

If you, Lord, were to mark what is done amiss,
O Lord, who could stand?
But there is forgiveness with you,
so that you shall be feared.   **R**

I wait for the Lord; my soul waits for him;
in his word is my hope.
My soul waits for the Lord,
more than the night watch for the morning,
more than the night watch for the morning.   **R**

O Israel, wait for the Lord,
for with the Lord there is mercy;
with him is plenteous redemption
and he shall redeem Israel from all their sins.   **R**   *Psalm 130*

Year 2

A reading from the Letter of Paul to the Ephesians.

Paul, an apostle of Christ Jesus by the will of God, to the saints who are in Ephesus and are faithful in Christ Jesus: Grace to you and peace from God our Father and the Lord Jesus Christ.

Blessed be the God and Father of our Lord Jesus Christ, who has blessed us in Christ with every spiritual blessing in the heavenly places, just as he chose us in Christ before the foundation of the world to be holy and blameless before him in love. He destined us for adoption as his children through Jesus Christ, according to the good pleasure of his will, to the praise of his glorious grace that he freely bestowed on us in the Beloved. In him we have redemption through his blood, the forgiveness of our trespasses, according to the riches of his grace that he lavished on us. With all wisdom and insight he has made known to us the mystery of his will, according to his good pleasure that he set forth in Christ, as a plan for the fullness of time, to gather up all things in him, things in heaven and things on earth.

This is the word of the Lord.   *Ephesians 1.1–10*

Responsorial Psalm

R **Sound praises to the Lord, all the earth;**
   [break into song and make music].   *cf Psalm 98.5*

Sing to the Lord a new song,
for he has done marvellous things.
His own right hand and his holy arm
have won for him the victory.   **R**

The Lord has made known his salvation;
his deliverance has he openly shown
in the sight of the nations.   **R**

He has remembered his mercy and faithfulness
towards the house of Israel,
and all the ends of the earth have seen
the salvation of our God.   **R**   *Psalm 98.1–4*

Year 1 and Year 2

Hear the Gospel of our Lord Jesus Christ according to Luke.

Jesus said, 'Woe to you! For you build the tombs of the prophets whom your ancestors killed. So you are witnesses and approve of the deeds of your ancestors; for they killed them, and you build their tombs. Therefore also the Wisdom of God said, "I will send them prophets and apostles, some of whom they will kill and persecute", so that this generation may be charged with the blood of all the prophets shed since the foundation of the world, from the blood of Abel to the blood of Zechariah, who perished between the altar and the sanctuary. Yes, I tell you, it will be charged against this generation. Woe to you lawyers! For you have taken away the key of knowledge; you did not enter yourselves, and you hindered those who were entering.'

When he went outside, the scribes and the Pharisees began to be very hostile towards him and to cross-examine him about many things, lying in wait for him, to catch him in something he might say.

This is the Gospel of the Lord.   Luke 11.47–end

Week 28: Friday between 14 and 20 October

Year 1

A reading from the Letter of Paul to the Romans.

What then are we to say was gained by Abraham, our ancestor according to the flesh? For if Abraham was justified by works, he has something to boast about, but not before God. For what does the scripture say? 'Abraham believed God, and it was reckoned to him as righteousness.' Now to one who works, wages are not reckoned as a gift but as something due. But to one who without works trusts him who justifies the ungodly, such faith is reckoned as righteousness. So also David speaks of the blessedness of those to whom God reckons righteousness irrespective of works:

'Blessed are those whose iniquities are forgiven,
    and whose sins are covered;
blessed is the one against whom the Lord will not reckon sin.'

This is the word of the Lord.   Romans 4.1–8

Responsorial Psalm

R **Be glad, you righteous, and rejoice in the Lord;**
   [shout for joy, all who are true of heart].   Psalm 32.12

Happy the one whose transgression is forgiven,
and whose sin is covered.
Happy the one to whom the Lord imputes no guilt,
and in whose spirit there is no guile. R

For I held my tongue;
my bones wasted away
    through my groaning all the day long.
Your hand was heavy upon me day and night;
my moisture was dried up like the drought in summer. R

Then I acknowledged my sin to you
and my iniquity I did not hide.
I said, 'I will confess my transgressions to the Lord,'
and you forgave the guilt of my sin. R

Therefore let all the faithful make their prayers to you
    in time of trouble;
in the great water flood, it shall not reach them.
You are a place for me to hide in;
you preserve me from trouble;
you surround me with songs of deliverance. R

'I will instruct you and teach you
    in the way that you should go;
I will guide you with my eye.
Be not like horse and mule which have no understanding;
whose mouths must be held with bit and bridle,
or else they will not stay near you.' R

Great tribulations remain for the wicked,
but mercy embraces those who trust in the Lord.
Be glad, you righteous, and rejoice in the Lord;
shout for joy, all who are true of heart. R   Psalm 32

Year 2

A reading from the Letter of Paul to the Ephesians.

In Christ we have also obtained an inheritance, having been destined according to the purpose of him who accomplishes all things according to his counsel and will, so that we, who were the first to set our hope on Christ, might live for the praise of his glory. In him you also, when you had heard the word of truth, the gospel of your salvation, and had believed in him, were marked with the seal of the promised Holy Spirit; this is the pledge of our inheritance towards redemption as God's own people, to the praise of his glory.

This is the word of the Lord.   Ephesians 1.11–14

Responsorial Psalm

R* Happy the nation whose God is the Lord:
[the people he has chosen for his own].   cf Psalm 33.12

Rejoice in the Lord, O you righteous,
for it is good for the just to sing praises.
Praise the Lord with the lyre;
on the ten-stringed harp sing his praise.   **R**

Sing for him a new song;
play skilfully, with shouts of praise.
For the word of the Lord is true
and all his works are sure.   **R**

He loves righteousness and justice;
the earth is full of the loving-kindness of the Lord.
By the word of the Lord were the heavens made
and all their host by the breath of his mouth.   **R***   Psalm 33.1–6, 12

Year 1 and Year 2

Hear the Gospel of our Lord Jesus Christ according to Luke.

When the crowd gathered in thousands, so that they trampled on one another, Jesus began to speak first to his disciples, 'Beware of the yeast of the Pharisees, that is, their hypocrisy. Nothing is covered up that will not be uncovered, and nothing secret that will not become known. Therefore whatever you have said in the dark will be heard in the light, and what you have whispered behind closed doors will be proclaimed from the housetops.

'I tell you, my friends, do not fear those who kill the body, and after that can do nothing more. But I will warn you whom to fear: fear him who, after he has killed, has authority to cast into hell. Yes, I tell you, fear him! Are not five sparrows sold for two pennies? Yet not one of them is forgotten in God's sight. But even the hairs of your head are all counted. Do not be afraid; you are of more value than many sparrows.'

This is the Gospel of the Lord.   Luke 12.1–7

Week 28: Saturday between 15 and 21 October

Year I

A reading from the Letter of Paul to the Romans.

The promise that he would inherit the world did not come to Abraham or to his descendants through the law but through the righteousness of faith.

For this reason it depends on faith, in order that the promise may rest on grace and be guaranteed to all his descendants, not only to the adherents of the law but also to those who share the faith of Abraham (for he is the father of all of us, as it is written, 'I have made you the father of many nations') – in the presence of the God in whom he believed, who gives life to the dead and calls into existence the things that do not exist. Hoping against hope, he believed that he would become 'the father of many nations', according to what was said, 'So numerous shall your descendants be.'

This is the word of the Lord. Romans 4.13, 16–18

Responsorial Psalm

R* **The Lord remembers his covenant:**
   [the promise he made for a thousand generations]. cf Psalm 105.8

O seed of Abraham his servant,
O children of Jacob his chosen.
He is the Lord our God;
his judgements are in all the earth. **R***

The covenant he made with Abraham,
the oath that he swore to Isaac,
which he established as a statute for Jacob,
an everlasting covenant for Israel. **R**

He opened the rock, and the waters gushed out
and ran in the dry places like a river.
For he remembered his holy word
and Abraham, his servant. **R**

So he brought forth his people with joy,
his chosen ones with singing.
He gave them the lands of the nations
and they took possession of the fruit of their toil. **R**

Psalm 105.6–10, 41–44

A reading from the Letter of Paul to the Ephesians.

I have heard of your faith in the Lord Jesus and your love towards all the saints, and for this reason I do not cease to give thanks for you as I remember you in my prayers. I pray that the God of our Lord Jesus Christ, the Father of glory, may give you a spirit of wisdom and revelation as you come to know him, so that, with the eyes of your heart enlightened, you may know what is the hope to which he has called you, what are the riches of his glorious inheritance among the saints, and what is the immeasurable greatness of his power for us who believe, according to the working of his great power. God put this power to work in Christ when he raised him from the dead and seated him at his right hand in the heavenly places, far above all rule and authority and power and dominion, and above every name that is named, not only in this age but also in the age to come. And he has put all things under his feet and has made him the head over all things for the church, which is his body, the fullness of him who fills all in all.

This is the word of the Lord.   *Ephesians* 1.15–end

Responsorial Psalm

R* **O Lord our governor,
        how glorious is your name in all the world!**   *Psalm* 8.1

Your majesty above the heavens is praised
out of the mouths of babes at the breast.
You have founded a stronghold against your foes,
that you might still the enemy and the avenger.   **R**

When I consider your heavens, the work of your fingers,
the moon and the stars that you have ordained,
what is man, that you should be mindful of him;
the son of man, that you should seek him out?   **R**

You have made him little lower than the angels
and crown him with glory and honour.
You have given him dominion over the works of your hands
and put all things under his feet.   **R**

All sheep and oxen,
even the wild beasts of the field,
the birds of the air, the fish of the sea
and whatsoever moves in the paths of the sea.   **R**   *Psalm* 8

Year 1 and Year 2

Hear the Gospel of our Lord Jesus Christ according to Luke.

Jesus said to his disciples, 'I tell you, everyone who acknowledges me before others, the Son of Man also will acknowledge before the angels of God; but whoever denies me before others will be denied before the angels of God. And everyone who speaks a word against the Son of Man will be forgiven; but whoever blasphemes against the Holy Spirit will not be forgiven. When they bring you before the synagogues, the rulers, and the authorities, do not worry about how you are to defend yourselves or what you are to say; for the Holy Spirit will teach you at that very hour what you ought to say.'

This is the Gospel of the Lord. Luke 12.8–12

Week 29: Monday between 17 and 23 October

Year 1

A reading from the Letter of Paul to the Romans.

No distrust made Abraham waver concerning the promise of God, but he grew strong in his faith as he gave glory to God, being fully convinced that God was able to do what he had promised. Therefore his faith 'was reckoned to him as righteousness.' Now the words, 'it was reckoned to him', were written not for his sake alone, but for ours also. It will be reckoned to us who believe in him who raised Jesus our Lord from the dead, who was handed over to death for our trespasses and was raised for our justification.

This is the word of the Lord. *Romans 4.20—end*

Canticle

R **Blessed be the Lord the God of Israel,**
   who has come to his people and set them free. *Luke 1.68*

Blessed be the Lord the God of Israel,
who has come to his people and set them free.
He has raised up for us a mighty saviour
born of the house of his servant David. **R**

Through his holy prophets God promised of old
to save us from our enemies,
from the hand of all that hate us,
to show mercy to our ancestors,
and to remember his holy covenant. **R**

This was the oath God swore to our father Abraham:
to set us free from the hands of our enemies,
free to worship him without fear,
holy and righteous in his sight
all the days of our life. **R** *Luke 1.68—73*

Year 2

A reading from the Letter of Paul to the Ephesians.

You were dead through the trespasses and sins in which you once lived, following the course of this world, following the ruler of the power of the air, the spirit that is now at work among those who are disobedient. All of us once lived among them in the passions of our flesh, following the desires of flesh and senses, and we were by nature children of wrath, like everyone else. But God, who is rich in mercy, out of the great love with which he loved us even when we were dead through our trespasses, made us alive together with Christ – by grace you have been saved – and raised us up with him and seated us with him in the heavenly places in Christ Jesus, so that in the ages to come he might show the immeasurable riches of his grace in kindness towards us in Christ Jesus. For by grace you have been saved through faith, and this is not your own doing; it is the gift of God – not the result of works, so that no one may boast. For we are what he has made us, created in Christ Jesus for good works, which God prepared beforehand to be our way of life.

This is the word of the Lord. *Ephesians 2.1–10*

Responsorial Psalm

R **Be joyful in the Lord, all the earth:**
   [give thanks and bless his name]. *cf Psalm 100.1a, 3b*

O be joyful in the Lord, all the earth;
serve the Lord with gladness
and come before his presence with a song.   R

Know that the Lord is God;
it is he that has made us and we are his;
we are his people and the sheep of his pasture.   R

Enter his gates with thanksgiving
and his courts with praise;
give thanks to him and bless his name.   R

For the Lord is gracious;
his steadfast love is everlasting,
and his faithfulness endures from generation to generation.   R

Psalm 100

Year 1 and Year 2

Hear the Gospel of our Lord Jesus Christ according to Luke.

Someone in the crowd said to Jesus, 'Teacher, tell my brother to divide the family inheritance with me.' But he said to him, 'Friend, who set me to be a judge or arbitrator over you?' And he said to them, 'Take care! Be on your guard against all kinds of greed; for one's life does not consist in the abundance of possessions.'

Then he told them a parable: 'The land of a rich man produced abundantly. And he thought to himself, "What should I do, for I have no place to store my crops?" Then he said, "I will do this: I will pull down my barns and build larger ones, and there I will store all my grain and my goods. And I will say to my soul, Soul, you have ample goods laid up for many years; relax, eat, drink, be merry." But God said to him, "You fool! This very night your life is being demanded of you. And the things you have prepared, whose will they be?" So it is with those who store up treasures for themselves but are not rich towards God.'

This is the Gospel of the Lord. *Luke 12.13–21*

Week 29: Tuesday between 18 and 24 October

Year I

A reading from the Letter of Paul to the Romans.

Sin came into the world through one man, and death came through sin, and so death spread to all because all have sinned.

But the free gift is not like the trespass. For if the many died through the one man's trespass, much more surely have the grace of God and the free gift in the grace of the one man, Jesus Christ, abounded for the many. If, because of the one man's trespass, death exercised dominion through that one, much more surely will those who receive the abundance of grace and the free gift of righteousness exercise dominion in life through the one man, Jesus Christ.

Therefore just as one man's trespass led to condemnation for all, so one man's act of righteousness leads to justification and life for all. For just as by the one man's disobedience the many were made sinners, so by the one man's obedience the many will be made righteous. But law came in, with the result that the trespass multiplied; but where sin increased, grace abounded all the more, so that, just as sin exercised dominion in death, so grace might also exercise dominion through justification leading to eternal life through Jesus Christ our Lord.

This is the word of the Lord.   Romans 5.12, 15, 17–end

Responsorial Psalm

R* **Have compassion on me, O Lord;**
  guard me with your love and faithfulness.   Psalm 40.12

Sacrifice and offering you do not desire
but my ears you have opened;
burnt offering and sacrifice for sin
you have not required.   **R**

Then said I: 'Lo, I come.
In the scroll of the book it is written of me
that I should do your will, O my God;
I delight to do it: your law is within my heart.'   **R**

I have declared your righteousness in the great congregation;
behold, I did not restrain my lips,
and that, O Lord, you know.   **R**

Your righteousness I have not hidden in my heart;
I have spoken of your faithfulness and your salvation;
I have not concealed your loving-kindness and truth
from the great congregation.   **R***   Psalm 40.7–12

A reading from the Letter of Paul to the Ephesians.

Remember that you were at that time without Christ, being aliens from the commonwealth of Israel, and strangers to the covenants of promise, having no hope and without God in the world. But now in Christ Jesus you who once were far off have been brought near by the blood of Christ. For he is our peace; in his flesh he has made both groups into one and has broken down the dividing wall, that is, the hostility between us. He has abolished the law with its commandments and ordinances, so that he might create in himself one new humanity in place of the two, thus making peace, and might reconcile both groups to God in one body through the cross, thus putting to death that hostility through it. So he came and proclaimed peace to you who were far off and peace to those who were near; for through him both of us have access in one Spirit to the Father. So then you are no longer strangers and aliens, but you are citizens with the saints and also members of the household of God, built upon the foundation of the apostles and prophets, with Christ Jesus himself as the cornerstone. In him the whole structure is joined together and grows into a holy temple in the Lord; in whom you also are built together spiritually into a dwelling-place for God.

This is the word of the Lord.   *Ephesians 2.12—end*

Responsorial Psalm

R **The Lord was gracious to his land;**
   and restored the fortunes of Jacob.   *cf Psalm 85.1*

Show us your mercy, O Lord,
and grant us your salvation.
I will listen
to what the Lord God will say.   **R**

For he shall speak peace to his people and to the faithful,
that they turn not again to folly.
Truly, his salvation is near to those who fear him,
that his glory may dwell in our land.   **R**

Mercy and truth are met together,
righteousness and peace have kissed each other.
Truth shall spring up from the earth
and righteousness look down from heaven.   **R**

The Lord will indeed give all that is good,
and our land will yield its increase.
Righteousness shall go before him
and direct his steps in the way.   **R**   *Psalm 85.7—end*

Year 1 and Year 2

Hear the Gospel of our Lord Jesus Christ according to Luke.

Jesus said to his disciples, 'Be dressed for action and have your lamps lit; be like those who are waiting for their master to return from the wedding banquet, so that they may open the door for him as soon as he comes and knocks. Blessed are those slaves whom the master finds alert when he comes; truly I tell you, he will fasten his belt and have them sit down to eat, and he will come and serve them. If he comes during the middle of the night, or near dawn, and finds them so, blessed are those slaves.'

This is the Gospel of the Lord.   Luke 12.35–38

Week 29: Wednesday between 19 and 25 October

Year 1

A reading from the Letter of Paul to the Romans.

Do not let sin exercise dominion in your mortal bodies, to make you obey their passions. No longer present your members to sin as instruments of wickedness, but present yourselves to God as those who have been brought from death to life, and present your members to God as instruments of righteousness. For sin will have no dominion over you, since you are not under law but under grace.

What then? Should we sin because we are not under law but under grace? By no means! Do you not know that if you present yourselves to anyone as obedient slaves, you are slaves of the one whom you obey, either of sin, which leads to death, or of obedience, which leads to righteousness? But thanks be to God that you, having once been slaves of sin, have become obedient from the heart to the form of teaching to which you were entrusted, and that you, having been set free from sin, have become slaves of righteousness.

This is the word of the Lord.   Romans 6.12–18

Responsorial Psalm

R* **Our help is in the name of the Lord,**
   [who has made heaven and earth].   Psalm 124.7

If the Lord himself had not been on our side,
now may Israel say;
if the Lord had not been on our side,
when enemies rose up against us.   **R**

Then would they have swallowed us alive
when their anger burned against us;
then would the waters have overwhelmed us
and the torrent gone over our soul;
over our soul would have swept the raging waters.   R

But blessed be the Lord
who has not given us over to be a prey for their teeth.
Our soul has escaped
as a bird from the snare of the fowler;
the snare is broken and we are delivered.   R*   Psalm 124

Year 2

A reading from the Letter of Paul to the Ephesians.

Surely you have already heard of the commission of God's grace that was given
to me for you, and how the mystery was made known to me by revelation, as
I wrote above in a few words, a reading of which will enable you to perceive
my understanding of the mystery of Christ. In former generations this mystery
was not made known to humankind, as it has now been revealed to his holy
apostles and prophets by the Spirit: that is, the Gentiles have become fellow-
heirs, members of the same body, and sharers in the promise in Christ Jesus
through the gospel.

Of this gospel I have become a servant according to the gift of God's grace
that was given to me by the working of his power. Although I am the very least
of all the saints, this grace was given to me to bring to the Gentiles the news
of the boundless riches of Christ, and to make everyone see what is the plan
of the mystery hidden for ages in God who created all things; so that through
the church the wisdom of God in its rich variety might now be made known
to the rulers and authorities in the heavenly places. This was in accordance with
the eternal purpose that he has carried out in Christ Jesus our Lord, in whom
we have access to God in boldness and confidence through faith in him.

This is the word of the Lord.   Ephesians 3.2–12

Responsorial Psalm

R* **Sound praises to the Lord, all the earth;
[break into song and make music].**   cf Psalm 98.5

Sing to the Lord a new song,
for he has done marvellous things.
His own right hand and his holy arm
have won for him the victory.   R

The Lord has made known his salvation;
his deliverance has he openly shown
in the sight of the nations.   R   →

He has remembered his mercy and faithfulness
towards the house of Israel,
and all the ends of the earth have seen
the salvation of our God.   R*

R* **Sound praises to the Lord, all the earth;
[break into song and make music].**

Make music to the Lord with the lyre,
with the lyre and the voice of melody.
With trumpets and the sound of the horn
sound praises before the Lord, the King.   R

Let the sea thunder and all that fills it,
the world and all that dwell upon it.
Let the rivers clap their hands
and let the hills ring out together before the Lord.   R

For he comes to judge the earth:
in righteousness shall he judge the world
and the peoples with equity.   R   Psalm 98

Year 1 and Year 2

Hear the Gospel of our Lord Jesus Christ according to Luke.

Jesus said to his disciples, 'Know this: if the owner of the house had known
at what hour the thief was coming, he would not have let his house be
broken into. You also must be ready, for the Son of Man is coming at an
unexpected hour.'

Peter said, 'Lord, are you telling this parable for us or for everyone?' And
the Lord said, 'Who then is the faithful and prudent manager whom his master
will put in charge of his slaves, to give them their allowance of food at the
proper time? Blessed is that slave whom his master will find at work when
he arrives. Truly I tell you, he will put that one in charge of all his possessions.
But if that slave says to himself, "My master is delayed in coming", and if he
begins to beat the other slaves, men and women, and to eat and drink and get
drunk, the master of that slave will come on a day when he does not expect
him and at an hour that he does not know, and will cut him in pieces, and
put him with the unfaithful. That slave who knew what his master wanted, but
did not prepare himself or do what was wanted, will receive a severe beating.
But one who did not know and did what deserved a beating will receive a
light beating. From everyone to whom much has been given, much will be
required; and from one to whom much has been entrusted, even more will
be demanded.'

This is the Gospel of the Lord.   Luke 12.39–48

Week 29: Thursday between 20 and 26 October

Year 1

A reading from the Letter of Paul to the Romans.

I am speaking in human terms because of your natural limitations. For just as you once presented your members as slaves to impurity and to greater and greater iniquity, so now present your members as slaves to righteousness for sanctification.

When you were slaves of sin, you were free in regard to righteousness. So what advantage did you then get from the things of which you now are ashamed? The end of those things is death. But now that you have been freed from sin and enslaved to God, the advantage you get is sanctification. The end is eternal life. For the wages of sin is death, but the free gift of God is eternal life in Christ Jesus our Lord.

This is the word of the Lord. Romans 6.19–end

Responsorial Psalm

R **The Lord knows the way of the righteous;**
[who delight in his law]. cf Psalm 1.6a, 2a

Blessed are they who have not walked
in the counsel of the wicked,
nor lingered in the way of sinners,
nor sat in the assembly of the scornful.
Their delight is in the law of the Lord
and they meditate on his law day and night.   R

Like a tree planted by streams of water
bearing fruit in due season,
with leaves that do not wither,
whatever they do, it shall prosper.   R

As for the wicked, it is not so with them;
they are like chaff which the wind blows away.
Therefore the wicked shall not be able to stand in the judgement,
nor the sinner in the congregation of the righteous.
For the Lord knows the way of the righteous,
but the way of the wicked shall perish.   R Psalm 1

Year 2

A reading from the Letter of Paul to the Ephesians.

I bow my knees before the Father, from whom every family in heaven and on earth takes its name. I pray that, according to the riches of his glory, he may grant that you may be strengthened in your inner being with power through →

his Spirit, and that Christ may dwell in your hearts through faith, as you are being rooted and grounded in love. I pray that you may have the power to comprehend, with all the saints, what is the breadth and length and height and depth, and to know the love of Christ that surpasses knowledge, so that you may be filled with all the fullness of God.

Now to him who by the power at work within us is able to accomplish abundantly far more than all we can ask or imagine, to him be glory in the church and in Christ Jesus to all generations, for ever and ever. Amen.

This is the word of the Lord. *Ephesians 3.14–end*

Responsorial Psalm

R **Rejoice in the Lord, O you righteous:**
   [it is good to sing his praises]. *cf Psalm 33.1*

Rejoice in the Lord, O you righteous,
for it is good for the just to sing praises.
Praise the Lord with the lyre;
on the ten-stringed harp sing his praise.   **R**

Sing for him a new song;
play skilfully, with shouts of praise.
For the word of the Lord is true
and all his works are sure.   **R**

He loves righteousness and justice;
the earth is full of the loving-kindness of the Lord.
By the word of the Lord were the heavens made
and all their host by the breath of his mouth.   **R** *Psalm 33.1–6*

Year 1 and Year 2

Hear the Gospel of our Lord Jesus Christ according to Luke.

Jesus said to his disciples, 'I came to bring fire to the earth, and how I wish it were already kindled! I have a baptism with which to be baptized, and what stress I am under until it is completed! Do you think that I have come to bring peace to the earth? No, I tell you, but rather division! From now on, five in one household will be divided, three against two and two against three; they will be divided:
     father against son
          and son against father,
     mother against daughter
          and daughter against mother,
     mother-in-law against her daughter-in-law
          and daughter-in-law against mother-in-law.'

This is the Gospel of the Lord. *Luke 12.49–53*

Week 29: Friday between 21 and 27 October

Year 1

A reading from the Letter of Paul to the Romans.

I know that nothing good dwells within me, that is, in my flesh. I can will what is right, but I cannot do it. For I do not do the good I want, but the evil I do not want is what I do. Now if I do what I do not want, it is no longer I that do it, but sin that dwells within me.

So I find it to be a law that when I want to do what is good, evil lies close at hand. For I delight in the law of God in my inmost self, but I see in my members another law at war with the law of my mind, making me captive to the law of sin that dwells in my members. Wretched man that I am! Who will rescue me from this body of death? Thanks be to God through Jesus Christ our Lord!

So then, with my mind I am a slave to the law of God, but with my flesh I am a slave to the law of sin.

This is the word of the Lord.   Romans 7.18–end

Responsorial Psalm

R **Teach me, O Lord, the way of your statutes:**
   [lead me in the path of your commandments].   Psalm 119.33a, 35a

Teach me, O Lord, the way of your statutes
and I shall keep it to the end.
Give me understanding and I shall keep your law;
I shall keep it with my whole heart.   **R**

Lead me in the path of your commandments,
for therein is my delight.
Incline my heart to your testimonies
and not to unjust gain.   **R**

Turn away my eyes lest they gaze on vanities;
O give me life in your ways.
Confirm to your servant your promise,
which stands for all who fear you.   **R**

Turn away the reproach which I dread,
because your judgements are good.
Behold, I long for your commandments;
in your righteousness give me life.   **R**   Psalm 119.33–40

Year 2

A reading from the Letter of Paul to the Ephesians.

I, the prisoner in the Lord, beg you to lead a life worthy of the calling to which you have been called, with all humility and gentleness, with patience, bearing with one another in love, making every effort to maintain the unity of the Spirit in the bond of peace. There is one body and one Spirit, just as you were called to the one hope of your calling, one Lord, one faith, one baptism, one God and Father of all, who is above all and through all and in all.

This is the word of the Lord. *Ephesians 4.1–6*

Responsorial Psalm

R **The earth is the Lord's, and all who dwell therein.** *cf Psalm 24.1*

The earth is the Lord's and all that fills it,
the compass of the world and all who dwell therein.
For he has founded it upon the seas
and set it firm upon the rivers of the deep. R

'Who shall ascend the hill of the Lord,
or who can rise up in his holy place?
Those who have clean hands and a pure heart,
who have not lifted up their soul to an idol,
nor sworn an oath to a lie. R

'They shall receive a blessing from the Lord,
a just reward from the God of their salvation.'
Such is the company of those who seek him,
of those who seek your face, O God of Jacob. R *Psalm 24.1–6*

Year 1 and Year 2

Hear the Gospel of our Lord Jesus Christ according to Luke.

Jesus said to the crowds, 'When you see a cloud rising in the west, you immediately say, "It is going to rain"; and so it happens. And when you see the south wind blowing, you say, "There will be scorching heat"; and it happens. You hypocrites! You know how to interpret the appearance of earth and sky, but why do you not know how to interpret the present time?

'And why do you not judge for yourselves what is right? Thus, when you go with your accuser before a magistrate, on the way make an effort to settle the case, or you may be dragged before the judge, and the judge hand you over to the officer, and the officer throw you in prison. I tell you, you will never get out until you have paid the very last penny.'

This is the Gospel of the Lord. *Luke 12.54–end*

Week 29: Saturday between 22 and 28 October

Year I

A reading from the Letter of Paul to the Romans.

There is now no condemnation for those who are in Christ Jesus. For the law of the Spirit of life in Christ Jesus has set you free from the law of sin and of death. For God has done what the law, weakened by the flesh, could not do: by sending his own Son in the likeness of sinful flesh, and to deal with sin, he condemned sin in the flesh, so that the just requirement of the law might be fulfilled in us, who walk not according to the flesh but according to the Spirit. For those who live according to the flesh set their minds on the things of the flesh, but those who live according to the Spirit set their minds on the things of the Spirit. To set the mind on the flesh is death, but to set the mind on the Spirit is life and peace. For this reason the mind that is set on the flesh is hostile to God; it does not submit to God's law – indeed it cannot, and those who are in the flesh cannot please God.

But you are not in the flesh; you are in the Spirit, since the Spirit of God dwells in you. Anyone who does not have the Spirit of Christ does not belong to him. But if Christ is in you, though the body is dead because of sin, the Spirit is life because of righteousness. If the Spirit of him who raised Jesus from the dead dwells in you, he who raised Christ from the dead will give life to your mortal bodies also through his Spirit that dwells in you.

This is the word of the Lord.   Romans 8.1–11

Responsorial Psalm

R   **The earth is the Lord's, and all who dwell therein.**   cf Psalm 24.1

The earth is the Lord's and all that fills it,
the compass of the world and all who dwell therein.
For he has founded it upon the seas
and set it firm upon the rivers of the deep.   **R**

'Who shall ascend the hill of the Lord,
or who can rise up in his holy place?
Those who have clean hands and a pure heart,
who have not lifted up their soul to an idol,
nor sworn an oath to a lie.   **R**

'They shall receive a blessing from the Lord,
a just reward from the God of their salvation.'
Such is the company of those who seek him,
of those who seek your face, O God of Jacob.   **R**   Psalm 24.1–6

A reading from the Letter of Paul to the Ephesians.

Each of us was given grace according to the measure of Christ's gift. Therefore it is said,

> 'When he ascended on high he made captivity itself a captive;
>> he gave gifts to his people.'

(When it says, 'he ascended', what does it mean but that he had also descended into the lower parts of the earth? He who descended is the same one who ascended far above all the heavens, so that he might fill all things.) The gifts he gave were that some would be apostles, some prophets, some evangelists, some pastors and teachers, to equip the saints for the work of ministry, for building up the body of Christ, until all of us come to the unity of the faith and of the knowledge of the Son of God, to maturity, to the measure of the full stature of Christ. We must no longer be children, tossed to and fro and blown about by every wind of doctrine, by people's trickery, by their craftiness in deceitful scheming. But speaking the truth in love, we must grow up in every way into him who is the head, into Christ, from whom the whole body, joined and knitted together by every ligament with which it is equipped, as each part is working properly, promotes the body's growth in building itself up in love.

This is the word of the Lord.   Ephesians 4.7–16

Responsorial Psalm

R **[I was glad when they said to me:]**
   Let us go to the house of the Lord.   Psalm 122.1

I was glad when they said to me,
'Let us go to the house of the Lord.'
And now our feet are standing
within your gates, O Jerusalem.   R

Jerusalem, built as a city
that is at unity in itself.
Thither the tribes go up,
the tribes of the Lord.   R

As is decreed for Israel,
to give thanks to the name of the Lord.
For there are set the thrones of judgement,
the thrones of the house of David.   R

O pray for the peace of Jerusalem:
'May they prosper who love you.
Peace be within your walls
and tranquillity within your palaces.'   R

For my kindred and companions' sake,
I will pray that peace be with you.
For the sake of the house of the Lord our God,
I will seek to do you good.   R   Psalm 122

Year 1 and Year 2

Hear the Gospel of our Lord Jesus Christ according to Luke.

There were some present who told Jesus about the Galileans whose blood
Pilate had mingled with their sacrifices. He asked them, 'Do you think that
because these Galileans suffered in this way they were worse sinners than all
other Galileans? No, I tell you; but unless you repent, you will all perish as
they did. Or those eighteen who were killed when the tower of Siloam fell
on them – do you think that they were worse offenders than all the others
living in Jerusalem? No, I tell you; but unless you repent, you will all perish
just as they did.'

Then he told this parable: 'A man had a fig tree planted in his vineyard;
and he came looking for fruit on it and found none. So he said to the gardener,
"See here! For three years I have come looking for fruit on this fig tree, and
still I find none. Cut it down! Why should it be wasting the soil?" He replied,
"Sir, let it alone for one more year, until I dig round it and put manure on it.
If it bears fruit next year, well and good; but if not, you can cut it down." '

This is the Gospel of the Lord.   Luke 13.1–9

Week 30: Monday between 24 and 30 October

Year 1

A reading from the Letter of Paul to the Romans.

So then, brothers and sisters, we are debtors, not to the flesh, to live according to the flesh – for if you live according to the flesh, you will die; but if by the Spirit you put to death the deeds of the body, you will live. For all who are led by the Spirit of God are children of God. For you did not receive a spirit of slavery to fall back into fear, but you have received a spirit of adoption. When we cry, 'Abba! Father!' it is that very Spirit bearing witness with our spirit that we are children of God, and if children, then heirs, heirs of God and joint heirs with Christ – if, in fact, we suffer with him so that we may also be glorified with him.

This is the word of the Lord. Romans 8.12–17

Responsorial Psalm

R* **God is the God of our salvation;**
 [the Lord who delivers from death]. cf Psalm 68.19

Let God arise and let his enemies be scattered;
let those that hate him flee before him.
As the smoke vanishes, so may they vanish away;
as wax melts at the fire,
so let the wicked perish at the presence of God.   R

But let the righteous be glad and rejoice before God;
let them make merry with gladness.
Sing to God, sing praises to his name;
exalt him who rides on the clouds.
The Lord is his name; rejoice before him.   R

Father of the fatherless, defender of widows,
God in his holy habitation!
God gives the solitary a home
and brings forth prisoners to songs of welcome,
but the rebellious inhabit a burning desert.   R* Psalm 68.1–6, 19

Year 2

A reading from the Letter of Paul to the Ephesians.

Be kind to one another, tender-hearted, forgiving one another, as God in Christ has forgiven you. Therefore be imitators of God, as beloved children, and live in love, as Christ loved us and gave himself up for us, a fragrant offering and sacrifice to God.

But fornication and impurity of any kind, or greed, must not even be mentioned among you, as is proper among saints. Entirely out of place is obscene, silly, and vulgar talk; but instead, let there be thanksgiving. Be sure of this, that no fornicator or impure person, or one who is greedy (that is, an idolater), has any inheritance in the kingdom of Christ and of God.

Let no one deceive you with empty words, for because of these things the wrath of God comes on those who are disobedient. Therefore do not be associated with them. For once you were darkness, but now in the Lord you are light. Live as children of light.

This is the word of the Lord.   Ephesians 4.32 – 5.8

Responsorial Psalm

R **The Lord knows the way of the righteous;
   [who delight in his law].**   cf Psalm 1.6a, 2a

Blessed are they who have not walked
in the counsel of the wicked,
nor lingered in the way of sinners,
nor sat in the assembly of the scornful.
Their delight is in the law of the Lord
and they meditate on his law day and night.   **R**

Like a tree planted by streams of water
bearing fruit in due season,
with leaves that do not wither,
whatever they do, it shall prosper.   **R**

As for the wicked, it is not so with them;
they are like chaff which the wind blows away.
Therefore the wicked shall not be able to stand in the judgement,
nor the sinner in the congregation of the righteous.
For the Lord knows the way of the righteous,
but the way of the wicked shall perish.   **R**   Psalm 1

Hear the Gospel of our Lord Jesus Christ according to Luke.

Jesus was teaching in one of the synagogues on the sabbath. And just then there appeared a woman with a spirit that had crippled her for eighteen years. She was bent over and was quite unable to stand up straight. When Jesus saw her, he called her over and said, 'Woman, you are set free from your ailment.' When he laid his hands on her, immediately she stood up straight and began praising God.

But the leader of the synagogue, indignant because Jesus had cured on the sabbath, kept saying to the crowd, 'There are six days on which work ought to be done; come on those days and be cured, and not on the sabbath day.' But the Lord answered him and said, 'You hypocrites! Does not each of you on the sabbath untie his ox or his donkey from the manger, and lead it away to give it water? And ought not this woman, a daughter of Abraham whom Satan bound for eighteen long years, be set free from this bondage on the sabbath day?' When he said this, all his opponents were put to shame; and the entire crowd was rejoicing at all the wonderful things that he was doing.

This is the Gospel of the Lord.   Luke 13.10–17

Week 30: Tuesday between 25 and 31 October

Year 1

A reading from the Letter of Paul to the Romans.

I consider that the sufferings of this present time are not worth comparing with the glory about to be revealed to us. For the creation waits with eager longing for the revealing of the children of God; for the creation was subjected to futility, not of its own will but by the will of the one who subjected it, in hope that the creation itself will be set free from its bondage to decay and will obtain the freedom of the glory of the children of God. We know that the whole creation has been groaning in labour pains until now; and not only the creation, but we ourselves, who have the first fruits of the Spirit, groan inwardly while we wait for adoption, the redemption of our bodies. For in hope we were saved. Now hope that is seen is not hope. For who hopes for what is seen? But if we hope for what we do not see, we wait for it with patience.

This is the word of the Lord.   Romans 8.18–25

R **Those who sow in tears
   shall reap with songs of joy.**   Psalm 126.6

When the Lord restored the fortunes of Zion,
then were we like those who dream.
Then was our mouth filled with laughter
and our tongue with songs of joy.   **R**

Then said they among the nations,
'The Lord has done great things for them.'
The Lord has indeed done great things for us,
and therefore we rejoiced.   **R**

Restore again our fortunes, O Lord,
as the river beds of the desert.
Those who sow in tears
shall reap with songs of joy.   **R**

Those who go out weeping, bearing the seed,
will come back with shouts of joy,
bearing their sheaves with them.   **R**   Psalm 126

Year 2

A reading from the Letter of Paul to the Ephesians.

Be subject to one another out of reverence for Christ. Wives, be subject to your husbands as you are to the Lord. For the husband is the head of the wife just as Christ is the head of the church, the body of which he is the Saviour. Just as the church is subject to Christ, so also wives ought to be, in everything, to their husbands.

Husbands, love your wives, just as Christ loved the church and gave himself up for her, in order to make her holy by cleansing her with the washing of water by the word, so as to present the church to himself in splendour, without a spot or wrinkle or anything of the kind – yes, so that she may be holy and without blemish. In the same way, husbands should love their wives as they do their own bodies. He who loves his wife loves himself. For no one ever hates his own body, but he nourishes and tenderly cares for it, just as Christ does for the church, because we are members of his body. 'For this reason a man will leave his father and mother and be joined to his wife, and the two will become one flesh.' This is a great mystery, and I am applying it to Christ and the church. Each of you, however, should love his wife as himself, and a wife should respect her husband.

This is the word of the Lord.   Ephesians 5.21–end

Responsorial Psalm

R **Blessed are those who fear the Lord,
[and walk in the ways of God].**   cf Psalm 128.1

Blessed are all those who fear the Lord,
and walk in his ways.
You shall eat the fruit of the toil of your hands;
it shall go well with you,
and happy shall you be.   R

Your wife within your house
shall be like a fruitful vine;
your children round your table,
like fresh olive branches.
Thus shall the one be blest who fears the Lord.   R

The Lord from out of Zion bless you,
that you may see Jerusalem in prosperity
all the days of your life.
May you see your children's children,
and may there be peace upon Israel.   R   Psalm 128

Year 1 and Year 2

Hear the Gospel of our Lord Jesus Christ according to Luke.

Jesus said to the crowd, 'What is the kingdom of God like? And to what
should I compare it? It is like a mustard seed that someone took and sowed
in the garden; it grew and became a tree, and the birds of the air made nests
in its branches.'

   And again he said, 'To what should I compare the kingdom of God? It is
like yeast that a woman took and mixed in with three measures of flour until
all of it was leavened.'

This is the Gospel of the Lord.   Luke 13.18–21

Week 30: Wednesday between 26 October and 1 November

Year 1

A reading from the Letter of Paul to the Romans.

The Spirit helps us in our weakness; for we do not know how to pray as we
ought, but that very Spirit intercedes with sighs too deep for words. And God,
who searches the heart, knows what is the mind of the Spirit, because the
Spirit intercedes for the saints according to the will of God.

   We know that all things work together for good for those who love God,
who are called according to his purpose. For those whom he foreknew he
also predestined to be conformed to the image of his Son, in order that he

might be the firstborn within a large family. And those whom he predestined he also called; and those whom he called he also justified; and those whom he justified he also glorified.

This is the word of the Lord. Romans 8.26–30

Responsorial Psalm

R **I trust in your steadfast love,**
and my heart rejoices in your salvation. cf Psalm 13.5

How long will you forget me, O Lord; for ever?
How long will you hide your face from me?
How long shall I have anguish in my soul
and grief in my heart, day after day?   R

How long shall my enemy triumph over me?
Look upon me and answer, O Lord my God;
lighten my eyes, lest I sleep in death;
lest my enemy say, 'I have prevailed against him,'
and my foes rejoice that I have fallen.   R

But I put my trust in your steadfast love;
my heart will rejoice in your salvation.
I will sing to the Lord,
for he has dealt so bountifully with me.   R Psalm 13

Year 2

A reading from the Letter of Paul to the Ephesians.

Children, obey your parents in the Lord, for this is right. 'Honour your father and mother' – this is the first commandment with a promise: 'so that it may be well with you and you may live long on the earth.'

And, fathers, do not provoke your children to anger, but bring them up in the discipline and instruction of the Lord.

Slaves, obey your earthly masters with fear and trembling, in singleness of heart, as you obey Christ; not only while being watched, and in order to please them, but as slaves of Christ, doing the will of God from the heart. Render service with enthusiasm, as to the Lord and not to men and women, knowing that whatever good we do, we will receive the same again from the Lord, whether we are slaves or free.

And, masters, do the same to them. Stop threatening them, for you know that both of you have the same Master in heaven, and with him there is no partiality.

This is the word of the Lord. Ephesians 6.1–9

R* **The Lord is righteous in all his ways**
and loving in all his works. *Psalm 145.18*

All your works praise you, O Lord,
and your faithful servants bless you.
They tell of the glory of your kingdom
and speak of your mighty power. **R**

To make known to all peoples your mighty acts
and the glorious splendour of your kingdom.
Your kingdom is an everlasting kingdom;
your dominion endures throughout all ages. **R**

The Lord is sure in all his words
and faithful in all his deeds.
The Lord upholds all those who fall
and lifts up all those who are bowed down. **R**

The eyes of all wait upon you, O Lord,
and you give them their food in due season.
You open wide your hand
and fill all things living with plenty. **R***

The Lord is near to those who call upon him,
to all who call upon him faithfully.
He fulfils the desire of those who fear him;
he hears their cry and saves them. **R** *Psalm 145.10–20*

Year I and Year 2

Hear the Gospel of our Lord Jesus Christ according to Luke.

Jesus went through one town and village after another, teaching as he made
his way to Jerusalem. Someone asked him, 'Lord, will only a few be saved?'
He said to them, 'Strive to enter through the narrow door; for many, I tell
you, will try to enter and will not be able. When once the owner of the house
has got up and shut the door, and you begin to stand outside and to knock
at the door, saying, "Lord, open to us", then in reply he will say to you, "I do
not know where you come from." Then you will begin to say, "We ate and
drank with you, and you taught in our streets." But he will say, "I do not know
where you come from; go away from me, all you evildoers!" There will be
weeping and gnashing of teeth when you see Abraham and Isaac and Jacob
and all the prophets in the kingdom of God, and you yourselves thrown out.
Then people will come from east and west, from north and south, and will
eat in the kingdom of God. Indeed, some are last who will be first, and some
are first who will be last.'

This is the Gospel of the Lord. *Luke 13.22–30*

Week 30: Thursday between 27 October and 2 November

Year I

A reading from the Letter of Paul to the Romans.

What then are we to say about these things? If God is for us, who is against us? He who did not withhold his own Son, but gave him up for all of us, will he not with him also give us everything else? Who will bring any charge against God's elect? It is God who justifies. Who is to condemn? It is Christ Jesus, who died, yes, who was raised, who is at the right hand of God, who indeed intercedes for us. Who will separate us from the love of Christ? Will hardship, or distress, or persecution, or famine, or nakedness, or peril, or sword? As it is written,

'For your sake we are being killed all day long;
we are accounted as sheep to be slaughtered.'

No, in all these things we are more than conquerors through him who loved us. For I am convinced that neither death, nor life, nor angels, nor rulers, nor things present, nor things to come, nor powers, nor height, nor depth, nor anything else in all creation, will be able to separate us from the love of God in Christ Jesus our Lord.

This is the word of the Lord.   Romans 8.31–end

Responsorial Psalm

R* **Help me, O Lord my God,
and save me for your mercy's sake.**   cf Psalm 109.25

Deal with me, O Lord my God, according to your name;
O deliver me, for sweet is your faithfulness.
For I am helpless and poor
and my heart is disquieted within me.   **R**

I fade like a shadow that lengthens;
I am shaken off like a locust.
My knees are weak through fasting
and my flesh is dried up and wasted.   **R**

I have become a reproach to them;
those who see me shake their heads in scorn.*
And they shall know that this is your hand,
that you, O Lord, have done it.   **R**

I will give great thanks to the Lord with my mouth;
in the midst of the multitude will I praise him;
because he has stood at the right hand of the needy,
to save them from those who would condemn them.   **R**

Psalm 109.20–26, 29–30

A reading from the Letter of Paul to the Ephesians.

Be strong in the Lord and in the strength of his power. Put on the whole armour of God, so that you may be able to stand against the wiles of the devil. For our struggle is not against enemies of blood and flesh, but against the rulers, against the authorities, against the cosmic powers of this present darkness, against the spiritual forces of evil in the heavenly places. Therefore take up the whole armour of God, so that you may be able to withstand on that evil day, and having done everything, to stand firm. Stand therefore, and fasten the belt of truth around your waist, and put on the breastplate of righteousness. As shoes for your feet put on whatever will make you ready to proclaim the gospel of peace. With all of these, take the shield of faith, with which you will be able to quench all the flaming arrows of the evil one. Take the helmet of salvation, and the sword of the Spirit, which is the word of God.

Pray in the Spirit at all times in every prayer and supplication. To that end keep alert and always persevere in supplication for all the saints. Pray also for me, so that when I speak, a message may be given to me to make known with boldness the mystery of the gospel, for which I am an ambassador in chains. Pray that I may declare it boldly, as I must speak.

This is the word of the Lord. *Ephesians 6.10–20*

Responsorial Psalm

**R* I will sing a new song to you, O God;
and praise you on a ten-stringed harp.** *cf Psalm 144.9*

Blessed be the Lord my rock,
who teaches my hands for war
and my fingers for battle.   **R**

My steadfast help and my fortress,
my stronghold and my deliverer,
my shield in whom I trust,
who subdues the peoples under me.   **R***

You that give salvation to kings
and have delivered David your servant.
Save me from the peril of the sword
and deliver me from the hand of foreign enemies.   **R**

Psalm 144.1–2, 9–11

Hear the Gospel of our Lord Jesus Christ according to Luke.

Some Pharisees came and said to Jesus, 'Get away from here, for Herod wants to kill you.' He said to them, 'Go and tell that fox for me, "Listen, I am casting out demons and performing cures today and tomorrow, and on the third day I finish my work. Yet today, tomorrow, and the next day I must be on my way, because it is impossible for a prophet to be killed away from Jerusalem." Jerusalem, Jerusalem, the city that kills the prophets and stones those who are sent to it! How often have I desired to gather your children together as a hen gathers her brood under her wings, and you were not willing! See, your house is left to you. And I tell you, you will not see me until the time comes when you say, "Blessed is the one who comes in the name of the Lord." '

This is the Gospel of the Lord.   Luke 13.31–end

Week 30: Friday between 28 October and 3 November

Year 1

A reading from the Letter of Paul to the Romans.

I am speaking the truth in Christ – I am not lying; my conscience confirms it by the Holy Spirit – I have great sorrow and unceasing anguish in my heart. For I could wish that I myself were accursed and cut off from Christ for the sake of my own people, my kindred according to the flesh. They are Israelites, and to them belong the adoption, the glory, the covenants, the giving of the law, the worship, and the promises; to them belong the patriarchs, and from them, according to the flesh, comes the Messiah, who is over all, God blessed for ever. Amen.

This is the word of the Lord.   Romans 9.1–5

Responsorial Psalm

R* **Sing praise to the Lord, O Jerusalem:**
    [praise your God, O Zion].   Psalm 147.13

The Lord has strengthened the bars of your gates
and has blest your children within you.
He has established peace in your borders
and satisfies you with the finest wheat.   **R**

He sends forth his command to the earth
and his word runs very swiftly.
He gives snow like wool
and scatters the hoarfrost like ashes.   **R**   →

He casts down his hailstones like morsels of bread;
who can endure his frost?
He sends forth his word and melts them;
he blows with his wind and the waters flow.   R

R* **Sing praise to the Lord, O Jerusalem:**
   [praise your God, O Zion].

He declares his word to Jacob,
his statutes and judgements to Israel.
He has not dealt so with any other nation;
they do not know his laws.   R   *Psalm 147.13–end*

Year 2

A reading from the Letter of Paul to the Philippians.

Paul and Timothy, servants of Christ Jesus, to all the saints in Christ Jesus
who are in Philippi, with the bishops and deacons: Grace to you and peace
from God our Father and the Lord Jesus Christ.

I thank my God every time I remember you, constantly praying with joy in
every one of my prayers for all of you, because of your sharing in the gospel
from the first day until now. I am confident of this, that the one who began a
good work among you will bring it to completion by the day of Jesus Christ. It
is right for me to think this way about all of you, because you hold me in your
heart, for all of you share in God's grace with me, both in my imprisonment
and in the defence and confirmation of the gospel. For God is my witness,
how I long for all of you with the compassion of Christ Jesus. And this is my
prayer, that your love may overflow more and more with knowledge and full
insight to help you to determine what is best, so that on the day of Christ
you may be pure and blameless, having produced the harvest of righteousness
that comes through Jesus Christ for the glory and praise of God.

This is the word of the Lord.   *Philippians 1.1–11*

Responsorial Psalm

R **The works of God are truth and justice:**
   [he is gracious and full of compassion].   *cf Psalm 111.7a, 4b*

I will give thanks to the Lord with my whole heart,
in the company of the faithful and in the congregation.
The works of the Lord are great,
sought out by all who delight in them.   R

His work is full of majesty and honour
and his righteousness endures for ever.
He appointed a memorial for his marvellous deeds;
the Lord is gracious and full of compassion.   R

He gave food to those who feared him;
he is ever mindful of his covenant.
He showed his people the power of his works
in giving them the heritage of the nations.   R

The works of his hands are truth and justice;
all his commandments are sure.
They stand fast for ever and ever;
they are done in truth and equity.   R

He sent redemption to his people;
he commanded his covenant for ever;
holy and awesome is his name.   R

The fear of the Lord is the beginning of wisdom;
a good understanding have those who live by it;
his praise endures for ever.   R   Psalm 111

Year 1 and Year 2

Hear the Gospel of our Lord Jesus Christ according to Luke.

On one occasion when Jesus was going to the house of a leader of the Pharisees
to eat a meal on the sabbath, they were watching him closely. Just then, in
front of him, there was a man who had dropsy. And Jesus asked the lawyers
and Pharisees, 'Is it lawful to cure people on the sabbath, or not?' But they
were silent. So Jesus took him and healed him, and sent him away. Then he
said to them, 'If one of you has a child or an ox that has fallen into a well,
will you not immediately pull it out on a sabbath day?' And they could not
reply to this.

This is the Gospel of the Lord.   Luke 14.1—6

Week 30: Saturday between 29 October and 4 November

Year 1

A reading from the Letter of Paul to the Romans.

I ask, then, has God rejected his people? By no means! I myself am an Israelite,
a descendant of Abraham, a member of the tribe of Benjamin. God has not
rejected his people whom he foreknew. Do you not know what the scripture
says of Elijah, how he pleads with God against Israel?

So I ask, have they stumbled so as to fall? By no means! But through their
stumbling salvation has come to the Gentiles, so as to make Israel jealous.
Now if their stumbling means riches for the world, and if their defeat means
riches for Gentiles, how much more will their full inclusion mean!

So that you may not claim to be wiser than you are, brothers and sisters,
I want you to understand this mystery: a hardening has come upon part of   →

Israel, until the full number of the Gentiles has come in. And so all Israel will be saved; as it is written,

'Out of Zion will come the Deliverer;
he will banish ungodliness from Jacob.'
'And this is my covenant with them,
when I take away their sins.'

As regards the gospel they are enemies of God for your sake; but as regards election they are beloved, for the sake of their ancestors; for the gifts and the calling of God are irrevocable.

This is the word of the Lord.   Romans 11.1–2, 11–12, 25–29

Responsorial Psalm

R **Justice shall return to the righteous,
[and the true of heart shall follow it].**   cf Psalm 94.15

For the Lord will not fail his people,
neither will he forsake his inheritance.
For justice shall return to the righteous,
and all that are true of heart shall follow it. **R**

Who will rise up for me against the wicked?
Who will take my part against the evildoers?
If the Lord had not helped me,
my soul would soon have been put to silence. **R**

And when I said, 'My foot has slipped',
your loving mercy, O Lord, upheld me.
In the multitude of cares that troubled my heart,
your comforts have refreshed my soul. **R**   Psalm 94.14–19

Year 2

A reading from the Letter of Paul to the Philippians.

Christ is proclaimed in every way, whether out of false motives or true; and in that I rejoice. Yes, and I will continue to rejoice, for I know that through your prayers and the help of the Spirit of Jesus Christ this will result in my deliverance. It is my eager expectation and hope that I will not be put to shame in any way, but that by my speaking with all boldness, Christ will be exalted now as always in my body, whether by life or by death. For to me, living is Christ and dying is gain. If I am to live in the flesh, that means fruitful labour for me; and I do not know which I prefer. I am hard pressed between the two: my desire is to depart and be with Christ, for that is far better; but to remain in the flesh is more necessary for you. Since I am convinced of this, I know that I will remain and continue with all of you for your progress and joy in faith, so that I may share abundantly in your boasting in Christ Jesus when I come to you again.

This is the word of the Lord.   Philippians 1.18–26

Responsorial Psalm

R* **As the deer longs for the water brooks**
so longs my soul for you, O God. Psalm 42.1

My soul is athirst for God, even for the living God;
when shall I come before the presence of God?
My tears have been my bread day and night,
while all day long they say to me, 'Where is now your God?' **R**

Now when I think on these things, I pour out my soul:
how I went with the multitude
and led the procession to the house of God,
with the voice of praise and thanksgiving,
among those who kept holy day. **R**

Why are you so full of heaviness, O my soul,
and why are you so disquieted within me?
O put your trust in God;
for I will yet give him thanks,
who is the help of my countenance, and my God. **R** Psalm 42.1–7

Year 1 and Year 2

Hear the Gospel of our Lord Jesus Christ according to Luke.

On one occasion when Jesus was going to the house of a leader of the Pharisees
to eat a meal on the sabbath, they were watching him closely.

When he noticed how the guests chose the places of honour, he told them
a parable. 'When you are invited by someone to a wedding banquet, do not
sit down at the place of honour, in case someone more distinguished than
you has been invited by your host; and the host who invited both of you may
come and say to you, "Give this person your place", and then in disgrace
you would start to take the lowest place. But when you are invited, go and sit
down at the lowest place, so that when your host comes, he may say to you,
"Friend, move up higher"; then you will be honoured in the presence of all
who sit at the table with you. For all who exalt themselves will be humbled,
and those who humble themselves will be exalted.'

This is the Gospel of the Lord. Luke 14.1, 7–11

Fourth week before Advent

Week 31: Monday between 31 October and 6 November

Year I

A reading from the Letter of Paul to the Romans.

The gifts and the calling of God are irrevocable. Just as you were once disobedient to God but have now received mercy because of their disobedience, so they have now been disobedient in order that, by the mercy shown to you, they too may now receive mercy. For God has imprisoned all in disobedience so that he may be merciful to all.

O the depth of the riches and wisdom and knowledge of God! How unsearchable are his judgements and how inscrutable his ways!
'For who has known the mind of the Lord?
Or who has been his counsellor?'
'Or who has given a gift to him,
to receive a gift in return?'
For from him and through him and to him are all things. To him be the glory for ever. Amen.

This is the word of the Lord. Romans 11.29–end

Responsorial Psalm

R* **The Lord listens to the needy,**
[he does not despise his captive people]. cf Psalm 69.35

As for me, I am poor and in misery;
your saving help, O God, will lift me up.
I will praise the name of God with a song;
I will proclaim his greatness with thanksgiving.   R

This will please the Lord more than an offering of oxen,
more than bulls with horns and hooves.
The humble shall see and be glad;
you who seek God, your heart shall live.   R*

Let the heavens and the earth praise him,
the seas and all that moves in them;
for God will save Zion and rebuild the cities of Judah;
they shall live there and have it in possession.   R Psalm 69.31–37

Year 2

A reading from the Letter of Paul to the Philippians.

If there is any encouragement in Christ, any consolation from love, any sharing in the Spirit, any compassion and sympathy, make my joy complete: be of the same mind, having the same love, being in full accord and of one mind. Do nothing from selfish ambition or conceit, but in humility regard others as better than yourselves. Let each of you look not to your own interests, but to the interests of others.

This is the word of the Lord. *Philippians 2.1–4*

Responsorial Psalm

R **O Israel, trust in the Lord,
from this time forth for evermore.** *Psalm 131.3*

O Lord, my heart is not proud;
my eyes are not raised in haughty looks.
I do not occupy myself with great matters,
with things that are too high for me. R

But I have quieted and stilled my soul,
like a weaned child on its mother's breast;
so my soul is quieted within me.
O Israel, trust in the Lord,
from this time forth for evermore. R *Psalm 131*

Year 1 and Year 2

Hear the Gospel of our Lord Jesus Christ according to Luke.

Jesus said to the one who had invited him, 'When you give a luncheon or a dinner, do not invite your friends or your brothers or your relatives or rich neighbours, in case they may invite you in return, and you would be repaid. But when you give a banquet, invite the poor, the crippled, the lame, and the blind. And you will be blessed, because they cannot repay you, for you will be repaid at the resurrection of the righteous.'

This is the Gospel of the Lord. *Luke 14.12–14*

Week 31: Tuesday between 1 and 7 November

Year 1

A reading from the Letter of Paul to the Romans.

We, who are many, are one body in Christ, and individually we are members one of another. We have gifts that differ according to the grace given to us: prophecy, in proportion to faith; ministry, in ministering; the teacher, in teaching; the exhorter, in exhortation; the giver, in generosity; the leader, in diligence; the compassionate, in cheerfulness.

Let love be genuine; hate what is evil, hold fast to what is good; love one another with mutual affection; outdo one another in showing honour. Do not lag in zeal, be ardent in spirit, serve the Lord. Rejoice in hope, be patient in suffering, persevere in prayer. Contribute to the needs of the saints; extend hospitality to strangers.

Bless those who persecute you; bless and do not curse them. Rejoice with those who rejoice, weep with those who weep. Live in harmony with one another; do not be haughty, but associate with the lowly; do not claim to be wiser than you are.

This is the word of the Lord.   Romans 12.5–16

Responsorial Psalm

R   **O Israel, trust in the Lord,**
    from this time forth for evermore.   Psalm 131.3

O Lord, my heart is not proud;
my eyes are not raised in haughty looks.
I do not occupy myself with great matters,
with things that are too high for me.   **R**

But I have quieted and stilled my soul,
like a weaned child on its mother's breast;
so my soul is quieted within me.
O Israel, trust in the Lord,
from this time forth for evermore.   **R**   Psalm 131

Year 2

A reading from the Letter of Paul to the Philippians.

Let the same mind be in you that was in Christ Jesus,
who, though he was in the form of God,
did not regard equality with God
as something to be exploited,
but emptied himself,
taking the form of a slave,
being born in human likeness.
And being found in human form,
he humbled himself
and became obedient to the point of death —
even death on a cross.

Therefore God also highly exalted him
and gave him the name
that is above every name,
so that at the name of Jesus
every knee should bend,
in heaven and on earth and under the earth,
and every tongue should confess
that Jesus Christ is Lord,
to the glory of God the Father.

This is the word of the Lord.   Philippians 2.5–11

Responsorial Psalm

**R* I will proclaim your name among the people:
[and praise you in the midst of the congregation].**   cf Psalm 22.22

Praise the Lord, you that fear him;
O seed of Jacob, glorify him;
stand in awe of him, O seed of Israel.   **R**

For he has not despised nor abhorred the suffering of the poor;
neither has he hidden his face from them;
but when they cried to him he heard them.   **R**

From you comes my praise in the great congregation;
I will perform my vows
in the presence of those that fear you.   **R**

The poor shall eat and be satisfied;
those who seek the Lord shall praise him;
their hearts shall live for ever.   **R**

All the ends of the earth
shall remember and turn to the Lord,
and all the families of the nations shall bow before him.   **R**

Psalm 22.22–27

Hear the Gospel of our Lord Jesus Christ according to Luke.

One of the dinner guests said to Jesus, 'Blessed is anyone who will eat bread in the kingdom of God!' Then Jesus said to him, 'Someone gave a great dinner and invited many. At the time for the dinner he sent his slave to say to those who had been invited, "Come; for everything is ready now." But they all alike began to make excuses. The first said to him, "I have bought a piece of land, and I must go out and see it; please accept my apologies." Another said, "I have bought five yoke of oxen, and I am going to try them out; please accept my apologies." Another said, "I have just been married, and therefore I cannot come." So the slave returned and reported this to his master. Then the owner of the house became angry and said to his slave, "Go out at once into the streets and lanes of the town and bring in the poor, the crippled, the blind, and the lame." And the slave said, "Sir, what you ordered has been done, and there is still room." Then the master said to the slave, "Go out into the roads and lanes, and compel people to come in, so that my house may be filled. For I tell you, none of those who were invited will taste my dinner." '

This is the Gospel of the Lord.   *Luke* 14.15–24

Week 31: Wednesday between 2 and 8 November

Year 1

A reading from the Letter of Paul to the Romans.

Owe no one anything, except to love one another; for the one who loves another has fulfilled the law. The commandments, 'You shall not commit adultery; You shall not murder; You shall not steal; You shall not covet'; and any other commandment, are summed up in this word, 'Love your neighbour as yourself.' Love does no wrong to a neighbour; therefore, love is the fulfilling of the law.

This is the word of the Lord.   *Romans* 13.8–10

R **Blessed are those
who delight in the commandments of the Lord.** cf Psalm 112.1

Blessed are those who fear the Lord
and have great delight in his commandments.
Their descendants will be mighty in the land,
a generation of the faithful that will be blest.   R

Wealth and riches will be in their house,
and their righteousness endures for ever.
Light shines in the darkness for the upright;
gracious and full of compassion are the righteous.   R

It goes well with those who are generous in lending
and order their affairs with justice,
for they will never be shaken;
the righteous will be held in everlasting remembrance.   R

They will not be afraid of any evil tidings;
their heart is steadfast, trusting in the Lord.
Their heart is sustained and will not fear,
until they see the downfall of their foes.   R

They have given freely to the poor;
their righteousness stands fast for ever;
their head will be exalted with honour.   R

The wicked shall see it and be angry;
they shall gnash their teeth in despair;
the desire of the wicked shall perish.   R   Psalm 112

Year 2

A reading from the Letter of Paul to the Philippians.

My beloved, just as you have always obeyed me, not only in my presence, but
much more now in my absence, work out your own salvation with fear and
trembling; for it is God who is at work in you, enabling you both to will and
to work for his good pleasure.

Do all things without murmuring and arguing, so that you may be blameless
and innocent, children of God without blemish in the midst of a crooked
and perverse generation, in which you shine like stars in the world. It is by
your holding fast to the word of life that I can boast on the day of Christ
that I did not run in vain or labour in vain. But even if I am being poured
out as a libation over the sacrifice and the offering of your faith, I am glad
and rejoice with all of you – and in the same way you also must be glad and
rejoice with me.

This is the word of the Lord.   Philippians 2.12–18

Responsorial Psalm

R **The Lord is my light and my salvation:**
 [he is the strength of my life]. cf *Psalm* 27.1

The Lord is my light and my salvation;
whom then shall I fear?
The Lord is the strength of my life;
of whom then shall I be afraid?   R

When the wicked,
even my enemies and my foes,
came upon me to eat up my flesh,
they stumbled and fell.   R

Though a host encamp against me,
my heart shall not be afraid,
and though there rise up war against me,
yet will I put my trust in him.   R

One thing have I asked of the Lord and that alone I seek:
that I may dwell in the house of the Lord
 all the days of my life,
to behold the fair beauty of the Lord
and to seek his will in his temple.   R *Psalm* 27.1–5

Year 1 and Year 2

Hear the Gospel of our Lord Jesus Christ according to Luke.

Large crowds were travelling with Jesus; and he turned and said to them, 'Whoever comes to me and does not hate father and mother, wife and children, brothers and sisters, yes, and even life itself, cannot be my disciple. Whoever does not carry the cross and follow me cannot be my disciple. For which of you, intending to build a tower, does not first sit down and estimate the cost, to see whether he has enough to complete it? Otherwise, when he has laid a foundation and is not able to finish, all who see it will begin to ridicule him, saying, "This fellow began to build and was not able to finish." Or what king, going out to wage war against another king, will not sit down first and consider whether he is able with ten thousand to oppose the one who comes against him with twenty thousand? If he cannot, then, while the other is still far away, he sends a delegation and asks for the terms of peace. So therefore, none of you can become my disciple if you do not give up all your possessions.'

This is the Gospel of the Lord. *Luke* 14.25–33

Week 31: Thursday between 3 and 9 November

Year 1

A reading from the Letter of Paul to the Romans.

We do not live to ourselves, and we do not die to ourselves. If we live, we live to the Lord, and if we die, we die to the Lord; so then, whether we live or whether we die, we are the Lord's. For to this end Christ died and lived again, so that he might be Lord of both the dead and the living.

Why do you pass judgement on your brother or sister? Or you, why do you despise your brother or sister? For we will all stand before the judgement seat of God. For it is written,

'As I live, says the Lord, every knee shall bow to me,
    and every tongue shall give praise to God.'
So then, each of us will be accountable to God.

This is the word of the Lord.   Romans 14.7–12

Responsorial Psalm

**R* I shall see the goodness of the Lord
    in the land of the living.**   Psalm 27.16

Teach me your way, O Lord;
lead me on a level path,
because of those who lie in wait for me.   **R**

Deliver me not into the will of my adversaries,
for false witnesses have risen up against me,
and those who breathe out violence.   **R***

Wait for the Lord;
be strong and he shall comfort your heart;
wait patiently for the Lord.   **R**   Psalm 27.14–end

Year 2

A reading from the Letter of Paul to the Philippians.

It is we who are the circumcision, who worship in the Spirit of God and boast in Christ Jesus and have no confidence in the flesh – even though I, too, have reason for confidence in the flesh.

If anyone else has reason to be confident in the flesh, I have more: circumcised on the eighth day, a member of the people of Israel, of the tribe of Benjamin, a Hebrew born of Hebrews; as to the law, a Pharisee; as to zeal, a persecutor of the church; as to righteousness under the law, blameless.

Yet whatever gains I had, these I have come to regard as loss because of Christ. More than that, I regard everything as loss because of the surpassing value of knowing Christ Jesus my Lord.

This is the word of the Lord.   Philippians 3.3–8a

Responsorial Psalm

R* **Remember the marvels the Lord has done:**
 [his wonders and the judgements he has given]. *cf Psalm 105.5*

O give thanks to the Lord and call upon his name;
make known his deeds among the peoples.
Sing to him, sing praises,
and tell of all his marvellous works.   **R**

Rejoice in the praise of his holy name;
let the hearts of them rejoice who seek the Lord.
Seek the Lord and his strength;
seek his face continually.   **R***

O seed of Abraham his servant,
O children of Jacob his chosen.
He is the Lord our God;
his judgements are in all the earth.   **R**   *Psalm 105.1–7*

Year 1 and Year 2

Hear the Gospel of our Lord Jesus Christ *according to Luke*.

All the tax-collectors and sinners were coming near Jesus to listen to him.
And the Pharisees and the scribes were grumbling and saying, 'This fellow
welcomes sinners and eats with them.'

So he told them this parable: 'Which one of you, having a hundred sheep
and losing one of them, does not leave the ninety-nine in the wilderness and
go after the one that is lost until he finds it? When he has found it, he lays it
on his shoulders and rejoices. And when he comes home, he calls together
his friends and neighbours, saying to them, "Rejoice with me, for I have
found my sheep that was lost." Just so, I tell you, there will be more joy in
heaven over one sinner who repents than over ninety-nine righteous people
who need no repentance.

'Or what woman having ten silver coins, if she loses one of them, does not
light a lamp, sweep the house, and search carefully until she finds it? When she
has found it, she calls together her friends and neighbours, saying, "Rejoice
with me, for I have found the coin that I had lost." Just so, I tell you, there is
joy in the presence of the angels of God over one sinner who repents.'

This is the Gospel of the Lord.   *Luke 15.1–10*

Week 31: Friday between 4 and 10 November

Year 1

A reading from the Letter of Paul to the Romans.

I myself feel confident about you, my brothers and sisters, that you yourselves are full of goodness, filled with all knowledge, and able to instruct one another. Nevertheless, on some points I have written to you rather boldly by way of reminder, because of the grace given me by God to be a minister of Christ Jesus to the Gentiles in the priestly service of the gospel of God, so that the offering of the Gentiles may be acceptable, sanctified by the Holy Spirit. In Christ Jesus, then, I have reason to boast of my work for God. For I will not venture to speak of anything except what Christ has accomplished through me to win obedience from the Gentiles, by word and deed, by the power of signs and wonders, by the power of the Spirit of God, so that from Jerusalem and as far around as Illyricum I have fully proclaimed the good news of Christ. Thus I make it my ambition to proclaim the good news, not where Christ has already been named, so that I do not build on someone else's foundation, but as it is written,

'Those who have never been told of him shall see,
    and those who have never heard of him shall understand.'

This is the word of the Lord. Romans 15.14–21

Responsorial Psalm

R* **Sound praises to the Lord, all the earth;**
    [break into song and make music]. cf Psalm 98.5

Sing to the Lord a new song,
for he has done marvellous things.
His own right hand and his holy arm
have won for him the victory. **R**

The Lord has made known his salvation;
his deliverance has he openly shown
in the sight of the nations. **R**

He has remembered his mercy and faithfulness
towards the house of Israel,
and all the ends of the earth have seen
the salvation of our God. **R***

Make music to the Lord with the lyre,
with the lyre and the voice of melody.
With trumpets and the sound of the horn
sound praises before the Lord, the King. **R** →

Let the sea thunder and all that fills it,
the world and all that dwell upon it.
Let the rivers clap their hands
and let the hills ring out together before the Lord. R

R* **Sound praises to the Lord, all the earth;**
   [break into song and make music].

For he comes to judge the earth:
in righteousness shall he judge the world
and the peoples with equity. R   *Psalm 98*

Year 2

A reading from the Letter of Paul to the Philippians.

Brothers and sisters, join in imitating me, and observe those who live according to the example you have in us. For many live as enemies of the cross of
Christ; I have often told you of them, and now I tell you even with tears. Their
end is destruction; their god is the belly; and their glory is in their shame;
their minds are set on earthly things. But our citizenship is in heaven, and
it is from there that we are expecting a Saviour, the Lord Jesus Christ. He
will transform the body of our humiliation so that it may be conformed to
the body of his glory, by the power that also enables him to make all things
subject to himself. Therefore, my brothers and sisters, whom I love and long
for, my joy and crown, stand firm in the Lord in this way, my beloved.

This is the word of the Lord.   *Philippians 3.17 − 4.1*

Responsorial Psalm

R **[I was glad when they said to me:]**
   Let us go to the house of the Lord.   *Psalm 122.1*

I was glad when they said to me,
'Let us go to the house of the Lord.'
And now our feet are standing
within your gates, O Jerusalem. R

Jerusalem, built as a city
that is at unity in itself.
Thither the tribes go up,
the tribes of the Lord. R

As is decreed for Israel,
to give thanks to the name of the Lord.
For there are set the thrones of judgement,
the thrones of the house of David. R

O pray for the peace of Jerusalem:
'May they prosper who love you.
Peace be within your walls
and tranquillity within your palaces.'   R

For my kindred and companions' sake,
I will pray that peace be with you.
For the sake of the house of the Lord our God,
I will seek to do you good.   R   Psalm 122

Year 1 and Year 2

Hear the Gospel of our Lord Jesus Christ according to Luke.

Jesus said to the disciples, 'There was a rich man who had a manager, and charges were brought to him that this man was squandering his property. So he summoned him and said to him, "What is this that I hear about you? Give me an account of your management, because you cannot be my manager any longer." Then the manager said to himself, "What will I do, now that my master is taking the position away from me? I am not strong enough to dig, and I am ashamed to beg. I have decided what to do so that, when I am dismissed as manager, people may welcome me into their homes."

'So, summoning his master's debtors one by one, he asked the first, "How much do you owe my master?" He answered, "A hundred jugs of olive oil." He said to him, "Take your bill, sit down quickly, and make it fifty." Then he asked another, "And how much do you owe?" He replied, "A hundred containers of wheat." He said to him, "Take your bill and make it eighty." And his master commended the dishonest manager because he had acted shrewdly; for the children of this age are more shrewd in dealing with their own generation than are the children of light.'

This is the Gospel of the Lord.   Luke 16.1–8

Week 31: Saturday between 5 and 11 November

Year I

A reading from the Letter of Paul to the Romans.

Greet Prisca and Aquila, who work with me in Christ Jesus, and who risked their necks for my life, to whom not only I give thanks, but also all the churches of the Gentiles. Greet also the church in their house. Greet my beloved Epaenetus, who was the first convert in Asia for Christ. Greet Mary, who has worked very hard among you. Greet Andronicus and Junia, my relatives who were in prison with me; they are prominent among the apostles, and they were in Christ before I was. Greet Ampliatus, my beloved in the Lord. Greet Urbanus, our co-worker in Christ, and my beloved Stachys. Greet one another with a holy kiss. All the churches of Christ greet you.

I Tertius, the writer of this letter, greet you in the Lord. Gaius, who is host to me and to the whole church, greets you. Erastus, the city treasurer, and our brother Quartus, greet you.

Now to God who is able to strengthen you according to my gospel and the proclamation of Jesus Christ, according to the revelation of the mystery that was kept secret for long ages but is now disclosed, and through the prophetic writings is made known to all the Gentiles, according to the command of the eternal God, to bring about the obedience of faith – to the only wise God, through Jesus Christ, to whom be the glory for ever! Amen.

This is the word of the Lord.   Romans 16.3–9, 16, 22–end

Responsorial Psalm

R* **I will exalt you, O God my King,**
   [and bless your name for ever].   *cf Psalm 145.1*

Every day will I bless you
and praise your name for ever and ever.
Great is the Lord and highly to be praised;
his greatness is beyond all searching out.   **R**

One generation shall praise your works to another
and declare your mighty acts.
They shall speak of the majesty of your glory,
and I will tell of all your wonderful deeds.   **R**

They shall speak of the might of your marvellous acts,
and I will also tell of your greatness.
They shall pour forth the story of your abundant kindness
and joyfully sing of your righteousness.   **R**   *Psalm 145.1–7*

A reading from the Letter of Paul to the Philippians.

I rejoice in the Lord greatly that now at last you have revived your concern for me; indeed, you were concerned for me, but had no opportunity to show it. Not that I am referring to being in need; for I have learned to be content with whatever I have. I know what it is to have little, and I know what it is to have plenty. In any and all circumstances I have learned the secret of being well-fed and of going hungry, of having plenty and of being in need. I can do all things through him who strengthens me. In any case, it was kind of you to share my distress.

You Philippians indeed know that in the early days of the gospel, when I left Macedonia, no church shared with me in the matter of giving and receiving, except you alone. For even when I was in Thessalonica, you sent me help for my needs more than once. Not that I seek the gift, but I seek the profit that accumulates to your account. I have been paid in full and have more than enough; I am fully satisfied, now that I have received from Epaphroditus the gifts you sent, a fragrant offering, a sacrifice acceptable and pleasing to God. And my God will fully satisfy every need of yours according to his riches in glory in Christ Jesus.

This is the word of the Lord. Philippians 4.10–19

Responsorial Psalm

R **Blessed are those**
 who delight in the commandments of the Lord. cf Psalm 112.1

Blessed are those who fear the Lord
and have great delight in his commandments.
Their descendants will be mighty in the land,
a generation of the faithful that will be blest. R

Wealth and riches will be in their house,
and their righteousness endures for ever.
Light shines in the darkness for the upright;
gracious and full of compassion are the righteous. R

It goes well with those who are generous in lending
and order their affairs with justice,
for they will never be shaken;
the righteous will be held in everlasting remembrance. R

They will not be afraid of any evil tidings;
their heart is steadfast, trusting in the Lord.
Their heart is sustained and will not fear,
until they see the downfall of their foes. R →

They have given freely to the poor;
their righteousness stands fast for ever;
their head will be exalted with honour.   R

R   **Blessed are those
who delight in the commandments of the Lord.**

The wicked shall see it and be angry;
they shall gnash their teeth in despair;
the desire of the wicked shall perish.   R   Psalm 112

Year 1 and Year 2

Hear the Gospel of our Lord Jesus Christ according to Luke.

Jesus said to the disciples, 'I tell you, make friends for yourselves by means
of dishonest wealth so that when it is gone, they may welcome you into the
eternal homes.

'Whoever is faithful in a very little is faithful also in much; and whoever is
dishonest in a very little is dishonest also in much. If then you have not been
faithful with the dishonest wealth, who will entrust to you the true riches?
And if you have not been faithful with what belongs to another, who will
give you what is your own? No slave can serve two masters; for a slave will
either hate the one and love the other, or be devoted to the one and despise
the other. You cannot serve God and wealth.'

The Pharisees, who were lovers of money, heard all this, and they ridiculed
him. So he said to them, 'You are those who justify yourselves in the sight of
others; but God knows your hearts; for what is prized by human beings is an
abomination in the sight of God.'

This is the Gospel of the Lord.   Luke 16.9–15

Third week before Advent

Week 32: Monday between 7 and 13 November

Year 1

Either

A reading from the Wisdom of Solomon.

Love righteousness, you rulers of the earth,
think of the Lord in goodness
and seek him with sincerity of heart;
because he is found by those who do not put him to the test,
and manifests himself to those who do not distrust him.
For perverse thoughts separate people from God,
and when his power is tested, it exposes the foolish;
because wisdom will not enter a deceitful soul,
or dwell in a body enslaved to sin.
For a holy and disciplined spirit will flee from deceit,
and will leave foolish thoughts behind,
and will be ashamed at the approach of unrighteousness.

For wisdom is a kindly spirit,
but will not free blasphemers from the guilt of their words;
because God is witness of their inmost feelings,
and a true observer of their hearts, and a hearer of their tongues.
Because the spirit of the Lord has filled the world,
and that which holds all things together knows what is said.

This is the word of the Lord.   Wisdom 1.1–7

Responsorial Psalm

R   **O Lord, you have searched me out and known me.**   Psalm 139.1a

O Lord, you have searched me out and known me;
you know my sitting down and my rising up;
you discern my thoughts from afar.   R

You mark out my journeys and my resting place
and are acquainted with all my ways.
For there is not a word on my tongue,
but you, O Lord, know it altogether.   R

You encompass me behind and before
and lay your hand upon me.
Such knowledge is too wonderful for me,
so high that I cannot attain it.   R   →

Where can I go then from your spirit?
Or where can I flee from your presence?
If I climb up to heaven, you are there;
if I make the grave my bed, you are there also.   R

R   **O Lord, you have searched me out and known me.**

If I take the wings of the morning
and dwell in the uttermost parts of the sea,
even there your hand shall lead me,
your right hand hold me fast.   R   Psalm 139.1–9

or the reading and psalm for Year 2 may be read.

Year 2

A reading from the Letter of Paul to Titus.

Paul, a servant of God and an apostle of Jesus Christ, for the sake of the faith
of God's elect and the knowledge of the truth that is in accordance with
godliness, in the hope of eternal life that God, who never lies, promised before
the ages began – in due time he revealed his word through the proclamation
with which I have been entrusted by the command of God our Saviour, to
Titus, my loyal child in the faith we share: Grace and peace from God the
Father and Christ Jesus our Saviour.

I left you behind in Crete for this reason, that you should put in order
what remained to be done, and should appoint elders in every town, as I
directed you: someone who is blameless, married only once, whose children
are believers, not accused of debauchery and not rebellious. For a bishop, as
God's steward, must be blameless; he must not be arrogant or quick-tempered
or addicted to wine or violent or greedy for gain; but he must be hospitable,
a lover of goodness, prudent, upright, devout, and self-controlled. He must
have a firm grasp of the word that is trustworthy in accordance with the
teaching, so that he may be able both to preach with sound doctrine and to
refute those who contradict it.

This is the word of the Lord.   Titus 1.1–9

Responsorial Psalm

R   **The earth is the Lord's, and all who dwell therein.**   *cf Psalm 24.1*

The earth is the Lord's and all that fills it,
the compass of the world and all who dwell therein.
For he has founded it upon the seas
and set it firm upon the rivers of the deep.   R

'Who shall ascend the hill of the Lord,
or who can rise up in his holy place?
Those who have clean hands and a pure heart,
who have not lifted up their soul to an idol,
nor sworn an oath to a lie.   **R**

'They shall receive a blessing from the Lord,
a just reward from the God of their salvation.'
Such is the company of those who seek him,
of those who seek your face, O God of Jacob.   **R**   Psalm 24.1–6

Year I and Year 2

Hear the Gospel of our Lord Jesus Christ according to Luke.

Jesus said to his disciples, 'Occasions for stumbling are bound to come, but woe to anyone by whom they come! It would be better for you if a millstone were hung around your neck and you were thrown into the sea than for you to cause one of these little ones to stumble. Be on your guard! If another disciple sins, you must rebuke the offender, and if there is repentance, you must forgive. And if the same person sins against you seven times a day, and turns back to you seven times and says, "I repent", you must forgive.'

The apostles said to the Lord, 'Increase our faith!' The Lord replied, 'If you had faith the size of a mustard seed, you could say to this mulberry tree, "Be uprooted and planted in the sea", and it would obey you.'

This is the Gospel of the Lord.   Luke 17.1–6

Week 32: Tuesday between 8 and 14 November

Year I

Either

A reading from the Wisdom of Solomon.

God created us for incorruption,
and made us in the image of his own eternity,
but through the devil's envy death entered the world,
and those who belong to his company experience it.

But the souls of the righteous are in the hand of God,
and no torment will ever touch them.
In the eyes of the foolish they seemed to have died,
and their departure was thought to be a disaster,
and their going from us to be their destruction;
but they are at peace.
For though in the sight of others they were punished,
their hope is full of immortality.   →

Having been disciplined a little, they will receive great good,
because God tested them and found them worthy of himself;
like gold in the furnace he tried them,
and like a sacrificial burnt-offering he accepted them.
In the time of their visitation they will shine forth,
and will run like sparks through the stubble.
They will govern nations and rule over peoples,
and the Lord will reign over them for ever.
Those who trust in him will understand truth,
and the faithful will abide with him in love,
because grace and mercy are upon his holy ones,
and he watches over his elect.

This is the word of the Lord.   Wisdom 2.23 – 3.9

Responsorial Psalm

R   **Taste and see that the Lord is good:**
    [happy are all who trust in him].   cf Psalm 34.8

I will bless the Lord at all times;
his praise shall ever be in my mouth.
My soul shall glory in the Lord;
let the humble hear and be glad.   **R**

O magnify the Lord with me;
let us exalt his name together.
I sought the Lord and he answered me
and delivered me from all my fears.   **R**

Look upon him and be radiant
and your faces shall not be ashamed.
This poor soul cried, and the Lord heard me
and saved me from all my troubles.   **R**   Psalm 34.1–6

or the reading and psalm for Year 2 may be read.

Year 2

A reading from the Letter of Paul to Titus.

As for you, teach what is consistent with sound doctrine. Tell the older men to be
temperate, serious, prudent, and sound in faith, in love, and in endurance.

Likewise, tell the older women to be reverent in behaviour, not to be
slanderers or slaves to drink; they are to teach what is good, so that they may
encourage the young women to love their husbands, to love their children, to be
self-controlled, chaste, good managers of the household, kind, being submissive
to their husbands, so that the word of God may not be discredited.

Likewise, urge the younger men to be self-controlled. Show yourself in all respects a model of good works, and in your teaching show integrity, gravity, and sound speech that cannot be censured; then any opponent will be put to shame, having nothing evil to say of us.

For the grace of God has appeared, bringing salvation to all, training us to renounce impiety and worldly passions, and in the present age to live lives that are self-controlled, upright, and godly, while we wait for the blessed hope and the manifestation of the glory of our great God and Saviour, Jesus Christ. He it is who gave himself for us that he might redeem us from all iniquity and purify for himself a people of his own who are zealous for good deeds.

This is the word of the Lord.   Titus 2.1–8, 11–14

Responsorial Psalm

R **The mouth of the righteous utters wisdom
[and their tongue speaks what is right].**   Psalm 37.31

Trust in the Lord and be doing good;
dwell in the land and be nourished with truth.
Let your delight be in the Lord
and he will give you your heart's desire. **R**

Commit your way to the Lord and put your trust in him,
and he will bring it to pass.
The righteous shall possess the land
and dwell in it for ever. **R**

The mouth of the righteous utters wisdom,
and their tongue speaks the thing that is right.
The law of their God is in their heart
and their footsteps shall not slide. **R**   Psalm 37.3–5, 30–32

Year 1 and Year 2

Hear the Gospel of our Lord Jesus Christ according to Luke.

Jesus said to his disciples, 'Who among you would say to your slave who has just come in from ploughing or tending sheep in the field, "Come here at once and take your place at the table"? Would you not rather say to him, "Prepare supper for me, put on your apron and serve me while I eat and drink; later you may eat and drink"? Do you thank the slave for doing what was commanded? So you also, when you have done all that you were ordered to do, say, "We are worthless slaves; we have done only what we ought to have done!"'

This is the Gospel of the Lord.   Luke 17.7–10

Week 32: Wednesday between 9 and 15 November

Year I

Either

A reading from the Wisdom of Solomon.

Listen, O kings, and understand;
learn, O judges of the ends of the earth.
Give ear, you that rule over multitudes,
and boast of many nations.
For your dominion was given you from the Lord,
and your sovereignty from the Most High;
he will search out your works and inquire into your plans.
Because as servants of his kingdom you did not rule rightly,
or keep the law,
or walk according to the purpose of God,
he will come upon you terribly and swiftly,
because severe judgement falls on those in high places.
For the lowliest may be pardoned in mercy,
but the mighty will be mightily tested.
For the Lord of all will not stand in awe of anyone,
or show deference to greatness;
because he himself made both small and great,
and he takes thought for all alike.
But a strict inquiry is in store for the mighty.
To you then, O monarchs, my words are directed,
so that you may learn wisdom and not transgress.
For they will be made holy who observe holy things in holiness,
and those who have been taught them will find a defence.
Therefore set your desire on my words;
long for them, and you will be instructed.

This is the word of the Lord.   Wisdom 6.1–11

Responsorial Psalm

**R* Arise, O God and judge the earth,
[and take the nations for your possession].**   cf Psalm 82.8

God has taken his stand in the council of heaven;
in the midst of the gods he gives judgement:
How long will you judge unjustly
and show such favour to the wicked?   **R**

You were to judge the weak and the orphan;
defend the right of the humble and needy;
rescue the weak and the poor;
deliver them from the hand of the wicked.   **R**

They have no knowledge or wisdom;
they walk on still in darkness:
all the foundations of the earth are shaken.   **R**

Therefore I say that though you are gods
and all of you children of the Most High,
nevertheless, you shall die like mortals
and fall like one of their princes.   **R***   Psalm 82

or the reading and psalm for Year 2 may be read.

Year 2

A reading from the Letter of Paul to Titus.

Remind everyone to be subject to rulers and authorities, to be obedient, to
be ready for every good work, to speak evil of no one, to avoid quarrelling,
to be gentle, and to show every courtesy to everyone. For we ourselves were
once foolish, disobedient, led astray, slaves to various passions and pleasures,
passing our days in malice and envy, despicable, hating one another. But when
the goodness and loving-kindness of God our Saviour appeared, he saved us,
not because of any works of righteousness that we had done, but according
to his mercy, through the water of rebirth and renewal by the Holy Spirit.
This Spirit he poured out on us richly through Jesus Christ our Saviour, so
that, having been justified by his grace, we might become heirs according to
the hope of eternal life.

This is the word of the Lord.   Titus 3.1–7

Responsorial Psalm

R   I will dwell in the house of the Lord for ever.   Psalm 23.6b

The Lord is my shepherd;
therefore can I lack nothing.
He makes me lie down in green pastures
and leads me beside still waters.   **R**

He shall refresh my soul
and guide me in the paths of righteousness
for his name's sake.   **R**

Though I walk through the valley of the shadow of death,
I will fear no evil;
for you are with me;
your rod and your staff, they comfort me.   **R**   →

You spread a table before me
in the presence of those who trouble me;
you have anointed my head with oil
and my cup shall be full.   R

R   **I will dwell in the house of the Lord for ever.**

Surely goodness and loving mercy shall follow me
all the days of my life,
and I will dwell in the house of the Lord for ever.   R   *Psalm 23*

Year I and Year 2

Hear the Gospel of our Lord Jesus Christ according to Luke.

On the way to Jerusalem Jesus was going through the region between Samaria
and Galilee. As he entered a village, ten lepers approached him. Keeping their
distance, they called out, saying, 'Jesus, Master, have mercy on us!' When he
saw them, he said to them, 'Go and show yourselves to the priests.' And as
they went, they were made clean. Then one of them, when he saw that he was
healed, turned back, praising God with a loud voice. He prostrated himself at
Jesus' feet and thanked him. And he was a Samaritan. Then Jesus asked, 'Were
not ten made clean? But the other nine, where are they? Was none of them
found to return and give praise to God except this foreigner?' Then he said
to him, 'Get up and go on your way; your faith has made you well.'

This is the Gospel of the Lord.   *Luke 17.11–19*

Week 32: Thursday between 10 and 16 November

Year I

Either

A reading from the Wisdom of Solomon.

There is in wisdom a spirit that is intelligent, holy,
unique, manifold, subtle,
mobile, clear, unpolluted,
distinct, invulnerable, loving the good, keen,
irresistible, beneficent, humane,
steadfast, sure, free from anxiety,
all-powerful, overseeing all,
and penetrating through all spirits
that are intelligent, pure, and altogether subtle.
For wisdom is more mobile than any motion;
because of her pureness she pervades and penetrates all things.
For she is a breath of the power of God,
and a pure emanation of the glory of the Almighty;

therefore nothing defiled gains entrance into her.
For she is a reflection of eternal light,
a spotless mirror of the working of God,
and an image of his goodness.
Although she is but one, she can do all things,
and while remaining in herself, she renews all things;
in every generation she passes into holy souls
and makes them friends of God, and prophets;
for God loves nothing so much as the person who lives with wisdom.
She is more beautiful than the sun,
and excels every constellation of the stars.
Compared with the light she is found to be superior,
for it is succeeded by the night,
but against wisdom evil does not prevail.

She reaches mightily from one end of the earth to the other,
and she orders all things well.

This is the word of the Lord.   *Wisdom* 7.22 − 8.1

Responsorial Psalm

R **Wisdom reaches from one end of the earth to the other:**
   [and orders all things well].   cf *Wisdom* 8.1

O Lord, your word is everlasting;
it ever stands firm in the heavens.
Your faithfulness also remains from one generation to another;
you have established the earth and it abides.   **R**

So also your judgements stand firm this day,
for all things are your servants.
If your law had not been my delight,
I should have perished in my trouble.   **R**

I will never forget your commandments,
for by them you have given me life.
I am yours, O save me!
For I have sought your commandments.   **R**

The wicked have waited for me to destroy me,
but I will meditate on your testimonies.
I have seen an end of all perfection,
but your commandment knows no bounds.   **R**   *Psalm* 119.89–96

or the reading and psalm for Year 2 may be read.

A reading from the Letter of Paul to Philemon.

I have received much joy and encouragement from your love, because the hearts of the saints have been refreshed through you, my brother.

For this reason, though I am bold enough in Christ to command you to do your duty, yet I would rather appeal to you on the basis of love – and I, Paul, do this as an old man, and now also as a prisoner of Christ Jesus. I am appealing to you for my child, Onesimus, whose father I have become during my imprisonment. Formerly he was useless to you, but now he is indeed useful both to you and to me. I am sending him, that is, my own heart, back to you. I wanted to keep him with me, so that he might be of service to me in your place during my imprisonment for the gospel; but I preferred to do nothing without your consent, in order that your good deed might be voluntary and not something forced. Perhaps this is the reason he was separated from you for a while, so that you might have him back for ever, no longer as a slave but as more than a slave, a beloved brother – especially to me but how much more to you, both in the flesh and in the Lord.

So if you consider me your partner, welcome him as you would welcome me. If he has wronged you in any way, or owes you anything, charge that to my account. I, Paul, am writing this with my own hand: I will repay it. I say nothing about your owing me even your own self. Yes, brother, let me have this benefit from you in the Lord! Refresh my heart in Christ.

This is the word of the Lord.   Philemon 7–20

Responsorial Psalm

R* **The Lord shall reign for ever,**
   [your God, O Zion, throughout all generations].   Psalm 146.10

Happy are those who have the God of Jacob for their help,
whose hope is in the Lord their God;
who made heaven and earth, the sea and all that is in them;
who keeps his promise for ever.   **R**

Who gives justice to those that suffer wrong
and bread to those who hunger.
The Lord looses those that are bound;
the Lord opens the eyes of the blind;
the Lord lifts up those who are bowed down.   **R**

The Lord loves the righteous;
the Lord watches over the stranger in the land;
he upholds the orphan and widow;
but the way of the wicked he turns upside down.   **R***   Psalm 146.4–end

Hear the Gospel of our Lord Jesus Christ according to Luke.

Jesus was asked by the Pharisees when the kingdom of God was coming, and he answered, 'The kingdom of God is not coming with things that can be observed; nor will they say, "Look, here it is!" or "There it is!" For, in fact, the kingdom of God is among you.'

Then he said to the disciples, 'The days are coming when you will long to see one of the days of the Son of Man, and you will not see it. They will say to you, "Look there!" or "Look here!" Do not go, do not set off in pursuit. For as the lightning flashes and lights up the sky from one side to the other, so will the Son of Man be in his day. But first he must endure much suffering and be rejected by this generation.'

This is the Gospel of the Lord. Luke 17.20–25

Week 32: Friday between 11 and 17 November

Year 1

Either

A reading from the Wisdom of Solomon.

All people who were ignorant of God were foolish by nature;
and they were unable from the good things that are seen
    to know the one who exists,
nor did they recognize the artisan while paying heed to his works;
but they supposed that either fire or wind or swift air,
or the circle of the stars, or turbulent water,
or the luminaries of heaven were the gods that rule the world.
If through delight in the beauty of these things
    people assumed them to be gods,
let them know how much better than these is their Lord,
for the author of beauty created them.
And if people were amazed at their power and working,
let them perceive from them
how much more powerful is the one who formed them.
For from the greatness and beauty of created things
comes a corresponding perception of their Creator.
Yet these people are little to be blamed,
for perhaps they go astray
while seeking God and desiring to find him.
For while they live among his works, they keep searching,
and they trust in what they see,
    because the things that are seen are beautiful.
Yet again, not even they are to be excused; →

for if they had the power to know so much
that they could investigate the world,
how did they fail to find sooner the Lord of these things?

This is the word of the Lord. *Wisdom 13.1–9*

Responsorial Psalm

R **The heavens proclaim the glory of God.** *cf Psalm 19.1a*

The heavens are telling the glory of God
and the firmament proclaims his handiwork.
One day pours out its song to another
and one night unfolds knowledge to another. R

They have neither speech nor language
and their voices are not heard,
yet their sound has gone out into all lands
and their words to the ends of the world. R *Psalm 19.1–4*

or the reading and psalm for Year 2 may be read.

Year 2

A reading from the Second Letter of John.

I was overjoyed to find some of your children walking in the truth, just as
we have been commanded by the Father. But now, dear lady, I ask you, not
as though I were writing you a new commandment, but one we have had
from the beginning, let us love one another. And this is love, that we walk
according to his commandments; this is the commandment just as you have
heard it from the beginning – you must walk in it.

Many deceivers have gone out into the world, those who do not confess
that Jesus Christ has come in the flesh; any such person is the deceiver and the
antichrist! Be on your guard, so that you do not lose what we have worked for,
but may receive a full reward. Everyone who does not abide in the teaching of
Christ, but goes beyond it, does not have God; whoever abides in the teaching
has both the Father and the Son.

This is the word of the Lord. *2 John 4–9*

Responsorial Psalm

R **Blessed are those who walk in the law of the Lord.** cf Psalm 119.1

Blessed are those whose way is pure,
who walk in the law of the Lord.
Blessed are those who keep his testimonies
and seek him with their whole heart. R

Those who do no wickedness,
but walk in his ways.
You, O Lord, have charged
that we should diligently keep your commandments. R

O that my ways were made so direct
that I might keep your statutes.
Then should I not be put to shame,
because I have regard for all your commandments. R

I will thank you with an unfeigned heart,
when I have learned your righteous judgements.
I will keep your statutes;
O forsake me not utterly. R   Psalm 119.1–8

Year 1 and Year 2

Hear the Gospel of our Lord Jesus Christ according to Luke.

Jesus said to the disciples, 'Just as it was in the days of Noah, so too it will be
in the days of the Son of Man. They were eating and drinking, and marrying
and being given in marriage, until the day Noah entered the ark, and the
flood came and destroyed all of them. Likewise, just as it was in the days of
Lot: they were eating and drinking, buying and selling, planting and building,
but on the day that Lot left Sodom, it rained fire and sulphur from heaven
and destroyed all of them – it will be like that on the day that the Son of
Man is revealed.

'On that day, anyone on the housetop who has belongings in the house
must not come down to take them away; and likewise anyone in the field
must not turn back. Remember Lot's wife. Those who try to make their life
secure will lose it, but those who lose their life will keep it. I tell you, on
that night there will be two in one bed; one will be taken and the other left.
There will be two women grinding meal together; one will be taken and the
other left.' Then they asked him, 'Where, Lord?' He said to them, 'Where the
corpse is, there the vultures will gather.'

This is the Gospel of the Lord.   Luke 17.26–end

Year 1

Either

A reading from the Wisdom of Solomon.

While gentle silence enveloped all things,
and night in its swift course was now half gone,
your all-powerful word leapt from heaven, from the royal throne,
into the midst of the land that was doomed,
a stern warrior
carrying the sharp sword of your authentic command,
and stood and filled all things with death,
and touched heaven while standing on the earth.

For the whole creation in its nature was fashioned anew,
complying with your commands,
so that your children might be kept unharmed.
The cloud was seen overshadowing the camp,
and dry land emerging where water had stood before,
an unhindered way out of the Red Sea,
and a grassy plain out of the raging waves,
where those protected by your hand passed through as one nation,
after gazing on marvellous wonders.
For they ranged like horses,
and leapt like lambs,
praising you, O Lord, who delivered them.

This is the word of the Lord.   Wisdom 18.14–16, 19.6–9

Responsorial Psalm

R* **Remember the marvels the Lord has done:**
[his wonders and the judgements he has given].   cf Psalm 105.5

O give thanks to the Lord and call upon his name;
make known his deeds among the peoples.
Sing to him, sing praises,
and tell of all his marvellous works.   **R**

Rejoice in the praise of his holy name;
let the hearts of them rejoice who seek the Lord.
Seek the Lord and his strength;
seek his face continually.   **R***

They ate every plant in their land
and devoured the fruit of their soil.
He smote all the firstborn in their land,
the first fruits of all their strength.   **R**

Then he brought them out with silver and gold;
there was not one among their tribes that stumbled.
Egypt was glad at their departing,
for a dread of them had fallen upon them.   **R**

He spread out a cloud for a covering
and a fire to light up the night.
They asked and he brought them quails;
he satisfied them with the bread of heaven.   **R**

He opened the rock, and the waters gushed out
and ran in the dry places like a river.
For he remembered his holy word
and Abraham, his servant.   **R**   Psalm 105.1–5, 35–42

or the reading and psalm for Year 2 may be read.

Year 2

A reading from the Third Letter of John.

Beloved, you do faithfully whatever you do for the friends, even though they
are strangers to you; they have testified to your love before the church. You
will do well to send them on in a manner worthy of God; for they began
their journey for the sake of Christ, accepting no support from non-believers.
Therefore we ought to support such people, so that we may become co-
workers with the truth.

This is the word of the Lord.   3 John 5–8

R **Blessed are those**
who delight in the commandments of the Lord. cf Psalm 112.1

or

R **Alleluia!**

Blessed are those who fear the Lord
and have great delight in his commandments.
Their descendants will be mighty in the land,
a generation of the faithful that will be blest.   R

Wealth and riches will be in their house,
and their righteousness endures for ever.
Light shines in the darkness for the upright;
gracious and full of compassion are the righteous.   R

It goes well with those who are generous in lending
and order their affairs with justice,
for they will never be shaken;
the righteous will be held in everlasting remembrance.   R

They will not be afraid of any evil tidings;
their heart is steadfast, trusting in the Lord.
Their heart is sustained and will not fear,
until they see the downfall of their foes.   R

They have given freely to the poor;
their righteousness stands fast for ever;
their head will be exalted with honour.   R

The wicked shall see it and be angry;
they shall gnash their teeth in despair;
the desire of the wicked shall perish.   R   Psalm 112

Year 1 and Year 2

Hear the Gospel of our Lord Jesus Christ according to Luke.

Jesus told the disciples a parable about their need to pray always and not to lose heart. He said, 'In a certain city there was a judge who neither feared God nor had respect for people. In that city there was a widow who kept coming to him and saying, "Grant me justice against my opponent." For a while he refused; but later he said to himself, "Though I have no fear of God and no respect for anyone, yet because this widow keeps bothering me, I will grant her justice, so that she may not wear me out by continually coming." ' And the Lord said, 'Listen to what the unjust judge says. And will not God grant justice to his chosen ones who cry to him day and night? Will he delay long in helping them? I tell you, he will quickly grant justice to them. And yet, when the Son of Man comes, will he find faith on earth?'

This is the Gospel of the Lord.   Luke 18.1–8

Second week before Advent
Week 33: Monday between 14 and 20 November

Year 1

Either

A reading from the First Book of the Maccabees.

There came forth a sinful root, Antiochus Epiphanes, son of King Antiochus; he had been a hostage in Rome. He began to reign in the one hundred and thirty-seventh year of the kingdom of the Greeks.

In those days certain renegades came out from Israel and misled many, saying, 'Let us go and make a covenant with the Gentiles around us, for since we separated from them many disasters have come upon us.' This proposal pleased them, and some of the people eagerly went to the king, who authorized them to observe the ordinances of the Gentiles. So they built a gymnasium in Jerusalem, according to Gentile custom, and removed the marks of circumcision, and abandoned the holy covenant. They joined with the Gentiles and sold themselves to do evil.

Then the king wrote to his whole kingdom that all should be one people, and that all should give up their particular customs. All the Gentiles accepted the command of the king. Many even from Israel gladly adopted his religion; they sacrificed to idols and profaned the sabbath.

Now on the fifteenth day of Chislev, in the one hundred and forty-fifth year, they erected a desolating sacrilege on the altar of burnt-offering. They also built altars in the surrounding towns of Judah, and offered incense at the doors of the houses and in the streets. The books of the law that they found they tore to pieces and burned with fire. Anyone found possessing the book of the covenant, or anyone who adhered to the law, was condemned to death by decree of the king.

But many in Israel stood firm and were resolved in their hearts not to eat unclean food. They chose to die rather than to be defiled by food or to profane the holy covenant; and they did die. Very great wrath came upon Israel.

This is the word of the Lord.   1 Maccabees 1.10–15, 41–43, 54–57, 62–64

Responsorial Psalm

R **Help us, O God, for the glory of your name;
[deliver us, and wipe away our sins].**   cf *Psalm* 79.9

O God, the heathen have come into your heritage;
your holy temple have they defiled
and made Jerusalem a heap of stones. **R**

The dead bodies of your servants they have given
to be food for the birds of the air,
and the flesh of your faithful to the beasts of the field. **R**

Their blood have they shed like water
on every side of Jerusalem,
and there was no one to bury them. **R**

We have become the taunt of our neighbours,
the scorn and derision of those that are round about us.
Lord, how long will you be angry, for ever?
How long will your jealous fury blaze like fire? **R**   *Psalm* 79.1–5

or the reading and psalm for Year 2 may be read.

Year 2

A reading from the Revelation to John.

The revelation of Jesus Christ, which God gave him to show his servants what
must soon take place; he made it known by sending his angel to his servant
John, who testified to the word of God and to the testimony of Jesus Christ,
even to all that he saw. Blessed is the one who reads aloud the words of the
prophecy, and blessed are those who hear and who keep what is written in
it; for the time is near.

John to the seven churches that are in Asia: Grace to you and peace from
him who is and who was and who is to come, and from the seven spirits
who are before his throne.

I heard a loud voice saying, 'To the angel of the church in Ephesus write:
These are the words of him who holds the seven stars in his right hand, who
walks among the seven golden lampstands:

'I know your works, your toil and your patient endurance. I know that you
cannot tolerate evildoers; you have tested those who claim to be apostles but
are not, and have found them to be false. I also know that you are enduring
patiently and bearing up for the sake of my name, and that you have not grown
weary. But I have this against you, that you have abandoned the love you had
at first. Remember then from what you have fallen; repent, and do the works
you did at first. If not, I will come to you and remove your lampstand from
its place, unless you repent.'

This is the word of the Lord.   *Revelation* 1.1–4, 2.1–5

R   **The Lord knows the way of the righteous;**
     [who delight in his law].   cf Psalm 1.6a, 2a

Blessed are they who have not walked
in the counsel of the wicked,
nor lingered in the way of sinners,
nor sat in the assembly of the scornful.
Their delight is in the law of the Lord
and they meditate on his law day and night.   **R**

Like a tree planted by streams of water
bearing fruit in due season,
with leaves that do not wither,
whatever they do, it shall prosper.   **R**

As for the wicked, it is not so with them;
they are like chaff which the wind blows away.
Therefore the wicked shall not be able to stand in the judgement,
nor the sinner in the congregation of the righteous.
For the Lord knows the way of the righteous,
but the way of the wicked shall perish.   **R**   Psalm 1

Year 1 and Year 2

Hear the Gospel of our Lord Jesus Christ according to Luke.

As Jesus approached Jericho, a blind man was sitting by the roadside begging.
When he heard a crowd going by, he asked what was happening. They told
him, 'Jesus of Nazareth is passing by.' Then he shouted, 'Jesus, Son of David,
have mercy on me!' Those who were in front sternly ordered him to be quiet;
but he shouted even more loudly, 'Son of David, have mercy on me!' Jesus
stood still and ordered the man to be brought to him; and when he came
near, he asked him, 'What do you want me to do for you?' He said, 'Lord, let
me see again.' Jesus said to him, 'Receive your sight; your faith has saved you.'
Immediately he regained his sight and followed him, glorifying God; and all
the people, when they saw it, praised God.

This is the Gospel of the Lord.   Luke 18.35–end

Week 33: Tuesday between 15 and 21 November

Year 1

Either

A reading from the Second Book of the Maccabees.

Eleazar, one of the scribes in high position, a man now advanced in age and of noble presence, was being forced to open his mouth to eat swine's flesh. But he, welcoming death with honour rather than life with pollution, went up to the rack of his own accord, spitting out the flesh, as all ought to go who have the courage to refuse things that it is not right to taste, even for the natural love of life.

Those who were in charge of that unlawful sacrifice took the man aside because of their long acquaintance with him, and privately urged him to bring meat of his own providing, proper for him to use, and to pretend that he was eating the flesh of the sacrificial meal that had been commanded by the king, so that by doing this he might be saved from death, and be treated kindly on account of his old friendship with them. But making a high resolve, worthy of his years and the dignity of his old age and the grey hairs that he had reached with distinction and his excellent life even from childhood, and moreover according to the holy God-given law, he declared himself quickly, telling them to send him to Hades.

'Such pretence is not worthy of our time of life,' he said, 'for many of the young might suppose that Eleazar in his ninetieth year had gone over to an alien religion, and through my pretence, for the sake of living a brief moment longer, they would be led astray because of me, while I defile and disgrace my old age. Even if for the present I would avoid the punishment of mortals, yet whether I live or die I will not escape the hands of the Almighty. Therefore, by bravely giving up my life now, I will show myself worthy of my old age and leave to the young a noble example of how to die a good death willingly and nobly for the revered and holy laws.'

When he had said this, he went at once to the rack. Those who a little before had acted towards him with goodwill now changed to ill will, because the words he had uttered were in their opinion sheer madness. When he was about to die under the blows, he groaned aloud and said: 'It is clear to the Lord in his holy knowledge that, though I might have been saved from death, I am enduring terrible sufferings in my body under this beating, but in my soul I am glad to suffer these things because I fear him.'

So in this way he died, leaving in his death an example of nobility and a memorial of courage, not only to the young but to the great body of his nation.

This is the word of the Lord. 2 Maccabees 6.18–end

R **The upright shall behold the face of the Lord.**   cf Psalm 11.8

In the Lord have I taken refuge;
how then can you say to me,
'Flee like a bird to the hills,
for see how the wicked bend the bow
and fit their arrows to the string,
to shoot from the shadows at the true of heart'?   R

When the foundations are destroyed,
what can the righteous do?
The Lord is in his holy temple;
the Lord's throne is in heaven.   R

His eyes behold,
his eyelids try every mortal being.
The Lord tries the righteous as well as the wicked,
but those who delight in violence his soul abhors.   R

Upon the wicked he shall rain coals of fire and burning sulphur;
scorching wind shall be their portion to drink.
For the Lord is righteous;
he loves righteous deeds,
and those who are upright shall behold his face.   R   Psalm 11

or the reading and psalm for Year 2 may be read.

Year 2

A reading from the Revelation to John.

I heard a loud voice saying, 'To the angel of the church in Sardis write: These
are the words of him who has the seven spirits of God and the seven stars:
    'I know your works; you have a name for being alive, but you are dead.
Wake up, and strengthen what remains and is at the point of death, for I have
not found your works perfect in the sight of my God. Remember then what
you received and heard; obey it, and repent. If you do not wake up, I will
come like a thief, and you will not know at what hour I will come to you. Yet
you have still a few people in Sardis who have not soiled their clothes; they
will walk with me, dressed in white, for they are worthy. If you conquer, you
will be clothed like them in white robes, and I will not blot your name out
of the book of life; I will confess your name before my Father and before
his angels. Let anyone who has an ear listen to what the Spirit is saying to
the churches.
    'And to the angel of the church in Laodicea write: The words of the Amen,
the faithful and true witness, the origin of God's creation: →

'I know your works; you are neither cold nor hot. I wish that you were either cold or hot. So, because you are lukewarm, and neither cold nor hot, I am about to spit you out of my mouth. For you say, "I am rich, I have prospered, and I need nothing." You do not realize that you are wretched, pitiable, poor, blind, and naked. Therefore I counsel you to buy from me gold refined by fire so that you may be rich; and white robes to clothe you and to keep the shame of your nakedness from being seen; and salve to anoint your eyes so that you may see. I reprove and discipline those whom I love. Be earnest, therefore, and repent. Listen! I am standing at the door, knocking; if you hear my voice and open the door, I will come in to you and eat with you, and you with me. To the one who conquers I will give a place with me on my throne, just as I myself conquered and sat down with my Father on his throne. Let anyone who has an ear listen to what the Spirit is saying to the churches.'

This is the word of the Lord.   *Revelation 3.1–6, 14–end*

Responsorial Psalm

R   **They shall dwell in your tabernacle, O Lord:**
    [those who do what is right].   *cf Psalm 15.1a, 2b*

Lord, who may dwell in your tabernacle?
Who may rest upon your holy hill?
Whoever leads an uncorrupt life
and does the thing that is right.   **R**

Who speaks the truth from the heart
and bears no deceit on the tongue;
who does no evil to a friend
and pours no scorn on a neighbour.   **R**

In whose sight the wicked are not esteemed,
but who honours those who fear the Lord.
Whoever has sworn to a neighbour
and never goes back on that word.   **R**

Who does not lend money in hope of gain,
nor takes a bribe against the innocent;
whoever does these things
shall never fall.   **R**   *Psalm 15*

Hear the Gospel of our Lord Jesus Christ according to Luke.

Jesus entered Jericho and was passing through it. A man was there named Zacchaeus; he was a chief tax-collector and was rich. He was trying to see who Jesus was, but on account of the crowd he could not, because he was short in stature. So he ran ahead and climbed a sycomore tree to see him, because he was going to pass that way. When Jesus came to the place, he looked up and said to him, 'Zacchaeus, hurry and come down; for I must stay at your house today.' So he hurried down and was happy to welcome him. All who saw it began to grumble and said, 'He has gone to be the guest of one who is a sinner.' Zacchaeus stood there and said to the Lord, 'Look, half of my possessions, Lord, I will give to the poor; and if I have defrauded anyone of anything, I will pay back four times as much.' Then Jesus said to him, 'Today salvation has come to this house, because he too is a son of Abraham. For the Son of Man came to seek out and to save the lost.'

This is the Gospel of the Lord. Luke 19.1–10

Week 33: Wednesday between 16 and 22 November

Year I

Either

A reading from the Second Book of the Maccabees.

It happened that seven brothers and their mother were arrested and were being compelled by the king, under torture with whips and thongs, to partake of unlawful swine's flesh.

The mother was especially admirable and worthy of honourable memory. Although she saw her seven sons perish within a single day, she bore it with good courage because of her hope in the Lord. She encouraged each of them in the language of their ancestors. Filled with a noble spirit, she reinforced her woman's reasoning with a man's courage, and said to them, 'I do not know how you came into being in my womb. It was not I who gave you life and breath, nor I who set in order the elements within each of you. Therefore the Creator of the world, who shaped the beginning of humankind and devised the origin of all things, will in his mercy give life and breath back to you again, since you now forget yourselves for the sake of his laws.'

Antiochus felt that he was being treated with contempt, and he was suspicious of her reproachful tone. The youngest brother being still alive, Antiochus not only appealed to him in words, but promised with oaths that he would make him rich and enviable if he would turn from the ways of his ancestors, and that he would take him for his Friend and entrust him with public affairs. Since the young man would not listen to him at all, the king called the mother to him and urged her to advise the youth to save himself. →

After much urging on his part, she undertook to persuade her son. But, leaning close to him, she spoke in their native language as follows, deriding the cruel tyrant: 'My son, have pity on me. I carried you for nine months in my womb, and nursed you for three years, and have reared you and brought you up to this point in your life, and have taken care of you. I beg you, my child, to look at the heaven and the earth and see everything that is in them, and recognize that God did not make them out of things that existed. And in the same way the human race came into being. Do not fear this butcher, but prove worthy of your brothers. Accept death, so that in God's mercy I may get you back again along with your brothers.'

While she was still speaking, the young man said, 'What are you waiting for? I will not obey the king's command, but I obey the command of the law that was given to our ancestors through Moses. But you, who have contrived all sorts of evil against the Hebrews, will certainly not escape the hands of God.'

This is the word of the Lord. 2 Maccabees 7.1, 20–31

Responsorial Psalm

R **I will offer to you a sacrifice of thanksgiving:**
 [and call upon the name of the Lord]. Psalm 116.15

or

R **Alleluia!**

How shall I repay the Lord
for all the benefits he has given to me?
I will lift up the cup of salvation
and call upon the name of the Lord.   R

I will fulfil my vows to the Lord
in the presence of all his people.
Precious in the sight of the Lord
is the death of his faithful servants.   R

O Lord, I am your servant,
your servant, the child of your handmaid;
you have freed me from my bonds.
I will offer to you a sacrifice of thanksgiving
and call upon the name of the Lord.   R

I will fulfil my vows to the Lord
in the presence of all his people,
in the courts of the house of the Lord,
in the midst of you, O Jerusalem.   R Psalm 116.10–end

or the reading and psalm for Year 2 may be read.

A reading from the Revelation to John.

I looked, and there in heaven a door stood open! And the first voice, which I had heard speaking to me like a trumpet, said, 'Come up here, and I will show you what must take place after this.' At once I was in the spirit, and there in heaven stood a throne, with one seated on the throne! And the one seated there looks like jasper and cornelian, and around the throne is a rainbow that looks like an emerald. Around the throne are twenty-four thrones, and seated on the thrones are twenty-four elders, dressed in white robes, with golden crowns on their heads. Coming from the throne are flashes of lightning, and rumblings and peals of thunder, and in front of the throne burn seven flaming torches, which are the seven spirits of God; and in front of the throne there is something like a sea of glass, like crystal.

Around the throne, and on each side of the throne, are four living creatures, full of eyes in front and behind: the first living creature like a lion, the second living creature like an ox, the third living creature with a face like a human face, and the fourth living creature like a flying eagle. And the four living creatures, each of them with six wings, are full of eyes all around and inside. Day and night without ceasing they sing,

'Holy, holy, holy,
the Lord God the Almighty,
who was and is and is to come.'

And whenever the living creatures give glory and honour and thanks to the one who is seated on the throne, who lives for ever and ever, the twenty-four elders fall before the one who is seated on the throne and worship the one who lives for ever and ever; they cast their crowns before the throne, singing,

'You are worthy, our Lord and God,
to receive glory and honour and power,
for you created all things,
and by your will they existed and were created.'

This is the word of the Lord.   Revelation 4

Responsorial Psalm

R   **Holy, holy, holy,
is the Lord God the Almighty.**   cf Revelation 4.8b

or

R   **Alleluia!**

O praise God in his holiness;
praise him in the firmament of his power.
Praise him for his mighty acts;
praise him according to his excellent greatness.   **R**   →

Praise him with the blast of the trumpet;
praise him upon the harp and lyre.
Praise him with timbrel and dances;
praise him upon the strings and pipe. R

R **Holy, holy, holy,**
   is the Lord God the Almighty.

   or

R **Alleluia!**

Praise him with ringing cymbals;
praise him upon the clashing cymbals.
Let everything that has breath
praise the Lord. R   *Psalm 150*

Year 1 and Year 2

Hear the Gospel of our Lord Jesus Christ according to Luke.

As the crowds were listening, Jesus went on to tell a parable, because he was
near Jerusalem, and because they supposed that the kingdom of God was to
appear immediately. So he said, 'A nobleman went to a distant country to
get royal power for himself and then return. He summoned ten of his slaves,
and gave them ten pounds, and said to them, "Do business with these until I
come back." But the citizens of his country hated him and sent a delegation
after him, saying, "We do not want this man to rule over us."

'When he returned, having received royal power, he ordered these slaves,
to whom he had given the money, to be summoned so that he might find
out what they had gained by trading. The first came forward and said, "Lord,
your pound has made ten more pounds." He said to him, "Well done, good
slave! Because you have been trustworthy in a very small thing, take charge
of ten cities." Then the second came, saying, "Lord, your pound has made
five pounds." He said to him, "And you, rule over five cities." Then the other
came, saying, "Lord, here is your pound. I wrapped it up in a piece of cloth,
for I was afraid of you, because you are a harsh man; you take what you did
not deposit, and reap what you did not sow." He said to him, "I will judge
you by your own words, you wicked slave! You knew, did you, that I was a
harsh man, taking what I did not deposit and reaping what I did not sow?
Why then did you not put my money into the bank? Then when I returned,
I could have collected it with interest." He said to the bystanders, "Take the
pound from him and give it to the one who has ten pounds." (And they said
to him, "Lord, he has ten pounds!") "I tell you, to all those who have, more
will be given; but from those who have nothing, even what they have will be
taken away. But as for these enemies of mine who did not want me to be king
over them – bring them here and slaughter them in my presence." '

After he had said this, he went on ahead, going up to Jerusalem.

This is the Gospel of the Lord.   *Luke 19.11–28*

Week 33: Thursday between 17 and 23 November

Year I

Either

A reading from the First Book of the Maccabees.

The king's officers who were enforcing the apostasy came to the town of Modein to make the people offer sacrifice. Many from Israel came to them; and Mattathias and his sons were assembled. Then the king's officers spoke to Mattathias as follows: 'You are a leader, honoured and great in this town, and supported by sons and brothers. Now be the first to come and do what the king commands, as all the Gentiles and the people of Judah and those that are left in Jerusalem have done. Then you and your sons will be numbered among the Friends of the king, and you and your sons will be honoured with silver and gold and many gifts.'

But Mattathias answered and said in a loud voice: 'Even if all the nations that live under the rule of the king obey him, and have chosen to obey his commandments, everyone of them abandoning the religion of their ancestors, I and my sons and my brothers will continue to live by the covenant of our ancestors. Far be it from us to desert the law and the ordinances. We will not obey the king's words by turning aside from our religion to the right hand or to the left.'

When he had finished speaking these words, a Jew came forward in the sight of all to offer sacrifice on the altar in Modein, according to the king's command. When Mattathias saw it, he burned with zeal and his heart was stirred. He gave vent to righteous anger; he ran and killed him on the altar. At the same time he killed the king's officer who was forcing them to sacrifice, and he tore down the altar. Thus he burned with zeal for the law, just as Phinehas did against Zimri son of Salu.

Then Mattathias cried out in the town with a loud voice, saying: 'Let everyone who is zealous for the law and supports the covenant come out with me!' Then he and his sons fled to the hills and left all that they had in the town.

At that time many who were seeking righteousness and justice went down to the wilderness to live there.

This is the word of the Lord. *1 Maccabees 2.15–29*

Responsorial Psalm

R **Remember us, O God,
and keep your covenant with us.** *cf Jeremiah 14.21*

'Many a time have they fought against me from my youth,'
may Israel now say;
'Many a time have they fought against me from my youth,
but they have not prevailed against me.' **R** →

The ploughers ploughed upon my back
and made their furrows long.
But the righteous Lord
has cut the cords of the wicked in pieces. R

R **Remember us, O God,
and keep your covenant with us.**

Let them be put to shame and turned backwards,
as many as are enemies of Zion.
Let them be like grass upon the housetops,
which withers before it can grow,
so that no reaper can fill his hand,
nor a binder of sheaves his bosom. R

And none who go by may say,
'The blessing of the Lord be upon you.
We bless you in the name of the Lord.' R   *Psalm* 129

or the reading and psalm for Year 2 may be read.

Year 2

A reading from the Revelation to John.

I saw in the right hand of the one seated on the throne a scroll written on
the inside and on the back, sealed with seven seals; and I saw a mighty angel
proclaiming with a loud voice, 'Who is worthy to open the scroll and break
its seals?' And no one in heaven or on earth or under the earth was able to
open the scroll or to look into it. And I began to weep bitterly because no
one was found worthy to open the scroll or to look into it. Then one of the
elders said to me, 'Do not weep. See, the Lion of the tribe of Judah, the Root
of David, has conquered, so that he can open the scroll and its seven seals.'
    Then I saw between the throne and the four living creatures and among
the elders a Lamb standing as if it had been slaughtered, having seven horns
and seven eyes, which are the seven spirits of God sent out into all the earth.
He went and took the scroll from the right hand of the one who was seated
on the throne. When he had taken the scroll, the four living creatures and the
twenty-four elders fell before the Lamb, each holding a harp and golden bowls
full of incense, which are the prayers of the saints. They sing a new song:
    'You are worthy to take the scroll
        and to open its seals,
    for you were slaughtered and by your blood you ransomed for God
        saints from every tribe and language and people and nation;
    you have made them to be a kingdom and priests serving our God,
        and they will reign on earth.'

This is the word of the Lord.   *Revelation* 5.1–10

R* Sing to the Lord a new song:
   [sing his praise in the congregation of the faithful].   *Psalm* 149.1

Let Israel rejoice in their maker;
let the children of Zion be joyful in their king.
Let them praise his name in the dance;
let them sing praise to him with timbrel and lyre.   **R**

For the Lord has pleasure in his people
and adorns the poor with salvation.
Let the faithful be joyful in glory;
let them rejoice in their ranks.   **R**   *Psalm* 149.1–5

Year 1 and Year 2

Hear the Gospel of our Lord Jesus Christ according to Luke.

As Jesus came near Jerusalem and saw the city, he wept over it, saying, 'If you, even you, had only recognized on this day the things that make for peace! But now they are hidden from your eyes. Indeed, the days will come upon you, when your enemies will set up ramparts around you and surround you, and hem you in on every side. They will crush you to the ground, you and your children within you, and they will not leave within you one stone upon another; because you did not recognize the time of your visitation from God.'

This is the Gospel of the Lord.   *Luke* 19.41–44

Week 33: Friday between 18 and 24 November

Year 1

Either

A reading from the First Book of the Maccabees.

Judas and his brothers said, 'See, our enemies are crushed; let us go up to cleanse the sanctuary and dedicate it.' So all the army assembled and went up to Mount Zion.

    Early in the morning on the twenty-fifth day of the ninth month, which is the month of Chislev, in the one hundred and forty-eighth year, they rose and offered sacrifice, as the law directs, on the new altar of burnt-offering that they had built. At the very season and on the very day that the Gentiles had profaned it, it was dedicated with songs and harps and lutes and cymbals. All the people fell on their faces and worshipped and blessed Heaven, who had prospered them. So they celebrated the dedication of the altar for eight days, and joyfully offered burnt-offerings; they offered a sacrifice of well-being and a thanksgiving-offering. They decorated the front of the temple with golden crowns and small shields; they restored the gates and the chambers for the   →

priests, and fitted them with doors. There was very great joy among the people, and the disgrace brought by the Gentiles was removed.

Then Judas and his brothers and all the assembly of Israel determined that every year at that season the days of dedication of the altar should be observed with joy and gladness for eight days, beginning with the twenty-fifth day of the month of Chislev.

This is the word of the Lord.   1 Maccabees 4.36–37, 52–59

Responsorial Psalm

R **[I was glad when they said to me:]**
   Let us go to the house of the Lord.   Psalm 122.1

I was glad when they said to me,
'Let us go to the house of the Lord.'
And now our feet are standing
within your gates, O Jerusalem.   R

Jerusalem, built as a city
that is at unity in itself.
Thither the tribes go up,
the tribes of the Lord.   R

As is decreed for Israel,
to give thanks to the name of the Lord.
For there are set the thrones of judgement,
the thrones of the house of David.   R

O pray for the peace of Jerusalem:
'May they prosper who love you.
Peace be within your walls
and tranquillity within your palaces.'   R

For my kindred and companions' sake,
I will pray that peace be with you.
For the sake of the house of the Lord our God,
I will seek to do you good.   R   Psalm 122

or the reading and psalm for Year 2 may be read.

Year 2

A reading from the Revelation to John.

The voice that I had heard from heaven spoke to me again, saying, 'Go, take the scroll that is open in the hand of the angel who is standing on the sea and on the land.' So I went to the angel and told him to give me the little scroll; and he said to me, 'Take it, and eat; it will be bitter to your stomach, but sweet as honey in your mouth.' So I took the little scroll from the hand of the angel and ate it; it was sweet as honey in my mouth, but when I had eaten it, my stomach was made bitter. Then they said to me, 'You must prophesy again about many peoples and nations and languages and kings.'

This is the word of the Lord.   Revelation 10.8—end

Responsorial Psalm

R   **Blessed are those who walk in the law of the Lord.**   cf Psalm 119.1

You have dealt graciously with your servant,
according to your word, O Lord.
O teach me true understanding and knowledge,
for I have trusted in your commandments.   **R**

Before I was afflicted I went astray,
but now I keep your word.
You are gracious and do good;
O Lord, teach me your statutes.   **R**

The proud have smeared me with lies,
but I will keep your commandments with my whole heart.
Their heart has become gross with fat,
but my delight is in your law.   **R**

It is good for me that I have been afflicted,
that I may learn your statutes.
The law of your mouth is dearer to me
than a hoard of gold and silver.   **R**   Psalm 119.65—72

Year 1 and Year 2

Hear the Gospel of our Lord Jesus Christ according to Luke.

Jesus entered the temple and began to drive out those who were selling things there; and he said, 'It is written,
    "My house shall be a house of prayer";
        but you have made it a den of robbers.'
Every day he was teaching in the temple. The chief priests, the scribes, and the leaders of the people kept looking for a way to kill him; but they did not find anything they could do, for all the people were spellbound by what they heard.

This is the Gospel of the Lord.   Luke 19.45—end

Week 33: Saturday between 19 and 25 November

Year 1

Either

A reading from the First Book of the Maccabees.

King Antiochus was going through the upper provinces when he heard that Elymais in Persia was a city famed for its wealth in silver and gold. Its temple was very rich, containing golden shields, breastplates, and weapons left there by Alexander son of Philip, the Macedonian king who first reigned over the Greeks. So he came and tried to take the city and plunder it, but he could not because his plan had become known to the citizens and they withstood him in battle. So he fled and in great disappointment left there to return to Babylon.

Then someone came to him in Persia and reported that the armies that had gone into the land of Judah had been routed; that Lysias had gone first with a strong force, but had turned and fled before the Jews; that the Jews had grown strong from the arms, supplies, and abundant spoils that they had taken from the armies they had cut down; that they had torn down the abomination that he had erected on the altar in Jerusalem; and that they had surrounded the sanctuary with high walls as before, and also Beth-zur, his town.

When the king heard this news, he was astounded and badly shaken. He took to his bed and became sick from disappointment, because things had not turned out for him as he had planned. He lay there for many days, because deep disappointment continually gripped him, and he realized that he was dying. So he called all his Friends and said to them, 'Sleep has departed from my eyes and I am downhearted with worry. I said to myself, "To what distress I have come! And into what a great flood I now am plunged! For I was kind and beloved in my power." But now I remember the wrong I did in Jerusalem. I seized all its vessels of silver and gold, and I sent to destroy the inhabitants of Judah without good reason. I know that it is because of this that these misfortunes have come upon me; here I am, perishing of bitter disappointment in a strange land.'

This is the word of the Lord.   1 Maccabees 6.1–13

Responsorial Psalm

R* **Our help is in the name of the Lord,**
   [who has made heaven and earth].   Psalm 124.7

If the Lord himself had not been on our side,
now may Israel say;
if the Lord had not been on our side,
when enemies rose up against us.   **R**

Then would they have swallowed us alive
when their anger burned against us;
then would the waters have overwhelmed us
and the torrent gone over our soul;
over our soul would have swept the raging waters.   R

But blessed be the Lord
who has not given us over to be a prey for their teeth.
Our soul has escaped
as a bird from the snare of the fowler;
the snare is broken and we are delivered.   R*   Psalm 124

or the reading and psalm for Year 2 may be read.

Year 2

A reading from the Revelation to John.

The two witnesses are the two olive trees and the two lampstands that stand
before the Lord of the earth. And if anyone wants to harm them, fire pours
from their mouth and consumes their foes; anyone who wants to harm them
must be killed in this manner. They have authority to shut the sky, so that no
rain may fall during the days of their prophesying, and they have authority
over the waters to turn them into blood, and to strike the earth with every
kind of plague, as often as they desire.

When they have finished their testimony, the beast that comes up from
the bottomless pit will make war on them and conquer them and kill them,
and their dead bodies will lie in the street of the great city that is prophetically
called Sodom and Egypt, where also their Lord was crucified. For three and a
half days members of the peoples and tribes and languages and nations will
gaze at their dead bodies and refuse to let them be placed in a tomb; and
the inhabitants of the earth will gloat over them and celebrate and exchange
presents, because these two prophets had been a torment to the inhabitants
of the earth.

But after the three and a half days, the breath of life from God entered
them, and they stood on their feet, and those who saw them were terrified.
Then they heard a loud voice from heaven saying to them, 'Come up here!'
And they went up to heaven in a cloud while their enemies watched them.

This is the word of the Lord.   *Revelation 11.4–12*

Responsorial Psalm

R* **I will sing a new song to you, O God;**
    and praise you on a ten-stringed harp.   *cf Psalm 144.9*

Blessed be the Lord my rock,
who teaches my hands for war
and my fingers for battle.   R   →

My steadfast help and my fortress,
my stronghold and my deliverer,
my shield in whom I trust,
who subdues the peoples under me.   R

**R* I will sing a new song to you, O God;
and praise you on a ten-stringed harp.**

O Lord, what are mortals that you should consider them;
mere human beings, that you should take thought for them?
They are like a breath of wind;
their days pass away like a shadow.   R

Bow your heavens, O Lord, and come down;
touch the mountains and they shall smoke.
Cast down your lightnings and scatter them;
shoot out your arrows and let thunder roar.   R

Reach down your hand from on high;
deliver me and take me out of the great waters,
from the hand of foreign enemies,
whose mouth speaks wickedness
and their right hand is the hand of falsehood.   R*   Psalm 144.1–9

Year 1 and Year 2

Hear the Gospel of our Lord Jesus Christ according to Luke.

Some Sadducees, those who say there is no resurrection, came to Jesus and
asked him a question, 'Teacher, Moses wrote for us that if a man's brother
dies, leaving a wife but no children, the man shall marry the widow and
raise up children for his brother. Now there were seven brothers; the first
married, and died childless; then the second and the third married her, and
so in the same way all seven died childless. Finally the woman also died. In
the resurrection, therefore, whose wife will the woman be? For the seven
had married her.'

Jesus said to them, 'Those who belong to this age marry and are given
in marriage; but those who are considered worthy of a place in that age and
in the resurrection from the dead neither marry nor are given in marriage.
Indeed they cannot die any more, because they are like angels and are children
of God, being children of the resurrection. And the fact that the dead are
raised Moses himself showed, in the story about the bush, where he speaks
of the Lord as the God of Abraham, the God of Isaac, and the God of Jacob.
Now he is God not of the dead, but of the living; for to him all of them are
alive.' Then some of the scribes answered, 'Teacher, you have spoken well.'
For they no longer dared to ask him another question.

This is the Gospel of the Lord.   Luke 20.27–40

Year I

A reading from the Book of Daniel.

In the third year of the reign of King Jehoiakim of Judah, King Nebuchadnezzar of Babylon came to Jerusalem and besieged it. The Lord let King Jehoiakim of Judah fall into his power, as well as some of the vessels of the house of God. These he brought to the land of Shinar, and placed the vessels in the treasury of his gods.

Then the king commanded his palace master Ashpenaz to bring some of the Israelites of the royal family and of the nobility, young men without physical defect and handsome, versed in every branch of wisdom, endowed with knowledge and insight, and competent to serve in the king's palace; they were to be taught the literature and language of the Chaldeans. The king assigned them a daily portion of the royal rations of food and wine. They were to be educated for three years, so that at the end of that time they could be stationed in the king's court. Among them were Daniel, Hananiah, Mishael, and Azariah, from the tribe of Judah.

But Daniel resolved that he would not defile himself with the royal rations of food and wine; so he asked the palace master to allow him not to defile himself. Now God allowed Daniel to receive favour and compassion from the palace master. The palace master said to Daniel, 'I am afraid of my lord the king; he has appointed your food and your drink. If he should see you in poorer condition than the other young men of your own age, you would endanger my head with the king.' Then Daniel asked the guard whom the palace master had appointed over Daniel, Hananiah, Mishael, and Azariah: 'Please test your servants for ten days. Let us be given vegetables to eat and water to drink. You can then compare our appearance with the appearance of the young men who eat the royal rations, and deal with your servants according to what you observe.' So he agreed to this proposal and tested them for ten days. At the end of ten days it was observed that they appeared better and fatter than all the young men who had been eating the royal rations. So the guard continued to withdraw their royal rations and the wine they were to drink, and gave them vegetables. To these four young men God gave knowledge and skill in every aspect of literature and wisdom; Daniel also had insight into all visions and dreams.

At the end of the time that the king had set for them to be brought in, the palace master brought them into the presence of Nebuchadnezzar, and the king spoke with them. And among them all, no one was found to compare with Daniel, Hananiah, Mishael, and Azariah; therefore they were stationed in the king's court. In every matter of wisdom and understanding concerning which the king inquired of them, he found them ten times better than all the magicians and enchanters in his whole kingdom.

This is the word of the Lord.   Daniel 1.1–6, 8–20

Canticle

R   **You are worthy to be praised and exalted for ever.**

Blessed are you, the God of our ancestors.   [R]
Blessed is your holy and glorious name.   [R]
Blessed are you, in your holy and glorious temple.   R

Blessed are you who look into the depths.   [R]
Blessed are you, enthroned on the cherubim.   [R]
Blessed are you on the throne of your kingdom.   [R]
Blessed are you in the heights of heaven.   R   *Song of the Three 29–34*

Year 2

A reading from the Revelation to John.

I looked, and there was the Lamb, standing on Mount Zion! And with him were
one hundred and forty-four thousand who had his name and his Father's name
written on their foreheads. And I heard a voice from heaven like the sound of
many waters and like the sound of loud thunder; the voice I heard was like
the sound of harpists playing on their harps, and they sing a new song before
the throne and before the four living creatures and before the elders. No one
could learn that song except the one hundred forty-four thousand who have
been redeemed from the earth. It is these who have not defiled themselves
with women, for they are virgins; these follow the Lamb wherever he goes.
They have been redeemed from humankind as first fruits for God and the
Lamb, and in their mouth no lie was found; they are blameless.

This is the word of the Lord.   *Revelation 14.1–5*

Responsorial Psalm

R   **The earth is the Lord's, and all who dwell therein.**   *cf Psalm 24.1*

The earth is the Lord's and all that fills it,
the compass of the world and all who dwell therein.
For he has founded it upon the seas
and set it firm upon the rivers of the deep.   R

'Who shall ascend the hill of the Lord,
or who can rise up in his holy place?
Those who have clean hands and a pure heart,
who have not lifted up their soul to an idol,
nor sworn an oath to a lie.   R

'They shall receive a blessing from the Lord,
a just reward from the God of their salvation.'
Such is the company of those who seek him,
of those who seek your face, O God of Jacob.   R   *Psalm 24.1–6*

Hear the Gospel of our Lord Jesus Christ according to Luke.

Jesus looked up and saw rich people putting their gifts into the treasury; he also saw a poor widow put in two small copper coins. He said, 'Truly I tell you, this poor widow has put in more than all of them; for all of them have contributed out of their abundance, but she out of her poverty has put in all she had to live on.'

This is the Gospel of the Lord.
Luke 21.1–4

Week 34: Tuesday between 22 and 28 November

Year 1

A reading from the Book of Daniel.

Daniel said to King Nebuchadnezzar, 'You were looking, O king, and lo! there was a great statue. This statue was huge, its brilliance extraordinary; it was standing before you, and its appearance was frightening. The head of that statue was of fine gold, its chest and arms of silver, its middle and thighs of bronze, its legs of iron, its feet partly of iron and partly of clay. As you looked on, a stone was cut out, not by human hands, and it struck the statue on its feet of iron and clay and broke them in pieces. Then the iron, the clay, the bronze, the silver, and the gold, were all broken in pieces and became like the chaff of the summer threshing-floors; and the wind carried them away, so that not a trace of them could be found. But the stone that struck the statue became a great mountain and filled the whole earth.

'This was the dream; now we will tell the king its interpretation. You, O king, the king of kings – to whom the God of heaven has given the kingdom, the power, the might, and the glory, into whose hand he has given human beings, wherever they live, the wild animals of the field, and the birds of the air, and whom he has established as ruler over them all – you are the head of gold. After you shall arise another kingdom inferior to yours, and yet a third kingdom of bronze, which shall rule over the whole earth. And there shall be a fourth kingdom, strong as iron; just as iron crushes and smashes everything, it shall crush and shatter all these. As you saw the feet and toes partly of potter's clay and partly of iron, it shall be a divided kingdom; but some of the strength of iron shall be in it, as you saw the iron mixed with the clay. As the toes of the feet were part iron and part clay, so the kingdom shall be partly strong and partly brittle. As you saw the iron mixed with clay, so will they mix with one another in marriage, but they will not hold together, just as iron does not mix with clay.

'And in the days of those kings the God of heaven will set up a kingdom that shall never be destroyed, nor shall this kingdom be left to another people. It shall crush all these kingdoms and bring them to an end, and it shall stand $\rightarrow$

Week 34: Tuesday 797

for ever; just as you saw that a stone was cut from the mountain not by hands, and that it crushed the iron, the bronze, the clay, the silver, and the gold. The great God has informed the king what shall be hereafter. The dream is certain, and its interpretation trustworthy.'

This is the word of the Lord. Daniel 2.31–45

Canticle

R **Sing God's praise and exalt him for ever!**

Bless the Lord all you works of the Lord. [R]
Bless the Lord you heavens. R

Bless the Lord you angels of the Lord; [R]
bless the Lord you waters above the heavens; [R]
bless the Lord all you his hosts. R Song of the Three 35–39

Year 2

A reading from the Revelation to John.

I looked, and there was a white cloud, and seated on the cloud was one like the Son of Man, with a golden crown on his head, and a sharp sickle in his hand! Another angel came out of the temple, calling with a loud voice to the one who sat on the cloud, 'Use your sickle and reap, for the hour to reap has come, because the harvest of the earth is fully ripe.' So the one who sat on the cloud swung his sickle over the earth, and the earth was reaped.

Then another angel came out of the temple in heaven, and he too had a sharp sickle. Then another angel came out from the altar, the angel who has authority over fire, and he called with a loud voice to him who had the sharp sickle, 'Use your sharp sickle and gather the clusters of the vine of the earth, for its grapes are ripe.' So the angel swung his sickle over the earth and gathered the vintage of the earth, and he threw it into the great wine press of the wrath of God.

This is the word of the Lord. Revelation 14.14–19

Responsorial Psalm

R **Sing to the Lord a new song;**
  [sing to the Lord, all the earth]. Psalm 96.1

Sing to the Lord and bless his name;
tell out his salvation from day to day.
Declare his glory among the nations
and his wonders among all peoples. R

For great is the Lord and greatly to be praised;
he is more to be feared than all gods.
For all the gods of the nations are but idols;
it is the Lord who made the heavens.   R

Honour and majesty are before him;
power and splendour are in his sanctuary.
Ascribe to the Lord, you families of the peoples;
ascribe to the Lord honour and strength.   R

Ascribe to the Lord the honour due to his name;
bring offerings and come into his courts.
O worship the Lord in the beauty of holiness;
let the whole earth tremble before him.   R

Tell it out among the nations that the Lord is king.
He has made the world so firm that it cannot be moved;
he will judge the peoples with equity.   R

Let the heavens rejoice and let the earth be glad;
let the sea thunder and all that is in it;
let the fields be joyful and all that is in them;
let all the trees of the wood shout for joy before the Lord.   R

For he comes, he comes to judge the earth;
with righteousness he will judge the world
and the peoples with his truth.   R   Psalm 96

Year 1 and Year 2

Hear the Gospel of our Lord Jesus Christ according to Luke.

When some were speaking about the temple, how it was adorned with beautiful stones and gifts dedicated to God, Jesus said, 'As for these things that you see, the days will come when not one stone will be left upon another; all will be thrown down.'

The disciples asked him, 'Teacher, when will this be, and what will be the sign that this is about to take place?' And he said, 'Beware that you are not led astray; for many will come in my name and say, "I am he!" and, "The time is near!" Do not go after them.

'When you hear of wars and insurrections, do not be terrified; for these things must take place first, but the end will not follow immediately.' Then he said to them, 'Nation will rise against nation, and kingdom against kingdom; there will be great earthquakes, and in various places famines and plagues; and there will be dreadful portents and great signs from heaven.'

This is the Gospel of the Lord.   Luke 21.5–11

Week 34: Wednesday between 23 and 29 November

Year I

A reading from the Book of Daniel.

King Belshazzar made a great festival for a thousand of his lords, and he was drinking wine in the presence of the thousand.

Under the influence of the wine, Belshazzar commanded that they bring in the vessels of gold and silver that his father Nebuchadnezzar had taken out of the temple in Jerusalem, so that the king and his lords, his wives, and his concubines might drink from them. So they brought in the vessels of gold and silver that had been taken out of the temple, the house of God in Jerusalem, and the king and his lords, his wives, and his concubines drank from them. They drank the wine and praised the gods of gold and silver, bronze, iron, wood, and stone.

Immediately the fingers of a human hand appeared and began writing on the plaster of the wall of the royal palace, next to the lampstand. The king was watching the hand as it wrote. Then the king's face turned pale, and his thoughts terrified him. His limbs gave way, and his knees knocked together.

Then Daniel was brought in before the king. The king said to Daniel, 'So you are Daniel, one of the exiles of Judah, whom my father the king brought from Judah? I have heard of you that a spirit of the gods is in you, and that enlightenment, understanding, and excellent wisdom are found in you. But I have heard that you can give interpretations and solve problems. Now if you are able to read the writing and tell me its interpretation, you shall be clothed in purple, have a chain of gold around your neck, and rank third in the kingdom.'

Then Daniel answered in the presence of the king, 'Let your gifts be for yourself, or give your rewards to someone else! Nevertheless, I will read the writing to the king and let him know the interpretation. You have exalted yourself against the Lord of heaven! The vessels of his temple have been brought in before you, and you and your lords, your wives and your concubines have been drinking wine from them. You have praised the gods of silver and gold, of bronze, iron, wood, and stone, which do not see or hear or know; but the God in whose power is your very breath, and to whom belong all your ways, you have not honoured.

'So from his presence the hand was sent and this writing was inscribed. And this is the writing that was inscribed: MENE, MENE, TEKEL, and PARSIN. This is the interpretation of the matter: MENE, God has numbered the days of your kingdom and brought it to an end; TEKEL, you have been weighed on the scales and found wanting; PERES, your kingdom is divided and given to the Medes and Persians.'

This is the word of the Lord.   *Daniel 5.1–6, 13–14, 16–17, 23–28*

Canticle

R Sing God's praise and exalt him for ever.

Bless the Lord sun and moon;   [R]
bless the Lord you stars of heaven;   [R]
bless the Lord all rain and dew.   **R**

Bless the Lord all winds that blow;   [R]
bless the Lord you fire and heat;   [R]
bless the Lord scorching wind and bitter cold.   **R**   *Song of the Three 40–45*

Year 2

A reading from the Revelation to John.

I saw another portent in heaven, great and amazing: seven angels with seven plagues, which are the last, for with them the wrath of God is ended.

And I saw what appeared to be a sea of glass mixed with fire, and those who had conquered the beast and its image and the number of its name standing beside the sea of glass with harps of God in their hands. And they sing the song of Moses, the servant of God, and the song of the Lamb:
'Great and amazing are your deeds,
    Lord God the Almighty!
Just and true are your ways,
    King of the nations!
Lord, who will not fear
    and glorify your name?
For you alone are holy.
    All nations will come
    and worship before you,
for your judgements have been revealed.'

This is the word of the Lord.   *Revelation 15.1–4*

Responsorial Psalm

**R* Sound praises to the Lord, all the earth;
[break into song and make music].**   *cf Psalm 98.5*

Sing to the Lord a new song,
for he has done marvellous things.
His own right hand and his holy arm
have won for him the victory.   **R**

The Lord has made known his salvation;
his deliverance has he openly shown
in the sight of the nations.   **R**   →

He has remembered his mercy and faithfulness
towards the house of Israel,
and all the ends of the earth have seen
the salvation of our God.   R*

R* **Sound praises to the Lord, all the earth;**
   [break into song and make music].

Make music to the Lord with the lyre,
with the lyre and the voice of melody.
With trumpets and the sound of the horn
sound praises before the Lord, the King.   R

Let the sea thunder and all that fills it,
the world and all that dwell upon it.
Let the rivers clap their hands
and let the hills ring out together before the Lord.   R

For he comes to judge the earth:
in righteousness he judge the world
and the peoples with equity.   R   *Psalm 98*

Year I and Year 2

Hear the Gospel of our Lord Jesus Christ according to Luke.

Jesus said to the disciples, 'They will arrest you and persecute you; they will
hand you over to synagogues and prisons, and you will be brought before
kings and governors because of my name. This will give you an opportunity
to testify. So make up your minds not to prepare your defence in advance; for
I will give you words and a wisdom that none of your opponents will be able
to withstand or contradict. You will be betrayed even by parents and brothers,
by relatives and friends; and they will put some of you to death. You will be
hated by all because of my name. But not a hair of your head will perish. By
your endurance you will gain your souls.'

This is the Gospel of the Lord.   Luke 21.12–19

Week 34: Thursday between 24 and 30 November

Year I

A reading from the Book of Daniel.

The conspirators against Daniel approached King Darius and said concerning
the interdict, 'O king! Did you not sign an interdict, that anyone who prays
to anyone, divine or human, within thirty days except to you, O king, shall
be thrown into a den of lions?' The king answered, 'The thing stands fast,
according to the law of the Medes and Persians, which cannot be revoked.'

Then they responded to the king, 'Daniel, one of the exiles from Judah, pays no attention to you, O king, or to the interdict you have signed, but he is saying his prayers three times a day.'

When the king heard the charge, he was very much distressed. He was determined to save Daniel, and until the sun went down he made every effort to rescue him. Then the conspirators came to the king and said to him, 'Know, O king, that it is a law of the Medes and Persians that no interdict or ordinance that the king establishes can be changed.'

Then the king gave the command, and Daniel was brought and thrown into the den of lions. The king said to Daniel, 'May your God, whom you faithfully serve, deliver you!' A stone was brought and laid on the mouth of the den, and the king sealed it with his own signet and with the signet of his lords, so that nothing might be changed concerning Daniel. Then the king went to his palace and spent the night fasting; no food was brought to him, and sleep fled from him.

Then, at break of day, the king got up and hurried to the den of lions. When he came near the den where Daniel was, he cried out anxiously to Daniel, 'O Daniel, servant of the living God, has your God whom you faithfully serve been able to deliver you from the lions?' Daniel then said to the king, 'O king, live for ever! My God sent his angel and shut the lions' mouths so that they would not hurt me, because I was found blameless before him; and also before you, O king, I have done no wrong.' Then the king was exceedingly glad and commanded that Daniel be taken up out of the den. So Daniel was taken up out of the den, and no kind of harm was found on him, because he had trusted in his God. The king gave a command, and those who had accused Daniel were brought and thrown into the den of lions – they, their children, and their wives. Before they reached the bottom of the den the lions overpowered them and broke all their bones in pieces.

Then King Darius wrote to all peoples and nations of every language throughout the whole world: 'May you have abundant prosperity! I make a decree, that in all my royal dominion people should tremble and fear before the God of Daniel:

For he is the living God,
    enduring for ever.
His kingdom shall never be destroyed,
    and his dominion has no end.
He delivers and rescues,
    he works signs and wonders in heaven and on earth;
for he has saved Daniel
    from the power of the lions.'

So this Daniel prospered during the reign of Darius and the reign of Cyrus the Persian.

This is the word of the Lord.   Daniel 6.12–end

Canticle

R **Sing God's praise and exalt him for ever.**

Bless the Lord dews and falling snows; [R]
bless the Lord you nights and days; [R]
bless the Lord light and darkness. R

Bless the Lord frost and cold; [R]
bless the Lord you ice and snow; [R]
bless the Lord lightnings and clouds. [R]
O let the earth bless the Lord. R   *Song of the Three 46–52*

Year 2

A reading from the Revelation to John.

I saw another angel coming down from heaven, having great authority; and
the earth was made bright with his splendour. He called out with a mighty
voice,
    'Fallen, fallen is Babylon the great!
       It has become a dwelling-place of demons,
  a haunt of every foul spirit,
     a haunt of every foul bird,
     a haunt of every foul and hateful beast.'

Then a mighty angel took up a stone like a great millstone and threw it into
the sea, saying,
    'With such violence Babylon the great city
     will be thrown down,
     and will be found no more;
  and the sound of harpists and minstrels
       and of flautists and trumpeters
     will be heard in you no more;
  and an artisan of any trade
     will be found in you no more;
  and the sound of the millstone
     will be heard in you no more;
  and the light of a lamp
     will shine in you no more;
  and the voice of bridegroom and bride
     will be heard in you no more;
  for your merchants were the magnates of the earth,
     and all nations were deceived by your sorcery.'

After this I heard what seemed to be the loud voice of a great multitude in
heaven, saying,
    'Hallelujah!
  Salvation and glory and power to our God,

for his judgements are true and just;
he has judged the great whore
   who corrupted the earth with her fornication,
and he has avenged on her the blood of his servants.'

Once more they said,
   'Hallelujah!
The smoke goes up from her for ever and ever.'

And the angel said to me, 'Write this: Blessed are those who are invited to
the marriage supper of the Lamb.' And he said to me, 'These are true words
of God.'

This is the word of the Lord.   Revelation 18.1–2, 21–23, 19.1–3, 9

Responsorial Psalm

R **Be joyful in the Lord, all the earth:**
   [give thanks and bless his name].   cf Psalm 100.1a, 3b

O be joyful in the Lord, all the earth;
serve the Lord with gladness
and come before his presence with a song.   R

Know that the Lord is God;
it is he that has made us and we are his;
we are his people and the sheep of his pasture.   R

Enter his gates with thanksgiving
and his courts with praise;
give thanks to him and bless his name.   R

For the Lord is gracious;
his steadfast love is everlasting,
and his faithfulness endures from generation to generation.   R

                                                        Psalm 100

Year 1 and Year 2

Hear the Gospel of our Lord Jesus Christ according to Luke.

Jesus said to the disciples, 'When you see Jerusalem surrounded by armies,
then know that its desolation has come near. Then those in Judea must flee
to the mountains, and those inside the city must leave it, and those out in
the country must not enter it; for these are days of vengeance, as a fulfilment
of all that is written. Woe to those who are pregnant and to those who are
nursing infants in those days! For there will be great distress on the earth
and wrath against this people; they will fall by the edge of the sword and be
taken away as captives among all nations; and Jerusalem will be trampled on
by the Gentiles, until the times of the Gentiles are fulfilled.   →

'There will be signs in the sun, the moon, and the stars, and on the earth distress among nations confused by the roaring of the sea and the waves. People will faint from fear and foreboding of what is coming upon the world, for the powers of the heavens will be shaken. Then they will see "the Son of Man coming in a cloud" with power and great glory. Now when these things begin to take place, stand up and raise your heads, because your redemption is drawing near.'

This is the Gospel of the Lord.   Luke 21.20–28

Week 34: Friday between 25 November and 1 December

Year 1

A reading from the Book of Daniel.

I, Daniel, saw in my vision by night the four winds of heaven stirring up the great sea, and four great beasts came up out of the sea, different from one another. The first was like a lion and had eagles' wings. Then, as I watched, its wings were plucked off, and it was lifted up from the ground and made to stand on two feet like a human being; and a human mind was given to it. Another beast appeared, a second one, that looked like a bear. It was raised up on one side, had three tusks in its mouth among its teeth and was told, 'Arise, devour many bodies!' After this, as I watched, another appeared, like a leopard. The beast had four wings of a bird on its back and four heads; and dominion was given to it. After this I saw in the visions by night a fourth beast, terrifying and dreadful and exceedingly strong. It had great iron teeth and was devouring, breaking in pieces, and stamping what was left with its feet. It was different from all the beasts that preceded it, and it had ten horns. I was considering the horns, when another horn appeared, a little one coming up among them; to make room for it, three of the earlier horns were plucked up by the roots. There were eyes like human eyes in this horn, and a mouth speaking arrogantly.

As I watched,
thrones were set in place,
      and an Ancient One took his throne;
his clothing was white as snow,
      and the hair of his head like pure wool;
his throne was fiery flames,
      and its wheels were burning fire.
A stream of fire issued
      and flowed out from his presence.
A thousand thousand served him,
      and ten thousand times ten thousand stood attending him.
The court sat in judgement,
      and the books were opened.

I watched then because of the noise of the arrogant words that the horn was speaking. And as I watched, the beast was put to death, and its body destroyed and given over to be burned with fire. As for the rest of the beasts, their dominion was taken away, but their lives were prolonged for a season and a time. As I watched in the night visions,

I saw one like a human being
   coming with the clouds of heaven.
And he came to the Ancient One
   and was presented before him.
To him was given dominion
   and glory and kingship,
that all peoples, nations, and languages
   should serve him.
His dominion is an everlasting dominion
   that shall not pass away,
and his kingship is one
   that shall never be destroyed.

This is the word of the Lord.   Daniel 7.2–14

Canticle

R   Sing God's praise and exalt him for ever.

Bless the Lord you mountains and hills;   [R]
bless the Lord all that grows in the ground.   **R**

Bless the Lord you springs;   [R]
bless the Lord you seas and rivers;   [R]
bless the Lord you whales and all that swim in the waters.   **R**

Bless the Lord all birds of the air;   [R]
bless the Lord you beasts and cattle.   **R**   *Song of the Three 53–59*

Year 2

A reading from the Revelation to John.

I saw an angel coming down from heaven, holding in his hand the key to the bottomless pit and a great chain. He seized the dragon, that ancient serpent, who is the Devil and Satan, and bound him for a thousand years, and threw him into the pit, and locked and sealed it over him, so that he would deceive the nations no more, until the thousand years were ended. After that he must be let out for a little while.

   Then I saw thrones, and those seated on them were given authority to judge. I also saw the souls of those who had been beheaded for their testimony to Jesus and for the word of God. They had not worshipped the beast or its image and had not received its mark on their foreheads or their hands. They came to life and reigned with Christ for a thousand years.   →

Then I saw a great white throne and the one who sat on it; the earth and the heaven fled from his presence, and no place was found for them. And I saw the dead, great and small, standing before the throne, and books were opened. Also another book was opened, the book of life. And the dead were judged according to their works, as recorded in the books. And the sea gave up the dead that were in it, Death and Hades gave up the dead that were in them, and all were judged according to what they had done. Then Death and Hades were thrown into the lake of fire. This is the second death, the lake of fire; and anyone whose name was not found written in the book of life was thrown into the lake of fire.

Then I saw a new heaven and a new earth; for the first heaven and the first earth had passed away, and the sea was no more. And I saw the holy city, the new Jerusalem, coming down out of heaven from God, prepared as a bride adorned for her husband.

This is the word of the Lord.   Revelation 20.1–4, 11 – 21.2

Responsorial Psalm

R   **How lovely is your dwelling place, O Lord of hosts!**   Psalm 84.1

How lovely is your dwelling place, O Lord of hosts!
My soul has a desire and longing
to enter the courts of the Lord;
my heart and my flesh rejoice in the living God.   **R**

The sparrow has found her a house
and the swallow a nest where she may lay her young:
at your altars, O Lord of hosts,
my King and my God.   **R**

Blessed are they who dwell in your house:
they will always be praising you.
Blessed are those whose strength is in you,
in whose heart are the highways to Zion.   **R**   Psalm 84.1–6

Year 1 and Year 2

Hear the Gospel of our Lord Jesus Christ according to Luke.

Jesus told his disciples a parable: 'Look at the fig tree and all the trees; as soon as they sprout leaves you can see for yourselves and know that summer is already near. So also, when you see these things taking place, you know that the kingdom of God is near. Truly I tell you, this generation will not pass away until all things have taken place. Heaven and earth will pass away, but my words will not pass away.'

This is the Gospel of the Lord.   Luke 21.29–33

Week 34: Saturday between 26 November and 2 December

Year I

A reading from the Book of Daniel.

As for me, Daniel, my spirit was troubled within me, and the visions of my head terrified me. I approached one of the attendants to ask him the truth concerning all this. So he said that he would disclose to me the interpretation of the matter: 'As for these four great beasts, four kings shall arise out of the earth. But the holy ones of the Most High shall receive the kingdom and possess the kingdom for ever – for ever and ever.'

Then I desired to know the truth concerning the fourth beast, which was different from all the rest, exceedingly terrifying, with its teeth of iron and claws of bronze, and which devoured and broke in pieces, and stamped what was left with its feet; and concerning the ten horns that were on its head, and concerning the other horn that came up, and to make room for which three of them fell out – the horn that had eyes and a mouth that spoke arrogantly, and that seemed greater than the others. As I looked, this horn made war with the holy ones and was prevailing over them, until the Ancient One came; then judgement was given for the holy ones of the Most High, and the time arrived when the holy ones gained possession of the kingdom.

This is what he said: 'As for the fourth beast,
   there shall be a fourth kingdom on earth
      that shall be different from all the other kingdoms;
   it shall devour the whole earth,
      and trample it down, and break it to pieces.
As for the ten horns,
   out of this kingdom ten kings shall arise,
      and another shall arise after them.
This one shall be different from the former ones,
      and shall put down three kings.
He shall speak words against the Most High,
      shall wear out the holy ones of the Most High,
      and shall attempt to change the sacred seasons and the law;
and they shall be given into his power
      for a time, two times, and half a time.
Then the court shall sit in judgement,
      and his dominion shall be taken away,
      to be consumed and totally destroyed.
The kingship and dominion
      and the greatness of the kingdoms under the whole heaven
      shall be given to the people of the holy ones of the Most High;
   their kingdom shall be an everlasting kingdom,
      and all dominions shall serve and obey them.'

This is the word of the Lord.

Daniel 7.15–27

Canticle

R **Sing God's praise and exalt him for ever.**

Bless the Lord all people on earth.   [R]
O people of God bless the Lord;   [R]
bless the Lord you priests of the Lord.   R

Bless the Lord you servants of the Lord;   [R]
bless the Lord all you of upright spirit;   [R]
bless the Lord you that are holy and humble in heart.   R

Song of the Three 60–65

Year 2

A reading from the Revelation to John.

The angel showed me the river of the water of life, bright as crystal, flowing from the throne of God and of the Lamb through the middle of the street of the city. On either side of the river is the tree of life with its twelve kinds of fruit, producing its fruit each month; and the leaves of the tree are for the healing of the nations. Nothing accursed will be found there any more. But the throne of God and of the Lamb will be in it, and his servants will worship him; they will see his face, and his name will be on their foreheads. And there will be no more night; they need no light of lamp or sun, for the Lord God will be their light, and they will reign for ever and ever.

And he said to me, 'These words are trustworthy and true, for the Lord, the God of the spirits of the prophets, has sent his angel to show his servants what must soon take place.

'See, I am coming soon! Blessed is the one who keeps the words of the prophecy of this book.'

This is the word of the Lord.   *Revelation 22.1–7*

Responsorial Psalm

R* **Come, let us sing to the Lord;
and rejoice in the rock of our salvation.**   cf Psalm 95.1

Let us come into his presence with thanksgiving
and be glad in him with psalms.
For the Lord is a great God
and a great king above all gods.   R

In his hand are the depths of the earth
and the heights of the mountains are his also.
The sea is his, for he made it,
and his hands have moulded the dry land.   R

Come, let us worship and bow down
and kneel before the Lord our Maker.
For he is our God;
we are the people of his pasture and the sheep of his hand.   R

Psalm 95.1–7

Year 1 and Year 2

Hear the Gospel of our Lord Jesus Christ according to Luke.

Jesus said to his disciples, 'Be on guard so that your hearts are not weighed down with dissipation and drunkenness and the worries of this life, and that day does not catch you unexpectedly, like a trap. For it will come upon all who live on the face of the whole earth. Be alert at all times, praying that you may have the strength to escape all these things that will take place, and to stand before the Son of Man.'

This is the Gospel of the Lord.   Luke 21.34–36

GOSPEL ACCLAMATIONS

Advent

Alleluia, alleluia.
Prepare the way of the Lord, make his paths straight,
and all flesh shall see the salvation of God.   cf Isaiah 40.3, 5
Alleluia.

Christmas

Alleluia, alleluia.
The Word became flesh and dwelt among us,
and we have seen his glory.   John 1.14
Alleluia.

Epiphany

Alleluia, alleluia.
Christ was revealed in flesh, proclaimed among the nations
and believed in throughout the world.   cf 1 Timothy 3.16
Alleluia.

Alleluia, alleluia.
We have seen his star at its rising,
and have come to pay him homage.   Matthew 2.2
Alleluia.

Ordinary Time

For Ordinary Time, see page 817.

Lent

Praise to you, O Christ, King of eternal glory.
The Lord is a great God, O that today you would listen to his voice.
Harden not your hearts.   *cf Psalm 95.3, 8*
Praise to you, O Christ, King of eternal glory.

Praise to you, O Christ, King of eternal glory.
Blessed are those who have endured temptation;
they have stood the test and will receive the crown of life.   *James 1.12*
Praise to you, O Christ, King of eternal glory.

Praise to you, O Christ, King of eternal glory.
I am the light of the world, says the Lord,
whoever follows me will have the light of life.   *John 8.12*
Praise to you, O Christ, King of eternal glory.

Praise to you, O Christ, King of eternal glory.
Your word is a lamp to my feet and a light to my path.   *Psalm 119.105*
Praise to you, O Christ, King of eternal glory.

Passiontide

Praise to you, O Christ, King of eternal glory.
Christ humbled himself and became obedient unto death,
even death on a cross.
Therefore God has highly exalted him
and given him the name that is above every name.   *Philippians 2.8–9*
Praise to you, O Christ, King of eternal glory.

Maundy Thursday

Praise to you, O Christ, King of eternal glory.
I give you a new commandment, says the Lord:
Love one another as I have loved you.   *cf John 13.34*
Praise to you, O Christ, King of eternal glory.

From Easter Day until the Eve of the Ascension

Alleluia, alleluia.
Jesus said to them, 'I am the bread of life.
Whoever comes to me will never be hungry,
and whoever believes in me will never be thirsty.'   *John 6.35*
Alleluia.

Alleluia, alleluia.
Jesus said, 'All who see the Son and believe in him
may have eternal life; and I will raise them up on the last day.'   *John 6.40*
Alleluia.

Alleluia, alleluia.
Jesus said, 'I am the resurrection and the life.
Those who believe in me, even though they die, will live,
and everyone who lives and believes in me will never die.'   *John 11.25–26*
Alleluia.

Alleluia, alleluia.
I am the first and the last, says the Lord, and the living one;
I was dead, and behold I am alive for evermore.   *cf Revelation 1.17–18*
Alleluia.

Jesus Christ is risen from the dead.
Alleluia.
He has defeated the powers of death.
Alleluia.
Jesus turns our sorrow into dancing.
Alleluia.
He has the words of eternal life.
Alleluia.

From the day after Ascension Day until the Day of Pentecost

Alleluia, alleluia.
Come, Holy Spirit, fill the hearts of your faithful people
and kindle in them the fire of your love.
Alleluia.

Alleluia, alleluia.
Go, and make disciples of all nations, says the Lord,
and remember, I am with you always, to the end of the age.
Alleluia.   *cf Matthew 28.19–20*

Ordinary Time

Alleluia, alleluia.
Speak, Lord, for your servant is listening.
You have the words of eternal life. *1 Samuel 3.9; John 6.68*
Alleluia.

Alleluia, alleluia.
I am the light of the world, says the Lord.
Whoever follows me will never walk in darkness
but will have the light of life. *John 8.12*
Alleluia.

Alleluia, alleluia.
My sheep hear my voice, says the Lord.
I know them, and they follow me. *John 10.27*
Alleluia.

Alleluia, alleluia.
I am the way, the truth, and the life, says the Lord.
No one comes to the Father except through me. *John 14.6*
Alleluia.

Alleluia, alleluia.
We do not live by bread alone,
but by every word that comes from the mouth of God. *cf Matthew 4.4*
Alleluia.

Alleluia, alleluia.
Welcome with meekness the implanted word
that has the power to save your souls. *James 1.21*
Alleluia.

Alleluia, alleluia.
The word of the Lord endures for ever.
The word of the Lord is the good news announced to you.
Alleluia. *cf 1 Peter 1.25*

From All Saints' Day until Advent

Alleluia, alleluia.
Blessed is the king who comes in the name of the Lord.
Peace in heaven and glory in the highest heaven.   *Luke 19.38*
Alleluia.

Alleluia, alleluia.
Blessed are the poor in spirit,
for theirs is the kingdom of heaven.   *Matthew 5.3*
Alleluia.

Alleluia, alleluia.
Jesus Christ is the firstborn from the dead;
to him be glory and power for ever and ever.   *cf Colossians 1.18*
Alleluia.

Alleluia, alleluia.
Stay awake, praying at all times
for the strength to stand with confidence before the Son of man.
Alleluia.   *cf Luke 21.36*

ACKNOWLEDGEMENTS

I am grateful to the following for permission to reproduce material:

the Daily Eucharistic Lectionary derives, with some adaptation, from the *Ordo Lectionum Missae* of the Roman Catholic Church and is reproduced by permission of the International Commission on English in the Liturgy; adaptations copyright © The Archbishops' Council of the Church of England, 1980, 2005;

the lectionary for Holy Week is from the Revised Common Lectionary copyright © The Consultation on Common Texts, 1992; used by permission;

scripture quotations, except for the psalms and canticles, from *The New Revised Standard Version of the Bible*, Anglicized Edition, copyright © 1989, 1995, by the Division of Christian Education of the National Council of the Churches of Christ in the USA;

the text of the psalms and the following canticles is from *Common Worship: Daily Prayer* (Church House Publishing), copyright © The Archbishops' Council 2005: Deuteronomy 32.3–4, 7–9; 1 Chronicles 29.10b–12; Jonah 2.2–4, 7; Tobit 13.1, 3–6a; Song of the Three 29–34; Song of the Three 35–65;

the text of the following canticles is based partly on canticles in *Common Worship: Daily Prayer*: Exodus 15.1–6; 1 Samuel 2.1, 4–8;

the text of the following canticles is adapted from a number of translations, mainly *The New Revised Standard Version of the Bible*: Exodus 15.8–10, 12, 17; Deuteronomy 32.18–21; Deuteronomy 32.35–36, 39, 41; Isaiah 38.10–16; Jeremiah 31.10–13;

the text of the *Magnificat* (Luke 1.46b–55) and *Benedictus* (Luke 1.68–79) is from *Praying Together*, © the English Language Liturgical Consultation, 1988;

the text of the Gospel acclamations is from *Common Worship: Services and Prayers for the Church of England* and from *Common Worship: Times and Seasons* copyright © The Archbishops' Council 2000 and 2006.

In addition my thanks are due to:

Dr Colin Podmore, Secretary of the Liturgical Commission, for his clarification of numerous lectionary details and many helpful suggestions;

the Revd Peter Allan CR and the Revd Professor Paul Bradshaw, for comments on the psalms and psalm responses;

Peter Owen and Simon Sarmiento, who have helped find and correct various errors and obscurities;

Karen, Jenny and Alexander, who once more have put up with the long hours spent editing and typesetting this book.

Any remaining errors and imperfections are the responsibility of the Editor.

SIMON KERSHAW
January 2008